DEMOCRACY IN SESSION

OHIO UNIVERSITY PRESS SERIES ON LAW,
SOCIETY, AND POLITICS IN THE MIDWEST
Series Editors: Paul Finkelman and L. Diane Barnes

The History of Ohio Law, edited by Michael Les Benedict and John F. Winkler

Frontiers of Freedom: Cincinnati's Black Community, 1802–1868, by Nikki M. Taylor

A Place of Recourse: A History of the U.S. District Court for the Southern District of Ohio, 1803–2003, by Roberta Sue Alexander

The Black Laws: Race and the Legal Process in Early Ohio, by Stephen Middleton

The History of Indiana Law, edited by David J. Bodenhamer and Hon. Randall T. Shepard

The History of Michigan Law, edited by Paul Finkelman and Martin J. Hershock

The Rescue of Joshua Glover: A Fugitive Slave, the Constitution, and the Coming of the Civil War, by H. Robert Baker

The History of Nebraska Law, edited by Alan G. Gless

American Pogrom: The East St. Louis Race Riot and Black Politics, by Charles L. Lumpkins

No Winners Here Tonight: Race, Politics, and Geography in One of the Country's Busiest Death Penalty States, by Andrew Welsh-Huggins

Democracy in Session: A History of the Ohio General Assembly, by David M. Gold

DEMOCRACY IN SESSION

A HISTORY OF THE
OHIO GENERAL ASSEMBLY

David M. Gold

OHIO UNIVERSITY PRESS

Athens

Ohio University Press, Athens, Ohio 45701
www.ohioswallow.com
© 2009 by Ohio University Press

To obtain permission to quote, reprint, or otherwise reproduce or distribute material
from Ohio University Press publications, please contact our rights and permissions
department at (740) 593-1154 or (740) 593-4536 (fax).

Printed in the United States of America
Ohio University Press books are printed on acid-free paper ⊗ ™

16 15 14 13 12 11 10 09   5 4 3 2 1

Library of Congress Cataloging-in-Publication Data
Gold, David M.
    Democracy in session : a history of the Ohio General Assembly / David M. Gold.
        p. cm. — (Ohio University Press series on law, society, and politics in the
Midwest)
    Includes bibliographical references and index.
    ISBN 978-0-8214-1844-4 (cloth : alk. paper)
    1. Ohio. General Assembly—History. I. Title.
    JK5566.G65 2009
    328.77109—dc22

                                                2008047576

TO THE PEOPLE OF OHIO

CONTENTS

Part Three: The Second Century

Part Four: The Third Century

FOREWORD

When I joined the Ohio House of Representatives in June 1992, its halls oozed history. Stories told by, and about, longtime members helped me learn institutional history as well as think about the kind of legislator I wanted to become. I learned the power of resourcefulness and creativity in overcoming setbacks by watching Mike Fox (R-Hamilton) at work. From Otto Beatty (D-Columbus) I learned how to withstand pressure and remain true to one's principles—an infinitely harder task as a member of the legislative majority. Bill Batchelder (R-Medina) told stories of debate in the pre–Vern Riffe legislature and taught me to value the persuasiveness of the argument over the status of the person making it. Although our stories would no doubt be different, all of my colleagues, whether Democrat or Republican, House or Senate, had similar opportunities to learn about the art of legislating.

Not only veteran legislators modeled a crucial appreciation for historical context. Members of the statehouse press corps also conveyed a strong sense of living history. I learned a great deal by listening to veteran statehouse reporters like Sandy Theis and Tom Suddes, both of the *Cleveland Plain Dealer,* and former statehouse reporters like Mike Curtin, who then headed the *Columbus Dispatch.* The rise of Internet journalism and the shrinkage of newspaper budgets have also changed the nature of statehouse reporting; all of these reporters have now moved on to pursue other opportunities.

The passage of legislative term limits in 1992, along with shifts in media coverage, has greatly diminished that sense of living history. Institutional memory became weaker with every retirement and defeat in the 1990s, culminating in the first forced, mass departure when term limits became effective for the entire House and half of the Senate in 2000. Two years later, the pre–term limits era truly came to a close with the retirement from the state Senate of Senate President Richard Finan (R-Evendale). A twenty-four-year member of the Senate who had previously served six years in the House, Finan was president of the Senate from 1997 to 2002. His personal integrity, pragmatic approach to governing, and principled dedication to long-term fiscal responsibility played a major role in shaping the views and ethics of many who work or have worked around Capitol Square, whether as legislative staff or members, including this writer.

In his honor, a group of statehouse participants and observers, contemplating the end of the pre–term limits era with the forced retirement of the second half of the Senate, and lamenting the tremendous loss of historical perspective, decided to commission this scholarly work, the first ever on the history of the Ohio General Assembly. We believe that this book will give scholars and the general public, as well as future state leaders, a perspective on Ohio history that has heretofore been available, if at all, primarily through the recollections of the individuals directly involved and the pages of Ohio newspapers. We hope that this book will be a starting point for additional efforts to study Ohio history, and in particular we strongly encourage the establishment of an oral history project while we still can learn from the major actors in the pre–term limits legislature.

As a student of, and participant in, that history and as chair of the committee that commissioned this work, I would first like to thank the author, David Gold, for his intense and prodigious effort in producing such a masterful book. Thanks and a great deal of admiration also go to the distinguished Ohio scholars who oversaw the work as members of the editorial board: Professors Herb Asher and David Stebenne, both of the Ohio State University; Professor Andrew Cayton of Miami University; Professor Barbara Terzian of Ohio Wesleyan; and Professor Alonzo Hamby of Ohio University. I also want to commend the work of the managing board, who assisted in fund-raising as well as in planning this project: former state Senate president Stan Aronoff, Herb Asher, Mike Curtin, then-state senator Eric Fingerhut, Joyce Garver-Keller, Victor Goodman, former state representative Keith McNamara, Tom Suddes, Paul Tipps, and former senator Nick Zimmers. Greg Saul from my Senate office staffed this project. Senate President Bill Harris and House Speaker Jon Husted provided important support as well. A final thank you is to the donors, without whom the project would never have been possible: our lead donor, the Institute for Collaborative Research and the Public Humanities at the Ohio State University; AT&T (both the "new" and the "old"); Altria Corporate Services, Inc.; the Ohio State University; the Ohio University Foundation; Wolfe Associates, Inc.; Matt and Nancy Diggs; Cox Ohio Publishing; and Keith McNamara.

In honor of Richard Finan, and the thousands of Ohioans who have served in or were employed by the General Assembly during the past two hundred years, we are proud to present their history.

State Senator Jeff Jacobson

PREFACE

ON JANUARY 4, 1804, an Ohio lawmaker rose in the grand jury room on the upper floor of the Ross County Courthouse and presented Hannah Willis's petition for divorce to the state Senate. Chillicothe, the chief settlement of the county, was then the temporary state capital. The new log courthouse, poorly heated and roughly furnished, served as the General Assembly's meeting hall. Mrs. Willis wanted the legislature to dissolve her marriage to her husband, Isaac, and to grant her guardianship of their two young children. The Senate referred Mrs. Willis's petition to a select committee of two for examination and report, "by bill or otherwise." The committee reported a bill to grant the petition. The committee of the whole—that is, the entire fifteen-member Senate sitting as a committee—discussed and amended the bill, and the Senate passed it. Senator Benjamin Tappan then carried the bill downstairs to the courtroom, where the House of Representatives met, and asked for the House's concurrence. Two days later the House passed the bill, freeing Hannah Willis from her husband, restoring to her the legal rights of a *feme sole* (an unmarried woman) and giving her guardianship of her two children. When the speakers of the two houses signed the bill, they transformed it into a law.[1]

One hundred years later, the General Assembly convened, as it had for nearly half a century, in the Greek Revival statehouse in Columbus, a thriving city of more than 100,000 souls. The lawmakers of that time rarely dealt with individual cases. If Hannah Willis had wanted a divorce in 1904 instead of 1804, she would have had no choice but to go to court. The legislature still passed laws involving marriage and divorce but not for the benefit of particular individuals. The manner in which the General Assembly handled legislation had also changed. For example, in 1904, Senator Lewis Houck introduced a bill to amend the section of the Revised Statutes that required marriage banns, the public announcement of an intended marriage. Instead of presenting a constituent's petition for relief, which an ad hoc committee might then turn into a bill, Houck filed an already prepared bill with the Senate clerk. The clerk numbered the bill so that its progress could be tracked. A member of the clerk's staff formally introduced the bill by reading the title when the introduction of bills came up in the regular order of business at a session of the Senate. The Senate clerk of 1804 may or may not have had helpers—a law passed in January of that year allowed the clerks of the two houses $1.50 per day for "clerk hire and incidental expenses"— but the twentieth-century clerk had a bevy of assistants to help him handle his responsibilities.[2]

The committee of the whole, which had discussed and amended Hannah Willis's bill in 1804, had practically disappeared by 1904. Houck's bill went to the Judiciary Committee, one of more than three dozen standing committees of the Senate that typically considered bills in particular subject areas. The Judiciary Committee amended the bill, and the full Senate passed it. Neither Houck nor any other senator deigned personally to inform the House that the bill had passed. Rather, the Senate clerk sent an employee to do the job. The House judiciary committee reported the bill favorably, the full House passed it, and Governor Myron T. Herrick, who could have vetoed the act, signed it into law.[3]

Fast-forward another century. From his office in the Riffe Center across the street from the statehouse, Representative William J. Seitz's aide sent to the director of the Legislative Service Commission (LSC) a request for a draft of a bill to declare same-sex marriage contrary to the public policy of the state. The director assigned an LSC lawyer to prepare the draft. Seitz filed six copies with the House clerk, who gave it a number and, after formal introduction, posted it on a public Web site. The House Rules and Reference Committee referred the bill to the Juvenile and Family Law Committee. LSC specialists provided the committee with an analysis of the bill and a fiscal note explaining what impact, if any, the bill would have on state and local government finances. The committee reported a substitute bill, which the House passed and sent to the Senate. The Senate Reference Committee referred the bill to a standing committee. The LSC staffers assigned to that committee provided an updated analysis and fiscal note. The committee reported another substitute bill, drafted by an LSC lawyer. The Senate passed the bill, a conference committee reconciled the differences between the House and Senate versions, both houses accepted the conference committee's report, and the governor signed the bill.[4]

The path followed by Seitz's bill bore some of the same earmarks of modernization as had Houck's a hundred years earlier. It first appeared in the General Assembly as a bill, not a petition. It was introduced by an individual member, not a committee. The clerk accepted the bill for filing and assigned it a number. Standing committees considered its merits, made changes, and recommended passage. The legislature presented it to the governor for his consideration. But there were remarkable differences, too. Advances in technology had made possible the filing of multiple copies, a phenomenon in its infancy in the early twentieth century. Modern technology also allowed the dissemination of the bill to the entire world via the Internet. A standing reference committee in each house directed the bill to a subject-matter committee. The committee hearings were open to the public, which was not legally required in 1904. All along the way, the sponsor, the committees, and every member of the General Assembly had the assistance of a full-time staff of attorneys, budget analysts, and other professionals. The General Assembly's basic functions in 2004 were much the same as they had been one hundred and even two hundred years earlier, but the institution had changed.

Alan Rosenthal, an eminent observer of modern state legislatures, wrote in 1981, "Legislatures are durable. They have persevered for over 200 years. Legislatures are significant. Their involvement in our lives runs the gamut from womb to tomb. Legislatures are fascinating. Although complex, and each with its own pattern and rhythm, they are very human institutions." Those are good reasons for studying legislatures, their evolution no less than their modern incarnations. Unfortunately, Rosenthal, a political scientist, has no counterpart among historians. Historians have paid some attention to colonial assemblies, but they have practically ignored nineteenth- and twentieth-century state legislatures.[5]

This book is an attempt to fill the gap. My charge in writing it was to produce a "comprehensive" history of the Ohio General Assembly. A truly complete history of a large state's most important political institution, one that is now more than two centuries old, would be a never-ending project. Every scholar, having only a limited amount of time, has to make hard decisions about what goes into a book and what gets left out. A few words ought to be said about the ground this book covers.

This is a history of the General Assembly as an institution, not as an arena in which political parties duked out their differences over policy and patronage. Raymond W. Smock, a historian of the U.S. House of Representatives, has offered this recipe for the institutional history of that legislative body: "[T]ake the Constitution, add House rules, slowly add committees, political parties, traditions, the biographies and personalities of members of the House, and parliamentary procedure—then mix these ingredients vigorously with United States history and a dash of world history and finally fold in the desires of the American people." I did not have this formula before me when I wrote this book, but if I had the result would have been the same. The book examines the constitutional parameters within which the General Assembly functioned, the development of legislative rules and procedures, and the physical setting in which the legislature operated. It looks at the legislators: who they were, how they got elected, how they interacted with other members and with interested nonmembers both inside and outside the statehouse, and what standards of conduct they maintained. It also considers the employees who made the institution function: clerks, doorkeepers, pages, porters, stenographers, legislative aides, and others. Employees have gotten short shrift from historians. I have attempted to give them their due.[6]

What of politics? A legislature is an inherently political institution, one of the main forums in which political parties contend for power. But political battles are fought everywhere, and political history can be and usually is written with little notice of the institutional aspects of a legislature. To venture into political history is to risk going far afield and losing the legislative focus. George B. Galloway's history of the U.S. House of Representatives, first published in 1962 and updated twice since then, barely mentions politics. Not wishing to go that far, I have taken account of partisan conflict in a selective but, I hope, revealing manner. Joel Silbey has described the period from the late 1830s to the 1890s as a golden age of political parties in which parties replaced personal relationships and family ties as the framework of politics and "the American political nation reflected the impulses of a unique, partisan era." In chapter 10, I look at the partisan battles of that age as they occurred in the General Assembly, particularly with regard to what may be called party-defining issues: banking and currency, race and sectionalism, and Prohibition. According to Silbey, electoral reforms, the rise of nonpartisan pressure groups, and other political and social changes beginning in the 1890s drained the dynamism from the party system. Despite the challenges they faced, Ohio's major political parties remained viable institutions in the twentieth century, but partisan divisions took on a different hue. In chapter 20, I examine the rise of peculiarly urban issues, the interplay between the urban-rural divide and party politics, and the partisan impact of two great changes in legislative apportionment.[7]

Then there is the subject of statutory law and public policy. Statutes are the chief work-product of a legislature and can hardly be ignored, although Galloway gave them scant notice. But to catalog all the laws passed over the course of two hundred years would be a mind-numbing job. The end product might be a reference work of some use to specialists, but no one would actually read it. Some histories of state legislatures concentrate on public policy, and do it reasonably well, but they do not tell us much about the legislatures themselves.

In the belief that the primary work-product of the General Assembly ought to be part of a history of the institution but not its centerpiece, I have examined some distinguishing characteristics of statutory law as it developed in the nineteenth and twentieth centuries. In the nineteenth century, the General Assembly, even as it enacted broad public policy in the form of general laws, passed thousands of "special" laws to grant divorces, change people's names, issue corporate charters, and perform other acts that later came to be regarded as more properly judicial or administrative in nature. In chapter 11, I examine both the creation of public policy regarding sexual morality, a subject that continues to agitate the Ohio legislature in the twenty-first century, and the rise and demise of special legislation. In the twentieth century, two significant developments curtailed the General Assembly's latitude in the enactment of statutory law. First, with the increasing complexity of life in a growing urban and industrial society came the need for the statewide implementation of policy. Accordingly, the General Assembly found itself establishing more and more agencies with the power not just to carry out legislative directives but also to create law in the form of administrative regulations. Second, the federal government—Congress, the courts, and federal agencies—imposed new mandates and limitations on the states. In chapter 21, I explore these trends, using environmental law as an illustration of how they came together.

As the preceding paragraphs suggest, this history is divided into two major parts, one on Ohio's first century and another on its second. That was not the original plan. The initial outline of the book called for four parts covering about fifty years each. As it turned out, though, chronological breaks that made sense from one perspective made no sense from another. For example, the adoption of a new constitution in 1851 and the nearly simultaneous breakup of the party system of Whigs and Democrats argue for a division at that point. But 1851 did not mark a new departure for legislative procedure, the electoral process, or other aspects of the General Assembly's evolution. After considerable cogitation, I settled on two century-long sections, along with an introductory chapter on the territorial background of the General Assembly and an epilogue on its future. The period around the turn of the century, roughly 1896 to 1912, was a time of transition for the legislature. During those years, power shifted from the legislature to the governor with the adoption of the executive veto and the rise of administrative agencies. A new method of apportioning representatives, one with long-term political consequences, went into effect. The direct primary changed the ways in which candidates were nominated and campaigned. Republicans embarked upon a long period of political dominance of the legislature. Manuals of legislative procedure for Ohio appeared for the first time. The General Assembly created the state's first legislative reference service. And although the constitution of 1851 remained in effect, it was heavily revised by the adoption of dozens of amendments.

Each of this book's two major divisions has both subject-matter and chronological elements. A strictly sequential account works only if the topics are limited, as for example in those histories of state legislatures that focus on public policy to the near exclusion of everything else. This book covers too much ground to adhere to an overall chronological narrative, but many distinct subjects are treated chronologically. The result will, I hope, give the reader both a feel for how the General Assembly looked, sounded, and functioned at different points in its history and a sense of its development over the course of two centuries.

A theme that runs throughout this work is the transformation of the General Assembly from a part-time body of citizen lawmakers into a full-time, professional legislature. There are different ways of measuring a legislature's professionalism. One set of indicia well-known to political scientists is the five S's: space, sessions, structure, staffing, and salaries. Does the legislature as a whole, and do committees and individual members, have adequate room and facilities to perform effectively? Does the legislature meet often enough and long enough to accomplish its objectives? Do the size and organization of the legislature and its committees allow for efficient functioning? Do the members have sufficient clerical, secretarial, and professional assistance to perform their jobs at a high level? Are legislative salaries and benefits high enough to attract capable candidates and to keep them independent? These benchmarks apply to the legislature as a body. Others apply to legislators as individuals. Does being a legislator take up all of a member's working hours? Do the members regard their legislative posts as their primary occupations? Do they expect to be career legislators and do they in fact stay on the job for many years?[8]

A movement in the 1960s and 1970s to reform state legislatures led to major changes in the General Assembly. Studies done in the latter decade concluded that Ohio's legislature had taken great strides in the direction of professionalism. Since the 1980s the General Assembly has been regarded as a "full-time, professional legislature." But while the transformation accelerated dramatically after 1965, it began long before then. In fact, as we will see, it had been going on almost from the start.[9]

ACKNOWLEDGMENTS

IN DEVELOPING this history of the General Assembly from its prestatehood days as a body of citizen-legislators to its twenty-first-century incarnation as a high-tech institution of full-time professionals, I incurred many debts. My thanks go first of all to Senator Jeff Jacobson and all those individuals and entities mentioned in his foreword for giving me the opportunity to write this book. The members of the editorial board read the manuscript at various stages in its progress and offered sage advice for its improvement. I also benefited from the wise counsel of Paul Finkelman, President William McKinley Distinguished Professor of Law and Public Policy at the Albany Law School and coeditor of the series of which this volume is a part. Dr. Susan A. Johnson, a graduate student at the Ohio State University when I started this project, was my research assistant. Her industry, creativity, and skill at hunting down and organizing information proved invaluable. Librarians at numerous institutions, most notably the Ohio Legislative Service Commission, *Columbus Dispatch,* Columbus Metropolitan Library, Ohio Historical Society, Ohio State University, State Library of Ohio, and Supreme Court of Ohio, all responded graciously to my requests for help.

Many people who have been connected with the General Assembly in one way or another, at one time or another, assisted me in assorted ways. Current and former staffers at the Legislative Service Commission, some of them well-seasoned repositories of institutional memory, reviewed portions of the manuscript and offered information, suggestions, and expertise. Legislators and members of the Ohio House and Senate staffs, past and present, provided me with the benefit of their experience. Individuals who gave their time for interviews, conversations, and e-mail communications include Stanley Aronoff, Lou Blessing, Jane Campbell, Bill Chavanne, Laura Clemens, Bill Cohen, Andy DiPalma, Ted Gray, Sandra Stabile-Harwood, Jeff Jacobson, Charles Kurfess, Lee Leonard, Keith McNamara, Priscilla Mead, Ben Rose, Bob Schmitz, and Dan Williamson.

Professors Michael F. Holt of the University of Virginia and Warren Van Tine of the Ohio State University furnished me with material that I would not otherwise have known about or been able to obtain. With Professor Michael Pierce of the University of Arkansas I had brief but enlightening discussions on Ohio's political history of the late nineteenth century. Professor Alan Rosenthal of the Eagleton Institute of Politics at Rutgers University read and commented on several chapters.

I regret that two of my former colleagues at the Legislative Service Commission, director Jim Burley and librarian Connie Yankus, did not live to see the completion of this work. Jim spent most of his professional career with the General Assembly and knew it well. He regarded the legislature not uncritically but with respect and affection. I shared bits and pieces of the book with him as it evolved and like to think that he would have approved of the finished product. Connie was an able researcher and an affable, obliging soul. Helping staff members with their personal projects was not part of her job, but she responded to my appeals for aid with unfailing good cheer.

If this book enhances the reader's understanding of the state legislature, one of the great institutions of American democracy, the credit is due largely to those persons, named and unnamed above, who generously shared with me their knowledge and insights.

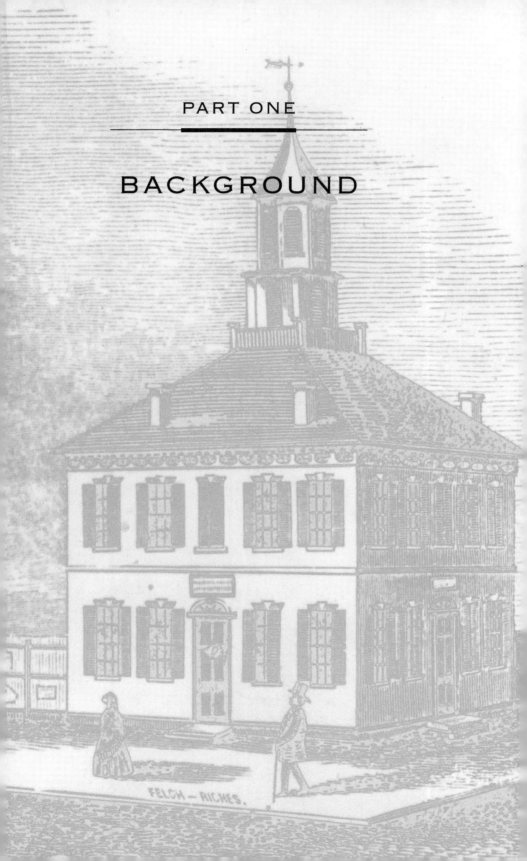

PART ONE

BACKGROUND

FELCH — RICHES.

1

THE NABOB AND
THE IGNORANT MULTITUDE

O HIO'S FIRST LEGISLATIVE AUTHORITY consisted of four unelected men who governed a region stretching from Pennsylvania to the Mississippi River and from the Ohio River to present-day Manitoba. The "Ohio country" occupied the southeastern portion of this immense Northwest Territory, between the Ohio River and Lake Erie. The end of the American Revolution had brought international recognition of American sovereignty over the area. Anxious to promote the settlement of the territory in an orderly fashion, Congress, in one of its last and best acts under the Articles of Confederation, passed the Northwest Ordinance. The Ordinance provided the framework of government for the Northwest Territory for the next eleven years.

While the Ordinance guaranteed individual rights and promised republican government and equality with the original states in the future, it did not provide for government by the consent of the governed, at least not initially and not entirely thereafter. Congress appointed all the chief territorial officials: the governor, the secretary, and three judges, all five of whom had to be substantial landowners, and all general officers of the militia. The governor in turn appointed magistrates and other local officials and militia officers below the rank of general. He also had the power to lay out counties and townships, subject to subsequent alteration by the territorial legislature, which consisted of the governor and the three judges appointed by Congress. The legislators had no power to make laws, but they could adopt any laws of the original thirteen states that they thought appropriate for the territory.[1]

The Ordinance looked forward to a more democratic government when the territory would have five thousand free male inhabitants. Even then, though, the government would resemble that of a British colony. A House of Representatives would be elected by men who met the residency and property qualifications, but Congress would still choose the governor, secretary, and other officers, as well as a five-member Legislative Council from a list of ten nominees selected by the representatives. The governor, Legislative Council, and House of Representatives together would make up the General Assembly. This body would be able to pass laws, but the governor would have an absolute veto and the power to dissolve the General Assembly at will.[2]

The term "general assembly" for a lawmaking body went back to the early days of English settlement in North America. The third (1611) charter of the "Knights, Gentlemen, Merchants, and other Adventurers" who made up the Virginia Company directed the company to meet at least once a week in "a Court and Assembly" to govern the day-to-day affairs of the colony. At least five members of a council appointed by the king and fifteen members "of the Generality of the said Company" would constitute a quorum. To make laws concerning more important matters and to select officers to manage company affairs, "one great, general, and solemn Assembly" would convene at four set times annually. In 1621, the company adopted an "Ordinance and Constitution" that created a government consisting of a small Council of State to assist the governor and a second body made up of the Council of State and representatives chosen by the inhabitants of the various towns and settlements. This second body, called the General Assembly, would meet annually to adopt laws for the colony by majority vote, subject to the governor's veto. The governing documents of several other colonies also provided for lawmaking institutions called general assemblies. By 1776, the term had become so familiar that a majority of the newly independent states referred to their legislatures as general assemblies.[3]

Until the population of the Northwest Territory reached the number required for the establishment of the General Assembly, the congressionally appointed legislature governed the territory with little partisan bickering but considerable personal friction. Governor Arthur St. Clair quarreled with the first judges over the extent of their joint legislative authority and disputed whether the judges, as a majority of the legislature, could adopt laws over the governor's opposition. The governor and judges had a hard time even getting together for legislative sessions. Travel and communication in the vast, sparsely settled territory were difficult enough under the best of circumstances, and circumstances were not the best. St. Clair and territorial secretary Winthrop Sargent, both great travelers themselves, complained about the peripatetic judges' inattention to duty. Early in 1793, Sargent wrote to the absent St. Clair of "the mortification of a vain Attempt to convene the Legislature" because Judge John Cleve Symmes had left the territory in defiance of Sargent's request for a meeting and both Symmes and Judge George Turner were pursuing their private interests. In July St. Clair issued a proclamation calling for a meeting of the legislature in Cincinnati on September 1, but he did not know where Symmes and Turner were and had to send copies of the proclamation to Secretary of State Thomas Jefferson in Philadelphia in the hope that he would know where to send them. The legislature did not actually meet again until two years after St. Clair issued the proclamation, and then three more years elapsed before the last legislative session of the governor and judges.[4]

Because the Northwest Ordinance provided only the bare outlines of a government, the legislators had much fundamental work to do. They established a militia system, created lower courts, provided for local government, passed tax laws, adopted a rudimentary criminal code, and regulated personal and commercial life in a variety of ways. They also established precedents for future legislatures: hiring a clerk and messenger, keeping a journal, opening their sessions to the public, making motions, debating, and voting.

The undemocratic nature of the territory's political arrangements displeased many of the settlers and contributed mightily to the drive for Ohio statehood. Pressure for representative government built throughout the 1790s. No sooner had a newspaper appeared in November 1793 than a disgruntled reader complained of "the oppressive hand of a legislature, in the formation or organization of which he was not consulted." Winthrop Sargent's arbitrary rule in St. Clair's absence provoked like cries of "tyranny and despotism." In the popular calls that led to the legislative session of 1795, demands for law reform were mixed with criticism of the tyrannical government of four unelected men.[5]

The Territorial General Assembly

The clamor for representative government spread with the rapid growth of population after General Anthony Wayne decisively defeated the Indians at the Battle of Fallen Timbers in 1794. In 1798, St. Clair, believing that the territory had the requisite number of inhabitants for the establishment of a General Assembly, set the third Monday in December as the date for the election of representatives. The Northwest Ordinance set property qualifications of two hundred acres to serve in the House of Representatives and fifty acres to vote. For every five hundred free male inhabitants, there would be one representative, to a maximum of twenty-five, after which the legislature would fix the number and proportion of members. St. Clair interpreted these provisions liberally, so that town dwellers who had houses but not much land qualified to vote if they possessed an estate equal in value to the average fifty acres of land in the same county. Even so, the franchise was more restricted than in any of the states.[6]

The first House of Representatives met on February 4, 1799, in Cincinnati. St. Clair had called the session for January 22, but delegates from distant areas—present-day Michigan, Illinois, and Indiana—found that traveling hundreds of miles through the wilderness in winter was no easy task. Even the members from Marietta had trouble getting to the session. They trudged through long stretches of dreary woods bearing no signs of human habitation, camping at night in the winter cold, swimming their horses across streams, traveling no roads except bridle paths or Indian trails.[7]

At the end of their journey the intrepid legislators found "a straggling and unprepossessing village" of 750 people, a garrison town that lacked "polished society" but not hard-drinking, hard-gambling soldiers. Winthrop Sargent complained that Cincinnatians were "very licentious and too great a portion indolent and extremely debauched." On February 4, 1799, the representatives finally met, nominated ten men for the Legislative Council, and adjourned to September 16 for their first real working session. When St. Clair declared the session over on December 19, the lawmakers expected to reconvene the following fall in Cincinnati. In May, however, in the act that carved the Indiana Territory out of the Northwest Territory, Congress, lobbied hard by St. Clair's political enemy Thomas Worthington of Chillicothe, made Chillicothe the seat of government.[8]

Although one of the chief settlements of the Northwest Territory, Chillicothe was just a little frontier town. In November 1800, the legislature met on the

Arthur St. Clair. *Reproduced by permission of the Ohio Historical Society*

lower floor of a small log structure that served as an all-purpose public building. Notwithstanding the legal prohibition of gaming devices, the upper floor housed "billiard tables and other appliances for the accommodation of those seeking recreation for either pleasure or profit." In 1801, the county completed construction of a new courthouse, which also served as the statehouse as long as Chillicothe remained the capital. A two-story, stone building with a cupola on which perched a gilt eagle on a ball, it was, said one observer, "very illy adapted" for legislative sessions. The House of Representatives met in the ground-floor courtroom, "a very uncomfortable, badly-lighted, and roughly-finished room," freezing in winter despite the large fireplace at each end. The second-story grand jury room would be occupied by the Senate after statehood. It was "a low room, with a platform for the Speaker's seat at one side, and long, roughly-made tables on the floor, with plain, Windsor chairs ranged behind them for the reverend senators."[9]

Representative Edward Tiffin and Council member Jacob Burnet emerged as the legislature's leading figures. Tiffin, a physician, Methodist deacon, and lay

An engraving of the Ross County courthouse in 1801, published in *American Pioneer* in June 1842. In 1800, before completion of the courthouse, the territorial General Assembly met in the log building behind the mound. The structure in the distance is the home of Edward Tiffin, Ohio's first governor. In reality, the log building and Tiffin home were several hundred feet off to the right. *Reproduced by permission of the Ohio Historical Society*

preacher, had been born in England in 1766, immigrated to Virginia as a teenager, and moved to Chillicothe in 1798. His friend Samuel Williams later recalled that Tiffin "selected a four acre out-lot at the upper end of the town for his residence, and built thereon the first house erected in town which was graced with a shingle roof." A short man with a large, bald head, vain and opinionated, Tiffin nevertheless quickly became and always remained extremely popular. He attended diligently to his patients through all kinds of weather, enduring "fatiguing rides on horseback, on dark nights over wretched roads, or, rather, no roads at all, crossing swollen streams with dangerous fords, and with full knowledge, frequently, that the patient was too poor to make him any remuneration for his services and medicines." Tiffin's fellow representatives unanimously elected him the first Speaker of the House and reelected him in the second territorial assembly.[10]

Tiffin, a good Jeffersonian, represented the political leanings of the population at large, but Jacob Burnet proved more important to the work of the legislature. A New Jersey lawyer who moved to Cincinnati in 1796, Burnet quickly rose to

Jacob Burnet. *Reproduced by permission of the Ohio Historical Society*

the head of the territorial bar. He lost his bid for election to the House of Representatives in 1798, but those who did get elected wisely nominated him for the Legislative Council, and Congress made the appointment. Burnet drafted numerous bills, the Council's rules of procedure, addresses to the governor and to President John Adams, and a memorial to Congress. His *Notes on the Early Settlement of the North-Western Territory*, written many years later, would be an unequaled source of information on the workings of the territorial legislature.[11]

Burnet belonged to the Federalist Party, one of two political parties that emerged in the 1790s. The other was the Jeffersonian Republicans, also called Democrats and Democratic-Republicans. Federalists believed in a strong national government and an executive authority with real power. Republicans like Tiffin remained skeptical of both, even after the adoption of the Bill of Rights in 1791 allayed some of their fears. Federalists distrusted democracy, a sentiment strengthened by their abhorrence of the French Revolution; Republicans believed in the virtue and good sense of the people, and for a long time they viewed the French Revolution as a continuation of the American. Many Federalists favored commercial development; for Republicans, the ideal society consisted of sturdy yeomen. These are generalizations, of course. Federalists John Adams and Alexander Hamilton disagreed over the advantages of a commercial republic, and Republican Thomas Jefferson knew that the people could be corrupted, especially if they congregated in cities. But for the most part, Federalists favored energetic government by the "better sort," while Republicans leaned toward agrarian democracy and limited government.[12]

The Federalists and Republicans of the 1790s lacked the organizational structure that later came to characterize parties. The physical and constitutional situation of the Northwest Territory retarded party development. Except for a few clusters in Marietta, Cincinnati, and Chillicothe, the population was scattered through a vast wilderness, with poor transportation and little communication. With no popular assembly before 1799 and governmental power concentrated in the hands of four federally appointed officials, the people had little opportunity to express themselves politically. Practical considerations also blurred political divisions. Frontier farmers who constituted a natural Republican constituency appreciated the protection the federal government afforded against Indian depredations. St. Clair's power of patronage and sectional rivalries, particularly over the location of the future capital, also inhibited partisan organization.[13]

The candidates for the House of Representatives in 1798 did not contest the election along party lines, and the House submitted to Congress a mixed list of nominees for the Legislative Council. There was, nevertheless, an "undercurrent of hostility" in the House toward the Federalist St. Clair. One representative wrote, "our Governor is cloathed with all the power of a British Nabob." Characterizing the opposing sides in the House as Court and Country, like the political factions of eighteenth-century Britain, historian Donald J. Ratcliffe has observed that an "informal grouping of interests opposed to the governor" made up "a 'Country' opposition pressing for the redress of grievances rather than endeavoring to win power in the name of a clearly defined national political party."[14]

St. Clair polarized the factions and radicalized the opposition at the end of the first territorial General Assembly by vetoing eleven of thirty laws passed. One veto prevented a census of the eastern section of the Northwest Territory. The census act would have been an important step on the road to statehood, which St. Clair wanted to forestall. In his message to the legislature St. Clair displayed a distinct lack of diplomacy by bluntly insisting on his prerogative. Some of St. Clair's opponents now argued that only statehood could rid them of arbitrary, undemocratic rule.[15]

Leadership of the statehood movement fell to a group of Chillicothe Republicans who opposed St. Clair on personal as well as political grounds. The Jeffersonian victory in the presidential and congressional elections of 1800 encouraged wavering Republicans in Ohio to declare openly their political allegiance. On May 7, 1800, Congress, urged on by Ohio Republicans, created the Indiana Territory, leaving the Northwest Territory to consist approximately of present-day Ohio. Republicans foresaw Ohio soon gaining admission as a state. But St. Clair doubted the Northwest Territory's capacity for self-government. The population, he wrote, consisted of a "multitude of indigent and ignorant people" who were "ill qualified to form a constitution and govern for themselves." He thought their remoteness from Washington made their loyalty to the U.S. government suspect. And Federalists feared, with good reason, that Ohio would be a Republican state.[16]

Despite widespread popular support for self-government, the election of 1800 produced a General Assembly dominated by Federalists. St. Clair's independence of the legislature, his patronage power, his influence on the election process, and his ability to exploit regional tensions proved important political advantages. In Cincinnati, previously the de facto territorial capital, resentment over the relocation of the seat of government to Republican-dominated Chillicothe significantly augmented Federalist strength.[17]

There was, of course, a great deal more to the General Assembly than political bickering and the developing movement for statehood. The people's elected representatives now had the duty to choose a nonvoting delegate to Congress and to enact laws for the territory. The first session in 1799 opened in a spirit of nonpartisanship, as St. Clair and the two houses exchanged flattering addresses and proceeded to organize. The House of Representatives submitted its nominees for the Legislative Council, and both chambers elected leaders, appointed employees, and adopted rules of procedure. The legislature elected Republican William Henry Harrison delegate to Congress. Because Harrison's only rival for the position was St. Clair's son, the election has been portrayed as a partisan victory for the Republicans, but it may have been more of a factional than an ideological triumph. In any case, the General Assembly went on to fulfill its lawmaking function with little party strife.[18]

The first law adopted by the General Assembly continued in force the acts of the governor and judges that established the basic framework of government: the militia law, the laws creating a judicial system, the criminal code, and a number of other statutes. Later in the session the legislature replaced the militia law with a more comprehensive statute. New tax laws set out detailed procedures for the levying and collection of territorial and county taxes. For territorial purposes, land continued to be divided into three classes and taxed according to its value. County taxes were imposed on town lots and on other real property valued at two hundred dollars and above; on able-bodied single men who did not have two hundred dollars' worth of taxable property; on horses, cattle, and bond servants; on watermills, windmills, and ferries; and on retailers of merchandise not produced in the territory. A small-claims act raised the monetary jurisdiction of justices of the peace to eighteen dollars, and an arbitration act authorized parties to resolve their differences through binding arbitration.[19]

Some laws reflected Ohio's rural conditions. There were new acts regulating fences, trespassing livestock, drifting canoes, and stray animals and offering bounties for the killing of wolves. To encourage social and economic growth, the General Assembly provided for the opening and maintenance of public highways, the costs of which would be paid for by a road tax, although anyone who did not pay taxes or who did not want to pay the road tax could work on the roads instead. In addition men from twenty-one to fifty years of age were subject to a work levy of two days per year. The courts could also contract for the construction of bridges at county expense. The road law required the erection of road signs at every fork "containing an inscription in legible characters, directing the way and mentioning the most remarkable places on each road, respectively." Graffiti writers could be fined.[20]

The General Assembly passed various acts of commercial regulation or promotion. One statute authorized local courts to license ferries and to regulate the rates of ferriage. Another required every gristmill operator to keep a county-sealed set of measures and limited the miller's compensation to a specified fraction of each type of grain ground. The legislature passed Ohio's first usury law, limiting the legal rate of interest to 6 percent. Two acts passed by the second territorial assembly authorized private parties to construct bridges and fixed the tolls for crossing, and another provided for inspection of agricultural products being exported and for the labeling of the packages as to the quality and quantity of their contents.[21]

Observing that "the increase of vice and immorality in a nation, eventually tends, by corrupting the human mind, to wound individual happiness, as well as to destroy national prosperity," the General Assembly took steps to safeguard the morals of the community. It prohibited many kinds of activity on the Sabbath, and profane swearing, public drunkenness, boxing, dueling, and gambling all the time.[22]

To improve the government of the territory the legislature adopted an election law, revised the law providing for a territorial treasurer, and directed the governor to appoint a territorial auditor. In its second session the first territorial General Assembly passed Ohio's first act of municipal incorporation, creating the town of Marietta. The act gave local voting rights to all adult male freeholders and taxpayers, recognized the town meeting as the main source of political authority, and authorized the election of various local officials and the levying of local taxes. Other municipal incorporation acts followed. Before long, rural townships too received powers of self-government.[23]

In addition to enacting legislation the General Assembly passed resolutions and issued addresses. For example, the House of Representatives unanimously rejected the petition of Virginia military officers to bring slaves into the territory, issued a request to the people of the territory for their patience in evaluating the system of taxation, and sent a complimentary address to President John Adams.[24]

The Drive for Statehood

In December 1801, St. Clair won a major victory when the General Assembly passed an act dividing the territory into two districts, with a boundary along the Scioto Valley and district capitals at Cincinnati and Marietta. St. Clair intended the act to delay statehood by making it harder for either of the smaller districts to get the necessary sixty thousand inhabitants and by splitting the Republican stronghold in half. Nevertheless, Chillicothe Republicans Thomas Worthington and Michael Baldwin, armed with petitions from around the territory against the division law and with fervor against the "tyrant" St. Clair, successfully lobbied Congress for a statehood act. "Attacking St. Clair and his 'tools' as obstacles to the open and rapid development of the West united a coalition of people— urban traders, large landholders, and small farmers—otherwise naturally divided by economic and regional differences," notes historian Peter Onuf. "They all shared the belief that statehood would place power in the hands of the people in their local regions and leave them free to promote their individual and group interests as they saw fit." In the winter and spring of 1802, Congress rejected the division law and passed an enabling act authorizing the people of the Northwest Territory to elect a constitutional convention as a prelude to statehood.[25]

The enabling act called for the election of convention delegates by adult male taxpayers who had been residing in the territory for at least one year before the date of the election. The act specified the number of delegates to be elected in each of the nine counties, for a total of thirty-five, in a ratio of one delegate for every twelve hundred inhabitants. Congress directed that the delegates first decide for or against statehood. Then, if they voted for statehood, they were to prepare a constitution to be submitted to Congress for approval.[26]

Some Republicans as well as Federalists opposed statehood on the grounds that the small, scattered population of Ohio could not afford the costs of state government. Privately, Federalists acknowledged that they wanted to prevent the creation of another Republican state. Although the Federalists carried their Washington County stronghold and put up a spirited fight in Hamilton County, where some Cincinnati Republicans supported St. Clair against his Chillicothe adversaries, the result was a foregone conclusion. The people overwhelmingly desired to replace the "colonial" territorial government with one responsible to themselves. Voters did not formally enroll in parties in those days, but participants in the convention agreed that the delegates included seven Federalists and between twenty-four and twenty-seven committed Republicans.[27]

The convention delegates gathered in Chillicothe on November 1, 1802. Many Federalists had realized during the election campaign that they could not win seats at the convention if they resisted the popular demand for statehood, and at the convention itself they believed they would have to vote for statehood if they were to have any influence in shaping the constitution. On the first day the delegates voted in favor of statehood 34 to 1. The high degree of consensus on statehood carried over to work on the constitution. Although the handful of Federalists frequently voted as a bloc, often in alliance with one or another faction of Republicans, they accepted the democratic principles on which the constitution rested. Afterwards, Federalists and Republicans agreed that party politics had not been prominently displayed at the convention. It helped that the delegates represented the best of a broad spectrum of Ohio society; one prominent Federalist remarked that they were, "with but few exceptions, the most intelligent men in the counties."[28]

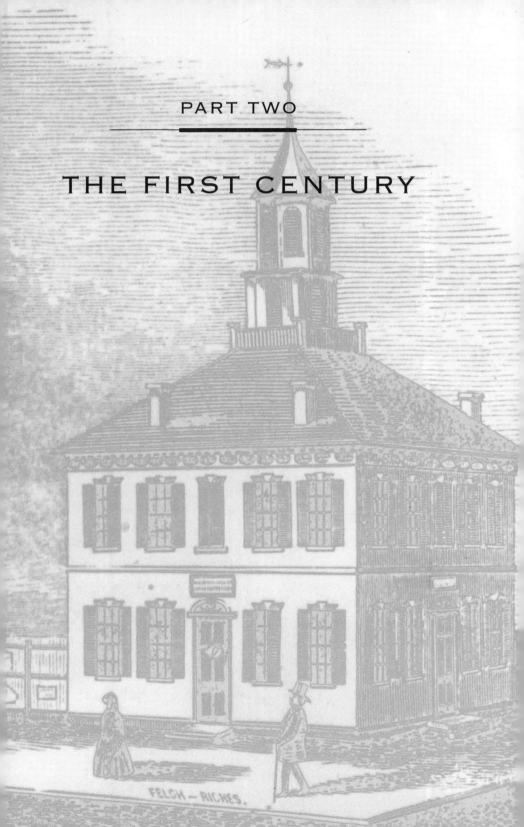

PART TWO

THE FIRST CENTURY

FELCH — RICHES.

2

REPUBLICANISM AND
REPRESENTATION

WITH THE COMING of statehood, a government dominated by the people's elected representatives replaced the "arbitrary" government of the Northwest Territory. The mechanics of representation was therefore a crucial matter for the members of Ohio's constitutional conventions. First, the conventions had to define the electorate, the group to whom legislators would be politically responsible. This proved to be a contentious question throughout the nineteenth century. Second, the framers of the constitutions had to decide whether representation would be based on geopolitical units, on population, or on some combination of the two. The 1802 convention settled rather easily on a familiar system of representation by county, with the number of representatives per county determined by population; however, the method of apportionment produced political controversy and greatly agitated the second constitutional convention a half century later.

Behind these issues lurked the fundamental question of the nature of representation. Were legislators in effect trustees for the people, with freedom to exercise their legislative powers as they saw fit? Or were they simply agents sent to the capital to carry out the people's will? The question received little explicit attention at the constitutional conventions. In theory Ohio's constitutions have always inclined toward the latter view by guaranteeing the people's right to instruct their representatives, but when the republican enthusiasm of the early years of statehood faded, so did the concern for the people's right of instruction. Only in the case of U.S. senators did the issue of instruction remain alive somewhat longer. In the nineteenth century, state legislatures elected the senators, and, until about 1840, the General Assembly occasionally issued instructions to Ohio's U.S. senators.

The Electorate

Defining the electorate in 1802 entailed two controversial issues: the enfranchisement of blacks and property qualifications. Racial matters occupied much of the convention delegates' time. A bloc of fourteen or fifteen delegates consistently opposed the interests of blacks, and enough other members often joined them to form an antiblack majority. At one point the delegates voted to prohibit blacks and mulattoes from holding civil or military offices and from testifying against whites in court, but they later struck these restrictions by the narrowest of margins. On the other hand, the delegates first voted to enfranchise the adult males of Ohio's small black and mulatto population, and then reversed themselves. (No one moved to grant suffrage to women, black or white.) The chief purpose of all the antiblack votes appears to have been to discourage blacks from the neighboring states of Kentucky and Virginia from emigrating to Ohio.[1]

The suffrage section, as reported by the committee of the whole, allowed all white males who met the age and residency requirements to vote if they "have paid or are charged with a state or county tax." A motion to strike the tax requirement failed, but the constitution as adopted did allow white males who labored on town or county roads to vote. This opened the franchise to people who did not own taxable property but who worked several days each year in lieu of paying taxes. Since the territorial laws already required all men aged eighteen to fifty-five to work two days on the public roads or procure a substitute, the constitution effectively ensured universal white male suffrage.[2]

The abolitionist crusade against slavery that began in the 1830s reawakened the issue of black suffrage. At Ohio's second constitutional convention in 1850–51, Norton S. Townshend, a member of the antislavery Free Soil Party, maintained that human governments could neither create nor destroy rights, which came from the Creator. The only purpose of government was to protect natural rights, which belonged equally to all men. Because government derived its power to render this protection from the consent of the governed, it could not legitimately impose taxes upon or demand obedience from any portion of the population without giving that portion a say in framing the laws. Townshend also condemned restrictions on suffrage as contrary to the egalitarian principles of democracy. Just as he would not vote for legislation that would confer special benefits on corporations or a privileged economic class, he declared, so he would not agree to any measure that placed any man below the common level. "Let us then have no limitations of suffrage," Townshend pleaded, "—for who does not know that all such limitations are anti-democratic?"[3]

Delegate Simeon Nash took issue with Townshend's natural rights argument. Suffrage, he asserted, was not a natural right but "a mere question of expediency," which was why minors and females could be excluded from the franchise. Other delegates insisted that Ohio was meant to be and ought to remain white man's country. The overwhelming majority evidently agreed, for only a handful supported a motion to strike the word "white" from the voting provisions.[4]

Immediately after the defeat of black suffrage, a delegate proposed deleting the word "male" from the report of the Elective Franchise Committee. The woman suffrage movement in Ohio had begun in earnest with the recent Salem women's rights convention, where orators had acclaimed universal suffrage as "a natural and inalienable right" and "the safeguard to liberty." Townshend again argued for the natural right to vote. He noted that women equaled men in intelligence and virtue and that their participation in politics would only improve political life. In view of the constant refrain sung by opponents of woman suffrage that women would neglect their domestic duties if they got involved in politics, Townshend felt constrained to point out that of the many female signatories to the women's rights petitions whom he knew personally, all faithfully discharged the responsibilities of home and family. No one else spoke for or against the motion, which lost 72 to 7. Five of the favorable votes came from men who had also voted for black suffrage, although several supporters of black suffrage opposed giving women the vote.[5]

Nine days after the defeats suffered by blacks and women, S. J. Andrews made one last, quixotic effort to change the convention's mind on black suffrage. Speaking in favor of a motion to recommit the committee's report, Andrews declared, "[T]he right to exercise the elective franchise cannot be made to depend upon caste or color. It may depend upon intelligence, upon attachment to free institutions, upon the relations su[s]tained to others, upon all the circumstances that go to make up the social condition; but a man's right to vote no more depends upon the color of his skin, than it does upon the color of his hair." But Andrews denied that suffrage was a natural right. When "sound policy" and the "public interest" required restriction of the right, then the majority might restrict it. "We exclude females," said Andrews, "upon considerations of public policy that look to their position—their happiness—the effect of marriage on their legal rights— and more than all, to the peace and harmony of the domestic relation." The motion to recommit lost overwhelmingly, and the new constitution went into effect without giving blacks or women the right to vote.[6]

Throughout the 1850s proponents of woman suffrage submitted numerous petitions with thousands of signatures to the General Assembly. A Senate select committee reported on them favorably and urged the legislature to submit a proposed constitutional amendment to the voters. The idea went no further, however, and at the end of the decade the House Judiciary Committee rejected female suffrage.[7]

At Ohio's third constitutional convention in 1873–74, the topic of woman suffrage occupied a great deal of the delegates' attention. It was no longer an appendage to the issue of black suffrage, which had been guaranteed by the Fifteenth Amendment to the U.S. Constitution in 1870. The debates, although extended, hot, and heavy, offered little that had not been said many times before. One new argument held that the right to vote was a privilege of citizenship protected by the recently adopted Fourteenth Amendment—and women were undoubtedly citizens. At one point the delegates present voted to submit the question of female suffrage to the voters, but the forty-nine favorable votes were less than a majority of all the delegates elected, and so, under the rules of the convention, the proposition failed.[8]

In 1889, the House voted 49 to 41 in favor of a joint resolution to put the issue of female suffrage on the ballot, but the forty-nine yes votes were far short of the three-fifths majority needed. A similar Senate resolution failed of adoption for the same reason. The *Ohio State Journal* thought the votes showed that woman suffrage was "nearer at hand than was supposed," but the paper's assessment proved overly optimistic. The most that advocates of female suffrage could achieve in the nineteenth century was a statute allowing women to vote in school elections. Americans regarded education as part of the nurturing, child-rearing role of women, and even if a state constitution did not allow women to vote for offices established by the constitution, it did not preclude them from voting for nonconstitutional offices such as school boards. When a school suffrage bill finally passed after several failed attempts, the sponsor telegraphed the woman suffrage association, "Woman suffrage bill a law; truth is mighty yet."[9]

Ohioans also argued over voting by aliens. The constitution of 1802 gave the franchise to white male "inhabitants," not white male "citizens." In 1809, the General Assembly required that judges of elections be satisfied that prospective voters were U.S. citizens. The citizenship requirement may have been the result of ethnocultural clashes resulting from the influx of settlers of Irish and German origin from Pennsylvania. Yankees in particular objected to the "dissolute vicious . . . wretches" among the Germans and to the Irish who threatened to gain control over local affairs around Youngstown. In 1827, a House committee recommended the calling of a constitutional convention in part to ensure that only citizens could vote. Ten years later another House committee thought it "very manifest" that the constitution allowed only citizens to vote.[10]

Nevertheless, aliens continued to cast ballots, often with the complicity of party organizations, judges of election, and the local population. The General Assembly criminalized voting by noncitizens in 1841, but enforcement must have been spotty at best. German immigrant Charles Reemelin argued briefly at the 1850–51 constitutional convention that Ohio should keep control over suffrage in the state's hands rather than allow Congress to say who could vote by defining U.S. citizenship; however, the delegates, without much debate, limited the franchise to U.S. citizens.[11]

But in a state where, in 1870, 14 percent of the inhabitants were foreign-born and another 13 percent had foreign-born parents, the issue would not stay squelched. At Ohio's third constitutional convention in 1873–74, the Committee on the Elective Franchise proposed extending the franchise to any man of foreign birth who declared his intention to become a citizen at least one year but not more than five years before offering his vote. Adolphus Kraemer noted that alien declarants voted in fourteen states. A German immigrant, Kraemer ardently defended the patriotism of immigrants and insisted that in a "great cosmopolitan nation" like the United States, they should not have to serve the five-year probationary period required by the federal naturalization law to vote. Other delegates, however, insisted that immigrants needed the years of probation to learn American ways. Pointing to the swarms of ignorant, destitute foreigners invading the country, they feared inundation and loss of control. Lewis D. Campbell, a former leader of the anti-immigrant Know-Nothing Party, even raised the specter of political domination by "foreign capitalists" such as Rothschild—code words for Jews—"colonizing" key districts with their immigrant minions. Campbell's motion to strike declarant suffrage from the committee report passed 39 to 29. Thus failed the last serious attempt to give aliens the vote, although the defeat hardly mattered since the voters rejected the proposed constitution. The loss foreshadowed a national trend, as new states rejected declarant suffrage in the late nineteenth century, and older states repealed laws that allowed it.[12]

Methods of Representation

Setting the qualifications of electors was only the first stage in establishing a system of representation. The framers of Ohio's polity also had to decide how the voters would be represented. Americans at the time of the Revolution rejected the British idea that all members of society were "virtually" represented by lawmakers they had had no say in electing. Virtual representation had led to the "rotten boroughs" of Britain, districts that had few residents but sent representatives to Parliament while some large cities sent no one. Americans could not accept the notion that members of Parliament elected in England could somehow know and care about the circumstances of colonists three thousand miles away. What Americans demanded was "actual representation"—representation by individuals who knew the interests of the electors and shared their concerns. And although Americans often established property qualifications for voting and excluded various categories of people from the franchise, they more and more thought of representation of people, not of property or geographical units such as boroughs. As egalitarian rhetoric and reform swept through America in the late eighteenth century, actual representation came to mean equal representation of people.[13]

Nevertheless, after the Revolution, states found it hard to part with traditional representation based on towns, parishes, or counties. In small states, the problem was not so bad. The population was more evenly distributed than in large states with vast, sparsely settled areas, people moved around less, and political units were more likely to be roughly equal in extent (and, incidentally, in population). Even if communities were not quite the coherent entities that the theory of corporate representation presumed, they were close enough that representation by political unit still made sense. In states with large territories and scattered, growing, mobile populations, where towns and counties were clearly collections of individuals rather than cohesive communities, the rationale for corporate representation broke down. There was no justification for the apportionment of legislative representatives on the basis of geography rather than people.[14]

Equal representation by population could be provided in at least three different ways. One way, at-large elections, never caught on with regard to state legislators, although it did gain currency for presidential electors and members of Congress. Another was election districts, with boundaries redrawn after each census. A third method involved weighted voting for geographical units: the number of representatives for each town or county would be a function of population and would be determined by formula.

The Northwest Ordinance used the latter method, and the first Ohio constitutional convention followed suit. Under the new constitution, a census of adult white males would be taken every four years. The General Assembly would then apportion representatives among the counties according to the census. Until the number of adult white males reached twenty-two thousand, the total number of representatives could not be less than twenty-four nor more than thirty-six; thereafter, the number of representatives could range from thirty-six to seventy-two. The General Assembly would also fix the number of state senators and apportion them by population among the counties or among senatorial districts created by law. The number of senators would be between one-third and one-half the number of representatives. The constitution left the General Assembly a great deal of discretion in filling in the details. It also imposed a serious burden and opened numerous opportunities for political wrangling and mischief by requiring a reapportionment every four years.[15]

Gerrymandering under the Constitution of 1802 and a particularly nasty apportionment battle in 1848–49 contributed significantly to popular support for a second constitutional convention. At that convention, Charles Reemelin, a radical Democrat from Cincinnati, set the terms of the apportionment debate by introducing resolutions aimed at taking away the legislature's power of apportionment. Under the existing constitution, he asserted, "Apportionments have been arranged by a very few men, perhaps very often by a single chairman of a committee, sitting in his room at a hotel, taking a map in his hand, not asking himself, what will be for the good of the people? . . . He asks himself no such question, but goes to marking upon the map his black lines, and red lines, and blue lines, to see how by an apportionment some particular party, or some favorite object can be best subserved and sustained." Others too railed at the corruption growing out of the General Assembly's apportionment power. In the vociferous arguments that ensued—over the retention of counties as a basis of representation, unicameral versus bicameral legislatures, large assemblies versus small, and so on—everyone seemed to agree that the General Assembly was not to be trusted with the authority to draw district boundaries.[16]

The delegates evinced a nearly universal belief that population ought to be the chief basis of representation, for unequal representation was "an outrage upon the principles of republicanism," reminiscent of the rotten boroughs of England. But attachment to the old idea of representation by territorial unit nevertheless remained strong. Delegates insisted that such venerable political divisions as counties could not be ignored in the creation of legislative districts. Reemelin proposed that every county have at least one representative so that the people would be represented by their neighbors, individuals who shared their "feelings and interests."[17]

Reconciling popular and geographical representation was not easy. Delegates floated a variety of ideas—one would have created House districts based on townships and wards rather than on counties because smaller units could more easily be arranged into equally populous districts—but no one seemed disposed to abandon political subdivisions altogether. Instead they focused their attention on single-member districts. Reemelin urged that there be one representative or senator for every so many people, the number to be fixed in the constitution. Making a rough estimate of the state's population and figuring on one representative for every 15,000 and one senator for every 30,000 inhabitants, Reemelin came up with a House of 126 members and a Senate of 65 to 75 members. As the population grew, so would the size of the General Assembly. Reemelin recommended a halt to the creation of new counties and the establishment of Senate districts in the constitution so that the number of districts would remain constant. He did not worry about the few small counties that lacked the requisite population because he assumed, incorrectly as it turned out, that they would all soon be big enough. When a unit grew large enough to have more than one representative or senator, the board of county commissioners or another local authority would divide it into single-member districts. Reemelin had opposed the division of Hamilton County into districts in 1848 (discussed in chapter 10), but his opposition, he explained, had been based on the wording of the old constitution, not on the concept of single-member districts.[18]

The notion of a legislature unlimited in size provoked debate over the relative merits of large and small assemblies. The rapid growth of the state, said some, would produce a huge, unwieldy legislature, a "mob" instead of a "deliberative as-sembly." Reemelin, however, insisted that good representation meant not repre-senting too many people. He and others asserted that the Ohio and U.S. senates were often more unruly than the larger houses of representatives. Reemelin's op-ponents proposed to fix the size of the General Assembly and allow the ratio of representation to change. Reemelin's objection to a variable ratio, aside from the possibility that it would create very populous districts, was that it would put some part of the apportionment power back into the legislature's hands and allow a General Assembly to legislate for its successor. Other delegates met this objec-tion by suggesting that the ratio be determined by executive officers.[19]

The idea of single-member districts met with general acclaim, but district lines would have to be drawn by someone, so that gerrymandering remained pos-sible. After the "scenes of anarchy and confusion" that had marked the General Assembly's exercise of the apportionment power, gerrymandering by the legisla-ture was an evil the convention intended to avoid. Some delegates thought that Reemelin's proposal to let local authorities create the districts simply transferred the power of abuse from the state to the local level. One declared that it was more republican to allow local officials to draw district lines because they were closer to the people, while another argued that the people and the press more closely scrutinized the actions of the General Assembly than those of local bodies.[20]

After much debate a badly divided convention finally settled on a scheme that combined representation by county and representation by population. The con-stitution fixed the ratio of representation, meaning that the size of the General Assembly would fluctuate. The population of the state would be divided by one hundred, and the quotient would be the ratio of representation for the House. Every county having at least one-half the ratio would have its own representa-tive; counties reaching higher thresholds would get more than one. For every fraction above a ratio that equaled one-fifth of a ratio, a county would get an additional representative for two years of the ten-year period between apportion-ments. A county that lost population might have to be combined with another. The population divided by thirty-five produced the Senate ratio. The constitution divided the state into thirty-three Senate districts, one consisting of Hamilton County and the others consisting of two or more counties. In the first Senate under the new constitution, Hamilton County would have three senators and each other district one. The constitution did not provide for single-member dis-tricts within any county or Senate district that had more than one representative or senator. The constitution implied, although it did not say so directly, that in both House and Senate districts, the legislators would be elected at large. A majority of the governor, auditor, and secretary of state would determine the ratio of representation every ten years according to the federal census and assign the appropriate number of representatives and senators to each county or district. Despite considerable grumbling, the system of apportionment created in 1850–51 remained in effect for the rest of the nineteenth century.[21]

The People's Right of Instruction

The constitutions of 1802 and 1851 both guaranteed the right of the people to instruct their representatives. Whether the lawmakers had to obey was another matter. Before the Revolution, Americans often told their representatives in colonial assemblies how to vote on particular issues. And many times the representatives, upon receiving instructions sent by town meetings or other public gatherings, felt bound to comply. But some agreed with Edmund Burke, who told his British constituents in 1774, "Your representative owes you, not his industry only, but his judgment; and betrays, instead of serving you, if he sacrifices it to your opinion." Advocates of virtual representation buttressed Burke's position by holding that a representative of the entire nation could not be bound by instructions from a single district. In America, the Revolution fostered the practice of instruction, and at least five early state constitutions explicitly recognized the right. Voters in the Northwest Territory sometimes instructed their representatives, and the General Assembly gave instructions to the territorial delegate to Congress. Ohio Federalists tended to agree with Burke, but they could not stem the democratic tide. The constitution of 1802 explicitly affirmed the right of the people "to instruct their representatives."[22]

In Massachusetts, where towns formed the basis of representation in the state legislature, the exercise of the right of instruction faded away as town meetings gave way to city government, and it largely vanished by the 1820s. In Ohio, which did not have the town meeting form of government, instructions generally came from mass meetings, a practice developed in colonies south of New England during the Revolutionary period. During a banking crisis in 1818, people at public meetings demanded that their state representatives reflect their antibank views. Some lawmakers actually complained about the lack of instructions on other matters. Republican politician John Sloane declared that "[t]he right of the people to instruct their representative, and his obligation to obey . . . is the essence of republicanism—destroy these, and you establish an aristocracy." Around the same time, during the uproar over Missouri's application to join the Union as a slave state, public meetings instructed members of Congress to vote against the spread of slavery. Nevertheless, even though Ohio did not experience the transition from town meeting to municipal government, the practice of instruction may have declined in Ohio when it did in Massachusetts. In 1820, a newspaper called for a resurrection of the right of instruction, which suggests that the practice was disappearing. It may be that the rapid growth of the state and the rise of party organizations rendered instruction impractical and ineffective. (As late as 1834, though, Congressman Robert Lytle resigned his seat because, he said, he could not vote in accordance with resolutions adopted at a mass meeting in Cincinnati.)[23]

The right of instruction remained controversial in another context. State legislatures elected U.S. senators until the twentieth century, and for many years they issued instructions to senators in the form of joint resolutions. Ohio's lawmakers generally agreed that they could not instruct U.S. representatives, who were elected directly by the people, but they did not hesitate to tell senators how they ought to vote. A typical resolution directed "That our Senators in Congress be instructed, and our Representatives be requested, to use their exertions to obtain from Congress" a donation of federal land for a road improvement project.[24]

In the 1830s, with the development of a fiercely competitive two-party system of Whigs and Democrats, the instruction of U.S. senators became a highly charged political issue. Whigs tended to believe, with their Federalist forebear Ephraim Cutler, that the instruction of U.S. senators was "indelicate and improper." Democrats had no such reservations. The parties clashed in December 1833 when the Ohio Senate adopted a resolution applauding certain policies of President Andrew Jackson. The resolution instructed Ohio's U.S. senators and requested the state's representatives in Congress to oppose any further attempts to recharter the Second Bank of the United States. When the House took up the resolution William V. H. Cushing, an anti-Jackson man, sought to amend the resolution by providing that nothing in it should "be construed as a request to any Representative in Congress to vote against the wishes of a majority of his immediate constituents." The amendment failed, and the Democratic majority passed the resolution.[25]

Following the Whigs' success in the 1834 election, Representative John P. R. Bureau moved to rescind the previous year's resolution on the grounds that "the right of instruction belongs properly to the People, and that it is an abuse of that right, whenever the Legislature instruct contrary to the popular will." After some debate in both houses, the General Assembly compromised. It rescinded the 1833 resolution, expressly withheld any opinion regarding the recharter of the Bank, and recognized "the doctrine that a Representative is bound by the will of his constituents, the people; and that in a correct discharge of his official duties, he should obey such will or resign his situation: *Provided,* Such will be ascertained and expressed in conformity with the Constitution." The resolution said nothing about the General Assembly's authority to instruct a U.S. senator. A proposed amendment stating that senators were bound by the will of the legislature when that will was in accord with the will of the people lost in the House by a vote of 39 to 31.[26]

The fuzziness of the rescinding resolution gave way in 1836 to a resounding reaffirmation of the right of instruction. After the U.S. Senate voted to censure Jackson for removing federal deposits from the Bank of the United States, the General Assembly, now firmly controlled by Democrats, instructed Ohio's senators to seek expungement of the censure from the record. The right of instruction, said the members, is "one of the fundamental principles of a Representative Government, and essentially necessary for the purity and stability of our republican institutions." If the "agents of the People" cannot comply, the resolution continued, they were duty-bound to resign. Of course, neither Ohio's Whig senator, Thomas Ewing, nor most other Whig senators subjected to similar resolutions gave up their seats.[27]

In 1838, the Whigs, once again in control of the General Assembly, called upon Ohio's members of Congress to oppose the subtreasury bill and public land policy of Jackson's handpicked successor, Martin Van Buren. The resolution "disclaim[ed] the power to give binding instructions" to members of Congress, but it asserted the legislators' right to declare the will of their constituents. That will, said the resolution, opposed Van Buren's proposals. Unable to command, the General Assembly commended its opinions to the federal senators and representatives "for their consideration and concurrence."[28]

The obvious futility of the Whig's declaration of sentiments signaled the decline of instruction as a political weapon in Ohio and elsewhere. Whig senators rejected "binding" instructions on principle, and Democratic senators often ignored them. The General Assembly took to making requests of senators rather than instructing them. In the session of 1844–45, for example, of the eight joint resolutions addressed to Ohio's senators, only one, on the vital subject of Texas annexation, actually instructed the senators on how to vote. A ninth resolution was addressed only to Ohio's representatives and therefore could not instruct, and a tenth expressed the sentiments of the General Assembly without either instructing or requesting. Scholars disagree over the extent to which the instruction of U.S. senators survived the Civil War in other states, but in Ohio the practice had all but disappeared before 1860.[29]

3

DEMOCRACY AND DISTRUST

Thomas Corwin, elected governor of Ohio in 1840, thought the state's chief executive was, politically speaking, "a mere dummy." Most delegates to the 1802 constitutional convention would have been pleased with the characterization. The first state constitution makers in the 1770s and 1780s, who had experienced the corruption of royal and aristocratic governors and judges, bequeathed to their successors a belief that the legislature ought to be the supreme branch of government. Although bills of rights provided protection against some legislative abuses of power, early state legislatures enjoyed very broad authority. Checks on that authority came not from governors or judges but from the people themselves, acting through frequent elections. Despite a trend toward more balanced government in the 1780s and 1790s, Americans, including the members of Ohio's first constitutional convention, remained committed to legislative superiority.[1]

Legislative Supremacy

In fixing the powers of the governor, the Ohio constitutional convention could look to two western states, Kentucky and Tennessee, for guidance. The second

Kentucky constitution, adopted in 1799, followed the trend toward a stronger executive by giving the governor a four-year term, the power to appoint public officers with the advice and consent of the Senate, the position of Speaker of the Senate (with the ability to break tie votes), and a weak veto (subject to override by a majority vote of each house). The Tennessee constitution of 1796 created a figurehead executive with no veto and the power to appoint only the adjutant general. The Ohio convention closely followed the Tennessee example. According to Ephraim Cutler, the delegates actually used the Tennessee constitution as a model. They gave the governor a two-year term and made him commander in chief of the state's military forces. The governor could grant reprieves and pardons, require written information from executive officers, supply vacancies in offices filled by the General Assembly, call special legislative sessions, and appoint the adjutant general. He had no other appointments at his disposal, no veto, and no major powers.[2]

The General Assembly, on the other hand, had extensive powers, limited primarily by the bill of rights. Early state bills of rights were often hortatory, declaring that certain rights "ought" to be respected. The Ohio bill of rights used obligatory language, substituting "shall" for "ought." It ranged widely, including not only freedom of religion and speech, the right to trial by jury, and other familiar guarantees, but also limitations on imprisonment for debt and prohibitions of poll taxes and transportation out of the state for the commission of crimes. The bill of rights required the legislature to ensure the fair disposition of land grant money to religious societies, and it secured the right of educational associations to incorporate.[3]

Aside from the bill of rights, the constitution contained few restrictions on the General Assembly's authority. The constitution bestowed on the General Assembly the power to appoint the secretary of state, the state treasurer and auditor, the judges of the supreme and common pleas courts, and major generals and quartermasters of the militia. It authorized the legislature to impeach and try the governor and all other civil officers and gave it considerable control over the salaries of executive officers and judges. The question of the salaries of public officials apparently generated much debate at the constitutional convention. The delegates at first agreed to set the compensation of members of the General Assembly but said nothing about the salaries of executive officers or judges. By their silence they would have left the compensation of such officials to the discretion of the legislature; however, they ultimately decided to cap the salaries of the governor, secretary of state, auditor, treasurer, supreme court judges, and presidents of the courts of common pleas, as well as the per diem compensation and travel allowances of legislators, at respectable but relatively modest levels until 1808. The General Assembly would retain the power to reduce executive and judicial salaries but not raise them above the stated ceilings.[4]

The sketchy convention journal reflects little controversy over the judiciary, but participants Ephraim Cutler and John Reily later recalled serious disputes concerning the courts. The delegates finally agreed upon a judicial system consisting of a supreme court, a court of common pleas for each county, and an undetermined number of justices of the peace. The jurisdiction of each court and the times and places of their meetings were, for the most part, left to the legislature. The General Assembly would elect the judges of the supreme and common pleas courts to seven-year terms. The constitution prohibited judges from holding any other state or federal office.[5]

While the constitution left the General Assembly with significant control over the judiciary, it said nothing about judicial checks on the legislature. Before long, a political firestorm blew up over the power of the courts to declare laws unconstitutional. The power had been advocated most famously by Alexander Hamilton in *The Federalist Papers* and had already been exercised by several state courts. In the very year of Ohio's statehood, the U.S. Supreme Court ruled in *Marbury v. Madison* that federal courts could strike down acts of Congress on constitutional grounds. But judicial review had its critics, particularly among Republicans. Federalists, less enamored of the people, tended more to believe that courts had the power to pass upon the constitutionality of acts of the other branches of government.[6]

The issue arose in Ohio with the passage in 1805 of the Fifty Dollar Act, which allowed justices of the peace to hear civil cases involving claims of up to fifty dollars. The previous limit had been twenty dollars. Justices of the peace heard cases without a jury. In 1806, in an opinion by Presiding Judge Calvin Pease, the common pleas court in Jefferson County held that the Fifty Dollar Act violated the constitutional right to trial by jury by allowing nonjury trials of claims for more than twenty dollars. In response, the House of Representatives, already concerned about the conduct of another common pleas judge, expanded its investigation to include Pease. The select committee appointed to examine Pease's conduct found that courts did have the right to pass upon the constitutionality of legislative acts. Attempts to revise the report narrowly failed in the committee of the whole house. That committee concluded that the legislature had no right to interfere with court decisions on the constitutionality of statutes unless such decisions resulted from corrupt motives, of which there was no evidence in Pease's case.[7]

But conflict over judicial review continued to roil Ohio politics. In August 1807 the Supreme Court of Ohio held in *Rutherford v. M'Faddon* that the Fifty Dollar Act violated the constitutional right to trial by jury. Judges Samuel Huntington and George Tod formed the majority; Daniel Symmes dissented, but there is no record of a dissenting opinion. Huntington and Tod conceded that many people entertained doubts about the power of courts to pass judgment on the constitutionality of legislative enactments. They maintained, however, that the General Assembly could not be the sole judge of the validity of its acts. The constitution placed limits on legislative power, but if no other body could check the power of the General Assembly, then the constitution was a "blank paper." The function of the courts, said the judges, is to say what the law is. The constitution is the supreme law, and if it conflicts with an act of the legislature, the courts have a duty to say that the act cannot be a valid law.[8]

Issued at a time of high political passions and ardent arguments over the powers of the different branches of government, the *Rutherford* decision excited politicians and the public alike. One newspaper reporter described life in Chillicothe as all "bustle and contradiction" over the conflict between court and legislature. "Legislators, governors, judges, lawyers, and farmers," he wrote, "are all together pell-mell." When the legislature convened in December, the House of Representatives, dominated by Democratic-Republicans, decided that judges did not, after all, have the authority to declare laws unconstitutional, and a member offered a resolution to appoint a committee to prepare articles of impeachment against Pease, Huntington, and Tod. The House proceeded no further in that session, and Huntington's election as governor that fall rendered any thought of his impeachment moot; however, in December 1808, the House impeachment committee reported charges against Pease and Tod. The House duly impeached both men.[9]

The impeachment charges alleged that the accused judges had set aside acts of the legislature to the detriment of justice and that they had acted from corrupt motives. At the Senate trial, Pease defended himself chiefly by asserting his honest conduct. Tod reiterated his reasoning from *Rutherford*. In response to Tod, the House managers adopted a Jeffersonian, strict constructionist approach to the constitution. The constitutional clause that reserved to the people "all powers, not hereby delegated," they argued, meant that no body could claim to have implied power. Since the constitution did not expressly grant to the courts the power of judicial review, that power did not exist. Only the people, not other branches of government, could check the power of the legislature. If the courts could exercise judicial review, then the judiciary had almost unlimited power.[10]

The Senate, which had never been as enthusiastic as the House about the impeachments, voted against Pease and Tod 15 to 9, one vote shy of the two-thirds necessary to convict. But the General Assembly thumbed its nose at the judges with a law that increased the jurisdictional limit of justices of the peace to seventy dollars. The legislators also retaliated against the offending judges, and asserted their control over the judiciary as a whole, the following December. In the "Sweeping Resolution," so called because it swept the judges out of office, the lawmakers interpreted the constitutional term limit of seven years for judges to mean that the term of a judge chosen to succeed an incumbent who had resigned should be measured from the beginning of the original term. Although Pease's term had begun in 1803, the legislature had elected Tod to succeed a judge who had resigned in 1806; the General Assembly replaced both men in 1810.[11]

In 1816, after the storm died down, the General Assembly elected Pease to the supreme court and Tod to the presidency of the court of common pleas for the third circuit. The appointments, wrote one historian, "would seem to be a vindication" for the courts. The real vindication, however, lay in the general acceptance of judicial review in Ohio. By the 1830s attorneys were regularly asking courts to declare statutes unconstitutional, and courts took for granted their right to do so. The supreme court, though, rarely struck down a law. In 1825, the court observed that the judiciary had a duty to refuse to enforce statutes that conflicted with the constitution but, to avoid usurping legislative power, only where the conflict was "plain and palpable." Not until 1843 did the supreme court declare another general statute unconstitutional, but by then the court felt no need to justify judicial review. Indeed, in what may be the supreme irony, the justices soon felt compelled to remind those who daily called upon the judiciary to restrain the legislature that courts, too, had to observe constitutional limitations on their power.[12]

Although the notion that the legislature would have to be restrained by another branch of government was alien to the majority of the framers of the 1802 constitution, distrust of the General Assembly set in early and reached serious proportions by the 1820s. In 1804, Edward Tiffin complained to Thomas Worthington about the "low, cunning, trifling, intrigueing conduct of a few restless, ambitious Spirits in our Legislature." Tiffin and other of Worthington's correspondents, sounding much like their old Federalist nemesis Arthur St. Clair, described the members of the House as inexperienced, ignorant, obstinate time wasters. During the frenzy of speculation and the banking crisis that followed the War of 1812, lawmakers, editors, and other concerned citizens fretted over the selfishness and dissipation sweeping the state and the rise of a "moneyed aristocracy." Federalists made political hay over evidence of corruption. They criticized pay raises that the Republican-controlled General Assembly and Congress gave themselves, denounced lawmakers who appointed themselves to other offices in defiance of the Ohio constitution, and decried abuses of the legislature's patronage power.[13]

The banking crisis passed, but agitation against banks and corporations generally—and with it denunciations of the General Assembly—reappeared with a vengeance in the 1830s. The storm grew out of the legislature's long-standing policy of encouraging certain types of business enterprise, originally with the purpose of establishing a foundation for community life in a frontier state. The policy accorded with a well-established American tradition embraced by both Federalists and Republicans. Legislative promotionalism started out slowly with occasional authorizations for the erection of milldams or toll bridges across navigable streams or for the construction of toll roads. Sometimes these grants of authority included the power of eminent domain (the right to take or use the land of others in return for compensation). By 1815, promotionalism had picked up considerable steam. The legislature granted numerous bank charters during the speculative whirl following the War of 1812. The first postwar General Assembly authorized the construction of nine toll bridges and a milldam, granted or extended the corporate charters of a dozen banks in a single act, and incorporated the Cleveland Pier Company, the Kendal Aqueduct Company, and the Zanesville Canal and Manufacturing Company. The Zanesville charter authorized the company not just to operate a canal but also "to erect and establish water works, and carry on manufactures and banking associations." The next legislature, displaying a similar zeal for chartering corporations, continued in force indefinitely a general incorporation law for manufacturing companies that had been passed in 1812 and was due to expire in January 1817. Under this law, various types of manufacturing enterprises, and any powered by steam, could become corporations by filing articles of association in the county recorder's office and sending a certified copy to the secretary of state. The same General Assembly also enacted a general law for the regulation of turnpike companies. The turnpike statute endowed every turnpike company with the right to lay out a road and to take land, gravel, sand, or timber for the road upon payment of compensation to the property owner. Twelve turnpike companies received corporate charters during the session, most of them under the new law. The legislature soon created a procedure by which anyone who proposed to build a "water grist mill, or other manufactory propelled by water," could, in exchange for compensation determined by a jury, obtain the right to build dams that would cause flooding on lands belonging to other people.[14]

In 1818, Governor Ethan Allen Brown called for improved "internal communications" that would "open a cheaper way to market" for Ohio's surplus produce and "raise the character of our State by increasing industry and our resources." Over the next several years, canal enthusiasts in and out of the legislature pressed their cause. In 1825, the General Assembly authorized the state to borrow money for canal construction and to pledge its full faith and credit for repayment. Canal advocates muted opposition from some quarters by endorsing tax reform. They quelled resistance from districts that the projected canals bypassed by appropriating money for roads in those areas but not for counties on the canal routes. The Miami Canal opened in 1829, the Ohio Canal in 1833. Salmon P. Chase declared with satisfaction that Ohio's internal improvements had given the state "a name and character of which her sons may be justly proud."[15]

In the next few years, however, the General Assembly expanded the internal improvements program beyond the state's capacity to pay. Everyone wanted a piece of the pie. With all parts of the state clamoring for internal improvements, the lawmakers authorized several major new canal projects and passed the Loan Law, which *required* the state to give financial aid to private canal, turnpike, and railroad companies. Railroads, a promising new form of transportation, could qualify for loans of state credit amounting to one-third of their authorized capital if private investors supplied two-thirds of the money needed for construction and the state canal board foresaw a 2 percent annual return on investment. Turnpike and canal companies could receive state subscriptions to large portions of their capital stock when private investors had taken the rest.[16]

All this economic activity on the part of the state helped shape the "second party system" of Democrats and Whigs. The first party system of Federalists and Jeffersonian Republicans ended in Ohio before 1820 as the Federalists, never strong in Ohio, faded away and the Republicans splintered into competing factions. The Whigs, who began party life as a coalition of opponents of President Andrew Jackson, generally favored active government and supported banks and soft (paper) money. Sometimes they enjoyed the cooperation of probank, soft-money Democrats who believed that banks and their notes were necessary for economic growth and, when properly regulated, benefited the whole population. Democrats tended to be more skeptical of both governmental and corporate power. Many favored hard money—gold and silver—and had no use for banks, which they characterized as mercenary, monopolistic corporations that oppressed the "producing classes." After the national financial crisis known as the Panic of 1837, hard-money, antimonopoly Democrats came to dominate the party, and Martin Van Buren proclaimed that "the less government interferes with private pursuits, the better for the general prosperity."[17]

Before the panic and ensuing depression hit, though, Democratic politicians had a hard time shaking the belief that the state should aid internal improvement projects that would serve their districts. In March 1837, Democrats and Whigs in the General Assembly united in their support of the Loan Law. Passed at a time when state funds were already heavily committed to public works, the law set no limit on the state's potential investment in private corporations. It mandated state assistance even to poorly planned enterprises, and it invited fraud. To make matters worse, the state acquired its Loan Law obligations on the eve of the great panic and depression. Scattered skepticism about public works and public aid to private enterprise soon turned into widespread revulsion against state involvement in economic affairs. As early as 1825, some Ohioans had been anxious about the increasing state debt and the imposition of taxes to pay for the canals. Between 1825 and 1830, the debt increased nearly elevenfold, from $400,000 to $4,333,000. With the inauguration of new public works in 1836 and aid granted under the Loan Law, the debt almost doubled again and by 1840 exceeded $12,000,000. The Loan Law came to be called the Plunder Law. In 1840, the General Assembly repealed the law except as to certain projects that had already begun, and, in 1842, it suspended aid under the exceptions. Skittish legislators backed away from further involvement in railroad and canal ventures, and a few radical Democrats even proposed repudiation of the state debt on the grounds that payment of the debt took money from the people's pockets and gave it to "the British lords and capitalists" who held canal bonds.[18]

Unlike some other states that had embarked on big internal improvement projects, Ohio finished its public works program without defaulting on bonds or repudiating its debt. Good fortune played a role—most canals were too close to completion to abandon, and operating canals were producing revenue—but so did the resolve of both parties in the General Assembly to maintain the public credit. The lawmakers pledged all the resources at the state's command—surplus funds distributed by the federal government in 1837, uncommitted canal lands, additional loans—to pay canal bonds. The canal fund commissioners used toll revenues to pay debts, and the state auditor, wielding authority granted by the 1825 canal law, raised canal taxes.[19]

Having survived with honor the fiscal crisis brought on by huge canal projects and mixed public-private enterprise, the General Assembly had no stomach for future state-financed internal improvements. However, with the return of prosperity in the mid-1840s, the legislature readily authorized local governments to issue bonds for or subscribe to the stock of railroad and turnpike companies. Local governments plunged headlong into railroad schemes, many of which proved worthless. The harsh experiences of state and local governments in aiding private corporations contributed significantly to the movement for a constitutional convention that would limit the ability of government to incur debt and aid private enterprise.[20]

Checks and Balances

Before 1846, calls for a constitutional convention, mostly motivated by the need to reform the judicial system or the desire to establish biennial legislative sessions, made little headway. But the combination of financial crises, bitter partisan conflicts over racial and sectional issues, the General Assembly's inability to deal with judicial backlogs, bribery and election scandals, clashes between the lawmakers and the press, and unseemly apportionment fights ratcheted up the demand. Between 1846 and 1848, resolutions in favor of a convention received majorities in one or both houses of the legislature but not the two-thirds required by the constitution. Proponents of a convention finally succeeded in 1849, when partisan passions had reached a fever pitch and popular disenchantment with government seemed deeper than ever. Whig representative Miller Pennington feared the consequences of a convention meeting under such circumstances. While judicial reform was the main reason urged for a convention, wrote Pennington, other issues such as black suffrage, bank charters, and corporations had been raised. "In the present state of party excitement," it would be impossible to get an unbiased convention. "We should not rush headlong upon the wild sea of experiment," especially when the legislature, in Pennington's view, had ample power to fix the courts. But Senator Edward Archbold, on behalf of the Senate Judiciary Committee, expressed the prevalent Democratic view when he denounced apprehensions about the "ghosts of anarchy and confusion and agrarianism and disorganization and civil strife." The constitution had many acknowledged defects that needed to be corrected, Archbold declared, and if the people could not be trusted to address them, the American adventure in popular government must be deemed a failure.[21]

In their quest for a constitutional convention, the Democrats got crucial help from Whigs and ex-Whigs associated with the Free Soil movement. As members debated the pros and cons of a convention, a bill to repeal an explosive apportionment law of 1848 was working its way through the legislature. That law, an attempt by Whigs to maintain their tenuous hold on the House by dividing Hamilton County into two election districts, raised legitimate constitutional concerns as well as political hackles. Democrats wanted its repeal. Free Soil representative Albert G. Riddle accommodated them by introducing a bill to that effect in January. On March 2, the House passed Riddle's bill by a close vote. Meanwhile, over in the Senate, only six members, all Whigs, voted against a bill to put the question of holding a constitutional convention before the people. Supporters of the measure included Whig Charles W. Goddard and ex-Whig Free Soiler Brewster Randall. But, on March 15, the House failed to muster the constitutionally required two-thirds majority for the bill. All the opposition came from Whigs. A frustrated Randall, and perhaps Goddard as well, then threatened to vote for repeal of the apportionment law if House Whigs didn't change their tune. Fearful Whig representatives quickly agreed to a deal. On March 20, the Senate, by one vote, refused to order a third reading of Riddle's bill, in effect defeating the effort to repeal the apportionment law. Both Randall and Goddard sided with the majority. The next day Goddard introduced a resolution in favor of a constitutional convention. It passed both houses easily, with only a handful of Whig diehards voting against it. In the end, the Democrats got the better of the bargain; not only did they get their convention, but in the next General Assembly, ten months after the adoption of Goddard's proconvention resolution, they and their Free Soil allies repealed the apportionment law.[22]

In May 1849, Samuel Medary, publisher of the leading Democratic newspaper in the state, established the *New Constitution,* a weekly paper meant to whip up enthusiasm for a convention. Under the motto "power is always stealing from the many to the few," the *New Constitution* identified five key goals for a convention:

sweeping reform of the judiciary, popular election of all public officers, limitations on the General Assembly's power to increase the state debt, an improved system of public schools, and authority in the people to "reform or annul" laws found to be injurious. By injurious legislation Medary probably meant special acts of incorporation and the "special privileges" they granted. In October, the people overwhelmingly approved the call for a convention, and the state plunged into "the wild sea of experiment."[23]

In 1850 and 1851, the elected delegates met to draw up a new fundamental law for the state. The document proposed by the convention and ratified by the voters did not shift power significantly from one branch of government to another, for the delegates as a whole were no more enamored of the executive or the courts than they were of the legislature; however, the new constitution did curtail the General Assembly's authority. "What kind of a General Assembly shall we have under the new Constitution?" asked a radical Democratic delegate early in the debates.

> [W]e must expect to have a General Assembly stripped of certain important powers which it before possessed; stripped of the power to enact special laws or creating special corporations; stripped of the appointing power; stripped of the apportionment power, and of the power of special legislation. We shall . . . thus take away from them as much as possible all temptation to the abuse of their powers. All this will be done with special reference to the complaints that we have too much legislation, which have come up from all quarters.[24]

In the minds of many, the legislature could no longer be trusted with the virtually unlimited power it had enjoyed under the 1802 constitution. One member of the convention declared his dismay at the evidence of "so much distrust of the legislative department." A stranger entering the convention hall, he said, "would suppose that we had lost all confidence in that department; and that we seem to be acting under the apprehension, that the entire body of our Senators and Representatives . . . wanted to trample upon the rights of the people." In fact, most of the delegates *had* lost confidence in the legislature. The new constitution drafted by the convention and approved by the people imposed major new restrictions on the power of the General Assembly.[25]

Believing that the world was "governed too much," the delegates decided upon two-year terms of office for both senators and representatives, biennial elections,

The First Century

and biennial sessions of the General Assembly (that is, sessions once every two years). Charles Reemelin bucked his fellow Democrats by arguing for annual elections and sessions. He and his allies, including prominent Whigs, feared that biennial sessions would destroy the equilibrium among the branches of government because the executive and the courts would, in effect, always be in session. The "safety of the republic" required frequent elections and annual meetings of the branch of government closest to the people. Advocates of annual sessions also maintained that the treasury needed constant watching and that appropriations for two-year periods would be difficult to calculate. They worried that biennial legislatures would stay in session longer and then rush through legislation in their anxiety to adjourn. And they predicted that special sessions would become more common.[26]

These arguments did not faze the proponents of biennial sessions. They noted, for example, that the General Assembly, convening annually, had not been very good at safeguarding the public treasury. They complained of the expense of annual sessions, the constant turmoil produced by annual elections, and the super-abundance of legislation. The people, they said, were sick and tired of all the lawmaking, logrolling, and partisanship such as had recently disgraced the General Assembly. Even the supporters of annual meetings had to acknowledge that the people wanted biennial sessions. The people got what they wanted, but biennial sessions did not work as intended. Instead of meeting every other year, every General Assembly but one before 1894 simply adjourned temporarily in the spring of its first year until the following fall or winter.[27]

The 1850–51 convention heard many tirades against banks and other corporations and fulminations against special legislation that benefited particular groups of people. Most delegates recognized the utility of corporations; they complained chiefly about the evils of special legislation and debated at great length the merits of general laws of incorporation. Opponents of a general law pointed out two potential problems: the inability of one law to address the differing needs of communities throughout the state and the legislature's loss of control over individual corporate charters. Advocates of a general law believed that a statute could be fashioned to meet these objections. More important, they saw special legislation as the source of incredible waste and corruption. Three-fourths of the laws passed by the General Assembly were special acts of incorporation, they complained. Most of them were dead letters, passed but never put into operation. Logrolling legislators rushed special laws through in a mass at the end of the session after giving them little or no consideration.[28]

Delegate G. Volney Dorsey expressed the prevailing view. Corporations brought together capital and labor in pursuit of enterprises "useful to the community," he said, "but the moment you allow your Legislature to grant special charters and to attach special privileges to individuals, then, all is wrong." Dorsey favored a general incorporation law not only to eliminate the nuisance of special laws but also "because it is more truly republican, to establish a general law, by which every association of individuals may be governed; for thereby you take away that corrupting influence always attendant upon the granting of special privileges by a Legislature, through which these 'special acts' are passed, as has been said, by a system of 'log-rolling.'"[29]

With a majority of delegates predisposed toward such views, the convention adopted constitutional provisions that prohibited special acts of incorporation, whether for business enterprises, municipalities, or nonprofit organizations; authorized the enactment of general incorporation laws; required taxation of the property of banks and other corporations to the same extent as individually owned property; and required a popular referendum on all acts that endowed associations with banking powers.[30]

The debates over legislation that conferred corporate powers inevitably involved the issue of state debt. Delegates angry over state subsidization of private companies that produced no public benefits and ran up huge public debts insisted that government "leave railroad, canal, turnpike and other corporate associations, to get along upon their own credit, without any connexion or partnership with the State whatever" and that "debt-contracting, loan laws, and money squandering may forever be put an end to—that the whole system may be dug up by the roots, and no single sprout ever permitted to shoot up again."[31]

These demands sparked debate among Democrats on the meaning of democracy. The report of the Committee on Finance and Taxation originally permitted the state to contract debts for specific internal improvements projects with the approval of the voters. The committee chairman insisted that the report embodied the principles of Jefferson and Jackson. "Who shall say," he asked, "that the voice of the people shall not be heard?" But appeals to majority rule could not overcome the animosity felt toward the General Assembly for what many delegates perceived as the enactment of special legislation for the benefit of a privileged elite. Delegates who denounced the executive veto as an obstacle to the will of the people voted overwhelmingly to take spending power away from the people's representatives. By huge margins, the convention put into the consti-

The First Century

tution severe restrictions on the General Assembly's power to spend the people's money. It imposed a state debt ceiling of $750,000 and prohibited the state from contracting any debt for internal improvements. It barred the state from lending its credit to "any individual[,] association or corporation whatever" and from becoming a joint owner or stockholder of "any company or association in this State or elsewhere, formed for any purpose whatever." It prohibited the state from assuming the debts of any political subdivision or corporation and forbade the General Assembly to authorize any subdivision to become a joint owner or stockholder of any company or to raise money for or loan its credit to any company.[32]

The executive veto received respectful consideration at the convention of 1850–51 such as would have been impossible fifty years earlier. The report of the standing Committee on the Executive Department stirred up a row by recommending the veto. A Democratic opponent declared that "the power which the people have to elect their representatives was wisely conferred for the purpose of enabling the people to direct and control all the subjects of legislation as they might desire. . . . I would rather the people should check the will of the Governor, than the Governor should check the will of the people." But a fellow Democrat denounced the "delusion" that the people's liberty consisted of their power to make laws. "Is it true," he asked, "that liberty resides with the government and proceeds from it, or is it true that in our government all liberty is possessed positively and absolutely by the masses, and can be obtained only, or taken away rightfully, by their free consent and will[?]" In his view, the executive veto was an instrument for the preservation of liberty, as its use by President Andrew Jackson had demonstrated. The convention struck the veto from the committee's report.[33]

Judicial review was not a major issue at the second constitutional convention, but the organization of the judiciary was, as it had been from the beginning of statehood. After extended debate and controversy, the delegates created a judicial system consisting of a five-member supreme court, district courts each made up of one supreme court judge and the common pleas judges of the district with appellate and limited original jurisdiction, common pleas courts, probate courts, justices of the peace, and such other courts as the legislature might create. The judicial article of the new constitution reflected the prevailing distrust of the General Assembly by transferring to an expanded electorate the power to choose judges.[34]

The new constitution restrained the General Assembly in other ways, too. It gave the job of electing the secretary, auditor, and treasurer of state, along with the new offices of lieutenant governor and attorney general, to the voters rather than the legislators. It placed restrictions on the creation and division of counties, a major activity of the General Assembly in the past. It banned retroactive laws. It required the General Assembly to appoint commissioners to reform legal procedure and to tax all real and personal property "by a uniform rule . . . according to its true value in money."[35]

The 1851 constitution did grant one new power to the legislature, although it was a power to propose and not dispose. The first constitution could be amended only by a convention called for by the voters upon the recommendation of two-thirds of the General Assembly. The new constitution still contemplated amendment by convention—indeed, it mandated that every twenty years the electorate have an opportunity to call another convention—but it also permitted amendment by resolution of the General Assembly, subject to approval by the voters.[36]

While the convention delegates came up with answers to such touchy political questions as apportionment, legislative sessions, the veto, and the selection of judges, they threw up their hands in frustration over two great social issues, education and temperance. The delegates readily acknowledged the miserable state of public education in many parts of the state. But, after extended arguments over funding, teacher education, the length of the school year, and the office of state superintendent of schools, they rejected attempts to write specific criteria into the constitution and explicitly or implicitly decided that these matters were best left to the discretion of the General Assembly. "Enjoin upon the Legislature the duty of establishing an efficient system," said one delegate, "and we shall have done our duty." Another declared that the convention "ought not by an iron rule, to determine absolutely with regard to this matter, what could be better done by the General Assembly." Rather, the convention should assert "the general principle that there should be schools; and that the means for supporting them should be provided; and that the details should all be left to the General Assembly." And so the convention simply directed the General Assembly to establish "a thorough and efficient system of common schools."[37]

Temperance proved equally perplexing to the members of the convention. Despite a barrage of temperance petitions, some delegates believed that the majority of voters opposed stricter regulation of liquor and would defeat the constitution if it included language that might lead to prohibition. Even professed friends of temperance objected to legislating morality. One delegate accused temperance crusaders of wanting to take away the General Assembly's power to license the liquor traffic in order to make the alcohol problem so bad that the legislature would enact prohibition. Too controversial for a definitive constitutional provision and too warmly advocated by a swelling temperance tide, restraint of the liquor trade wound up as a separate proposition on the ballot. The proposition, reported by a special committee, read: "No license to traffic in intoxicating liquors shall hereafter be granted in this State, but the General Assembly may by law, provide against evils resulting therefrom." No doubt to the surprise of many delegates, it passed easily. Some realized that the wording was ambiguous and could lead to trouble, which in fact it did.[38]

The new constitution revealed the progress of the "American principle," as one delegate called it, "to gradually take more and more power from the government and leave more to the individual man." People simply did not trust the government as much as they had in the early days of the republic, when rule by the people was seen as the remedy for the corruption of power. Commenting on the convention's handiwork, Cincinnati lawyer Rutherford B. Hayes wrote, "Government no longer has its ancient importance. . . . The people's progress, progress of every sort, no longer depends on government."[39]

"A Necessary Evil"

It was not long before the General Assembly started considering constitutional amendments that might restore some of its lost authority. In 1856, the legislature appointed a joint committee to recommend changes. The committee pointed to one chief source of the document's defects: "*legislating in the Constitution.*" In a rapidly growing and changing state, it reported, no one ought to presume to know what laws should or should not be passed for the public good, yet the constitution of 1851 sought "to regulate the detailed action of the government throughout all coming time." Pursuant to the committee report the General Assembly proposed five constitutional amendments that would have removed some of the "fetters" placed upon the legislature by the constitution. The amendments called for single-member districts, annual sessions, the power to enact special laws for the benefit of corporations "in peculiar cases," and the power to moderate some of the effects of the uniform rule of taxation. A fifth proposed amendment would have modified the district courts. In each case, a huge majority of those voting on the issue favored adoption; however, the constitution required that amendments be approved by a majority of the total votes cast at the election. Because more than

40 percent of the electors who went to the polls ignored the constitutional issues, no amendment received a majority of all the votes cast. As a result, all the amendments failed.[40]

In 1871, impelled by temperance agitation, never-ending complaints about the judicial system, and popular demand for closer regulation of railroads, the electorate seized the opportunity to call a constitutional convention. By the time the convention met in 1873, a depression had also revived the old fears of government-backed internal improvement projects. The convention's Committee on Public Debt and Public Works recommended allowing political subdivisions greater authority to aid the construction of railroads and other public improvements, but opponents fought it fiercely. Existing constitutional language was bad enough, they said; it fostered waste and corruption as "[c]unning men, anxious for jobs and plunder," lobbied for legislation such as the Ferguson Law, "enacted to enable [Cincinnati] to build a railroad in the State of Kentucky," and the Boesel Law, "enacted to enable everybody to build railroads anywhere." The convention voted to keep existing prohibitions and to further prohibit political subdivisions from owning or helping to construct railroads or canals.[41]

Besides refusing to expand legislative authority with regard to the financing of internal improvements, the convention acknowledged the importance of the judicial and executive branches of government as checks on legislative power. Judicial review had long since become a generally accepted fact as well as theory of governmental life; in the 1850s alone the Ohio Supreme Court struck down statutes relating to taxation, juries, eminent domain, legislative appointments, and other matters. Advocates of longer judicial terms of office at the convention referred to the judiciary as the "most important" branch of government and as the shield of the people against their oppressors (the great corporations, against which the legislators were too inexperienced and unsophisticated to offer protection).[42]

The convention also adopted the executive veto. The subject engendered lengthy and vituperative debates. Proponents differed on the form the veto should take, but most agreed that the General Assembly had demonstrated the need for it. They pointed to a history of "acts of questionable constitutionality and doubtful expediency"; to the "superabundance of legislation," much of it poorly drawn and hastily considered; to legislative corruption, partisanship, and, in the growing urban centers where many people crowded into small districts, the influence of passion and prejudice. Opponents predicted that the governor would use the veto for partisan purposes, to override the will of the majority, and to block good legislation as well as bad. The governor, they said, was not better qualified than the majority of the legislature to decide what ought to be law, and he was just as likely to be corrupt. As in 1850–51, there were those who argued that the veto strengthened democracy and others who insisted that it was undemocratic.[43]

A long, drawn-out affair, the convention failed to satisfy temperance advocates or to rouse popular enthusiasm; its proposed constitution and three separate proposals suffered a resounding defeat at the polls. In 1891, the voters refused to call another convention. Perhaps they recalled the futility of the previous one, or they may have felt that the constitution's amending process provided a sufficient avenue for change.

Aside from the amendments proposed in 1857 and the products of the 1873–74 constitutional convention, only two amendments made the ballot before 1875. Then, between 1875 and 1900, the General Assembly placed twenty amendments before the voters. They dealt with everything from a tax on dogs to the organization of the judiciary. About half of these late-nineteenth-century proposals failed only because so many electors who turned out to vote for governor or president did not vote on them. Of those that passed, none enhanced the General Assembly's power. Despite periodic bursts of enthusiasm—during the opening days of the Civil War, for example, or the postwar railroad boom— the public generally took a dim view of the legislature. That substantial segments of the public may have bellowed for laws that later turned sour made little difference, especially when corruption, absenteeism, and inefficiency plagued the legislature. After the wasted convention of 1873–74, the General Assembly continued to decline in public esteem until it came "to be regarded as a kind of necessary evil, to be patiently endured until such time as a satisfactory substitute can be agreed upon."[44]

4

DELEGATES FRESH
FROM THE PEOPLE

O N MAY 28, 1850, John L. Green, representing Ross County at Ohio's second constitutional convention, declaimed against a proposal to increase the terms of state senators from two years to four, with half the senators elected every other year. Green preferred that all senators go before the voters every two years, so that the whole body would come "fresh from the people." Thirteen years later, Ohio congressman Samuel S. Cox, nicknamed "Sunset" from his fulsome description of a sunset in the *Ohio Statesman*, declared that Republicans would not run roughshod over the Democratic minority in the House. "You forget," he cautioned his adversaries, "that we come fresh from the people, covered all over with their generous approbation." In nineteenth-century America, the "fresh infusion of public sentiment" into legislative bodies was the essence of representative government.[1]

The Legislators

Who were these delegates who came "fresh from the people" to speak for their fellow Buckeyes in the General Assembly? And how did the people choose them?

Most were obscure even in their own lifetimes and are completely unknown today. Senate clerk William A. Taylor compiled a session-by-session list of members in 1891, giving the names of the members and the districts they represented. Others updated and revised Taylor's work, adding an alphabetical roster that included each member's dates of service. The *Hundred-Year Book*, published on the occasion of Ohio's statehood centennial, purported to list every legislator to that time. Unfortunately, errors and omissions abounded. Moreover, neither Taylor nor his successors provided any biographical information about the members other than their names and dates of service.[2]

Beginning in the 1850s, some House and Senate journals included rosters of the members. The rosters varied in content but might include such information as the members' ages, occupations, party affiliations, and places of residence. From these rosters and material gleaned from county histories it is possible to paint a rough collective portrait of Ohio's nineteenth-century legislators. The profiles presented here are not the result of scientific sampling or exhaustive research, and the less-than-exacting standards of some nineteenth-century historians require that their information be taken with a dose of skepticism. But they will have to suffice until some dedicated scholar comes along to dig out the data and subject them to rigorous scrutiny.[3]

The early legislatures had few native Ohioans, and even after the passage of more than half a century a majority of lawmakers came from other states or countries. Most belonged to the great westward migration of the American people. Pennsylvania and other eastern states provided a large proportion of Ohio's lawmakers, and Ohio supplied many of Indiana's. Nearly one-fifth of Indiana's legislators from 1851 to 1889 were born in Ohio. Of the fifty-nine members of Ohio's Tenth General Assembly (1811–12) whose birthplaces have been discovered, not one was born in the Northwest Territory, which was first settled just twenty-three years before that legislature met. About one-quarter came from Pennsylvania and another quarter in equal parts from Maryland and Virginia. (In those days, Virginia included what is now West Virginia and bordered Ohio.) Seven hailed from Ireland, one from Wales, and one from France. Fifteen years later, the legislature still contained almost no home-grown Ohioans, but the foreign-born cohort dropped from 15 percent to 4 percent of the total, and one of the foreigners was born in Spanish Louisiana, which had since become U.S. territory. Pennsylvania supplied nearly one-third of the members, Virginia and Maryland a quarter (mostly from Virginia), and New England a quarter. As Ohio grew, the picture changed radically. In 1856, natives made up more than three-fifths of the state's population and nearly half the legislature. The disparity may be owing to a higher percentage of youngsters among the Buckeye-born. Over time, the difference disappeared. By the end of the century, about three-quarters of both the population of Ohio and the membership of the General Assembly were born in Ohio.[4]

The typical nineteenth-century lawmaker was young or middle-aged by modern standards. The vast majority were in their thirties and forties, with senators usually averaging a year more in age than representatives. Before 1850, the members averaged about forty-three years old. There are no statistics for life expectancy in Ohio in 1850, but males born in Massachusetts that year, if they survived the dangers of childhood then so prevalent and made it to age twenty, could expect to live to be sixty. By 1896, the life expectancy of twenty-year-olds in Massachusetts had improved by only a year, but the average age of Ohio legislators had risen to forty-seven in the House and forty-eight in the Senate. Throughout the century, members in their fifties, who in those days would have been regarded as senior citizens, always outnumbered members in their twenties in both houses.[5]

Determining the occupations of members before 1850 is difficult because legislators did not report their jobs for publication in an official roster. Other sources such as county histories sometimes provide occupational information, but they do not always say whether an individual engaged in a particular pursuit before, during, or after his service in the legislature. Some members had multiple occupations. Taking into account the vagaries of labeling under such circumstances, it seems clear that, throughout the nineteenth century, farmers and lawyers held more seats in the General Assembly than did men who worked in any other field. Farmers, some of whom were also millers or merchants, constituted a third of the membership of the Tenth General Assembly. At least six lawmakers were attorneys and perhaps another half dozen had judicial experience beyond the level of justice of the peace. About a dozen legislators were businessmen of some sort, but this category covers a lot of ground: merchant, banker, hotel and tavern keeper, locksmith, distiller. At least four appear to have owned mills without having been farmers. A few physicians, clergymen, and surveyors and at least one teacher also sat in the Tenth General Assembly. Several members had held local public office, such as justice of the peace, sheriff, or court clerk. The Twenty-fifth General Assembly (1826–27) had a similar makeup. Farmers and lawyers predominated, with most of the rest being businessmen or tradesmen of one sort or another.

In 1856, farmers and lawyers still constituted over half the membership of the General Assembly. The proportion of farmers rose to nearly one-third of the members—more than one-third if we include those who listed dual occupations. Farmers gained at the expense of attorneys, but the latter still approached one-quarter of the total. Almost one-fifth of the members were professionals of some kind other than lawyers: physicians (10 percent of the total), ministers, a teacher, an editor, an engineer. About 10 percent of the members, all in the House, were craftsmen or workers. There was one law student and one "citizen." The legislature of 1896 reflected the spectacular growth of cities, industry, and commerce in Ohio after the Civil War. Lawyers had held their own, making up over a quarter of the membership; however, farmers had dropped to just under 20 percent, or a little more if those with dual occupations are counted. Businessmen—merchants, bankers, manufacturers, grain dealers—now accounted for almost one-third of the members. Doctors, teachers, writers, newspapermen, and other professionals and white-collar workers made up another 16 percent. The rest were a hodge-podge of artisans, workers, and retirees.

Lawyers played an important role in the operation of the General Assembly. The public often regarded lawyers as shysters and charlatans, and in fact some attorneys had little legal learning. In 1845, John Brough, a future governor who was already well-known as a politician and newspaper editor, did not know much about the law, but he added attorney-at-law to his résumé by treating the court-appointed examining committee to the best bourbon in town. Some leading legislators had no legal training at all, but the legislature would have been hard-pressed to function effectively without lawyers, especially since the members had no professional staff to assist them. David Purviance, a nonlawyer who served in the General Assembly for many years in the first half of the century, later recalled that while there was "much talent and good judgment among the farmers and mechanics," few of them could draft a bill properly. A legislature could have too many lawyers, thought Purviance, but it needed some "as they were generally well qualified to bring up business correctly."[6]

All the members of the General Assembly had one thing in common throughout the nineteenth century: they were men. Until the last two decades of the century, they were all *white* men. Between 1880 and 1900, a handful of black Republicans sat in the House and one, a member of Cleveland's light-skinned African American elite, held a seat in the Senate. All but one represented either Hamilton or Cuyahoga County. Their nominations generally involved racial politics: the balancing of votes to be gained and lost by black candidates, promises not to support antidiscrimination legislation, the number of blacks one county could run at a time. But the election of blacks cannot be attributed to the black vote, however important that may have been in close contests. Hamilton and Cuyahoga counties elected their big legislative delegations on an at-large basis, and African Americans made up a small percentage of the total vote. John P. Green of Cleveland, who served in both houses, estimated that blacks constituted only 1 or 2 percent of Cuyahoga's electors; census returns suggest a far lower percentage than that. Benjamin Arnett, a mulatto, represented Greene County, which in 1880 was about 15 percent black.[7]

Turnover among the legislators was high throughout the century, but rapid turnover coexisted with considerable experience. More than three-quarters of the Tenth General Assembly—twenty-one of twenty-two senators and thirty-one of forty-six representatives—had previously sat in the state legislature. Although only sixteen of the representatives had served in the House of the Ninth General Assembly, making for a turnover from one session to the next of about 78 percent, most of the representatives had prior or subsequent service in the House. The Senate enjoyed more stability. Of the twenty-two senators, fifteen had served in the Senate of the Ninth General Assembly. Because senators had two-year terms and only half were up for election each year, a comparison of nonconsecutive legislatures provides a better idea of the turnover rate in the Senate. Only eight men sat in the Senate of both the Eighth and Tenth General Assemblies, for a turnover rate over the two-year period of 73 percent. But the Senate, like the House, had a great deal of experience; seventeen senators had been elected to the House or the Senate, or both, of legislatures before the Ninth General Assembly.

Some members of the Tenth General Assembly had extensive legislative careers. Thomas Kirker served in either the House or the Senate in every General Assembly but one from 1803 through 1817 and then again from 1821 through 1825. Eight times he was elected Speaker of either the House or Senate. Robert F. Slaughter won election to five terms in the House and three in the Senate between 1803 and 1832. Joseph Foos, one of the founders of Columbus, sat in the Senate for seven terms between 1808 and 1828. William Gass served numerous times in both houses over a thirty-year period beginning in 1803. David Purviance spent many years in the Kentucky legislature before moving to Ohio, where he won election once to the House and three times to the Senate. Only half a dozen members made the Tenth General Assembly their sole stop in the legislature.

In the Twenty-fifth General Assembly, too, the great majority of the members had been there before: more than three-fifths of the representatives and more than three-quarters of the senators. Many served again in subsequent legislatures. Some had long legislative careers. James Shields served almost continuously from 1806 through 1828. John McLaughlin had a couple of hiatuses, but he sat often in either the House or the Senate between 1804 and 1835. Robert F. Slaughter and Joseph Foos of the Tenth General Assembly were back for the Twenty-fifth. A significant gap often separated years of service. Fisher Blocksom, elected to four terms in the House before 1833, won election to the Senate in 1846. Philip Lewis left the House in 1808 but returned for three terms beginning in 1824 and subsequently served two terms in the Senate. Twenty years separated William Coolman's penultimate and final years in the legislature. For George House the gap was twenty-six years. More than 80 percent of the members of the Twenty-fifth General Assembly had been elected before or would be again.

There was a common though not universal custom of relinquishing an office after two terms—a sort of informal term limit. The results were especially glaring in the House, where the entire membership was elected every year. For example, while thirty-two House members elected in 1822 were reelected in 1823, only sixteen representatives elected in 1822 were also elected in 1824, and nine of those had not served in the intervening year. These numbers equate to a turnover rate of more than 50 percent from 1822 to 1823 and about 75 percent from 1822 to 1824. Only 10 percent of the House members served in all three terms.

Calculating and comparing turnover rates over the course of the nineteenth century—indeed, until 1966—is complicated by the fluctuating sizes of the House and Senate and by electoral changes wrought by the constitution of 1851. Under the new constitution, representatives as well as senators served two-year terms. House terms all expired at the same time, but half the Senate was elected every other year. Nevertheless, one thing is clear: at some point, the turnover rate increased. The change may have been due to the growing and changing nature of the state's population, the rise of the cities, the development of highly competitive political parties, the new constitution, or some combination of these and other causes. Whatever the reasons, the percentage of members who retained their seats from one General Assembly to the next, and from one legislature to the second succeeding legislature, dropped dramatically. Fewer than 40 percent of the representatives in the Sixty-fourth General Assembly, elected in 1879, belonged to the Sixty-fifth House. The Senate retention rate was less than 30 percent. Between the Sixty-third and Sixty-fifth General Assemblies, there was almost a 100 percent turnover. The seesawing of political control in the 1880s cannot entirely account for this phenomenon. Republicans controlled both houses of the General Assembly from 1896 through 1900, but the legislatures that convened in those two years had just two members in common, and one of those had not served in the intervening legislature.

The General Assembly naturally had a wide assortment of luminaries and mediocrities between 1803 and 1900. The membership included two future presidents of the United States (Garfield and Harding) and many individuals who later served in Congress or other high positions in the state or national government. But these members did not necessarily stand out as state legislators. Garfield might have, but he left after one term to fight in the Civil War and then went on to national prominence as a congressman and president. Thomas Kirker, on the other hand, set a nineteenth-century record for holding speakerships, but he "remains a rather obscure figure" who may have been either a dominating politician or a popular figurehead.[8]

Alfred Kelley was arguably the most influential member of the General Assembly before 1900. Neither Kelley's son-in-law, who privately published an appreciative biography in 1888, nor modern-day historian Harry N. Scheiber, who wrote a lengthy article on Kelley, provides much detail on Kelley's legislative career. But Kelley the lawmaker had an enormous impact on public policy. Born in Connecticut in 1789, Kelley accompanied his uncle to Cleveland in 1810 and soon became that settlement's first lawyer. In 1814, he was the youngest member of the House of Representatives. It was the first of his dozen terms in the General Assembly. Kelley pioneered the abolition of imprisonment for debt, worked to secure rights for blacks, and sought to improve the system of public schools. He also pushed for internal improvements, acquired expertise in canal construction and finance, and, as a canal commissioner in the 1820s, was instrumental in bringing Ohio's canals into being. When the state overextended itself, against Kelley's advice, in building canals, he negotiated financial deals that kept the state from defaulting on its obligations. Back in the legislature in 1844, Kelley wrote and shepherded through the Senate legislation that salvaged Ohio's banking system and revamped its tax laws. As the leading Whig in the legislature, Kelley roused the ire of Democrats. One groused that controversial resolutions had been "rushed through under the dictation of Alfred Kelley, by those who bow to his dictation." To his opponents, Kelley was the head of a "corrupt clique,—the pliant tools of a horde of swindlers and stock-jobbers." After the 1846 session, he left the legislature for good to become the chief builder of railroads in Ohio.[9]

Alfred Kelley. *Reproduced by permission of the Ohio Historical Society*

Kelley at least remains known to modern scholars. Others who were prominent in their day are now mere asides, if that. Consider Thomas Kirker, the oft-elected Speaker. He was nineteen years old when, in the midst of the American Revolution, he emigrated with his family from Ireland to Pennsylvania. Around 1790, he married, moved to Kentucky, and a few years later settled in what later became Adams County, Ohio. In territorial days he served as a judge and a Republican member of the constitutional convention. Kirker was elected to the House in the first state General Assembly and then to the Senate, where he remained until 1815. Seven times he was Speaker of the Senate. After a break of one session, the voters sent him back to the House, where he was elected Speaker, for a single term and then to the Senate again from 1821 to 1825. In 1807, Senate Speaker Kirker became acting governor when Edward Tiffin resigned, and the next year Kirker ran for governor as the candidate of Republicans who had had enough of Thomas Worthington and the political dominance of the Scioto valley. Kirker and Worthington split the Republican vote and lost to Samuel Huntington, a nominal Republican who ran with Federalist support. Notwithstanding

this record, modern histories of early Ohio barely mention Kirker and tell us nothing of him as a legislator.[10]

Seabury Ford has faded into oblivion altogether. Ford served in the General Assembly almost continuously from 1835 through 1848, held the speakership in both houses, and won a contentious gubernatorial race in 1848. According to Albert G. Riddle, Ford's onetime law student and longtime friend, Ford thoroughly prepared himself for legislative work, assiduously gathered facts and figures from official reports and other available sources, "and brought to the discharge of his duties a carefully-acquired fund of information, such as few men, even of that time, were masters." Riddle attributed to Ford more than any other individual the Whig reforms of the state banking, taxation, and common-school systems of the 1840s. But the major American biographical dictionaries do not include entries on Ford, and modern histories of Ohio mention him only as the man whom the General Assembly finally declared governor during the turbulent session of 1848–49.[11]

Total obscurity envelops many once-important lawmakers. Edward Archbold is a prime example. Representing Monroe County as a Democrat in both the House and the Senate in the 1840s, Archbold contributed importantly to the de-

Seabury Ford. *Reproduced by permission of the Ohio Historical Society*

bates over major issues. He served on either the House or the Senate Judiciary Committee in each of his four terms in the General Assembly and chaired the Senate committee in his last term. He wrote thoughtful standing and select committee reports, and sometimes lengthy minority reports, on a wide range of subjects: the repeal of the Black Laws (which he opposed), capital punishment (which he defended), the principles of taxation, and other matters. When most Senate Democrats "absquatulated" in an attempt to prevent a quorum during the great apportionment ruckus of 1848, Archbold refused to bolt. After leaving the General Assembly he took a leading part in the constitutional convention of 1850–51. In short, Archbold seems to have been a key Democratic figure in the legislature. Yet he is now unknown. Even a history of Monroe County tells us only that Archbold published a newspaper for a few months in 1836, served for a time as the county prosecuting attorney, was at some point one of thirteen lawyers in Woodsfield, and represented Monroe County in the legislature.[12]

Then there were the run-of-the-mill members who appeared briefly, made no impact, and went home. Abraham Hegler, a Whig who served one term in the House shortly before Archbold's first election, is as unknown as Archbold but more deservedly so. He is surely more typical of the thousands of men who sat in the General Assembly during the nineteenth century. A prosperous Ross County farmer who eventually owned five thousand acres of land, he migrated from Virginia to Ohio in 1809 and within a few years was a militia officer and justice of the peace. His surviving letters suggest that he was a reasonably intelligent but not highly educated man who took a lively interest in his surroundings in the capital but not much in legislation. The roll-call votes recorded in the 1838–39 House journal reveal Hegler's diligent attendance at the daily sessions, but his name rarely appears in other contexts. Hegler served on the Committee on Agriculture and Manufacturing, for which he made one report on a minor matter to the House. He presented several petitions on behalf of constituents, including two in favor of temperance and one to repeal racially discriminatory laws. He also introduced at least one bill, which sought to amend the statute that regulated tavern licenses. The bill must have been innocuous because it did not go to a standing committee and it passed the House without a recorded vote. The Senate postponed the bill indefinitely at the end of the session, as Hegler's short and uneventful legislative career came to a close.[13]

The years after the Civil War seem to have produced few notable legislators. The high turnover in membership, growing influence of lobbyists, and increase in corruption no doubt made the General Assembly a less attractive arena than the exciting new worlds of business, big-city government, and higher education for men of talent and knowledge. But the legislature was not entirely bereft of accomplished individuals. For example, James R. Garfield, the murdered president's son, in two Senate terms at the end of the century established himself as a Progressive reformer, although his condescending criticism of "kindergarten politics" didn't win him any friends in the legislature. Garfield would later be the U.S. secretary of the interior, a member of the federal Civil Service Commission, and the Progressive candidate for governor of Ohio. But if fellow Progressive Frederic C. Howe's assessment is correct, the turn-of-the-century members of the General Assembly were for the most part an unimpressive lot.[14]

Getting Elected

We turn now from the question of who the people sent "fresh" to sit in the General Assembly to how the people chose them. For starters, would-be members had to be eligible for office under the Ohio constitution. The constitution of 1802, which remained in effect for almost half a century, required that every

James R. Garfield. *From the George Grantham Bain Collection, Library of Congress*

member be a citizen of the United States, a resident of the county or district he represented, and a taxpayer. A member of the House had to be twenty-five years old, of the Senate thirty. The constitution did not explicitly exclude blacks or women from public office, but everyone took their exclusion for granted. The constitution adopted in 1851 retained a residency requirement but otherwise simply required that every officeholder be qualified to vote. Since electors did not have to be taxpayers, neither did legislators. But electors, and therefore members, did have to be white male citizens at least twenty-one years of age. The Ohio Supreme Court held in 1842 and reaffirmed after the adoption of the second constitution that "white" meant "nearer white than black." In theory, then, individuals who had some African ancestry could hold seats in the legislature. The federal constitutional amendment of 1870 that prohibited racial discrimination in state voting laws incidentally made Ohio's African American men eligible to serve in the General Assembly regardless of the shade of their skin.[15]

In early Ohio, candidates for the General Assembly emerged in various ways. The names of nominees began to show up in newspapers in the summer, often as a brief announcement that so-and-so "is a candidate" for a particular office or "will serve if elected." Sometimes newspapers published the names of supposed candidates heard around the courthouse or local tavern, occasionally to the surprise of the persons named. If a candidate was not well-known, the announcement might include a bit of background. Describing the nomination process to his father back in Vermont, a resident of Urbana wrote in 1818 that everyone who wanted to run for the legislature "Declares himself a candidate in the Public print or Hand Bills" and stoops "to the turpitude of self praise, so much, as to declare 'that he thinks himself amply qualified to represent his constituents & can do it better than any other man.'" Because self-nominations smacked of bad taste, if not downright antirepublicanism, they sometimes appeared in humorous form or with apologies for their "indelicacy."[16]

Anonymous individuals might propose slates of candidates, but these slates carried less weight than tickets adopted at meetings, whether of small groups of influential men, public gatherings, or county conventions. Township meetings, often advertised in advance by handbills or newspaper notices, were common but not as significant as countywide assemblies that could claim to represent the wishes of a larger constituency and a consensus that transcended local differences. Actual attendance might be low, perhaps only a couple of dozen men. The resulting tickets were published in the newspapers without much detail about the meeting, giving an impression of broad support and unanimity. A less flattering truth sometimes surfaced when disgruntled electors alleged that a meeting had been rigged in favor of a particular candidate by such tricks as limiting the circulation of notice of the meeting or packing the meeting with paid bystanders or a candidate's employees.[17]

Dissatisfaction with public meetings led to the wider use of county nominating conventions in which the number of delegates from each township reflected the township's population. Pioneered in territorial days by Hamilton County Republicans, conventions appealed to voters who believed they provided more equitable representation and to party leaders who thought they fostered party discipline. It took some time for the convention system to become firmly established. Dissident factions sometimes broke away and nominated "independent" tickets. Challenges to the official Republican ticket rarely succeeded, in part because the dissidents usually had to rely on Federalist support, which left them open to charges of political impurity. Republicans also had to deal with the infiltration of individuals who got elected to county conventions without intending to support the ticket if it did not suit them. Any insistence on party discipline, however, ran up against a well-entrenched feeling that parties and partisanship were bad things. Most Federalists and many Republicans deplored parties as antithetical to republican liberty.[18]

Federalists also charged that Republican party managers secretly chose their candidates in advance and then used popularly elected conventions to ratify their choices. By the mid-1820s, delegate conventions had in fact become the tools of party leaders, enabling Federalists, who had stopped contesting elections in their own name and no longer felt compelled to ape Republican political tactics, to criticize the delegate system as "aristocratic." Proconvention Republicans argued in reply that popularly elected conventions, meeting in public and deriving their authority from the people, gave voice to the wishes of the community, including those humbler members of society who might otherwise not be heard. They also insisted that by settling on a single candidate for each office behind whom the party could unite, the convention system reduced the "jargon and discord" that a multiplicity of candidates produced.[19]

For a time, nominating conventions fell into disrepute. Private nominations by would-be officeholders or their friends gained respectability. Other nominations came from groups of men such as grand juries and assemblies of militia officers who normally met for other purposes. Delegate conventions continued to meet in some counties, but nomination by a convention could hinder more than help a candidate, and rival nominations might be made by general public meetings, gatherings of reformist "mechanics," or dissident convention delegates.[20]

The convention system recovered its vigor with the rise of party spirit in the late 1820s. Counties began to cooperate with each other in coordinating their nominations. Jacksonians were particularly active in party organization at all levels and in calling for county, congressional district, and state nominating conventions. The use of conventions spread, albeit unevenly, during the decade after 1826. Not every county held one, and among those that did, not all nominated a candidate for every office. Candidates continued to be nominated by other methods in different parts of the state. As late as 1855, a mass meeting in Elyria nominated James Monroe to be a Senate candidate of the new Republican Party. But when the Democrats and Whigs crystallized as parties in the 1830s, they developed sophisticated party organizations, with state central committees, party newspapers, and networks of correspondents, and both parties adopted the convention as the chief method of nominating candidates. In many multicounty legislative districts, each county sent delegates to a district nominating convention. When district conventions were not held, the county conventions typically nominated candidates separately. In many instances, one county convention took the lead and the conventions of other counties in the district endorsed its choice.[21]

Nomination by convention involved two stages. Local party leaders would call a meeting of party supporters, trumpeted in the local party organ, where the call would be accompanied by exhortations to the faithful to attend. This meeting, known as a caucus or primary, might take place in a private home or some public forum such as a meeting hall. In small towns, or in years when there was little political excitement, the caucus could be tiny. Three times a fellow in Wood County's Perry Township made up a caucus of one. The caucus elected delegates to a county or district convention (or, for the selection of gubernatorial or other statewide officers, a state convention). The convention delegates then nominated the candidates. County conventions nominated those members of the General Assembly who represented single counties, while district conventions made nominations for multicounty districts. In 1859, for example, fifty-five Republicans from townships in Portage and Summit counties met to choose a senatorial candidate. When two or more counties made up a House or Senate district, it was not uncommon, and indeed was sometimes required by law, for the counties to take turns choosing a candidate. In 1859, Portage County had the choice. After four ballots taken in a separate caucus, the Portage delegates settled on James A. Garfield. They returned to the convention hall, offered their man, and instantly received the Summit delegates' consent.[22]

The preconvention caucus or primary, which predominated throughout the nineteenth century, was not a direct primary. The voters did not vote directly for nominees for state office, although they did usually directly nominate candidates for local office, such as sheriff or mayor, and there may have been exceptions even with regard to candidates for state representative. Warren G. Harding's nomination for the Ohio Senate in 1899 illustrates the working of the system. Shortly before that year's meeting of the Marion County Republican convention, Harding announced his candidacy in his newspaper, the *Star*. The Senate district included four counties, and it was Marion's turn to choose a nominee. Republican caucuses met in each of the City of Marion's nine precincts to choose delegates to the county convention. The race was hotly contested and the caucuses well attended. Amid the noise and confusion of the next day's convention, Harding triumphed by one vote and then picked his delegates to the district convention, which ratified the Marion County convention's selection.[23]

There was more to the caucus-convention system than the formal nominating procedure. A potential candidate's friends might prepare for the primary by holding a "parlor caucus" in someone's home and mapping out a strategy for getting supporters to the official caucus; or they might arrange to have ballots printed with various combinations of names, all of them including that of their favorite. In 1877, for example, the black Independent Union Club met shortly before the Republican Hamilton County convention to agree on candidates whom black convention delegates would support. (In this instance, the club's preconvention preparations proved fruitless; the convention nominated a black candidate for the House, but not the one the club had recommended.)[24]

One problem with the convention system was that there was no way to compel a convention delegate to vote for the candidate preferred by the primary voters. The primary voters might adopt a resolution instructing the delegates to support a particular candidate, but they could not enforce it. Another, more serious problem was the ease with which party bosses controlled both caucuses and conventions. The "machine" often selected the candidates "before the people had thought much about the question of who should be nominated." Reformers pushed for direct primaries in which the voters voted directly for candidates rather than for convention delegates. They urged, for example, that all the ballots cast throughout the county for a state representative be collected and tallied by party workers; the candidate with the most votes would be the party's nominee. Democrats in Columbiana, Stark, and Wayne counties used the direct primary as early as the 1840s, and the system may have been in vogue in other rural Ohio counties by the 1880s. Cleveland Republicans experimented with direct primaries in the 1890s, but contemporary critics complained that the city was too large for voters to know the candidates and that the candidates spent too much money on advertising, which resulted in candidates being chosen on the basis of their ads rather than their ability. Moreover, party bosses still seemed to control candidate selection by deciding on candidates in advance and vigorously promoting them.[25]

In 1871, the General Assembly for the first time attempted to ensure the integrity of primary elections by passing the Baber Law. Although it applied to conventions as well, the newspapers referred to it as the primary law. A city, county, or township party committee that wished to assure voters of the honesty of its procedures could elect to operate under the law. The committee would call for party elections by publishing a notice stating that the call was made under the law and setting forth the qualifications of voters. The law provided for the selection of election clerks and for criminal penalties for offering rewards in exchange for votes. The Baber Law was a "half-way measure," typical of primary election laws of the late nineteenth century. It was optional, it left the selection of election clerks to the parties, and it allowed the parties to determine who would vote in the primaries. In other words, the law left control of the primaries in the hands of party bosses.[26]

The Australian ballot law, passed in 1891 and amended significantly in 1892, reformed the nominating process more thoroughly. Named for the country where it first appeared, the Australian ballot was a ballot printed by the government and distributed by election officials. For the first time, Ohio parties and candidates had to qualify for an official ballot instead of handing out tickets of their own. A candidate nominated by a party, whether by convention or otherwise, could appear on the ballot if the party had received at least 1 percent of the total vote at the previous general election. The party could request that the ballot include a party symbol, such as a star or an eagle, at the top of the party's column on the ballot. Below the symbol the ballot included a circle that a voter could check to vote a straight ticket. A candidate could also qualify for the ballot by filing with the secretary of state a nominating petition signed by a specified number of individuals (in the case of candidates for the General Assembly, a number equaling 1 percent of the votes cast in the district at the preceding election). The official ballot was intended to eliminate the control of the nominating process by party operatives and allow anyone who could obtain a relatively small number of signatures to secure a place on the ballot; however, it could be a disadvantage for fledgling third parties that now had to get on the official ballot rather than hand out tickets of their own. In 1897, the Negro Protective Party, a short-lived party formed by disaffected black Republicans, lost its bid to have a symbol placed on the ballot because it had had to nominate its candidates by petition.[27]

After nomination came the campaign for office. For much of the nineteenth century, political campaigns had a highly personal flavor. In the days before mass entertainment, organized sports, and rapid communication, politics was a form of social activity and entertainment as well as a civic concern. People discussed the candidates in taverns, marketplaces, and other gathering places. Many voters knew the candidates personally or had heard about them from mutual acquaintances. They read the numerous handbills passed out by the candidates' friends announcing rallies, extolling the candidates' virtues, and denouncing their adversaries. Newspapers often published correspondence or reprinted articles from other papers discussing a candidate's fitness or unfitness for office. Many of the handbills, letters, and articles were scurrilous beyond the worst excesses of contemporary journalism, full of gross exaggerations and outright lies about a candidate's character, personal history, or political positions. Sometimes outrageous handbills would be circulated or defamatory letters printed on the eve of the election, when the victim had no time to respond. In 1822, Ephraim Cutler's opponents tried unsuccessfully to defeat his candidacy for the House of Representatives by handing out a broadside just before the election announcing that he was not running—a tactic that his backers averred "outstrips all the electioneering tricks that can be met with in the annals of Jacobin perfidy." Although treating electors to food or drink in exchange for votes had been outlawed since territorial days, candidates often offered voters dinners, whiskey, or tobacco in the days before an election.[28]

One disappointed novice candidate for state representative in 1818 learned how not to campaign. He wrote to his uncle, "I had devoted all my leisure time during the summer, being perfectly confident of success in the election, to reading Adam Smith, Ganilh, Algernon Sydney & other economists & politicians, in order to qualify myself in some manner for the seat—my successful opponents, the Lord knows, did not trouble themselves with these things the while." Another candidate learned the perils of stumping a large, rural district when he got lost at night in a forest infested by wildcats and found his way out only by following the far-off sound of a barking dog to a log cabin.[29]

As party organization developed and a competitive, two-party system evolved, campaigns grew simultaneously more organized and more boisterous. The hard cider campaign of 1840 is the prime example, but, except for its excesses, it typified the era. In 1844, Democrats contemptuously dismissed the Whigs' "silly, absurd, and ridiculous mode of reaching the intellect and reason of their hearers, by a Kickapoo array of Indian banners, cider barrels, doggerel songs, ginger bread etc." According to one historian, "Although the campaign was not as interesting from the spectator standpoint as had been the one in 1840, a good many of the same props were used by both sides in an attempt to catch the applause—and votes—of their spectators." In Wayne County, the parties organized political clubs, held parades and rallies, set up meetings in each township, and provided speakers and even glee clubs for the meetings. Rival mass meetings occasionally convened at the same place simultaneously, and Whigs and Democrats sometimes engaged in public debates. Kenneth J. Winkle has noted that the ballyhoo often masked "the real business of politics." He describes how, during the 1840s, the small group of party leaders making up the Whig central committee of Wayne County chose campaign officers, selected candidates, sent messengers to the townships to learn and report on election returns, and checked the returns for irregularities.[30]

Campaigning could be hard on the candidates. A contender for office might try to schedule daytime meetings for farmers and evening meetings for business-men and laborers, squeezing in smaller encounters with voters as circumstances permitted. In tough campaigns, the candidates endured grueling schedules. After his nomination for the House in July 1879, George Washington Williams "cov-ered Cincinnati and Hamilton County quite systematically, speaking in public halls, on fairgrounds, and on street corners." In September, he rarely missed a day and frequently spoke more than once. Often party stalwarts appeared together, as when Williams, Garfield (then a congressman), and other Republicans addressed the crowds at the Hamilton County fairgrounds. Campaigning had its personal elements, too. One representative acknowledged helping an old farmer milk his cow while out soliciting votes. And of course partisan newspapers indulged in vit-riol and hyperbole, although the late nineteenth century witnessed the rise of independent papers and a growing concern for objectivity.[31]

Campaigning retained much of the Jacksonian-era hoopla throughout the 1800s, but toward century's end, alongside the old-fashioned parades and rallies, there arose a new style of campaign managed by professionals and geared more toward the intellect. The old methods brought out the party faithful and lent en-thusiasm to campaigns, but prohibitionists and other crusaders weakened party loyalties with their appeals to ethnocultural ties, and reformers disgusted with Gilded Age corruption attacked unthinking devotion to political organizations. The parties now had to do more than fire up the troops. Campaign managers sought to educate voters, especially wavering or undecided voters, about their po-sitions on the issues. Democrats in Ohio decided in 1892 that the way to carry the state that fall was "to do it by a quiet and vigorous organization and active campaign work, and not with a bluster of brass horns and blazing torches, but by seeing that every voter . . . has placed in his hands such papers as the New York Weekly and other documents relating to Tariff Reform and [President Grover Cleveland's] late administration." Campaign committees began to shift money away from bummers, banners, and brass bands to mass mailings, the printing and distribution of fliers and pamphlets, doorbell ringers, and speakers, all designed to educate the public on the issues of the day. The rise of commercial advertising at the end of the nineteenth century foreshadowed another innovation in political campaigning: the selling of candidates as "products," with slogans and images intended to appeal to the voter-consumer in a simple and personal way.[32]

The ever-increasing influence of money on campaigns, whether in advertising, currying favor, or outright vote-buying, led reformers to demand financial accountability from candidates and party committees. In 1896, the General Assembly passed the Corrupt Practices Act. The law prohibited a variety of activities, including vote selling as well as vote buying. It limited campaign expenditures for both the nomination contest and the general election and required candidates to report campaign receipts and expenses. It also made violators ineligible to hold elective office and nullified their elections if they won. The nullification provision could not apply to members of the General Assembly because the constitution made each house the judge of the qualifications of its members, but the law did authorize any elector to bring an election contest on the grounds that the apparent winner of a seat in the General Assembly had violated the law. Sponsored by Senator James R. Garfield, the act passed with little dissent. By one account, the members were tired of being importuned for money. The General Assembly repealed the law in 1902, however, in part, it seems, because local officials found the law too burdensome to observe.[33]

The ballots that electors cast for most of the nineteenth century bore no governmental seal of approval. Party supporters often handed out ballots just before or even during the voting. A ticket might be handwritten or printed, or a voter could cut one out of the newspaper. In 1824, Jackson supporter Joseph Kerr advertised in a Ross County paper that like-minded electors who lived in towns without printing presses could call on him for printed tickets. Voters had to inspect their ballots carefully, for an ambitious office-seeker might print up his own tickets reproducing the party slate but replacing the name of one of the nominees with his own. A voter could cross out a name on a ticket or write one in, but it was easier to simply drop a ticket as received into the ballot box. This may have reinforced the political allegiances that developed at an early date in Ohio. Straight-ticket voting, at least for state and federal offices, was common in 1803 and stayed so for decades afterward. Sometimes, however, coalitions offered mixed tickets. In the closely fought Wayne County contest of 1846, for example, there were straight Whig and Democratic tickets, mixed tickets of Whigs and soft-money Democrats, and in some townships separate tickets of softs who called themselves Independent Democrats. Not until the 1890s did the law require a standardized official ballot.[34]

Voting and vote counting changed greatly from the beginning to the end of the nineteenth century. Even before Ohio became a state, the General Assembly had abandoned voice voting for written ballots and provided for judicially established election districts with centrally located polling places. The first General Assembly to meet under the constitution brought the polling places even closer to the voters by making each township an election district. It also stiffened the penalty for bribery or treating to a fine of up to five hundred dollars for each offense; bribe-takers could be fined up to a hundred dollars. The new law also provided for fines for anyone who gave a ticket to an illiterate voter and told him that the names written on it were different from what they actually were.[35]

Over the years, the General Assembly tried to tighten up the voting laws to ensure the "purity" of elections. Early laws first recommended and then prescribed the form of the poll book. They required that after the election one poll book "must absolutely be put under cover and sealed before the judges disperse" and "be delivered to one of the judges and by him personally carried to the clerk of the court of common pleas of the proper county." They gave more authority to local officials, allowing township trustees to choose the polling places and making them the judges of election. Later laws established rules and procedures for determining a voter's residence; penalized multiple voting, voting by an unqualified person, and voting in a ward or county where the voter did not reside; and required that ballot boxes be opened publicly and turned upside down to ensure that all ballots were counted. They obliged naturalized citizens to provide proof of their citizenship, although anyone who claimed to have lost his certificate could swear to that fact and be allowed to vote. Finally, the General Assembly established a primitive form of voter registration so that judges of election could post lists of qualified voters and allow for corrections in advance of an election. The registration law did not apply statewide, however, and it was not well enforced. Passed by a Whig legislature, it seems to have been aimed at areas with high rates of transience, which tended to vote Democratic.[36]

The law did not prescribe precisely how voting was to take place. Often, the voters handed their tickets to the judges of election through a window; they could not actually see if the judges put the tickets into the ballot box. The judges generally knew how a person intended to vote, even if they did not know the man personally, for the tickets handed out by party workers were usually identifiable by their size, shape, or color. In 1844, the House instructed its Judiciary Committee to look into measures "to prevent the coloring of tickets, or any other shift or device whereby the political character of the voter may be known," but the committee quickly dropped the matter. Nor could the electors always be certain that the polls would stay open for the hours required by law. A voter in Mohicanville in 1846 found the window closed at what seemed an early time, but he had no watch and couldn't challenge the judges.[37]

Judges of election had to resolve numerous complaints about the qualifications of voters. John Mercer Langston, who in 1855 won election as a town clerk in the Western Reserve and thereby became the first African American in the country elected to public office, said in 1865 that the folks near Lake Erie and on the Reserve would let any man vote who swore to being more than half white, regardless of how black he was. But he also noted that poll watchers sometimes hung around the polls waiting to challenge dark-skinned voters. Lack of citizenship could also be a ticklish subject because so many immigrants voted Democratic. Many a nonnaturalized immigrant who had lived in a town for long time voted with the tacit acquiescence of the populace. Residence, too, could be a tricky issue because of Ohio's growing and highly mobile society. In 1837, the House Judiciary Committee recommended against enactment of a voter registration law because registration would be "impracticable in a new and rapidly settling country" where the population was constantly changing. Uncertainty over the criteria of residence gave the judges a great deal of latitude, which could be used to partisan advantage. More surprisingly, the age qualification caused trouble. Many people simply didn't know how old they were. When challenged at the polling place, a would-be voter had to produce evidence in the form of testimony from his parents, a record in the family Bible, a doctor's account book, or some other proof. The General Assembly resolved the age issue in 1841 when it allowed any voter to overcome a challenge on grounds of age by swearing under oath that he was at least twenty-one.[38]

Election officials often bent or broke the rules. Nevertheless, when losing candidates took their cases to the House or Senate, the lawmakers let the election results stand more often than not. In one case, for example, Jefferson County sent an alien to the Senate; the Senate promptly naturalized him and let him take his seat. County judges, who participated in making the official abstracts from township pollbooks, sometimes rejected pollbooks because they were improper in form, not signed, not delivered on time, or otherwise deficient. Most of the time, the rejections did not affect the outcome. When they did and an election challenge followed, the House or Senate generally turned away the challengers. Not counting the wholesale unseating of the Hamilton County House and Senate delegations in 1886, the two houses between them sustained twenty-four election challenges in the nineteenth century, about 28 percent of the total. Despite the occasional abuse of power and unintentional violations by election officials, most elections—if not necessarily the campaigns leading up to them—seem to have been conducted as fairly as possible under the circumstances.[39]

During and after the Civil War, the process of voting changed. The question of voting by soldiers led to the first absentee ballots, passed by the Unionist General Assembly in 1863. The law provided for the collection of soldiers' ballots in the field and their transmission to Ohio for counting. The supreme court upheld the law over Democratic objections that the constitution required voting to take place in the state. Then there was the matter of eligibility. In the mostly rural Ohio of the Jacksonian era, judges of election could usually rely on firsthand knowledge—their own or that of someone in the community—to determine whether a prospective voter met age, citizenship, or residency requirements. In rapidly growing cities full of anonymous migrants and immigrants, the judges simply couldn't know. The absence of an official voter list opened the door to massive fraud.[40]

The idea of voter registration to combat illegal voting spread westward from New England after 1860. Some scholars maintain that Republicans pushed registration laws as a way of cutting down Democratic strength among immigrants and workers in the big cities. The Democratic *Cleveland Plain Dealer* opposed registration on the grounds that it would actually increase fraud in the cities, where it would be easy "to fill the registry list with fictitious names and names of dead men, and then have gangs of repeaters vote under them." That there was in fact considerable illicit voting was undeniable. The General Assembly adopted a limited precursor to registration in 1845 to prevent alien voting, and in 1870 the House Judiciary Committee reported a voter registration bill. Not until 1885, though, did the General Assembly pass a more stringent law designed to crack down on large-scale fraud in the biggest cities. The law provided for bipartisan boards of elections in Cincinnati and Cleveland and charged them with the creation of election precincts and the appointment of precinct registrars. No one could vote in a general election in those cities without first registering two to four weeks beforehand. (The law did not apply to primaries.) A person convicted of falsely registering faced one to three years in the penitentiary. In a case brought after the 1885 election, the Ohio Supreme Court rejected an argument that the law added an unconstitutional qualification to the right to vote; however, the court invalidated the law for providing an unreasonably short time in which to register. The General Assembly addressed the problem with a revised registration statute the next year.[41]

The registration law did not prevent gross election fraud in Cincinnati in 1885. The Republican members of the Senate Committee on Privileges and Elections excoriated Democratic "conspirators" who had "debauched police officers" and "selected corrupt men as officers of the election, that they might switch tickets, stuff the ballot-boxes, falsify the returns, receive the votes of repeaters, and refuse the votes of honest men who were not in political sympathy with them." The Democratic members of the committee also found a general disregard of the election laws and "a resort to questionable, illegal, and fraudulent methods," but they blamed both parties. The *Weekly Law Bulletin* credited the registration law with "furnish[ing] evidences of fraudulent voting which could never have been so apparent before."[42]

But the law applied only to general elections, not primaries, and only in the largest cities. In 1887, the General Assembly extended registration to Toledo, Columbus, and Dayton, and a Columbus paper applauded the law for helping to produce a trouble-free election that year. "Does it not keep away from the ballot-boxes on election day imported heelers and repeaters from other states who formerly made elections in our large cities a sham and a farce?" asked the Republican *Ohio State Journal* in 1889. But the Democratic *Mansfield Shield* still regarded registration laws as "monstrosities." Whatever its impact in the cities, the registration statute did nothing for such notorious scenes of voting fraud as rural Adams County, where commerce in votes was a way of life. Annual registration, thought necessary because of the highly mobile population of the cities, was an administrative nightmare. Registrars could not effectively investigate so many registrants, and the registration lists were outdated by the time primary or special elections rolled around the next year. Moreover, the office of precinct registrar represented a new source of patronage for big-city bosses.[43]

Another, more effective election reform of the same period was the Australian ballot. As noted earlier, voters traditionally had received ballots from party workers, friends of the candidates, or the candidates themselves, or cut them out of partisan newspapers. An observer could easily see how a person voted by the size or color of his ballot. Sometimes the friends of a candidate distributed tickets identical in every respect to the regular ticket of a major party, listing a full slate for local, state, and federal offices, except for the name of their favorite. To remedy these evils, the General Assembly had tried standardizing ballots by requiring that they be made of plain white paper with black ink, specifying the size of the ballot and the spacing between lines of print, and prohibiting the use of any distinguishing marks. However, the parties evaded the law by varying the color— bright white for Republicans, cream for Democrats—and local parties printed their own tickets substituting their preferred candidates for some offices for the regular party nominees.[44]

Reformers insisted on the need for an Australian-type ballot, officially printed and distributed, to eliminate the intimidation of workers by employers and the rampant bribery of voters. The General Assembly passed an Australian ballot law in 1891. But the Australian ballot had shortcomings. If it listed all candidates for all offices on a single paper, it could overwhelm voters with its length and complexity. One observer attributed light voter turnout in 1891, notwithstanding the "unusual political excitement" in Ohio, to the unwillingness of voters to wade through a baffling ballot. Critics claimed that a long ballot that could only be obtained at the polling place encouraged straight-party voting rather than "intelligent individual choice" by eliminating the opportunity for thoughtful voters to study and carefully mark the ballot in advance. It also allowed pollwatchers to guess whether a voter split his ticket by seeing how long he took to mark his ballot. Finally, the Australian ballot law helped the established parties by limiting the printed names on the ballot to party nominees and by saving them the cost of printing and distributing their own ballots.[45]

The new ballot law gave to the secretary of state the duty of preparing official ballots, the forms of poll books, certificates of nomination, and other election documents. An election officer would supply the voters with the ballots. The statute required that every polling place have a shelf or booth where the voter could mark his ballot confidentially. It allowed any voter who had trouble marking his ballot to have the assistance of the election judges. In 1896, though, the General Assembly prohibited poll workers from helping any person who was not physically disabled. Because the law threatened to disenfranchise illiterates, Cleveland's first assistant city attorney told the city's board of elections that the law imposed an unconstitutional educational qualification for voting. One court agreed in principle, but the supreme court later upheld the restriction.[46]

The atmosphere on election day may have depended on the provenance of a district's early settlers. New England generally enjoyed orderly and tranquil elections; southern elections tended to be boisterous if not bloody. Tales of election-day rowdiness in Ohio emanated from areas settled by southerners. In 1818, Vermont emigré Calvin Fletcher witnessed a two-month election campaign in Urbana marred not only by slander and intrigue but also by roaming mobs, vicious fights that made Fletcher's "blood freeze in [his] veins," and threats of armed conflict on election eve. Election-day crowds around the polling places were often tumultuous and sometimes intimidating. Because distinctive paper tickets made a mockery of the secret ballot, voters could be bullied into casting a particular ticket by threats to their persons or their businesses or bribed into a vote by a free trip to the tavern. The *Village Register* of Adams County in southern Ohio described election day of October 1823 "as one of fear and anxiety":

> The friends of many of the candidates are using their last efforts to draw the unguarded citizen in their noose. While one is parading a squad, with a jug of whiskey in his arms, exclaiming with a huzza for his favorite candidate, and treating those only who agree in opinion another, his coadjutor, is employed in distributing tickets, or rather forcing them into the hands of the already intoxicated multitude. In this way, we are creditably informed, have the previous elections been conducted in this county.

In Cincinnati the election-day outrages of 1885 included widespread "intimidation of voters and personal assaults upon unoffending citizens."[47]

Scottish geographer John Melish recorded a totally different scene in Zanesville in 1811. There, he wrote, the election "was conducted with the greatest imaginable harmony." Another European traveler who happened to stop in Springfield on election day two decades later described another tranquil contest: "The voters gathered in groups before the assembly hall while their carriages lined the streets with horses tied to fence posts or other carriages. . . . No noise, no tempered squabblings, no violent clashes. When his turn came, the registered voter calmly entered the ballot room and calmly cast his vote into the ballot box. That was the end of the great thing." Pennsylvanians and other Northeasterners predominated in Zanesville. Virginians and Kentuckians founded Springfield, but after 1825, immigrants from New York and New England established themselves in the town. Perhaps the Northerners' penchant for orderliness accounts for the peaceable polls of 1811 and 1831.[48]

Election day in Centerburg, 1863. *Courtesy of the Local History Center, Centerburg Public Library*

The election-day atmosphere in Ohio probably did not change much before 1900, except perhaps in Cincinnati and Cleveland, where boards of elections had been created in an effort to combat dishonesty and prevent a repeat of the violence and fraud that marked the election in Cincinnati in 1885. Party loyalists arose bright and early and hurried to the polling place—"almost always located in the back room of some neighborhood drugstore or barbershop or what have you"—to ensure that one of their own was chosen as chief election judge. The parties ran buggies all day ferrying supporters to the voting booths; sometimes paid contractors rounded up voters at so much per head. Before adoption of the Australian ballot ticket, peddlers tried to induce voters to take their ballots. Often, they had "tickets to suit"; if an elector hesitated to use the regular party ticket because he didn't like the party's nominee for, say, sheriff, the peddler had one at hand with a different candidate for that position. Party workers kept an eye out for cheating by their opponents, ever ready to challenge illegal ballots or ineligible voters. As closing time approached, the judges might start counting the ballots early, or the party with the most bodies at the polling station might crowd the window and allow only its friends through to cast ballots.[49]

One old-timer, reminiscing about election day in Columbus in the late nineteenth century, recalled: "After supper everybody gathered downtown or at the

The First Century

City Hall . . . where the election returns were received and read. Saloons were opened all day and night. When the successful candidates were pretty well assured, the real celebration was started, ending up with a huge bonfire at the corner of Broad and High. . . . A good time was had by all except the defeated candidates." Columbus saloons weren't always open on election day. In 1887, the mayor ordered the saloons closed, and some liquor sellers were arrested. But the gaffer accurately recalled the crowds, fires, and general tumult. The faithful packed the rooms where the party committees took up quarters to hear announcements of returns as they came in during the night, both local returns and those telegraphed in from other counties and states. On the streets, crowds might gather to see the returns displayed in front of a newspaper office "by means of a powerful oxy-hydrogen light" or cast onto a building wall by a stereopticon.[50]

Notwithstanding the rowdiness of election night, elections seem to have gone smoothly in Columbus in the late nineteenth century. The registration law cut down on the number of challenges, and a law prohibiting electioneering within 100 feet of a polling place, enacted after the Cincinnati vote-fraud scandal of 1885, theoretically kept hired hectorers at a distance. Violations of the election laws, voter intimidation, and fighting still occurred—Cincinnati was again the scene of election abuses in 1910—but such incidents appear to have been occasional exceptions to an otherwise orderly process.[51]

The constitution made each house the "judge of the election, returns, and qualifications, of its own members." The first General Assembly had hardly convened when it confronted a batch of election challenges. On March 2, the Speaker of the House presented a memorial from Israel Donelson complaining of "many and great improprieties" in the January election in Adams County and asking that the election be set aside. Other protests came from Jefferson County. The Senate received similar complaints about the "fraudulent and corrupt proceedings" in Adams and Jefferson counties. The elections committees of the two houses studied the remonstrations and issued reports. Before the week ended, the Senate unseated a senator in favor of his challenger. The House rejected all the challenges. The Jefferson County petitions led to the General Assembly's first recorded division on any issue; by a vote of 15–10, the House upheld the elections of Zacheus A. Beatty and Thomas Elliot.[52]

A candidate for the General Assembly, or an elector of the county for which the candidate stood, could contest an election by giving written notice to the declared winner of the basis for the contest and the names of two justices of the peace to take testimony. The justices then forwarded the written evidence to the appropriate house of the General Assembly for decision. The House and Senate decided scores of election contests during the nineteenth century. The battles could be long, drawn-out affairs, involving dozens of witnesses. After the raucous 1840 election, for example, when Whig John C. Wright challenged the election of Democratic senator George W. Holmes of Hamilton County, the Senate Committee on Privileges and Elections did not issue the report of its investigation until March 4, 1841, twenty-five days before the end of the legislative session. The report and exhibits took up 420 pages of an appendix to the Senate journal. The committee's Democratic majority concluded that the Whigs of Cincinnati had brought in men from Kentucky and from several Ohio counties to vote the Whig ticket. Although each party accused the other of importing illegal voters, the majority found no evidence that Democrats had engaged in the practice. Simeon Nash, a staunch Whig, issued a seventy-three-page minority report blasting the majority for relying exclusively on "hearsay, and rumor, and suspicion" and charging a Democratic judge of elections with counting double ballots ("two tickets rolled up together") instead of rejecting them as required by law.[53]

The electoral contest following the surprise, one-vote victory of Democrat Joseph Willford in the 1846 senatorial contest in Wayne County produced another voluminous record. With the Senate evenly divided between the parties, the outcome was crucial. Willford maintained the 17-to-17 tie in the Senate by insisting on voting in his own case. He dared his colleagues to remove him from the chamber by force and announced that if there was anything personal between him and his opponent in the race for Senate, "there was a way of settling that too." The crisis was soon resolved when another Democratic senator resigned due to illness and Willford, threatened by the now-majority Whigs with prosecution, also resigned as of the end of the session.[54]

The election process, from nomination through election contests, looked rather different at the end of the nineteenth century from how it appeared at the beginning. Nomination by newspaper announcement of one's availability or by the acclamation of one's friends had given way to candidate selection by delegate conventions controlled by well-organized political parties or, in a few instances, by direct primaries. Campaigns full of bombast and ballyhoo aimed at rallying the party faithful were beginning to yield to educational campaigns meant to inform the voters on the issues and to advertising campaigns designed to sell candidates to the electorate at large. Statutes provided an optional scheme for conducting elections of convention delegates, prohibited corrupt campaign practices, required candidates to disclose campaign receipts and expenditures, provided for limited voter registration and an official ballot, and gave the secretary of state more control over elections. Most of the laws were limited in scope and effectiveness, but, along with changes in the methods of appealing to the electorate and in the electorate itself, they foreshadowed the modern system of choosing the people's representatives.

5

A DELIGHTFUL CAPITAL

O n Christmas Day, 1834, James Loudon sat at his desk in the House chamber writing letters to his family and constituents. During his long legislative career, Loudon often wrote letters from the statehouse about both personal and public matters. The statehouse, the quintessential public building, was also in a sense Loudon's home away from home. More permanent than a room in a boardinghouse, which might change from session to session, the statehouse, ironically, could also be more private. In this chapter, we will examine the personal side of legislative life: travel, living arrangements, social activities. But since no clear boundary existed between the private and public sides of a lawmaker's time when the General Assembly was in session, we will also look at the anchor of his life in Columbus, the statehouse.[1]

Traveling to Columbus

The General Assembly convened for a new session in early December under the first Ohio constitution, in early January under the second. The legislator's first and last task was traveling. Getting to and from the capital was not easy given the horrid state of transportation. The General Assembly passed numerous laws incorporating turnpike and bridge companies, granting ferry licenses, and allocating federal money from the sale of public lands for road building, but travel remained difficult. Lawmakers sometimes had to resort to extraordinary measures to get back and forth. When heavy rains made the roads impassable at the time of adjournment in 1827, Thomas Morris and Robert Lytle, both of southwestern Ohio, refused to be trapped in Columbus. They canoed one hundred miles down the swollen Scioto River, reached Portsmouth in a few days, and took an Ohio River steamboat the rest of the way home.[2]

The roads of early Ohio beleaguered travelers with an "endless succession of stumps and mud holes" and sometimes paused at unbridged streams. Ohio had few regular stage routes before 1815, and the federally financed National Road, which ultimately ran alongside Capitol Square on its way from Maryland to Illinois, did not reach Columbus until 1833. After 1829, when Ohio's first canal opened, some legislators may have journeyed partway to Columbus on canal boats. The canals did not extend throughout the state, but they connected with stage and steamboat service. Railroads began to spread in the 1840s, but Columbus had no passenger train service until 1850.[3]

In 1842, Charles Dickens, traveling by stagecoach from Cincinnati to Sandusky, complained of "dirty, sullen, and taciturn" coachmen and melancholy roadside inns. The road to Columbus at least was macadamized, a "rare blessing," but from Columbus north, the coach alternately jolted the passengers enough "to have dislocated all the bones in the human body" and threatened to leave them mired in mud. Ohio's roads did not rattle the sensibilities of famous English visitors only. In December 1842, Representative John Armstrong Smith, on arriving in Columbus, wrote to his wife, "I am here but in no very comfortable plight, I assure you. The roads were in such condition, that after remaining in Bainbridge until 10 am Tuesday morning, I have been bouncing on a stage every hour since." At the end of that session another lawmaker, noting the thick snow and ice, wrote, "when it does break up it will be awfully muddy and if the break up should take place about the time of our adjournment, it may take me a day longer to get home."[4]

Crossing streams could be perilous. In 1846, Representative William P. Cutler had several crossing adventures. At one place his stagecoach traversed a bridge that was under high water. At another, "we found the plank afloat, and the driver and myself waded in and spent half an hour in the water loading the plank down with stones."[5]

Getting to the capital was much easier after 1850, as railroads brought Columbus within easy reach of most parts of the state. By 1853, the trip from Cleveland to Columbus, which formerly had taken two days by stage, could be made by rail in five hours at a cost of four dollars (and exposure to jolts, smoke, cinder, noise, and wrecks). But travel could still be dangerous. In 1852, the year Congress passed a steamboat safety act, a state senator died and two representatives and a clerk suffered serious injuries in a steamboat explosion on the Muskingum River while journeying to Columbus for the adjourned session of the legislature. In 1865, Senator Thomas Whetstone was killed when his train plunged into a gorge. A month later, a Senate committee reported that train accidents were an "every day occurrence" in Ohio.[6]

The Capital City

During the first thirty years of statehood, when the legislators arrived at the capital they found little more than a small frontier town. The constitution established Chillicothe as the seat of government until 1808. One of early Ohio's leading settlements, Chillicothe was nevertheless small and unprepossessing. In 1807, the village had 1,200 inhabitants and boasted 14 stores, 6 inns, 2 newspaper printing offices, 2 churches, and 202 dwelling houses. The statehouse was the same inadequate building used in territorial days. There was little the General Assembly could do about it; the constitution forbade them to spend any money on a building for the legislature until 1809.[7]

Chillicothe neared the end of its constitutional status as the seat of government during the political controversy over judicial review. Legislators from eastern Ohio who resented the political dominance of Chillicothe and Cincinnati succeeded in having the capital moved temporarily to the small but rapidly growing village of Zanesville. Some lawmakers may have backed the move in exchange for election to offices made available by the Sweeping Resolution; others thought that the citizens of Chillicothe were not committed to building an adequate statehouse and that the village did not offer enough decent housing for the legislators. The General Assembly met for two sessions in Zanesville, holding sessions in the brand-new, two-story brick courthouse. Some folks thought the legislature would make the village its permanent home, but the members never intended to stay. As soon as they got there, they started investigating the location

The Zanesville courthouse. The wings were added after the building had served as the state capitol. *Reproduced by permission of the Ohio Historical Society*

of a permanent capital and soliciting proposals from interested communities and developers. The intense competition badly divided the legislators, who could agree only that the capital should be centrally located.[8]

The General Assembly decided that the capital should be no more than forty miles from the geographical center of the state. The winning bidders offered a site a bit further off center than the places proposed by some of their competitors, but they put together a promising package. Indeed, it was more promise than anything, for in 1812 the location was a wilderness. The successful lobbyists, four owners of wooded land on the high, east bank of the Scioto River, agreed to provide not only land but also a statehouse, public office building, and penitentiary. Chillicothe beat out Lancaster for the honor of temporary capital while the new town of Columbus rose out of the forest, and, in 1812, the General Assembly returned to its Ross County quarters.[9]

On receiving the good news from Zanesville, the Columbus proprietors set out to build their town. They auctioned off the first private lots in June 1812 and cleared land for the public buildings. Within a year, Columbus had three hundred residents. By 1815, the public buildings had been erected. Dr. John Cotton of

Massachusetts was not impressed with the settlement. In his diary, he wrote, "The streets are filled up with stumps and environed with woods, which gives the town the appearance of having just emerged from the forest. . . . The people are collected from every quarter and exhibit great diversity of habits and manners; of course, they are not very agreeable companions." The town's government found it necessary to pass ordinances to prevent hogs from running at large, to require the speedy removal of animal carcasses, to prevent the obstruction of streets by "manure from stables, lumber from workshops, materials for building," and to compel people with infectious diseases to move away from the inhabited parts of town.[10]

Over the next three decades, Columbus grew from a village in the woods to a city of more than seventeen thousand, with restaurants, theaters, lyceums, a botanical society, a stratified social structure, and a varied economy. Visitors in the early 1830s described Columbus as "the most delightful town in the State" and noted that it "had an air of neatness and substantial comfort." The broad sidewalks, paved with brick, "present[ed] quite a busy scene." A newly arrived immigrant from Massachusetts, though, prayed that improved transportation would soon bring "enterprizing Eastern capitalists thronging to this quarter with Croesian gold and the nobility and gentry of Boston, New York, and Philadelphia gaily careening in their gilded carriages through this blossoming wilderness, bringing with them elegant manners and courtly deportment, and God grant that the variety of Ohio may catch some of them." In 1832, the Eagle Coffee House opened a public bathhouse with warm, cold, and medicated baths. The National Road reached the capital in 1833, and the General Assembly incorporated the City of Columbus in 1834. In the 1840s, Columbus acquired gas lighting, telegraph service, a sewer, and a new market house.[11]

Columbus also had a fair number of hotels and boardinghouses where members of the General Assembly stayed during sessions. In the early years especially, some members took rooms in private homes. In 1819, Colonel Abner Lord welcomed newly elected representative Ephraim Cutler to Columbus and invited him to board at the Lord home. "I am, accordingly," wrote Cutler, "at his house, which is very pleasantly situated, and have a room, elegantly furnished, entirely to myself." A few years later, Cutler, having been elected to the Senate, boarded with Representative William Skinner at the home of the wealthy Dr. Lincoln Goodale, "where we have an abundance of company, and a pleasant room by ourselves."[12]

Most members had less commodious accommodations. Columbus had some fine hotels, most notably the Neil House. Even Charles Dickens appreciated the Neil House's "excellent apartments . . . which were richly fitted with polished wood of the black walnut, and opened on a handsome portico and stone veranda, like rooms in some Italian mansion." But Robert Russell's tavern at the corner of High and Rich streets was more typical. Abraham Hegler, a prosperous Ross County farmer, boarded there during his single term in the legislature in 1838–39. "I meet with a great many friendly people in Columbus," he wrote soon after his arrival, "and all quiet and comfortable so far. I room with Messrs A. Waddle and William H. Creighton very agreeable room mates, and I have Messrs Vanmeter and Genl Green for near neighbors who are also very Sociable, I lodge at Mr. Russel's (room No. 16,) Boarding $5, per week, every thing plenty except milk." Hegler probably ate well at Russell's, where one could get a breakfast of "good coffee and eggs, and delightful bread." By February, Hegler had gained five pounds.[13]

Restaurants and coffeehouses sprang up around Capitol Square. The popular Eagle Coffee House, a "plain, two story, brick building" on High Street opposite the public buildings, served the "choicest game" in season and "Old Bourbon, Sour Mash, Kentucky Rye, and the best of wines." Frequented by lawyers and judges who had business in the nearby state and federal courthouses, it became the Whig Party's unofficial headquarters. There these eminent gentlemen not only drank but gambled regularly. "In broad daylight, in open sight of the public eye, the most prominent men and ablest statesmen, with white fixed faces bent over the green cloth."[14]

Democrats, too, had their favorite haunts. For some time they congregated at the Tontine Coffee House, later called the Tin Pan from its oyster-laden chafing dishes, on Market Square. (One long-ago member recalled in 1886 that a Whig had once derisively called the Tontine the Tin Pan and that the nickname had stuck.) The Tin Pan gained such notoriety for its "secret caucuses and sly partisan manipulation" that its very name became synonymous with "caucus dictation and clandestine politics." In 1836, Whig representative Alfred Kelley, accusing the Democrats of choosing a U.S. senator by fiat, sardonically offered a resolution that "the Van Buren party, at the place usually known as the *Tin Pan* . . . on Friday night next, between the hours of seven and eleven in the evening," convene to issue their decree. Another Whig denounced the Democrats' "secret meetings, and one-sided proceedings" at the Tin Pan as "destructive of every principle of correct legislation . . . and false to the purposes of free and open discussion."[15]

Some observers were highly critical of the dissipated lives many of the legislators seemed to be leading. Cincinnati lawyer I. A. Jewett wrote to a relative in Boston in 1833:

> As to their morals, they do not invariably furnish the purest models of propriety. Nay, it is a fact that they grossly violate in the evening and livelong night the very laws which they were enacting during the day. You may perhaps be surprised when I inform you that in this village of the West, the capital of our State, are supported two billiard tables open continually to the public, two roulette tables expressly for gambling, and at the first hotel a room is occupied by a stranger who is risking his thousands, or rather hundreds, every night at the game of faro. Now it is a difficult matter to enter any of these hells between the hours of six and twelve P.M., without meeting Representatives "fresh from the people," or the most grave and reverend Senators. True, we have gaming prohibitions, but they are quietly reposing on the shelf. The games are too captivating and the green ones are duped. The citizens are pleased to have the salaries of the members untransferred from this city.[16]

During his trip across Ohio in 1842, when the temperance crusade was in high gear, Dickens complained about the unavailability of alcoholic beverages. The General Assembly had passed many laws over the years outlawing public intoxication, making habitual drunkenness grounds for divorce, and otherwise expressing disapproval of intemperance. But until 1851, legislative committees regularly rejected petitions to prohibit the manufacture or sale of liquor. Liquor laws could not be effective, they declared, until public sentiment had turned decisively against drinking. The committees urged moral suasion rather than legislation as the appropriate means of fighting intemperance. In the meantime, the members often enjoyed "wine parties" and "other festal occasions." If ladies happened to be present, "[y]our member almost invariably . . . retires into an adjacent apartment where he recreates himself with liquor and those delectable ditties '[Jump] Jim Crow' and 'Clar De Kitchen,' or perhaps he rends his flanks shouting merriment at the facetious stories of a celebrated German Doctor who, although obscure in the 'House,' is a prime Hero at these gatherings."[17]

But the temperance crusaders had some impact on the public behavior of legislators. Joshua Giddings, who had served in the House in 1827, reported from the capital a decade later that Columbus had "greatly changed": "No member or other gentleman is willing now to be seen with Liquor on his table whereas in old times no one was willing to be seen without it. The subject of temperance has certainly made great progress in this place." On the other hand, Giddings thought that the "vice of profanity has much *increased*." (Earlier in the century a traveler claimed to have heard no swearing in Ohio, a phenomenon he attributed to strict enforcement of the law prohibiting oaths.) Giddings may have been deceived about the drinking, or perhaps the progress was only temporary. In 1853, as the temperance campaign tore apart the party system of Whigs and Democrats, a Columbus newspaper described Ohio's state senators as "better drinkers than thinkers." An offended senator retorted that "a more orderly and temperate body of Senators" had never convened.[18]

In any case the members had options other than gambling, drinking, and swearing to occupy their nonworking hours. Legislators had a great fondness for the theater. Theatrical performances of widely varying quality took place at different venues, including the Eagle Coffee House and the market house, in the 1820s and 1830s. A real theater opened in 1835. Although the theater offered a good deal of Shakespeare, sometimes by well-known actors, legislator John Carey crabbed about one performance that it was a "gorgeous display of nonsense and mockery set forth by a set of knaves for the amusement of fools." Columbus hosted concerts, lectures, circuses, and minstrel shows, too. The theater often attracted a rowdy crowd, but when Representative John Armstrong Smith went to hear the English tenor John Braham sing, he found "the *Elite* of the city" in attendance.[19]

Lawmakers often attended elegant parties given by the city's leading lights. Dr. Goodale entertained the members lavishly at soirees with hundreds of guests. Many social gatherings took place at the Neil House. Smith dropped in on one in 1842. "I was there about 20 minutes," he wrote, "—house crowded with all the youth & beauty of the City—rooms furnished in splendid style. It was a perfect light, and in one apartment they were doing things up on the 'light fantastic.' I walked through with Alex Waddle to see what was to be seen, then left. The whole Legislature was there. I was almost sorry I left so soon, for they say there is much fun in seeing the *Menagerie* fed. I mean the *Members*."[20]

Socializing on a smaller scale occurred continuously during the session. Cutler, living in Colonel Lord's home, noted that "No other person boards with me, but there are fifty members within a few steps, so that I have the benefit of retirement in the midst of bustle and noise." Representative Henry Stoddard, who boarded nearby, and Senator David Jennings "spend much of their time with me; Col. Lord also spends a part of every evening." A few years later, boarding with Goodale, Cutler noted that he had "an abundance of company."[21]

Legislators who lived in boardinghouses shared a peculiarly male and in some ways almost military society. The members and employees of General Assembly were all men. Except for the few who represented local districts, the members lived with each other, apart from their families. Within each house, they shared rooms and dined at a common mess. Having no offices, they worked at their desks in the statehouse or in their rooms, so there was no clear demarcation between business and personal time. Politics, like war, was regarded as a masculine profession, involving campaigns, strife, and coarseness. And the associated pastimes— drinking, gambling, and, in the eyes of some, the theater—were seen as particularly unsuited for feminine delicacy. As a delegate to Ohio's third constitutional convention in 1874 contended, nature had confided to man "the rough duties appertaining to war and politics." Governmental matters were "rough, rude and inconsistent" with woman's amiable and gentle character.[22]

Even battle-hardened soldiers, though, miss home and fireside. In the early days, sessions might run until late January or early February, but by the 1830s they typically lasted into March. With no easy way to get home, members might be away from their families and businesses for more than three months. In their letters they asked for news about their children's schoolwork, their families' health, the well-being of the livestock, and other matters of vital concern. They lamented the slowness of the mails and wrote tenderly of the domestic joys they missed.[23]

Historians have noted that the conventions of nineteenth-century politics required candidates and public officials to deny any personal ambition in seeking or holding office, but many of Ohio's legislators seem truly to have served from a sense of public duty. After only a month in Columbus, Abraham Hegler wrote that he "would be very glad to be at home in a social family circle Which would be far more pleasure to me, than to be here working for other people. But so it is someone has to do this, and I am willing to take my turn in the service of the publick, for the general good. I am not any more dissatisfied than I expected, but happy is the man who can stay home with an agreeable family." After three months, he noted that "the greater portion of the members are getting very anxious to get away from here."[24]

John A. Smith, also after just one month away, wrote to his wife, "I am sincerely anxious to be with you all again. Yes *Love*, one kind *Kiss* from your sweet *self* and I would feel that I was once more myself again." Smith wondered whether his little son would remember him by the time session ended. In Columbus again for a rare summer session, Smith, like Hegler, thought of public office as more a burden than an honor. "I am really sick of being away from you, and this sacrafis-ing so much of my happiness for the Sake of a temporary elevation," Smith wrote to his wife. "The glory of my place is truly an empty shade, a thing not worth struggling to attain, and though I think, sometimes, that it is creditable to be es-teemed by my friends; and honorable to be deemed worthy of the confidence of our people, yet I do not think that there is the least honor, to holding a place among such men, as most here in like capacity with myself. Hence, you may infer that should it be the good pleasure of the people to select another in my place, instead of giving me displeasure, it would, 'my *love*,' afford me happiness. There is but few among us have any wish to come back, if we speak the true lan-guage of our feelings." Neither Hegler nor Smith ever sat in the General Assem-bly again, although, many years later, Smith did serve two terms in Congress.[25]

Alfred Kelley wrote to his wife in 1820 that "if kind Providence ever again restores me to your faithful affectionate arms . . . I do not believe anything but dire necessity will ever tempt me, to leave you so long again." Unlike Hegler and Smith, Kelley continued to serve in the legislature and other public offices in Columbus. He eventually solved his separation problem by moving his family to the capital, first as boarders and later as the inhabitants of one of the city's finest residences. As homeowners, the Kelleys often entertained other legislators and invited colleagues to enjoy dinner at a private home. The Kelleys once hosted a lawmaker's wife for a month because she could not get a hotel room.[26]

The Statehouse

When legislators who did not reside in Columbus needed privacy, they occasionally resorted to that most public of buildings, the statehouse. There, after the House and Senate had adjourned for the day, a member might find quiet time in the main hall or a committee room to write a letter home or to meet someone for a confidential conversation. Sometimes, though, members attended to personal affairs in the midst of public business. As his colleagues debated a bill, Represen-tative Seabury Ford wrote to a friend, "I wish I had commenced writing sooner whilst I have been sitting here wasting time to hear their nonsense."[27]

In 1812, on selecting the site for the new state capital, the General Assembly resolved that the statehouse should be a brick building 75 feet by 50 feet. And so it was. Erected on the southeast corner of the Columbus public square in 1814,

The Alfred Kelley home in 1959, two years before being dismantled. *Courtesy of the* Columbus Citizen-Journal *Collection, Scripps-Howard Newspapers/Grandview Heights Public Library/Photohio.org*

it had two stories and a steeple that rose to 106 feet above the ground. The bricks were made in part from an ancient Indian mound at the intersection of High and Mound streets. A bell in the spire notified members when session was about to begin. (Misuse of the bell eventually led the Senate to allow its ringing only to call the members to business or in case of fire.) The main entrance, on State Street, opened into a small hall from which a door led to the House chamber on the north side of the building. Stairways led to the House gallery and to the Senate chamber on the second floor. The Senate had no gallery. Each floor had two committee rooms. The House chamber had a west door opening onto High Street and an east door leading to a woodyard, a situation that one visitor regarded as "very unsuitable for silence, deliberation or convenience." According to an early historian of Columbus, "The halls were of good size and respectable with wooden finish" with large wooden columns "painted in imitation of clouded marble." "The speakers' desks were upon the 'old-fashioned' plan of high pulpits with the members' seats facing them."[28]

The First Century

The "new" statehouse on the southwest corner of Capitol Square in 1816. To its left are a state office building and the federal courthouse. *Reproduced by permission of the Ohio Historical Society*

The statehouse sat on the northeast corner of State and High streets, which present-day pedestrians know as a windy spot. The wind may be due in part to the configuration of the structures in the area, but even in the early nineteenth century, it could be severe. Senator Allen Trimble wrote to his brother in 1820, "We are all well after a tremendous gale of wind which has done much harm to the buildings. The Senators scampered out of the Senate Chamber like rats out of a feed-building; the motion was so great as to move my chair several inches."[29]

By the time young Cyrus P. Bradley of New Hampshire visited in 1835, the floor of the House was "well carpeted" and the members had moveable desks and more elbow room than New Hampshire's legislators. Nevertheless, the statehouse did not impress Bradley. The General Assembly had directed that the building be proportioned "according to the most approved models of modern architecture, so as to combine, as far as possible, elegance, convenience, strength and durability." Bradley described it simply as "a small, square, temporary, brick building . . . surmounted with a patriotic extract from Barlow" that Bradley thought much too long for good taste. Barlow's poem included a reference to the United States as a "federal band," and that is what the workman, copying from a book, cut into the stone. This was too much for William Ludlow, the superintendent of

An inscription above one of the doors to the first Columbus statehouse. *Reproduced by permission of the Ohio Historical Society*

construction and a staunch Democrat. He had *federal* filled in and *Union* cut over it. Eventually, the filler fell out and *federal* reappeared.[30]

Fifty or sixty feet north of the statehouse, along High Street, stood the new state office building and, beyond that, the U.S. courthouse. A rail fence surrounded the public square until the fence became dilapidated. Jarvis Pike, Columbus's first mayor, cleared the square of trees around 1816 and for several years raised wheat and corn there. Thereafter it became a public common. When Cyrus Bradley saw the square, it was covered with clover in which pigs were "rioting at pleasure." Not long before, the state had erected a "neat and substantial fence of cedar posts and white painted palings" and transplanted young elms to the square. Unfortunately, the neat paling fence gave way in 1839 to a tall, ugly board fence to keep in the inmates of the state penitentiary who were to work on a new statehouse. Construction of the new edifice took so long that a generation of Columbusites grew up regarding the eyesore as a permanent fixture.[31]

In 1887, forty years after he served there, Albert G. Riddle remembered the old statehouse as a "dingy, lonely brick edifice." The corner of the House chamber to the Speaker's left, he recalled, was nicknamed the chuckery in tribute to "two or three gray headed marmot-like Whigs who once burrowed there."[32]

By 1837, the Senate Committee on Public Buildings thought the need for a new statehouse was "manifest." The existing capitol was too small for the conduct of official business in the rapidly growing state, and the calamitous loss of public records to fire was a real possibility. The committee also believed that state pride demanded a more imposing edifice, and it reported a bill to construct

The First Century

one. The need for a new statehouse was not manifest to all—fourteen senators voted against the measure—but the bill passed and construction soon began. Hard economic times and a dispute over whether Columbus should even remain the capital of the state brought the work to a halt in 1839, but, in 1845, the House Committee on Public Buildings recommended that construction resume. Everyone could see that the current structure was "entirely inadequate," the committee declared; it was "inconvenient, uncomfortable, and greatly liable to fire." The shortage of committee rooms caused constant complaint and slowed work down. Committees needed space to store their papers and meet without interruption. The hall of the House was too small. So were other public offices. The secretary of state had to rent space elsewhere, and the library could barely accommodate new acquisitions. A minority of the committee objected to spending money on a statehouse when the state carried an enormous debt and the citizens groaned under oppressive taxation. A smaller fireproof building would suffice for the public records, said the minority report, and repairs would keep the capitol going for another fifteen years while the state accumulated money for a new building. The state followed the majority's advice; construction began again in 1846.[33]

The 1851 constitution made Columbus the state capital until the legislature decided otherwise, which it never did. Construction of the new statehouse proceeded fitfully, delayed by political disputes, changes on the board of commissioners appointed to oversee the project, and a cholera epidemic. It was not ready for occupation on Sunday, February 1, 1852, when the old statehouse burned to the ground. The House sergeant at arms and his assistants saved most of the books and papers, furniture, and even carpeting from the representatives' chamber, but the Senate, on the upper floor, was a near-total loss. The Senate clerk reported the next day that files going back twenty or thirty years had been destroyed. The bill book and manuscript journals for the current session had been saved, however, and all Senate bills but the most recent had been printed and distributed. Petitions that had been referred to committees had been sent to the committee chairs, so the clerk had no way of knowing which of them had survived.[34]

Since the House records had been saved and the Senate's work could be reconstructed from what remained of its papers, the General Assembly could carry on without a break if only it had a place to meet. The city of Columbus and town of Mount Vernon offered space free of charge. So did the Starling Medical College, the federal court, and the proprietor of the Odeon Hall. The House immediately took up residence at the Odeon, where it remained until 1857. (Not for free, though. The House paid rent after 1852.) The Senate finished the spring session at the federal courthouse, but its presence there proved a great inconvenience to the court. When the General Assembly reconvened in November, the Senate contracted with Peter Ambos for the rental of his new hall. The senators hired carpenters and purchased carpet to fit out the hall as a Senate chamber and moved in during January 1854.[35]

Numerous vicissitudes continued to impede progress on the new capitol. Political partisanship intruded into the work as the General Assembly replaced the statehouse commissioners twice in four years. In 1853, the House committee on the penitentiary charged prison guards in the statehouse yard with "gross neglect of duty" for talking with the convict laborers, "encouraging them in the exhibition of various tricks of sleight of hand for their amusement," using profane language, and generally subverting discipline. To make matters worse, free laborers at the site were providing the prisoners with alcohol. In 1854, after arguing with the commissioners, the architect resigned in a huff. The new architect found "a radical defect in the entire absence of any means for ventilation" and poor interior lighting. He proposed corrective measures for these and other problems; other architects hired to review the plans suggested further changes.[36]

The General Assembly moved into the still uncompleted statehouse on January 6, 1857. Five or ten thousand people—estimates varied—attended the opening ceremonies, which included a banquet in the rotunda and dancing in the Senate chamber. The structure was finally finished in 1861, at a cost of three times the original estimate. The dome, however, remained a bone of contention; in 1892, Columbus historian Alfred Lee asserted that "the Capitol of Ohio remains to this day surmounted by an incomplete, nondescript structure, wholly out of keeping with its general style."[37]

At 184 feet wide and 304 feet long, including the porticos on each side, the new structure occupied two acres of land and rose 61 feet high to the base of the cupola. The executive branch occupied the twenty-eight first-floor rooms. On the north side of the second floor, the Senate enjoyed a chamber measuring 49 feet by 57 feet, plus lobbies on three sides. The House chamber, on the south side, measured 55.5 feet by 82.5 feet. The House had just one lobby, but it featured a gallery running its entire width. The second floor also housed the supreme court, the state library, a law library, a supply room, and a room for military trophies. Committee rooms were on the third floor. The building had twelve water closets and five washrooms.[38]

The completed statehouse in the 1860s. *Reproduced by permission of the Ohio Historical Society*

The "Lincoln" chair behind the Speaker's desk in the House of Representatives. Statehouse lore long held that Abraham Lincoln had sat in this chair during a stop en route to Washington for his inauguration in 1861, but in fact the chair was not made until 1879. *Courtesy of the Ohio Legislative Service Commission*

A crowd waits to pay its respects to the murdered President Lincoln, April 29, 1865.
Reproduced by permission of the Ohio Historical Society

Lincoln lying in state in the statehouse rotunda, April 29, 1865. *Reproduced by permission of the Ohio Historical Society*

The House chamber in the 1870s. *Reproduced by permission of the Ohio Historical Society*

The formal completion of the statehouse hardly ended the legislature's tribulations with its new home. The roof leaked. Poorly designed heating and ventilation systems caused serious discomfort. Dirt and dust from the coal-fired boilers in the basement floated into the rooms upstairs. By 1870, the building needed major repairs. The House Committee on Public Buildings, in addition to recommending interior painting and the installation of lighting by "cone reflectors," urged that the "warm, moist-air furnaces" of Peter Martin of Cincinnati be purchased to replace the existing steam boilers. Representative Thomas J. Haldeman objected. He had visited numerous public buildings in and around Cincinnati, he said, and found that while most had satisfactory steam-heat systems, Martin's boilers had a history of trouble. Haldeman urged that the statehouse's expensive steam boilers be moved outside, under the House terrace.[39]

The next year the committee reported that the necessary maintenance and repairs, including removal of the boilers as Haldeman recommended, had been done. However, the committee complained about the "loose manner in which all matters appertaining to the State House are conducted." Lighting had been installed without a contract and at too high a price. Some of the ventilation work had been performed without a contract or competitive bidding. Record keeping for the purchase of furniture had been sloppy. General neglect on the part of the statehouse superintendent had cost the state a lot of money.[40]

The new heating and ventilation systems didn't help. The air in the basement, befouled by leaking furnace gas and waste from water closets and horse stables, had no outlet but the ducts that led to the chambers and meeting rooms. It was also very dry, causing, thought the Committee on Public Buildings, numerous colds and sore throats among House members. The architects urged many changes, including a new boiler. The legislators ordered the construction of new fireplaces, prohibited the stabling of animals in the basement, and appointed a committee to oversee improvements in the water supply, but whatever was done wasn't enough. In 1892, a joint committee excoriated the "absolutely criminal" sanitary conditions in the statehouse: "poisoned air," uncontrollable temperatures, poor ventilation, excessive heat in the winter (which caused the members to open the windows), horrible drainage, and so on. Lighting, provided by windows and gas lamps, also remained inadequate. The lawmakers had skylights installed in the House and Senate chambers, but the senators complained of the harsh light and directed the sergeant at arms to shade the skylight. The Senate also ordered electric lighting, for which the comptroller of the treasury, then in charge of the statehouse, contracted in 1876. At some point within the next few years the capitol acquired an electrical system based at least partially on the Ruhmkorff coil, an early type of transformer. It's not clear how much electricity the General Assembly used in the next decade and a half, but, in 1891, the legislature appropriated $13,000 for an electric lighting system. A committee reported in 1894 that the 1,023 incandescent lamps and 12 arc lights weren't enough and recommended the installation of hundreds more lamps, a new wiring system, and the establishment of a power plant at the statehouse.[41]

Even jobs well done did not always turn out as planned. In 1882, the House had its finance committee room "painted and frescoed most elegantly" to please

Representative James Scott, who all assumed would be the next chairman of the finance committee, but by the time the work was done, Scott was not even on the committee. In 1890, the members met for a special session on bare floors because the statehouse carpets had been taken up for cleaning and repair.[42]

Beyond all that, the state government outgrew the capitol in one generation. By the 1880s, the building was overcrowded, and the statehouse superintendent had taken to creating new offices by partitioning hallways. A joint committee of the legislature concluded that the increase in the size of government stemming from Ohio's growth in population and industry made enlargement of the statehouse imperative. Finally, in 1897, the General Assembly approved the construction of an annex to house the supreme court, the law library, the attorney general's office, and several other departments of state government. But the annex, completed in 1899, provided only partial and temporary relief.[43]

Life in Columbus after 1850

Life outside the statehouse also changed significantly for legislators during the second half of the nineteenth century. Already by 1850, Columbus was no longer the "pleasant little village" that visitor Cyrus Bradley had seen in 1835. With a population of 18,000, it had developed distinctive neighborhoods—fashionable districts not far from the statehouse, the working-class west side, the German settlement to the south. The Germans established Capital University in 1850, America's first kindergarten in 1858, and Columbus's first Catholic church and Jewish congregation. Irish immigrants built the city's second Catholic church between 1852 and 1855. Never a great industrial center, Columbus enjoyed a diversified economy of small-scale manufacturing, commerce, and, of course, government.[44]

By 1870, the population exceeded thirty thousand. The city boasted thirty-one churches, many medical and law offices, and all kinds of commercial establishments—hotels and restaurants, bookstores, groceries, tanneries, and more than one hundred saloons. It would soon have to the north of the city a state university. The Ohio Agricultural and Mechanical College opened with twenty-four students in 1873; in 1897, enrollment at the renamed Ohio State University exceeded one thousand. As the century moved toward its end, the city paved its streets and sidewalks, expanded outward with the advent of streetcars, witnessed the growth of factories and incidents of labor violence, and saw the erection of

Columbus in 1855. *Courtesy of the* Columbus Citizen-Journal *Collection, Scripps-Howard Newspapers/Grandview Heights Public Library/Photohio.org*

the ten-story Wyandotte skyscraper. Columbus acquired its first public telephone in 1880, electric street lighting in 1890, the ornate Southern Theater in 1896, and an amusement park in 1899. The population in 1900 surpassed 125,000.[45]

Lawmakers generally continued to live as before, boarding in homes or hotels near the statehouse. In 1882, Representative William Bloch boarded with Martha Bailey at 49 East Town Street. Representatives Benjamin Brownfield, William Wright, and David Yates and Yates's teenaged son boarded with Alice Jane George at 88 West Gay Street. James Garfield, elected to the Senate in 1859, had the good fortune to reside in the home of William Bascom, chairman of the state Republican Central Committee, just two blocks from the capitol, though he had to share a bed with fellow senator Jacob Cox. Unhappily married, Garfield dissuaded his wife from coming along. The expense of boarding may also have discouraged family living. Senator David A. Hollingsworth found that his pay of five dollars per diem did not cover the cost of boarding for himself and his family. (Hollingsworth could have saved money by not staying at the fanciest hotel in Columbus, the Neil House.) On the other hand, George Washington Williams, Ohio's first black legislator, rented a house on Third Street in 1879 for himself and his family.[46]

In a way, the legislator's private life in Columbus after the Civil War was less important than it had been before. Members spent less time in the capital than their predecessors had and more going home. Improvements in transportation meant that lawmakers were no longer stuck in Columbus. Sessions grew longer, extending into May, but the official work week grew shorter and absenteeism ran high. At the end of the century, the General Assembly went to biennial sessions; once the legislature adjourned for good in the spring, the members were

The First Century

The corner of Broad and High streets, Columbus, in 1880. *Courtesy of the* Columbus Citizen-Journal *Collection, Scripps-Howard Newspapers/Grandview Heights Public Library/Photohio.org*

home free for eighteen months or more. Columbus was no longer a home away from home. The members were transients rather than temporary residents.

The legislators still had a social life, of course. They enjoyed the restaurants, bars, and theaters of the growing capital. In 1879, a Republican paper, noting that the Democrats had postponed a caucus so that its members could attend a minstrel show, commented, "When negro minstrels prove to be an impediment to the machinations of designing Democratic politicians, it is high time to organize more minstrel troupes." Another paper complained that too many members "run after the sinful amusements of the world and help swell the audience that crowds the Atheneum matinees." It recommended that rural members in particular spend their Saturday afternoons visiting the state-supported benevolent institutions located in Columbus. Many members in fact did just that. A few months later, the same paper bewailed "the absenteeism and junketing about visiting Benevolent Institutions," which had become "a crying evil in legislative bodies" and "reduced the working force below a quorum most of the time."[47]

There were parties, too, sometimes at the benevolent institutions. In the 1880s, the *Ohio State Journal* reported that "quite a number" of legislators had attended a masquerade ball at the insane asylum and that the members had responded with "fervor" to an official reception by the governor. The paper thought that the reception indicated "the importance of continued social greetings" that brought "the members who sojourn here during the winter months into closer communion with the capital city and her citizens." The citizens may have paid for this entertainment more often than they cared to. In 1876, for example, Columbus City Hall hosted a lavish "citizens' reception," a banquet and ball, for the General Assembly and the rest of the state government. Of course, a good time could be had without such formality. Temperance advocates might be astonished, wrote one reporter, to see members who had so passionately presented their petitions "surrounding a gin-sling or a brandy-smash, when the toils of a day is over and the over-worked statesman has hied himself to the nearest cognac conservatory." When Representative Frank Owen introduced a bill to strengthen the penalties for being found in a state of intoxication, statehouse wits asked what Owen had against the other members, newspapermen, and clerks.[48]

Toward the end of the nineteenth century, lobbyists assumed a larger and more pernicious role in entertaining the lawmakers. Politician Allen O. Myers, who thought that Ohio government was riddled with corruption, asserted acidly that the Speaker of the House "doubted the presence of such a thing as a lobby, even when he sat in a poker game with the agents and was permitted to win." A Columbus paper noted one year that the Park Hotel had "become quite a center of members of the General Assembly, lobbyists and others" and that "a conspicuous circle of public men," including leading legislators, were concentrating at the hotel. The observation, innocuous on its face, portended the unhealthy mix of lobbyists and lawmakers that would scandalize reformers in the twentieth century.[49]

Evolution of the Statehouse in the Twentieth Century

The Broad Street entrance to the statehouse in the early twentieth century. *Reproduced by permission of the Ohio Historical Society*

The statehouse and annex in 1963, with the underground parking garage under construction. *Courtesy of the Columbus Citizen-Journal Collection, Scripps-Howard Newspapers/Grandview Heights Public Library/Photohio.org*

Downtown Columbus with Capitol Square at its center, 1968. *Courtesy of the Columbus Citizen-Journal Collection, Scripps-Howard Newspapers/Grandview Heights Public Library/Photohio.org*

The construction of state office buildings
shown in the next three photographs
relieved the space crunch in the statehouse.

The Ohio Departments Building (*right*) opened in 1933, housed the House of Representatives during the statehouse renovation of the 1990s, and was itself renovated to become the Ohio Judicial Center in 2004. *Courtesy of the* Columbus Citizen-Journal *Collection, Scripps-Howard Newspapers/Grandview Heights Public Library/Photohio.org*

The Rhodes State Office Tower opened in 1974, freeing up space in the annex for Senate offices. *Courtesy of the* Columbus Citizen-Journal *Collection, Scripps-Howard Newspapers/Grandview Heights Public Library/ Photohio.org*

Representatives got their own offices in 1988 with the completion of the Vern Riffe Center for Government and the Arts. *Courtesy of the Ohio Legislative Service Commission*

The reading room of the state library, located in the statehouse, in 1901. The library moved to the Ohio Departments Building in 1933. *Reproduced by permission of the Ohio Historical Society*

The Ohio Supreme Court room in the annex in the early twentieth century The bottom
photograph on page 114 shows the same room after the renovations of the 1990s.
Reproduced by permission of the Ohio Historical Society

The Senate chamber around 1910. Note the spittoons and the balcony. The balcony was built in the early part of the century. According to statehouse lore, Senate clerk Tom Bateman ordered it removed in the 1940s to prevent unruly spectators from throwing things onto the senators below. *Courtesy of the* Columbus Citizen-Journal *Collection, Scripps-Howard Newspapers/Grandview Heights Public Library/ Photohio.org*

The Senate chamber, minus the balcony, in 1949. *Courtesy of the* Columbus Citizen-Journal *Collection, Scripps-Howard Newspapers/Grandview Heights Public Library/Photohio.org*

The House in session, 1951. Papers piled up in the days before the representatives had offices or computers. *Courtesy of the* Columbus Citizen-Journal *Collection, Scripps-Howard Newspapers/Grandview Heights Public Library/Photohio.org*

A fish-eye view of the House in 1984. The House seems not to have worried about missiles being launched from the balconies. *Courtesy of the Ohio Legislative Service Commission*

The House post office, located at the rear of the House chamber, in 1984. Representatives now send and receive mail on the twelfth floor of the Riffe Center. *Courtesy of the Ohio Legislative Service Commission*

Repeated divisions of statehouse space over the years produced not only new rooms but whole new floors. The upper staircases shown here led to the House clerk's office and the House chamber. They were removed during the renovation of the 1990s. *Reproduced by permission of the Ohio Historical Society*

On the now removed fifth floor of the statehouse, formerly occupied by Legislative Service Commission staff, yet another stairway led to more offices.
Courtesy of the Ohio Legislative Service Commission

From 1983 to 1985, the author shared this office with another staffer and once climbed out onto the statehouse roof to clean the grime off the window. *Courtesy of Joe Aninao*

Courtesy of the Ohio Legislative Service Commission

The "bullpen" in the statehouse basement, which LSC staff members shared with cockroaches and mice. *Courtesy of the Ohio Legislative Service Commission*

Bad air in the statehouse basement remained a problem into the late twentieth century, as this LSC memo attests. *Courtesy of the Ohio Legislative Service Commission*

TO: Basement and Library LSC Staff

FROM: Bev

DATE: March 15, 1976

RE: Basement odors, or, Something is rotten in Denmark

      Last week, Mr. Hursch from the Environment section of the Department of Industrial Relations, made various tests of the air quality in our basement offices.

      In a few days, I will receive a detailed, written report of our test results--which will, in effect, "break down" our air composition and tell us just what we're breathing.

      Mr. Hursch phoned me today, however, and indicated that a preliminary screening of our air samples revealed no evidence of any toxicity (poisonous or harmful elements). Accordingly, the only other problem left to alleviate is the <u>stink</u> of our non-toxic air, and Mr. Hursch will be back next Monday with a machine that, hopefully, will identify the source or sources of the basement office odors.

      One more point--even though the basement air is "non-toxic", Mr. Hursch commented that the nausea and headaches that a few of you have experienced is probably real, and not imagined, because odor-laden air can and does cause such discomfort for some people.

Senator Richard Finan, the moving force behind the statehouse renovation, points to the crumbling interior of the annex in 1985. *Courtesy of the* Columbus Citizen-Journal *Collection, Scripps-Howard Newspapers/Grandview Heights Public Library/Photohio.org*

The renovated House chamber. *Courtesy of the Ohio Legislative Service Commission*

The South Hearing Room in the Senate Building (annex), formerly the room in which the supreme court heard cases. *Courtesy of the Capitol Square Review and Advisory Board*

A House committee room, after the renovation. *Courtesy of the Ohio House of Representatives*

Newly elected members of the 127th General Assembly enjoy dinner in the statehouse atrium, November 29, 2006. *Courtesy of the Capitol Square Review and Advisory Board*

The Veterans Plaza on Capitol Square, created as part of the renovation. *Courtesy of the Capitol Square Review and Advisory Board*

6

THE RULES OF PLAY

DISPUTES OVER INTEREST RATES flared up occasionally throughout the nineteenth century. What ceiling, if any, should the legislature place on the rate of interest a lender could charge a borrower? What should be done when a lender and borrower agreed to a rate above the legal limit? In 1804, the General Assembly enacted the state's first usury law, setting an interest rate ceiling of 6 percent and providing that a lender who exceeded the limit forfeited the debt. The statute originated as the recommendation of a joint committee of senators and representatives appointed to revise the laws of Ohio, many of which had been inherited from the Northwest Territory and were manifestly inadequate for a new and rapidly growing state. On December 22, the joint committee presented a usury bill to the Senate for a first reading. Two days later, the bill went to the committee of the whole, consisting of all the senators. That committee reported the bill back to the Senate without amendment. On Christmas day, the bill was "amended by way of rider at the clerk's table" and passed. The Senate immediately sent the bill to the House, which proceeded with its first reading on December 26, second reading and report by the committee of the whole on December 27, and third reading and amendment on December 28. The Senate promptly concurred in the House amendments, and both Speakers signed the enrolled bill on December 29.[1]

This mode of proceeding was familiar to those members of the General Assembly who had served in the territorial House of Representatives or in the legislatures of other states. Although Ohio's constitutions, like the constitutions of other states, provided little guidance for the exercise of legislative power, they authorized the House and Senate to adopt rules of procedure by which they would conduct their affairs. At the beginning of every session, the presiding officer of each house appointed a committee to draft the rules, which the members then approved by resolution. (After 1851, when the lieutenant governor presided over the Senate and might not be of the same party as the majority, the Senate itself sometimes named the committee.) Although the full body could amend the committee's report or amend the rules after adoption, the rules seldom stirred controversy. Sometimes the House or Senate simply readopted its rules from the previous General Assembly. But the rules were not a matter of mere housekeeping. Thomas Jefferson regarded legislative rules as an assurance of "order, decency and regularity" and a shield for the minority party. The parliamentary practice embodied in the rules, explained a nineteenth-century political scientist, was "an important guarantee of liberty. . . . It is not only a guarantee of the free share of every representative in the legislation of his country, but it is also . . . a guarantee, for the people, that its legislature remain in its proper bounds, and that laws be not decreed as the effects of mere impulse and passion."[2]

The General Assembly's first rules rested on the experience of the Northwest Territory, which in turn drew on the practice of Parliament, the colonies, and the first states. The rules spoke to many matters, such as the duties of the Speaker, the making of motions, the manner of addressing fellow members, and decorum on the floor. The House always adopted more detailed rules than did the Senate, although in most matters the practice in the two chambers was similar. Over time, the rules of both bodies became more comprehensive, dealing with the number and size of standing committees, the privileges of newspaper reporters, the functions of the clerks, and a host of other subjects. When a question arose that the rules did not cover, the members could look elsewhere for direction. The rules themselves usually designated a procedural manual to be used in such cases. For many years, it was Thomas Jefferson's *Manual of Parliamentary Practice*, published in 1801 for use by the U.S. Senate; later it was Luther Cushing's popular handbook of the same name, supplemented by Cushing's magisterial treatise on the subject.[3]

The Stages of Legislation

The constitution of 1802 established a few basic guidelines for the legislature. For example, it provided that bills might "originate in either house" and required that every bill "be read on three different days in each house, unless, in case of urgency, three-fourths of the house where such bill is so depending, shall deem it expedient to dispense with this rule." But the constitution did not say how bills originated or what a reading consisted of.[4]

In the early days, most bills "originated" in the reports of temporary select committees appointed to propose revisions of the existing statutes, to consider issues raised in the governor's annual message to the legislature, or to address matters of public interest otherwise brought to the attention of the lawmakers. As time went on, citizens increasingly took to petitioning their representatives and senators for the enactment of legislation. Often the petitions involved matters of purely local concern, but crusaders for causes learned to use the petition process to get the General Assembly's notice. Individual members presented the petitions, and the Speaker referred them to select committees. Regardless of how legislation originated, the Speaker usually appointed a committee, typically consisting of one, three, or five members, to prepare, amend, or consider each bill.

Members did not have a right to introduce legislation. From the beginning of statehood through the 1850s, when Cushing published his treatise, the House rules allowed for the introduction of measures by motion for leave to introduce a bill or on the report of a committee. A motion for leave had to be made on one day's notice. The Senate rules ignored the subject but arrived at the same result by resorting to guides to parliamentary practice. After the rules began fixing the order of business in the 1820s, a member who wished to present a bill had to wait until the journal had been read, petitions presented, and committee reports submitted. The rules did not detail the process of introduction. Jefferson and Cushing differed slightly in their descriptions. According to Cushing,

> the ceremony of presenting a bill is attended with little or no formality. The member who is about to present a bill, whether as the report of a committee or otherwise, rises in his seat, and having obtained possession of the floor for the purpose, proceeds to inform the house that he has a report and bill, from such a committee or source, which he reads, if he thinks proper, and thereupon offers to present the bill to the house. If no objection is made, the bill is of course presented and received.

Jefferson recorded that when a bill was presented,

> the clerk reads it at the table, and hands it to the Speaker, who rising, states to the House the title of the bill, that this it the first time of reading it, and the question will be whether it shall be read a second time? Then sitting down to give an opening for objections, if none be made, he rises again and puts the question whether it shall be read a second time? . . . A bill cannot be amended at the first reading . . . nor is it usual for it to be opposed then: but it may be done and rejected.

A bill that had been passed by one house would be introduced in the other by a message sent from the first house.[5]

Rarely did either branch of the General Assembly deny a motion for leave to introduce legislation. One such instance occurred in 1827, when the Senate refused to allow James B. Gardiner to introduce a bill to fix the compensation of members of the legislature. The subject had been fought over for years, with disastrous results for the members' public image. In 1825, Gardiner won election to the House from Greene County on a promise to reduce the members' per diem compensation by a dollar or, if that failed, to donate his extra dollar to the county treasury. The House expelled him, declaring that his campaign promise amounted to a bribe to the voters. Greene County promptly sent him back in a special election, but the House refused to seat him because the constitution prohibited bribe-givers from serving for a period of two years. In 1827, Gardiner won election to the Senate, where he persisted in his efforts to reduce the members' pay; however, his fellow senators denied him leave to introduce his bill. A Columbus newspaper commented, "We have no doubt that the indefatigable mover would prefer that his favorite measure should die a natural death, rather than consume the time of the Legislature, disturb their harmony, and be fairly smothered by obliging friends, with the weight of amendments, for additional retrenchments in other departments of Government."[6]

If the introduction of bills was not a perfunctory matter from the beginning, it became one as the business of the legislature increased. By the 1860s, the rules of both the House and Senate either explicitly or implicitly permitted individual members to introduce bills without leave of the house, and a bill was as likely to be introduced by an individual as by a committee. The House and Senate journals also show a growing propensity to introduce bills and refer them to committee en masse: four or five at a time in the 1860s, dozens at a time by the 1880s.

The first reading of a bill was "for information." If any member opposed the bill, the house could reject it on the spot. That did not happen often, but in 1870 the House rejected a bill to put to the women of the state the question of whether they wanted the right to vote. (The House reconsidered the vote and reversed itself, but the bill died quietly thereafter.) If no one opposed the bill at this stage, or if the chamber did not reject it, the bill went to a second reading. At that time, the presiding officer announced the bill as ready for commitment or engrossment. Engrossment, the preparation of a clean copy of a bill in official form, including any amendments made up to that time, rarely if ever occurred at this stage. Commitment meant referral of a bill to a committee for consideration of its form and merits. Cushing noted that public bills, which involved matters of general concern, typically went to the committee of the whole, whereas private bills, which affected only particular individuals, usually went to a select committee. The committee of the whole consisted of all the members of the House or Senate, but discussion was freer than when the members sat as a house. As the business of the legislature increased, select committees and then standing subject-matter committees (on agriculture, roads, and other topics) proved more practical for consideration of a bill in detail.[7]

How bills got referred to a committee is not clear. The rules were silent on the subject throughout the nineteenth century, and the journals reported the act of referral in the uninformative passive voice. Technically, referral seems to have been the duty of the chamber as a whole, on motion of a member, but the presiding officer probably exercised the power in fact. On one day in 1868, when standing committees were well-established, more than two dozen House bills and two Senate bills were "read" the second time in the House and each was referred to a particular committee on motion of a member. In some cases, the person who moved the referral was the bill's sponsor. The House referred most of the bills to standing committees but a few to select committees, which the Speaker named at the time. On the same day, members presented petitions from groups of constituents urging the passage of laws for favored purposes: to establish a reform school for girls, to "protect" dental surgery, to repeal a road law, and so on. Most were referred to standing committees, some to select committees. According to a later House parliamentarian, in the early twentieth century, the sponsor would routinely ask that the bill be referred to a specific committee; if another member asked to have the bill go to a different committee, the Speaker would put the question to the house. This description of the process suggests that the Speaker had the initial power of referral.[8]

If, on the second reading of a bill, the house voted for engrossment, a clerk wrote out the bill and scheduled it for a third reading. The British Parliament continued to require engrossment on parchment in the old black letter (Gothic) script to provide permanence, uniformity, and protection against falsification, but Ohio followed the American practice of engrossing bills in a plain round hand. A bill sent to a committee would be engrossed after receiving a favorable committee report, but it could be recommitted at any time before passage. Once a bill was engrossed, it was not supposed to be changed. In many states an engrossed bill could not be amended. In Ohio, however, amendment on third reading, after engrossment, became common. A separate sheet of paper called a rider, often used to correct inadvertent errors, would be attached to the engrossed bill. For a time in the 1840s, the House prohibited the use of riders to amend bills on third reading, although not without objection from a large minority of members. The representatives must have found the prohibition to be impractical, for it soon disappeared from the rules.[9]

The early rules said almost nothing about third readings. In Parliament and most state legislatures, the third reading was chiefly for an up-or-down vote on passage; debate and amendment had occurred on second reading in the committee of the whole, where every member had had a chance to participate. Jefferson described the process as a full reading of the bill by the clerk; three readings of any riders presented to insert essential provisions left out during engrossment; the admission of amendments, but only with "almost invincible reluctance" because of the dangers of erasures and interlineations; debate; and the vote on passage. In 1856, Cushing noted that amendment on third reading was allowable but inappropriate and that the U.S. House of Representatives had prohibited amendment by rider at this stage. In Ohio, where the committee of the whole was fading away by then, third reading was the only chance for most members to debate a bill and offer amendments. Ohio's legislative rules eventually addressed third readings briefly, but they offered little insight into actual practice.[10]

Reading the Bills

Whether the clerk really read each bill in full at any time in Ohio's history is probably an unanswerable question. According to one scholar, "Undoubtedly bills were read at length in the American assemblies of the colonial period and for some time after. The documents were almost invariably short, and seldom if ever printed at the time of discussion." By the late eighteenth century, though, the practice, if it had ever been followed, may have disappeared. In Jeremy Bentham's day, the clerk in Parliament read only the title and the first few words of the body of the bill. A traditional explanation for three full readings—to ensure that lawmakers knew the contents of bills when printing was not widely practiced and some legislators were illiterate—did not apply in Ohio. It is doubtful that many, if any, members of the General Assembly were illiterate even in 1803. The rules themselves were printed even in territorial days, and they soon called for the printing of bills early in the legislative process. The constitutional requirement that bills be read on three different days guarded against hasty action, but that purpose could be accomplished without reading the bills in full.[11]

When the General Assembly generated relatively few bills, most of them short, three full readings would not have been too burdensome. But one wonders whether the House and Senate clerks really read the militia bill, which took up fifty printed pages in the 1804 session laws, three times in its entirety. It may be that in early statehood days, members heard bills read from top to bottom in the committee of the whole, where, according to the House rules, the clerk read the entire bill through and then read it again, clause by clause, for the purpose of debate. In any case, the members learned to avoid tedious first and second readings by suspending the rule. By 1841, the rules themselves provided for first and second readings by title only.[12]

The 1851 constitution required that every bill be "fully and distinctly read" on three different days, unless three-fourths of the members of the house in which the bill was pending voted to dispense with the rule. (This meant three-fourths of the members present, assuming a quorum, not three-fourths of the members elected to the house.) The legislators were not happy with the prospect of reading every bill from beginning to end three times. Not disposed to engage in the absurdities practiced elsewhere, such as the reading of several bills simultaneously by different clerks or flat-out lying about the readings in the journals, they resorted to the old practice of suspending the rule. Sometimes they dispensed with the reading on three different days, a practice also used occasionally under the first constitution; on other occasions, they voted to read a bill by title only. At some point, probably not long after the new constitution went into effect, first and second readings by title only again became customary. When the lawmakers developed the habit of introducing bills in batches, sometimes dozens at a time, full readings became practically impossible.[13]

At the 1873–74 constitutional convention, delegate Peter Hitchcock noted that the three-readings rule had been adopted "to prevent the hasty action of the General Assembly" but that "in practice the rules have been suspended, as we suspend them here from day to day on the various readings, by consent, without any vote." The clerk was supposed to read the bill distinctly, but just as nobody in the convention listened to the reading of a proposition the second time, no one in the General Assembly paid any attention to a second reading of a bill. That was why both bodies typically dispensed with second readings. Delibera-tions could not be secured "by these rapid readings." In fact, Hitchcock noted, the general practice of both houses had been to read bills by title only on all three readings. Another delegate recalled that the entire municipal code had been read three times from beginning to end, although he conceded that atten-dance had not been "very full" for the first two readings. A few years later, the *Cincinnati Enquirer* reported that a number of codification bills, totaling over 1,200 pages, had been "read section by section in Select Committee, Committee of the Whole and in open session." A high school civics book published in 1901 asserted flatly that when a bill came up for third reading it was "read in full for the first time," but that seems unlikely. Perhaps some important bills received the constitutionally required treatment, but most bills must have gone through with no more than one full reading and probably not even that.[14]

The 1851 constitution also required that every bill deal with only one subject clearly expressed in its title. The one-subject rule, which dates back to ancient Rome, first appeared in this country in the New Jersey constitution of 1844. The concept of clear title grew out of the Yazoo land scandal of 1795, when bribery induced the Georgia legislature to pass a law with a deliberately misleading title, obscuring the fact that the lawmakers were selling enormous tracts of public land to private parties at ridiculously low prices. The purpose of the one-subject and clear-title rules, and to some extent the three-readings rule as well, was to pre-vent "legislation by stealth," that is, the sneaking of proposals into law without adequate notice or deliberation. The Committee on the Legislature at Ohio's second constitutional convention copied all three clauses almost verbatim from the California constitution. Outside of committee, they occasioned no debate.[15]

Within a few years of the constitutional convention, the Ohio Supreme Court essentially gave the General Assembly the authority to disregard these new rules by declaring them to be "directory" only. Observance of the three-readings rule, said the justices in 1855, had to be "secured by [the legislators'] sense of duty and official oaths, and not by any supervisory power of the courts." As long as the journal indicated that three readings had occurred, the court would presume that the readings had met the constitutional requirements. Two years later, the court held the clear-title and one-subject rules to be directory as well.[16]

"The Laborious Part": Committees

The legislative rules had surprisingly little to say about committees, considering the importance of those bodies in the legislative process. The rules included guidelines for procedure only in the committee of the whole. Emphasizing the section-by-section reading, debate, and amendment of bills, the rules for the committee of the whole remained basically the same throughout the century, even as the use of that committee faded away. For a time, the House required that all committees observe the rules of the House "as far as may be applicable." Once standing committees became common, the House limited the requirement to the committee of the whole, as the Senate had always done.[17]

Although the House and Senate rules said little about committee procedure, committee chairmen apparently set down rules of their own. In 1839, according to James Welch, the chairman of the Committee on New Counties, the "common rules of the committee" established a fixed time for regular committee meetings in the west committee room and provided for meetings at the call of the chair. However, the committee often had no business "ripe for action" at the set meeting time, and the designated committee room was "thronged with the business of the clerks." Welch therefore called meetings at appropriate times, at first upon oral notice to the committee members and then by leaving notes on their desks to meet at Welch's seat on the floor of the House. Because the members often could not all get together because of illness, attendance at other committees, or other reasons, Welch would solicit their views individually if the matter was of minor import or had already been considered by the committee. This too he originally did orally but later by notes handed to the members or left on their tables. Under Welch's "rules of the chair," whenever he gave any kind of notice to one member, he gave the same notice to all the members. He did not necessarily feel impelled to convene the committee upon receiving papers related to some matter before the committee, unless requested to do so by a member, but, he insisted, if "new matter came to hand," he advised the members and "obtained their consent and instructions before reporting." According to Welch, "[T]he chair is but the mouthpiece of the committee, or an instrument in their hands which they use to put into effect their will."[18]

During the period of the first constitution, the Speaker of each house had the power to appoint all committees other than the committee of the whole, unless the house directed otherwise. Under the second constitution, which made the lieutenant governor the presiding officer of the Senate, the Senate rules flip-flopped, sometimes conferring the power to appoint standing committees on the lieutenant governor, who served as president of the Senate, and sometimes on the body as a whole. The Senate Republican caucus caused a stir one year by taking the appointing power away from the lieutenant governor–elect after he had already doled out committee seats. At some point, probably after the rise of the vigorous two-party system of Whigs and Democrats, there arose a custom of giving the parties proportional representation on key committees. In 1884 House Republicans protested that the Democratic Speaker had violated this "heretofore uniformly prevailing" practice by depriving them and their constituents of "fair representation upon all the important committees."[19]

Both chambers routinely prohibited committees from meeting during sittings of the full house without special permission. The earliest rules of each house provided for only one standing committee, the committee of privileges and elections, charged with examining the credentials of members and other election-related matters. However, both houses created several additional committees, such as a committee on claims and a ways and means committee, that were in name or effect standing committees. The two chambers adopted joint rules that provided for conference committees to work out differences between the House and Senate when they could not agree on a single version of a bill and a standing enrollment committee to ensure that bills that passed were correctly written in their final form. The two houses also appointed a number of other joint committees.[20]

By the 1820s, the growing importance of standing committees was evident. In 1826, the House and Senate rules provided for the appointment of nine and eight standing committees, respectively, most of them dealing with substantive matters such as finance, the judiciary, or roads. The number of standing committees grew to twenty in the House and seventeen in the Senate in 1837 and twenty-seven in the House and twenty-five in the Senate in 1847. These committees did not only consider bills. They also issued narrative reports, some brief but others quite lengthy, on banking, women's rights, the law of evidence, and other controversial subjects. Sometimes committee members based their reports on personal knowledge of and ruminations on the issue; on other occasions, they gathered evidence from official or commercial documents and the testimony of witnesses.[21]

The General Assembly's action on usury legislation illustrates the uses of committees in the 1830s and 1840s, a transitional period in which the committee of the whole, select committees, and standing committees might all have a hand in shaping a single bill. At that time, and for years afterwards, both the House and Senate rules required that, on second reading, bills go to the committee of the whole unless a motion to do otherwise was adopted. In 1835, the House took up a Senate usury bill in the committee of the whole, which reported an amendment to raise the maximum legal rate of interest. When the representatives reverted to their roles as members of the House rather than members of a committee, however, they rejected the amendment and voted to postpone further consideration of the bill to the meeting of the next General Assembly in December. A few days later, the House reversed itself and recommitted the bill to a select committee of five. After a week, the committee reported back a new amendment, which the House approved. On the day appointed for the third reading, however, the House, after defeating a motion to postpone the bill indefinitely, voted once again to postpone consideration to December.[22]

Postponement either indefinitely or to the next General Assembly effectively killed a bill. However, a measure postponed to the next General Assembly, which before the advent of biennial sessions in 1852 might be only a few months away, was regarded as unfinished business that might be resurrected. As it happened, the 1835 House Committee on Unfinished Business did not include the usury bill in its report to the new House in December, so the bill stayed dead. But the General Assembly often referred unfinished business to a committee for action. In 1844, for example, the House passed a contentious bill to establish Wyandot County. In February, the Senate narrowly rejected a motion to postpone the bill indefinitely but agreed to postpone further consideration until the next legislature convened in December. In December, the new Senate referred the bill to a standing committee, which reported a bill to erect the county. The measure might have been identical to the one postponed in February, but technically it was a new bill that had to go through the whole legislative process. This time the bill became law.[23]

In the decade after it killed the interest rate bill of 1835, the General Assembly defeated repeated attempts to amend the usury law. Some usury bills were introduced upon report of a committee, others by individuals upon notice previously given. Most went to the committee of the whole. Sometimes that committee reported a bill without amendment and the House recommitted the bill to a standing committee. In those instances, the committee of the whole may have functioned as a committee of reference. At other times, the committee of the whole reported a bill with amendment, after which the bill went to a standing committee. The standing committees that considered usury bills in the 1840s took various actions: reporting a bill without amendments; reporting a bill without amendments but recommending indefinite postponement; reporting a bill with amendments, regardless of whether the committee of the whole had already done the same. In one case, the Senate referred a bill to a select committee of one with instructions on amending the bill. Because of the traditional bar on the amendment of a bill by a standing committee or individual member after it had been read a third time, amendments at that stage had to be accomplished by a motion to refer the bill to a select committee of one with explicit instructions on how to amend the bill. If the full house agreed, the person making the motion was appointed as the select committee. The member would instantly report that he had amended the bill as instructed and the clerk would insert the amendment into the bill.[24]

The instant reporting of amendments, a practice not confined to last-second changes, continued well into the twentieth century, sometimes accompanied by other questionable practices. During debate on one usury bill, Representative Peyton Hord proposed a substitute bill by way of amendment. The legislature did not then use the term "substitute bill." Rather, Hord moved that the bill be recommitted to a select committee of one, with instructions to amend by striking everything after the enacting clause in the first line and substituting all new language (a practice at one time prohibited by the Senate rules if the amendment contained entirely different subject matter). The motion passed, and the bill was recommitted to Hord as the select committee. Hord immediately "reported" a bill "amended by substitute, as instructed." The House then passed Hord's entirely new bill and sent it on to the Senate. Robert Luce criticized this method of amending a bill on third reading, so common in Ohio and possibly unique to the Buckeye State, as a "farce" designed to evade the deliberative process. The procedure was indeed farcical, but it was often used for minor changes that did not require extensive deliberation. Even in Hord's case, where the amendment consisted of four significant paragraphs, the members had been exposed to considerable discussion of the issues and probably knew what Hord sought to accomplish.[25]

Some special committees, even committees of one, had more serious func-tions. In 1848, Senator Edward Archbold submitted thoughtful and informative reports on usury law, capital punishment, and the principles of taxation. A spe-cial committee on the repeal of the Black Laws, a subject of intense political in-terest that year, produced majority and minority reports that clearly laid out the opposing positions. Notwithstanding the proliferation of standing committees, the legislature continued to create special committees to deal with topics of ex-traordinary concern, and these sometimes functioned as new standing commit-tees. In 1868, in what appears to have been an organized campaign, advocates of interest rate reform flooded the legislature with petitions to amend the usury law. The House at first referred usury bills to the Finance or Judiciary Committee, but when it became apparent that usury would command an unusual amount of attention during the session, the House appointed a seven-member special Com-mittee on Interest. The Senate, too, used a special committee for at least one usury bill.[26]

The number and size of standing committees continued to grow in the second half of the nineteenth century, reflecting both the growth in business handled by the legislature and the increased use of committee seats as political rewards. In 1850, the Senate had 25 standing committees and 79 places on those commit-tees, for an average of just over 3 members per committee and 2.2 places for each senator. The House had 132 places on 27 standing committees, for an average of 4.9 seats per committee and 1.8 places per representative. Fifty years later, the Senate had 40 standing committees averaging 7.2 members apiece, with approxi-mately 9.3 committee places available for each senator. There were more stand-ing committees than there were senators. No senator could serve effectively on 9 different committees. The House, more than three times as large as the Sen-ate, had 44 standing committees and 322 places on those committees. House committees averaged 7.3 members, and there were approximately 3 places for each representative.[27]

Long before the end of the nineteenth century, standing committees had become the locus of the most important legislative work. In 1847, the *Wooster Democrat* urged the members to spend less time "letting off gas" in their daily sessions and saving their energy for committee work. "For it is in the committee rooms really that the laborious part of the Legislator's duties are performed," the paper asserted. "It is there that he must examine his subject, and prepare himself if need be, to bring forth his strong reason. It is there the bill must be drafted, and its several provisions cautiously examined." The paper also recommended that fixed times be set aside for committee meetings and that "peering and pestiferous" lobbyists be made to understand "that *this time belongs to the committee*."[28]

Toward the end of the century, Henry L. Dawes, a man of vast legislative experience, observed that "[a]lmost the entire consideration and shaping of the most important measures which now come before legislative bodies is done in the committee room before they are reported for action. Little more than ratification of committee work remains after a measure leaves the committee room." The dominance of committees made their defects all the more critical. There are no official records to show how the committees of the General Assembly actually functioned. (Or deliberately failed to function. A committee chairman could tie up legislation he opposed through "masterly inactivity.") In Congress and other state legislatures, committees operated in an unregulated and often secretive fashion. Critics complained that committees were not responsible to the public. Committees frequently met in private, without notice even to the authors of the bills under consideration. "[H]earings are of the 'snap' variety, no one but professional lobbyists knowing the time and place in advance," wrote one observer. Committees could act or not act on bills as they, or their autocratic chairmen, chose. In 1860, the Ohio Senate Judiciary Committee recommended the indefinite postponement of so many bills that it came to be called the slaughterhouse. (According to an anonymous commentator, possibly Senator Jacob D. Cox, most members thought this wholesale butchering of bills served the "true interests of the State.") Committees did not report their proceedings, and newspapers did not get news of committee work until after bills had been reported out, by which time it was too late for effective action by anyone who disagreed. Critics demanded "open and public sessions" of committees "at stated periods." Every proponent or opponent of a measure, they said, should have a "fair opportunity on public notice to present his views," so that the arguments pro and con could be set forth "free from secret influence." In the early nineteenth century, closed committee meetings probably caused little unease. Most committees were appointed on an ad hoc basis to draft bills that would then be debated publicly by the committee of the whole. The rise of the standing committee, with ongoing authority over a particular area of policy, and the decline of the committee of the whole made the closed nature of committee work a matter of public concern.[29]

Overcrowding in the statehouse made some committee meetings public by necessity. In 1837, a House committee insisted that a new statehouse with adequate committee rooms had to be built. The lack of rooms in which committees could meet without interruption and safely keep their files forced committees to convene in members' hotel rooms, "where they are constantly liable to interruption, and where neither the books nor papers to which it is necessary to refer can be kept," or in the legislative halls, where anyone could wander in at any time and several committees might be meeting simultaneously. Either situation caused delay and inaccuracy and waste of time later on in the preparation and discussion of amendments. The General Assembly got its new statehouse, but it didn't help much. A special joint committee noted in 1886 that the House, with forty standing committees, had just four committee rooms, while the Senate, with thirty-five committees, had none. Senate committees still considered bills in the Senate chamber, "amidst the confusion and interruption that cannot be avoided in a public hall." Similar complaints two decades later helped bring about a remodeling of the Senate chamber and a carving up of statehouse space to provide more committee rooms.[30]

Given the large number of committees, shrinking session week, and prohibition on meeting while the house was in session, it seems likely that in Ohio many committees either met rarely or rushed through business. Except for a few key committees, perfunctory meetings may have been the rule. (A member of Congress complained in 1918 that "two thirds of our committees are useless and instead of being really busy the majority of our congressmen down here are telling stories and practising to see who can spit the farthest.") But sometimes, when important bills were being heard, newspaper stories included notice of committee hearings. In 1892, for example, the *Ohio State Journal* noted that "next Tuesday night" the Senate Committee on Railroads would be hearing arguments "pro and con" on a controversial fare bill. (Meeting at night was a common, perhaps general, committee practice.)[31]

Committees probably did not have formal agendas, and it seems that for a long time the sponsors of bills could not even be sure they would get a chance to appear at a committee hearing to discuss their handiwork. In 1872, a senator proposed that each committee chairman notify a bill's author of a time when he could explain the bill to the committee before the committee reported on it. Other senators wanted to require notification to the sponsor only if the committee desired instructions related to the bill or opposed all or part of the bill. The original proposal passed both houses as a joint rule, but within a few years the joint rules called for notification only if a committee member objected to the bill or offered a material amendment.[32]

Perhaps the General Assembly abolished the 1872 notification rule because it went unheeded. State legislatures often ignored their own procedural rules; according to a Columbus newspaper, "the rules of both houses are violated or ignored every day, and frequently twenty times a day." Nevertheless, changes in the rules reflect trends in legislative practice and reveal problems that legislators believed needed to be considered. As time went on, the number of rules, the matters addressed by them, and the amount of detail they contained steadily increased. In 1850, the rules of the Ohio Senate numbered thirty-five, and in 1898, ninety. Although the legislative process in 1900 resembled that of 1850 in many ways, the rules evinced a growing concern, at least in theory, for orderly procedure.[33]

In 1900, assistant Senate clerk Eliot H. Gilkey, under the direction of a joint committee, arranged the House, Senate, and joint rules and pertinent constitutional and statutory provisions into a comprehensive *Manual of Legislative Practice*. The General Assembly had been publishing legislative practice manuals for years, but, before 1900, such handbooks just reprinted the rules and related legal provisions in separate sections. Gilkey integrated the rules and laws into one coherent document, but his *Manual* never went into effect. The Senate approved it two days before adjourning sine die. It was printed in both journals for the benefit of the next General Assembly, but in 1902 the two houses adopted separate rules, as always. But the *Manual* was a laudable effort to systematize procedure and perhaps accord it greater respect.[34]

The *Manual* included some significant rules that were not in the House or Senate rules of 1850, although most had appeared in the rules of at least one of the chambers since then. The *Manual* required that the clerks print and distribute a daily calendar before the opening of business each day, an idea that went back at least to 1860. Bills up for second reading had to be read in the order in which they were introduced. Bills scheduled for third reading had to be read in the order in which they were sent to the calendar. Other rules were meant to ensure that members would know about changes that had been made to a bill. If a bill was amended before its third reading, the clerk had to indicate that fact on the calendar by designating the bill "Amended H.B." or "Amended S.B." The *Manual* included detailed requirements for the engrossment and reengrossment of bills and resolutions. If one house passed a bill and the other amended it, the clerk of the second house had to engross the amendments on a separate piece of paper, reengross the bill, and return both the amendments and the reengrossed bill to the first house along with the original bill. The title of every bill had to list any section of law to be amended or repealed, and new matter contained in the bill had to be underlined (or, when printed, italicized). These and related rules put legislators and the public on notice as to what was happening and when, so that they could less easily be intentionally hoodwinked or inadvertently deceived. But the *Manual* still had little to say about committees, where so much of the most important legislative work occurred. Many years would pass before the functioning of committees would be satisfactorily reformed.[35]

7

THE WORKING LIFE

THE FORMAL LEGISLATIVE PROCESS described in chapter 6 was only part of a nineteenth-century legislators' working life, and for some not the most important part. Many members, knowing and caring little about parliamentary procedure, contented themselves with following their leaders in committee or on the floor. But every lawmaker had an interest in the length of the session, the workweek, and the workday; in standards of decorum; in compensation; and in other aspects of his job not directly related to the passage of legislation.

Sessions

Under the constitution of 1802, the legislature convened on the first Monday in December and adjourned anywhere from late January to late March. The long-term trend was toward longer sessions. The members usually sat as a body Monday through Saturday, including, until the late 1830s, Christmas and New Year's Days. In the early years, the House and Senate generally met around 9:00 A.M., although later on they typically began at 10:00 in the morning, broke for lunch, and re-convened at 3:00 in the afternoon. Sometimes that schedule proved inadequate. In 1839, for example, the House rejected an early-session motion to hold regular evening sessions as an economizing measure and voted instead to get together at 10:00 A.M. and 3:00 P.M. By February, the representatives were often reconvening at 2:00 P.M., occasionally starting the day at 9:00 A.M., and holding evening sessions as well. Not infrequently, especially toward the end of a session, the law-makers met after dinner. Committees often, perhaps usually, met in the evening. Joshua Giddings wrote in 1837 that the members seemed "more [attentive] to their business than formerly. they rise at breakfast, sit around & read the news till half past ten oclock then go to the house & sit about one hour and adjourn to three oclock at which time they again repair to the state house & remain an-other hour & adjourn over to the next day." On one very special day, the last day of the session, the members met very early: 6:00 A.M. in 1803, but after 1830 anywhere from 2:00 to 5:00 in the morning. It may be that they were already in the chambers following a frenzied late-night session to wrap up business.[1]

As Ohio moved from an agricultural economy to an industrial economy less dependent on the seasons, and as improvements in transportation allowed mem-bers to take trips home during session, the General Assembly shortened its work-week and lengthened its sessions. By the 1870s, Saturday meetings had become rare, and the members frequently took three-day weekends. (In 1884, a Repub-lican newspaper, complaining that the Democratic caucus made all the impor-tant decisions on legislation in advance, suggested acidly that the caucus sit daily and the House and Senate meet just once a week to ratify the caucus's decrees.) Sessions usually ran into April or early May, although the Sixty-third General Assembly, which dealt with the arduous task of codifying the state laws, did not adjourn until June 23, 1879.[2]

Many Ohioans doubted the need for longer sessions. Indeed, they thought the legislators ought to go home and stay home. The 1851 constitution provided for biennial sessions, by which the delegates intended that the General Assembly hold one session every other year. But, as we saw in chapter 3, the constitutional provision did not work as planned. Every General Assembly but one before 1894 simply adjourned in the spring of its first year until the following November, December, or more typically January. At the 1873–74 constitutional convention, the delegates again vigorously debated the merits of biennial sessions, which got tangled up with the issue of terms of office. Advocates of longer terms sought to reduce the political agitation and expense entailed in frequent elections and to provide experience and continuity in the legislature. They also hoped to attract better men as candidates, reduce turnover, and add "tone and dignity" to the General Assembly. One delegate, complaining that good men often failed of re-election because merit carried little weight in local politics, blamed the inexperience of legislators for the prevailing "political degeneracy," "evil enactments," and "corrupt influence" of "soulless corporations."[3]

Opponents of longer terms insisted that decent men did get reelected, that the legislature had always had its share of experienced members, and that longer terms would induce legislators to pay less attention to the wishes of their constituents. Some zealous democrats urged a return to annual elections. Since the General Assembly was meeting almost every year anyway, why not go back to "first principles"—short terms of office and annual elections? The convention settled on annual sessions but provided for two-year terms for both senators and representatives.[4]

The voters rejected the constitution proposed by the convention, and public respect for the General Assembly continued to fall. Progressive commentators added to the chorus of complaints about "overlegislation," and, in 1894, Governor William McKinley called for biennial sessions. The General Assembly complied. It resolved to adjourn sine die at the end of its session in the first year of the biennium. The Speaker of the House claimed that it did so in part because of "a wide and increasing public opinion that the people are governed too much." (The members continued to receive their full compensation, which since 1880 had been a salary for the term of office rather than a daily rate while the legislature was in session.)[5]

Late-nineteenth-century critics of state legislatures often complained of "overlegislation." When the Sixty-third General Assembly finally adjourned in June 1879, the Speaker noted that in addition to codification, the legislature had had to deal with nearly 1,500 bills. He might have added that the members of the two houses also introduced 256 joint resolutions and 304 House and Senate resolutions, and that in the House alone members had presented 925 petitions, memorials, and remonstrances. One Speaker thought the "vast mass of legislation" was a sign of progress in the great state of Ohio, but not many agreed with him. The move to biennial sessions succeeded in reducing the number of bills. In each of the Sixty-ninth (1890–91) and Seventieth (1892–93) General Assemblies, lawmakers introduced over 2,500 bills and passed nearly 1,600; in the Seventy-first

(1894) and Seventy-second (1896) General Assemblies, they introduced 1,543 and 1,378 bills, respectively, and passed 928 and 691.[6]

Several times under the first constitution, the General Assembly met in special session after the regular session had adjourned, usually to draw congressional district lines. In 1835, Governor Robert Lucas called the lawmakers together to deal with the Toledo War, an ongoing boundary dispute with the Territory of Michigan during which Michigan authorities arrested Ohio boundary commissioners. At the special session, the General Assembly created Lucas County, including the disputed area. It also appropriated funds for running the boundary line and outlawed the kidnapping of white citizens of Ohio. In 1836, the Democratic majority in Congress, anxious to secure Ohio's electoral votes in the approaching presidential election, resolved the controversy in Ohio's favor. Under Ohio's second constitution, the General Assembly met in a contentious special session in 1890 at the call of Governor James E. Campbell, a reform-minded politician who demanded action to deal with "the deplorable condition of public affairs" in Cincinnati. After a nasty intraparty battle between Campbell and Hamilton County Democrats, the legislature abolished Cincinnati's corrupt board of public improvement and authorized the mayor to appoint a new board to function until the next election. However, the supreme court nullified Campbell's victory, declaring the law to be unconstitutional special legislation.[7]

Almost all sessions, regular and special, were open to the public. At times of great political excitement, the public crowded the galleries to observe the proceedings. At the opening of the tumultuous session of 1848–49, when members of the short-lived Free Soil Party held the balance of power, the galleries and lobbies were "packed to suffocation." Albert G. Riddle recalled that "a noisy, and in the main, good-natured mob" took possession of the lower half of the building, in which the House met. They showed "not the least respect to the presence of the representatives, taking up and repeating the cries of the members, all shouting, yelling and swearing at once," so that the member "shouting to his speaker could not hear his own voice."[8]

The constitution allowed for secrecy when either house thought it necessary. The first secret session came in 1806 thanks to the machinations of former vice president Aaron Burr, who visited Ohio and other western scenes in 1805 and 1806. Rumors abounded that Burr hoped for hostilities between the United States and Spain along the Mexico-Louisiana border in order to detach New Orleans from the United States and set up an independent country. Burr denied it, and his friend, U.S. senator John Smith of Ohio, defended him. But President Jefferson's agent convinced Governor Tiffin that the danger was real. Tiffin sent the General Assembly a confidential message relating that "an agent of a gentleman late high in office in the United States" was raising men and building boats in the Muskingum River area for the purpose of seizing New Orleans. Several times between December 2 and December 6, each house cleared the lobby and closed its doors to consider Tiffin's message. According to Tiffin, an intoxicated Representative Nathaniel Massie objected so vehemently to the first secret session that the House adjourned in disorder, allowing two of Burr's cohorts to escape Ohio jurisdiction. On December 6, the General Assembly enacted legislation prohibiting anyone from building boats, recruiting individuals, or marching forces in or through Ohio with the intent to act against the peace of the United States. The lawmakers authorized the governor to call out the militia to enforce the new law. Tiffin alerted the militia, the boats were seized, and the conspiracy, insofar as Ohio was concerned, came to an inglorious end.[9]

For Senator Smith, Burr's shenanigans had disastrous political consequences. Smith had defended Burr in good faith. When he learned of Burr's deception, Smith, who had business interests and army supply contracts in Louisiana, took steps to arm the woefully equipped Ohio militia and then brought military supplies to U.S. forces in New Orleans. Nevertheless, Smith's political opponents in Ohio used his defense of Burr and absence from the Senate as an excuse to get rid of him. On December 23, 1806, the General Assembly demanded Smith's resignation. Jefferson's allies in the U.S. Senate hounded Smith and came within one vote of expelling him before Smith, seeing that his political career was ruined, resigned.[10]

The General Assembly held secret sessions again in December 1814, prompted as in 1806 by a confidential message from the governor. This time the governor, unaware that the War of 1812 was drawing to a close, informed the legislators that military posts along Ohio's northwestern frontier were sadly undersupplied. The General Assembly could think of nothing better to do than offer to loan the U.S. government twenty to thirty thousand dollars to pay the supply contractors (which turned out to be unnecessary). At least once during the Civil War, the House went into secret session, and the Senate used executive sessions to consider the governor's nominations to public offices that required Senate approval. In 1870, leaks to the governor and the press of secret proceedings to consider nominations infuriated some senators, but the Senate refused to appoint a committee of investigation.[11]

Rituals

Some aspects of the legislator's working life had less gravity than the duration or openness of sessions but nevertheless carried some weight with men who had to endure them for months on end. Consider, for example, the matter of seating in the chambers. (Actually, seating arrangements may have had political implications. Studies of the General Assembly around 1970, before most members had much in the way of staff, found that "seat contiguity" affected members' votes.) How the lawmakers chose their seats, especially during Ohio's first half century, is not clear. In 1857, the General Assembly's first year in the new statehouse, a House member proposed that the clerk draw a ballot from one box with a member's name and a ballot from another box with a seat number and thus match the member with the seat. Instead, the House formally resolved to have the clerk draw ballots with just the representatives' names; as each member's name was called, he would choose his seat. The House may have copied the seat selection procedure from other states or from the U.S. House of Representatives, which began drawing lots for seats in 1845. For more than a century thereafter, according to the House journal, representatives chose their seats by lot, with exceptions noted for members with seniority or physical infirmities. The House embellished the ritual by having a blindfolded page rather than the clerk draw the ballots. Members who got stuck in the back rows had to deal with the noise and confusion created by lobbyists and other visitors in that part of the hall. Those unhappy with the drawing might have exchanged seats with other representatives, perhaps with a cash incentive for the swap, as legislators in other states sometimes did. One year, some disgruntled members moved their desks to the open space near the clerk's table, and the House had to instruct the sergeant at arms to put them back where they belonged. Senators began choosing their seats by lot in 1860, at least according to the Senate journal; James Monroe's biographer states that, in 1860, Monroe, Jacob D. Cox, and James A. Garfield sat next to each other in the Senate because they represented contiguous districts.[12]

Although the House seating resolutions of 1857 said nothing about the subject, seating by party seems to have been an established tradition by then. A seating chart for the House of 1848–49 shows almost all the Whigs seated to the Speaker's left as he faced his colleagues from the front of the hall and almost all the Democrats on the Speaker's right. A member recalled that the east half of the hall was the Whigs' "by prescription." In 1894, Republican Speaker Alexander

Boxwell, at the close of the session, thanked his colleagues, including his "friends who occupy the southeast corner" of the hall, the minority Democrats, for their cooperation.[13]

Another early-session event that changed over time was the election of the Speaker, clerk, and other officers of the House and Senate. In 1841 and 1842, the House broke with tradition and elected its officers by voice vote rather than by secret ballot. A large minority of members resisted the innovation, and in 1843 the House reverted to the old practice. At the midcentury constitutional convention, however, the committee on the legislature recommended viva voce elections. Supporters of the proposal argued that the people had a right to know whether their servants voted in accordance with the will of their constituents. Opponents complained that members would be "compelled to vote under the party lash." The convention adopted the measure by a wide margin, and, from 1852 on, the House and Senate chose their officers by voice vote.[14]

Seat selection and the election of officers were welcoming ceremonies of sorts for the members. The General Assembly also had ritualistic leave-takings: resolutions of thanks to leaders and employees and closing speeches by the presiding officers, but also farewells to colleagues who died during their terms of office. Before the Civil War, when living and working conditions drew the members into close social relations and travel was slow and difficult, the House or Senate would appoint a committee to arrange Columbus funerals for deceased lawmakers. The lawmakers typically resolved to attend the services and wear black crepe armbands ("the usual badge of mourning") for thirty days or the remainder of the session, and they might even appropriate money to pay for funeral expenses. In the latter part of the century, railroads and easy getaways weakened the forced intimacy among legislators and with it their involvement in the goodbyes. The House and Senate still adopted resolutions of respect, and they draped the deceased legislators' desks in mourning and lowered the chamber's flag to half-mast. But the crepe armbands disappeared, funerals took place in the deceased members' districts, and specially appointed committees rather than the entire body usually went to the services.[15]

Opening the daily sessions with prayer became a ritual in the 1840s, but not without controversy. Legislative prayer dated back to colonial days and was common in state legislatures and Congress. In the 1830s, though, it stirred noisy disputes in some states, particularly where assemblies had paid legislative chaplains. The Workingman's Advocate, a labor newspaper whose ideas the Democratic Party generally absorbed, agitated against prayer in the legislature, arguing for a complete separation of church and state and pointing out that most members skipped the prayer anyway. *Niles' National Register,* a Whig paper, defended legislative chaplains, relying on the authority of no less a skeptic than Benjamin Franklin. In December 1844, Democratic representative Israel Brown introduced and the Ohio House passed a resolution to have Columbus clergymen send one of their number to begin session each morning with a prayer. Perhaps Brown meant his resolution to be a dig at the Whigs, whose recently defeated presidential candidate, Henry Clay, belonged to no church and had a reputation for loose morals. Another Democrat, Charles Reemelin, denounced opening prayers by regular clergymen as an "antiquated, merely ceremonious, and therefore really irreligious" practice, but the House journal does not record any discussion of or vote on the resolution and it may be that few members seriously objected. The next day, though, the representatives adopted a Whig-sponsored resolution to commence their daily sessions in the *afternoon,* ostensibly to give standing committees time to prepare their reports. The Democratic *Ohio Statesman* called the resolution a Whig trick to enable members to avoid the daily prayer. The paper credited Democrats with properly interpreting the prayer resolution as a call to start each day's session with prayer regardless of when it began, which is what the House did.[16]

The senators, faced with a similar prayer resolution, voted as might have been expected. A Whig introduced the resolution. A Democrat promptly moved to table it. The senators, by a nearly straight party-line vote, refused to table. The Senate then amended the resolution to request each member to contribute one dollar from his private funds to compensate the clergymen and to have the sergeant at arms collect the money. The requisition was a Democratic idea, perhaps intended to embarrass the Whigs by forcing them to put their money where their mouths were or to forestall any attempt to appropriate money for the ministers. After defeating motions to delay or kill the resolution, the Senate passed it, with Whigs supporting the resolution 16 to 3 and Democrats opposing it 9 to 6. Both Whigs and Democrats had second thoughts about the private contribution, though, and, on reconsideration, the Senate struck it out. Then, with a second chance to vote on the prayer resolution itself, the Senate adopted it on a party-line vote, only four members of either party breaking ranks.[17]

For several years, resolutions to start the daily sessions with prayer encountered the opposition of a diminishing minority in each house. Radical Democrats objected to legislative prayer on constitutional grounds. Adverting to the Ohio constitution's guarantee of religious freedom, Charles Reemelin complained that public prayer turned the Senate chamber into a house of worship that he could be compelled by the sergeant at arms to attend upon a call of the Senate. It reminded him of the dangerous affiliation of church and state in his native Germany. "Connect religion with state affairs," Reemelin warned, "and you have a connection *beneficial to neither party, and injurious to both.* Governments will corrupt religion, and a corrupted religion will ultimately subvert a free government." A religious paper claimed in 1847 that the clergymen in Columbus had arranged among themselves to exclude Universalist ministers from the clerics who offered prayer in the legislature and that the Senate had responded by appointing a Universalist preacher as its chaplain, but there is no evidence in the Senate journal that the senators took such action. The journal does show that nine senators opposed opening that session's meetings with prayer; one of them, later in the session, would present a petition from a constituent for the incorporation of the Infidel Church. In 1852, Senator Jonathan Tod, after voting against the prayer resolution in vain, offered a resolution instructing the presiding officer, if he could not find a clergyman to give the opening prayer the next day, to appoint one of the senators to do so. That senator was to offer a prayer "so pointedly and impressively addressed to the Ruler of the Universe, that no further prayers particularly intended for the benefit of the Senate shall be necessary during the balance of this session." Tod's acerbic suggestion appears to have been the last gasp of the opposition. From then on, both the House and the Senate adopted prayer resolutions as a matter of routine, with no division on the question.[18]

Some members thought their fellows were in need of prayer. After the General Assembly repealed a law favored by Catholics that allowed prison inmates to have clergymen of their own faiths, Senator Edward Lewis offered a resolution recognizing that the lawmakers had "torn from the statutes of this State all laws favoring liberty of conscience in matters of religion." Lewis, supported by I. T. Monahan, proposed to invite the famous evangelists Dwight L. Moody and Ira D. Sankey to open the daily sessions for a week with "supplications particularly addressed to the demise of this great principle." Other senators then suggested that the supplications be directed especially toward Lewis and Monahan and that Monahan be substituted for Moody and Sankey. The exchange seems to have been a bitter one, not at all taken in good fun.[19]

The First Century

Conduct Unbecoming a Legislator

Blatant hostility occasionally leaps off the pages of the journals. In 1843, a bill to prohibit the firing of cannon in public streets came up for a final vote on the floor of the House. Representative Legrand Byington and his allies tried various parliamentary tactics to amend the bill or delay the vote. At length, Speaker John Chaney ruled Byington out of order. After the bill passed, with Byington's support, Byington introduced a resolution declaring that Chaney had "forfeited all confidence, as an impartial presiding officer, either from stupid ignorance of parliamentary law, or from a wilful maladministration of it." This was not a partisan affair; Chaney and Byington were both Democrats. Whig Simeon Fuller moved to expel Byington "for his contumacious and disorderly conduct, in making reiterated motions, to delay business and prevent legislative action," but quickly withdrew the motion. After much bickering and several attempts to defuse the situation, the House finally crushed the no-confidence resolution and censured Byington "for his unprovoked insult to the Speaker."[20]

The official House and Senate journals are mostly dull chronicles of legislative proceedings, notwithstanding the inclusion of bitter or humorous resolutions and the sometimes fascinating committee reports on controversial political issues or election contests. The journals contain no record of debates or committee hearings and of course nothing on party caucuses. (A caucus consisted of all the senators or representatives or both of a single party.) In 1884, the Republican *Ohio State Journal* published an extensive report on an acrimonious "joint Democratic secret caucus" that the paper described as "a regular slaughter-pen." For all their importance, though, caucus meetings remained outside the formal legislative process and seldom received such detailed coverage.[21]

Published accounts of legislative debates are also rare and of committee meetings almost nonexistent. The quality of debate in the General Assembly probably would have disappointed scholars of rhetoric. In 1843, three New England professors, in the introduction to a book of essays on classical studies, deplored what they saw as a "coarseness and vulgarity of sentiment, a disregard or ignorance of the proprieties of speech, an utter insensibility to the elegances of letters, and to the humanizing influences of the arts" among American legislators. The aim of legislators, as well as preachers and writers, they claimed, was "the production of immediate practical effect. Hence, there is a struggle for the boldest figures and the most passionate oratory. . . . Passion; over-statement; ridiculous conceits; the introduction of terms that have no citizenship in any language on earth; a disregard of grammar; an affected smartness" were employed in an effort to carry the human heart "by storm."[22]

If the scholars could complain of the vulgarity of debate in the East, including the halls of Congress, what could be the state of the art out in the Old Northwest? Alluding to his days as a territorial legislator, Edward Tiffin regretted the "unguarded expressions which escaped me in the heat of debate." Even Ephraim Cutler sometimes faulted himself for overheated statehouse oratory. "I sometimes get excited in debate, perhaps too much so," he wrote, "but I believe I have never descended from a dignified course."[23]

What passed for dignity in Ohio did not satisfy fastidious New England critics. Isaac Appleton Jewett, born in Vermont, educated at Harvard, and offended by the "rank democracy" exhibited in the halls of the General Assembly, described Buckeye legislators as "ignoble specimen of mental [S]aharas—no eloquence— no splendid bursts—no masterly elucidation of momentous subjects—no statesman like deportment . . . Common place thoughts, given in common place language, and delivered in common place manner. . . . Never was English grammar so unpardonably mangled." What's more, wrote Jewett, "[o]ur Legislature are a shabby looking set of fellows. Indeed a ragged coat is the best passport to office and immortality in Ohio, and on meeting an apparent object of charity in the Streets, it is necessary to take heed, or we shall present our voluntary alms to a representative." Cyrus Bradley, the young traveler from New Hampshire, remarked upon the lack of decorum in 1835: members smoking, their legs on their desks, their manner careless, and their conversation profane. One permanently intoxicated member, wrote Bradley, "reeled into the house and undertook to say something, but was pulled down by his friends." About all that can be said in defense of such behavior is that it was no worse than what occurred in many legislatures, including Congress, for much of the nineteenth century. Besides, conceded Jewett, underneath that crude exterior lay "the soul, the enterprize, the pride, the resolution which have made Ohio what she is, and will make her."[24]

The General Assembly never formally prohibited alcohol in the legislative chambers in the nineteenth century; the lawmakers apparently took it for granted that they were not supposed to drink while on duty, even if some of them did. (When the House sought new cloakrooms in 1884, a newspaper commented, "The cloak-rooms will never harbor jugs of good bourbon. Perish the thought!") Smoking was another matter. In 1857, a member of the House offered a resolution requesting members to refrain from smoking in the representatives' hall, whether or not the House was in session, and directing the sergeant at arms to prevent others from smoking. The resolution went nowhere. In 1870, though, the Senate banned smoking in the chamber during session, and the House eventually barred smoking "in the body of the hall of the house." That either house enforced the ban is doubtful. A few years after the Senate formally prohibited smoking, a senator asked that the ban be strictly enforced. His colleagues moved to adjourn, to amend the resolution, to send the sergeant at arms to round up absentees, and resorted to other parliamentary evasions before finally adjourning without acting on the proposal.[25]

The General Assembly remained a rough-and-tumble arena long after Ohio passed the frontier stage. Although the House Speaker or Senate president might close a session with a little speech lauding the cooperation of the opposition party and the friendships made during the previous year or two, sweetness and light often seemed in short supply. Tensions boiled over into name-calling, charges of corruption, and even fisticuffs. In 1845, Representative Jacob Flinn of Cincinnati *"took off his coat and laid it on his desk,* swearing that he would *lick the first three men"* who voted for the engrossment of a bill to which he objected. A Columbus newspaper, noting that this was Flinn's second "outbreak of bullyism" of the session, urged that Flinn be expelled from the House. Exactly one year later, Flinn menaced another member during debate and then attacked his adversary on the street. The two men, both armed with knives, had to be pulled apart by bystanders. The House declined to expel Flinn, but it did censure him. A few years after that, House clerk Mahlon H. Medary's office upset Representative George Barnum when it failed to have Barnum's pet bill engrossed in time for a scheduled third reading and the bill got placed behind another one in the order of business. Barnum declared on the floor of the House that the failure was due to Medary's "hocus pocus" and that Medary was either dishonest or grossly incompetent. The clerk, irate that no one spoke up to defend him, advanced to the Speaker's chair to proffer his resignation. There he encountered Barnum, and instead of tendering his resignation, grabbed another member's crutch and whacked Barnum on the head, drawing blood. In the investigation that followed, all the witnesses testified to Medary's general courtesy and effectiveness, but the House could hardly keep a clerk who assaulted the members. It quickly replaced him.[26]

In 1857, Representative Darius Cadwell called one of Representative John P. Slough's proposals foolish, whereupon Slough, taking the remark as a personal insult, struck Cadwell in the face. Slough refused the House's invitation to dismiss the matter with an apology and a promise of good behavior—the most Slough would do was acknowledge a breach of propriety—and the House expelled him. In 1864, Representative William H. Free, who had served more than two years in the Union army, took offense at Representative Archibald Mayo's intemperate denunciation of the government for suppressing opposition newspapers, and he assaulted Mayo on the floor of the House. Free apologized for his conduct, which the House condemned without actually censuring Free. The House did, however, censure Mayo for his "disloyal and morally treasonable sentiments." A group of Democrats promptly protested the censure as a tyrannical punishment for the expression of opinion and a threat to freedom of debate in the legislature.[27]

Physical violence faded from the legislative scene after the Civil War, although, as late as 1878, the state railroad commissioner threw down and choked a senator on the floor of the Senate. Emotions could still run high, however, especially over war-related matters. In 1878, Democratic representative John O'Connor, a resident of the national soldiers' asylum in Dayton, was made chairman of the House Military Affairs Committee. After two and a half months, Republican James M. Dalzell and two other members of the committee, believing that O'Connor had deserted during the Civil War and prompted "by a sense of self-respect," asked to be excused from further service as long as O'Connor held the chair. O'Connor resigned as chairman, but he insisted that he was the victim of mistaken identity. An investigating committee exonerated O'Connor and the House accepted the committee's report, refusing even to print Dalzell's minority report. Two months later, Dalzell, a zealous advocate for ex-soldiers popularly known as Private Dalzell, was waving his own discharge papers on the floor of the House, defending himself against charges made in the Democratic *Ohio Statesman* that he himself had been a deserter.[28]

O'Connor's troubles did not end with the favorable committee report. The House appointed another committee to investigate charges that O'Connor had been convicted of a felony in Michigan, which would have made him ineligible to hold a seat in the General Assembly. The committee found that he had indeed been convicted of larceny in 1869 and served three years in a Michigan prison. The House duly expelled him. Later that year, O'Connor, having gained national notoriety as a criminal and wartime bounty jumper, was arrested in Dayton on a federal warrant, convicted of forgery, and sent to prison.[29]

Violence may have diminished in the General Assembly, but, in an age of high party tensions and seesawing control of the legislature, civility still suffered. A newspaper noted in 1873 that "liar" had become a "common epithet" in the General Assembly. Ten years later, the Speaker of the House and another representative engaged in "a loud and boisterous exchange of words, the unfortunate and in some degree disgraceful feature being that such a scene should be precipitated and enacted in the presence of the speaker's wife and her mother, who sat within a few feet of the combatants . . . Several members remarked they had never witnessed such a scene in the House." In addition, if the highly partisan newspapers are to be believed, the occasional inebriated member still roamed the halls of the legislature. One Democratic editor, conscious of his party's opposition to the gathering prohibition crusade, commented in 1874 upon the remarkably temperate habits of most members of both parties, although another paper noted at the opening of that session that "[m]embers would occasionally withdraw themselves from the political excitement about them to break a friendly bottle at Ambos' or to smack their lips over a convivial glass of 'something strong.'"[30]

Not every breach of decorum stemmed from intoxication or personal animosity. In 1880, the Speaker of the House had to "read the riot act" almost daily to noisy, inattentive members who were "addicted to grouping." The members sometimes engaged in conduct astonishing for its puerility, especially on the day of adjournment. The custom of convening at the unholy hour of two or three in the morning on the last day of session disappeared in the mid-1850s, apparently leaving the members with sufficient energy to celebrate by throwing wads of paper. Sometimes the frivolity got out of hand. One year the members of the House "engaged in a general scrimmage, throwing paper balls, books and heavy cushions from their chairs in all directions." A flying cushion smashed a gas lamp, sending shards of glass flying and driving the iron stem of the lamp into the face of an elderly representative who had been minding his own business. At least the Ohio General Assembly was not alone in its indecorousness. "I shall never forget," wrote writer and former Toledo mayor Brand Whitlock in 1914, "those scenes of riot, the howling and drunkenness and confusion and worse I have witnessed in the legislatures of Illinois and of Ohio on the last night of the session."[31]

The end of session was the prime time, but not the only time, for such antics. One midsession day in 1885, when business was slow because of the lack of a quorum, the Speaker pro tem of the House "got on the floor to play the buffoon in a manner that would shock a variety show. While the officers of the House were out scouring the salons and dives for absentees, members indulged in throwing paper balls, yelling, tearing maps from the wall and conducting the worst beer-garden frolics that were even seen in public places."[32]

Taking the Job Seriously

Lest one conclude from all these descriptions of inelegant speech, inebriation, and indecorous behavior that the General Assembly was nothing but a home for elected delinquents, it would be well to remember that many lawmakers brought talent, education, and a deep respect for republican institutions to their work. Ephraim Cutler may have been cranky at times, but he was the scion of an old New England family, the son of a founder of Ohio University, himself a founder of the first public library in the Northwest Territory, and a prominent player in the establishment of Ohio's public school system. One may readily believe that he "never descended from a dignified course" in the legislature.

Cutler was hardly unique. There were others of all parties and backgrounds who acted creditably. Clement Vallandigham, remembered now as the fiery Copperhead whom President Lincoln ordered deported to the Confederacy, entered the General Assembly in 1845 as a serious young man determined to "bear in mind the dignity and responsibility of [his] station." The rules of conduct he set for himself included "speak[ing] but rarely, and never without having made myself complete and thorough master of the subject—so that when I rise, every one may expect to hear something worth listening to." When one of Vallandigham's fellow Democrats chided him for being overly courteous toward a Whig, he replied that he "hoped always so to be a Democrat as not to forget that he was a gentleman."[33]

In the years leading up to the Civil War, the Western Reserve in northeastern Ohio sent several antislavery intellectuals to the legislature. In 1848, the Reserve elected Free Soilers Albert G. Riddle, a lawyer, novelist, biographer, and historian, and Norton S. Townshend, a physician and professor of agriculture. In 1855, Oberlin professor James Monroe, formerly an abolitionist lecturer, won a seat in the Ohio Senate. He would be joined in 1859 by Republicans James A. Garfield, professor of ancient languages and president of Hiram College, and Jacob D. Cox, superintendent of schools in Warren and future lawyer, author, university president, and winner of a gold medal for photomicroscopy.

Toward the end of the nineteenth century, a number of gifted African Americans sat in the legislature, beginning with George Washington Williams. Raised poor and poorly educated in Pennsylvania, Williams enlisted in the Union army as an underage soldier in 1864. Later, despite inadequate preparation, he enrolled in the Newton Theological Institution in Massachusetts and proved to be an

George Washington Williams. *Reproduced by permission of the Ohio Historical Society*

excellent student. He served as a Baptist minister in Boston and edited a weekly newspaper in Washington, D.C., before moving to Cincinnati in 1876. There Williams wrote newspaper columns, studied law, and became an active member of the Republican Party. After a term in the House as Ohio's first black state legislator, Williams took to lecturing and to writing about the history of blacks in America. To many blacks and whites alike, writes historian John Hope Franklin, Williams "possessed a curious combination of rare genius, remarkable resourcefulness, and an incomparable talent for self-aggrandizement."[34]

Williams and his fellow African American legislators do not seem to have encountered much overt bigotry from their colleagues. When a restaurant refused to serve Williams, the House appointed a committee to investigate. The committee condemned the insult to "a gentleman of intelligence, culture, and high moral worth" and rejected the proprietor's public apology as insincere. The House adopted the committee's report and denounced the treatment of Williams as "an insult to this House as well as the whole people of the State of Ohio." John P. Green, who on February 21, 1882, became the first African American to preside over the House, recalled in his memoirs that he had been treated without dis-crimination in the General Assembly. However, the black legislators, all Repub-licans, met resistance from "lily white" Republicans as well as Democrats when they tried to enact antidiscrimination laws or other legislation of special interest to blacks. When they persisted, as in their fight for an antilynching bill and for an end to legally segregated schools, they usually got their way.[35]

The General Assembly always had members like Cutler, Townshend, Garfield, and Williams, but they were atypical. Tomfoolery, drunkenness, and assaults upon legislators and language alike may not have been the norm, but neither was close adherence to the standards of decorum preferred by critical New Eng-landers. Perhaps the democratization of public life contributed to the shortage of dignity in legislative councils, for it brought to the capital many men of modest education and limited political experience and forced even better-equipped men to appeal to the masses to get elected. Fatigue and frustration may also have ac-counted for some departures from decency. A handful of men often carried the burden of the work, as Jacob Burnet did in territorial days. Indeed, one could hardly expect the general run of legislators, who served in Columbus for one or two terms of a few months each, to produce much of substance in the absence of clerical, research, and bill-drafting assistance. Ephraim Cutler, who could and did perform these essential legislative tasks, often complained of the difficulties of his work. Less than three weeks after taking his seat in the House of Repre-sentatives for the first time, Cutler wrote to his wife, "I came from the house this evening wearied. I had made a speech, in which I felt considerably animated, and now experience the consequent exhaustion." By February of that term, having served on committees, drafted bills, and carried the burden of debate for his side on school, taxation, and canal legislation, Cutler was nearing exhaustion. "I expect to have one more tiresome day when [the canal bill] comes up," he wrote. "It makes my head and back ache to discuss these tough questions. . . . It cost me a day's most fatiguing labor when it was before the committee of the whole house. To support every proposition, and rebut every cavil, single-handed, is, indeed, a task." During the session of 1824–25, when he served in the Senate, Cutler re-peatedly wrote home about the effects of his labors on the school and tax issues. For weeks, he reported in January 1824, he had slept no more than four hours a night and subsisted on coffee, tea, and light meals. His friends thought he looked sick. As chairman of the Revenue Committee, he wrote, "it has devolved upon me to prepare an entirely new system of revenue for the state. . . . Not only my reputation, but the good of my country is at stake, and much depends upon how I am enabled to discharge my duty. This, with the necessity of close application in reading, and intense thinking, in order to digest a subject so difficult and interesting, which has for years appalled the best talents of the state, has become a burthen almost too much to bear." Cutler's only assistance came from a visiting acquaintance who helped him copy bills.[36]

Other conscientious lawmakers also put in long hours. Lawyer Alexander Long, who represented Hamilton County at midcentury, remembered laboring "day and night." In his first term he drafted and introduced thirty-six bills. The next year, he "was not only required to draft and present, act after act, for the county of Hamilton, but was applied to from other sections of the state to do the same thing." James A. Garfield found that, toward the end of session, the work became "more laborious. Events crowd upon each other rapidly and it requires all of one's energies to keep the run of business and act intelligently." Seabury Ford, elected in 1835, set to work so diligently that he lost forty pounds in four months, and the next year he complained that his constant exertions in connection with a railroad bill were affecting his health.[37]

Earning One's Pay

Members received modest compensation for their services. The constitution limited their pay until 1808 to two dollars per day during session and two dollars per twenty-five miles in traveling between home and the capital. In 1816, the legislators raised their pay to three dollars per day and increased the salaries of other public officials as well. The raise led to a storm of protest, although it was overshadowed by the even more hated federal Compensation Act of that same year. During the financial crisis of the early 1820s, the members reduced their compensation, but, in the 1823–24 session, they sparked an outcry by again raising their pay "from the constitutional and ample amount of two dollars per day to the more liberal and *gentlemanly sum of three dollars per day.*" The controversy over the salaries of legislators, in both Columbus and Washington, fueled the suspicions of those who thought the legislatures had become sinks of corruption.[38]

With the return of prosperity, the compensation controversy died down, but it revived during the depression of the 1840s. With the economy suffering and the state deeply in debt, "retrenchment" became the General Assembly's watchword.

The House and Senate each had a standing Committee on Retrenchment. The Senate committee reported that a decrease in legislative compensation would have an insignificant effect on the state's financial troubles, but it acknowledged that a "reduction of unimportant items may bear upon the face of it a disposition to lighten the burdens of the people."[39]

In a separate report, committee chairman David T. Disney compared legislative compensation in Ohio with the compensation in more than a dozen other states. He found that only two states paid less than Ohio, while six others paid more. On a per capita basis, Ohioans paid their legislators far less than did the citizens of other states. With regard to legislative expenses in general, Disney concluded that, so far as he had investigated, "with reference to population alone, the legislative expense incurred by the people of Ohio, is far less than that of the people of any State in the Union." Three dollars per day, he said, was reasonable compensation. Legislators had to "avoid an appearance of meanness by which their constituents would feel themselves disgraced." "The calls upon their hospitality, by their constituents, the high rates of boarding, and a just regard for their own personal appearance, can easily exhaust" three dollars a day. Legislators received their compensation for only three months of the year, during which time they had to neglect their usual business or leave it in the hands of others. A reduction would exclude the poor man from public service and "throw your lawmaking power . . . exclusively into the hands of the rich."[40]

Disney's argument may have conflicted with a more general belief that the purpose of compensating legislatures was to provide them with room and board, not to enable them to keep up appearances. The fact that legislators in the 1820s could board comfortably for four dollars per week perhaps contributed to the outcry over the 1824 pay increase to three dollars per day. Republican James Monroe, elected to the Senate in 1855, recalled that his "corrupt" Democratic predecessors had increased the daily pay to four dollars, "not more than half of which was charged at the hotels for their board." Whatever the reason, Disney failed to sway a majority of the members. The General Assembly reduced legislative compensation to two dollars per day and two dollars per twenty-five miles traveled. In 1847, it reinstated the three dollars per diem rate for the first sixty days of session, made the pay one dollar per day thereafter, and restored the mileage allowance to three dollars per twenty-five miles, "the distance to be reckoned by the most convenient route of public conveyance."[41]

The First Century

The members' compensation was not great in any case. Looking back on his four years as a legislator, James M. Dalzell recalled his initial decision to run for office as a foolish mistake. Until then, he had been doing well as a lawyer and farmer, with money in the bank and no debts. Later, when he "looked into an empty flour-barrel and hungry children's faces," he understood his "folly." Dalzell got more caught up in the "maelstrom of politics" than most legislators, writing innumerable letters and stumping for other candidates in and out of state, but his experience illustrated one of the major problems of a part-time, citizen legislature: ordinary men with families to support could not afford to devote much time to politics, even if they were elected to office. "It is a grand game," wrote Dalzell, "and none but grand men need try to play it."[42]

The members undermined their case for higher pay by neglecting their duties. Absenteeism was a minor problem in the first half of the nineteenth century, but it worsened as transportation improved and escape from the capital got easier. Roll-call votes for the third, midsession, and third-to-last weeks of the 1819–20 session of the General Assembly show an average attendance in each house of about 96 percent. By 1830, a clear trend toward lower attendance had set in. In the General Assembly of 1834–35, attendance averaged 90 percent in the House and 92 percent in the Senate. Five years later, the House average slipped to 83 percent. During the turbulent year of 1845, when the Texas and Oregon controversies aggravated racial, sectional, and partisan anxieties, House attendance rebounded, averaging 88 percent during the third-to-last week. (Senate attendance averaged 96 percent during the same period.) But, after 1850, attendance dropped precipitously. In the tense months of January through April 1861, as the looming Civil War riveted the people's attention on public affairs, the legislators might reasonably be expected to have been in their seats. Yet in two-thirds of the votes during the three weeks studied, fewer than thirty of the thirty-five senators registered their presence, and, for one-quarter of the roll-calls, fewer than twenty-five voted. The members of the House were similarly derelict.

In 1862, Representative Myron C. Hills offered a resolution decrying absenteeism as "a prolific source of evil" and an "abuse which destroys the efficiency of this body." Hills proposed that no one be excused from attendance on session days except when absolutely necessary. He also urged that every fourth Friday the House adjourn until the following Tuesday, probably to allow the members to go home at regularly scheduled times and thus eliminate a common excuse for absences. Another member recommended that the Speaker dock members' pay for each day of unexcused absence (an idea voiced by 1852, if not earlier). The reporting committee rejected the resolution, remarking that the ultimate sanction for a representative's absences rested with his constituents.[43]

After the Civil War, the frequency with which the House and Senate failed to get a quorum became both a joke and a matter of grave public concern. In 1871, the *Ohio State Journal* observed that absentees averaged twenty-five or more members and that getting a quorum in the House had proved difficult. "If the private affairs of the members are so urgent, and their private business so absorbing that they cannot give attention to their legislative duties," griped the paper, "they should by all means resign, in order that the vacancies which practically exist, may be filled." The *Statesman* complained about the many lawmakers who took public money for "go[ing] about their private business . . . sparing only enough time to draw their pay; while others come here, but spend their nights in carousal and their days in dozing." The General Assembly was taking three-day weekends once or twice a month, but still some members seemed to "run home every time there is a recess of ten or fifteen minutes." The most frequent absentees, asserted the *Journal*, were "the most prompt when it comes to drawing the five dollars [per diem pay] which the State is beat out of."[44]

Since 1866, members had been paid five dollars for each day of "actual attendance," up from four dollars for each day "attended" in 1852. (Pay had temporarily dropped to three dollars per day during the Civil War.) The General Assembly switched to a flat salary of twelve hundred dollars per two-year term in 1880, with a deduction of five dollars for each day's absence, but it didn't help because, as in Congress and other states, the law was not enforced. The annual reports of the state auditor show that every member got paid the full amount every year. Attendance in each house in January 1881 was around 65 percent. The highest participation rate for any of the numerous roll-call votes in either house was 83 percent.[45]

Matters did not improve as the decade wore on. Absences sometimes put the minority party in temporary control. When the Democrats got a Senate majority owing to Republican absences, the Republican *Ohio State Journal* griped that the enemy "came near playing smash with the power at their command." On February 18, 1885, with Republicans in the majority and the controversial liquor question scheduled to be heard, the *Journal* observed, "Every effort has been exhausted by the leaders of the House to get the absentees here by this noon. It was expected that most of the members would be here yesterday, yet a call of the House showed but 57 members present. Of the 47 absentees, 27 were Democrats. Had the Republicans all been present they could have done as they pleased; as it was they had to take their medicine." Sometimes bills that had broad support failed for lack of a quorum. In 1889, the voter registration and Australian ballot bills lost, said a *Journal* headline, "Because of the Usual Lack of Votes."[46]

On occasion, absenteeism was a matter of strategy. In 1886, Democratic senators absconded en masse in an attempt to prevent a quorum and a decision on the contests of four seats following the corrupt elections in Cincinnati the previous fall. The Republican *Ohio State Journal* eschewed the old label "absquatulators" for the missing Democrats in favor of the more politically charged "secessionists." Even Democrats attacked the runaway senators for their "weak and cowardly conduct," which only left the Republicans in uncontested control. When the Republicans went ahead and unseated the four Hamilton County Democratic senators, the Democrats assailed the action as invalid for lack of a quorum, but the decision stood and the fugitives returned for the adjourned session in January 1887.[47]

Aid and Comfort

The members had no personal assistants, but, from 1817 on, they at least had access to a library. Governor Thomas Worthington founded the state library, which at first served the General Assembly almost exclusively. Using money from his contingency fund, Worthington purchased "a small but valuable collection of books" so as to place "within reach of the representatives of the people, such information as will aid them in the discharge" of their duties. The books dealt mostly with history, biography, politics, and law, but they included Robert R. Livingston on sheep-raising and woolen manufactures, Owen Biddle on architecture, and other miscellaneous items. Worthington's initial rules for the library called for it to be open Monday through Saturday from 9:00 A.M. to 1:00 P.M. and from 5:00 P.M. to 9:00 P.M. during session, and they set time limits on borrowing and fines for late returns. The General Assembly appointed a librarian, who before long acquired from the sergeant at arms the job of maintaining the statehouse between sessions and seeing that it was aired out, cleaned, and kept in repair. In 1845, the legislature placed the library under a board of commissioners

The state library in the old statehouse around 1850. *Courtesy of the State Library of Ohio*

consisting of the governor, secretary of state, and state librarian and opened it to the public, although only members and former members of the General Assembly, judges, and state officers had borrowing privileges. Unfortunately, until 1854, the librarians were political hacks who knew little about librarianship.[48]

New technology appeared in the capitol, sometimes to the puzzlement of members. In 1884, the House authorized the sergeant at arms to put a telephone in the clerk's office for the use of members and officers of the General Assembly. The device eventually became so popular that the House empowered the Speaker to appoint a "telephone boy" to take charge of it and see that only members used it. The House's call box, used by newspaper correspondents to summon messenger boys, mystified new representatives from rural areas who had never seen such a contraption. The sergeant at arms was said to have designated one of his porters "instructor of string pulling" for the benefit of the "cornstalk brigade."[49]

Over time, the members enjoyed simpler amenities as well. In 1867, the House directed the sergeant at arms to procure a coat rack or wardrobe for the members and, seventeen years later, ordered the construction of two cloak rooms. In 1860, the House instructed the sergeant at arms to furnish ice for the water cooler, and, in 1898, it authorized a Columbus woman to operate "a fruit, confectionary and cigar stand" in the statehouse. Until then, members who wanted refreshments without leaving the building relied on mobile vendors. For a time, a teenaged girl named Ettie roamed the building selling oranges from a basket, but she fell in love with a visiting Tennessee legislator and left with him for southern climes.[50]

8

WELL-FED POLITICIANS,

LITTLE BOYS, AND

OTHER EMPLOYEES

THE CONSTITUTION OF 1802 required the House and Senate to keep and publish journals of their proceedings and empowered them to compel the attendance of absent members, punish members and nonmembers for disorderly conduct, and close the chamber doors for secret sessions. In accordance with the traditions of Parliament and the practice of the legislature of the Northwest Territory, the General Assembly hired employees to carry out these and other clerical and law-enforcement functions. It could hardly have operated without them.

Historians of state legislatures have paid virtually no attention to the employees whose daily chores translated the actions of lawmakers into law. Even the most comprehensive histories shed almost no light on the work of the clerks, sergeants at arms, pages, stenographers, and other employees who did the paperwork, kept order in the chambers, delivered messages, lit the fires, and performed the many other tasks necessary to keep a legislature in operation. Evidence on the subject for the nineteenth century is slim, but enough fragments exist to provide a general idea of the work and its changing nature during Ohio's first century of statehood.

At first, a handful of employees sufficed to handle the work of a small legislature that met for short sessions and passed relatively few laws. A hundred years later, the staff had grown and adjusted to meet the legitimate needs of a bigger and busier legislature, the questionable needs of patronage, and the changing needs of a technologically advancing society.

From the beginning, the Ohio House and Senate each had a clerk and a doorkeeper. The very first enactment of the General Assembly after statehood established per diem rates of $4 for the former and $1.50 for the latter. The compensation rose and fell with the daily rates for members. It peaked at $6 for the clerks and $3 for the doorkeepers in 1816, but the public outcry over pay increases for Ohio and federal lawmakers forced a retreat. When the humble doorkeeper became the more imposing sergeant at arms, his pay equaled that of the clerk. At midcentury, the clerks, sergeants at arms, assistant clerks, and assistant sergeants at arms all received $4 per diem. They lost a dollar per day during the Civil War, but, in 1866, the General Assembly increased their daily compensation to $5, where it remained into the twentieth century.[1]

Legislation of the Northwest Territory referred to the sergeant at arms and doorkeeper as distinct individuals, but for nearly twenty years after the beginning of statehood neither the House nor the Senate elected an officer known as a sergeant at arms. The House rules of 1803 listed the doorkeeper's duties: "to notify the house of all messages from the governor and senate; to carry all messages the house may require, private as well as public; when any person requires him to call a member of the house, he shall call such member by name, without title other than mister; he shall have the house kept clean, and a good fire made therein, by the hour of eight o'clock in the morning, when the weather requires it." For a time, the legislature used "doorkeeper" and "sergeant at arms" interchangeably, as when the Senate "proceeded to the election of a door keeper (or sergeant at arms)," but the first term eventually gave way to the second. (Doorkeepers would eventually reappear, but as ordinary employees, like porters and attendants, and not as officers of the House or Senate.) After statehood, the lawmakers did not spell out the duties of the sergeant at arms in statutes, resolutions, or rules. Traditionally, the sergeant at arms was a law-enforcement officer charged with maintaining order in the legislative chamber and, on instructions from the members present, compelling absentees to attend to make up a quorum. The rules of the territorial House of Representatives reflected this customary role, but in the State of Ohio the sergeant at arms also took on the old doorkeeper's jobs. He acquired various administrative duties as well. In 1849, the House sergeant at arms reported that he had ten men and boys working under him: one to "attend to the post-office," one to distribute documents to the members, three to keep the House clean and orderly, one to bring in wood and make fires, and four to serve as messengers.[2]

The territorial legislature first provided itself with a clerk in 1791 and charged him with "engrossing all acts or laws which the said legislature may pass," procuring authenticated copies of acts for publication in the counties, providing fair and accurate copies of the acts to the governor and judges, and performing such other duties as might be assigned. (Engrossment usually means the preparation of a bill for consideration by a legislative body by incorporating changes made to that point into a clean copy. The clerk of the territorial legislature may have been responsible for engrossing bills, but the 1791 statute actually required enrollment, which is the preparation of a final, postpassage version for the required signatures.) For a time during the early years of statehood, the clerk's duties grew to include taking inventory of items purchased by the General Assembly and depositing whatever was on hand at the end of a session with the secretary of state until the legislature reconvened. By 1836, the clerks had to provide certified copies of the journals to the state printer, keep records of committee reports, and index the journals.[3]

In 1804, the General Assembly gave the clerks money "for clerk hire and incidental expenses," but typically the House or Senate authorized the hiring of assistant clerks by resolution when the need arose. In 1836, the lawmakers gave the clerk of each house the power to employ assistants as necessary, but at the next session they thought better of bestowing such broad discretion and instead allowed the clerks to apply for extra help when the work became "unreasonably burdensome." At the same time, the General Assembly established by law the offices of chief clerk, assistant clerk, and clerk for recording and enrollment in each house.[4]

In 1849, House clerk Charles W. Blair had a staff of nine assistants. The first assistant clerk made up the journal pages from notes taken by Blair. The message clerk kept track of bills, kept the orders of the committee of the whole, and copied and transmitted messages to the Senate, to House committees, and to executive departments. Two journal clerks copied the first assistant's daily journal leaves into a permanent book. Another man oversaw the "general labor" of the clerk's office. He and the remaining four clerks saw to "the enrolling, engrossing, copying of resolutions, reports, and whatever and all that is necessary to be done."[5]

The House Committee on Retrenchment objected to the size of the staffs of the clerk and sergeant at arms. In December 1849, the committee recommended that the clerk limit himself to four assistants. The clerk complied, but, in January, the House approved three more. In February, Blair, noting that the assistant clerks were "compelled to work until after midnight very frequently, and that even then, the business could not be completely finished up," hired an eighth assistant, so that he was almost back to where he had started in December. The sergeant at arms eliminated three positions by order of the House, although he later reinstated one man by having him split the per diem pay with another assistant.[6]

"Retrenchment" in state government was always a popular political theme. In 1873, a House investigating committee found that, during the recent Fifty-eighth and Fifty-ninth General Assemblies, House clerk Amos Layman had been paid five dollars per day for 2,441 days, the extra compensation being given pursuant to resolutions. That was a lot of duplication. The committee believed that the clerk's work could be done more cheaply. Two members of the committee also expressed concern about nepotism in Layman's office, which they declared was "incompatible with economy and the public interest."[7]

Despite the prominence of the clerks' positions, the actual functioning of their offices remains obscure. Some details emerge from contentious episodes in the 1850s. House clerk Mahlon H. Medary had a rough session in 1852–53. As of December 10, 1852, the journal had not been recorded since February 20, and a member moved to terminate him for being "notoriously incompetent." Medary defended himself with a description of his office's work. He had one assistant "constantly employed at the desk in keeping the daily minutes of the proceedings, and making up the current journals for each day therefrom, and frequently superintending the work in the engrossing and enrolling room." He had two other assistants occupied with "engrossing and enrolling; also in copying resolutions, reports, amendments, and transcribing generally." It would be impossible, said Medary, to comply with the statutory requirement of recording the journal in a book every day without the hiring of an additional clerk for just that purpose. He would need yet another assistant to meet the law's mandate of recording committee reports and special reports to the General Assembly from executive departments and public institutions. Moreover, the clerk had previously employed someone "at the desk, whose duty it was to make out messages from the House to the Senate, and to take charge of the *bill book* duties, both important and responsible, and on days of general business, very laborious." Medary did not think it necessary to detail "his own immediate duties, believing that the committee are fully apprised of his labors from his voice, which is almost constantly heard at the reading stand." He concluded by requesting three additional assistants.[8]

The House kept Medary on the job—until, as we saw in chapter 7, he assaulted Representative George Barnum on the House floor—and authorized him to hire two recording clerks, one to bring the journal up to date and the other to record the current journal. The House also directed Medary promptly to deliver the original sheets, after being approved each day and conformed to the record, to the printer.[9]

Another revealing episode involved Senate clerk Charles B. Flood, whom Dr. W. D. Ide accused in a newspaper article of receiving more money than Flood was entitled to. The article seems to have been payback for a piece written more than four years earlier in which Flood had cast aspersions on Dr. Ide's work during the cholera epidemic of 1849. Flood demanded an investigation. A Senate committee cleared him, but it recommended a revision of the laws that governed the recording of legislative journals and reports.[10]

The committees in the Medary and Flood cases called members of the clerks' staffs and other state employees to describe aspects of their work. The witnesses generally agreed that the clerks were neither underworked nor overpaid. Until recently it had been the secretary of state's custom, in certifying the clerks' work for payment, to count six pages written as a day's work. Seeing the possibility of abuse in such a system, since "there might be much of little matter on a page," the first clerks of the secretary of state's, auditor's, and treasurer's offices determined that three thousand words "were a fair day's work for a good clerk" and adopted that as a basis in auditing the accounts of the House and Senate clerks. Counting by words rather than pages produced significant savings.[11]

A legislative clerk agreed that three thousand words in six hours was "an average day's work for the majority of men who follow clerking for a livelihood." "Six hours," he continued, "is enough for a man to sit half bent over a table, with a pen in his fist, one day with another." But, at that rate, there were not enough clerks to keep the books and papers up to date. Describing his work in the session of 1852–53, a clerk testified:

> Mr. Price and myself done all the engrossing, copying and a great part of the message writing until the last week of the session, when with three additional clerks we worked at least 18 hours per day, Sundays included, in order to keep up the engrossing and enrolling of bills in time for the use of the

Senate. Mr. Price and myself worked many nights during the session. The Senate never waited on the clerks for any work which it ordered, and it was a common remark by old Legislators that the clerical labor was never more promptly and correctly done.[12]

But the clerk's work was not over at the end of the session. It sometimes took weeks afterward to bring the journal up to date, and then weeks more to index the printed journals.[13]

The record in Medary's case shows how the clerk physically handled bills. Representative Barnum complained that the clerk had taken bills out of order. In fact, Medary had tried to accommodate Barnum. His sole engrossing clerk was desperately trying to finish another bill in time for an ordered third reading, so Medary had set his journal recording clerk and a newly hired clerk to engrossing. As it happened, although the House had first ordered Barnum's bill to be engrossed, and bills were normally engrossed in the sequence ordered by the House, the two bills were finished and placed in the "third reading box" at the same time. Once the bills were in the box, there was no regular order of reading. Similarly, in the Senate bills ready for third reading were placed in a desk pigeonhole labeled "third readings," but with no particular order of precedence. Flood, still the Senate clerk, testified that when he had numerous bills he might place them in numerical order, but members often came in to look at the bills and disarranged them. At other times, a bill that was expected to generate a lot of debate would be put at the bottom of the pile, so that while that bill was under discussion the clerks could catch up on other work.[14]

With overworked clerks toiling late into the night to keep up with the paperwork, errors sometimes crept into the law. A House committee in 1856 complained about "the manner in which bills have been engrossed, or rather *not-engrossed*; for a bill partly written, partly printed, and defaced by interlineations and erasures, cannot be said to be *engrossed* in any proper sense of the term." It was not the first time the committee had complained of the practice of reading and voting upon bills in this lamentable condition, which, it said, violated parliamentary usage and invited fraud. The committee urged the adoption of a resolution directing the clerk, when the House ordered a bill to be engrossed, "accurately to copy the same in a uniform, large, distinct and legible handwriting, which copy shall thereafter be substituted for the original bill."[15]

The clerks had charge of the journals, but others had access to them. In 1863, Amos Layman, then a reporter for the *Ohio Statesman*, on his own initiative inserted into the House journal a few words that the clerk had omitted. When the tampering was discovered, the House appointed a three-man committee to investigate. Two members of the committee, asserting that "the Journals of this body are of so high and sacred a character, that any unauthorized interpolation therein, although of an exact truth, deserve the strongest expression of disapproval," recommended that Layman be excluded from the floor of the House and from access to the journal. The third member urged that Layman be given an opportunity to be heard, which the House agreed to. More than six weeks went by before the issue was resolved. On April 11, the committee reported that Layman had appeared and stated that he understood there was a long-standing custom for reporters to correct the journal. He offered to bring in other reporters to support his contention. The committee scheduled another hearing, but Layman failed to show up and never offered anything further in his defense. The majority therefore repeated its recommendation that Layman be barred from the floor. After some parliamentary maneuvering designed to avoid a vote, the House rejected the committee's recommendation. Ironically, when Democrats gained control of the House in 1869, they elected Layman clerk. It would be interesting to know how Layman felt then about reporters tampering with the journal.[16]

For most of the second half of the nineteenth century, the statutes provided for a clerk and sergeant at arms, each with a first and second assistant, in each house. The laws authorized the Senate president to appoint three pages, the Speaker of the House five. The House or Senate could authorize additional legislative personnel by resolution. Toward the end of the century, the statutes designated the assistant clerks with more precision. Each house had a journal clerk, message clerk, engrossing clerk, enrolling clerk, and recording clerk. In addition, the House had three assistant sergeants at arms, the Senate two. As before, either house could authorize additional employees by resolution.[17]

The rosters published in the House and Senate journals of 1900, which may be incomplete, list both statutory and nonstatutory employees. Besides those employees expressly mentioned in the Revised Statutes, the House had an auditing clerk, eight stenographers, and seventeen porters. The auditing clerk seems to have been a new position. In 1898, the House empowered the Speaker to appoint an auditing clerk "whose duties shall be the making out of vouchers of the members, officers, clerks, porters, and pages of the House, and to assist in performing the clerical work of the House." The Senate roster included two "assistant clerks," an assistant engrossing clerk, six assistant sergeants at arms (rather than the two provided for by statute), eleven porters, two doorkeepers, two cloak room custodians, and an assistant postmaster. The House had a dozen pages, the Senate ten.[18]

Getting a job with the legislature was always a matter of political connections. When a new General Assembly came to Columbus, a scramble for jobs ensued, especially if the party in power changed. The "voice of the beseecher" was everywhere: in the statehouse, the hotels, the taverns, and the streets. But, as the *Ohio State Journal* observed, the "fat offices" generally went to "sleek and well fed professional politicians." The House and Senate clerkships in particular were positions of importance, fought over, sometimes bitterly, by the parties and occupied by men of current or future political significance. In 1829, William Larwill, of a prominent political family in Wooster, wrote to his brother how his election as Senate clerk after a hard-fought battle "had given my Jackson friends and acquaintances cause for rejoicing." "I find it will require great exertions to re-elect God," Larwill continued. "He ought to come down and show that he is not the drunken sot his enemies represent him to be."[19]

Thirty years later, William Dean Howells, then a reporter for the *Ohio State Journal*, sought advice from both the editor of his paper and the secretary of state on how his abolitionist father could best line up support for the Senate clerkship. The elder Howells did not get the job, but the House elected him official reporter, a position that existed for a time in both houses in the second half of the nineteenth century and was sometimes referred to as reporting clerk. His job, it seems, was to provide a summary of each day's proceedings for the newspapers. In 1876, the Senate described the reporter's duties as "furnish[ing] a full and complete report of the proceedings of this body, and also a synopsis of the remarks of Senators upon all matters eliciting general discussion."[20]

Just what the rest of the growing host of legislative employees did is not clear. The General Assembly often imposed special duties on the sergeant at arms, usually with regard to maintenance of the chambers or the purchase, care, and custody of books, furniture, and other property, and the members in attendance frequently sent him out to round up absentees. But did the Senate of 1898, with fewer than three dozen members, really need six assistant sergeants at arms? And all those porters? The journals refer to porters at least as early as 1878, when the Senate authorized the sergeant at arms to employ two, but without a job description. They may have been general, unskilled assistants. In 1892, the House authorized the sergeant at arms to hire six additional porters, to be known as doorkeepers, to preserve order in the galleries. Maybe the House attracted particularly rowdy visitors that year.[21]

Some of these employees probably did next to nothing. In 1896, a Columbus newspaper "easily explained" why nineteen porters had been appointed for the House when the chamber had only eighteen spittoons to be washed: "One is to do the work while the other 18 look on." The resolutions naming specific individuals as pages, porters, or assistant sergeants at arms suggest that Ohio's lawmakers saw the positions as opportunities to dole out patronage. So too does the 1892 House resolution authorizing the hiring of more porters and specifying that one had to be from the minority party. But state legislatures of the late nineteenth century were notorious for padding their payrolls, and Ohio's was hardly the worst of the lot. In any case, the growing volume of work eventually justified an increase in the workforce, if not the incompetence of some of those who obtained sinecures.[22]

The horde of employees included numerous pages, once referred to as messenger boys. The pages were typically boys from twelve to fifteen years of age. At the close of one General Assembly, the House Speaker thanked the "little boys who have so readily sprang at the clap of the hands or ring of the bell to do our bidding." If any further descriptions of the page's functions in the Ohio General Assembly exist, they are too obscure to be found. Ohio's messenger boys probably performed the same tasks as pages in the U.S. Senate. There the pages delivered messages, retrieved documents, kept the legislators supplied with paper and ink, swept up around the desks, and kept the fires going. Edmund Alton, who served as a U.S. Senate page in the 1870s, recalled how the fourteen pages sat on the steps leading up to the presiding officer's chair, waiting to the called by a crooked finger or a handclap to run an errand. When things got quiet in the Senate, the boys sometimes played marbles, to the annoyance of only a few of the august members. If they had time in the morning before the start of business, the pages might impersonate their employers in mock sessions. If one of their number fell asleep in an unused room during a late-night session, he might awaken to find his face spotted with ink; on occasion, a mischievous senator might tell the pranksters where they could find a victim. Even the senators could find themselves on the receiving end of a practical joke, such as a salted rather than sweetened lemonade.[23]

In 1880, Ohio's House pages made a poor impression on the *Cincinnati Gazette* when they accompanied the members on a "big oleomargarine junketing tour" to the Queen City. "It is pleasant to know that the pages are so far away," sniffed the paper, "for a more ill-mannered lot than the majority of them never infested a State House or a street corner." A Columbus paper acknowledged that some of the boys had misbehaved and that one in particular was "too mean for the place," but it thought that in general the Gazette's "slur . . . was unjust and uncalled for." Some of the members must have agreed with the Gazette, though, for a resolution defending the pages' zeal and ability ran into considerable opposition before it finally passed.[24]

Another category of employees, stenographers, became important toward the end of the century. Modern stenography (shorthand, or, as it was sometimes called, phonography) was a mid-nineteenth-century invention. The General Assembly sometimes allowed investigative committees to hire stenographers. In 1878, for example, the legislature authorized a joint committee looking into affairs at the penitentiary to retain a "phonographic reporter." In 1896, the House permitted the Committee on Elections to hire a stenographer to take and transcribe testimony.[25]

Stenographers probably first appeared as regular legislative employees in the mid-1890s. Early in the 1896 session, the House authorized the Speaker to appoint four "accountants and stenographers" to act as committee clerks and to assist members with their official correspondence. These four employees may have constituted the first committee staffs and the first steno pool. In 1898, the House dropped accountants from the resolution and provided for the appointment of six "clerks or stenographers" for committee work and the steno pool. Initially, the House wanted to pay these employees at the same rate as porters, $3.50 per day, but it soon agreed to the $5 daily rate that the other clerks received.[26]

Although stenography is technically the taking of notes in shorthand, some of the "stenographers" may actually have been typists. The typewriter came into use as a practical office machine in the 1870s. Its great attribute was speed. The clerk who copied three thousand legible words per day with quill pen and ink averaged only eight or nine words per minute. A fast typist could do ten times as much. In 1898, the Senate authorized the clerk to procure two "type writing machines."[27]

Typing was a new, open field not associated with male employment, and many young women who aspired to white-collar work rushed in to fill it. Already known as copyists in the business world before the Civil War, women took up stenography and typing with alacrity afterwards. Of the dozen employees listed as stenographers in the House and Senate rosters for 1900, half were women. It may be that the attempt to pay stenographers less than other clerks in 1896 stemmed from the prominence of women in the field. As shorthand and typing came to be seen as women's work, and as the job came to be viewed as a specialty that did not fit the typist for other jobs in the increasingly hierarchical world of the office, the pay scale, too, became differentiated.[28]

Although stenographers and temporary clerks made up the large majority of early female legislative workers, the General Assembly's first regular woman employee may have been an engrossing clerk for the Senate, Lillie C. Darst. A frail but energetic woman, Darst wrote for several leading newspapers and edited a weekly. Selected as engrossing clerk in 1879, she died in 1883 at the age of thirty-seven. In the proceedings held on her passing, Senator Coates Kinney took pains to stress that Darst had earned her clerkship. "There was no talk or thought of woman's rights," he said. "There needed none. She was fit to be Clerk of the Senate. She could do the work and do it thoroughly. She knew she could, and we knew she could, and she did." Her fellow clerks, all males, also paid tribute to Darst as an efficient coworker and beloved friend. The House employed a woman as recording clerk during Darst's tenure in the Senate. Thereafter, each house reserved an assistant clerkship for a woman until 1898, when a man won the House recording clerkship over a woman who had formerly held the position. In 1900, Ella Sohn, formerly the House recording clerk, had the dubious distinction of losing both the House and Senate elections for recording clerk to men. In 1902, for the first time in a generation, no one in either house nominated a woman for a clerkship.[29]

It is not known when the General Assembly first hired black employees. There may have been blacks in menial positions from an early date. In 1876, the House and Senate elected as their engrossing clerks African Americans James Seneca Tyler and W. Scott Thomas. Upon the Republicans' nomination of "two able-bodied negroes over one-armed and crippled Republican soldiers," Democratic representative James A. Norton, an officer in a black regiment during the Civil War, offered a resolution demanding that the House "take immediate action to recognize the existence of this evil, and place wounded soldiers in place of the men named." The House referred the resolution to a committee, where it languished. By 1886, the General Assembly had hired its first black page, and black assistant clerks had become common. When a Democratic legislature offered the position of porter to a black attorney and the attorney accepted, the African American *Cleveland Gazette* complained about both of them. But, as the *Gazette* reported, the same legislature elected a black man engrossing clerk of the House. Within a few years, the paper could report that the engrossing clerkship of the House was "usually conceded to some Afro-American." Blacks also served in other responsible positions from time to time. The *Gazette*, acutely conscious of the conspicuousness of the black clerks, applauded when Representative Jere Brown told an unqualified black aspirant to a clerkship "to go home and go to school." "To have one of our race elevated to a position he was not capable of filling," wrote the paper, "would be worse than not having it."[30]

Blacks participated enthusiastically in the rush for jobs. "They were here, there and everywhere, flitting among the members, buttonholing this and that member and impressing him with his worth and ability," wrote one reporter in the early days of a session. "If any one has heretofore thought the colored man modest about asking for office, they should have been in Columbus this week and they would have concluded at once that the colored man, like the white man, wants the earth, too."[31]

9

STATEHOUSE SCANDALS

I N 1836, SAMUEL STRONG went to Columbus at the behest of numerous citizens of Lorain County to collect and disseminate facts and arguments in support of a canal bill. Not being up to the job, however, he offered Representative William V. H. Cushing of Clark County one thousand dollars to perform these "extra services," but only, he later claimed, if Cushing felt he could conscientiously support the bill. It just so happened that Strong and his friends stood to gain between sixty and ninety thousand dollars if the bill passed. From the time Strong approached Cushing, the latter "suspected from [Strong's] deportment, in the lobbies of both Houses, he would be troublesome." The lawmaker reported the attempted bribe offer to the House, and the House put Strong on trial for contempt.[1]

Witnesses for Strong testified to his good character. Indeed, according to one, when Strong's Lorain County friends named him their agent, some "expressed fears that Samuel Strong would be too zealous and too *frank, odd* and *honest* to make a good lobby member." The representatives were not convinced; they found him guilty and subjected him to a public reprimand by Speaker William Medill.

Strong, said Medill, seemed "to have ascribed to money a power which it has lost in America," for America's legislative councils had been rendered "inaccessible to corruption." Cushing seems to have been resistant to corruption, but Medill's sanctimonious speech conflicted with the implied opinions of those who thought Strong was too honest to make a good lobbyist and with the unfortunate reality of corruption in American legislatures.[2]

The widespread belief that money and offers of position had corrupted Parliament beyond repair encouraged and justified the American Revolution. But legislatures in the independent American nation also proved susceptible to improper influence. The Georgia legislature succumbed to wholesale bribery in the great Yazoo land fraud of 1795. In the 1810s and 1820s, many congressmen took money from corporations in exchange for votes on legislation or other actions to promote corporate interests. Between the 1830s and the 1850s, high-pressure lobbying of the Pennsylvania legislature turned into outright corruption.[3]

As we saw in chapter 7, Representative David T. Disney justified the members' pay in the 1840s in part by pointing to the "calls upon their hospitality" by constituents. How much hospitality the legislators had to provide is unclear. No doubt they occasionally hosted folks from back home who had personal business in the capital or were just passing through, and they may have had visits from travelers such as Charles Dickens and Cyrus Bradley. They quite reasonably wanted to present a respectable if not ostentatious and unrepublican appearance. But what constituents did the lawmakers have to entertain? Neither the historical literature nor the surviving correspondence of the members answers the question.

On the other hand, some constituents may have had something to offer the members—publicity, votes, even money—in exchange for favorable consideration of legislative measures. These constituents came to be called lobbyists, after the anterooms outside legislative chambers where people who sought to influence the votes of their representatives congregated. Lobbying is often seen as a derivation of the constitutional right of petition, a right that Americans exercised freely from the beginnings of their governments. Ohioans inundated the General Assembly with petitions for laws on a wide range of public and private matters: the creation of new counties, the repeal of the Black Laws, the enactment of prohibition, the payment of claims, the incorporation of seminaries and academies, of turnpike, railroad, banking, and manufacturing companies, and on and on. But lobbying involved something more than written communication. In the words of one historian, "lobbying occurs when some group or individual, typically a private economic interest seeking benefits or protection, makes its case *personally* to government decision makers, often but not necessarily through some sort of specially deputed emissary."[4]

True lobbying existed at an early date in Ohio, as evidenced in the fight over the location of the state capital, when landowners from different areas besieged the legislators in an effort to secure their votes. Similar lobbying took place in the early 1840s during a debate over the possible relocation of the capital and at various times when interested parties sought the removal of county seats. In 1818, landowners in Huron County paid an agent one hundred dollars for successfully lobbying the General Assembly to move the county seat to a place more convenient to themselves. A "seat in the lobby," averred an observer in 1820, was almost as important as one in the legislature itself. In the early days, though, there were few organized interests, and government was small enough that petitions could capture the attention of the members. It may have been only in the 1830s, with the rise of business corporations and, in the absence of general incorporation laws, their need for special legislation, that modern lobbying was born. In 1842, when hard-money Democrats tried to wipe out banking in Ohio, one of their number complained that it seemed

> almost impossible for the people to secure a faithful representative of their principles and wishes in the halls of the Legislature. You may send men here, culled fresh from the ranks of the people . . . devoted in their professions and promises, but in five or six weeks they begin to fall off, to become pliant and yielding, to swerve from their duty, the victims of the seductions of bank officers with the corruption of hell, who hovered round the Legislature, to defeat by their sinister appliances the wants and wishes of the people.[5]

A number of scandals shook the statehouse in the decade or so after the Samuel Strong trial. Eighteen forty proved particularly fruitful for outrages. In that year the House attempted to expel Whig representative William B. Lloyd of Cuyahoga County for altering the record of his account at a Cleveland hotel. The Whig minority of the select investigating committee disparaged the evidence against Lloyd and accused Democrats of trying to oust him for political reasons. A majority of the representatives found Lloyd guilty, but they lacked the two-thirds vote constitutionally required to throw him out.[6]

During the same session, a disgruntled printer who had unsuccessfully sought the state printing contract charged in a Whig newspaper that state printer Samuel

Medary had sold newsprint to a third party after charging the state for it. Medary was a staunch Jacksonian and publisher of the Democratic *Ohio Statesman*. Democrats called for a committee of investigation. The committee exonerated Medary on the grounds that the newsprint he sold had been damaged and, as was customary in the trade, could be disposed of by the printer as he saw fit. The post of state printer was a lucrative patronage plum; the legislature tried to take the politics out of it in 1852 by requiring that the job be put out for bid.[7]

Also in 1840, the House revoked the privileges of William Penn Clark, a reporter for the *Cincinnati Daily News*. It had become usual for the House, early in a session, to grant reporters the privilege of the House floor; however, Clark angered representatives by publishing letters critical of them in the newspaper. The House acted peremptorily against Clark, condemning him quickly and without a hearing. Thirteen members, almost all Whigs, issued a protest denouncing the denial of due process and the invasion of liberty of the press.[8]

With all the bitter partisan conflict of the late 1830s and the 1840s spilling over into bribery charges, the importation of out-of-state voters, the attempted expulsion of Lloyd, conflicts with the press, apportionment fights, and absquatulation, it is no wonder some legislators as well as the public grew disgusted with the atmosphere at the capital. Representative Seabury Ford repeatedly groused that self-interest and partisan advantage prevailed over the public good. "[N]o argument, no reason, no sense of justice, no glaring exposition of the most open violation of the constitution can avail any thing against the determination to make place for offices," he wrote. John Armstrong Smith wrote to his wife that "the flummery of politicks and party management as displayed in this House, has given me a disgust for such a life. It is all a grand scheme of intrigue, where honesty of heart and rectitude cannot flourish." Ford and Smith, both Whigs, issued their indictments in years when their opponents controlled the General Assembly, but, as the Democratic attacks on the legislature in the 1850–51 constitutional convention demonstrated, the dissatisfaction knew no political bounds.[9]

The constriction of legislative power by the 1851 constitution failed to prevent suspicions of corruption in the General Assembly. The General Assembly's reputation for integrity, like the reputations of legislatures all over the country, suffered acutely after the Civil War. In 1873, Vermont congressman Luke P. Poland, chairman of the committee investigating the Crédit Mobilier scandal, declared, "This country is fast becoming filled with gigantic corporations wielding and controlling immense aggregations of money and thereby commanding great influence and power. It is notorious in many State Legislatures that these influences are often controlling, so that in effect they become the ruling power of the State." That same year two Cincinnati newspapers accused Ohio state senators of gambling and taking bribes in connection with a lottery bill. When the Senate appointed a committee of investigation, though, the reporters quickly backed away from their charges.[10]

Another Senate bribery investigation in 1888 came to naught when reporters refused to identify their sources. Newspapers alleged that several senators had solicited bribes from Chicago meat shippers to vote against the Geyser Meat Bill. The senators vehemently denied the charges. With nothing more to go on than unsubstantiated rumors, the committee exonerated them. A House bribery investigation a few years later also foundered for lack of evidence, although this time sloppy coverage rather than the honor of the journalistic profession was at fault. The Democratic *Columbus Post* published several articles accusing Republican representative Harry N. Daugherty of taking money to support John Sherman rather than Joseph B. Foraker for U.S. Senator. Daugherty, who would later become notorious as a member of the "Ohio gang" surrounding President Harding, had perfectly legitimate reasons for supporting Sherman, but there were suspicious circumstances nonetheless. The committee called several *Post* reporters and editors to testify. None even claimed to have a solid basis for the stories. They had relied on the word of strangers as well as supposedly reliable sources, on rumor and snippets of overheard conversation. Everyone—the manager, the editor, the managing editor, the city editor—professed ignorance as to how some of the stories appeared.[11]

Some legislative investigations of corruption had more serious consequences. The House censured Representatives William Bloch and William Wright for consorting with unsavory lobbyists and listening to their schemes to purchase the members' votes. Despite incriminating evidence, the committee did not think there was enough proof to find them guilty of taking bribes. The committee did, however, recommend that the prosecutor charge the chief lobbyists with offering bribes. In an exceedingly rare use of the bribery law, a grand jury indicted Bloch, Wright, and lobbyist J. D. Watson. The members got off, but Watson was convicted and sent to prison. On another occasion, a House investigating committee let Representative James A. Spear off the hook even though the evidence showed plainly that he had offered to obtain jobs at the penitentiary for several men in exchange for money. The majority report concluded lamely that Spear's acts did not fall within the statutory definition of bribery. A dissenting committee member thought Spear should have been expelled from the House for farming out offices. In 1896, a grand jury indicted five former senators for taking or soliciting bribes for their votes on legislation or in contested election cases. Juries returned guilty verdicts against two, but appellate courts ordered new trials and none of the ex-senators ended up with convictions.[12]

Charges of corruption regularly plagued the election of U.S. senators in the late nineteenth century. When James Garfield campaigned for the position, to be chosen by the General Assembly in 1880, he disavowed "the shameful methods that have characterized the last two or three" elections. He preferred an indirect approach that encouraged the members' constituents to let the legislators know that they wanted Garfield. Garfield backer Representative Freeman Thorpe (also spelled Thorp), better known as a portrait artist than as a politician, gave his candidate grief by going "boldly" among Republican members with a pencil and paper seeking written pledges of support. A political ally told Garfield that "something must be done with Thorpe. . . . I am in favor of almost anything short of poisoning, and I don't know but that would be justifiable on the ground of public interest." Almost a year later, he was still pleading, "You *must* bottle Thorpe."[13]

Garfield's scruples would soon become quaint. Allegations that the Standard Oil Company had purchased the nomination of Henry B. Payne over incumbent George Pendleton by the Democratic caucus in 1884 had been rife at the time; since the Democrats controlled the General Assembly, nomination was tantamount to election. Representative Allen O. Myers, who was on the rules committee for the joint caucus, later claimed that the price per member ranged from $1,200 to $8,000. To avoid revelations of bribery, the caucus resolved to settle all questions without debate. According to Myers, a roll-call vote that pitted Payne men against anti-Payne men "was used as the pay-roll in settling the accounts and making the final payments."[14]

The lawmakers elected Payne on the morning of January 16. That afternoon, with accusations of corruption being openly hurled, Representative George W. Love introduced a resolution to have a committee appointed to investigate Payne's election. Myers sought to amend the resolution to add an investigation of former governor Charles Foster, a Republican whom Myers blamed for introducing huge sums of money into Ohio political campaigns for corrupt purposes. Another member then demanded that Myers himself be investigated for stuffing the ballot box at his own election. Myers agreed, but "[b]oodlers of both parties were opposed to investigation," he wrote, and the amended resolution went down to defeat.[15]

In 1886, following an exposé in a Cincinnati newspaper that named names, a House committee investigated charges that four representatives had been bribed to vote for Payne. The committee exonerated the accused members and found no legal proof of wrongdoing, but both houses passed resolutions asking the U.S. Senate to investigate. On the basis of hearsay evidence of large-scale bribery, two members of the federal committee to which the case was referred wanted to pursue the matter further, but the majority refused.[16]

In 1890, the Democratic General Assembly sent Calvin S. Brice, another friend of Standard Oil, to the U.S. Senate. Myers claimed that Brice and Standard Oil had outbid Brice's rival for the post with large campaign contributions and had bought off opposition newspapers. For the second time in six years, he wrote, "the Senatorship from Ohio, had sold to the highest bidder." At the Democratic state convention a few years later, a speaker lamented that "[w]hen a Senator is to be elected by a legislature, the question is no longer asked . . . what is *his* worth, but what is *he* worth."[17]

The tactics used by Brice and his Democratic supporters blunted their criticism of Republican Mark Hanna's election to the U.S. Senate in 1898. Hanna, a Cleveland businessman, was close to President McKinley and a power in the Republican Party. Named reluctantly by Governor Asa Bushnell to fill temporarily the vacancy left by John Sherman's appointment as U.S. Secretary of State, Hanna sought election to the remainder of the term and to the next full term as well. But Hanna had enemies within his own party, and they combined with Democrats to threaten his election. The contest turned into a public spectacle of the first magnitude, as the opposing sides marshaled all their forces. A contemporary critic described how newspaper correspondents "swarmed from every direction," how mobs of men who owed their positions to Hanna "surged about members of the house and senate, at their hotels, on the streets, even at their very seats in their separate legislative chambers," and how political operatives importuned the families of recalcitrant legislators, even holding the wife of one unreliable member "prisoner" for several hours. For the first time, claimed the writer, a U.S. Senate seat was openly "auctioned off" with money and promises of jobs. Hanna's sympathetic biographer Herbert Croly attributed much of the excitement to public indignation over the attempt to deprive Hanna of a seat that most voters, who had elected the Republican legislature, had clearly ex-

Calvin S. Brice. *Courtesy of the State Library of Ohio*

pected him to receive. But he, too, painted a picture of confusion and mischief, with mobs roaming the streets, armed guards everywhere, the statehouse "full of desperate and determined men," rumors of bribery on both sides, and the rivals fighting for custody of a doubtful member who was drugged or drunk. The General Assembly elected Hanna to both terms by a three-vote margin.[18]

The Senate, which had voted 19 to 17 for Hanna's opponent, promptly appointed a committee of investigation. Chaired by a Republican whom Croly described as Hanna's "one personal enemy in the Senate," the committee claimed that Hanna's agents had attempted to bribe a member of the House. To permit Hanna to hold his seat, proclaimed the committee, "would go far toward legalizing corruption and bribery." The committee urged the U.S. Senate to conduct its own investigation of the election and to expel Hanna from Congress. As in the Payne case, the U.S. Senate committee found insufficient evidence to justify a full-fledged inquiry. Hanna kept his seat, but the history of the General Assembly's elections of U.S. senators since 1884 helped mobilize support for the federal constitutional amendment that provided for direct elections by the people.[19]

Notwithstanding these lurid tales of corruption, it is impossible to say how widespread the bribery of Ohio's legislators was in the late nineteenth century. Rumors

Marcus Alonzo "Mark" Hanna.
*Reproduced by permission of the Ohio
Historical Society*

circulated constantly, and newspapers irresponsibly fanned the flames. But some bribery clearly existed. In several investigations, members of the General Assembly testified that they had been approached with offers, which of course they had spurned. Robert Luce, a lawmaker himself and a close student of legislative affairs, thought the low point of legislative dishonesty in both Congress and the states had been reached around 1873 and that matters had slowly improved thereafter. Political scientist Paul S. Reinsch agreed that "direct money bribery" had become less common, but only because the "great interests" controlled the legislatures and therefore had no need "to buy support on individual measures." On the other hand, when, in 1898, a House committee investigating allegations of corruption asked Myers whether his experience in the General Assembly fourteen years earlier led him "to think that members of the legislature have their prices," he answered with an unequivocal yes.[20]

Bribery was an obvious form of corruption and clearly regarded as such. But there were other practices that drew complaints and that today would be regarded as unethical and illegal. Witnesses at investigative hearings testified to political junkets, lavish entertainments, and special trains and railroad passes for legislators. (In 1902, before the General Assembly enacted legislation on the subject, the railroads east of Chicago agreed among themselves to stop issuing free passes to government officials.) Lobbyists frequently thronged the floors of the legislative chambers. Then there was blackmail. In 1898, a newspaper correspondent reported that some rural members had been taken out "to see the town"—that is, to places "where exhibitions of vice and degradation are given than cannot even be hinted at in the columns of a paper." The members were then told to vote as ordered or risk being exposed. Some practices that today are considered unethical may not have been thought so in the nineteenth century. The political parties routinely assessed their members who held local office for contributions to the party coffers. In 1851, an agent for persons interested in establishing a new county more or less promised Representative Samuel Gilcrest a town lot and money for a house if he supported the bill. The witness who reported the agent's conversation to a committee of investigation said, "I did not . . . understand him as attempting to corrupt Mr. Gilcrest."[21]

Thanks to the proliferation of special legislation and the scandals associated with illegal and unethical practices, lobbyists acquired a bad name. Even representatives of interest groups who tried, by perfectly legitimate means, to persuade legislators to vote for or against particular bills, denied that they were lobbyists. The desire to free lawmakers from their reliance on lobbyists contributed to the creation of legislative reference services, a cherished Progressive reform and a key step on the path to the professionalization of state legislatures.[22]

10

BANKS, RACE, AND

DEMON RUM

AROUND 1830, WHILE SOJOURNING in Ohio, Englishwoman Frances Trollope remarked to a local citizen upon the great amount of time Americans devoted to their newspapers, which brimmed with political news. "And I'd like you to tell me how we can spend it better," replied the Buckeye. "How should freemen spend their time, but looking after their government, and watching that them fellers as we gives offices to, doos their duty, and gives themselves no airs?" To Mrs. Trollope's suggestion that roads and fences might be kept in better repair if folks spent less time on politics, the citizen retorted, "The Lord! to see how little you knows of a free country! Why, what's the smoothness of a road, put against the freedom of a free-born American? And what does a broken zig-zag signify, comparable to knowing that the men what we have been pleased to send up to Congress, speaks handsome and straight, as we chooses they should?" A quarter century later, the American passion for politics astounded another visiting Englishwoman. "Party spirit pervades the middle and lower ranks," wrote Isabella L. Bird. "[E]very man, almost every woman, belongs to some party or other, and aspires to some political influence." And what an amazing array of political groups to choose from: "Whigs,

Democrats, Know-nothings, Freesoilers, Fusionists, Hunkers, Woolly-heads, Dough-faces, Hard-shells, Soft-shells, Silver-greys, and I know not what besides; all of them extremely puzzling to the stranger, but of great local significance."[1]

Both Trollope and Bird took a jaundiced view of American democracy. The United States, thought Bird, had been placed "under a tyranny as severe as that of any privileged class—the despotism of a turbulent and unenlightened majority." Public officers, and none more than state legislators, were the "servile tools" of the populace, "the *delegates* of a tyrannical majority rather than the *representatives* of the people. The million succeeds in exacting an amount of cringing political subserviency, in attempting to obtain which, in a like degree, few despots have been successful."[2]

The Rise of Political Partisanship

Given the popular ardor for politics and the subservience of legislators to the people's will—however deplorable in the eyes of those genteel Englishwomen—the General Assembly could not help being a highly partisan body. In the nineteenth century's golden age of parties, legislative politics reflected the political rivalries that dominated public life. However, the actors and issues changed over time. The first half of the century saw the rise and fall of two party systems. The first, consisting of Federalists and Jeffersonian Republicans, effectively ended before 1820 when most Federalists conceded that they could not compete in Jeffersonian Ohio. With the demise of the Federalists as an organized opposition, the Republicans splintered into competing factions until the polarizing figure of Andrew Jackson fostered the formation of two distinct parties, the pro-Jackson Democratic Republicans and the anti-Jackson National Republicans. The Antimasons spiced up the political scene by electing fifteen members to the General Assembly in 1831 and 1832, but they quickly disappeared. Crushing defeats in the 1832 and 1833 federal and state elections killed off the National Republicans, but soon afterward a broad coalition of Jackson's opponents united in the Whig Party. The Whigs and their Jacksonist adversaries, who came to be known as Democrats, made up the ferociously competitive second party system. The antislavery Liberty and Free Soil parties that arose in the 1840s did not seriously challenge the Whigs or Democrats, but the Free Soilers held the balance of power in the General Assembly for two rumbustious sessions.

At midcentury, the Whigs disintegrated, destroyed by slavery expansion and the sectional conflict, according to some historians, or by the rise of ethnocultural issues, especially temperance, according to others. For a time, it appeared that the nativist Know Nothing Party might replace them as the Democrats' chief rival, but the revival of the slavery issue with the passage of the Kansas-Nebraska Act in 1854 gave rise to a new Republican Party that proved more durable. The Civil War split the Democrats into a War faction, which cooperated with Republicans under the Unionist label, and a Peace faction that formed the loyal or disloyal opposition, depending on one's perspective. After the war, most Democrats returned to the party fold. Notwithstanding the postbellum emergence of nettlesome third parties—the Greenback, Prohibition, and People's parties—the Republicans and Democrats made up a third party system that endured without major disruption for the rest of the century.

In Ohio, party conflict emerged in territorial days. Republican and Federalist "protoparties," although not highly organized, expressed contrasting visions of Ohio's future. Federalists wanted to create "an orderly society based on equality and security of property, and on the institutions of school, church, and government, all firmly entrenched in the purity of a natural, regular setting." They distrusted the squatters and backwoodsmen from Pennsylvania and Kentucky who seemed to have little regard for authority or for the property of others. But while Federalists generally favored the restrained development of the Ohio country by men appointed by the national government, Republicans smiled upon the "social scramble" of new settlements and endorsed popular elections as the legitimate means of obtaining political authority.[3]

Notwithstanding these contrasting visions, early Ohio lacked serious partisan competition. Ohio was overwhelmingly Jeffersonian. Around 1816, Ohio Federalists, recognizing the futility of formal opposition, gave it up. When the Republicans succumbed to the pressure of ethnic, economic, and sectional tensions and fractured into competing factions, the Federalists gained the chance for influence by supporting one or another group of Republicans, but they never reconstituted themselves as an effective party.[4]

The rise of Andrew Jackson sharpened the lines dividing Republicans and brought about hotly contested political races. The election of U.S. senators, a function of state legislatures throughout the nineteenth century, illustrated the new political reality. There were hard-fought contests before Jackson's presidency —in 1825, the candidates lobbied the members "as if their salvation depended on their efforts," and the 1827 election went to twenty-four ballots—but only in 1829 did true party candidates square off.[5]

Senatorial elections remained intensely partisan ever after. In 1832, the Democratic General Assembly chose Thomas Morris, a good Jacksonian. Six years later, Morris informed a Democratic committee that slavery was "wrong, in principle, in practice, in every country and under every condition of things." Morris's antislavery radicalism, at odds with his party's position, doomed his chances of re-election. The Democratic legislature chose another solid Jacksonian, Benjamin Tappan, the brother of New York antislavery activists but not himself deeply involved in the antislavery cause. By this time, party identification was becoming ingrained among voters and politicians, and senatorial elections had acquired a permanently partisan cast. So strong did party feeling become that, in the 1848–49 session, antislavery Whigs in the General Assembly refused to send their like-minded former colleague Joshua Giddings to the U.S. Senate because they thought him a traitor for joining the Free Soil Party; their stubbornness got them instead Salmon P. Chase, a Free Soil Democrat.[6]

The Whigs and Democrats, like the Federalists and Republicans before them, had distinctive political outlooks. Mass parties that drew support from all social classes and all walks of life, they differed most significantly in their general attitude toward government. Whigs viewed government as a positive good, especially when controlled by educated men devoted to public order, while Democrats generally saw government as a necessary evil that had to be limited as much as possible so that it could not be manipulated by powerful men for selfish ends.

Bank Wars

The transition to passionate political partisanship during the Jacksonian era, culminating in the clash of these two distinct attitudes, can be seen in the long fight over banking and currency. On these and other economic issues, Whigs and Democrats tended strongly to vote along party lines. Until about 1815, Ohioans harbored little animosity toward banking and other corporations. A banking crisis that year caused some people to grumble about "moneyed aristocracies" and to demand tighter state control over banks. The General Assembly responded with regulatory legislation that included taxation of banks, state ownership of bank stock, inspection of the banks' books, and limitations on bank debt. The law also granted a dozen new bank charters and extended to January 1, 1843, the charters of existing banks that agreed to the new regulations. But popular demands for more money and credit in the rapidly growing state swamped the efforts of the regulators. The Second Bank of the United States (BUS), chartered in 1816, added to the speculative delirium by offering easy credit. Ohio bankers had other grievances against the BUS, including the fact that the BUS claimed exemption from state taxation. Influential Ohioans believed the state had to assert control over the Bank.[7]

The speculative bubble burst in 1818; panic and depression followed. The BUS, having encouraged a reckless economic expansion, found it necessary to call in loans, foreclose mortgages, and present state bank notes for redemption. State banks that could not redeem their notes failed, and economic disaster ensued, accompanied by deep anger toward the BUS. Popular pressure to tax the BUS proved irresistible. In 1819, the General Assembly levied an annual tax of fifty thousand dollars on each branch of the BUS in Ohio. Within a month, however, the U.S. Supreme Court ruled in *McCulloch v. Maryland* that the BUS was constitutional and, as a creature of the federal government, exempt from taxation by the states. In the ensuing five-year legal battle, which Ohio lost, Federalists and Republicans stood shoulder-to-shoulder in their anti-BUS stand.[8]

By 1824, Ohio's financial crisis had passed and the animus against banks, including the BUS, had largely dissipated. In 1829, after an eleven-year hiatus, the General Assembly resumed chartering banks. But Henry Clay revived the bank battle in 1832 by shepherding through Congress an act to renew the charter of the BUS four years before it was due to expire. President Jackson vetoed the act with a populist, egalitarian message declaring the Bank's "powers and privileges" to be "unauthorized by the Constitution, subversive of the rights of the States, and dangerous to the liberties of the people." Notwithstanding the great Democratic victory in that fall's elections, Clay spoke for many when he declared that Jackson's actions in replacing National Republican federal officeholders with Democrats, running roughshod over the Indians, vetoing internal improvements bills passed by Congress, and undermining the currency all demonstrated that the United States was "in the midst of a revolution, hitherto bloodless, but rapidly tending towards a total change of the pure and republican character of the Government, and to the concentration of all power in the hands of one man."[9]

Between 1833 and 1836, Jackson's opponents coalesced into the Whig Party, a name that recalled the seventeenth-century fight for liberty against the Stuart kings of England and the eighteenth-century American Revolution. The Whigs generally supported banks and paper money. Sometimes they enjoyed the cooperation of probank, soft-money Democrats who believed that banks and their notes were necessary for economic growth and, when properly regulated, benefited the whole population. The majority of the Democrats moved toward a preference for hard money—gold and silver—and an antipathy toward banks, which they increasingly characterized as mercenary, monopolistic corporations that oppressed the "producing classes." In Ohio in the mid-1830s, a General Assembly controlled by Democrats brought the chartering of banks to a near halt. After the Panic of 1837, "the hard money, antimonopoly, anticorporation principles of the antibank Democrats became official Democratic dogma both in the states and at the national level."[10]

In the General Assembly, the old bipartisan, or nonpartisan, attitude toward banks and currency evaporated. When Whigs assumed control, and especially when Democratic "softs" broke party ranks, the laws usually favored banks and paper money. When Democrats took over, the laws went the other way. In 1841, when Whigs and Democrats each held a house of the General Assembly, nothing could be done, even though money was in short supply and the looming expiration of most state bank charters threatened a banking crisis. Thirteen charters lapsed on January 1, 1843, and two more on January 1, 1844, leaving just eight banks in the state.[11]

The public revolt of probanking Democrats against their party's assault on the banks led to an acrimonious internecine quarrel. By 1844, with business still slow, public opinion had turned decisively against the hards, and the Whig General Assembly passed major banking reform legislation. Although the new act contributed significantly to the improved health of Ohio's economy, hard Democrats would not concede the point. In 1846, radical Democrats in Hamilton County began agitating for a new constitution that would prohibit new banks. The convention, meeting in 1850, had a Democratic majority that included a vocal, antibank contingent. Eager to establish more banks before it was too late, the probank majority in the General Assembly passed a free banking law allowing any three or more individuals to go into business as a bank under stipulated conditions. The new banks would not need acts of incorporation; they would simply have to file papers with the secretary of state. Thirteen banks organized under the free banking law before the attorney general ruled in 1852 that the new constitution prohibited the formation of any more new banks under the statute. A few years later, the supreme court overruled the attorney general, opening the door again to the creation of new banks.[12]

According to one student of the long battle over banks, "The defeat of the hard-money Democrats on the free-banking bill marked the end of the banking controversy in Ohio. The growing industry, agriculture, and commerce of the state, and the accompanying needs for banks and credit, made the hard-money notions of the Democrats quaint relics of the past." In fact, the bitter partisan division over banking and currency continued. But the new constitution's restrictions on the General Assembly's power removed some of the most controversial economic issues from the legislative arena, and, by the mid-1850s, other matters, including the fight over slavery, were pushing the economic questions of the Jacksonian era off center stage.[13]

Black and White, North and South

Ohio was an antislavery state, but its constitution and laws institutionalized racism. The constitution restricted suffrage to white males. The General Assembly, at its first full session, passed the first of the Black Laws, prohibiting blacks from settling in Ohio without a certificate of freedom from a court, prohibiting the hiring of blacks and mulattoes who already lived in Ohio unless they had a certificate of residence from the county clerk, and penalizing anyone who assisted runaway slaves. Other early Black Laws presented additional obstacles to black immigration, prohibited blacks from testifying against whites in court, and excluded blacks from the militia. Statutes that required jurors to have the qualifications of electors excluded blacks from juries. The immigration and residency laws were rarely enforced, but they remained a threat and an insult.[14]

Missouri's application for admission to the Union as a slave state in 1819 galvanized antislavery sentiment, but it did not spark much sympathy for blacks. The General Assembly passed a law to protect blacks in Ohio from kidnapping by slave catchers, but most Ohioans still wanted to keep any more of them from moving in. In 1824, the House of Representatives passed a set of resolutions urging the federal government to emancipate the slaves, on condition that the owners be compensated and the freedmen colonized overseas. The preamble to the resolutions condemned the barbarities of slavery and extolled the Jeffersonian principle "that all men were created free and equal." The Senate passed the resolutions but unanimously rejected the preamble. The House acceded to the Senate amendment. In 1828, the House passed a bill to restrict the future immigration of blacks and mulattoes into the state; the Senate killed the bill by a single vote. In 1829, the legislature exempted blacks from the school tax and excluded them from the public schools. Although under subsequent, ambiguous laws, some school districts admitted black pupils, not until 1848 did the General Assembly provide for a system of schools for black children, supported by taxes on property owned by blacks.[15]

Antislavery agitation remained low-key until the Missouri crisis. The prospect that slavery would spread to the Louisiana Purchase provoked great consternation, and public meetings instructed congressmen to prevent the westward expansion of slavery. The General Assembly registered its protest in a resolution that, as introduced, called slavery "a great moral and political evil" and its extension a threat to "the permanency and durability of our republican institutions." After some dispute over the vigor of the language, the House and Senate agreed on a version of the resolution that objected to the introduction of slavery into any new state or U.S. territory.[16]

President Jackson received the unanimous approbation of the General Assembly when he denied South Carolina's right to nullify the protective tariff and threatened to implement the tariff with military force. The controversy did not on its face involve slavery, but it aggravated southern fears that the North would use the power of the federal government to override states' rights and abolish slavery. Indeed, some southern states had excoriated Ohio's colonization resolution of 1824 because it posed that very danger. During the fight over Ohio's taxation of the Bank of the United States, both Republicans and Federalists had advocated state sovereignty; however, in 1828, the General Assembly rejected South Carolina's states' rights arguments against the tariff, and, in 1833, the legislature once again denied that a state could nullify a federal law it considered unconstitutional. Even as it denounced nullification, though, the General Assembly sought to assure the South that it had no wish to interfere with slavery where it existed. Although the legislature had once urged Congress to pay for the emancipation and colonization of slaves, the lawmakers now found it "inexpedient" to express an opinion on the constitutionality of doing so.[17]

Throughout all the controversy over slavery in the 1830s, Whigs tended to be more antislavery than Democrats. The Western Reserve in northeastern Ohio was a particular stronghold of Whig abolitionism. During the 1838–39 session of the General Assembly, Whig senator Benjamin F. Wade of Geauga and Ashtabula counties fought doggedly to have a committee consider his memorial on the power of Congress to take antislavery measures. Whigs squared off against Democrats over the right of blacks to testify against whites in court. House Whigs fought unsuccessfully against resolutions offered by Democrat George H. Flood that condemned abolitionism, opposed congressional measures against slavery, and denied the right of blacks and mulattoes to present petitions to the General Assembly. Senate Whigs led by Wade tried to prevent passage of a bill for the more effective return of fugitive slaves, literally keeping the Senate in session all night, but to no avail. When Whigs regained control of the General Assembly, they repealed the fugitive slave law and reinstated an antikidnapping law that the Democrats had repealed.[18]

Of course, most Whigs were not abolitionists. Whigs outside the Western Reserve grew increasingly wary of measures that might alienate a touchy South and imperil the Union. The fugitive slave law passed both houses of the General Assembly by huge margins, and its repeal may have been due as much to the unconstitutionality of its procedural protections for fugitives as to the politics of slavery. The Flood resolutions also passed the House overwhelmingly. Attempts to insert declarations in favor of free speech and the right of petition into the resolutions lost resoundingly. (The Senate tabled the resolutions and ordered them printed but took no further action.) In 1841, a standing committee report in the Whig-controlled House found that it would be "impolitic" to repeal the Black Laws, censured abolitionists for provoking violence, and praised the majority of Ohioans for their determination "to respect the rights of their brethren of the south." Any attempt by the people of one state "to interfere, even indirectly, with the domestic institutions of another," said the committee, threatens the Union.[19]

The question of slavery extension, first in Texas and then in territories taken from Mexico, turned Ohio decisively against the South. Texas sought annexation to the United States soon after winning its independence from Mexico in 1836. In 1838, Wade, on behalf of a Senate select committee, reported an antislavery tirade asserting that the people of Ohio would not be bound by any agreement of annexation between Congress and a foreign state. It stood no chance of acceptance. Wade then proposed a milder report stressing the danger of war; it passed the Senate but not the House. Finally, a resolution "solemnly protest[ing]" annexation passed both chambers unanimously.[20]

By 1845, the annexation of Texas had become a real possibility. Public sentiment in Ohio favored leaving slavery alone where it already existed but opposed its extension. In January, the Whig legislature denounced annexation as a step toward war with Mexico, a financial liability, an extension of the "great social, political and moral evil" of slavery, and an enhancement of the South's political power.[21]

The closely contested elections of the 1840s gave committed antislavery voters a degree of power well beyond their numbers. Whigs often accused the Liberty Party, founded in 1840 by religiously motivated abolitionists who could not abide the sin of slavery, of playing into the hands of Democrats by drawing off Whig votes. Whig leaders vilified Liberty men as "fanatics" and "mercenary, corrupt scamps, whose only object is office." The Liberty Party was too sectarian to succeed politically, but more practical abolitionists proved the political potency of antislavery sentiment with the Free Soil Party. Although the Free Soilers included abolitionists and sought to improve the lot of free blacks in Ohio, they emphasized the rights of whites and the threat to white opportunities presented by the westward spread of slavery. The Free Soil appeal to the economic and political interests of northern whites attracted far more support than had the Liberty Party's denunciation of slavery as a sin.[22]

The combination of Free Soil sentiment and abolitionism pushed both parties, but especially the Whigs, toward more problack, antislavery, antisouthern positions. After years of halfhearted attempts to repeal the Black Laws, in 1847 a House select committee condemned the laws as unequal and unconstitutional. At the same time, after long urging the federal government to annex Oregon with no mention of slavery, the General Assembly demanded that slavery be excluded from Oregon and any other territories the United States might annex. In 1848 and 1849, the legislature finally enacted laws—severely defective but still an improvement—for the establishment of public schools for blacks. In 1849, the lawmakers asked Ohio's congressional delegation to seek an end to slavery in the District of Columbia and resolved that the federal government had an obligation to help oppressed blacks, perhaps by giving them free land in the Mexican cession and providing them with schools and a government.[23]

The Mexican War itself was a highly partisan issue in Ohio. Ohio's Whigs saw the war as a southern conspiracy, led by President James K. Polk of Tennessee, to extend the area of slavery. In December 1846, Democratic representative Clement Vallandigham introduced a series of resolutions defending the war as constitutional, "justifiable and necessary," expressing complete confidence in Polk, thanking the men in the field, and offering sympathy to the widows and children of fallen soldiers. The Whig majority bottled up the resolutions for nearly two months, then, on a party-line vote, adopted a set of substitutes that eliminated any defense of the war and praised Whig ex-governor Mordecai Bartley instead of Polk. When Whig U.S. Senator Thomas Corwin denounced the war in February 1847 and voted against a military funding bill, Vallandigham offered a resolution condemning Corwin for giving aid and comfort to the enemy. Another party-line vote postponed the resolution indefinitely.[24]

The powerful partisanship of the Jacksonian era, illustrated by the controversies over banking and slavery extension, often tempted the majority party in the General Assembly to gerrymander legislative districts. In March 1836, the Democratic majority passed an apportionment bill that gave Democratic counties a disproportionately large number of representatives. As a result of this "nefarious project to enable a minority to control a majority," the Democrats secured a small majority in the General Assembly that fall even though the Whigs won the gubernatorial race and carried the state in the presidential election. On December 8, when a Democrat offered the standard resolution to provide for the election of a U.S. senator, Whig Alfred Kelley moved the following substitute: "That the members belonging to the party, self-styled *democratic party* . . . shall meet in secret conclave . . . and . . . designate, determine on and *decree* who shall be the Senator in the Congress of the United States" and that the Whigs shall be required to attend a joint meeting of the General Assembly to give legal sanction to the decree. House Whigs managed to delay until December 13 passage of a resolution for a joint meeting on January 14, 1837. After the Senate concurred on January 12, House Whigs fought the customary message to invite the senators to the House chamber for the vote. Through an "organized system of speech making" and "real *down-easter, yankee quibbling*"—a Democratic slap at the New England background of so many Whigs—the Whigs succeeded in delaying the joint meeting, and thereby disgusting the public, until January 18, when the Democratic candidate finally prevailed on the thirteenth ballot.[25]

The lawmakers fought another apportionment battle at the contentious special session of 1842, when partisan feeling was running high over banking, currency, and the depressed state of the economy. The General Assembly had been unable to deal with the "multiplicity and magnitude of interests" during the regular session. The "heat and dust" of a Columbus summer no doubt exacerbated the bad temper of members called away from home once again. And then the Whigs carried out a "revolution" that made the whole session for naught.[26]

Congressional redistricting headed the list of topics on the agenda of the special session. The Democrats, in control of the General Assembly, proposed a

map of congressional districts that Whigs condemned as an outrageous gerrymander. One critic mocked the shapes of the districts in verse, likening them to
kangaroos, giraffes, and other animals. Lacking the votes to defeat the plan, Whig
members of both houses absconded en masse to prevent a quorum. The Speakers
ordered the sergeants at arms to round up the "absquatulators," but the Whigs
claimed that they had resigned and could not be compelled to attend. Fuming
over the "mad infatuation of the ambitious leaders of the federal party" (a Democratic epithet for the Whigs), the Speaker of the House denounced the Whigs
as "enemies of freedom," but there was nothing he could do. On August 12, pow-
erless even formally to adjourn, the General Assembly simply disbanded.[27]

The fight continued into the next legislature. In 1843, the Democrats, still in
the majority, introduced a bill "to preserve the constitutional quorum of the General Assembly." The bill made a resignation tendered by a member while the legislature was in session ineffective unless a majority of the member's house accepted
the resignation. Whigs sought unsuccessfully to amend the bill to punish any state
lawmaker who "corruptly and wilfully" attempted to apportion representation "so
as to deprive any of the free electors of the State of their equal and fair proportion
of Representatives in Congress, or in the General Assembly." In other words,
the Whigs tried to criminalize gerrymandering. The bill became law, without the
penalty provision, on party-line votes in both the House and the Senate.[28]

The most notorious gerrymander occurred in 1848–49. Previous gerrymandering had always involved the combination of different counties, never the division
of individual counties. In 1848, with the parties at nearly equal strength and bitterly at odds over slavery and the Mexican War, Senate Whigs tried to pad their
slim legislative majority with a bill that divided Democratic Hamilton County
into two electoral districts, one of which would be predominantly Whig. The
House then passed an amended version of the bill. Decrying the legislation as unconstitutional, Democratic senators sought to forestall Senate concurrence in
the House amendments by leaving the chamber to prevent a quorum, but the
House receded from its amendments and the bill passed.[29]

The novel method of apportionment stirred up a constitutional controversy.
The constitution required that representation be apportioned "among the counties." For Democrats this provision precluded the partitioning of individual counties. Whigs countered that they had given Hamilton County its due representation;
the creation of districts, they said, simply affected the manner of election.[30]

The fall elections produced a General Assembly in which Democrats and
Whigs had nearly equal strength in both the House and the Senate. In each

chamber, the Free Soil Party held the balance of power. The eight Free Soilers in the House and three in the Senate were in a position to exact concessions from the Democrats and Whigs in return for their support. Ironically, some of this leverage resulted from the Whig gerrymander, which not only had divided Hamilton County but also had increased the representation of supposedly safe Whig counties in the Western Reserve. A hotbed of abolitionism, the Reserve elected Free Soilers. The fall elections also produced two competing sets of representatives from Hamilton County. Democrats there, insisting that the apportionment act was unconstitutional, had voted on a countywide basis for five of their own for the House, while Whigs claimed to have elected two representatives from one of the new districts.[31]

On the first day of the session, the Democrats got to the House chamber first, swore in their members, including the five Democrats from Hamilton County, and elected a Speaker, who occupied the Speaker's chair. Then the Whigs entered, took their seats on the opposite side of the hall, swore in their members, and elected their own Speaker. "[B]oth organizations," recalled a participant, "continued to call the roll of counties, marking each other absent alternately; the Democrats kept up the session constantly day and night for five weeks never allowing the chair to be vacated and never adjourning except on Sunday; the Whigs came in generally once and twice a day, called the roll and adjourned." Without Free Soil help, neither party could take undisputed control.[32]

The Free Soilers in the General Assembly wanted two things: the U.S. Senate seat and the repeal of Ohio's Black Laws. According to historian Michael F. Holt, the major parties were prepared to bargain on these issues in exchange for support on "what really mattered": "control of the state legislature, the state jobs at its disposal, and the policies it might enact for Ohio concerning banks, corporations, taxes, constitutional revision, and other subjects" unrelated to slavery. Unfortunately for the Whigs, their former colleagues who made up the majority of the Free Soilers insisted on Joshua Giddings, an ex-Whig whom the Democrats abhorred on policy grounds and whom the Whigs regarded as a traitor. As a result, two Free Soilers, Norton S. Townshend and John Morse, were able to unite with the Democrats behind Salmon P. Chase and to agree to repeal most of the Black Laws. The two Free Soil votes sufficed to ensure the seating of all the Hamilton County Democrats, Democratic control of the legislature, and Democratic appointees as state printer and various judgeships (including two on the Ohio Supreme Court).[33]

The same session saw a vicious fight over the closest gubernatorial election in the state's history. The constitution required that the vote returns be sealed and brought to the Speaker of the Senate, who would open them before a joint convention of the two houses and announce the winner. In January 1849, this normally routine procedure produced two or three days of "intense excitement." When the Free Soil Whig Speaker Brewster Randall began reading the returns, Democrats interrupted and demanded that a committee be informally appointed to assist in counting the returns. (Randall had been elected Speaker as a compromise candidate on the sixteenth ballot. The senators took even more ballots, 54 and 121, respectively, to elect the sergeant at arms and clerk.) Randall appointed the committee, then ruled its report out of order. There followed a tumult over who would be heard, what would be entered on the journal, what returns should be disqualified, and who had been elected governor. Democratic senator Edward Archbold shouted at the Speaker, "God damn your perjured soul." Another Democrat, Henry C. Whitman—"with his tall, lithe person, aboriginal face, weak beard, and long never-cut hair . . . a rather bad copy of John Randolph of Roanoke"—shook his fist at Randall, denounced him as a "miserable coward" who had violated his oath of office, and "threateningly commanded" the clerks not to enter the Speaker's remarks in the journal. When the senators finally went back to their own hall and the House Speaker called for order, Representative Luther Monfort, waving his cane, expostulated "Order, hell! order, hell!" Bad feelings between the parties simmered. Days after the worst of the outbursts, one member called another to order for using "indecorous language in referring to the members on this side of the House in the manner in which they said their prayers this morning." Not until January 22, after weeks of investigation and parliamentary maneuvering, did the legislature finally declare Whig Seabury Ford governor.[34]

The election of 1849 produced another closely divided General Assembly, with Free Soilers again holding the balance of power in each house. Cooperation between Democrats and Free Soilers gave Democrats control of the House fairly quickly. Democrats prevailed in the Senate, too, but only after weeks of wheeling and dealing; it took 301 ballots to elect a Speaker. The victorious Democrats repealed the division of Hamilton County into two election districts.[35]

The Democrats' collaboration with Free Soilers and willingness to repeal the Black Laws reflected the sprouting of a commitment to racial justice in Ohio that would deepen during the Civil War era. So too did the General Assembly's adoption of a resolution in 1851 declaring that the people should not voluntarily cooperate in the enforcement of the federal Fugitive Slave Law and the legislature's appropriation of money for legal action to recover the children and a grandchild of freed slave Peyton Polly, who had been abducted from Ohio and sold into slavery. But Ohio still had a long way to go. Various forms of racial discrimination remained in the constitution and statutes. Revulsion against slavery and kidnapping and resentment at being told by southerners and the federal government what to do within Ohio's borders contributed far more than a belief in racial equality to the adoption of the resolutions on the Fugitive Slave Law and the Polly abductions. The Polly resolution as passed by the General Assembly omitted language in the original version that demanded a criminal investigation of the seizures and that called upon all citizens to help enforce the state antikidnapping act. And the lawmakers still clung to the hope that free blacks would move to Liberia. Ohioans' ambivalent attitude toward racial equality portended legal turmoil in the future.[36]

Ethnocultural Issues and the Midcentury Shakeup

The second party system suddenly collapsed in 1851 when the Democrats won a crushing victory in the gubernatorial and legislative elections. "We know that the Whigs are used up, here as elsewhere in the state," lamented the Whig *Cincinnati Gazette*. "There is no denying the fact, by compromise, coalition, or otherwise." In 1853, the Whig candidate for governor received just 30 percent of the vote; the Democrats that year gained a huge majority in the General Assembly. The Whig Party was dead.[37]

Why such a successful mass political party came to so swift and shattering a demise, not just in Ohio but throughout the nation, is not entirely clear. Other parties have suffered equally disastrous defeats and lived to fight another day. Many scholars blame the sectional crisis. Whigs were generally more antislavery than Democrats, less committed to the idea of a party, and more likely to desert in a crisis. The crisis came with the fight between free and slave states over the extension of slavery into the western territories. Some analysts date the death of the Whig Party as a national organization to the passage of the Kansas-Nebraska Act of 1854, when congressional Whigs split along sectional lines. According to Stephen E. Maizlish, though, Ohio's Whig leaders already sensed the dissolution of their party by early 1847. Indeed, the inability of both major parties to satisfy their antislavery wings effectively destroyed the Jacksonian party system. The shaken Democratic Party survived, but the Whigs' nomination of Zachary Taylor, a slaveholding political parvenu from Louisiana, as their presidential candidate in 1848, opened wounds in the party that could not be healed. In the words of another historian, the defection of antislavery radicals in 1848 "dealt the Whig organization in Ohio a blow from which it never recovered."[38]

An alternate interpretation of the Whigs' disappearance plays down the influence of slavery and the election of 1848. Ohio's Whigs stayed reasonably close to the Democrats in electoral strength until 1853. From 1849 to 1852, Whigs and Free Soilers cooperated in the General Assembly to defeat Democratic proposals on banking, currency, shareholder liability, and business incorporations. Intraparty tussles over sectional issues weakened the Whigs, but their evaporation as a party was due more to the fading significance of economic issues that had formed the centerpiece of the Whig program, the rising importance of an ethnocultural issue (prohibition), and the ease with which voters who were disillusioned with existing parties could start new ones.[39]

The party system of Whigs and Democrats may or may not have remained viable after the sectional conflict of 1846–48, but it certainly failed to survive the outburst of prohibitionism in the early 1850s. The Ohio constitutional convention of 1851–52 energized anti-alcohol activists, and the liquor issue divided both major parties. In 1853, Whigs and Democrats alike avoided the divisive subject in their state party platforms. Nevertheless, prohibition dominated the campaign. "Wets," including many Whigs, generally voted for Democratic candidates, who had traditionally been more inclined to oppose governmental intervention in the moral life of the citizenry. "Drys" had an alternative, the Free Soil Party, which took a firm stand against alcohol. The Free Soil candidate for governor received 17.5 percent of the vote. The Whig candidate pulled in only 30 percent, and the Whigs elected just seven senators and seventeen members of the House.[40]

Prohibition divided voters along ethnic and cultural lines. German and Irish voters resented the attempts of priggish Yankees to impose their teetotalism on them. Charles Reemelin, a leading spokesman for the Germans of Cincinnati, declared, "there are *some* subjects unfit for legislation, and among them is 'what we shall eat and what we shall drink and wherewithal we shall be clothed.'" A Democratic paper in Marietta defended beer as "the healthful German beverage" and condemned a local ordinance that required the closing of "lager beer establishments" at 10:00 P.M. as "an unwarrantable interference in private affairs."

Other issues divided voters along religious lines. The archbishop of Cincinnati sparked a furor in 1853 by asking that parochial schools receive a share of state school funds. "*This is the time,*" responded the nativist *Cincinnati Dollar Times*, "to give a blow to priestly arrogance and foreign dictation." Sometimes religion and ethnicity worked at cross-purposes and confused the electoral scene. Some Protestant German refugees from the European revolutions of 1848 brought with them a strident anti-Catholicism, which reinforced a long-standing American suspicion that Catholics were too subservient to pope and priest to be good, independent-minded republicans. But, in 1853, the German Protestants of Cincinnati joined with German Catholics in support of the Democratic Party, the traditional home of Catholic voters, because the Democrats opposed prohibition. The next year some German Protestants voted for the nativist Know Nothing Party because the party's chief bogeymen were Catholics; the Know Nothings carried the municipal elections. When the party turned virulently anti-immigrant over prohibition, its German support disappeared.[41]

Democrats had a long history of appealing to Catholic and immigrant voters. In the early 1850s, the Whigs tried to revive their fortunes by appealing to them too, an about-face made easier by the order-loving Whigs' opposition to the militant bigotry that animated many anti-immigrant activists. At a time when the old issues that had separated the parties were losing their relevance, this competition for the foreign and Catholic vote convinced many nativists that a new party was needed to represent their interests. A widespread repugnance toward established party politics, "a general disgust with the powers that be," aggravated the political confusion. James Garfield wrote in his diary in 1852, "I am exceedingly disgusted with the wire-pulling of politicians and the total disregard for truth in all their operations."[42]

In this atmosphere of ethnic and religious strife and dissatisfaction with existing political parties, there arose the nativist American or Know Nothing Party, so called because it grew out of a secret organization whose members, when questioned, claimed to know nothing about it. Nativists portrayed the immigrants who flooded Ohio at midcentury as slum-dwelling drunkards and Sabbath-breakers who crowded the prisons and poorhouses, drove wages down and food prices and rent up, and corrupted the political system by voting in readily manipulated blocs.

Starting the new party was easy. Candidates did not have to "get on the ballot"; they simply had to hand out tickets to voters for deposit into the ballot box. In April 1855, they carried the municipal elections in Cincinnati. But despite its broad appeal, Know Nothingism quickly burned out in Ohio because of a revulsion against the antiforeign violence during the Cincinnati municipal elections, a belief that anti-immigrant sentiment was too narrow a basis for a political party in a nation of immigrants, and the revival of the sectional crisis.[43]

The Civil War Era

The Kansas-Nebraska Act of 1854 invigorated the antislavery movement throughout the North by opening up the possibility of slavery in Kansas and other territories where freedom had formerly been ensured. A fusion convention of Anti-Nebraska men—Whigs, Democrats, and Free Soilers—met in Columbus in July and nominated a Whig and a Democrat for the two state offices to be filled that year. The *Ohio State Journal* referred to the nominees as Republicans, a name that had already been used in Vermont and Michigan. In October, the fusionists won a thumping victory, taking the two state offices by a wide margin. Anti-Nebraska candidates won all twenty-one congressional districts.[44]

In 1855, the fusionists officially became the Republican Party. The Republican state convention nominated Salmon P. Chase for governor. The Know Nothings had already decided against putting up their own slate of candidates. The Republicans co-opted them by naming Know Nothings for all statewide offices other than governor. Dissident Know Nothings and old Whigs who could not stomach Chase held a separate convention and nominated their own candidate for governor, as, of course, did the Democrats. Chase won easily, and the Republicans carried both houses of the General Assembly by a wide margin.[45]

The Republicans and Democrats offered sharply different positions on the racial and sectional issues that dominated the legislative agenda for the next fifteen years. In April 1857, for example, the Republican General Assembly passed three personal liberty laws designed to hamper enforcement of the federal Fugitive Slave Act in Ohio. Although tame in comparison with the personal liberty laws of some other northern states, they did not all stay on the books long. Chase won a narrow victory in the 1857 gubernatorial election, but the Democrats, aided by the failure of the mammoth Ohio Life Insurance and Trust Company, a nationwide financial panic, and an embezzlement scandal in the state treasurer's office, recaptured both houses of the General Assembly. The legislature repealed two of the personal liberty laws and, in defiance of supreme court decisions holding that men more than half white could vote, passed a law directing election judges to reject the vote of anyone having "a distinct and visible admixture of African blood."[46]

The deepening sectional crisis, which in Ohio featured the dramatic Oberlin-Wellington fugitive slave case in 1858–59, produced a wave of anti-Southern sentiment across the North and Republican victories in the 1859 fall elections in Ohio. But a bloc of conservative House Republicans allied with Democrats on key issues to obstruct radical measures, such as repeal of the Visible Admixture Law, reenactment of the personal liberty laws, and a resolution condemning slavery in the wake of John Brown's raid on Harpers Ferry. During the session, Democrats harped on the prospect of mass black immigration into Ohio, a favorite theme throughout the coming war, but failed to pass legislation on the subject.[47]

The Senate of 1860 included a remarkable "radical triumvirate" from the Western Reserve. That part of the state had a history of sending powerful anti-slavery voices to the legislature: Benjamin F. Wade, who would be a leading radical Republican in the U.S. Senate during Reconstruction; Norton S. Townshend, the physician and former Free Soiler who had helped send Salmon Chase to the U.S. Senate, had fought for black and female suffrage at the 1850–51 constitutional convention, and would for many years be a professor of agriculture at Ohio State; Albert G. Riddle, a lawyer, politician, and writer who prosecuted one of the accomplices in Lincoln's assassination and worked to get women admitted to the bar. James Monroe, the senior radical triumvir of 1860, had been a lecturer for the American Anti-Slavery Society, Oberlin professor, and state senator since 1856. In 1859, the Western Reserve elected James A. Garfield and Jacob D. Cox to join him. Garfield was a professor of ancient languages and the very young president of Hiram College. Cox, an Oberlin graduate and Garfield's roommate in Columbus, was a school superintendent and future lawyer, scientist, author, and railroad corporation and university president. All of these Western Reservists but Cox eventually served in Congress. Garfield went on to become president of the United States, while Cox would be a postwar governor of Ohio and U.S. secretary of the interior.[48]

Secession and the threat of war in late 1860 and early 1861 induced a spirit of compromise among Republicans as well as Democrats. The General Assembly adopted a series of resolutions that, while not as conciliatory as the Democrats would have liked, nevertheless stood foursquare against "meddling with the internal affairs of other states" and for the repeal of any laws that might render

James A. Garfield and Jacob D. Cox,
two-thirds of the "radical triumvirate" of the Ohio Senate on the eve
of the Civil War. The photograph of
Garfield is contemporaneous with
their Senate service. Cox appears in
his Civil War army uniform.

James A. Garfield. *Reproduced by permission of the Ohio
Historical Society*

Jacob D. Cox. *Reproduced by permission of
the Ohio Historical Society*

"less efficient" the Constitution and laws of the United States. (Personal liberty laws, designed to hamper enforcement of the federal Fugitive Slave Act, were prime examples of legislation that would make a law of the United States "less efficient.") For good measure, many Republicans, not wishing to be seen as more problack than pro-Union, acceded to a Democratic bill forbidding interracial sex and marriage.[49]

All these measures were too little too late. When the war erupted in April 1861, a surge of patriotic, pro-Union feeling swept through the North. The General Assembly, still in session, unanimously appropriated one million dollars for war purposes, half of that amount to pay for the president's requisition of troops. The lawmakers also passed a treason law forbidding anyone to give aid and comfort to the enemy and prohibiting unauthorized military expeditions against any other state. Cox and Garfield terminated their brief state legislative careers and went off to war.[50]

Before the fall elections, Republicans and prowar Democrats resolved to put aside party labels for the duration and cooperate as the Union Party. Democrats who refused to go along maintained a separate Democratic organization and referred to themselves as Peace Democrats. The Unionists won a smashing victory in the 1861 election, but old differences quickly surfaced in fights over patronage, resolutions against slavery and in favor of the Lincoln administration, and bills to provide relief for soldiers' families and to allow troops in the field to vote. The new alliance nearly disintegrated over the election of a U.S. senator. The Unionists, burdened with military failure and dissension within their ranks, lost the congressional and state elections of 1862. They still had control of the General Assembly, but emboldened Democrats attacked the Lincoln administration without restraint, so much so that Ohio army officers in the field complained about the fire in their rear.[51]

In July 1862, on the recommendation of Ohio governor David Tod, the secretary of war ordered the arrest of Edson B. Olds, a former Speaker of the Ohio House, former congressman, and outspoken opponent of the war. In characteristically intemperate language, Olds had publicly denounced the war, called Lincoln a tyrant for his arbitrary arrests and suppression of free speech, and predicted that Democrats would resist the draft and defeat the administration at the polls. Federal authorities arrested him, along with ten other antiwar speakers and editors in Ohio. The best known of the arrestees, Olds remained in federal custody until December. While imprisoned, he was elected to fill a vacancy in the Ohio House of Representatives, whereupon the secretary of war ordered his release.[52]

After Olds's triumphant return to Columbus, his ally Representative Otto Dresel of Franklin County demanded a legislative investigation of military arrests in Ohio. After a month of haggling over Dresel's resolution, the House agreed. The committee of investigation completely exonerated the administration, declaring that, "in its effort to restrain the rage of sedition and violence, which are the beginnings of anarchy," the country provided "an example of power tempered with clemency, without a parallel in the annals of civil wars."[53]

Dresel suffered tribulations of his own. On March 19, 1863, he offered a series of resolutions avowing that "the liberties of the people are menaced by Congressional and Federal usurpations," that the newly enacted national banking system was "covertly designed to establish a vast central money power," and that the Emancipation Proclamation, the result of "pandering to the insane fanaticism of the Abolition faction," threatened to "carry lust, rapine and murder into every house of the slaveholding States." The resolutions indicted the government for establishing a "military despotism," creating a system of secret police to spy on the people, arbitrarily arresting and detaining citizens without charge, depriving them of trial by jury, transporting them to faraway places, answering their petitions for redress with "repeated injury and insult," suppressing freedom of speech, and other violations of constitutional rights. The indictment read like the list of accusations against the British monarchy in the Declaration of Independence.[54]

No sooner had Dresel's resolutions been defeated than a Unionist representative called for Dresel's expulsion from the House. A proposed substitute would have declared Dresel "an unfit associate for loyal men" and recommended that the members withhold "all fellowship" from him. In the end, the House satisfied itself with censuring Dresel as "a promoter of sedition and disunion, and an enemy to his country."[55]

A few months later, the tide of battle, and with it the tide of politics, turned in the Union's favor. The Union Army won the pivotal battles of Gettysburg and Vicksburg, and a vigorous Unionist campaign produced a decisive political victory. The General Assembly formally repealed the Visible Admixture Law, revoked a statute that made blacks ineligible for poor relief, and ratified the Thirteenth Amendment abolishing slavery. But black suffrage proved unattainable. The question continued to roil Ohio politics after the war. The Western Reserve strongly favored equal voting rights, but conservative Unionists equivocated and

Democrats maintained their outright hostility. The Democratic state executive committee condemned the "monstrous scheme of the radicals to place negroes upon a footing of perfect political and social equality with the whites and to govern the country in all time to come by means of negro votes."[56]

The 1865 elections produced a 2 to 1 Unionist majority in each house of the General Assembly, but neither the governor nor most Unionists favored an amendment to eliminate the word "white" from the Ohio constitution. Blacks formed equal rights leagues, bombarded the General Assembly with petitions, and convened in Columbus to make their case to the legislature in person, but to no avail. The General Assembly ratified the Fourteenth Amendment to the U.S. Constitution, which reduced the representation in Congress of any state that denied the franchise to blacks, but it refused to endorse federal laws that gave the vote to blacks in the District of Columbia and that required Negro suffrage as a precondition for restoration of southern state representation in Congress. Debates over proposed suffrage amendments to the Ohio constitution attracted large crowds to the House of Representatives. The lawmakers adopted a compromise amendment that tied black suffrage to the disenfranchisement of rebels, deserters, and draft dodgers. Intended to attract support in cities where black suffrage held no allure, the disenfranchisement strategy backfired. Thousands of Ohioans had deserted after Lee's surrender. During the election campaign the Democrats not only pledged to free Ohio "from the thralldom of niggerism," but also to oppose "the disenfranchisement of those soldiers who did faithful service throughout the actual continuance of the war, but returned home before receiving an official discharge." Congress mitigated the effect of the disenfranchisement clause on July 17 by exempting servicemen who went AWOL after Appomattox from the charge of desertion, and after a hard-fought campaign filled with vituperation and, in Democratic parades, wagonloads of young girls holding banners that pleaded, "Fathers, save us from negro equality," Republican Rutherford B. Hayes won a narrow victory for governor. But the voters gave both houses of the General Assembly to the Democrats and defeated the suffrage amendment.[57]

The new General Assembly rescinded the ratification of the Fourteenth Amendment, investigated charges of illegal voting by blacks and mulattoes, overturned a senatorial election on the grounds that only men who were "pure white, unmixed" could vote, and enacted a new Visible Admixture Law. The supreme court, still in Republican hands, declared the new statute unconstitutional. The same legislature refused to ratify the Fifteenth Amendment to the U.S. Constitution, which prohibited racial discrimination in voting laws. The next General Assembly just barely approved it in 1870. The amendment, which took effect later that year, nullified the Ohio constitution's racially restrictive voting provision, but as late as 1912 the voters refused to repeal it; it remained in the constitution until 1923.[58]

The Fifteenth Amendment drained race of its force as a political issue. Racial prejudice remained powerful; Ohio witnessed lynchings and race riots into the twentieth century. But in law, at least, blacks secured equality. Clement Vallandigham helped pave the way with his "new departure" for the Democrats. In resolutions prepared for the Montgomery County Democratic convention in 1871, Vallandigham accepted the recent federal constitutional amendments as facts of life and pledged the party to "secure equal rights to all persons under [the Constitution], without distinction of race, color, or condition." In 1878, the General Assembly unanimously voted to remove the word "white" from the militia law. After the U.S. Supreme Court declared the federal Civil Rights Act of 1875 unconstitutional in 1883, the General Assembly passed a state civil rights act and repealed the last of the Black Laws, which provided for segregated schools and prohibited interracial sex and marriage. In 1889, the legislature unanimously outlawed "riotous conspiracy" (conspiracy by three or more people to commit misdemeanors while wearing white caps or other disguise) and, with just one dissenting vote, prohibited discrimination in the sale of life insurance. Black lawmakers required perseverance to secure antilynching legislation, but that too passed in 1896.[59]

Prelude to Prohibition

As racial issues faded in importance, the ethnocultural controversies that had dominated state politics before 1854 returned. It would be overly simplistic to say that ethnic background or religious bent determined one's political attachment. As one historian has explained, "church affiliation was itself a reflection of class standing and aspiration, so that cultural and economic concerns were closely intertwined in the creation of party loyalties." But culture proved a remarkably potent factor, perhaps more important than class, in determining party ties.[60]

In 1873, with the nation in the throes of an economic depression and the Grant administration rocked by scandals, the Democrats captured the governorship and both houses of the General Assembly. Democratic representative John J. Geghan of Cincinnati introduced a bill to protect inmates of jails and asylums from being forced to attend religious worship or instruction and to require the directors of institutions to provide equal facilities for inmates of all religions. In a letter that became public while the bill was pending, the Catholic Geghan referred to his bill as an act of justice to Catholics and payment of an obligation to Catholics for supporting the Democrats. The letter induced a sometimes hysterical response from Republican newspapers.[61]

Democrats deplored the power of prison and asylum authorities to retain ministers of one sect to the exclusion of others and urged that employed chaplains be dispensed with altogether. They accused Republicans of using the Geghan bill "to work upon the passions and prejudices of the anti-catholic and anti-foreign element of our people." After public opinion had been whipped up, the Republican Ohio State Journal observed that "[i]nstead of being an advantage to the Democracy this most unnecessary piece of legislative bunkum has aroused and alarmed the people of the entire State, and is alienating from the Democratic fold hundreds of conscientious voters who cannot submit to sectarian dictation and who will not act with a priest-ridden party." Republicans regained control of the General Assembly in the 1875 elections and promptly introduced a repealer of the Geghan law. When the repeal bill passed the Senate, one Democrat moved to amend the title by adding that one of its purposes was "to deprive the people of Ohio of impartiality in legal matters in religious affairs."[62]

No ethnocultural issue proved more disruptive to politics than prohibition. Finding it hard to stake out their positions without alienating important groups of voters, the parties often skipped lightly over the issue in their statewide campaigns. In the General Assembly, though, liquor was one of the few subjects that provoked party-line votes in the late nineteenth century. According to one student of Gilded Age state politics, "The repeated divisions along party lines that occurred over liquor issues in most of the northern legislatures were often replicated on other social issues such as restrictions on activities on Sundays, prostitution, gambling and racing, the use of tobacco by minors, and obscenity." In Ohio, that wasn't the case. The General Assembly prohibited the sale of tobacco to children under fifteen by a total vote in the House and Senate of 88 to 2. It outlawed opium dens by a combined vote of 87 to 3 and banned the publication and distribution of obscene materials by votes of 90 to 1 and 81 to 1. A bill to prohibit public theatrical performances, minstrel shows, baseball playing, circuses, and other activities on Sunday ran into some opposition, passing by a combined vote of 87 to 35. There was a partisan flavor to the vote, as House Republicans supported the measure 50 to 7 and Democrats opposed it 21 to 10. But the partisanship may have stemmed from a provision that increased the penalty for Sunday liquor sales. A bill to prohibit barbering on Sunday, with no liquor issue attached, originally passed the House 66 to 19 and the Senate 20 to 0. When the Senate, on reconsideration, increased the penalty, just one Democrat and one Republican voted against the bill.[63]

Republicans and Democrats did line up against each other on national issues, such as the protective tariff, the nomination of former slaveholder and Confederate army officer Lucius Q. C. Lamar to the Supreme Court, and congressional control of federal elections; but the votes on most types of legislation—election reforms, tax laws, labor laws, business regulations, morals legislation—tended to be lopsided. When there was significant opposition to a measure, Republicans and Democrats could be found on both sides. In his study of populism in Ohio, Michael Pierce found that in voting on legislation of interest to farmers and workers, the lawmakers usually divided into urban and rural camps rather than along party lines. Even on the bill that raised the penalty for Sunday liquor sales, every Republican representative who voted no represented a populous county with a large city, and every House Democrat who voted yes came from a county with fewer than fifty thousand people.[64]

Although the gubernatorial candidates tried to brush prohibition aside in their campaigns, legislators simply could not withstand the popular pressure to confront it. Prohibitionists flooded the 1873–74 constitutional convention with petitions. The Women's Christian Temperance Union organized in Cleveland in 1874 and the Anti-Saloon League in Oberlin in 1893. The national Prohibition Party held its conventions in Ohio in the 1870s. Politicians ignored the power of prohibition sentiment at their peril. In the 1880s, the General Assembly passed a series of laws designed to discourage the sale and consumption of liquor by taxing retail dealers, prohibiting Sunday sales, and allowing local-option elections. In 1883, the General Assembly placed on the ballot alternative constitutional amendments, one to allow the legislature to regulate and tax traffic in intoxicating liquor and the other to prohibit commerce in booze altogether. A majority of the voters approved one or the other, and most of those favored outright prohibition; but neither proposition individually received a majority of all votes cast at the election, so both failed.[65]

Women kneeling outside a Bucyrus saloon during the Women's Temperance Crusade of 1873–74. *Reproduced by permission of the Ohio Historical Society*

Roll-call votes on liquor measures reveal a gulf between the parties. Between 1882 and 1886, the General Assembly passed the Pond, Scott, and Dow laws, each of which taxed liquor dealers and imposed conditions on their trade. (The lawmakers had to revisit the issue twice because of unfavorable supreme court decisions.) In 1882, Republican senators supported Pond's bill 17 to 4; Democratic senators opposed it 10 to 0. In the House, four-fifths of Republicans favored the measure, while four-fifths of Democrats rejected it. The votes on the Scott legislation the next year followed a similar pattern. In 1886, only three House Republicans voted against the Dow bill and no House Democrats voted for it. The Dow bill passed the Senate almost unanimously, but that was because most Democratic senators had walked out during the feud over the seating of senators from Hamilton County.[66]

Notwithstanding this impressive party solidarity, liquor bills eventually caused serious intraparty dissension. When local-option legislation came under discussion in 1884, a Columbus paper reported that some rural Democrats "threaten to pulverize the caucus if it attempts to force them further, while the city members know that sure destruction awaits them if nothing more is done." For Republicans, who relied more heavily on the antiliquor vote, the division between urban and rural members was even more troubling. An amendment to the Dow Law passed in 1888 on a party-line vote. The combined vote of House and Senate Republicans was 74 to 9 in support of the bill. All forty-four Democrats who voted on the bill voted against it. Significantly, all nine Republican no votes came from large-county representatives. That same year the General Assembly passed a local-option bill giving to residents of townships outside municipal corporations the power to vote their territories dry. Republicans voted overwhelmingly for the bill, Democrats overwhelmingly against. But "urban" Republicans—those from counties having populations over 100,000—split 16 to 10 against the bill. All thirteen members from Hamilton County, the heart of Republican opposition to prohibition, voted no.[67]

These votes were portents of things to come. As in the 1850s, moral issues cast a shadow over party loyalty. A Republican temperance activist declared in 1886 that "when it comes to the temperance question, I am ready to see any party go down, if prohibition will result." Prohibitionists gave the Republicans migraines; the Grange and Greenback movements induced annoying if less serious headaches among Democrats. In a highly competitive political environment, both major parties sought to broaden their appeal without endangering their bases. For Republicans, this meant reaching out to Catholics and German Lutherans, a strategy that caused major defections of pietists to the Prohibition Party. (Pietist sects, such as Methodists and Quakers, emphasized right behavior—personal piety and evangelical action to bring one's self and others from sinfulness to salvation. Ritualists, including most Catholics, stressed right belief—adherence to formal doctrine and established rituals—and acceptance of God's imperfect world.) But the Republican-passed liquor laws, while less than what prohibitionists demanded, pushed German Lutherans into the arms of the Democrats. Republicans might have made headway among Grangers—farmers who sought railroad regulation and other legislation that ought to have aligned them with the Democrats—because Grangers tended to be pietists who favored temperance and moral reform. But the Republicans weakened their moral stance by courting Catholics. The Democrats had similar though shorter-lived problems with pietist Greenbackers, who stood close to the Democrats on currency and other matters but had a moral fervor that sat poorly with Democratic Catholics and German Lutherans.[68]

The upshot was that party loyalties began to crack. The new Anti-Saloon League, headed by Howard Russell, put cause above party. Russell molded the League into a well-organized entity along the lines of a modern corporation, directed from the top down, with a central office, specialized departments, and local but not autonomous branches. The League's legislative department monitored political activity, drafted bills, and lobbied the lawmakers. Although deliberately

The Prohibition Party holding its national convention in Cincinnati in 1892. *From the Prints and Photographs Division, Library of Congress*

political, the League was consciously nonpartisan, willing to work with any politician who supported the cause. As the League gathered strength, its single-minded devotion to prohibition gave Republicans fits. Most drys remained within the Republican ranks, but the party could no longer count on the loyalty of the most active and energetic prohibitionists.[69]

For much of the nineteenth century, party affiliation was intimately connected to personal identification. People were intensely loyal to their parties; being a Democrat, Whig, or Republican was a large part of who a person was. In the Ohio of the 1870s and 1880s, party membership "was not a matter of intellectual choice, it was a process of biological selection." An out-of-state politician declared, "We love our parties as we love our churches and our families." Many Republicans viewed defection to the Prohibition Party as not just a sign of disagreement but an act of betrayal, similar to the treachery of Joshua Giddings when he deserted the Whigs for the Free Soilers. But change was in the air. The rise of the educational and merchandising styles of campaigning, with their emphases on the substance of issues and the individual virtues of candidates, contributed to the decline of party devotion. So, too, did the official, secret ballot, which made voters less susceptible to tests of party fealty. Third parties often stimulated party sentiment, but voter registration laws and ballot regulations, intended to reduce election fraud, threw obstacles in their way. Whether the major parties would withstand these challenges was a question for the twentieth century.[70]

The First Century

11

LEGISLATION AND

THE PUBLIC GOOD

THE GENERAL ASSEMBLY that met in 1849–50 passed laws to tax banks, modify judicial procedures, amend the poor relief statutes, prescribe the width of roads and the powers of turnpike companies, and deal with other issues of concern to the citizens at large. These "acts of a general nature" occupied ninety-six pages in the published session laws. The same General Assembly also found time for "local laws" that affected one county or township, one road, one corporation, or one person. The lawmakers prohibited cranberry picking in Lucas County from July 1 through October 1. They authorized the state auditor to pay the funeral expenses of Representative Joseph W. Ross, who died just before the session ended. They provided for the appointment of guardians for the minor legatees of Lyne Starling. They penalized fast driving over bridges in Ashtabula County. They passed one special act of incorporation after another, chartering turnpike companies, railroad companies, cemetery associations, libraries, academies, organizations of every description. The local enactments took up 707 pages in the printed session laws.[1]

In 1904, as Ohio embarked upon its second century of statehood, the General Assembly was still passing both general and local laws, but the ratio had changed.

The 1904 session laws contained 614 pages of general acts and nine pages of local laws. The nature of the legislature's work product had undergone a dramatic transformation since 1850.[2]

The General Assembly of the early nineteenth century had a monumental task: to provide for the organization, support, defense, and growth of the state. Initially these matters of an obviously general character engaged most of the legislators' attention. In its first two sessions, those that convened in March and December 1803, the General Assembly passed laws that organized the state judiciary, overhauled the militia system, provided for the incorporation and government of townships and counties, regulated elections, established a criminal code, and addressed other vital concerns. By the end of its second session, the General Assembly, in the opinion of Salmon P. Chase, had produced a "tolerably complete system of statute law."[3]

Some issues proved intractable. The constitution of 1802 limited the legislature's power to modify the structure of the court system, and the General Assembly never found an adequate solution to the backlogs and delays that plagued the judiciary for the next half century. Nor could constant legislative tinkering turn the militia into an effective military force. On the other hand, in the remarkable year of 1825, the General Assembly enacted crucial tax, canal, and school laws because the interested parties worked out compromises palatable to all. Representative Ephraim Cutler of Washington and Athens counties had two legislative passions: reform of the tax system and the establishment of a tax-supported system of free public schools. The state relied for revenue on an antiquated land tax based on soil quality. Education, notwithstanding the constitutional requirement that "schools and the means of instruction shall forever be encouraged by legislative provision," was abysmal and public education virtually nonexistent. Cutler had no particular interest in canals, but other prominent Ohioans wanted the state to finance artificial waterways to open up cheap and reliable trade with the east.[4]

Supporters of legislative action in these three areas sometimes clashed. The canals being proposed would serve the well-off Miami and Scioto valleys; citizens from other parts of the state saw no reason to bear the cost. Many opponents of public support for canals also opposed public schools, for both meant increased taxation and state power. On the other hand, the overtaxed New Englanders of Cutler's region, who had nothing to gain from the canals, shared with prominent canal advocates a wish for public education. It seemed only fair that the areas to be benefited by the canals pay for them, and that would happen only if land were

Ephraim Cutler. *Reproduced by permission of the Ohio Historical Society*

taxed according to its value. Furthermore, the commissioners appointed to investigate the feasibility of canals recognized that taxation of both real and personal property according to its value would be necessary to raise enough revenue to build the canals. In the meantime, a joint legislative committee on education urged the establishment of a "truly republican" system of free schools in which the children of the rich and poor would meet "upon a footing of perfect equality." Recognizing that the proposed canals would also require increased taxes, the committee shrewdly recommended only a "slight ad valorem assessment" sufficient to get a decent school system started. Once the people got used to the idea, the state could improve upon it.[5]

Clearly, a deal was in order. When canal advocates endorsed tax reform and agreed to appropriate money for roads in areas not on the canal routes, Cutler and his cohorts dropped their opposition to the canals. The General Assembly easily passed both tax reform and the canal project. By abolishing the tax classification of real property according to soil quality, taxing personal property used in business, and basing taxation on the monetary value of the property being taxed, the lawmakers took a long step toward the general property tax, that is, a tax on all property within a taxing district at the same, uniform rate. In subsequent legislation, the General Assembly moved closer to that ideal until it was embodied in the

1851 constitution. The canal law authorized the state to borrow money for canal construction and to pledge its full faith and credit for repayment. Within a few years, two major canals, the Miami and the Ohio, opened for business.[6]

The school law mandated the organization of districts and the establishment of schools (although it left the execution of the mandates in local hands), levied a statewide property tax for the support of schools, and required that teachers receive certificates of qualification from court-appointed examiners. The law had its defects: no state and only limited local supervision of the schools, no reporting of information on the performance of the schools, inadequate enforcement. Nevertheless, as Cutler's daughter wrote many years later with pride and some exaggeration, the law of 1825 created "a *system*," including "the power and duty to lay taxes . . . to organize districts, elect directors, build houses, employ teachers, and impose qualifications, and the legal machinery for collecting and applying funds."[7]

The rising Jacksonians would question the merits of all this legislation, but there is no denying its significance. Historian Daniel Ryan wrote in 1912 that the legislature of 1824–25 "stands in the history of the State as one that accomplished more for the public good and posterity than any which preceded or succeeded it."[8]

Special Legislation

The public good, of course, was supposed to be the object of all legislation. The political thought of the republic's founders drew on the writings of radical English Whigs who lamented the corruption of Parliament by a power-hungry ministry. With offers of bribes, titles, and preferments of various kinds, charged the Whigs, the ministry prostituted the members of Parliament, who then acted not for the good of the country but for the benefit of themselves and their ministerial masters. By the time of the Revolution, many Americans felt sure that evil ministers, a greedy "monied interest," and a "junto of courtiers and state-jobbers" had gotten the king's ear and gained control of the legislature "by power, interest, and application of the people's money to *placement* and *pensioners*." These malefactors sought to obliterate liberty and establish ministerial tyranny. But as Gordon Wood has observed, the Revolution destroyed "archaic ideas of personal monarchical government. Public power was to be used for the public good, not for benefit of special interests or private individuals. In republican America government would no longer be merely private property and private interests writ large as it had been in the colonial period. Public and private spheres that earlier had been mingled were now to be separated."[9]

Nevertheless, there persisted a very old tradition that citizens had a right to petition their government for the redress of private grievances. At first, Englishmen addressed their petitions to the king, but petitions later came to dominate Parliament's legislative agenda. English settlers in America brought the petitioning habit with them. The historian of the Maryland General Assembly attributed the astonishing "number and variety of petitions" submitted to that body in the late eighteenth century in part to "the absence of laws of general application and of agencies of government which could handle the requests without recourse to the Legislature." But appeals to the legislature rested less on practical necessity than on the nature of government at the time. The concept of separation of powers, so central to the American constitutional order today, was not then highly developed. Courts had legislative and administrative as well as judicial functions. Some courts levied local taxes, saw to the maintenance of roads, or supervised assistance to the poor. The courts of quarter sessions of the Northwest Territory, for example, divided counties into townships, appointed township constables, clerks, and overseers of the poor, heard petitions for the laying out of roads, appointed highway superintendents, and determined the need for and estimated the cost of major bridges. In some parts of the country, the nonjudicial functions of courts persisted well into the nineteenth and even twentieth centuries. American legislatures, for their part, had always entertained petitions of a judicial nature. According to Wood, "[T]he assemblies in the eighteenth century saw themselves, perhaps even more so than the House of Commons, as a kind of medieval court making private judgments as well as public law. . . . The assemblies constantly heard private petitions, which often were only the complaints of one individual or group against another, and made final judgments on these complaints."[10]

Citizens also submitted petitions of a nonjudicial character to their legislatures. These petitions often sought authority to engage in some activity that would not otherwise be permitted, to establish corporations for business, religious, literary, or other purposes, or to alter the powers of local political units (which might themselves be corporations). In England, requests for corporate charters were usually directed to the sovereign, the crown; in the American colonies, petitioners sought authority from governors acting as agents of the crown or, in some colonies, from assemblies that derived their authority from charters granted by the crown. After the Revolution, when the people were sovereign, petitioners generally submitted their requests to the state legislatures. In the decade or so after the end of the Revolution, the Maryland General Assembly received petitions for authority to extend streets, divide counties, hold fairs, lay out towns, operate stage lines, build warehouses, erect bridges, construct mill dams, and do a variety of other things that were not strictly private in their effect but that affected only one community.[11]

Much of the legislation produced by the Ohio General Assembly, especially in the first half of the nineteenth century, originated with petitions. Petitioners wanted to construct roads, lease public lands, change their names, get divorced, receive payment for claims against the state, build bridges, form corporations, have individuals admitted to state institutions. Crusaders for causes pressured lawmakers with petitions for the enactment of general laws or the amendment of the constitution. They flooded the General Assembly with petitions, signed by dozens if not hundreds of citizens, for temperance laws and for black and female suffrage. Some petitions the legislature granted by joint resolution; others required passage of a statute. "Special," "private," or "local" acts passed in response to petitions far outnumbered acts of a general nature. Even when the lawmakers denied a petition, they still took up time in presenting, reading, and reporting on it.

The most notorious cases of special legislation involved the creation of corporations by special acts that granted corporate charters, the sole method of forming corporations in the early nineteenth century. During the American Revolution, the passion for equality had led to attacks on acts of incorporation as grants of special privilege by the government. In Pennsylvania, for example, legislator William Findley argued against rechartering of the Bank of North America by declaring that the legislature had no right "to give monopolies of legal privilege —to bestow unequal portions of our common inheritance on favourites."[12]

This Revolutionary legacy of opposition to special legislation coexisted with an old notion that government had the duty to promote private endeavors for the benefit of the public. From the beginning of settlement, American colonial governments offered loans, land grants, tax abatements, and other inducements to various types of enterprises, including sawmills, fulling mills, iron works, and gristmills. One means of promoting the public welfare was the grant of corporate charters by special acts of the legislature. Both the idea that government had the obligation to foster the general welfare and the practice of doing so through the encouragement of private enterprise, corporate and noncorporate, remained common currency when Ohio attained statehood.[13]

Business incorporations in Ohio grew by leaps and bounds after the War of 1812. The General Assembly's zest for granting charters to banking and other business corporations, its enthusiastic extension of state aid to private corporate enterprise, and the disastrous consequences following the Panic of 1837 have been described in chapter 3. Andrew Jackson's war on the Bank of the United States, the rise of laissez-faire thought, and the popular reaction against corporations following the panic eventually ended the practice of incorporating businesses by special acts. Indeed, they destroyed the whole pattern of special acts of incorporation for charitable, educational, and religious organizations and municipalities as well, although, as we will see, the affinity for special municipal corporation laws took a long time dying.

Of the countless petitions the General Assembly received on matters unrelated to incorporation, those for divorce were especially bothersome. The highly mobile Americans of the early nineteenth century moved often, fast, and far, sometimes as families, sometimes as individuals, married or unmarried. Sometimes they deliberately moved to states with more liberal divorce laws or abandoned their spouses without regard to divorce laws at all. Ohio had an especially peripatetic population before 1850. Starting with the squatters of the 1780s, people arrived in a swelling westward tide. Many kept going across the Indiana border, but immigration and natural increase produced a demographic boom in a restless people.[14]

Marital stability could be hard to maintain under such circumstances, and the law had to take account of this reality. The General Assembly steadily liberalized the divorce statute. The laws of the Northwest Territory allowed for absolute divorce on grounds of bigamy, impotence, and adultery and for divorce from bed and board (in effect, separation) for extreme cruelty. State laws enacted between 1805 and 1834 added as grounds for absolute divorce extreme cruelty, willful absence of a spouse for five (later three) years, imprisonment of one's spouse in the penitentiary, fraudulent contract, gross neglect of duty, and, in deference to the mounting temperance crusade, habitual drunkenness.[15]

Alongside the procedure for judicial divorce stood the phenomenon of the legislative divorce, the exclusive method of obtaining a divorce in England and some of the American states. Unhappy spouses might petition the legislature because they did not have grounds for divorce under the general divorce statutes, because they could not afford a court proceeding, or because they could influence the votes in the legislature. In Ohio, petitioners sometimes complained of judicial backlogs. In his application to the General Assembly in 1835, Lewis Myers stated that he had filed for divorce in Monroe County in 1833 but that the supreme court, which had jurisdiction and was supposed to sit annually in each county, had not met there since and no one knew when it would.[16]

Despite the liberalization of the divorce laws and the increasing percentage of divorce petitions granted by the courts, by 1840, petitions for legislative divorce had become a serious nuisance. In its first half century, the General Assembly passed approximately one hundred special acts dissolving marriages, nineteen of them in 1843 alone; however, these figures are only for acts passed, not for applications considered. In the session of 1839–40, for example, at least forty-three unhappy spouses submitted petitions for divorce, but the General Assembly granted only four. Often the judiciary committees tried to get rid of petitions by noting that the courts had the power to grant relief under the circumstances alleged. The Senate Judiciary Committee told Lewis Myers that he would just have to wait for the court to sit in his county; if the legislature started granting petitions on the same grounds as the courts, there would be no end to them. Meritorious or not, divorce petitions took up time in committee, sometimes on the floor, and sometimes in both houses. Where the supreme court had jurisdiction, legislative investigations of petitions were a "great waste of time and money."[17]

As the concept of separation of powers evolved and lines between the branches of government sharpened, questions arose about the propriety of legislative divorces. The General Assembly granted Jacob Overmire's petition for a divorce in 1814, but some senators sought to reject the petition and instead expand the grounds for judicial divorce to include force and gross fraud. During the 1847–48 legislative session, the House Judiciary Committee announced in its report on Horace P. Dunbar's divorce bill that legislative divorces were unconstitutional, although a subsequent select committee report disagreed. On the floor, the representatives defeated a motion to refer the question to the state attorney general and then narrowly passed the bill, but the Senate refused to go along. Soon afterward, the supreme court held that the power to grant divorces was judicial in nature and that legislative divorces were therefore unconstitutional. Thus ended the phenomenon of legislative divorces in Ohio, probably to the relief of many of the lawmakers. The House Judiciary Committee's report and the supreme court's decision reflected the ongoing transformation of the General Assembly from a quasi-judicial, quasi-administrative body absorbed in private and local affairs into a modern legislature concerned with statewide policy and statutes of general application.[18]

But the transformation took a long time to complete. Despite the end of legislative divorces, the General Assembly continued for a time to pass special laws relating to family matters. For example, the common law did not recognize adoption, but informal adoptions sometimes received legislative recognition through special acts to change the adoptee's name or to make the child the legal heir of the parents. At least one Ohio change-of-name act expressly referred to the child as an adopted son. In an industrializing society with a growing urban population of poor immigrants, the increasing difficulty of apprenticing orphaned or neglected children or placing them with relatives helped pave the way for a general adoption law. Public poorhouses did not do a good job of caring for children, private orphan asylums could not pick up all the slack, and apprenticeship was on the wane. Adoption looked like a more satisfactory way of dealing with dependent children. In 1854, a bill to change the name of Margaret J. Martin to Margaret J. Watkins and to make her the legal heir of Christopher Watkins mutated into a general law allowing anyone to designate an heir at law who could inherit the same as a child of marriage. The supreme court later referred to this law as an adoption statute. In 1859, in tune with a national trend that had recently begun in Massachusetts, the General Assembly enacted a true adoption law.[19]

The 1851 constitution outlawed legislative divorces, prohibited special acts of incorporation, and authorized the General Assembly to enact general corporation laws. The corporation provisions applied to all types of corporations: business, not-for-profit, and municipal. Moreover, the constitution required that laws of general nature operate uniformly throughout state. But notwithstanding these constitutional requirements and the enactment of general incorporation laws, an adoption law, and, before 1851, a law empowering courts of common pleas to grant changes of name, the General Assembly continued to devote considerable time to the needs and desires of individuals. Petitions kept pouring in. In 1870, for instance, members of the House presented well over 300 petitions, plus forty-four memorials and twenty-eight remonstrances—all this in one house and one year of the biennium. Probably most petitions asked for the enactment of general laws, but others sought local laws or individual relief of various sorts. By joint resolution, the General Assembly continued to direct the state insane asylum and other public benevolent institutions to accept particular persons as patients. As late as 1896, the legislature passed eleven local laws changing the names of individuals.[20]

Members took a proprietary interest in local laws. When the House passed a bill to erect a new jail in one member's county even though his opposition to the bill was known, the representative protested the House's disregard of the "honored custom . . . of referring all local matters to, and following the judgment of, the member whose county is affected." It did not help the member's mood that the House took up the bill out of order in his absence and that the clerk recorded him as voting no.[21]

The General Assembly continued to enact special laws in defiance, if not of the letter of the constitutional inhibitions, then certainly of their spirit. In 1851, Ohio's school districts outnumbered New York's by more than one thousand. One-third had been organized under special laws. Even after 1851, the General Assembly continued to create new districts via special acts and to redraw the boundaries of many others. Some laws carved well-to-do districts out of townships, leaving poorer subdistricts geographically divided and financially strapped. In 1882, the Ohio Supreme Court held that special-district laws violated the constitutional requirement that laws of a general nature have a uniform operation throughout the state; however, most of the already-created special districts continued to function, and in 1889 the court reversed itself. The latter decision opened the floodgates to a torrent of special laws, until, in 1902, the court once again slammed them shut. Twelve years later, in a general redesignation of school districts, the lawmakers abolished all special districts.[22]

Subterfuge by Classification

Classification, too, bedeviled school legislation. In 1873, the General Assembly divided school districts into five types: city districts of the first and second classes, as determined by the city's population, and village, township, and special districts. By 1898, the two classes of city districts had become five. Only in 1904 did the General Assembly end the proliferation of city district classifications by putting all city districts into a single class.[23]

When applied to municipal corporations, classification became special legislation by another name and a scandal of the first order. Before 1817, the General

Assembly incorporated two dozen towns by special acts, but then the rapid growth of settlement induced the lawmakers to pass the first general municipal incorporation law. Despite the 1817 law and another general law adopted in 1838, the legislature devoted much time before 1851 to passing and amending special acts incorporating towns, villages, boroughs, and cities. The delegates to the second constitutional convention, disgusted with all types of special in-corporations, declared municipal corporations to be of two types, city and village, and prohibited the General Assembly from passing special acts to incor-porate municipalities.[24]

In 1852, the General Assembly enacted a general law for the incorporation of villages and the organization of cities. The law classified existing municipali-ties into villages, villages for special purposes (road districts), cities of the second class (having a population of between five and twenty thousand), and cities of the first class (having a population over twenty thousand). It established a pro-cedure whereby the voters of an unincorporated area could petition county officials for the creation of a village and provided for the transition from one category to another as population changed. The statute spelled out the powers shared by all municipal corporations—to lay out streets and regulate traffic, suppress disorder, control animals, create a water supply, regulate taverns and theaters, and so on—and those that belonged only to cities. Every city could, for example, establish a police force and fire company; cities of the first class could also establish houses of refuge and police courts. The structure of municipal government under the law grew more complex with size.[25]

This laudable attempt to recognize the needs of differently sized municipalities while keeping within the constitutional confines of general legislation soon gave way to a constitutional subterfuge: the use of general language to cover specific cities or villages. In 1869, the General Assembly authorized every city that met certain criteria to issue bonds to complete a sewer project. The criteria were that the city be of the first class, have a population over 150,000, have established an unimproved public avenue ninety feet wide, and have a partially constructed sewer. Of course, only one city fit the bill: Cincinnati. Three laws passed in 1890 au-thorized villages having populations 1,046, 1,560, and 1,268, respectively, to issue sewer bonds. The General Assembly passed well over a thousand such laws in the second half of the nineteenth century.[26]

Even municipal corporation laws that could more plausibly be characterized as general approached special status. The four municipal categories of 1852 grew to more than a dozen by century's end, many of them deliberately drawn to include a single city. For example, cities of the first grade of the second class were those with between 30,500 and 31,500 inhabitants. The only rationale for such a category was to apply a particular rule to a specific city (in this case, Columbus).[27]

The increasingly detailed classification of cities reflected the General Assembly's ever-growing interference in municipal affairs. The original municipal law of 1852 seemed designed to establish the general structure and powers of municipal government and then to let villages and cities govern themselves. But the lawmakers could not shake their addiction to special legislation. As a student of municipal affairs in Ohio wrote, "The General Assembly determined for Cleveland, Cincinnati, Toledo, Dayton, and nearly every other city in the state, as well as for particular villages of even the smallest population, what officers they should elect, what salaries they should pay them, what parks, streets, and hospitals they should build or improve, what their tax limits would be, what bonds they should issue, and what powers each and every department of the municipal government should possess."[28]

Special legislation for municipalities grew out of political as well as structural considerations. The dominant party in the legislature would pass special laws to keep political brethren in power or to enhance their chances of getting it. Such "ripper" legislation, so called because it ripped apart constitutional and legal provisions for partisan advantage, played havoc with city government. Cincinnati underwent six rearrangements of its chief administrative boards between 1885 and 1891 as control of the General Assembly changed hands.[29]

For years, the Ohio Supreme Court turned aside challenges to special legislation for municipalities, but, in the 1890s, as the scandals of municipal government gave birth to the Progressive urban reform movement, the justices changed their views. In 1892, they struck down a law authorizing one village to assess property owners for the costs of constructing sidewalks. In 1896, they invalidated a law requiring fire escapes on buildings in Cincinnati, lamenting the General Assembly's "growing tendency" to ignore constitutional limitations on its powers. In 1901, the court announced that it would no longer tolerate sham classifications.[30]

A series of similar decisions announced during the regular legislative session of 1902 instilled caution in the lawmakers. They refused to pass a number of special acts and adopted several laws of a general nature relating to municipal powers. Then on June 26, after the legislature had adjourned sine die, the court rendered two opinions that essentially declared the whole scheme of municipal classification unconstitutional and strongly suggested that the legislature do something about it immediately. The decisions precipitated a crisis; they threatened to put every municipal government in the state out of business. As if this were not enough, the public learned that, in May, the General Assembly had inadvertently taken away virtually all of the supreme court's appellate jurisdiction.[31]

To deal with these two emergencies, Governor Nash called a special session of the legislature. Summoning his municipal law experts, the state bar association, the attorney general, and legislative leaders of both parties, Nash had a bill prepared by the opening of the special session. After much debating, amending, and conferencing, the bill passed on October 22. Among its many other reforms, the new municipal code gave cities a large measure of home rule and applied uniformly throughout the state, thereby promising an end to logrolling and ripper legislation. Home rule, the power of municipalities to govern local affairs without interference from state lawmakers, would be enshrined in the constitution a decade later. As late as 1994 and 2003, the General Assembly passed laws aimed at the tiny villages of Linndale and New Rome, notorious speed traps that seemed to exist for the sole purpose of collecting fines from unwary motorists; however, the supreme court declared the first statute unconstitutional, and New Rome, under siege by the attorney general and other officials as well as the *Columbus Dispatch*, faced dissolution anyway. Special legislation, if sufficiently general in form, might still pass muster, but home rule had done away with old-fashioned direct intervention by the General Assembly in the business of municipal governments.[32]

Legislating Morality

The demise of special legislation, it will be recalled, was rooted in the revolutionary notion of a separation of the public and private spheres. Radical Democrats of the Jacksonian era challenged the traditional belief that government had a responsibility to promote economic development for the welfare of the community. The *Washington Globe*, Jackson's unofficial mouthpiece, proclaimed in its masthead that "the world is governed too much." The *Cleveland Plain Dealer* declared, "Governments have no right to interfere with the pursuits of individuals" by "granting privileges to any particular class of industry, or any select bodies of men." The argument was not limited to economic matters. Opponents of tax-supported public schools tended to be Democrats who believed that the state had no business telling a man how to educate his children. Democratic foes of prohibition insisted that what a man ate and drank was not the government's concern.[33]

Notwithstanding the success of the radical Democratic viewpoint at the 1850–51 constitutional convention, the idea that government should stay out of people's lives as much as possible did not win easily and never prevailed completely, even with respect to economic affairs. Indeed, writes historian William Novak, few Americans regarded the relationship between the state and the economy as adversarial until the latter half of the nineteenth century, and even then the traditional view of the regulated, "well-ordered market" yielded only grudgingly to the notion that government and society occupied separate spheres, one public, the other private. The success of the prohibition and public-school movements testify powerfully to the limits of individualism. Nowhere do these limits appear more dramatically than in the campaign for sexual morality.[34]

The General Assembly had always attempted, mostly ineffectually, to control behavior in the interest of morality. Early statutes outlawing blasphemy, Sabbath-breaking, gambling, and fornication remained on the books throughout the nineteenth century. After the Civil War, the General Assembly, along with legislatures elsewhere, intensified its efforts to regulate sexual conduct. Historians have attributed the moral crusade to a variety of causes: the attempt by "transplanted provincials" to impose their old, small-town moral order on great urban centers filled with rootless workingmen; the spread of scandalous literature through cheap, mass-market books and magazines; a masculine reaction against the new female assertiveness; the fight by females against the degradation of women; a desire to preserve the family against increasing social pressures. Probably all played a role. Whatever the cause, the increase in legislation is undeniable.[35]

The newly invigorated campaign for sexual morality in Ohio can be traced at least back to 1834, when the General Assembly adopted an antiabortion statute. At the time, abortion was dangerous and as much a matter of public health as morality. Neither abortion nor any other aspect of medicine was highly regulated. Beginning in 1811, at the urging of a member who was also a doctor, the General Assembly passed a series of laws dividing the state into medical districts and establishing criteria for the practice of medicine. The experiment proved a "dismal failure." In 1833, the legislature gave up the attempt at regulation for a generation and did not enact anything effective until 1896.[36]

While the General Assembly stopped saying *who* could practice medicine, it started saying *how* people could practice. In 1834, the lawmakers provided penalties for prescribing medicines while drunk and for refusing to divulge the composition of "secret" nostrums. The same law criminalized attempted abortion, whether by drugs or instruments, and made causing the death of either the mother or the fetus (after quickening) a felony. The statute foreshadowed the convergence of two concerns: medical quackery and a dramatic increase in abortions, particularly among married women and Protestants, often procured by patent remedies and untrained practitioners.[37]

After 1840, the antiabortion movement grew and spread, spearheaded by regular doctors concerned about both public safety and the competition from charlatans. In the 1850s, the General Assembly considered but failed to agree on legislation to regulate the sale of nostrums. By then the moral element in the antiabortion argument had gathered strength. A select House committee consisting of three physician-representatives defended the role of the state as the protector of public safety and morals, called on doctors to fight quackery, railed against the unholy alliance of humbugs and newspapers that profited from the pervasive advertising for patent medicines, and decried the "filthy notices" for contraceptive potions, cures for sexual diseases, and concoctions to induce miscarriages, all of which encouraged illicit sexual activity. Noting the legislature's penchant for passing laws to regulate the liquor traffic and to ensure the "purity of elections," the committee thought "it may be necessary to do something for the purity of morals." The bill urged by the committee died on a tie vote in the House.[38]

Opponents of abortion achieved legislative success in 1862; this time the vote was not close. By a combined vote of 90 to 5 in the two houses, the General Assembly passed a law "to prevent publication and circulation of obscene advertisements and books." The statute prohibited the publication of any account or description of "any drug, medicine, instrument, or apparatus" used to terminate a pregnancy or to prevent conception. The law also banned the advertisement or sale of abortifacient and contraceptive nostrums. When purveyors tried to evade these prohibitions with ads for "secret drugs" exclusively for female use, the General Assembly prohibited those too.[39]

With abortion and contraception attended to, the lawmakers attacked other issues of sexual morality. They prohibited indecent exposure and the use of obscene language in the hearing of a female. They outlawed the printing, circulation, and sale of "obscene, lewd, and lascivious" material, a prohibition soon expanded to include the possession or sale of items used for abortion, contraception, or "self-pollution," the mailing of prohibited items, and even telling someone where such items could be obtained. Male teachers risked imprisonment for having consensual sex with a student. So did anyone who enticed a female into "illicit carnal intercourse" or who permitted such activity on his premises. Even publishing a notice for the purpose of procuring a divorce could lead to a fine and up to six months in jail.[40]

All these laws passed in the 1860s and 1870s, but the crusade for sexual purity and defense of the family continued unabated. Before passage of the first anti-pornography law in 1872, the House Judiciary Committee reduced the fines by a factor of ten and the possible term of imprisonment from between ten days and six months to "not less than thirty days." Within the next twenty-five years, though, the General Assembly increased the penalties for most sexual-morality violations and added new prohibitions. Serving wine to a female in order to weaken her resistance to sexual overtures could get the server three years in the penitentiary. Making, publishing, or exhibiting "indecent" pictures, or present-ing indecent exhibitions of the human form, was prohibited. Sodomy carried a penalty of up to twenty years' incarceration.[41]

The degree of concurrence among the lawmakers on morals legislation is as-tounding. After the Judiciary Committee reduced the penalties, the 1872 anti-pornography bill passed the House 63 to 1. A few years later, just one member of the General Assembly opposed the bill to strengthen the antipornography law. The bill to protect feminine ears from lewd language passed by a combined vote of 110 to 4. The prohibition on advertising to procure a divorce ran into some opposition in the Senate, but it passed the House unanimously. In 1885, barely more than a majority of representatives attended the House session in which the sodomy bill came up for a vote, but since every single member present supported it, as had every senator present a week earlier, the bill passed.[42]

The General Assembly's persistent attention to sexual morality reveals more than the limits of individualism under Ohio's statutory law. It also illustrates a change in the focus of lawmaking and in the role the General Assembly played in the lives of the citizenry. In regulating sexual behavior, the General Assembly was formulating public policy on the basis of social values. It was not dealing with individual or local problems. Notwithstanding the continued use of peti-tions and the enactment of numerous local laws throughout the nineteenth cen-tury, the public perception of the legislative function was changing. We saw at the beginning of this chapter the precipitous decline in the number of local laws after 1900, prompted in part by the supreme court's more vigorous application of constitutional strictures against special legislation. Petitioning too dropped sharply in the early twentieth century. In 1921, the 162 members of the General Assembly presented a grand total of sixty-four petitions, memorials, and remonstrances. Over 80 percent of the members presented none at all. By 1930, Robert Luce could write that the right of petition had come to be "only a right to an idle form, a waste of time and energy for both the petitioner and the petitioned." Petitions were typically referred to a committee and then ignored. The General Assembly's role as a quasi-judicial forum in which individuals sought redress of personal grievances or communities looked for assistance with purely local matters had lost its prominence. Twentieth-century developments—the decline of voter turnout, the rise of administrative agencies, the growth of cities, the increasing influence of the federal government on state legislation—would just about finish it off.[43]

PART THREE

THE SECOND CENTURY

FELCH — RICHES.

12

DIRECT DEMOCRACY

AMERICANS HELD THEIR legislatures in low regard in the late nineteenth and early twentieth centuries. An eminent attorney noted that "the citizen too often distrusts, fears and is ashamed of his representatives." A governor remarked that popular distrust of the legislature had "almost ripened into open hostility" and in many states had "grown into open contempt." The founder of the reform magazine the *Arena* thought that the elections of U.S. senators Henry Payne and Mark Hanna by the Ohio legislature and the control of the General Assembly by public utility corporations presaged a bleak future for America. Wealth and corruption seemed to be destroying the American republic, as they had ruined the republics of Greece, Rome, and Florence.[1]

The influence of corporations and party bosses over the General Assembly drew cries of outrage from many quarters. Lawyer and politician Frederic C. Howe of Cleveland decried the power of urban political bosses "who selected members of the House of Representatives and candidates for the courts as they would select clerks in their offices." A Cleveland businessman declared that he had "seen men come in here to the city of Columbus . . . and with their boodle in gripsacks buy legislators of the state of Ohio as you would buy cattle in the stock yard." Cincinnati pastor Herbert S. Bigelow launched his crusade for political reform with a denunciation of legislators who had to be begged "to protect the public interest against the monopolies."[2]

Howe went to the Ohio Senate in 1906 with high hopes of enacting reform legislation. Three years' experience convinced him that the system was corrupt. The most capable members, Howe found, were insurance company agents and lawyers for steam railroads, interurban railways, and banks. They were devoted to the well-being of their clients and employers rather than to the general welfare and in many cases took their instructions from out of state. These able legislative leaders ruled over ignorant members who, lacking opinions of their own, "did quite honestly and naturally as they were told." Bankers, intimately connected by business to powerful corporations and often active in local party organizations, exerted tremendous influence over the legislature. "The county banker was a person of local distinction, active in the church, identified with good works," wrote Howe. "Members of the Assembly honestly relied on him for advice." Lobbyists for important business interests, many of them former state officeholders, knew everyone and knew how members could be reached. Newspapermen took their cues from party leaders. "Ohio, in short, was not ruled by the people," wrote Howe. "It was ruled by business. Not by all business, but by bankers, steam-railroads, public-utility corporations. Representative government did not represent the people; it represented a small group, whose private property it protected."[3]

What was to be done about the dishonesty and inefficiency of government? In an earlier age, reformers had concluded that government could not be trusted with power and therefore had to be narrowly confined. By the late nineteenth century, notwithstanding all the complaints about overlegislation and corruption in government, people wanted government to do things. With the depression of the 1870s, writes historian Morton Keller, "the state activism of the post-Civil War years" came to an end, and "[o]ld traditions of localism, individualism, and hostility to government reasserted themselves. . . . But beneath its surface desuetude, state government was beginning to respond to the new conditions of American life." Even as antipathy toward active government appeared in many state constitutional conventions, state assemblies, with the approval of large segments of the public, passed more and more social, economic, and fiscal legislation.[4]

The demands for governmental action stemmed from dramatic social changes in the last quarter of the nineteenth century. Abetted by a surge of immigration,

Ohio's population grew by 30 percent between 1880 and 1900. The number of rural folks declined slightly in those years, while the urban population almost doubled. By the turn of the century, Cleveland and Cincinnati each had well over 300,000 inhabitants, Toledo and Columbus over 100,000. The growth of the cities went hand in hand with Ohio's transformation into a leading industrial state. Urbanization and industrialization strained municipal services, created health hazards, aggravated relations between labor and management, and opened new opportunities for corruption.[5]

To many reformers, the solution to venality in government and to the distortion of the popular will could no longer be the contraction of governmental authority. Rather, it was to assert popular control over government. If there were flaws in the representative system of government, then government had to be made more representative or representation had to be replaced with direct action by the people. Rumination on his experiences in the General Assembly led Frederic Howe to embrace three fundamental political principles: "Government should be easily understood and easily worked; it should respond immediately to the decision of the majority; the people should always rule." From these principles, Howe developed an eight-point program that included the nomination of political candidates by direct primaries rather than conventions, the printing of a candidate's platform on the ballot, the short ballot, the recall of elective officials, the initiative and referendum, municipal home rule, a small unicameral legislature that stayed in continuous session for a four-year term, and the abolition of judicial review of legislation. It was a typical program of the Progressive era.[6]

Some parts of the Progressive agenda received major attention at the Ohio constitutional convention of 1912. The constitution of 1851 required that the question of calling a convention appear on the ballot every twenty years. In 1891, the voters had not found a convention necessary, but, in 1910, there seemed to be a widespread if amorphous sentiment that the constitution needed an overhaul. The strongest advocates of a convention included tax reformers, liquor interests who wanted to license saloons, and proponents of the initiative and referendum. Popular interest also ran high in woman suffrage, protection of workers, judicial reform, and municipal home rule. Contemporary observers disagreed over the extent of the demand for a convention. Critics argued afterwards that the convention had been the work of activists who had pushed it through in the face of hostility or indifference on the part of most Ohioans. One scholar asserted that, notwithstanding the ratification of most of the amendments proposed by the convention, "there is a prevalent idea of the whole business having been railroaded through in the interest of radical changes, which a naturally conservative state would be cautious in adopting." Be that as it may, those citizens who took the trouble to vote on the amendments responded to complaints about the General Assembly by giving the electorate a more direct role in the selection of candidates and the enactment of legislation.[7]

At the convention, the deplorable state of representative government in Ohio elicited from delegate J. W. Tannehill a call for reform before it was too late. Referring to the scandals of 1911, when the secret recording of conversations between legislators and lobbyists had helped indict at least nineteen individuals for bribery, Tannehill declared that "with a few more dictograph-pursued and corruption-enmeshed sessions of the legislature as we witnessed a year ago an outraged public will arise in its might and wipe representative government from the state, and we will revert to the rule of the mob." Tannehill urged a two-part solution to the peril. First, every "friend of representative government" had to favor the initiative and referendum. The initiative would allow voters, through petitions signed by a small percentage of their numbers, to put proposed laws and constitutional amendments on the ballot. The referendum, through a similar petition process, would give voters the opportunity to reject acts passed by the General Assembly. Second, said Tannehill, to prevent the overuse of direct legislation, it was necessary to restore public confidence in representative government by giving the people a greater role in choosing candidates. That could be done by replacing nominating conventions with direct primaries.[8]

Direct Legislation

The direct legislation movement in Ohio began in the 1890s. In 1893 and again in 1894, before any state had yet adopted direct democracy in any form, Representative John W. Winn of Defiance County introduced resolutions to provide for the referendum in Ohio. The proposals received scant consideration at the time, but the movement picked up steam after the turn of the century. The Ohio Senate approved a direct legislation constitutional amendment in 1906, and the Senate and House passed differing versions of an amendment in 1908. The first died in the House and the second in conference committee. In the meantime, the movement met success elsewhere. Fourteen states adopted some form of direct democracy before 1912.[9]

Opponents of the reform claimed that it would wreak havoc on representative government. "To indulge in the practice of *referendum*," declared New Jersey governor and soon-to-be U.S. attorney general John W. Griggs in a speech in Cleveland, "would tend to destroy confidence in our representative system and produce the highest degree of instability, subjecting [*sic*] the judgment of the un-informed and the passionate for that of the selected and reasonable representa-tives." (These were the same legislators whom Governor Griggs had shortly before condemned for sloppy, inexpert lawmaking that was subject to too many political and personal influences.) At the Ohio constitutional convention, op-ponents lauded representative government as a more deliberative vehicle for law-making than direct legislation. They also displayed a deep distrust of the people, whom they described as impulsive, incompetent, and corrupt. Daniel J. Ryan, for-mer state representative and secretary of state, prophesied after the convention that the initiative and referendum would wreck the representative character and independence of the General Assembly. "This," he declared, "is government of the crowd with a vengeance."[10]

Although some advocates of the initiative and referendum sought to replace representative government with direct democracy, most insisted that the reform would improve, not abolish, the system of representation. The weakness of rep-resentative government in the United States, editorialized the *Independent*, was "the absolute lack of control by the people over those to whom they have dele-gated legislative functions." To protect themselves against the misuse of legis-lative authority by their delegates, the people needed to have the power to initiate laws that they wanted but the legislature would not pass and to veto laws that the legislature passed but the people did not want. In addresses to the Ohio constitutional convention of 1912, William Jennings Bryan com-plained of "representatives [who] mis-represent their constituents" and "embez-zle power" for personal advantage, while Theodore Roosevelt spoke of the need to make government more "responsive to the popular will." Both men insisted that the initiative and referendum would correct rather than destroy represen-tative government and that direct democracy would not become the usual way of enacting laws.[11]

After a great deal of acrimonious debate over the shape of the reform—whether the General Assembly should get first crack at passing a law proposed by an initiative petition, how many signatures should be necessary, whether sig-natures should be required from different parts of the state—the convention adopted a compromise measure that gave the people a direct voice in legislation.

The voters ratified the amendment handily. Under the new amendment, adoption of a law by initiative was a two-step process. First, proponents had to try the indirect initiative; that is, they had to submit a petition, with enough valid signatures, to the General Assembly for the lawmakers' consideration. If the General Assembly did not adopt the law as proposed, a second, direct-initiative petition could bring the law before the voters at the next election. The initiative could also be used to put constitutional amendments on the ballot. And through the petition process, opponents of a law enacted by the legislature in the usual manner could have the law placed on the ballot for a referendum by the people.[12]

Some reformers saw the initiative and referendum as ways to exercise the constitutional right of citizens to instruct their representatives. Progressives who sought direct democracy as a tool for making legislators more responsive to the will of the electorate occasionally urged voters to question candidates closely and to obtain pledges of support for particular reforms, including in the first place the initiative and referendum. In earlier times, when most people lived in small towns and nominated their candidates at public meetings, the voters might instruct candidates through resolutions adopted at those meetings. Now, as the Anti-Saloon League had demonstrated, an organized interest group could pressure candidates with questionnaires on issues of concern to them and publicize the results. Once direct democracy took effect, the interest group could fall back on the initiative or referendum if its legislative demands were not met. Some Progressives objected to the initiative and referendum for just this reason, fearing that legislators would lose all sense of judgment and simply parrot the popular opinion of the moment.[13]

The General Assembly's right to instruct Ohio's U.S. senators fell victim to another Progressive reform. The theoretical right of instruction had not had any practical effect at least since the 1850s, although the lawmakers issued instructions to the senators as late as 1892. Beginning in 1891, the General Assembly repeatedly adopted resolutions favoring a constitutional amendment to provide for the election of U.S. senators directly by the people instead of by the state legislatures. In 1913, the Seventeenth Amendment to the U.S. Constitution did just that, wiping out even the theoretical basis for the legislature's right to instruct senators. The amendment, favored by reformers as the best way to eliminate the purchase of Senate seats by big corporations, removed from the state legislatures one of their chief partisan functions.[14]

The Second Century

Direct Primaries

The second half of Tannehill's cure for the ills of representative government was the direct primary, which Howe called "the fountainhead of democracy." Conventions, critics alleged, had come under the control of party bosses; the direct primary, in which party members chose their candidates by direct election, was a popular reform intended to put control of the party back into the hands of the people. Tannehill and Howe surely knew that a Republican experiment with the direct primary in their own city of Cleveland had failed in the 1890s. The voters often did not know the candidates, so they tended to support those who had the slickest advertising or the most personal charm. Political cliques had no trouble controlling the nominations; they simply decided on their candidates and then used their wherewithal to help their men win. Primary races brought out many inferior candidates, produced hard feelings among the candidates, and cost a lot of money. About their only advantage seemed to be a growing turnout at the polls. But advocates thought the system could be fixed. They argued that, to be effective, a direct primary had to be mandatory, use the Australian ballot, and be held under state regulation at public expense, and all parties had to hold their primaries at the same time and place.[15]

The General Assembly enacted three direct primary laws before 1900. A general law passed in 1871 gave political parties the option of conducting primaries under the law's provisions. The other statutes, passed in the 1890s, required direct primaries in Butler and Hamilton counties. In 1899, the Cincinnati Superior Court found the Hamilton County law (and, by implication, the Butler County law) to be unconstitutional special legislation. Ohio State University professor A. H. Tuttle observed that the parties in most counties were happy to conduct primaries under the general law because it left the time, place, and manner of the election, the qualifications of voters, and the choice of election supervisors to the parties, while the public picked up the tab.[16]

In 1904, Representative Hiram S. Bronson, a former member of the Franklin County Board of Elections, introduced a bill to clean up primaries. Bronson proposed to have mandatory primaries, conducted by all parties on the same day under the supervision of local boards of elections. Only voters who were enrolled as members of a party would be able to vote in that party's primary. Names could be put on the ballot by petition. Party leaders, who would have lost control of the primaries, objected to the bill, which the House Elections Committee obligingly eviscerated. The bill that finally passed, without dissent in either house, was, wrote Tuttle, "little better than no law at all." Its one redeeming feature, he thought, was the requirement that each voter be registered in the precinct where he voted. Until then, "In Columbus wagon loads of men might be seen at any primary being carried from one voting place to another, voting as many times as there were primaries."[17]

Bronson had more success in 1908, when the General Assembly passed a mandatory direct-primary law applicable to candidates for Congress and other public elective offices, including the controlling committees of the major parties; however, the primary requirement did not apply to candidates for statewide offices or for district offices in multicounty districts. Those candidates would still be selected by nominating conventions, although the convention delegates would be chosen at primaries. This was a huge exception that exempted from participation in primaries not only the governor and other top executive officers but also most senators; without the exemption, the Senate would not approve the bill. A person could still get on the general election ballot via a nominating petition, but he would not run on a party ticket. To get onto the primary ballot, a candidate had to file nominating papers signed by 2 percent of the party's voters in the last election in the political subdivision for which the nomination was made. The parties had to hold separate primaries, and only self-declared party members could vote in a party's primary. The public would bear the expense of primary elections.[18]

At the 1912 constitutional convention, advocates of the direct primary sought to extend its reach to cover all state officers and senators. Conventions, asserted Tannehill, were boss-controlled and unrepresentative. They consisted of the same crowd year after year: "A lot of two-by-four editors like myself, a lot of one-horse lawyers and a bunch of county officials." Not everyone agreed. One delegate favored conventions because they required "consultation and conference between the best citizens of the community," whereas primaries meant "bossism all of the time." Another contended that no one beat the political machines for getting out primary voters to support candidates chosen by "little cliques" in "back rooms." Despite such objections, the convention adopted the mandatory direct primary and the voters ratified it by a wide margin.[19]

The Fruits of Reform

The initiative and referendum and direct primary were major innovations in representative government in Ohio, but they did not work out as well as reformers hoped or as badly as opponents feared. The initiative and referendum got off to an inauspicious start when people hired to circulate referendum petitions doctored the documents. The Equity Association of Cleveland, an organization created by liability insurance companies that opposed compulsory workers' compensation legislation, conducted a petition drive in 1913 to defeat several recently enacted laws. An investigation by the attorney general found that the individuals hired to circulate the petitions engaged in massive fraud, forging signatures and smudging petitions to make them look well-used. The General Assembly reacted by penalizing as corrupt practices the misrepresentation of the contents of a petition, alteration of signatures, payments to obtain signatures, and other acts that threatened the integrity of petitions. Governor James Cox wanted to outlaw the use of paid solicitors of signatures, but he yielded to the argument that the collection of tens of thousands of signatures would be impossible without them.[20]

Daniel Ryan feared that the initiative and referendum would send Ohio down the road to socialism. Advocates of radical measures, including the Socialist Party, had supported the movement for the initiative and referendum in Ohio. The campaign had been secretly funded by a British proponent of Henry George's single-tax plan. Ryan knew the power of a well-organized minority in the face of an apathetic electorate. To submit a bill to the General Assembly, he noted, the bill's supporters had to get signatures totaling just 3 percent of the number of votes cast for governor in the last election. If the General Assembly refused to pass the bill, another 3 percent could put the bill on the ballot. A petition to subject a regularly passed bill to the referendum required signatures equaling 6 percent of the number of votes cast for governor. Based on the 1910 election, said Ryan, 3 percent came to 27,733. The Socialist Party candidate that year got 60,637 votes. The danger was clear.[21]

In practice, however, the initiative and referendum turned out to be rather tame monsters. As soon as the General Assembly met in 1913, it faced five laws proposed by initiative petitions. One, wrote Ryan, "provides practically for the suppression of a free press." The General Assembly passed two of the five, including the one denounced by Ryan. Over the next ninety-four years, however, initiative drives brought only fifteen more proposed statutes before the legislature; the General Assembly passed two, one in amended form. The House and Senate passed different versions of another initiative bill, a Depression-era measure providing for old-age assistance, but they never came to an agreement, while the repeal of prohibition rendered another bill moot. Of the sixteen measures begun through the initiative process that the General Assembly either failed to consider or declined to pass, eleven eventually appeared on the ballot because advocates secured enough signatures on a second petition. Only three passed: the old-age relief bill, a bill allowing the sale of colored oleomargarine, and a ban on smoking in public places. In sum, over the course of nearly a century, the initiative process has produced a grand total of seven laws, four adopted by the legislature and three by the voters.[22]

The referendum proved slightly more potent. Only twelve laws and one joint resolution adopted by the General Assembly in the regular course of business have been subjected to the referendum, eight of them between 1913 and 1923. Since then, just five laws have been put on the ballot by the referendum process. Some of the thirteen measures dealt with major issues such as congressional re-districting, woman suffrage, prohibition, taxation, and the civil service. The voters killed every one except a 1920 bill enacting statewide prohibition. Still, the exceedingly rare use of the referendum—for one stretch of nearly sixty years, no use at all—proved Ryan's fears to be unfounded.[23]

Although the initiative and referendum turned out to have little impact on legislation, activists for various causes have used the initiative process to propose more than five dozen constitutional amendments. Voters have approved sixteen, about half of them dealing with taxation. One allowed for the taxation of different classes of property at different rates, an idea with broad support in the General Assembly. However, the supreme court ruled that it could not take effect because the voters had simultaneously approved by a larger margin another amendment to the same section of the constitution and put on the ballot by a joint resolution of the legislature. Other significant tax amendments adopted via the initiative limited the tax rate the state or any local government could apply to real property without the approval of the voters and earmarked motor vehicle fuel taxes for highway-related purposes. An important nontax amendment required the use of the office ballot rather than the party-column ballot at elections. In grouping candidates by office rather than listing them in columns under the party label, the office ballot made it harder for electors to vote a straight ticket.[24]

Notwithstanding the bounds that some of the initiative amendments put on the lawmaking power of the General Assembly, only one seriously affected the workings of the legislature. In 1992, the voters approved four initiative amendments that limited the number of consecutive terms that could be served by the state's top executive officers other than the governor (who was restricted to two

(Signatures from......*Noble*......County).   No. *10*

Amendment to the Constitution

Proposed by Initiative Petition to be submitted directly to the electors.

NOTICE

Whoever knowingly signs this petition more than once, signs a name other than his own or signs when not a legal voter, is liable to prosecution.

Be it Resolved by the People of the State of Ohio:

That section 1 of Article V of the Constitution be amended so as to extend the suffrage to women.

We hereby designate from our number

W. O. Thompson
Pres. Ohio State University.

Thomas McKinnon

W. B. Kilpatrick
Chm. Judiciary Committee
House of Representatives.

Attorney-at-Law.

A. R. Hatton
Prof. Economics Western Reserve University.

F. G. Taber
Lecturer Ohio State Grange.

as a committee to represent us in all matters connected with this petition.

SIGN IN INK. NAME, DATE AND RESIDENCE, WARD AND PRECINCT MUST BE GIVEN.

If Living in a Municipality fill in SIGNATURE / If Living Outside a Municipality fill in SIGNATURE	STREET & NO. / TOWNSHIP	City or Village and County / COUNTY	WARD	PRECINCT	MONTH	DAY	YEAR
C. O. Brown	Belford St	Caldwell Noble Co. O.	1		June	10	1914
J. J. McAdams	North St.	Caldwell Noble Co.	1		June	10	1914
H. F. Evans	Belford	Caldwell Noble Co.	1		June	10	1914
H. B. Hume	North St	Caldwell Noble Co. O.	2		June	10	1914
W. S. McCleary	Cumberland St	Caldwell Noble Co.	1		June	10	1914
C. M. Ructter	North St	Caldwell Noble Co.	1		June	10	1914
H. B. Wycoff	North St	Caldwell Noble Co.	1		June	10	1914
Geo. W. Rice	North St	Caldwell Noble	2		June	11	1914
H. E. Danford	North St.	Caldwell Noble	2		June	11	1914
L. B. Walters	North St.	Caldwell Noble Co	2		June	11	1914
J. M. Combs	North St	Caldwell Noble Co.	2		June	11	1914
W. S. Hague	North St	Caldwell Co			June	11	1914
E. E. Stouffer	North St.	Caldwell Noble Co	2		June	11	1914
B. J. Brossard	North St	Caldwell Noble Co	2		June	11	1914
J. S. Danford	North St.	Caldwell Noble Co.	2		June	12	1914
C. L. Walls	North	Caldwell	2		June	12	1914

An initiative petition for a constitutional amendment granting woman suffrage, 1914.
Reproduced by permission of the Ohio Historical Society

successive terms in 1954), by Ohio's U.S. senators and representatives, and by state legislators. In 1995, the U.S. Supreme Court struck down state-passed term limits on members of Congress, but the other limits have gone into effect. The very serious consequences of the limits on state legislative terms are discussed in chapter 22.[25]

Of course, every proposed constitutional amendment, whether it originates in the General Assembly or a popular initiative, is subject to a referendum. Because of constitutional constraints on legislative action put in place in 1851, there have been many referenda on proposals that are constitutional amendments in form but more akin to ordinary legislation in substance. The constitutional convention of 1851, with its deeply cynical view of the General Assembly, severely restricted the state's ability to incur debt or assist private enterprise. For better or worse, programs that before 1851 could have been implemented by legislation have since then required voter approval. Beginning with the granting of bonuses to World War I veterans, the General Assembly has put on the ballot a host of amendments to allow the state to incur debt beyond the general constitutional limit, to lend its aid and credit to private businesses, or both. The proposed programs have included highway repair and construction, job creation, cleanup of hazardous waste sites, and so on. Most of the amendments are so detailed that they are more like statutes than constitutional provisions. The voters have approved many such proposals but not all. In 2003, for example, they rejected Governor Bob Taft's "Third Frontier" program, which would have authorized the state to issue $500 million worth of bonds to finance the development of high-tech industries in Ohio. In 2005, a similar program, but coupled with funding for roads and bridges, passed. At least when it comes to spending on public infrastructure and economic development, the referendum is alive and well.

Ultimately, the initiative and referendum disappointed the hopes of its early advocates. Some Progressives had been skeptical from the first, but most saw the reform as a powerful tool for cleaning up representative government and enacting a liberal or even radical program. But as one commentator noted in 1927, "in Ohio, which is a typical state, the electorate is not eager for innovation." A historian of the initiative and referendum has concluded that direct democracy "has not empowered ordinary citizens, it has not increased political awareness or participation, it has produced few significant public policy achievements, and it has not reduced the power of special interests."[26]

The direct primary, like the initiative and referendum, has worked out quite differently from how its early supporters anticipated. In 1913, a skeptical George

Kennan, noting the low voter turnout for the election of constitutional convention delegates in Ohio and for ratification of the proposed amendments, warned that "[n]o machinery of any sort, whether by direct primary, referendum, initiative, or recall, will accomplish any real reform, unless the individual citizen himself is stirred to a better performance of his duty as a voter and as a member of his party." If the people continued in their neglect, he warned, "the new machinery will grind out crooked bosses and crooked business just as the old machinery did."[27]

In the 1920s, a widespread reaction against the direct primary set in, not so much among the people at large to whom the direct primary seemed fair on its face, but among party activists. One Progressive confessed to having changed his mind about the direct primary because "[i]t makes men who are elected to represent all the people truckle to every little superficial ripple of popular hysteria, to support what they know to be false because they think it to be popular." He thought the Ohio elections of 1914, in which the number of dry counties rose to seventy-seven but the state as a whole voted for a wet amendment, illustrated the "inability on the part of the people to see things clearly enough to justify their having direct control." Warren Harding believed "that the results of the direct primary system are not good. . . . [I]t is actually easier to corruptly manipulate a primary than a convention." The historian of Ohio Progressivism concluded that while the direct primary "has had the virtue of eliminating the most grievous abuses of the convention method, i.e., clique-domination and bribery," it disappointed the naive hope of its advocates by failing "to bring forth consistently candidates strong in their devotion to the general public interest."[28]

At the 1912 constitutional convention, a delegate foresaw that direct primaries would produce such scattered voting for so many candidates that a party nominee might have the support of only a small percentage of the primary voters. Combined with voter apathy, the scattering of votes meant that "aggressive and determined minorities" who could deliver even a small bloc of votes could make or break a candidacy. Organized interest groups led by the Anti-Saloon League quickly learned to take advantage of these weaknesses of the system. They turned the people's right of instruction into an interest group's power to control: Promise to do our bidding *or else*.[29]

The direct primary also turned out to be expensive. A candidate had to get onto the primary ballot by gathering signatures on a petition. Then he had to conduct two campaigns, one against several members of his own party and another against the nominee of the other party. The government bore the cost of two elections. The direct primary, wrote Richard Hofstadter, "put a new premium on publicity and promotion in nominating campaigns, and thus introduced into the political process another entering wedge for the power of money." Although the money problem existed with regard to legislative and other district or local offices, it was worse where statewide offices were concerned. Robert A. Taft complained in 1926 that "[t]he quality of the candidates and officials has steadily deteriorated since [the statewide direct primary] was instituted. To be nominated for any State office requires a campaign extending over many months and involving the expenditure of thousands of dollars, or as in the recent case in Pennsylvania of millions of dollars. No man except one who has no business or one who is very rich can afford to enter a campaign."[30]

Because the direct primary allowed candidates to get onto the ballot without party backing, individuals unknown even to party committee members, let alone the voters, wound up on the list. The problem was particularly bad in big cities, where ballots had to be huge to accommodate all the candidates. Cleveland became notorious for its "bedsheet ballots." In 1922, voters taking part in the Cleveland Republican primary had to choose six senatorial candidates out of twenty-four on the ballot and sixteen representatives out of eighty candidates. All told, about 175 candidates had offered themselves for forty-three different offices. How was a voter to make an intelligent choice in the few minutes allotted? Forty years later, some observers reckoned the Cuyahoga County ballot to be the largest ballot in the world and "the champion frustrator of the democratic process." The bedsheet ballot continued to plague Cleveland voters until the apportionment revolution of 1966 ended the election of state legislators on a countywide basis.[31]

Critics of the direct primary also believed that it had a detrimental effect on party organization and policy, making politics more personal and less issue-oriented. Taft remarked that "it is exceedingly distasteful to many men to make a Statewide campaign which can have no possible issue except a personal one, and no possible argument except the claim that the speaker is himself the best man available." He moaned that the direct primary had "made impossible the existence of a State Party organization, and the result is that no State Party in recent years has initiated or carried through any important policy of State government." As Speaker pro tempore of the House in 1925, Taft chafed at the independence of many nominally Republican legislators.[32]

The direct primary may also have contributed to the rise in the number of uncontested legislative races, especially in rural counties. In 1908, when party conventions chose the nominees, few legislative seats went by default. In 1948, when the voters chose the nominees in primary elections, nearly one-fifth of all races and one-third of those in single-member districts had but a single major-party candidate. In most rural counties, the great majority of primary elections also went uncontested, so that in many instances the voters had no choice of candidates at either the nominating stage or in the general election. Political scientist V. O. Key suggested that the primary system, by weakening local party organizations, had helped reduce the number of contested legislative elections.[33]

Despite doubts and disappointments, opposition to the direct primary faded away during the 1930s. The full impact of the direct primary hit only in the 1960s, though, when television allowed candidates to sidestep the parties and appeal directly to the voters and when money proved more important to political campaigns than the labor of party workers. At the same time, the apportionment revolution, with its single-member districts, reinforced the decline of party control and the increasing need for money. When candidates were nominated on an at-large basis, any of the unknowns on an outsized ballot might squeak by. In 1960, twenty-eight-year-old Cincinnati lawyer Stanley Aronoff threw his hat into the ring because the mayor suggested that the race might generate good publicity for Aronoff's firm. The future Senate president did not campaign much and finished ninth out of ten in the primary voting, just high enough to secure the last spot on the Republican ticket for representative from Hamilton County. In the general election, active traditional campaigning and party support won him a seat at relatively little financial cost. The single-member districts that came along a few years later created head-to-head competition in both the primary and general elections in those districts that had contests. The campaigns grew more personal, intense, and expensive. Candidates for the General Assembly became increasingly dependent on legislative leaders who could raise and distribute large sums of money. The parties lost much of the remaining control they had over the candidates.[34]

The direct primary was intended to put control of nominations into the hands of the people rather than party workers, the many instead of the few, but the people have not shown much inclination to take it. Voter turnout for primary elections has been notoriously low. In 1960, almost a million fewer electors participated in the primaries than in the general election. In 1980, the first presidential election year following the inauguration of statewide voter registration, about 74 percent of registered voters in Ohio took part in the general election;

only 39 percent of registered voters voted in the primaries. These numbers understate the extent of voter apathy because many people who are eligible to vote do not even register.[35]

Even if the voters cared more about the primaries, many have not had much choice regarding the nomination of candidates for the General Assembly. In 1960, with half the Senate up for grabs, 11 races went uncontested in the Democratic primary and 8 in the Republican. With the entire House at stake, each party put up only one candidate in nearly 60 House primary elections. The situation was even worse in 1980: 16 Senate seats and all 99 House seats had to be filled. That made for 115 potential contests in each party's primary, or 230 in all. A grand total of 44 featured more than one candidate; 18 had no candidates at all. The direct primary produced chaos in Cuyahoga County for a long time, and although it initially boosted turnout, in the long run and in most of the state it failed to stimulate voter participation in the nomination process and did nothing to expand the voters' choice of candidates.[36]

Nonlegislative Events at the People's House

The inauguration of Governor George K. Nash in the rotunda in 1902.
Reproduced by permission of the Ohio Historical Society

The dedication of the McKinley memorial in 1906. Ohioans sincerely mourned the assassination of President William McKinley, a native son, in 1901. However, the big attraction on dedication day was featured speaker Alice Roosevelt Longworth, daughter of President Theodore Roosevelt and wife of congressman and former Ohio state legislator Nicholas Longworth. *Reproduced by permission of the Ohio Historical Society*

The opening of the fourth Ohio constitutional convention in the House chamber in 1912.
Reproduced by permission of the Ohio Historical Society

Suffragettes demonstrate on the statehouse steps in 1914. *Reproduced by permission of the Ohio Historical Society*

Feeding pigeons near the statue of Christopher Columbus at the statehouse, 1940s. *Courtesy of the Columbus Citizen-Journal Collection, Scripps-Howard Newspapers/Grandview Heights Public Library/Photohio.org*

Demonstration in favor of welfare increases at the McKinley memorial in front of the statehouse, 1966. *Courtesy of the Columbus Citizen-Journal Collection, Scripps-Howard Newspapers/Grandview Heights Public Library/ Photohio.org*

President Gerald Ford addresses a crowd outside the statehouse a few days before the 1976 election. *Courtesy of the* Columbus Citizen-Journal *Collection, Scripps-Howard Newspapers/Grandview Heights Public Library/Photohio.org*

A festival on the statehouse grounds, 1984. *Courtesy of the* Columbus Citizen-Journal *Collection, Scripps-Howard Newspapers/Grandview Heights Public Library/Photohio.org*

13

THE BALANCE

OF POWER

T HE MEMBERS OF OHIO's first constitutional convention, who had guarded
so carefully against executive "tyranny," would have been shocked to learn
that the legislature's "loss of parity with the governor" was "the outstanding fact
of twentieth century state politics." And the authors of the Sweeping Resolution
would have been equally outraged by the audacity of twentieth-century judges
who denounced legislators for engaging in constitutional interpretation, a power
the judges claimed for themselves alone. Ohio's founding fathers could not
have fathomed an American state government in which the legislature did not
reign supreme.

After several decades of disappointment with the General Assembly's performance under the 1802 constitution, Ohioans took away much of the legislature's
power. However, they did not transfer it to the other branches of government.
Under the constitution of 1851, the General Assembly could no longer allow the
state to incur debt above $750,000, except to suppress insurrection or repel in-
vasion. It could not authorize any state debt for internal improvements. It could
not assist private enterprise, or permit local governments to do so, as it had in

the past. The legislature lost flexibility in the creation of new counties and in levying taxes, and the constitution forbade it to confer corporate powers by special legislation. Most significantly for its relationships with the other branches of government, the General Assembly lost the power to appoint judges and the major executive officers of the state. But except for a slight increase in gubernatorial patronage—the governor gained the power to appoint the trustees of state benevolent institutions, subject to the advice and consent of the Senate—the executive and judiciary acquired no new authority. The general thrust of the new constitution was toward limited government and more popular control of government through the direct election of judges and executive officers.

Yet a shift in power did occur. It began slowly soon after the new constitution took effect, gathered steam in the late nineteenth century, and became an accomplished and decisive fact of political life in the twentieth.

The Veto

The General Assembly's "loss of parity" with the governor began in the nineteenth century with the governor's growing powers of patronage. It accelerated in the early twentieth century with the veto, the governor's authority and responsibility to prepare a state budget, and the expansion of government by administrative agencies. Moreover, the governor retained his traditional advantages of being the center of political attention in state politics, a person who could set a legislative agenda with his annual message to the legislature, who spoke with one voice to and for the entire state rather than a single district, and who commanded the constant attention of the press. Notwithstanding the creation of legislative research and bill-drafting agencies, state legislatures remained for much of the century inadequately housed, staffed, and paid; they simply could not compete with a governor determined to control state government. Of course, not all governors exploited their positions to the fullest, and they could be frustrated when faced by a legislature completely controlled by the opposite party— a common phenomenon in Ohio.[1]

An enormous change in the relationship between the governor and the legislature came in 1903 when the voters approved a constitutional amendment giving the governor the veto power. Shortly before the election, the *Columbus Dispatch* reported that there was "a very general sentiment in favor of the amendment." Opponents later claimed that there had been no popular demand for the veto and that it had been "gotten through by designing politicians." The amendment did in fact benefit from the short-lived Longworth Law of 1902, by which the General Assembly meant to prevent proposed amendments from failing simply because so many voters ignored amendments when they cast their ballots. The Longworth Law authorized political parties to take an official position on a proposed amendment and to indicate that position on the ticket in such a way that anyone who voted a straight ticket automatically voted on the amendment in accordance with the party's position. The Republican and Prohibition parties officially endorsed the veto amendment. A badly divided Democratic state convention rejected it, but leading Democrats came out in support. The amendment passed by more than 120,000 votes.[2]

The new constitutional provision required at least a two-thirds majority of each house to override a veto—and no fewer than the number of votes the bill had received on its original passage—and it allowed the governor to veto individual sections of bills or appropriations of money. It gave the governor tremendous power over legislation. One newspaper exclaimed that the clause setting the number of favorable votes needed to override a veto gave the governor "almost a death grip on the General Assembly." The lawmakers soon had misgivings. In 1906, the General Assembly almost unanimously voted to put a modified veto on the ballot, one that required a straight two-thirds vote of each house for an override and eliminated the governor's authority to veto parts of bills other than appropriations. Before the next general election, which would not be until 1908 because the legislature was moving its regular sessions to odd-numbered years, the General Assembly repealed the Longworth Law. Reverting to their old habit, the voters approved the amendment by a resounding margin, but too few of them voted on the issue to adopt it.[3]

The veto occasioned some discussion at the 1912 constitutional convention, but the delegates displayed little inclination to revoke it. They did, however, agree to lower the majority necessary to override from two-thirds of each house to three-fifths, to abolish the requirement that a bill receive the same number of votes on repassage as on its original passage, and to remove the governor's ability to veto sections of bills other than appropriation line items. The voters ratified the amendment.[4]

Ohioans adopted the veto during the rise of Progressivism, and some Progressives favored a strong executive as a counterbalance to powerful corporations and unrepresentative legislatures. Nevertheless, the veto was not necessarily a Progressive reform. Cleveland mayor and Democratic gubernatorial candidate Tom Johnson and his city solicitor Newton D. Baker, who were then emerging as leading Ohio Progressives, favored the veto; but so did big business. The veto checked the lawmaking power of the people's elected representatives and could easily be abused. On the other hand, because the legislators being checked were often venal or incompetent, the veto could be a safeguard of the people's rights and pocketbooks. Either way, no one denied the veto's importance. Myron T. Herrick, the first governor to have the veto power, alienated key interest groups by both threatening to veto legislation and actually doing it. He lost his bid for reelection. In 1911, when the governor could still reject parts of bills, Governor Judson Harmon vetoed numerous sections of law that the General Assembly had passed in the end-of-session whirl. Of one he noted acerbically, "If whoever framed the bill really meant this, he does not belong in Ohio. If he did not, our language becomes a dangerous weapon in his hands." In the 1920s, Democratic governor Victor "Veto Vic" Donahey rejected well over one hundred acts and appropriations, though he failed to derail the Republican agenda because the Republicans had veto-proof majorities in both houses of the General Assembly and repassed their chief measures. In 1925, the General Assembly overrode thirty-four of Donahey's forty-six vetoes.[5]

Veto Vic was not the last governor to make liberal use of the veto. Not surprisingly, the veto came into play most frequently when one party held the governor's office and the other controlled both houses of the legislature. During the session of 1931–32, for example, Democratic governor Myers Y. Cooper vetoed 30 of the 192 bills passed by the Republican General Assembly. Lacking a veto-proof majority, the Republicans failed to override a single veto. In 1975–76, Republican governor James A. Rhodes vetoed 23 of 474 acts, not an inordinate percentage (4.8 percent), but 22 more than his Democratic predecessor had vetoed during the previous session when each party controlled one chamber.

The pattern did not always hold. During the five sessions from 1941 through 1950, when Republicans dominated the General Assembly, Republican governors John Bricker and Thomas Herbert and Democratic governor Frank Lausche displayed a remarkable consistency, vetoing 2 or 3 percent of the acts each session. During the first three sessions of the 1950s, however, Lausche sent back 6.5 percent of the acts passed by the Republican legislature. After a brief Republican interlude, when the Republican governor vetoed just 1 percent of the Republican

Myron T. Herrick. *Reproduced by permission of the Ohio Historical Society*

Victor "Veto Vic" Donahey being sworn in as governor, 1923. *Reproduced by
permission of the Ohio Historical Society*

legislature's acts, the Democrats regained the governor's office and Governor Michael DiSalle returned to the consistency of the 1940s. He vetoed 5.6 percent of the bills passed by the Democratic legislature of 1959–60 and 5.8 percent of the bills passed by the Republican legislature of 1961–62.

Rhodes's use of the veto clearly demonstrates its partisan value. During the 1960s, he rarely rejected acts of the Republican General Assembly. Of the more than 1,000 bills passed by the legislature from 1967 through 1970, Rhodes vetoed just 2. As noted above, when Rhodes faced a Democratic legislature in 1975–76, he vetoed 23 of 474 acts. In one long-playing drama, he thwarted Democratic efforts to enact legislation granting collective bargaining rights to public employees for years.[6]

The Rise of the Administrative State

The veto was only one of the tools that enhanced the governor's clout in the twentieth century. By 1900, the governor was becoming the head of a powerful administrative state. After the adoption of the 1851 constitution, the state's chief role in economic affairs became regulatory rather than promotional. Because the legislature lacked the ability to closely regulate a complex economy, it created administrative bodies to do the job. Railroads prompted the first serious attempts to control business through bureaucratic means. In 1857, Governor Salmon P. Chase recommended the creation of a railroad commission with "general supervision over the construction and operation" of railroads. In 1867, the legislature created the office of state commissioner of railroads and telegraphs with power to investigate safety conditions on the railroads, gather information and report on railroad operations, set speed limits or prevent trains from running altogether if conditions were unsafe, and prosecute violations of law. Over time, the commissioner gained additional powers, including the authority to investigate citizens' complaints and to regulate crossing gates and other safety devices.[7]

Other administrative agencies and officers followed: the inspector of mines, the superintendent of insurance, the inspector of workshops and factories, and so on. The General Assembly also resumed regulation of the practice of medicine and established boards to determine the fitness of candidates for dentistry, pharmacy, and other professions. While health and safety predominated as subjects of administration, the state also intruded into more purely business affairs through railroad rate regulation and the Board of Arbitration (established to help resolve industrial strikes and lockouts). The appropriations acts of the late nineteenth century reflect the growth of the bureaucracy. In 1898, appropriations for the commissioner of railroads and telegraphs included salaries for the commissioner himself, three clerks, an inspector, and a statistician. For the inspector of workshops and factories, they included salaries for thirteen district and bakeshop inspectors and a high explosives inspector and additional money to hire clerks. A student of administration in Ohio complained in 1903 that the legislature chronically underfunded the state's administrative agencies and gave them inadequate authority. Nevertheless, the creation of state regulatory authorities represented a dramatic shift: from local to state control, from regulation by common law to regulation by statute, and from legislative to administrative responsibility.[8]

In 1904, Professor Samuel P. Orth called for greater "centralization of administration" in Ohio. Orth noted that recent years had witnessed significantly increased state control over elections and corporations and broader authority given to the state treasurer, secretary of state, attorney general, and auditor; however, he thought that Ohio's "progress toward efficient administrative authority" was far too slow for a large commercial state. The General Assembly was too reticent to hand over power to administrative bodies. Instead, it established numerous boards and commissions with inadequate powers and funding. The legislature's more recent creations, such as the State Board of Health, were better, but Orth saw the rise of public sentiment in favor of increased administrative centralization as the prerequisite for an impartial and efficient administration of a great state.[9]

Orth and his fellow Progressives got their wish. In 1906, the General Assembly abolished the first statewide regulatory office it had ever created, that of commissioner of railroads and telegraphs, and replaced it with a three-member railway commission. The old commissioner had very little power. His chief function was to gather information and report to the governor and legislature. The new commission, which had authority over express and freight car companies as well as railroads, could hear complaints and issue orders concerning rates and service and could establish rates on its own initiative. In 1911, after a two-year fight in which public utility companies lobbied furiously against the legislation and several lawmakers from both parties went to prison for soliciting bribes, the General Assembly launched the Public Service Commission, soon renamed the Public Utilities Commission of Ohio. The commission had regulatory authority, which in some instances it shared with municipalities, over telephone, electric, and gas companies, railroads, commodity pipelines, and waterworks. Its powers extended to accounting, securities, mergers, rates, discrimination, property valuation, and other matters. In the 1920s, motor bus companies and trucking fell under the commission's jurisdiction.[10]

Centralization meant not only the consolidation of existing state functions in a given area, such as utility regulation, in a single agency, but also the augmentation of state powers in that field. Consider, for example, developments in public education. A student of education legislation wrote in 1930:

> In spite of the glaringly evident decentralized state of the Ohio schools for the larger part of the period [1851–1925], the unmistakable tendency of the period was toward a more centralized administrative and uniform school system. This tendency was translated into fact with the general reorganization of the school system in 1913–1914. At that time a unified, closely coördinated county system of schools was created. The office of State Superintendent of Public Instruction was made a vital factor in the state educational scheme. With a staff of supervisor inspectors clothed with authority through his office, education in Ohio took on the appearance of a state system of education. It was quite thoroughly coördinated from the top down.[11]

By centralizing authority in administrative agencies, the General Assembly significantly enhanced the power of the executive branch of government. Before 1921, there existed numerous boards, commissions, and officers, from the state geologist and Meteorological Bureau to the Board of State Charities and the Department of Health, most of them appointed by the governor. In 1921, a joint legislative committee found such a welter of administrative offices that the governor could not possibly "exercise supervision and control over this large number of independent and unrelated departments. . . . If the governor is to be made responsible for the administration of state affairs the organization of the state should be simplified and the number of boards and commissions reduced." The General Assembly responded with an administrative code that reorganized the execu-tive agencies and gave the governor broad authority to approve changes within departments.[12]

The creation of a state budget system in 1913 further enlarged the power of the governor. The haphazard methods of public accounting that had prevailed in simpler times no longer sufficed in the age of administrative government, and the part-time citizen legislature lacked the time and expertise to handle the job.

The Second Century

Legislative finance committees had inadequate information and typically gave the most money to those state agencies that had the "best talkers." Appropriation bills, said one knowledgeable critic, "were absolutely beyond the comprehension of any person who tried to digest or analyze the financial acts of any session." Under the new budget law, each state agency had to submit an itemized statement of its monetary needs for the next fiscal biennium, and the governor had to prepare a biennial budget for presentation to the legislature. The law empowered the governor to appoint a state budget commissioner to examine all administrative agencies for ways to improve efficiency and cut waste. In 1914, the General Assembly adopted an alphanumeric code to identify budget items. A professional budget, prepared by a central office in the executive department, was a powerful tool that could, "in effect, create a coherent and self-conscious executive branch where before there had been only individual bureaus and departments." With the executive budget and a staff of budget experts, the governor acquired a control over the state's financial information that the General Assembly could not hope to crack, at least not until it developed independent sources of information and analysis later in the century.[13]

Republicans denounced the 1913 budget law for enhancing the "dangerous and autocratic power" of the governor, but they never tried to repeal it. In fact, a heavily Republican General Assembly passed a comprehensive administrative reorganization act in 1921 that strengthened the governor's hand even more. Together the budget law and the reorganization act created a strong, unitary executive branch and the "most powerful governor Ohio has had since the time of Territorial Governor St. Clair."[14]

As the executive branch grew, it assumed more and more lawmaking power. For example, the State Board of Health, created in 1886, had been chiefly an information-gathering body that reported annually to the governor, while local boards of health had made and enforced "sanitary rules and regulations." The Public Health Council of the Ohio Department of Health, which replaced the board in 1917, had the power to adopt a statewide sanitary code. Agencies having such rule-making power in essence shared legislative authority with the General Assembly. In theory, only the General Assembly could pass laws; it could not constitutionally "delegate" its lawmaking authority to an independent or executive agency. The legislature could, however, confer "an authority or discretion as to [a law's] execution, to be exercised under and in pursuance of the law." In 1922, a unanimous supreme court relied on this theoretical distinction to uphold the statute creating the Department of Health and giving the Public Health Council the authority to adopt a sanitary code. In practice, the distinction between making and executing the law was often so blurry as to be fictional.[15]

By 1930, the state had a significant number of regulatory state agencies and offices with rule-making authority. The Industrial Commission of Ohio had wide-ranging powers to make health and safety rules for many branches of industry, to investigate violations, and to conduct hearings. The Division of Securities administered the Ohio Securities Law. The State Board of Optometry made rules governing the practice of optometry. The Department of Public Welfare regulated state mental hospitals, reformatories, and other state institutions. The State Board of Agriculture established standards for food and feed stuffs and regulated other matters relating to agriculture. During the Great Depression, the number of administrative agencies "multiplied by leaps and bounds," so that, by 1937, at least twenty-eight had rule-making power.[16]

The growing muscle of the bureaucracy raised fears in some quarters that it threatened democratic government. Concerned about the arbitrary power of agencies to issue orders or to grant or withhold licenses, with no uniformity of procedure and sometimes with no recourse to the courts for aggrieved parties, Governor John Bricker complained that "[a]dministrative agencies have brought the tendency to substitute government of men for government of laws." In 1943, the General Assembly addressed these concerns by adopting an administrative procedure act that required license-issuing agencies to publish their rules and to provide hearings for licensees. The act also guaranteed an opportunity for judicial review of licensing decisions. The legislature soon expanded the act to cover most agencies that had authority to promulgate rules or make adjudications.[17]

Restoring the Balance

The steady growth of the executive branch gave it an ever-increasing advantage over the legislature in the contest to determine state policy. But the General Assembly did not lack resources of its own. As will be described in chapter 18, the General Assembly created a number of agencies between 1910 and 1950 to provide itself with research and bill-drafting services. The lawmakers raised executive hackles in 1953 by consolidating the functions of several of these agencies in the new Legislative Service Commission (LSC). The governor, who had representation in most of the LSC's predecessor agencies and dominated the Ohio Program Commission, had no say in the LSC's operations. Governor Frank Lausche saw the new agency as a potential rival in the development and execution of public policy; only the General Assembly's agreement to maintain the Legislative Reference Bureau as a separate entity saved the LSC from a veto. Even when he retired a few years later, Lausche described the LSC as a "mongrel satellite government" used by the legislature to thwart the governor, and he urged that it be abolished. Instead, the General Assembly, as it evolved into a full-time, professional legislature, added to its institutional capital. In the 1950s, the LSC began hiring fiscal analysts to perform research and analysis of bills and agency budget requests. In 1963, the General Assembly created the position of legislative auditor to supply the lawmakers with information on state finances on a regular basis, and, in 1973, it established the Legislative Budget Office with liaisons to the majority and minority caucuses in each house.[18]

All these fiscal resources further reduced the General Assembly's reliance on the executive branch, but not enough to suit some members. In 1970, Republican House Speaker Charles Kurfess argued the need for independent legislative staffs, adequate office space and equipment for legislators and employees, "respectable" salaries, and involvement of the rank and file in policy making. He called for improvement of the General Assembly's stature in the eyes of the public through the formation of citizens' committees to recommend reforms, the restructuring of legislative procedures, and the adoption of ethical standards. Kurfess believed that these measures would strengthen the legislature's hand in dealing with the executive. Democrat Vernal G. Riffe Jr., who began his long tenure as House Speaker in 1975, recalled years later, "What I saw back in the '60s was that the executive branch of government had more say than the legislative branch, and that's wrong. I made up my mind I was going to regain some of the power and authority that we lost." He did that in part by increasing the size of the House staff from 276 in 1975 to 379 in 1994 and by increasing the House operating budget in those years from $3.35 million to $17.45 million.[19]

In 1977, the General Assembly created the Joint Committee on Agency Rule Review (JCARR), a permanent committee of House and Senate members with the power to review and overturn rules made by administrative agencies in the executive branch. One commentator characterized the bill as a "classic power play" on the part of a Democratic legislature against a Republican governor, but there was more to the story than partisan politics. JCARR was the legislature's response to Ohio Supreme Court decisions that restricted judicial review of administrative rulemaking. The General Assembly first tried to establish JCARR in 1975 in an attempt to place some check on agencies' rule-making power. The bill passed both houses with broad bipartisan support. Governor Rhodes vetoed it, declaring first and foremost that he could not abide "the obliteration of the historical distinction between administrative functions of executive departments, agencies and commissions and the legislative functions of the legislature." The House promptly repassed the bill over the veto; in the Senate, more than a year later, the minority Republicans, who had split almost evenly on the original vote, rallied behind the governor to prevent an override. In 1977, the General Assembly again enacted a JCARR bill. This time Rhodes let it become law without his signature.[20]

Rhodes's confrontation with the legislature over JCARR was just part of a highly partisan "two-year war" he fought against the Democratic legislature in the 1970s. More often than not, however, relations between the General Assembly and the governor depended less on the political coloration of the two branches than on the personality of their leaders. Moderate Democratic governor Frank Lausche usually worked smoothly with the Republicans who controlled the General Assembly during four of Lausche's five terms in the 1940s and 1950s. In the early 1990s, Republican Governor George Voinovich tussled with both Democratic House Speaker Vern Riffe and Republican Senate president Stanley Aronoff; Riffe and Aronoff got along better with each other than either did with the governor.[21]

The bitterest confrontation between a governor and a legislative body occurred during the Great Depression when Democratic governor Martin Davey, who also fought the Roosevelt administration over control of relief in Ohio, squared off against an overwhelmingly Democratic Ohio Senate over allegations of corruption in state agencies. The battle began with the development of an antitax group in the Senate that came to be called "hatchet men" because they wanted to cut Davey's budget. The protax faction won the fight for majority floor leader and chairmanship of the Finance Committee, but their adversaries, with a small group of Republican allies, impeded the governor's program and secured the appointment of a special committee to investigate rumors that the Davey administration was awarding state contracts to political friends and otherwise misusing state funds and employees for political purposes.[22]

Davey refused to cooperate with the Senate investigation. He called for a joint meeting of the legislature so that he could deliver a "bombshell" message,

Martin L. Davey. *Courtesy of the* Columbus Citizen-Journal *Collection, Scripps-Howard Newspapers/Grandview Heights Public Library/Photohio.org*

to be broadcast by more than a dozen radio stations. The Senate ignored his request, but most senators joined the throng in the House gallery on January 3, 1938, to hear the attack. Davey did not disappoint. He lambasted the Senate committee for subjecting him to abuse "too raw" to endure in silence. "Anyone would be supremely stupid," he declared, "who could think this hatchet investigation would be fair and honest." He accused several senators by name of being puppets of Republican businessmen and Democratic bosses, having "loose public morals," and other offenses. The Senate fought back. The investigating committee found the Department of Liquor Control "so shot through with forgery, corruption, graft, false reports, faked statistics, pretended 'buys' and maladministration, as to be hopeless of cure"; the Highway Department to present "the sad spectacle of almost gleeful waste of taxpayers' money"; and the Purchasing Department to be operating "plainly in defiance of the law." The committee laid the blame for it all at the feet of Governor Davey. "[I]f political achievement and political ambitions become the guiding light of a chief executive," it intoned, "then, unfortunately, too many employees walk in that path, with the result that real public service lags and withers and wanes."[23]

Davey struck again in another speech to the House, likening the Senate investigation to a "Russian inquisition," a "sinful game," and a "hypocritical and malicious persecution." He promised "a fight to the finish." He lost. After a bitter primary campaign in which he could not shake the stigma of corruption, Davey became the first Ohio governor to be denied renomination by his party.[24]

The Legislature versus the Courts

The relationship between the legislative and judicial branches also had its up and downs in the twentieth century, but no single outstanding event comparable to the adoption of the executive veto altered that relationship. Since the 1830s, the courts had enjoyed a rarely questioned "judicial veto" in the form of judicial review. The Ohio Supreme Court wielded this weapon in stunning fashion in 1902 when it condemned the General Assembly's municipal classification scheme, forcing a special session of the legislature and hastening the reform of municipal government. Progressive urban reformers welcomed the decision, but they could not have been happy with the judiciary's recent history of striking down labor and tax legislation. In 1887, the General Assembly required that certain miners and industrial workers be paid every two weeks. In 1889 and 1890, the lawmakers strengthened the statute. On each occasion, the law passed overwhelmingly, the last time by a combined House and Senate vote of 97 to 2. The Ohio Supreme Court declared the laws unconstitutional. In 1890, the General Assembly, by a combined vote of 116 to 1, passed a law regulating the hours of railway workers; an appellate court struck it down. Between 1894 and 1902, Ohio courts invalidated other acts, most of which had passed by wide margins, regulating hours or wages, protecting the right of workers to join unions, authorizing mechanics' liens, authorizing a joint public-private venture to create a city water supply system, and imposing an inheritance tax.[25]

The constitutional convention of 1912 adopted at least eight amendments for the specific purpose of undoing judicial decisions that had struck down or cast doubt upon legislation. These amendments provided for mechanics' and materialmen's liens, graduated estate and income taxes, the Torrens system of recording deeds, the regulation of hours and wages of workers, a compulsory workers' compensation system, investigative powers for committees in each legislative chamber, and the regulation of billboards. The voters approved seven of these amendments and barely defeated the eighth (billboard regulation).[26]

Some convention delegates sought more general restrictions on the judiciary's power to interfere with legislation. One delegate introduced a proposal instructing judges to liberally construe statutes in derogation of the common law, which would have reversed traditional practice. Another moved to forbid courts from exercising any power not expressly conferred by law; his aim, he said, was "to stop the judges from making any more law." One member of the convention urged instead that judicial review be abolished entirely. A proposal that gained a more respectful hearing would have required a unanimous decision of the supreme court to hold a statute unconstitutional unless a court of appeals had already declared the statute invalid. The convention finally adopted and the voters ratified an amendment requiring the concurrence of all but one of the supreme court justices to declare unconstitutional any statute that had been upheld by a court of appeals.[27]

The restriction on the supreme court's power to overturn legislation allowed a statute to be upheld in one appellate district and struck down in another, a situation that in 1928 the chief justice denounced as "deplorable." Nevertheless, the provision remained in the constitution for another forty years. In 1967, the General Assembly had under consideration the Modern Courts Amendment, the product of several years' work on judicial reform by the bar, judges, and legislators. The amendment included restoration of the supreme court's authority to resolve all constitutional questions by a simple majority. Once a controversial provision for the appointment rather than election of judges was dropped, the amendment passed the General Assembly with little opposition and received the voters' endorsement the next year.[28]

The supreme court promptly took advantage of its new power and, with two justices dissenting, struck down a criminal procedure statute that the court of appeals had upheld. Another, more controversial example of the court's greater authority came in 1997 when just four members of the court declared the state's school funding formula unconstitutional after a divided court of appeals had sustained it. That decision, which would not have been possible under the old rule, led to a bitter six-year dispute between the majority and dissenting justices and between the supreme court and the General Assembly.[29]

The Modern Courts Amendment also strengthened the supreme court vis-à-vis the General Assembly by giving the justices the power to make rules of procedure for the courts and control over admission to the bar and the practice of law. The General Assembly had always governed these areas to some extent by statute, and, although it had often deferred to the supreme court by granting the court authority to regulate judicial procedure and the legal profession, it had never surrendered its own theoretical right to control courts and lawyers by legislation. By the twentieth century, though, Ohio courts were claiming an inherent power to adopt procedural rules and to govern the legal profession. The Modern Courts Amendment resolved the conflict in the judiciary's favor. It placed the authority to adopt rules of procedure in the supreme court, subject only to the General Assembly's right to disapprove a proposed rule within a few months after the court files it with the House and Senate clerks. Once a rule or amendment takes effect, it overrides any conflicting statutes. The supreme court's rights to regulate admission to the bar and to discipline attorneys are not subject to even that much legislative oversight.[30]

The concept of judicial review is so firmly entrenched in legal and political thought that neither the impeachment of judges nor the limitation of their jurisdiction has been seriously proposed since the 1912 constitutional convention, even under the greatest provocation. Between 1997 and 2003, a bitterly divided Ohio Supreme Court struck down far-reaching tort reform and school funding legislation, the majority of the court accusing the General Assembly of "boldly seiz[ing] the power of constitutional adjudication" and "threaten[ing] the judiciary as an independent branch of government." The dissenters charged the court majority with "usurp[ing] the legislative function," "cloak[ing] judicial legislation in the guise of constitutional scholarship," and "claim[ing] veto power over policy determinations made by the General Assembly." One constitutional scholar urged the General Assembly to oust offending supreme court justices under a constitutional provision that allows the removal of judges upon a two-thirds vote of each house. The purpose of the provision, adopted at the 1850–51 constitutional convention, seems to have been to provide a means of removing judges who had become grossly immoral or incompetent after taking office but who had not committed impeachable offenses. No one adopted the scholar's suggestion or pursued impeachment. Opponents of the supreme court majority sought instead to defeat the offending justices in elections, not to alter the institutional relationship that had developed between the legislative and judicial branches of government.[31]

The supreme court's activism has not always placed it at odds with the legislature. The court has often repeated the maxim that statutes are entitled to a presumption of validity, and at times it has enhanced legislative power by practically draining constitutional limitations on that power of all meaning. A classic example is the court's virtual abolition of the constitutional requirement that all real property be taxed by a uniform rule. The uniform-rule provision, adopted as part of the new constitution in 1851, originally applied to all types of property, although by 1973 constitutional amendments had carved out exceptions for personal property and agricultural land. The uniform rule required that all property within a taxing district be assessed in the same manner and at the same rate. The supreme court punched a big hole in the rule in 1965 by holding that the General Assembly could grant tax exemptions for all kinds of real property, not just property used for cemeteries, schoolhouses, and other public purposes listed in the constitution. After a long, noisy fight involving commercial developers, county auditors, farmers, and homeowners and featuring a "tax revolt" and a constitutional revolution, the supreme court effectively abolished the uniform rule in 1980 by characterizing a legislative "rollback" of taxes on homesteads (that is, a reduced tax rate) as a tax exemption.[32]

In 2001, former Senate president Richard Finan complained that the "three-legged stool" of Ohio government had become unbalanced. He blamed legislative term limits for shifting power to the governor by causing a loss of experience and institutional memory in the General Assembly, and he blamed an arrogant supreme court majority for disregarding the leeway usually given to legislative judgment and for using inflammatory rhetoric to disparage the General Assembly. It was probably too soon to know whether term limits had shifted power to the governor. During the gubernatorial tenure of Bob Taft, who was in office when Finan penned his complaint, the legislature proved to be notably independent of the executive, while the supreme court, thanks to a change in personnel, became distinctly more cordial toward the lawmakers. But Finan's instincts were right. Great institutional changes had occurred in the preceding hundred years. The executive and judicial branches had assumed expanded roles in the formulation and execution of policy and had acquired powers that, in the hands of strong-willed users, could thwart the legislative will.[33]

14

MIGHTY TRUTH AND
THE PURITY OF ELECTIONS

"WOMAN SUFFRAGE BILL a law; truth is mighty yet." So telegraphed Ohio state senator William T. Clark to a woman suffrage association in 1894. The great testament to truth was a law allowing women to vote in school board elections. In retrospect, the accolade seems a bit overblown. Ohio women would wait another quarter century for full suffrage. When they finally got it, though, they got something else too: eligibility to sit in the General Assembly. The composition of the legislature changed in various ways during Ohio's second century—by race, occupation, age, and experience—but in no manner more sudden or more obvious than by the addition of women.[1]

The New Face of the Legislature

The voters elected six female lawmakers, two senators and four representatives, in 1922, eight in 1924. Altogether, seventeen different women served in the General Assembly in the 1920s, but only thirteen women won election during the 1930s, none of them to the Senate. In the 1935–36 session, just three women sat in the House. By virtue of their small numbers, if nothing else, women remained a breed of lawmaker apart, not just in Ohio but nationwide. In 1938, they formed their own organization, the National Order of Women Legislators, and the Ohio House voted to send its female members to the order's first national conference in Washington.[2]

Republicans had always been more favorably inclined than Democrats toward woman suffrage. That, combined with the party's domination of the legislature in the 1920s, ensured that almost all the women legislators of the 1920s would be Republicans. Most of them represented counties with big cities. When Democratic fortunes revived in the 1930s and the party began drawing more and more urban votes, the group political profile of the female legislators changed. Among women legislators in the 1940s, big-county Democrats outnumbered rural Democrats, rural Republicans, and urban Republicans combined. One small-county female won the popular vote for representative in 1940 but never got to serve. A committee of the Republican-controlled House confirmed that Democrat Gladys E. Davis had beaten Republican Orin L. Graves in Scioto County, but it refused to unseat Graves because, it said, Davis had not followed proper procedures in contesting the election.[3]

Like most of their male colleagues, the women elected to the General Assembly in the first half of the twentieth century typically served for just a few years. Two, though, had remarkable careers. Anna F. O'Neil represented Summit County in the House in 1933–34, lost her bid for reelection in 1935, and won again in 1937. This time she stayed through 1954. O'Neil, a founder and president of the National Order of Women Legislators, in 1949 became the first woman to chair the House Finance Committee. Margaret A. Mahoney of Cleveland sat in the House from 1939 through 1942 and in the Senate from 1943 through 1950. Despite the law degree she had earned in 1929, Mahoney was working as a secretary and serving on the legislative committees of women's organizations when she decided to quit her job and run for the House in 1936. She just missed election to the eighteen-member Cuyahoga County delegation that year, but in 1938 she led the ticket. After two terms, Mahoney moved to the Senate, where in 1949 her colleagues elected her president pro tempore. She retired from the General Assembly at the end of the term because of the low salary and spent the rest of her working life practicing law and holding cabinet posts in the administrations of Governors Lausche and DiSalle.[4]

The first class of women legislators in Ohio, 1923: (1) Senator Maude C. Waitt;
(2) Senator Nettie P. Loughead; (3) Representative Nettie M. Clapp; (4) Representative
May Van Wye; (5) Representative Adelaide S. Ott; (6) Representative Lulu T. Gleason.
Reproduced from James K. Mercer, Ohio Legislative History (Columbus: F. J. Heer [1925?]), 5:360

Margaret A. Mahoney.
Courtesy of the Columbus Citizen-Journal *Collection, Scripps-Howard Newspapers/Grandview Heights Public Library/Photohio.org*

Mahoney had a sense of humor, but she demanded respect. Criticized during one campaign for venturing outside a woman's proper place, the home, Mahoney offered to quit if someone would marry her. Apparently, she had no takers. In 1943, upset about the treatment accorded one of her bills, she staged a three-day walkout from the legislature. The committee hearing the bill issued this poetic report:

> Where, oh where, can Margaret be,
> And what makes her so blue?
> Come back, beloved senator.
> We've recommended Bill 272.[5]

Notwithstanding Mahoney's pioneering leadership role, women remained a small contingent in the General Assembly until the late twentieth century. In 1981–82, the General Assembly still had just ten female members, nine in the House and one in the Senate. From then on, the number of women in the legislature grew steadily, reaching twenty in 1991–92 and thirty-two in 1995–96, just under a quarter of the total membership. Thereafter, the figure dropped some-what but remained at least double the number of 1985. From 1969 through 1982, when there were never more than ten female legislators, women made up a higher percentage of the combined House and Senate Republican caucus than of the Democratic. From 1983 through 1996, the Democratic percentage ex-ceeded the Republican, although, at the end of that period, women were almost exactly one-quarter of each combined caucus. After that, a decline in the number of female legislators set in. Early in 2007, when the dust had settled from resigna-tions and appointments, just twenty-two women held seats in the General Assem-bly. They still made up a quarter of the Democratic members but just 8 percent of the Republicans.[6]

Blacks, like women, became more conspicuous in the General Assembly in the second half of the twentieth century. Before 1966, only twenty-eight African Americans had served in the Ohio legislature. All were men, all but one were Republicans, and all but one came from populous counties. Most had professional careers (law, medicine, or the clergy). The movement of blacks into the Demo-cratic Party and the one-man, one-vote reapportionment revolution of the 1960s brought about dramatic change. When Carl Stokes of Cleveland, the first black Democratic representative, won a seat in the House in 1962, the only other African American in the General Assembly was Republican representative David Albritton. As soon as Ohio's one-man, one-vote apportionment plan took effect, the number of black legislators jumped to eleven. Stokes and the new members, all Democrats, soon formed a black legislative caucus, originally called the Black Elected Democrats of Ohio. Since Albritton's retirement in 1972, almost every black in the General Assembly has been an urban Democrat.[7]

Black legislators usually voted as a bloc and usually in accord with the major-ity of Democratic representatives, although one student of the legislature be-lieved that the unity of the early black caucus was based more on the similarity of the districts they represented than on racial identity. Sometimes the caucus found itself at odds with the rest of the party. In one notable case, caucus mem-bers, acting as an "impenetrable block" [sic], absented themselves from the vote on the state budget, preventing its passage two days before the constitutional dead-line. Their surprise action and refusal to comment on the boycott angered the Democratic leadership, which feared that any compromise would set a trouble-some precedent. Speaker Vern Riffe announced that there was only one Demo-cratic caucus. Riffe met privately with the black members, lambasted their ingratitude for his role in making Martin Luther King Day a state holiday, and

Carl B. Stokes. *Courtesy of the* Columbus Citizen-Journal *Collection, Scripps-Howard Newspapers/Grandview Heights Public Library/Photohio.org*

threatened to throw them out of the party caucus. The renegades recanted, and the budget passed on time.[8]

With their increased presence in the General Assembly, African Americans advanced to leadership positions. Albritton became the first black to chair a House committee, in 1969. In 1975, House Democrats chose William Mallory to be majority leader, the third-ranking position in the House and one he held for nineteen years. Before Mallory retired, another black man, Ben Espy, rose to minority leader in the Senate. African American women first got their seats in the House and Senate as appointed replacements, Helen Rankin in 1978 for her deceased husband and Rhine McLin in 1994 for a senator who had resigned. But McLin, the daughter of longtime representative C. J. McLin Jr., had already won election for the ensuing General Assembly at the time of her appointment, and Rankin went on to be elected in her own right eight times. In 2006, both houses had black women as minority leaders, C. J. Prentiss in the Senate and Joyce Beatty in the House.[9]

Mighty Truth and the Purity of Elections

C. J. McLin Jr. *Courtesy of Rhine McLin*

Of all the black members, none had a more impressive legislative career in the General Assembly than the Dayton mortician C. J. McLin Jr. Others had broader reputations—Carl Stokes, for example, gained national fame or notoriety, depending on one's point of view, as mayor of Cleveland, and later served as a television news anchor in New York, general counsel to the United Auto Workers in Cleveland, judge, and ambassador—but none accomplished more as a legislator than McLin. With his low-key personality, strong work ethic, and belief in politics as the art of the possible, McLin made many friends and few enemies in his two decades in the House. It didn't hurt that his friends included Speaker Riffe, the most powerful politician in the state. Elected with the reapportionment class of 1966, McLin's lasting accomplishments included the organization of the black caucus.[10]

The Changing Profile of the Membership

Sex and race aside, what kind of individuals did the voters choose to represent them in Columbus? In the early twentieth century, Senator Frederic C. Howe described his fellow legislators as mostly older men—"insurance agents, real-estate

The Second Century

men, farmers"—who were not unintelligent but who also were not very thought-ful or independent. According to Howe, "They would get their orders from the county committee, the court-house crowd, whom they did not wish to offend." Over the course of the century, the profile of the typical legislator slowly changed. Describing state lawmakers across the country, in Ohio no less than elsewhere, Alan Rosenthal wrote in 1981, "There is a new breed, unlike the old timers—the court house politicians, the representatives of malapportionment, the old county board members, the slow-witted and cigar-smoking politicians. The new breed is young, well-educated, bright, hard-working, aggressive, and sometimes zealous."[11]

Youth, of course, is relative. For a while, the General Assembly continued to get grayer. In 1911, the average age of both senators and representatives was a bit over forty-five. Twenty and forty years later, representatives averaged over forty-eight years of age, senators almost fifty-two. At the same time, though, life expectancy for white males, who made up the great majority of legislators, jumped sharply. Those who survived to age twenty could expect to live to be sixty-three in 1911 and seventy in 1951. The number of legislators who were under thirty, always higher in the House than in the Senate, rarely if ever exceeded 10 percent of the total, but the proportion of members sixty and older rose steadily from less than one-tenth to just under one-quarter. By the middle of the century, the number of members in their seventies surpassed the number in their twenties. Later on, members started getting shy about reporting their ages, but it appears that the size of the midrange cohort, those between thirty and fifty-five years old, grew at the expense of the extremes. The average age dropped a bit, fluctu-ating between 43.5 and 49.5 from 1969 through 1996. Interestingly, it was about three years lower in the first half of that period than in the second. Perhaps the reapportionment revolution of 1966 caused the loss of older members who had long held secure seats, bringing down the average age until the new crop of leg-islators settled in. Senators were usually older than representatives, in one session by five years, but not always.[12]

The election of many inexperienced lawmakers in the era of term limits helped create the impression that the General Assembly was getting younger. In the first session after term limits took effect, the average age of both senators and represen-tatives actually did decline, but the aura of youthfulness might have lasted longer than the reality of it. In 2006, Representative Lou Blessing, who had been in one house or the other for over twenty years, remarked, "Everybody's younger, that's for sure. . . . When I first went to the House there were people that had been there 30–40 years. People now don't have the experience." Term-limited legislatures really are younger than legislatures without term limits, the Ohio General Assembly more so than most; however, the average age of those members of the 2005–6 General Assembly who reported their ages was 47.8, right about where it had been for a hundred years. The very presence of Derrick Seaver, beginning his third House term at the ripe old age of twenty-two, no doubt enhanced the feeling of general youth, but Seaver was the only member in his twenties. The next youngest was thirty-three.[13]

The occupational profile of the General Assembly changed far more than the average age of members during Ohio's second century. The percentage of lawyers and individuals involved in the business world remained stable or grew, while the number of farmers declined. Ohio's economy had become highly industrialized by 1900. Agriculture remained important, but the number of people engaged in agricultural pursuits continued to fall, while the number working in commerce and industry swelled. Farmers enjoyed a short-lived upsurge in seat-holding during the 1920s. An analysis of the 1929 General Assembly revealed that 18 percent of the members were farmers, while 8.2 percent listed themselves as farmer-teachers or other hyphenated agriculturalists. The lawmakers, it seemed, liked to emphasize any connections they had with farming. The temporary increase in the number of farmers may have been due to the delayed effect of the constitutional amendment of 1903 that gave rural areas representation far above their share of the population. The rise in farmer representation may also have stemmed from the improved political organization, at least among better-off farmers, that accompanied the decline in the agricultural population in the early twentieth century. The official history of the Ohio Farm Bureau Federation, which was formed in 1919, boasts of the organization's influence on politics and legislation. But Ohio's changing demographics made the near disappearance of the farmer from the General Assembly inevitable. By the middle of the twentieth century, farmers constituted less than 10 percent of the membership; in 1971 they were 3 percent.[14]

Attorneys had their ups and downs, too. In 1900, they made up 48 percent of the Senate. That was an unusually high percentage, but, for most of the twentieth century, roughly a third of the General Assembly consisted of lawyers. With the rise of the law school and the growing stringency of requirements for admission to the bar, the large number of attorneys meant an increasingly educated General Assembly. Many of the Senate lawyers of 1900 may have received their legal preparation in whole or in part as apprentices in law offices. Those who did attend law schools did not necessarily have college degrees. As the century wore on, university law schools more and more came to dominate training for the bar, and the curriculum grew more rigorous. The large number of lawyers in the General Assembly therefore guaranteed a substantially educated legislature. But nonlawyers also brought increasingly impressive academic credentials to the General Assembly. In the first decade of the twentieth century, just over two-thirds of the members claimed some college education. In 1957, almost all the members had been to college, compared to less than 15 percent of the general population.[15]

A steep decline in the number of lawyer-legislators began in 1983, when attorneys constituted about 22 percent of the General Assembly's membership. At times since then, the figure has been even lower. The Ohio State Bar Association, calling the lawyer-legislator a "vanishing breed," attributed the drop to several factors. Attorneys found it hard to make time for both lawmaking and legal practice. Conflict-of-interest laws jeopardized relationships between lawyer-legislators and their clients, and financial disclosure laws caused wariness. Participation in the legislative arena increased exposure to the ever-popular sport of lawyer bashing. Term limits, adopted in 1992, also discouraged lawyers from running for office; the prospect of a short legislative career made the cost of disrupting a law practice too high. Why the sharp decline in Ohio should have begun in 1983 and not a few years sooner or later is not clear. Legislating was already pretty much a full-time job before 1983, and term limits were not yet in view. Whatever the reasons, the bar association regarded the threatened disappearance of the lawyer-legislator as a calamity because it diminished the availability of legal and analytical skills needed to deal with complex and technical issues. The organization urged more lawyers to run for legislative office, and the number of attorneys in the General Assembly did increase after 2000. The biggest jump came with the 2006 election, which produced a legislature with thirty-five attorneys, 27 percent of the total membership. Whether the rising numbers in the twenty-first century signaled the end of a long-term downward trend remained to be seen.[16]

Attorneys and agriculturalists were replaced to a large extent by professional lawmakers—that is, by people whose main job was being a full-time legislator. For official directories, the members supplied their own biographical information, including their occupations. Until the second half of the twentieth century, "legislator" was not one of them. In 1973, just thirteen members reported legislator as their livelihood; one listed legislator along with another job. Those fourteen people constituted just over 10 percent of the members. In 2005, notwithstanding the implementation of term limits, fifty-seven members (43 percent) listed legislator as their sole employment. Former House Speaker Vern Riffe declared that term limits had destroyed legislating as a career, but he was only partly right. A member could no longer count on endless reelections, but being a state legislator remained a full-time position, with a respectable salary and good health and retirement benefits. It was real job, worth keeping for as long as possible.[17]

Nothing resembling the career legislator existed in 1900. The high rate of turnover that characterized the General Assembly in the late nineteenth century continued into the twentieth, accompanied by a decrease in the amount of state legislative experience that members brought to the legislature. Sixty-five percent of the representatives and 73 percent of the senators in 1900 had never before sat in the General Assembly; over 90 percent had not had more than a single prior term. In 1915, the *Ohio State Journal* complained acerbically that "[i]n charge of the work of the 156 members are 92 Republicans, of whom all but 24 are without legislative experience and are just learning the difference between a legislative bill and a bill for goods sold." The *Journal* blamed the voters for this sad state of affairs, for they had developed the "distressing habit" of voting against incumbents and sending to Columbus new "members pledged to do their will and knowing as little how as they do themselves." There was also the "rule of rotation, contrived by the politicians for division of the honors." In most Senate districts, said the paper, "either the one or two-term rule is as inflexible, and as worthless, as an ancient pair of suspenders."[18]

The *Journal* did not offer an explanation for the falling level of experience among legislators. Perhaps the air of corruption discouraged some public-spirited men from running for the General Assembly. Certainly the late nineteenth and early twentieth centuries offered many other outlets for men's energy and talent, some of which seemed more important and vital than government: the expanding world of business corporations; the increasingly organized and prestigious professions, including law, medicine, engineering, and accounting. Even within the sphere of politics, municipal government and the executive branch of state government drew in gifted or ambitious men who might otherwise have seen service in the General Assembly as either a civic responsibility or an opportunity for personal advancement.

The early years of the twentieth century brought some notable Progressives to the General Assembly, but they didn't stay any longer than anyone else. The

Robert A. Taft. *Courtesy of the Columbus Citizen-Journal Collection, Scripps-Howard Newspapers/Grandview Heights Public Library/Photohio.org*

best-known was Frederic C. Howe, an attorney in James R. Garfield's firm and an authority on tax law. He enlisted in the ranks of reformist, good-government activists, served a term on the Cleveland city council, and ardently supported Cleveland's Progressive mayor Tom Johnson. Elected to the Ohio Senate in 1905 with high hopes for enacting Progressive reforms, he left disillusioned after one term and soon departed Ohio altogether. Howe remained active in public life and held several appointive positions, but he never again ran for elective office.[19]

For the first third of the twentieth century, few members of the General Assembly lingered long enough to have a significant impact. Robert A. Taft, a son of former president William Howard Taft who served in both houses between 1921 and 1932, may have been the most notable legislator of the period. A Cincinnati lawyer who had worked for the federal Food Administration during and after World War I, Taft was a diligent and independent-minded Republican who bucked the party on prohibition, Bible reading in the schools, and other issues yet won election as majority floor leader and Speaker of the House. He more than any other member brought about tax reforms for the benefit of Ohio's financially strapped cities. In 1938, Taft went to the U.S. Senate and soon became a regular contender for the Republican presidential nomination. He never won it, but he was influential enough to be known as "Mr. Republican."[20]

During Taft's time in the General Assembly, legislative tenures started to grow longer. Lengthening tenures brought significant changes, for they made seniority an important consideration in everything from the choice of seats in the chambers to the appointment of committee chairs to the allocation of offices (when members finally got offices). Improved salaries, benefits, and working conditions no doubt contributed to the careerism that eventually became evident, but the change began long before the improvements occurred. It may be that Progressive-era developments, such as constitutional reforms and the bribery convictions of several bad apples, made the General Assembly a more attractive place to stay. Whatever the reason, the period saw a revival of the old practice of serving many terms and the end of the informal limit on consecutive terms. Of the members of the 1911 General Assembly, only 4 percent served as many as five terms, and of those just half served all their terms consecutively. For 30 percent, the 1911 General Assembly was the only one in which they would ever participate. By contrast, 14 percent of the members of the 1931 General Assembly won election to the legislature five or more times. Several had careers of eight to twelve terms, and a few served for ten or more years in a row. Only 12 percent made the 1931 session their sole stop in the legislature. Twenty years later, the number of five-termers exceeded half the membership, and careers of ten or more terms had become common. Moreover, many members had long years of consecutive service. Ted Gray began his astonishing run of forty-three straight years in the Senate in 1951. Over 90 percent of the members that year had served before or would serve again. One, Senator Robert A. Pollock, first entered the legislature in 1900; he wouldn't depart for good until 1956.[21]

Rookies made up just over one-quarter of the senators and one-third of the representatives in 1951. These numbers were about the same in 1960, but in 1980 only 9 percent of the senators and 13 percent of the representatives had not had prior experience. The occasional change in party control and the reapportionment of 1966 produced spikes in the number of freshmen, but the long-term trend was clear until term limits intervened. A constitutional amendment adopted in 1992 limited both senators and representatives to eight years. A member could return after a four-year hiatus or could go to the other house without a break, but

Theodore W. Gray. *Courtesy of the* Columbus Citizen-Journal *Collection, Scripps-Howard News-papers/Grandview Heights Public Library/Photohio.org*

no one could hold the same seat indefinitely. The eight-year count started in 1992, so the full effects of the amendment were first felt in 2000. The proportion of newcomers rose back to one-third. "When you consider the number of term-limit freshmen, appointees who replaced resigning members, and candidates who upset incumbents," one newspaper found, "about half of the House started this year with zero or near-zero prior legislative experience." After the dust settled, the number fell again to about one-fifth in the subsequent General Assembly, still higher than before term limits. But even the novices have brought relevant experience to their legislative jobs. Over half have held elective office at the local level.[22]

Not that experience at the local level necessarily helped. An ineffective and obnoxious city councilman could become an equally unproductive, unpopular legislator. Consider Gus Kasch, one of the most colorful, cantankerous men ever to sit in the General Assembly. First elected to the Akron city council in 1919, Kasch made himself a nuisance by sponsoring four hundred resolutions in a single term. Later, as a member of the school board, he bombarded his colleagues with so many measures that they required every resolution to be seconded before it could be discussed; no one seconded Kasch's proposals. In the legislature, "Kasch built up the all-time high record for the number of bills and resolutions introduced and the all-time low record for bills passed." He offered resolutions to bar attorneys from membership in the General Assembly, to unite the United States and Canada, to establish a model cooperative colony, and to deny a seat in the House to anyone who had not abstained from alcohol for the preceding year. The House ordered at least one of his resolutions expunged from the record.[23]

A House rule of long standing, rarely invoked, allowed the members to reject a bill or resolution when it was offered for introduction. Kasch undoubtedly holds the record for rejected legislation. In 1933, the representatives served notice that if Kasch continued to take up their time with frivolous matters, they might expel him. The undaunted "perpetual rebellion expert" later made such derogatory remarks about the Speaker that the House, by a vote of 80 to 4, demanded an apology. When he refused, the House ordered the sergeant at arms to bar him from the chamber until he complied. Kasch missed the rest of the regular session, being readmitted only when the General Assembly met in special session later that year. In 1945, back in the House after a five-year absence, Kasch provoked new threats of expulsion by refusing to sit in his assigned seat. The obstreperous old buzzard finally left his fellow lawmakers in peace when he died in 1946.[24]

Making a Difference

The lengthening of legislative tenures in the middle of the century gave members time to make an impression on the politics and law of the state. Time alone is not enough, though, and an impact made may not be for the better. In ratings of legislators by *Columbus Monthly* and *Ohio Magazine*, longtime members regularly ranked among the worst. Statehouse insiders regarded one member as "unknowledgeable, uninterested, unconcerned and unfathomable" even after twelve years. In 1978, *Columbus Monthly* declared that Senator Anthony O. Calabrese, then nearing the end of nearly three decades in the General Assembly, would without doubt appear on any list of the worst state legislators. Citing his "coziness with lobbyists," his highly questionable claim for workers' compensation benefits based on a fall in the statehouse parking lot, "his malapropisms, [and] his coarse battles for leadership and recognition," the magazine called him an anachronism. Even in an affectionate column written years later on the occasion of Calabrese's passing, statehouse reporter Lee Leonard recalled Calabrese's loyalty, style, and bonhomie but acknowledged that he was "a throwback to the free and easy days when legislating was a good-old-boy network of back-scratching and palm-greasing."[25]

Calabrese at least had influence. Many long-serving lawmakers were simply "furniture." On the other hand, relative newcomers could be effective even in the days before term limits, when seniority counted. The same issue of *Columbus Monthly* that put Calabrese at the bottom of the barrel ranked first-term senator Anthony J. Celebrezze Jr., a member of one of Ohio's most prominent political families, near the top. According to the magazine, "Celebrezze entered the Senate at full gallop, paused to learn the mechanics, and has been going at top speed ever since." A few years later, *Columbus Monthly* cited Representative David Leland as one of the "rookies of the year" for his long hours, personal contact with his constituents, and success in getting bills enacted. Ironically, neither Celebrezze nor Leland ever served in the General Assembly again.[26]

Celebrezze and Leland were exceptions. Usually a member required more than one term to become an effective legislator. "Eight years may not be enough time for the methodical building of a solid reputation," observed a political reporter in 2003. Members who might have developed into first-rate legislators in an earlier era now got overlooked, especially if they belonged to the minority party. With term limits, "you've got to announce your presence with authority or you may never get noticed." In the 2003 *Columbus Monthly* survey, House Speaker Larry Householder received far and away the most votes for "most effective legislator," largely because he made his presence known with too much authority for some of his colleagues. As one survey respondent remarked, "If heavy-handed, brutal political tactics are considered 'effective,' Larry Householder takes the cake."[27]

For the way Householder ruled as Speaker, some commentators compared him to Vern Riffe, who led the House from 1975 through 1994. Riffe was unquestionably the most powerful member of the General Assembly in the second half of the twentieth century and probably in the history of the institution. Other men—rarely women—have been described as powerful, but none transformed the legislature as Riffe did. Riffe used the Speakership to fullest advantage. The Speaker had always had great formal authority, particularly in appointing committees and acting as traffic cop during sessions. But often the real power lay

Vernal G. Riffe Jr. *Courtesy of the* Columbus Citizen-Journal *Collection, Scripps-Howard Newspapers/Grandview Heights Public Library/Photohio.org*

elsewhere, with other members, businessmen, or interest groups who controlled the caucus or pulled strings behind the scenes. Men with minimal experience and little real influence might become Speaker of the House. And even when an experienced and respected lawmaker took over, he might be more interested in friendly persuasion, conciliation, and freedom of debate than in enforcing his will. Riffe had different ideas. "Riffe's rapid-fire gavel, which brooks little philosophizing or classic debating on the floor, will often hammer 10 bills to passage inside of a half hour," wrote Lee Leonard. "The bills are assembled in committee, the script is written in tight little leadership meetings, sometimes comprising only Riffe and his opposite number, House minority leader Corwin Nixon." Anyone who crossed him could expect to lose a committee chairmanship, have his or her bills ignored, or see pet appropriations cut.[28]

But Riffe was not simply a dictator. He was loyal to members who played by his rules. Of all the things that enabled the Democrats under his leadership "to deliver on practically any issue," he wrote after his retirement, "no factor was more important than loyalty. None." Back in his day, House Democrats "would fall on a sword for the caucus if necessary," even when they disagreed with the caucus position, "because they knew over time the caucus would be there for them and their constituents when they needed it." Riffe didn't mention the fear members had that they would be rendered impotent as legislators and denied campaign funds if they crossed the Speaker. Riffe blamed the weakening of loyalty on term limits and on news media that cared more about "controversy and con-flict" than news. "What you end up with," said Riffe, "are too many legislators who are too impatient to learn and compromise, and too eager to make headlines rather than do the kind of trench work that really makes a difference." Riffe viewed the decline of loyalty with regret, for it handicapped the caucus and made it tough to get things done.[29]

Riffe's critics complained about his authoritarian style. Some Republicans were particularly vexed by their own leader's acquiescence in Riffe's every demand. Corwin Nixon and Riffe, card-playing pals from southern Ohio, were both moderate, pragmatic politicians. Nixon's supporters maintained that Nixon did his work quietly behind the scenes and that his friendship with the Speaker won concessions for his caucus. Other Republicans complained that their caucus had become meaningless and unwilling to fight for anything. Nixon's agreement to clear with Riffe the names of Republicans who would speak on disputed measures and the substance of what they would say angered them. "Isn't that great?" said one member. "In the House of Representatives—the body that represents the people—that we're not going to have people allowed to talk about the issues before the House! I thought, 'Gee, what happened to freedom?'" To make matters worse, in the minds of the disgruntled, the Republicans got little in return for their subservience.[30]

But Riffe's great objective was not the implementation of a program; it was efficiency. Unlike influential lawmakers before him who were associated with particular areas of policy—Alfred Kelley with banking law, the "radical triumvirate" with antislavery, Robert Taft with taxation—Riffe is remembered mostly for his impact on the process rather than the substance of legislation. He had no use for the hours-long floor debates that some bills provoked. As Speaker, he refused to tolerate "knock-down, drag-out fights" or "arguing and finger pointing." When a controversial issue came up, he insisted that the interested parties work out a compromise so that "if one side or the other came running in afterwards

Representative William G. Batchelder protesting the "muzzling" of Republican members by Speaker Riffe in 1983. *Courtesy of the* Columbus Dispatch *Archives*

complaining about the law, I'd simply say: 'Wait a minute. You supported that. You signed off on that.'" Riffe didn't like much debate within the Democratic caucus either. Previous leaders had sometimes downplayed the caucus, especially before the apportionment revolution of 1966, when the House was larger and the majority caucus could be too big for collegiality. But Riffe had little use even for a much smaller caucus because of leaks and "grandstanding," and toward the end of his reign he rarely called his members together. While he ran the show in the House, Riffe had a profound impact on the way the legislature functioned. As long as term limits last, it is doubtful that there will be another like him.[31]

The Expanding Electorate

Riffe had a big impact on election campaigns, too, but the story of elections in Ohio's second century must begin with statutory and constitutional changes. The General Assembly has a long history of revising Ohio's election laws. Probably not a session has gone by since 1803 in which the legislature has not passed

The Second Century

a law modifying some aspect of the electoral process. Occasionally a new statute is important for political reasons (witness the enactment and repeal of the Visible Admixture Law in the Civil War era) or because it attempts to rationalize the jumble of confusing and inconsistent laws enacted over the course of decades (for example, the 1953 revision of the election law, adopted along with the Revised Code). More commonly, the statutes represent legislative tinkering with the composition and pay of boards of elections, the forms of nominating petitions, the counting of ballots, or other details of the process.

Major reforms have not been spread evenly over time. A flurry of legislative and constitutional activity in the early 1900s was followed by a long period of relative stability punctuated by an occasional significant event. Then came another burst of activity in the 1970s, which has sputtered and flared ever since. The most significant legal changes have been in the areas of suffrage, voter registration, nominations (discussed in chapter 12), campaign finance, and the form and method of casting the ballot. In addition, the growth and urbanization of the population and technological advances altered the way candidates campaigned.

Of all the legal changes, the expansion of the elective franchise had the greatest impact on the most people. Thanks to the Fifteenth Amendment to the U.S. Constitution, blacks had been able to vote since 1870, even though the Ohio constitution had a racially discriminatory suffrage provision until 1923. Female suffrage was another matter. In accordance with a nationwide trend, Ohio women received the right to vote in school elections in 1894. People saw education as part of the nurturing, child-rearing role of women. Women might not have been able to vote for offices established by the constitution, but nothing prevented the legislature from allowing them to vote for nonconstitutional offices such as school boards.[32]

At the 1912 constitutional convention, proponents of female suffrage appealed to democracy, fairness, and the tendency of the times. They maintained that women's participation in politics would result in industrial reform and better municipal government. Over the opposition of "wets," who feared that women would vote overwhelmingly for prohibition, the convention decided to submit a female suffrage amendment to the electorate. The voters rejected it easily.[33]

In the meantime, suffragists had come up with the idea of "presidential suffrage." If women could be made eligible to vote for president, they could pressure the national political parties for a general suffrage amendment to the U.S. Constitution. The General Assembly passed a presidential suffrage statute in 1917, but opponents organized a referendum on the law and soundly defeated it. In 1919, Congress passed the Nineteenth Amendment, prohibiting sex discrimination in voting laws, and the General Assembly ratified it. Beginning in 1920, all adult citizens who met the residency requirements, except for "idiots," insane persons, and felons who had forfeited their franchise by their illegal conduct, had a constitutional right to vote.[34]

Another significant expansion of the electorate occurred a half century later, again under the impetus of a federal constitutional amendment. In 1970, Congress lowered the voting age to eighteen in federal and state elections. The U.S. Supreme Court upheld the law insofar as it gave eighteen-year-olds the right to vote in federal elections but declared that Congress had no authority to set a minimum voting age in state elections. As a result, Ohio and most other states faced the administratively horrifying prospect of dealing with two sets of voters, with insufficient time to fix the problem with constitutional amendments before the 1972 election. But amendments to the U.S. Constitution could be adopted more quickly. Congress swiftly passed the Twenty-sixth Amendment lowering the voting age to eighteen in all elections; it sailed through the states in record time.[35]

All the new voters had to register if they wanted to take part in elections. Voter registration laws applicable to Ohio's largest cities had been enacted in the nineteenth century, but they were not terribly effective and did not address problems of vote fraud in the smaller cities and rural areas. When the General Assembly revamped the election laws in 1904, it required voter registration in all cities of fourteen thousand or more inhabitants, but a truly effective registration provision came only in 1929 with another overhaul of the election code, which Governor James M. Cox had previously described as "a confused jumble of legislative piecework." The updated code enhanced the secretary of state's authority to regulate elections and investigate fraud, required voters to sign the poll lists before receiving their ballots, simplified procedures for recounting ballots and contesting elections, included optional provisions for the use of voting machines, and increased the penalties for violation of the election laws. It also required that voters in cities of more than sixteen thousand people be registered. Smaller cities and villages could adopt registration voluntarily. Registration was permanent; a voter who moved or changed his or her name had to inform the board of elections, but the law no longer required a periodic general registration of voters. The code directed registrars to check the accuracy of voter registration lists periodically and to purge the names of individuals who had not voted for two years. Those people would have to reregister if they wanted to vote.[36]

In 1977, the Democratic General Assembly passed a law allowing permanent, election day registration, a pet idea of President Jimmy Carter. The law required all voters to register, authorized registration by mail, made available election day registration at the voter's polling place, provided for registration when an elector applied for or renewed a driver's license, and eliminated the purge from registration lists of voters who hadn't voted for two years. Opponents of instant registration argued that it would increase fraud, cause confusion at polling places, and require the hiring of thousands of election day registrars. Republican governor James A. Rhodes vetoed election day registration, motor-voter registration, and the elimination of the purge for nonvoting, but the General Assembly overrode the vetoes.[37]

Opponents of instant registration organized a successful initiative petition drive and put before the voters a constitutional amendment to require that individuals register at least thirty days before an election in which they desired to vote and to reregister if they failed to vote for four years. The vote on the amendment was widely regarded as a referendum on Carter's project. Notwithstanding the vigorous opposition of the Democratic Party and labor unions, the amendment passed without difficulty. The next year, the General Assembly conformed the election law to the new amendment by requiring registration at least thirty days in advance as a condition of eligibility to vote and cancellation of the registration of a voter who failed to vote for four years. Rhodes had not vetoed mail-in or motor-voter registration, and those provisions remained on the books.[38]

The federal National Voter Registration Act of 1993, the motor-voter law, required some changes in Ohio's registration laws. Beginning in 1995, applicants for driver's licenses had to be offered the chance to register to vote on the license application form. Libraries, schools, and other public agencies also had to make voter registration forms available. The law provided for mail-in registration and prohibited public officials from removing voters from registration lists just because they had not voted. The law applied only to federal elections, but no state was going to have two sets of registration laws. Ohio already had mail-in and motor-voter registration, but the General Assembly passed legislation to conform the details to federal requirements for state as well as federal elections.[39]

Ironically, as the size of the electorate grew, turnout at the polls fell. According to historian Michael McGerr, the rise of the educational and advertising styles of campaigning, the advent of reformist interest groups more committed to a cause than to a party, the Australian ballot, and voter registration laws all contributed to the waning of partisanship. The new style of politics had less appeal for new voters—women, young adults, immigrants, and the children of immigrants—than had the old ballyhoo style. New voters in the twentieth century did not undergo the "intense partisan socialization of older members of the electorate." As a result, voter turnout fell precipitously, raising fears that "aggressive and interested minorities" or political radicals were getting control of the government. A study of voter turnout in Delaware, Ohio, in 1924 suggested that these fears were groundless. Although the study showed that the children of foreign-born parents were somewhat more likely to vote than the children of natives, it also found that voter turnout increased with education, wealth, and church affiliation. But even among the best-off members of the electorate, a quarter of eligible voters did not vote.[40]

After reaching a low point in the 1920s, voter turnout began to rise in 1928. A Columbus newspaper reported a turnout in that city in the 1928 general election of more than 86 percent. Nationally the Great Depression and the New Deal brought out the electorate, but the 1940s witnessed another reversal before turnout increased once more. But turnout never again reached the levels seen in the latter half of the nineteenth century. Since the 1960s, notwithstanding some upward blips, popular participation in the political process, along with party commitment, has trended downward.[41]

Running for Office

The shift in campaign style from ballyhoo to education that began in the late nineteenth century continued after 1900. The complexity of the issues, the rise of the independent voter, and the growth of organized interest groups caused many politicians to focus on informing as many voters as possible about the issues rather than rallying the party faithful. Tom Johnson, the progressive mayor of Cleveland, said of his 1903 gubernatorial campaign, "I always discouraged brass bands, red fire [sic] and the usual artificial paraphernalia of political contests. We relied entirely on the merits of the questions we were presenting. The cost of tent and other meetings and of literature represented our outlay."[42]

Johnson was famous for his tent meetings, which he believed lent an air of freedom to the events that was absent in an indoor hall, and for his mode of travel, his "Red Devil" automobile. For a time, politicians found the interurban electric railways that flourished throughout Ohio in the early twentieth century

a great means of getting about the countryside to meet the voters, but competition from automobiles killed off the interurbans. In 1915, Joseph Foraker noted
the change that cars had made in political campaigns. They enabled candidates
to travel to small towns and crossroads, to have ten to twenty small meetings across
a county in a day rather than one or two large ones. The candidates reached
more people, but had less to say in the limited time available. Instead of having
"three or four thousand people in one mass meeting, with time and opportunity
for a logical, thorough-going speech," a candidate might have "fifteen or twenty
audiences each day, composed of from only fifteen to two or three hundred persons each . . . assembled at out-of-the-way places, to be there hurriedly and
briefly addressed."[43]

Not every candidate had a car. In 1927, seventy-two-year-old L. P. Vandament
of Clermont County walked from ten to thirty miles a day throughout the county,
accepting rides when he could get them but sometimes traveling country roads too
rough for automobiles. A Democrat running in a Republican county, Vandament
had no platform and made no promises, but he "literally walked his way into the
legislature." Forty-five years later, Representative Howard A. Knight of north-
central Ohio, running for the Senate, chose to hike 205 miles through his district
despite cold, rainy weather and unfriendly dogs.[44]

Other technological innovations besides the automobile helped change the
way candidates campaigned. The mass production and rapid distribution of newspapers and other printed material brought the written word, in the form of educational articles, editorials, and advertisements, to voters in every corner of a
state or district. Radio and motion pictures gave an immediacy to political propaganda that newspapers lacked, and, as early as 1932, the future importance of
television was obvious. Sound trucks cruised through residential neighborhoods
as election day approached, urging voters to support one party or another (or one
candidate or another, for photographs, radio, and other technological advances, together with the merchandising style of campaigning, pushed personalities rather
than parties to the fore). Direct contact remained important—indeed, the automobile made it possible for a candidate to see more people—but the demands
on a candidate's time and stamina became daunting. Much of the contact, especially in the big cities, was therefore made by canvassers under the supervision
of precinct captains.[45]

The new style of campaigning was expensive. By the 1920s, political campaigns had become selling campaigns, heavily dependent on costly advertising

and public relations efforts. Campaign expenditures, observed a political scientist in 1932,

> are characterized by infinite variety. No longer do political managers limit their activities to meetings and torchlight processions. Elaborate headquarters are set up; "organizers" speed hither and yon; tons of letters, pamphlets and dodgers are distributed; bands play, flags wave, billboards, radios, and other advertising media, as well as speakers, preach the gospel on all sides; and campaign buttons and lithographs familiarize the public with glorified likenesses of the respective candidates.[46]

The new approach to campaigning, with its increased costs, affected primary as well as general elections. Indeed, one of the arguments against the direct primary was that it increased the influence of money in politics. An aspirant for office had to conduct a full-blown campaign just to get the nomination. Money's impact on primaries may have been particularly pernicious because candidates often had to rely on their own resources or the generosity of friends rather than on county or state party committees. On the other hand, money probably made little difference in many contests, particularly in the smaller counties. In 1946, law student and future U.S. senator and attorney general William B. Saxbe ran unopposed in his first race for public office, the Republican primary for representative from Champaign County. He ran unopposed again two years later. Even in his first general election, Saxbe faced only nominal competition. The number of uncontested seats has fluctuated wildly since Saxbe's time, but it has often been high. In 1944, twenty House and four Senate races were uncontested, and in other races the eventual winner did not face serious opposition. In 1952, twenty-three House and three Senate races went by default. The raw numbers were similar more than a half century later, but in the smaller legislature that meant a higher percentage of uncontested races. In 2004, twenty-two of ninety-nine House candidates (22 percent) and two of sixteen Senate candidates (14 percent) had no opposition.[47]

Studies of political campaigns usually focus on federal, gubernatorial, and big-city mayoral elections. It's hard to tell how much the changes in campaign style affected races for the General Assembly, particularly the House of Representatives, which generally took place on a much smaller canvas. The automobile no doubt affected the number and size of meetings and the style of oratory, but many candidates for local office did not indulge in the expensive, high-profile campaigns that often characterized statewide and federal races. Frederic C. Howe's campaign for Cleveland city council in 1901 probably typified the big-city campaign for a seat in the General Assembly at the time. Howe "was out every night, making speeches in the saloons, visiting from house to house." He had his "photograph taken in a frock coat, and liked to see it on telegraph-poles, in shops, and in the windows of private homes." Because campaign financing statements have not been preserved, it is hard to know how much state legislative candidates spent or where they got campaign funds. The candidates themselves may not always have known. Howe remembered that ward politicians distributed his literature and set up meetings without asking him for money. Only later did he learn that utility companies had bankrolled his campaign in the expectation of favorable votes in the council.[48]

Outside the big cities, most legislative campaigns must have been low-key, low-budget affairs, as they often were in other states. Official records of expenditures do not exist for most of the twentieth century. The campaign finance laws were not enforced, and, in any case, records had to be retained for only four years. During the 1920s, however, the Columbus *Ohio State Journal* occasionally noticed the campaign contributions and expenditures reported by General Assembly candidates. Some spent nothing. Most others reported amounts of less than $200 for such items as postage and gasoline. In 1926, three successful candidates from Franklin County said they shelled out $342.38, $130.60, and $79, respectively. On the other hand, in 1924, Senate candidate Ralph J. Bartlett spent $1,000, more than five times his receipts, in a losing cause.[49]

County party committees also reported campaign contributions and expenditures. In 1924, the Franklin County Republican and Democratic organizations reported receipts of $30,117 and $11,149, respectively, all from contributions, mostly from the candidates. Expenditures fell just short of receipts for both parties, with the biggest items being advertising and campaign literature. The Republicans reported spending $12,424 for literature, $1,287 for office supplies, and $2,324 for meetings. In 1926, the single biggest contributor to the Franklin County Democratic campaign chest was the county auditor's office, which gave $3,084. (It would be interesting to know who in the office contributed the money and how they did it. In 1913, the General Assembly prohibited the solicitation of political assessments from civil servants.)[50]

For presidential, congressional, and gubernatorial candidates, methods of campaigning and the costs of running campaigns changed significantly in the second half of the twentieth century. The changes affected state legislative candidates, too, but more slowly and to a lesser degree. Candidates for federal and statewide offices hired political consultants and public relations experts, who sold their clients like merchandise on radio and television. Few state legislative candidates could afford such expensive sales campaigns. They relied instead on old-fashioned techniques: coffee klatches in constituents' homes, appearances before church groups and at picnics, visits to newspaper offices in search of endorsements, handouts of cards with the candidate's name, attendance at as many covered-dish suppers and dinners of as many organizations as possible, and door-to-door campaigns. Nevertheless, the new methods filtered down to the local level, and the high cost of campaigning began to affect state legislative races as well. In his first campaign for the House, Vern Riffe bought radio and newspaper ads and mailed literature directly to likely supporters. He spent around $1,800, a substantial sum in 1958.[51]

Major changes came with the rising costs of campaigns in the 1960s and 1970s. Until the early 1970s state legislative candidates were, in the words of Bill Chavanne, the "orphans of candidates," left by the party organizations and legislative caucuses to fend for themselves. Then Ted Gray started holding caucus fundraisers to help Republican senatorial candidates pay for television spots. Chavanne, the Democratic Senate clerk from 1975 through 1978, spent most of his time gathering and tracking information for Senate races and doling out money to his party's candidates, who found themselves dependent on party leaders for financial support. Vern Riffe, who began his record-setting tenure as Speaker of the House in 1975, built his awesome power in part on his ability to raise prodigious amounts of money. He organized the first fund-raising dinner for the Democratic caucus in 1973. A few years later, he instituted another big event, his own "birthday party," which anyone who wanted anything from the legislature would skip at his or her peril. The first birthday fundraiser brought in $165,000. By the time he retired, Riffe's cash presents topped $1.5 million per celebration. Riffe would distribute much of the money to House Democratic candidates. Along the way, he hired a marketing firm to see that the candidates spent the money he gave them effectively.[52]

By one calculation, the average cost of a House campaign in Franklin County rose from $4,564 in 1974 to $84,207 in 1992. In the latter year, a single House race in Summit County cost each side nearly half a million dollars. After his retirement from politics, Riffe, saying "don't blame me for the outrageous cost of state campaigns today," called campaign demands on a candidate's time and wallet "obscene" and declared that "something should be done about it." In fact, attempts to limit the influence of money on politics in Ohio went back to the eighteenth century, when territorial laws prohibited bribery and "treating" of voters. The Garfield Corrupt Practices Act of 1896 imposed on candidates for the General Assembly a campaign spending limit of $500, including the campaign for nomination, and required candidates and political committees to file campaign finance reports. The legislature repealed the Garfield Law after six years, but, in 1911, when a grand jury exposed the buying and selling of votes on a breathtaking scale in Adams County and a House committee found widespread treating, bribery, and vote buying in Hamilton County, the General Assembly enacted a campaign finance law that required public accounting of campaign expenses, specified the purposes for which contributions could be used, and limited the amount a candidate could spend. Around the same time the General Assembly prohibited corporate campaign contributions.[53]

The next several decades saw no major modifications of the campaign finance laws or improvement in their enforcement; however, as campaign costs rapidly escalated in the 1950s, lawmakers and good-government groups throughout the nation became increasingly concerned about the impact of money on democracy. They got a boost from the Watergate scandal, which fostered the enactment of campaign finance laws at both the federal and state levels. In 1974, the General Assembly attempted to control spending on political campaigns by limiting the amount that candidates for different offices or their campaign committees could spend or that others could spend on their behalf. The spending limits were based on population. A candidate for the Ohio Senate could spend no more than 12¢ times the population of the state (10,657,423 in 1970) divided by the number of Senate districts, or $38,754. A candidate for the House could spend 15¢ times the population divided by the number of House districts, or $16,148. The law set a cap of $100 on the cash contributions any person could make to any candidate in each primary, special, or general election; prohibited individuals from pressuring public employees into making campaign contributions; required more frequent and more detailed reporting of contributions and expenditures; and in other respects tried, in the words of the old nineteenth century statutes, to ensure "the purity of elections."[54]

The 1974 act also created the Ohio Elections Commission. The commission consisted of five members: four appointed by the secretary of state (two from each major party from lists of names submitted by the parties) and a fifth chosen by the first four. The members received per diem pay of $50. The commission's job was to investigate complaints of violations of the campaign finance law and to report findings of violations to the appropriate prosecuting attorney.[55]

In 1976, the U.S. Supreme Court threw a monkey wrench into the General Assembly's regulatory scheme. In *Buckley v. Valeo*, the Court held limitations on campaign spending unconstitutional. The General Assembly duly repealed the expenditures limitation. During the next decade and a half, it altered the campaign finance laws in other ways. For example, the legislature prohibited the diversion of campaign funds for the personal use of the candidates. It required door-to-door solicitors to file reports listing those who donated along with the amounts and required the solicitors to inform prospective donors of the reporting requirement. The lawmakers authorized corporations to establish political action committees (PACs) and to seek contributions from shareholders and employees, but they also required the corporations to report to the PACs the extent to which their employees or equipment were used for political purposes (information that the PACs would then have to include in reports filed with the secretary of state). They regulated the manner in which contributions could be solicited and prohibited reprisals against employees who declined to contribute. The General Assembly also ventured into the public financing of elections by allowing a taxpayer to check a box on the individual tax return directing a dollar of his or her taxes—two on a joint return—to a state fund in which the state and county committees of the major parties would share. The money could be not be used to support or oppose candidates or issues, but it could help defray the cost of operating party headquarters, of registration drives, or of get-out-the-vote campaigns.[56]

Despite these changes, many people believed that more serious reform was needed, particularly in light of the fund-raising scandals of the 1980s and early 1990s, discussed in chapter 19. In 1994, two political scientists complained that Ohio's "rather free-and-easy campaign regulations invite very large infusions of political money into Ohio elections." There were, they noted, no limits on how much money a campaign could collect and spend. (The $100-per-person limit apparently applied only to cash in the form of legal tender.) The Citizens League Research Institute of Cleveland complained that the "[c]ontributions from some sources . . . can total tens of thousands of dollars in an election, in some cases for a single candidate. The United Auto Workers Ohio State Political Action Committee, for example, reported campaign expenditures of $730,000 during

1987–88, including $120,000 to the state Democratic Party and $84,650 to the Ohio Democratic Senate Campaign Committee." Champion fund-raisers such as Democrat Vern Riffe and Republican Stanley Aronoff raised huge sums of money, far more than they needed for their own elections, and they could induce legislators to follow their line with infusions of much-needed funds.[57]

By the 1990s, reform was in the air. Senator Robert Cupp, chairman of a Senate task force on campaign finance reform, noted the widespread public belief that big campaign contributors determined public policy. "We may protest that it isn't so—and it generally isn't," said Cupp, "—but appearance IS the voter's reality." Notwithstanding Cupp's disclaimer, members of his own party complained that government was for sale. One said that "if you want a bill passed into law, all you've got to do is pay the right price to the right person in the right campaign." Another griped that the merits of proposed legislation were incidental to its prospects for success; the key was money. Secretary of State Bob Taft, testifying before the Senate task force, declared that "[t]oo many Ohioans feel their voices cannot be heard against the roaring tide of big money flowing into campaigns from special interest groups and wealthy contributors. Too many candidates feel that campaigns have become competitions for dollars, rather than contests of ideas." Organizations such as the League of Women Voters and Common Cause called for legislation that would limit campaign contributions, encourage voluntary limits on campaign spending, require full disclosure of contributions and expenditures, and provide for public financing of political campaigns. Taft also advocated reform of the Ohio Elections Commission, likening that body to "the cowardly lion in the Wizard of Oz," "rough and gruff" at first glance but "not equipped to adequately fight its battles."[58]

The General Assembly enacted legislation to tighten the campaign finance law and to strengthen the Elections Commission. The laws limited the amount of money an individual, a political action committee, or a campaign committee could make to candidates, campaign committees, and campaign funds. They sought to keep campaign committees from building up big postelection surpluses for use in future campaigns. They prohibited anyone from intimidating potential contributors, including public employees, into making or not making contributions. They required detailed reporting of contributions and expenditures, including aggregate contributions from donors, thus outlawing pancaking to evade the limits (see chapter 19). Some of the limits covered in-kind contributions. The laws required that campaign funds be kept in separate accounts and not commingled with the personal or business accounts of a candidate or campaign committee. They transformed the Elections Commission into an independent body of salaried members appointed for the most part by the governor, provided for detailed procedures for hearing complaints, authorized the commission to refer cases to a prosecutor or to levy fines, and increased the penalties a court could impose.[59]

The "centerpiece" of the new campaign finance law was the limit on donations. For General Assembly races, that limit was $2,500. While the limits were significant for statewide and federal races, which attracted big donors, they meant little in many legislative races, where most contributions fell well below the cap. The law did not limit in-kind contributions by parties or legislative caucuses, so those entities could still provide important aid to individual legislative candidates. Nor did the law limit spending.[60]

After years of complaints, and impelled by campaign finance controversies involving gubernatorial aides and legislative leaders and a hard-hitting advertising campaign against a supreme court justice running for reelection, the General Assembly earnestly set to work on a reform bill in 2004. Late in the year, when House and Senate leaders could not agree on a number of other measures, the Senate adjourned sine die, leaving work on campaign finance reform unfinished. Governor Bob Taft called a special session to avoid having to start all over in the next General Assembly. In the special session, the legislature passed a wide-ranging act that limited issue-oriented ads within thirty days of an election, restricted the transfer of funds among local party committees, increased reporting requirements, and directed the secretary of state to make more reported information publicly available through the Internet. The law also prohibited per-signature or per-volume payments to people who circulated election petitions and made numerous other changes, large and small, to the campaign finance law.[61]

The act's most notorious provisions quadrupled contribution limits, allowing individuals and political action committees to donate $10,000 to a candidate during an election period. Because separate election periods existed for primary and general elections, the contribution limit for a complete election cycle became $20,000. Democrats fumed over the increase in contribution limits even as state and federal investigations of statehouse fund-raising scandals were taking place. Republicans argued that responsibility for the scandals lay with unreasonable limits and that full disclosure rather than severe limits was the best way to ensure fair elections. The law did not take effect until after the 2004 election, but, by the end of 2005, Common Cause was claiming that the law had "opened the floodgates to more money in Ohio politics and more influence for fewer wealthy donors." After analyzing information available on the secretary of state's Web site, the organization reported that individual and PAC donations to candidates for state office in the first six months of the 2006 election cycle (January through June 2005) more than doubled the amount contributed in the same period in 2003, with many of the donations exceeding the previous cap of $2,500. Common Cause thought the increased contribution limits would have an especially harmful effect on state legislative races, which cost much less than statewide races and could therefore be funded by a relatively small group of donors. Candidates for the General Assembly, it predicted, would "rely less on grassroots support and the power of their ideas and more on gaining the support of a small handful of wealthy supporters." The organization urged voters to approve a constitutional amendment on the November 2005 ballot that would have imposed drastic limits on campaign contributions, as well as other changes in the regulation of elections, but the voters overwhelmingly turned it down.[62]

Voting

All the voter registration, fund-raising, campaigning, and spending culminated in election day, when the voters at last got to cast their ballots. The form of the ballot provoked controversy for much of the twentieth century. When the General Assembly adopted the Australian ballot in 1891, it chose to require the party-column format, which featured side-by-side columns of the candidates of each party. At the top of each column were the party name and emblem and a circle that a voter could check if he wanted to vote the straight party ticket. Progressive reformers disliked the party-column ballot, especially when, as in Ohio after 1906, it allowed a candidate's name to appear more than once if he was nominated by more than one party. ("Fusion" nominations were not uncommon, especially for local offices.) The ballot could be long and confusing, and its facilitation of straight ticket voting discouraged thoughtful independence on the part of the electors. Progressives preferred the office-group ballot on which all the candidates for a particular office would be listed together, with the whole group blocked off from the candidates for other offices and a candidate's name appearing just once. They also favored making more positions appointive rather than elective, which would produce a shorter ballot. The 1912 constitutional convention made a start toward the short ballot by eliminating some elective positions and making others appointive, but the ballot remained long, and it retained the party-column format.[63]

More than three decades later, the *Columbus Citizen* complained that the long, party-column ballot encouraged voters to "clos[e] their eyes and vot[e] straight" with a simple X at the top of the column rather than consider the merits of each of dozens of candidates. "Straight ticket voting," grumbled the paper, "helps the party bosses, but it hurts the people." The *Citizen* recommended that some elective offices be eliminated and that the candidates be grouped on the ballot by office rather than listed under party column.[64]

The office-type ballot finally came to Ohio in 1949. Republicans were preparing for the reelection of U.S. senator Robert A. Taft in 1950. The election law required that candidates for various offices be listed in a specified order, beginning with governor; candidates for U.S. senator sat in seventh place. Many voters never read that far down the list. Taft's backers worried that their man would be swamped by Democratic straight ticket voting, which in Cleveland alone had been averaging 61,000 per election. They pushed the office-type ballot in an effort to force voters actually to look at the names of the candidates for each office. Democrats and labor organizations vigorously opposed the amendment, but it passed easily.[65]

Voters continued to cast paper ballots well into the twentieth century. The General Assembly first authorized cities, towns, and villages, on the approval of their voters, to use voting machines in 1898. The new machines were mechanical devices with push buttons or levers and automatic counters. Reformers regarded them as safeguards against fraud; however, in 1909, the Ohio Supreme Court held the use of voting machines unconstitutional because the constitution said elections had to be by ballot, which in the court's view meant a paper ballot. The 1912 convention tried to overrule the court with a constitutional amendment. The voters rejected the proposal, but the issue refused to die. A student of Ohio elections noted that voting machines "are used in a number of states and cities and are giving full satisfaction," that they saved money and presented "no danger of fraud." In 1921, a majority of House members present voted for a joint resolution to amend the constitution to allow the use of voting machines, but they were far fewer than the required three-fifths of the whole body, so the resolution failed. Voting machines remained off limits until the supreme court overruled itself in 1929.[66]

The Second Century

Republican presidential nominee Warren G. Harding enters a voting booth in Marion to mark his paper ballot in the 1920 election. *Reproduced by permission of the Ohio Historical Society*

Even after 1929, hand-marked paper ballots remained in use for a long time. In some Columbus districts in 1944, election officials handed voters a paper ballot of four pages listing seventy-two candidates and a number of issues presented in tiny print. In the 1952 general election, more voters in Mahoning County cast papers ballots than voted by machine. But voting machines were the wave of the future. Punch-card voting, invented in Ohio, spread after the secretary of state approved its use in 1960. Turn-of-the-century elections made it clear, though, that punch-card voting machines did not give "full satisfaction." The system used by the vast majority of Ohio voters in the 2000 and 2004 elections proved contentious, but so did attempts to make the costly switch to electronic voting machines. In 2005, Ohio was still "behind the curve when it [came] to voting technology," but, by the 2006 primary elections, the entire state had been converted to touch-screen or optical-scan devices.[67]

Some voters could not avoid using paper ballots, at least until the Internet raised the theoretical possibility of long-distance voting by computer. The General Assembly authorized absentee voting for soldiers in the field during the Civil War, but that was an expedient to meet a temporary emergency. In 1915, Governor Frank Willis urged the General Assembly to permit registration and voting by mail so that the thousands of people who were kept from voting "by the exigencies of their circumstances" would be able to participate. The General Assembly did not act on his recommendation, but the next year the issue gained salience when President Woodrow Wilson called up thousands of Ohio National Guardsmen to quell the commotion raised by Mexican revolutionary Pancho Villa along the southwestern border. In January 1917, a senator introduced a resolution urging Wilson to recall the troops, who had been away far longer than expected. Both Willis and incoming governor James M. Cox called for an absentee voter law. It was bad enough, said Cox, that Ohio's servicemen had had to leave their families and businesses; they should not also lose the opportunity to vote. In March, the General Assembly passed a law permitting anyone who would be "unavoidably absent" from his home precinct on the day of a primary, special, or general election to cast an absentee ballot. When the legislature rewrote the election code in 1929, it made specific provision for military personnel on active duty away from home and allowed voters who could not get to the polls because of illness or physical disability to vote by absentee ballot. In 2005, the General Assembly extended the right to cast an absentee ballot to all Ohio voters.[68]

For a surprisingly long time, boards of elections could not use schoolhouses or other public buildings for elections. Not until 1915 did the General Assembly authorize school districts to permit schoolhouses to be used as polling places. In 1917, the legislature required schools districts to allow the use of schoolhouses upon request and payment of a janitor fee. When schools were not used, voting often took place in unsuitable locations. A House committee investigating the election scandal in Hamilton County in 1911 recommended the use of portable voting booths, probably because so much voting had taken place illegally in and around saloons. In some cities, election officials set up voting booths on street corners, obstructing traffic and costing the taxpayers roughly $250 per year per booth. James Thurber recalled his experience as a Republican election official in Columbus, sitting in a stuffy "voting booth on wheels" with his Democratic counterpart, the two men sustained by coffee as they sat late into the night counting votes and debating the validity of ballots marked in red crayon rather than pencil or enhanced by expressions of opinion ("Nuts!" or, referring to Woodrow Wilson, "À bas le professeur").[69]

Election night was still an exciting time in 1920. Bracing for a huge down-town crowd, the Columbus police chief had most of his force on hand. He excluded street cars from the main road in front of the statehouse and prepared to ban all vehicular traffic as well. The *Ohio State Journal* kept the throngs informed by displaying returns on a giant screen on the statehouse lawn. "If the interest taken in the campaign holds out until returns are in and the battle settled tonight," predicted the *Journal* on election day, "it will be one howling hulla-baloo." Ten years later, the exciting election night scenes were gone. "Time was when election night in Columbus was a festive occasion and people from the city and from the rural sections near the city congregated in the downtown streets, mainly in front of the newspaper offices, to watch the results of the election, which was flashed upon large screens," a writer for the *Journal* recalled in 1930. But radio had changed all that. Now people received news of the returns at home. The crowds, the cheers and hisses, the street fights were things of the past.[70]

15

LIVING IN COLUMBUS

I N 1923, A DEMOLITION CREW brought down the Neil House. The imposing hostelry had stood on the site opposite the statehouse for sixty-one years
after fire destroyed the original Neil House, the one that had so impressed
Charles Dickens. President Harding regarded the demise of the hotel, which
"might fairly have been called the real capitol of Ohio," with regret. "On its
floor," he wrote, "I first saw and felt the pulsing movement of the political
throng. If windows were eyes, and walls had tongues, what a story the old
Neil House could tell of the public life of Ohio, indeed, in no small way of
the nation, for two generations!" But the Neil House saga wasn't over yet.
Columbus boomed in the 1920s, and a third, even more magnificent Neil House
rose in place of the second. Lawmakers and lobbyists congregated there for
another half century. As long as downtown Columbus thrived, and laws and life-
styles kept legislators in close proximity to both lobbyists and the statehouse, the
Neil House lived on, with a plausible claim to the title of Ohio's "real capitol."[1]

The "old" Neil House, razed in 1923. *Courtesy of the* Columbus Dispatch *Archives*

The "new" Neil House in 1977. *Courtesy of the* Columbus Dispatch *Archives*

A Thriving Metropolis

Downtown Columbus, along with the rest of the city, flourished in the first half of the twentieth century. The capital's population tripled to 375,000 by 1950. A midwestern crossroads, served by more than twenty railroads, the city developed into an important manufacturing and distribution center. The rise of the automobile caused a decline in rail service, but, in 1929, 160 passenger trains still entered Columbus daily. At the same time, nearly 20,000 cars and trucks passed through the city on eleven major highways, and transcontinental air service began at a new airport. The great flood of 1913 led to a thorough renovation of the Scioto riverfront, about three blocks west of the statehouse. The 1920s and 1930s saw the construction there of a new city hall (following the destruction by fire of the old "tawdry, crowded, and unsafe" city hall located on State Street across from the statehouse), central police station, federal building, U.S. courthouse, state office building, and the fifth tallest structure in the world, the fifty-five-story American Insurance Union Citadel, later known as the LeVeque Tower. The city enjoyed several daily newspapers, two universities, an art museum, a number of theaters near the statehouse, and other cultural attractions and popular entertainments.[2]

During Prohibition, wrote a journalist at the time, Columbus also had "about one thousand speakeasies and beer flats and approximately four thousand bootleggers—and that is a conservative estimate if bellboys, taxi drivers and colored hip-pocket vendors are included. Hotel attendants specialize in quick service and provide fairly good liquor, too." Hooch and football proved a troublesome mix. After one Ohio State–Michigan game, carousing students smashed hotel furniture and dumped the feathers from hundreds of pillows out of hotel windows. Police removed almost 150 inebriated students from one hotel alone.[3]

Columbus took on a shabby air during the Great Depression and by the end of World War II was in a "state of ramshackle disrepair"; however, the combined efforts of an energetic city government and a group of well-to-do private citizens organized as the Metropolitan Committee secured voter approval for the issuance of bonds to spruce up the capital and improve public services. At midcentury, novelist George Sessions Perry described Columbus as a bustling, thriving, yet "homey" city lying "gracefully along the Scioto and Olentangy rivers." Travel writer John Gunther called Columbus "a spacious and friendly town; a big issue is whether or not to cut down the trees and so make a street broader." Prohibition and the speakeasies had vanished, but Columbus remained "a fanatic and frenzied football town; if you don't go to football games on Saturday, people think you're an odd fish and a pariah." Gunther found Columbus to be a strongly religious city with an active community life. He noted the PTAs, church groups, African American organizations, and "great numbers of patriotic, Masonic, fraternal, neighborhood, and other units, like the Columbus Council for Democracy, the Columbus Town Meeting and the Council for Social Agencies."[4]

Unlike Ohio's other big cities, whose populations peaked before 1970, Columbus continued to grow throughout the second half of the twentieth century. While other cities lost people to the suburbs, Columbus annexed surrounding areas. Between 1955 and 1960, it doubled in size to eighty-nine square miles. In the next fifteen years, Columbus's territory nearly doubled again, and the population surpassed a half million. The size of the city surprised journalist Neal Peirce, who wrote in 1972 that "[w]ell-scrubbed, provincial, and complacent" Columbus still had "the old rural flavor." This, despite the interstate highways running through and around the city. A historian commented in 1979 that a "healthy mix of federal, state, city, and county government offices; universities and colleges; research facilities; as well as diversified industries and business, have created a stable community with a built-in financial resiliency." But people left downtown Columbus. Notwithstanding the growth of cultural organizations and redevelopment efforts, the city center became a "daytime town."[5]

The Transient Legislator

Although the modern metropolis of Columbus had more to offer in the way of culture, entertainment, business, and just about every other sphere of human endeavor than had the village and small city of the nineteenth century, the character of the town probably had less significance for the legislators. They were not tied to it as they had been during pre–Civil War sessions. In the early days of statehood, men came to Columbus in December and stayed put for months on end. They fretted about their families and businesses and longed for letters and the occasional visitor from home. If they met in session every weekday, Saturdays included, perhaps it was to help fill the time. The railroad in the second half of the nineteenth century and the automobile in the twentieth gave lawmakers much greater freedom—and an inducement to limit formal legislative affairs to the middle of the week.

High Street looking north from Broad Street around 1910–20. *Reproduced by permission of the Ohio Historical Society*

High Street, 1940. *Courtesy of the Columbus Citizen-Journal Collection, Scripps-Howard Newspapers/Grandview Heights Public Library/Photohio.org*

Columbus looking east from the Scioto River, 1968. The statehouse is in the upper center of the picture. The large building in the center of the picture, across the street from the river, is the Ohio Departments Building, now the Ohio Judicial Center. The tall building to the left, across Broad Street, is the LeVeque Tower, formerly the American Insurance Union Citadel. *Courtesy of the* Columbus Citizen-Journal *Collection, Scripps-Howard Newspapers/Grandview Heights Public Library/Photohio.org*

The statehouse overshadowed by sky-scrapers, including the Rhodes Tower on the right-hand side of the picture, in 1984. The Huntington Bank Building, in the upper left of the picture directly across High Street from the statehouse, sits in the spot once occupied by the Neil House. *Courtesy of the* Columbus Citizen-Journal *Collection, Scripps-Howard Newspapers/Grandview Heights Public Library/Photohio.org*

Getting into and out of Columbus got easier as highways spread throughout the state and automobile travel became routine. Automobiles caught on fast. In 1923, the number of registered automobiles in Ohio topped one million. By 1935, the state highway system exceeded 12,000 miles, and many more miles of county and township roads were constructed or paved. So many legislators drove to Columbus in the 1940s that parking at the statehouse became a thorny issue. Still, the trip to the capital could be tricky. In 1950, a member-elect was injured in an automobile accident shortly before the beginning of session and had to be sworn in by a judge at home. A legislator from Akron recalled that the journey in those days followed "two-lane roads bordered by deep ditches and took three and a half to four hours on Route 5 by way of Johnson's Corners in Barberton, Doylestown, Smithville, and a treacherous gully on the outskirts of Wooster, then Route 3 from Wooster through Loudonville (Harriet's Restaurant), over a roller coaster with banked turns, past a stand still selling trail bologna at the top of a hill, and on to Mount Vernon (the Alcove Restaurant), Centerburg, Gahanna, and Columbus." Sharing rides with fellow lawmakers, reporters, or others who had business in Columbus made the trip easier. The construction of the interstate highway system, beginning in the mid 1950s, and the development of faster, safer, and more comfortable cars soon made travel to and from the capital a breeze.[6]

The ease of transportation affected living arrangements and personal relations among legislators. Streetcars in the late nineteenth century and automobiles in the twentieth nurtured suburbs that were easily accessible from downtown. The old-fashioned accommodations—boardinghouses and hotels, located within walking distance of the statehouse, in which members messed together and shared rooms and even beds—gave way to more private and sometimes more distant accommodations.[7]

Representative Frances McGovern stayed at the Deshler-Hilton Hotel opposite the statehouse for her three terms in the 1950s. The room plus tips for the doorman, bellman, and maid cost her less than $35 per week, which struck McGovern as a good deal. (That figure most likely covered a weekly stay of three nights, Monday, Tuesday, and Wednesday.) Not all of her colleagues agreed. When hotels changed their customary discount for legislators from 20 percent to a flat $1.25 per day, some members squawked and threatened "retaliatory legislation— such as requiring hotels to have rest rooms immediately adjacent to their liquor permit areas, instead of several corridors away." One senator suggested converting

The Chittenden Hotel, three blocks north of the statehouse on High Street, in an undated photograph that appears to be from the late nineteenth or early twentieth century. The hotel was razed in 1973. The site is now part of Nationwide Plaza. *Courtesy of the* Columbus Citizen-Journal *Collection, Scripps-Howard Newspapers/Grandview Heights Public Library/Photohio.org*

The Deshler Hotel on Broad and High, diagonally across from the statehouse, in 1968, the year it closed. A private office building now occupies the site. *Courtesy of the* Columbus Citizen-Journal *Collection, Scripps-Howard Newspapers/Grandview Heights Public Library/Photohio.org*

The Great Southern Hotel, three blocks south of the statehouse on High Street, in the early twentieth century. *Reproduced by permission of the Ohio Historical Society*

the old governor's mansion into a dormitory for lawmakers. Another noted that the Senate's new carpeting might be soft enough to sleep on. A few years earlier young representative William Saxbe might have appreciated such ideas. A law student, Saxbe could not afford a hotel room, so he usually drove back home to Mechanicsburg when the day's work was done. Inclement weather occasionally forced him to sleep on a cot in the Columbus Athletic Club's gym, and now and then he shared a bed with another member in one of the downtown hotels.[8]

By the 1970s, a significant number of legislators were choosing not to stay at the hotels near Capitol Square. In January 1971, the venerable Neil House expected to house about fifty members for the upcoming session, some in single rooms, others in doubles. The Sheraton anticipated fifteen or so members, the Downtown Holiday Inn a handful. A few would be staying at the Columbus Athletic Club, although presumably not in the gym. The high cost of hotel rooms, even with the traditional legislative discount, encouraged lawmakers to

The Second Century

The Athletic Club of Columbus, just east of the statehouse on Broad Street, in an undated photograph that appears to be from the 1930s. *Courtesy of the Columbus Citizen-Journal Collection, Scripps-Howard Newspapers/Grandview Heights Public Library/Photohio.org*

The Athletic Club of Columbus gymnasium, where Representative William Saxbe sometimes spent the night during session. *Courtesy of the Columbus Citizen-Journal Collection, Scripps-Howard Newspapers/Grandview Heights Public Library/Photohio.org*

Representative Thomas Kindness during the 109th General Assembly (1971–72). While in
Columbus Kindness lived in his motor home, which he parked in the statehouse lot. *Courtesy
of the* Columbus Citizen-Journal *Collection, Scripps-Howard Newspapers/Grandview Heights Public Library/
Photohio.org*

make other arrangements. Some lived in trailers. Others opted for apartments,
either downtown or out in the suburbs. Apartments offered more peace and quiet
than hotels, which sometimes hosted noisy conventions, and more protection
from lobbyists and constituents. In 1970, Senator Stanley Aronoff shared a furnished two-bedroom apartment in Grandview with three other legislators. "You
need enough people to get total maid service," he said, "and then you share the
other details just like the Army." Soon apartments and condominiums in the
suburbs would become the norm.[9]

The demise of the Neil House in 1980 signaled the end of the old way of life.
The Neil House had not only housed members during session, it had been an
after-hours hangout, a meeting place for legislators and lobbyists, the scene of legislative wheeling and dealing. One lawmaker recalled, "You could walk in there
[the Neil House bar] at 6 pm and see almost everyone you had to see about a bill.

Republicans and Democrats drank together and ate together. A collegiality developed that has been missing since the Neil House was torn down." Speaker Vern Riffe kept some of the old spirit of the Neil House alive by moving his after-hours headquarters to the Galleria Tavern just east of the statehouse, but the scattering of lawmakers in living spaces away from downtown, ethics laws that kept lobbyists from picking up tabs, and the professionalization of the legislature all helped bring down the traditional nighttime hobnobbing. After Riffe and the Galleria ended their runs in the 1990s, "there were several places where people got watered, [but] there was no watering hole as such." The new generation of legislative leaders was more likely to take work home at night than to hold court.[10]

Social Life

Although legislators were no longer stuck in the capital as they had been in the nineteenth century, they might still find themselves at loose ends during session. Some helped fill the hours by visiting state institutions. Before the Civil War, when the capital was small and public establishments were nearby, members visited penal or benevolent institutions, sometimes to inform themselves on matters pertaining to legislation or committee investigations, but occasionally as a matter of curiosity. Visiting public institutions was a form of tourism. In 1839, Representative Abraham Hegler stopped by the school for the blind, where a ten-year-old boy impressed him with his mathematical skills. In the twentieth century, penitentiaries, mental hospitals, and schools for the disabled were no longer innovations—although the Ohio Penitentiary still attracted out-of-towners—and many of the institutions had moved beyond walking distance of the statehouse. Official visits and "junkets" still occurred, but private visits actuated by an active curiosity like Hegler's probably became rare. Even group excursions to the institutions lost their allure. In 1921, eighty members of the House visited the experimental prison farm in London, Ohio, to see if the project should be continued. In 1973, only two legislators showed up for a bus trip to the Orient State Institute for the Mentally Retarded fifteen miles from Columbus, with some members complaining that the tour was just a poorly planned exercise in lobbying. A more conveniently scheduled cocktail party given by the institute at the Neil House drew over one hundred lawmakers. Some visits were mere time-fillers, at least according to the

Columbus Citizen. During the very slow opening weeks of the 1953 session, said the paper, members took trips to state institutions just to have something to do.[11]

Lobbyists supplied much of the social life of the members, especially the "playboys" among them. Even Progressive reformers ate and played cards with lobbyists. Until the overhaul of the lobbying laws in the post-Watergate era, lobbyists routinely provided free food and drink for the members. Each January, they had hotels stock up on steaks and liquor; at session's end they held farewell parties; and, in between, they invited particularly important legislators to private dinners. The Ohio Trucking Association maintained an open bar for members at the Neil House. "If you had no one else to buy you a drink," recalled one lawmaker, "you were always welcome at the OTA." In 1959, a newspaper reported the circulation of rumors "too ugly to repeat" concerning the type of entertainment being offered to some legislators. The members knew how to milk the system. In the 1950s, Cuyahoga County Democrats held weekly meetings at upscale restaurants and clubs. Before each meeting, they would "invite" a lobbyist to "sponsor" the event by picking up the tab. "So far," reported the *Columbus Citizen*, "no lobbyist has turned down an 'invitation.'" At least one lobbyist was always ready to play poker with and lose to any legislator, although an unwritten code of ethics prohibited a legislator from winning more than he needed. Real ethics laws later drained much of the entertainment value out of members' relationships with lobbyists, but, as we will see in chapter 19, dubious connections never completely disappeared.[12]

Some legislators were perfectly capable of entertaining themselves in questionable ways without prompting from lobbyists. Even the presence of legislative wives could not keep the boys from being boys. Florence Harding, a rare bird among the spouses, accompanied her husband to Columbus early in the century. She kept a close eye on Warren, living with him in a suite at the Great Southern Hotel, watching legislative proceedings from the gallery, and going with him on day excursions. And she watched with misgivings as Warren drank, smoked, and played poker in their suite with back-slapping politicos and lobbyists. For all her attentiveness, she could not keep her husband from becoming popular "in certain pleasantly unmentionable places."[13]

"Unmentionable" activities held their allure for some lawmakers well after Harding's day. In 1959, a sting operation by the Columbus police vice squad netted a prostitute who claimed to cater "mainly to state legislators and other high type and high paying men." She usually charged $50, but one lawmaker who was "a good friend" got a special rate of $30. Poker also remained a popular pastime.

In 1953, the senators gave their majority leader a birthday present of chewing to-bacco and a deck of cards. Representative C. J. McLin and House Speaker Vern Riffe, fellow Democrats who served together for two decades beginning in 1967 and for a time lived in the same apartment complex, cemented their political al-liance with poker games.[14]

Official and quasi-official events, such as luncheons given by the governor and open houses by the attorney general, gave members a chance to be amused in respectable fashion, to build relationships, and maybe to learn something useful to them as lawmakers. For many years, legislators held "reunions" between sessions. One summer they enjoyed "a two-day round of entertainment and education" as guests of the Cleveland Chamber of Commerce and other local organizations. Members from other parts of the state received firsthand exposure to conditions in Cleveland, which their hosts hoped would produce a sympathetic response when the city sought assistance from the General Assembly in the future. The Chamber often hosted Great Lakes cruises with plenty of good food and drink. During the 1954 excursion, the ship had to anchor for eight hours in a heavy fog, prompting someone to remark: "Typical condition for legislators. They stay up all night and are in a fog all day."[15]

Many members appreciated baseball and football, especially when they had access to free passes. So many members attended the opening game of the base-ball season in Cincinnati or Cleveland that legislative business slowed to a crawl on those days. Eventually, the leadership just gave up holding session on opening day. Legislators who had business in Columbus in the fall might arrange their meetings around the Ohio State football schedule. In 1955, the members of the Legislative Service Commission decided to meet on Fridays so they could be in town for Buckeye games the next day. A Columbus paper noted wryly, "Members of the commission get their expenses, including hotel, for attending meetings. And all legislators get two tickets each for all OSU home football games." When ethics rules grew more stringent, the failure of several members to report a gift of free luxury box seats for a Cincinnati Bengals football game brought them a reprimand from the Joint Legislative Ethics Committee.[16]

On occasion, the members held their own athletic events, with one house or party inviting the other to a competition. In 1910, the House appointed a com-mittee to challenge the Senate to a baseball game. The next year Democratic lawmakers pummeled their Republican colleagues 15–4 in a baseball game held at Neil Park. Neither side could field, and both ran wild on the bases. A Columbus paper reported that once a man got to first, "all that was needed to get [him] home was to compel the other side to throw the ball to a few infielders." In 1911, the House declared in a resolution that whereas some senators *thought* they could bowl and a number of representatives *knew* they could bowl, a contest ought to be held to determine who was better. Even the capitol press corps got into the act. In 1970, the House defeated the reporters in a basketball game 33–26. A few years later, the Senate commended "the Senate Slammers for slamming the House basketball team, and demonstrating Senate superiority." Statehouse sports challenges remained popular into the twenty-first century. In 2001, House Republicans defeated their Democratic colleagues 13–4 in a softball contest that apparently stayed friendly despite the beaning of the Republican Speaker by a Democratic pitcher.[17]

The Statehouse

Notwithstanding the completion of the statehouse annex in 1901 and repeated attempts to repair the capitol's heating and ventilation systems, the statehouse remained an unpleasant place to work. An investigation by the State Board of Health in 1906 confirmed that the air in the building was indeed unhealthful. Members complained about cold drafts, overheated galleries and committee rooms, and foul air at least into the 1930s. They appointed committees and directed their officers to investigate the problems and recommend solutions, but nothing seemed to help. In 1915, Representative John Cowan, believing the House to be "the worst ventilated room west of the Allegheny Mountains," offered a facetious resolution calling on the Speaker to appoint a Grand and Exalted Ventilator in Chief to take sole charge of atmospheric conditions in the House. If the Ventilator could not rectify the conditions that filled the hall with "foul air, surface gas and profanity," causing all manner of illness and mental stupor, he could at least take the brunt of the members' complaints. As late as 1933, grumbling about poor temperature control and ventilation in the House chamber and committee rooms led the House reference committee to the unusual step of referring a resolution on the matter directly to the House custodian. Resolutions on the subject disappear from the journals after that. Either the custodian found a cure or the members gave up in despair.[18]

One thing the custodian could not do was control the lengthening regular sessions and numerous special sessions that caused the General Assembly to meet in the sweltering Columbus summer. In 1941, the General Assembly appropriated money to air-condition the Senate, but for some reason, perhaps the diversion of resources to military purposes with the approach of World War II, the system was not installed. After the war, however, the lawmakers decided to treat both houses to a more comfortable atmosphere. Whether this was a cause or effect of longer sessions is not clear. The *Columbus Citizen* reported in June 1953 that the air conditioning was "working beautifully." The paper suggested that the members "stir themselves out of their air-cooled chambers" and visit the Columbus State School, where the patients baked in the hot weather.[19]

A description of the statehouse in 1953 skipped lightly over the exterior—the writer likened the building to "a straw hat perched on a mashed-down silo"—but lingered over the interior. The halls, he observed, "seem papered with oil paintings. These are portraits of the governors, and the curve of whiskers is interesting. They start clean-shaven and gradually work up to a climax in which the portraits seem to be made only of hair and eyes in the 1870s and 1880s. Then back down again into the bare-faced 20th century." The rotunda, lined with cases of historical flags, was "really impressive. High, hushed, and with soft light filtering down through the colored glass far above, there's a beauty about it which is more than the sum of its parts."[20]

To reach the Senate chamber, the writer climbed the stairs and passed unquestioned through "a darkish room containing a few clusters of men with their heads together, talking in low voices"—apparently "one of those horrible lobbies we've been taught to shudder at." The Senate chamber beyond was "a much larger room, filled with desks, and on the far side, an official-looking rostrum with flags. . . . The green walls and filtered light make it a lovely room. On the floor proper, surrounded by a railing and with a runway down the middle, are the senators' desks, each with swivel chair." The writer took just a quick peek at the House from the "small gallery" that ran "around three sides of a wall. Far below there's a semicircle of seats, looks like two or three hundred."[21]

The senators had better accommodations than the representatives. One reporter thought the senators were coddled with their "big, leather covered, softly padded," adjustable armchairs, lush carpeting that extended under the desks and chairs, and spacious desks "with scrolled carvings and a fine finish." The Senate, he wrote, was "quiet, like a rich man's club." The House chamber sported more pedestrian furnishings: plain wooden armchairs "with a wafer thin pad on the back and detachable rubber pads on the seats—blue, green and candy striped"; a garish carpet in the aisles and linoleum under the desks; small but serviceable desks. House members sat "in close communion whether they get along with each other or not. The chairs and desks huddle together chummily even if their occupants aren't speaking." The spaciousness of the Senate allowed "a snub to be thrown with a full windup." Ironically, most House members considered their hall adequate for conducting business, at least after the installation of microphones, while half the senators complained about their chamber's lighting, acoustics, or galleries.[22]

Overcrowding afflicted the General Assembly endlessly. The clerks and stenographers worked in cramped quarters. The newspapers needed a press room and a telegraph office. The members wanted a telephone room, cloakrooms, and smoking rooms. The handful of committee rooms could not meet the needs of dozens of committees. In 1900, the Senate gave a stenographer permission to work in the Senate smoking room when it was not occupied by a committee. The action reflected a longstanding state of affairs. For years, the Senate lamented the lack working of space for stenographers and clerks. The House complained about the sharing of rooms by clerks and committees and the distance between the clerks' file room and their work space. Meanwhile, the expanding state bureaucracy occupied much of the statehouse. The House and Senate took to dividing up existing space, converting light courts into rooms, putting committees in underutilized rooms assigned to state agencies, and even kicking agencies out of coveted space. In 1913, a Senate select committee reported that many departments, including the new Legislative Reference Department, had to rent space in private office buildings. The committee recommended construction of a state office building. Erected twenty years later, the structure finally provided some relief, but the problem of overcrowding would persist until the construction of new state office towers in the last quarter of the twentieth century.[23]

Working space was at a premium until the 1970s. In the 1950s, House members used the small openings between the corners of their desks, arranged in a semicircle facing the Speaker, as storage spaces. By the end of session, Frances McGovern recalled, "dynamite would have been the best, if not the most acceptable, way to free up the accumulations." Only legislative leaders and some committee chairmen got their own offices. In McGovern's case, the extra room only helped her accumulate more paper. The demand for space led the custodians of the statehouse to divide large rooms into small ones and to create whole new floors. The original fifty-three rooms turned into 317. As early as 1904, ten-year-old James Thurber got lost in the "stony labyrinth" for an hour while looking for his father in the pressroom. By midcentury, he wrote, it was "almost impossible to find the governor's office, or any other, unless you have been accustomed for years to [the statehouse's] monumental maze of corridors and rooms. Even the largest rooms seem to have been tucked away in great, cool, unexpected corners by an architect with an elephantine sense of humor."[24]

The completion of state office buildings in 1932 and 1974 freed up some space in the statehouse, but not enough, especially after legislators started getting their own offices. David Johnston, director of the Legislative Service Commission, waged an ongoing battle for more and better accommodations in the early 1970s. Only his agency, he noted, was statutorily required to be located in the statehouse, but the shortage of space forced him to place some of his staff in rented offices across the street. Some authorized positions went unfilled because there was no place to put new employees. The exiles on West Broad Street may have been better off than their statehouse colleagues. In the statehouse, the occupants of adjacent rooms might be in different climate zones, one freezing and the other sweltering. Johnston managed to wangle some spots in the basement, but the staffers there had to endure musty odors, cracked walls, and, when the air conditioning broke down, intolerable heat even in winter. Cockroaches flourished everywhere.[25]

The statehouse underwent some refurbishment in the 1920s, 1930s, and 1960s, but the space problem remained unresolved. An inviting target of expansion opened up when the supreme court and the attorney general moved out of the statehouse annex in 1974. The annex had been criticized from the start for spoiling the east view of the statehouse, and by 1974 it was in bad shape. There was talk of razing it and giving the General Assembly space in the new state office tower. Instead the legislators decided to renovate the annex and move in. A few members set up shop there in the 1970s, and, eventually, with the huge statehouse restoration project of the 1990s, the annex became the Senate office building. House members got new facilities with the construction of the Vern Riffe Center for Government and the Arts on the northwest corner of State and High streets. In 1988, the representatives, the Legislative Service Commission, the governor, and many state agencies relocated to the Riffe Center. This office tower provided much improved physical facilities and incidentally allowed historic restoration and renovation of the capitol.[26]

In the meantime, the members had another space shortage, this one outside the statehouse. The automobile age created a demand for parking space. By mid-century, the deficiency of parking places at the statehouse and in Columbus generally had become acute. Members and employees of the General Assembly used a lot that ran along the front and sides of the annex, but lax enforcement of parking restrictions allows outsiders to take up members' spots. The lot was too small, anyway, and members so often parked on the sidewalks that the House wanted to extend the lot all the way to the northeast and southeast corners of Capitol Square. The city meanwhile considered building a parking garage under the statehouse lawn. In 1955, the General Assembly created an underground parking commission and authorized the construction of a parking garage, to be open to the public, under the statehouse grounds. After years of study, construction finally got under way in 1963 and the garage opened the next year. The surface lots remained in use until the statehouse restoration project.[27]

The construction and expansion of legislative facilities could not be avoided, but they had some unfortunate side effects. When members had no private offices to retreat to after a day's session, they tended to hang around the House or Senate chamber and talk. One longtime member recalled that there was "a lot more camaraderie" in the old days; members of opposing parties got to know each other better.[28]

In 1986, a writer called the statehouse "the jewel of Columbus." The roof had been redone a few years earlier. Senator Charles Horn had personally planted flower beds on the east side of the annex. The "gleaming" rotunda floor featured a "dazzling pattern" of marble blocks from Vermont, Portugal, and Italy. The Senate was sprucing up its office doors, and the House was updating electrical wiring. Mary's lunchroom in the statehouse basement provided a congenial place for lawmakers, lobbyists, and legislative employees to meet. The article said nothing about the cockroaches, labyrinthine arrangement of the building's hundreds of rooms, lack of temperature control, or any of the numerous other problems troubling Columbus's "jewel."[29]

Meanwhile, Richard Finan, who came to the General Assembly in 1973, brooded over the deterioration of the statehouse: the faded paintings, dirty and damaged tile flooring and marble staircases, dropped ceilings, leaky roofs, dead-end corridors, inefficient heating and cooling systems. "I'd be in here at night," he recalled, "so I would wander around these buildings. I'd look up at the ceilings or at those beautiful torchieres, and it just seemed to me that it was such a waste, that there was still so much beauty in this place, that something could be done." Finan rounded up support inside and outside of government for a restoration project. The legislature appropriated money for a master plan, which was published in 1989.[30]

Construction on the annex in the early 1990s forced the senators into cramped statehouse offices. Even before the senators moved back to their spiffed-up old quarters in 1993, statehouse employees started moving out of the main building. Denizens of the basement vacated the premises at the end of 1992. The governor and his staff, most of whom had already relocated to the Riffe Center, left the space they still occupied soon afterward, followed by the press corps. Finally, in September 1993, the House moved its chambers to the Ohio Departments Building, later the Judicial Center, on Front Street. The Senate held its sessions in the old law library room in the annex.[31]

Seven years and $121 million after the restoration project began, the statehouse had been transformed into a magnificent edifice based on the original and, wherever possible, historically faithful. The restorers removed well over 200 rooms, reopened light courts, reproduced the original color and carpeting schemes, restored or reproduced the furniture of an earlier era, replicated early light fixtures, restored grand murals of scenes from Ohio's history, and reproduced the original stained-glass state seal in the rotunda skylight. Workers also modernized the antiquated heating, ventilation, and air-conditioning systems, installed sprinklers, removed asbestos, and added facilities for public information and access. The renovated statehouse basement featured a marble map of the state set into the floor, historical exhibits, a museum shop, and a cafeteria. The George Washington Williams room commemorated Ohio's first black legislator. Improvement of the statehouse grounds included a Veterans' Plaza featuring curved limestone walls inscribed with dozens of letters home from military personnel serving in different wars. Everything in and around the statehouse, even the restrooms with their classy brass-and-marble look and the glass-enclosed elevators in the light courts, seemed old yet at the same time shiny and new. To ensure that the statehouse would retain an aura of history, the General Assembly put the buildings and grounds under the aegis of the Capitol Square Review and Advisory Board.[32]

In addition to improving the grounds and renovating the statehouse and annex, the restoration project linked the two buildings with an atrium available for public events. Although not historically accurate, the atrium fit well with the overall plan of restoration and provided an attractive arena for press conferences, luncheons, and special events. It also relieved senators from exposure to pigeon bombardments while walking between their offices and the statehouse. In 1957, the mess created by the pigeons induced Senator Robert Shaw to introduce a bill authorizing the destruction of pigeons on the statehouse grounds. The committee on state government reported the bill, but the full Senate defeated it by six votes. Some senators regarded Shaw's bill as a joke, beneath the dignity of their august body, but one made an emotional speech on behalf of the "defenseless bird." (The floor debate revealed another problem around the statehouse when a senator moved to strike "pigeons" from the bill and replace it with "rats.") The next General Assembly addressed the issue by eliminating the protection pigeons enjoyed as nongame birds. The pigeon plague persisted, however, until the construction of the atrium. Even the atrium, though, did not protect the cupola skylight and stained-glass Great Seal of Ohio from the droppings of pigeons rousted from their roosts across the street by the collapse of a billboard in 2005. To fix that problem, the keepers of the statehouse installed a sound system that mimicked pigeon distress calls and the sounds of predators.[33]

The statehouse reopened on July 5, 1996, with a luncheon in the rotunda for 500 current and former legislators and other dignitaries. Two days later, the public rededication, a "Picnic with the Past," drew twenty thousand visitors who settled, apparently with good grace, for hot dogs and ice cream rather than the fancy luncheon enjoyed by the legislators or the sumptuous feast of the 1857 grand opening.[34]

The General Assembly resumed regular business in the statehouse in January 1997, although the legislators met in their newly elegant halls a few times before then. After restoration, the capitol was a delight to work in. The House and Senate chambers and the committee rooms had adequate light, heat, and ventilation, new carpeting, fresh paint, and polished woodwork. The Senate offices and hearing rooms in the annex had the tony look that the blend of history and money provides. Life was good.[35]

16

GLASNOST AND
PERESTROIKA

M IKHAIL GORBACHEV, the last leader of the Soviet Union, tried to save his crumbling empire with perestroika (restructuring) and glasnost (openness). Perestroika was Gorbachev's plan to restructure the torpid Soviet economy by weakening the grip of government on the activities of producers. Gorbachev combated corruption and the resistance of hardliners to perestroika with glasnost, the freedom to criticize public officials and policies. His daring program failed to prevent the disintegration of the Soviet Union, but it did win him the Nobel Peace Prize.

The Ohio General Assembly experienced its own glasnost and perestroika in the twentieth century. Cries for a more open process rang throughout the Progressive era and beyond. Indeed, as we will see, in 1951, a legislator compared the secretive Senate Rules Committee to the Soviet Politburo, the Political Bureau of the Communist Party. The restructuring of legislative procedure in the interests of openness, efficiency, and modernization occurred in fits and starts throughout the century.

The Path of Legislation

On February 4, 1937, Senator W. J. Zoul introduced Senate Bill 100 to amend the hunting license law. Ten years earlier, Zoul could still have filed a "legibly written" bill; in 1937, though, the bill had to be typed or printed and submitted to the Senate clerk in quadruplicate. The clerk probably sent the original to a committee after the bill was referred, kept one copy for his files, made one available to the press, and had one extra for inspection by lobbyists or other interested parties. The joint rules required that the bill be printed after its first reading and distributed to the members. The clerk would not send bills to the printer unless they conformed to criteria set forth in the rules for showing changes to existing sections of law. Statutory standards for the printing of bills, such as type size and lines per page, went back at least to 1852, but by Zoul's time the printers had to use italics and asterisks to show new and deleted matter, respectively.

Four days after its introduction, Senate Bill 100 had its second reading by title only, and, on Zoul's motion, the Senate referred it to the Conservation Committee. Three days after that, the committee reported the bill without amendment and without any narrative report on the merits of the bill. In the 1920s, the clerk could have engrossed the bill for third reading "in plain handwriting, in printing or in typewriting." Now the rules required engrossment by typewriting or printing. On February 17, the Senate passed the bill unanimously.

The House received Zoul's bill that same day. Introduction and placement on the calendar constituted the bill's first reading. The Reference Committee then recommended that the bill be read a second time and assigned to the Conservation Committee. On March 4, the Conservation Committee reported the bill, and, a week later, the House passed it unanimously. The governor signed the act on March 25.[1]

Senate Bill 100's journey through the General Assembly in 1937 followed a distinctly modern path. Some features of the trip had appeared during the nineteenth century: routine filing with the clerk by an individual sponsor rather than introduction on notice or by a special committee; numbering by the clerk; placement on the calendar; printing in accordance with statutory criteria; referral to a standing committee. Other features were twentieth-century innovations, some of them reflecting the influence of the typewriter, which had inaugurated the age of mechanical document production and duplication: the filing of multiple typed or printed copies, printing in a manner that showed changes to existing statutes proposed by the bill, referral in the House by a standing committee of reference, engrossment by typing or printing. In addition, Zoul had access to the services of professional draftsmen employed by the General Assembly. He may not have used those services, but the creation of a professional staff was a landmark in the modernization of the legislature.

Flouting the Rules

The constitution required that every bill be read "fully and distinctly" three times in both the Senate and House unless a three-fourths majority of the chamber considering the bill voted to suspend the rule. In accordance with common practice, the Senate formally dispensed with a full reading of Zoul's bill when it came up for a second reading. The journals do not mention any other suspensions of the rule for Senate Bill 100, but the bill undoubtedly received the same perfunctory treatment on all its readings. Observance of this impractical constitutional mandate had long since been abandoned. The theoretical justification for disregarding the three-readings rule was that if no one objected to a reading by title only, unanimous consent could be assumed. The real reason was that no one wanted to sit through the readings, distinct or otherwise. What was the point when a printed copy sat on everyone's desk? In 1933, the House's standing irritant Gus Kasch condemned the custom of reading bills by their titles because it "depriv[ed] members of an opportunity to question any point that might arise or occur to them during the proper reading of a bill." His complaint had no effect. In 1950, a state senator could write simply that first and second readings were by title only, and he did not suggest that bills were read in full even on third reading.[2]

In 1906, the General Assembly voted almost unanimously for a constitutional amendment that would have prohibited the House and Senate from dispensing with the reading of a bill on its final passage (the third reading). Why the lawmakers would endorse a constitutional amendment to require them to do what they could more easily have accomplished through their rules is a mystery. The proposed amendment, which also would have modified the procedure for repassing an act over the governor's veto, received little attention from the press or the voters. A huge majority of those voting on the issue favored the amendment, but because only one-third of the voters bothered to vote on the issue at all, the amendment failed, and the General Assembly continued on as before.[3]

Eventually, the constitution recognized reality. By 1973, the three-readings rule had long been a dead letter, although for some time both houses went through the formality of suspending the rules on second reading and occasionally on the other readings as well. The practice was inconsistent and capricious. One day in 1973, for example, the Senate, on motion, dispensed with a full and distinct first reading upon introduction of a list of over one hundred bills, but the journal records no motion to suspend for the second reading of the same bills. On occasion, the minority party would refuse to provide the supermajority necessary to suspend the rule. One year, the Senate minority insisted that a lengthy appropriations bill be read the third time "fully and distinctly" in order to gain time to negotiate a compromise. After the reading clerk had droned on for some time, the parties worked out an agreement and relieved the weary clerk of his task. A 1973 constitutional amendment finally abolished the fiction of three readings and required only three "considerations," so that no legislator would, even theoretically, be required to read any bill, or hear it read, even once.[4]

The General Assembly also frequently flouted the constitutional provision that limited every bill to one subject. In 1857, the supreme court had held the rule to be "directory" rather than mandatory, except in the unlikely event of a "manifestly gross and fraudulent violation." In other words, the General Assembly could pretty much ignore it. In the late twentieth century, though, the court began to invalidate legislation that it believed dealt with multiple subjects. The resuscitation of the rule did not prevent members from disregarding it, particularly when they wished to expedite the enactment of a pet idea by adding it to a bill that had already begun its way through the process or by burying it in the huge budget bill. However, the court's decisions did make some lawmakers more conscious of the rule. In at least one instance, a senator who approved the substance of a bill voted against it, and put his formal protest on the record, because the bill involved more than one subject.[5]

The political brouhaha known as the Six Day War in 1975 ended with the supreme court establishing as mandatory another constitutional rule governing the legislative process. In 1974, Democrat John Gilligan sat in the governor's chair, Republican John W. Brown was lieutenant governor, and the Republicans and Democrats each controlled one house of the General Assembly. In that year's election, Republican James A. Rhodes defeated Gilligan, Democrat Richard Celeste defeated Brown, and the Democrats won both houses of the legislature for the first time since 1958. The new General Assembly convened on January 6,

1975, but Rhodes would not succeed Gilligan until January 13. That gave the Democrats one week in which to pass highly partisan legislation without fear of a veto by a Republican governor. In short order, they passed six bills of an indisputably partisan nature. Republicans expressed their feelings about the legislative railroad by playing the sound of a train over the House sound system and calling out "all aboard" during the roll call.[6]

The only obstacle for the Democratic juggernaut was Lieutenant Governor Brown. Since 1851, the constitution had required that every bill passed by the General Assembly be presented for signing to the presiding officer of each house —in the Senate, the lieutenant governor. In 1973, on the recommendation of the Constitutional Revision Commission, the voters amended that provision but did not remove the presentation and signature requirement. Democratic leaders, afraid that Brown would hold the bills until Rhodes took office, gave him copies on the Friday before the gubernatorial inauguration, promising to deliver the originals when Brown agreed to sign. Brown insisted on his unconditional right to the originals. To deprive the Democrats of an opportunity to claim that he was absent and that therefore they could present the bills to the Democratic president pro tempore, Brown hunkered down in his office for the weekend. Out of options, the Democrats tracked down Gilligan at a friend's house on Friday evening, and Gilligan signed the bills despite the absence of the lieutenant governor's signature.[7]

Republican senator Michael J. Maloney quickly brought suit to have the six Democratic bills declared unconstitutional. The Democrats argued that the Constitutional Revision Commission intended by the 1973 amendment to make the presentation and signature rule directory only. The Democratic clerk and message clerk of the Senate bolstered the argument with testimony that Brown had routinely signed bills perfunctorily, so that the lieutenant governor's signature was a mere formality of no substantive significance. The supreme court's Republican majority disagreed. The rule, they said, was mandatory; a bill could not become law without the signature of the presiding officer of each house.[8]

A few days after Rhodes and Celeste took office, the Senate adopted a rule authorizing either the president or the president pro tempore to sign bills. The rule served little purpose because Celeste, the new Senate president, was a Democrat. An appellate court declared the rule unconstitutional, holding that the president pro tem could sign bills only if the president were absent, impeached, or serving as governor. The issue became moot with a constitutional amendment in 1979 that took the Senate presidency away from the lieutenant governor.[9]

The three-readings, one-subject, and presentation controversies involved procedural rules contained in the constitution. There was always something anomalous about the argument, especially when made in a court of law, that a constitutional provision was not binding on the legislature. Not so with regard to rules that the House or Senate itself adopted at the beginning of a session to govern its own procedures. One could plausibly argue that what a legislative body did about such rules was not the courts' concern, and that's what the Ohio Supreme Court held. The lawmakers could and often did ignore the rules without fear of rebuke from the courts. In his memoirs, House Speaker Vern Riffe admitted to ruling a member out of order to ensure passage of a controversial measure even though "I didn't even know what I was talking about."[10]

In the first half of the twentieth century, a striking indifference to the rules prevailed when adjournment approached. The House and Senate both attempted to deal with the end-of-session madness (described in chapter 17) by prohibiting the introduction of bills without the consent of the body after a specified date, but the Senate typically ignored that rule too. Later on, after the General Assembly became a full-time enterprise, a looming long recess might prompt a frenzy and a cavalier disregard of the rules. Representative Diane Grendell's protest of a conference committee's indifference to the rules, discussed below, occurred as the legislature was trying to wrap up business before a summer break.[11]

The lawmakers disobeyed the rules most flagrantly in the waning days of a session, but they strayed from the straight and narrow at other times as well. Sometimes their nonchalance delayed rather than expedited business. For example, a member might file a bill in which he had no real interest "by request" of a constituent. Many such bills were inexpertly prepared by the constituents themselves, resulting in delay when presented to the clerk because they did not conform to the rules. Longtime parliamentarian Edward Wakefield Hughes found the frequent disregard of rules relating to the preparation of bills "very annoying and inexcusable."[12]

Even if courts refused to invalidate statutes that had been enacted in defiance of the rules, disdain for the rules offended notions of fair play. In 1941, during the tension-filled months preceding America's entry into World War II, the Senate took from the Judiciary Committee a bill to bar "un-American" parties from the ballot and suspended the rules to allow immediate consideration on the floor. Neither action had the support of enough members under the rules. Senator William M. Boyd blasted the "un-American and un-democratic procedure in the wholesale and roughshod violation of our parliamentary rules" as "a lasting shame in the annals of a legislative body of a free people." In 1999, Representative Diane Grendell protested when a conference committee removed from a budget bill an appropriation that had passed both houses and was not in dispute. The joint rules allowed conference committees to deal only with differences between the House and Senate versions of a bill. If six committee members could delete provisions not in question, Grendell asked, "Why do we bother with legislators in this process?" After both houses accepted the conference committee report, Grendell took her complaint to the Ohio Supreme Court, but to no avail. As long as no constitutional violation is involved, said the justices, it is none of a court's business whether the legislature complies with its own rules.[13]

New Practices for New Times

During Ohio's second century, the operation of the General Assembly also changed in ways not directly related to the enactment of legislation. The election of officers assumed a new character. In the early 1900s, the parties put forward opposing candidates for clerkships and other offices and held roll-call votes because the members thought the constitution required such contests. In 1906, for example, the House conducted contested elections for Speaker, four assistant clerks, sergeant at arms, and two assistant sergeants at arms. Only Ed Doty, the respected clerk; Fred Blankner, who had effectively acquired life tenure as third assistant sergeant at arms; and the journal clerk received the unanimous endorsement of the representatives. In the Senate, where Republicans and Democrats each had eighteen members and a lone Independent Democrat held the balance of power, everyone from the president pro tempore to the third assistant sergeant at arms won election by a 19-to-18 vote, although the senators unanimously approved resolutions naming a doorkeeper, stenographers, porters, pages, and other employees. By the 1920s, both houses had given up the charade of elections, except for Speaker of the House, president pro tem of the Senate, and chief clerk, and even these offices the members sometimes filled without a formal challenge. Typically, at first in the House and later in the Senate, once the few contested elections were over, a member of the majority party would offer a resolution nominating the other officers and chief employees and the body would adopt the resolution without dissent. Finally, the uncontested election of even the top officers became routine. In 2007, the opening-day bonhomie reached such heights that the House assistant minority leader seconded the nomination of the majority's candidate for Speaker.[14]

Usually, neither the election of officers nor the appointment of subordinate legislative employees offered any surprises because the candidates and the distribution of patronage had been worked out in advance in party caucuses. In 1935, a rare surprise enlivened the election of officers in the House. Republicans held a one-vote majority, but Republican representatives Edmund H. Deibel and E. R. King, asserting that "selfish interests" had dictated the caucus nominee for Speaker, voted with the Democrats. The Republicans then conceded the position of Speaker pro tempore to the Democrats, although Deibel and three others voted for a Republican. King returned to the Republican fold for the election of the clerk, but Deibel did not vote and the Democratic candidate won 67 to 66. The Republicans then defeated a routine Democratic resolution nominating the assistant clerks and the sergeant at arms and his assistants 68 to 67 and adopted their own resolution doling out the offices to their friends, including a new journal clerk named James A. Rhodes.[15]

The formal process of legislation also underwent significant revision. In the remarkable session of 1913, when the Progressive movement reached its zenith, the House experimented with a few radical changes in its rules, apparently aimed at promoting efficiency. No member except the author of a bill or resolution could speak more than once per day on any one measure on the floor of the House, and then was limited to fifteen minutes. The author could speak once for thirty minutes and a second time, solely to explain the legislation, for ten minutes. If a representative was absent without leave when his bill came up for third reading, the bill would go to the bottom of the calendar. The rules moved the printing and distribution of bills from after consideration by a standing committee to before, which perhaps alerted attentive members to referrals of bills to inappropriate committees. (The joint rules before, during, and after 1913 required that bills be printed and distributed after their first reading, which makes one wonder whether anyone actually read the joint rules.) The new House rules required that any bills containing appropriations be sent to the Finance Committee before rather than after their second reading. They placed debate and amendment at the second-reading stage and required that, when the debate was over, the bill go to a standing Committee on Phraseology for the correction of any errors of spelling, grammar, or punctuation. The rules flatly prohibited any further debate or amendment of a bill once it had emerged from the Phraseology Committee, although in practice the House could evade the prohibition by suspending the rule. The primary purpose of all these alterations seems to have been to make the members thresh out their differences in committee and have finished products presented on the House floor. Speaker Vern Riffe would adopt a similar policy, by fiat rather than a change in the rules, later in the century. However, the House of 1915 dropped most of the innovations. The only one to reappear, in modified form, was the limitation of speaking time. In 1931, the House instituted a limit of twenty minutes per speaker per day on any one measure, a restriction that remains in effect.[16]

The working environment on the chamber floors changed significantly over the course of the twentieth century, as we will see in the next chapter, but formal procedure remained much the same. The presiding officers retained their traditional powers. They called the chambers to order, ruled on procedural questions, and recognized members who wished to speak. For half a century, House members, following an old custom, introduced bills according to an alphabetical roll call by counties. When the clerk called the name of his county, a representative would hand his bill to a page. The page brought the bill to the clerk, who read the title, thereby introducing the bill. The House abandoned this quaint procedure in the 1950s and instead required the clerk to read the titles of bills that had been filed in his office when the House reached introduction of bills in the regular order of business. The Senate did not adopt a similar method of introduction until 1971.[17]

Anyone who wants to evaluate the quality of debate on the House or Senate floor since 1997 can go to the General Assembly's Web site and search the video-recorded archive of sessions. We have little information about floor debate before then. Commentators in the first half of the twentieth century observed that state legislatures in general were not really deliberative bodies and that oratory had gone out of fashion. Charles Gongwer, who published a newsletter on Ohio legislative proceedings, gave an example of senatorial speechmaking in 1935 when he quoted W. J. Zoul's maiden speech in the Senate. The subject under discussion was the exemption from the sales tax of liquor sold by the glass. According to Gongwer, Zoul said:

> With all due respect to the gentleman from—from (out of the righthand corner of his mouth to Foss "where's he from")—to the gentleman from Muskingum, I want to say that I'm in favor of this bill. It ain't what it should

be but it's a step in the right direction. When we get back to the days when a man can go in and buy a shot for 10¢ then we'll be accomplishing something. When a man can buy a shot of good liquor for 10¢ he ain't goin' to patronize no bootlegger. And I'm tellin' you. This is a good bill. And everybody here ought to vote for it.[18]

Zoul's grammar could have been better, but the senators probably appreciated his pithiness. The General Assembly no doubt had members then, as it does now, who can deliver cogent and even moving arguments in correct English, but twentieth-century legislators were more interested in efficiency than in eloquence. Both houses allowed members to read from books, papers, or documents, which may have blunted the need, if need there had been, to make original speeches. The House's adoption of the twenty-minute limit suggests that some representatives had been exasperating their colleagues with long-winded commentary. If speechifying got out of hand, a majority of members could terminate it with the Ohio tradition of moving the previous question, a procedural device that cut off debate. The problem with the previous question motion was that it prevented members who had not yet been recognized from speaking at all. Opponents of the motion, who had tried to limit its effectiveness at least as early as 1846, decried it as an undemocratic "gag rule."[19]

The method of voting on the House floor became a subject of interest thanks to the invention of electrical devices for recording roll-call votes. Voice roll-call votes wasted a great deal of time and money and were notoriously used by dissenters to obstruct business. Inventors of roll-call machinery, including Thomas Edison, thought they had the solutions to these problems and started getting patents for their creations in 1848. A House committee appointed to investigate the feasibility of one such contrivance in 1880 concluded that it would be practicable but expensive, and a late-session resolution to purchase the device fizzled. Thirteen years later, the House authorized a committee to spend up to $1,000 on an electrical roll-call system, but the committee apparently could not find a suitable system for the price. The Wisconsin legislature installed a vote-counting apparatus to general acclaim in 1917, but subsequent repeated calls in Ohio for investigations and trial demonstrations of similar machinery fell flat. Finally, in 1929, the House adopted a joint resolution to have a committee investigate the installation of a mechanical voting device for the General Assembly. The Senate, one-fourth the size of the House and therefore less trou-

bled by the traditional roll call, agreed only after deleting itself from the resolution. Nothing came of that effort. In 1947, a House committee report noted
the spread of electric voting machinery and the huge savings of time it produced: thirty-second votes in Michigan instead of five to fifteen minutes as before; ten days out of a sixty-day session saved in Florida. Electric voting was
accurate; it promoted independent judgment because members had to be at
their seats to vote, and everyone voted simultaneously; it promoted decorum;
it saved money by shortening sessions. The committee noted some objections—
the high cost of installation, the risks of hasty voting and of voting by nonmembers on the floor—but, by its tone if not by explicit endorsement, clearly
supported the change.[20]

The House finally installed electric voting equipment for the 1955 session. A
Columbus newspaper likened the vote-recording board, with its flashing red and
green lights, to a pinball machine. As predicted, the system saved considerable
time and tedium, reducing the time for a roll-call vote from between eight and
twelve minutes to six seconds, but it was not perfect. Seventeen years after its inauguration, the system broke down, and for the first time in memory the House
clerk had to call the roll.[21]

The installation of roll-call equipment in the House reflected a long-standing
difference between the House and Senate. An article on life in the statehouse
in 1986 described the House style as "Next, next, next!" Debates never got
"windy" and were not recorded. The Senate, with its greater elbow room, manual
roll calls, and more rambling debate, was more "laid-back." The theoretical importance of Senate debate was reflected in the tape recordings made of floor sessions since 1977; perhaps revealing their practical lack of importance, the tapes
were simply filed away in a drawer. Sometimes a speaker won the careful attention of his colleagues; more typically, some senators read and others wandered
around talking to each other or went out for a smoke or phone call. The article's
author did not mention that the House's accelerated pace might have been due
in part to Speaker Vern Riffe's distaste for floor debate—Riffe wanted controversies resolved in committee—but Riffe notwithstanding, the Senate did in fact
have a history of being slower and more deliberative in its work. The House acknowledged the difference when it honored Tom Bateman on his retirement as
Senate clerk in 1971. "Tom has always looked upon House members as strange
animals," read the resolution, "somewhat out of place in the sober and dignified
legislative process."[22]

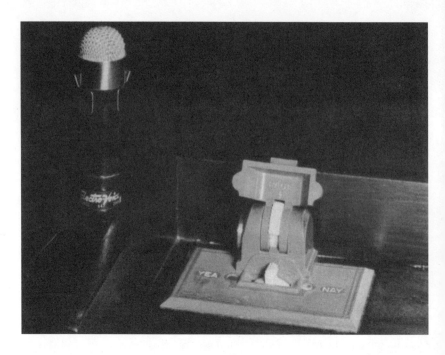

The House's electric voting apparatus, as shown in the 1959–60 House brochure.
Courtesy of the Ohio House of Representatives

Committees

Committee work continued throughout the twentieth century to be the most crucial and controversial stage of the formal legislative process, although critics complained that the real work usually took place in bars, restaurants, hotel rooms, or closed meetings of party leaders. The House Speaker's greatest power derived from his domination of committees. The Speaker appointed committees and from 1915 served ex officio as chairman of the Rules Committee, a key position because of the committee's control of the agenda for floor votes. The lieutenant governor, who was president of the Senate until 1979, lacked the power to appoint standing committees because the senators would not entrust such authority to the hands of an officer who was not one of them and might not even belong to the majority party. Even after 1979, the Senate rules continued to give the Senate as a whole the authority to appoint standing committees, although, in accordance with long-standing practice, it exercised the power on the "recommendation" of a select committee on committees consisting of the leadership of the two parties. Only during the 1983–84 General Assembly did the rules give the Senate president the authority to appoint standing committees—until 2003, when he reacquired it. Furthermore, the 2003 rules did not list the standing committees, something the rules had done for over a century and half. The president could now name the standing committees, decide their size, and appoint their members. For the first time, at least on paper, the president of the Senate had greater power over committees than the Speaker of the House.[23]

The House Speaker, in addition to chairing the all-important Rules Committee and appointing the members of the standing committees, for many years referred bills and resolutions to standing committees. This authority, not explicitly granted in the rules but wielded by long custom, gave the Speaker enormous power. Having appointed the committees, he knew where his friends were and could direct measures to committees that could be counted on to act in accordance with his wishes. In most cases, no doubt, the Speaker sent bills and resolutions to the committees he thought best suited to deal with them. In view of the large number of measures and the short time between first and second readings, however, his snap decisions might often be inappropriate. Particularly important bills would get more considered treatment. Every legislature had its committee of executioners—a committee that could be relied on to smother a bill. These were known as "pickling committees" or "legislative morgues." By the simple act of referring a bill to the morgue, the Speaker could ensure that it would not see the light of day.[24]

In 1921, the House established a standing Reference Committee, possibly the nation's first. The Reference Committee reduced the power of the Speaker at least formally and helped ensure more satisfactory referrals. Before 1915, the House rules provided that, on a bill's second reading, the Speaker would proclaim it ready for commitment or engrossment. If no one offered a motion to the contrary, the bill was supposed to go to the committee of the whole. In practice, however, the Speaker referred the bill to a subject-matter standing committee. In 1915, the House transferred the power to refer bills from the Speaker to the whole body, but in 1921 the House rules directed that every bill, after its first reading, go to the new Reference Committee. If the committee found that the bill was frivolous, a duplication of another bill, or improper in form, it returned the bill to the sponsor. The committee didn't do this often, but, in 1929, it sent back forty-five bills, about 8 percent of the total. By that time, the committee was more commonly suggesting that a bill not be printed because, for example, it duplicated a Senate bill or could be handled as an amendment to another measure. In 1939, more than one-fifth of all House bills, 150 in number, received this recommendation, which saved the taxpayers a considerable sum. The House could override the Reference Committee's counsel by a majority vote, but that rarely happened. In most cases, the Reference Committee reported a bill to the House with a recommendation of referral to a subject-matter committee. Of course, the Reference Committee, itself appointed by the Speaker, could refer a bill to any committee to ensure friendly or less-than-friendly treatment. In 1929, the Reference Committee sent most labor bills to the Insurance Committee rather than the Labor Committee. The Insurance Committee "proved to be a death-house for labor legislation." Beginning in 1925, a standing committee that wanted to send a bill on to the full House for a vote first had to return it to the Reference Committee for review as to form and legal effect. The subject-matter committee could reject the Reference Committee's suggestions, but its report had to state that the suggestions had been considered or had not been received in time for the report. The Reference Committee generally worked as intended. Nearly two decades after its initial appearance, a political scientist concluded that the committee had "proved a positive force for economy and efficiency in the legislature."[25]

The Reference Committee wielded a powerful club known as the "pigeonhole veto." Rather than send a controversial bill to an unfriendly committee, it could refrain from referring the bill at all, in disregard of a longtime House rule, no longer extant, requiring a referral to be made within six or eight legislative days. An aggrieved representative protested in 1957 that the Reference Committee had sat on one of his bills for two months, despite repeated requests to have it referred to the Tax Committee, and then the Tax Committee had refused to hold a hearing on it even when the bill was on the committee agenda. On the other hand, sponsors occasionally asked that their bills be held. Sometimes a member didn't really care about a bill and wanted to be able to blame the awful Reference Committee for not getting it passed. In other cases, circumstances had changed since the bill was introduced or the political situation made passage unlikely.[26]

The Senate rules made no mention of a reference committee until 1971, when they alluded to a select committee of reference appointed, as were all select committees, by the president (then still the lieutenant governor) with the advice and consent of the president pro tempore. From then on, the Senate traveled a convoluted path toward centralization of the power of reference. Sometimes the rules explicitly created a reference committee. At other times, they simply assumed its existence. Sometimes the whole Senate, at other times the Senate president, appointed standing committees, including a reference committee. For a while, the Senate appointed standing committees but the president referred every bill himself in the absence of a motion to the contrary. In the twenty-first century, the Senate seems to have settled on a reference committee appointed, along with every other committee, by the president.[27]

Legislative leaders could effectively veto a bill at other stages besides reference. After a standing committee reported a bill, the measure went to the Rules Committee to be scheduled for consideration on the floor. There was no way to force the Rules Committee to put a bill on the calendar. In 1951, a disgruntled Senator Carl Sheppard complained that the Senate Rules Committee had indefinitely postponed one of his bills after the Judiciary Committee had conducted full hearings and recommended its passage. Sheppard argued that the rules of the Senate limited the Rules Committee to arranging the calendar and prescribing the order of business; they did not authorize the committee to usurp the functions of other committees and kill bills that had been favorably reported. To make matters worse, he said, the Rules Committee operated in secrecy, meeting behind closed doors and failing to keep records of its votes, again in violation of the rules. Another senator likened the Rules Committee to a politburo. But

Sheppard failed to force the Rules Committee to retract its action and to conduct its business in public. A member of the committee, calling the business interests behind Sheppard's bill a "selfish group" that had pushed the measure with unprecedented pressure, declared that the committee's "action served due notice to the well-financed lobby to call off their wolves." Years later, when the House Rules Committee bottled up a bill, the sponsor moved that the House convene as a committee of the whole to consider the measure. Calling a recess to consult the rules, Speaker Riffe and his majority floor leader discovered that a motion to adjourn took precedence, and they promptly brought the session to an end. The sponsor didn't try that tack again, Riffe recalled, "because he knew I wouldn't recognize him until I was sure he had dropped the issue."[28]

"Legislative morgue," "pigeonhole veto," and "politburo" hardly exhausted the epithets used to describe committees and their methods during the twentieth century. Even Robert Luce, the scholarly Massachusetts lawmaker who thought the criticisms overblown, conceded that the complaints often had merit. In the selection of committee members, he wrote in 1922, "[p]residing officers, ostensibly exercising initiative, may be really puppets, with strings pulled by a party leader." The proliferation of committees put legislators under tremendous time pressure and created conflicts, aggravating tardiness and absenteeism. "Invariably," said Luce, "a quorum is not present at the appointed hour." Limited notice provisions meant that the author of a bill "gets no chance to protect his offspring, at least in its infancy, unless he happens to be a member of the committee to whose mercies it is entrusted."[29]

Emmet O'Neal, the progressive-minded governor of Alabama, believed that the way committees operated contributed greatly to the lack of public confidence in legislatures. In 1914, he urged that all committee hearings be open to the public, that committee journals be kept to record who testified for or against a bill and how committee members voted, and that the common rule that only a two-thirds vote of the House or Senate could recall a bill from committee be amended so that committees could not thwart the will of the public.[30]

Some committee chairmen in Ohio conducted business openly and fairly. Judge Milton Clark, chairman of the Judiciary Committee in 1915, managed meetings as if they were judicial proceedings, with posted agendas, due notice to the authors of bills, and careful hearings. But Ohio's legislative leaders acknowledged the prevalence of problems. House Speakers, in their remarks upon being elected, sometimes adverted to the need for public committee hearings. They urged that committee rooms be open "for the fullest possible discussion from all interested parties" and that ordinary citizens receive the same courtesies as the representatives of great corporations. In 1931, Speaker Arthur Hamilton pointed out that the public's only opportunity to express its views on pending legislation was at committee hearings; it was therefore important that committees meet at regular, convenient times.[31]

The House rules adopted a few weeks later must have made Hamilton's remarks look disingenuous in retrospect. The rules of the previous General Assembly had required that "due notice" be given "to all committee meetings" and that they "be open to the public." As the *Ohio State Journal* reported, "'Star chamber' sessions were abolished in the Ohio Legislature in 1913 as an aftermath of the legislative bribery scandals of 1911 when several members of the General Assembly were sent to the penitentiary." The 1931 rule, however, called for notice of all committee *meetings*, while requiring that only committee *hearings* be public. House leaders had reportedly admitted to making the change deliberately so that a committee could clear the room after a hearing and conduct its deliberations in secret. In 1933, the House restored the old rule, but the all-important Rules Committee remained a de facto exception, meeting behind closed doors and keeping no records until the late twentieth century.[32]

The Senate went the other way, at least on paper. Its 1939 rules required committee meetings to be open *unless the committee voted to close them.* More than thirty years afterward, no one could recall when a Senate committee had ever closed a meeting, although, as late as 1991, Senate subcommittees seem to have done their key budget work in secret. House rules called for open meetings, without exception, until 1971. The issue of closed meetings arose in 1970 after a joint committee investigating campus riots met behind closed doors. The chairman of the House Rules Committee thought that college officials would have been more reticent in their testimony if they had been compelled to testify in public. Under the new rule adopted by the House in 1971, committee meetings had to be public unless the rules provided otherwise in accordance with the constitutional mandate that legislative proceedings "shall be public, except in cases which, in the opinion of two-thirds of those present, require secrecy." It is doubtful that a House committee ever invoked the rule. In 1993, the General Assembly put the question to rest with a statute requiring that all legislative committee and subcommittee meetings, except for certain meetings of the Joint Legislative Ethics Committee, be open to the public.[33]

House leaders of the early twentieth century repeatedly complained about the inefficiency of committees. One Speaker urged committees to consider and report the most important bills first "and not encumber our calendar at the start with an endless procession of bills of only local or minor interest." Others observed that the prompt attendance of committee members would speed up the work of committees and that quick committee action on bills would accelerate the work of the General Assembly as a whole. A Progressive-era Speaker demanded that the "vicious" practice of pigeonholing bills be abolished. Subsequent Speakers lauded the committee system as "the workable plan for a representative government" but acknowledged the need for committees to pay closer attention to both the form and substance of bills. One recommended that every committee include an expert on language and assign one member the task of checking bills against existing laws to avoid duplication and unintended consequences.[34]

Occasionally, rebels could force a change in the rules. In 1949, the united Republican minority in the House found enough Democratic allies to attack the power of committees to pigeonhole bills. Traditionally, the seldom-used motion to discharge a committee of further consideration—that is, to take a bill from a committee and bring it to the floor—could not be made until the committee had had the bill for thirty days, and then the motion required the signatures of a majority of the members elected to the House. During the Depression, the House used the discharge procedure to take from a committee a bill related to mortgage foreclosures. In 1949, the Republican and dissident Democratic representatives eliminated the thirty-day waiting period and allowed the motion to be made in the names of five representatives. The rule change attacked not only the power of committees but also the power of legislative leaders who sent measures they didn't like to the morgue. The amendment also allowed any five members to force their colleagues to take a stand on a bill they might prefer to ignore. It's hard to know how much difference the amendment made; a majority of all the members of the House was still needed to adopt the motion. In any case, the experiment proved short-lived. In the next General Assembly, the House reverted to the old rule.[35]

The number of standing committees trended downward in both houses for much of the twentieth century. House standing committees dropped from forty-five in 1911 to thirty-six in 1931 to twenty-two in 1951. The corresponding numbers for the Senate were thirty-nine, twenty-one, and eleven. In 1971, the House had thirteen standing committees and seven standing subcommittees; the

Senate had ten standing committees. But, in 1973, the General Assembly passed a law giving extra compensation to committee chairs, and the number of committees began to grow. Subsequent laws increased the bonuses substantially and provided additional pay for ranking minority members of committees and for subcommittee chairs as well. By 1985, the number of House committees had doubled. The Senate had more moderate increases, but, in 1995, the number reached fourteen. Riffe attributed the rise to the General Assembly's increased workload, but he conceded that all those chairmanships also strengthened his control over the members.[36]

After Riffe left office, another downward movement in committee numbers set in, unless one accounts for subcommittees. The General Assembly that took office in 2005 created nineteen standing committees and nine subcommittees in the House and fourteen standing committees in the Senate. In addition, there existed under statutory law a half dozen permanent joint legislative committees and a slew of commissions, boards, task forces, and similar entities on which legislators served.[37]

The size as well as the total number of committees affected the average number of committee assignments per member. In 1911, most House committees had 7 or 9 members, while Senate committees typically had 7. Twenty years later, House committees averaged 13 members, Senate committees 9. However, because the number of committees kept falling, the average number of committee assignments per member dropped too, from 8 or more in each house in 1911 to about 2.5 in the House and 3 in the Senate in 1951. Even the reapportionment revolution of the 1960s, which led to a reduction in the size of both chambers, did not reverse the trend. In 1971, the Senate's 10 standing committees each had 8 or 9 members, giving senators an average of 2.6 committee assignments. House committees were twice as large, but there were so few of them that the representatives averaged just 2.3 committee assignments apiece. When the number of committees started to go up again, so did the number of committees on which each member sat. By 1991, the average number of committee assignments for senators had gone from 2.6 to 3.6; for representatives, the number had nearly doubled to 4.5. Fifteen years later the Senate had the same number of committees, but because they had grown in size the senators were up to 4.4 committee places each. House committees got bigger too, but their number dropped from 27 to 19 so representatives had on average one fewer committee seat than the senators.

The committee of the whole largely disappeared from the General Assembly. In 1925, the House used it on the third reading of the general appropriations bill for what was then a rare floor debate on the budget and again during the Depression to consider a major tax program. But these were unusual events. A senator asserted in 1950 that the Senate still frequently debated legislation in the committee of the whole, but the journals do not reflect such usage. In many other states, a chamber sat as a committee of the whole to debate and consider amendments after the second reading of a bill. In Ohio, debate and amendment by the whole house took place on third reading, when the House or Senate acted as a "quasi committee of the whole" before putting a bill "on passage."[38]

The General Assembly continued to use special committees to conduct investigations, to study important legislative issues, or both. The Depression spawned an unusually high number of special committees. A sampling, just from 1935, includes joint committees to study the financing and needs of the public schools, to examine the administration of public relief in the state, and to inquire into the means of funding old-age pensions and poor relief; House committees to look into the use and abuse of state-owned vehicles by state employees and to consider the desirability of extending the life of the milk commission; and Senate committees to investigate the supply and cost of natural gas in Ohio and to study the operations of the Ohio securities laws. One reason for the creation of the Legislative Service Commission in 1953 was to provide for the in-depth study of issues facing the legislature without the appointment of so many special committees and commissions.[39]

In 1919, the General Assembly established a joint committee on German propaganda to investigate evidence of disloyalty in Ohio and to recommend legislation "whereby our institutions and laws may become thoroughly American." This action presaged a new departure for the legislature, for it was prompted not by a particular incident or issue but by a conglomeration of political, social, and security concerns that coalesced into a general fear of un-American ideas and that could not be resolved by a single resolution or act of the General Assembly. Although the committee did not do much investigating—the legislature soon transformed it into the Joint Americanization Committee, with a focus on patriotic education—the idea of probing disloyalty and the propagation of un-American doctrines would return with force thirty years later. In the meantime, the Americanization Committee expired in 1923 and anxiety about dangerous foreign influences waned. Indeed, as World War I and the postwar "red scare" receded in time, the General Assembly took a more pacific turn. It accepted the offer of the women's auxiliary of the Grand Army of the Republic, an organization of Civil War veterans, to erect a peace memorial on the statehouse grounds, and it asked the U.S. Senate to ratify the Kellogg-Briand Pact, which renounced war as a means of solving international disputes. In 1925, the Ohio Senate urged its federal counterpart to approve American participation in the Permanent Court of International Justice; eight years later, the General Assembly recommended that the U.S. Senate ratify the treaties that would make such participation possible.[40]

By 1939, though, with the world teetering on the brink of war and with fascism and communism threatening to destroy democracy, the xenophobia had revived. Declaring that "in this country anti-American forces are striving to discredit the ideals and institutions symbolized by the American flag," the House and Senate separately endorsed a national plan for a "patriotic revival" and the celebration of flag week. Senator Robert Pollock offered a resolution to invite the Dies Committee of the U.S. House of Representatives, then investigating communist influence in America, to visit Ohio. That resolution did not get far, but another of Pollock's proposals, to establish a committee to investigate the alleged teaching of un-American doctrines at the Ohio State University and in the public schools, caused a stir in the Senate. Senator Horace Kiefer denounced it as a threat to freedom of speech, and newspapers derided the proposed "red hunt." The Senate first adopted the resolution, then reconsidered and referred it to the Military Affairs Committee. Kiefer and a number of other senators who had voted against the resolution sat on that committee. After a few days' fuss, Pollock withdrew his proposal.[41]

During World War II, the United States allied itself with the Soviet Union, the world's sole communist power, to fight a common enemy, but, after the war, Americans worried again about the spread of an ideology that threatened American security and values. For a few years, the concern in Ohio remained muted. In 1945, the House asked the superintendent of public instruction to look into the teaching of un-American theories of government (that is, socialism) in the public schools, and four years later the General Assembly required recipients of unemployment compensation to take a loyalty oath. In the interim, though, only a few anticommunist measures were proposed and they all failed. Then, in 1950, U.S. Senator Joseph McCarthy of Wisconsin launched his anticommunist crusade; the *Cincinnati Enquirer* published a multipart exposé of communist influence in the Cincinnati area; the House Un-American Activities Committee (HUAC), successor to the Dies Committee, visited Ohio; and communist North Korea invaded South Korea, bringing the United States into armed conflict with communist forces. The anticommunist fever rose. Ohio's lawmakers responded with a number of anticommunist measures, including one that required the dismissal of any public employee or teacher affiliated with any communist or other subversive organization and another that made a public employee's refusal to testify about his or her affiliations prima facie evidence of an illegal affiliation. Even so, the legislature rejected other anticommunist proposals and those that got enacted were not enforced.[42]

The legislature's most significant anticommunist measure was the creation of the Ohio Un-American Activities Commission (OUAC). In March 1951, the General Assembly, concerned about revelations in the HUAC hearings of communist activity in Ohio, set up a joint antisubversive investigating committee to determine whether communist influence was pervasive enough to require a more substantial investigative body. The committee recommended the establishment of an entity modeled on HUAC, and the lawmakers obliged. Passed over the unanimous opposition of Democratic legislators but signed by Democratic governor Frank Lausche, the law created the OUAC and gave it two years to conduct its investigations and report back to the General Assembly. (Its name notwithstanding, the commission was actually a joint legislative committee.) Democratic opposition to the commission crumbled in 1953, when the General Assembly extended the commission's life to January 31, 1954. The commission held hearings throughout the state in 1952 and 1953, calling witnesses suspected of being or consorting with communists, probing their political associations, and citing for contempt forty-two individuals who refused to answer questions in reliance on the Fifth Amendment's privilege against self-incrimination. A conviction for contempt carried a maximum penalty of ten days in jail and a $500 fine on each count. The U.S. Supreme Court overturned several convictions, but some defendants ended up with jail terms and fines and a few lost their jobs. By the end of 1953, public interest in the commission's hearings had waned. The General Assembly, over Lausche's veto, outlawed membership in subversive organizations, but prosecutions seem to have been rare. McCarthy's disgrace in the famous Army-McCarthy hearings in Congress in 1954, when the Ohio legislature did not meet, took some steam out of the national anticommunist campaign. The new General Assembly that convened in 1955, almost a year after the OUAC wound up business and turned its files over to the state attorney general, showed no inclination to revive the commission.[43]

The General Assembly created another wide-ranging investigatory committee in the wake of the Kent State tragedy of 1970. In the 1960s, demonstrations and riots over civil rights, the Vietnam War, governance in higher education, and sometimes over nothing more than youthful exuberance enhanced by alcohol swept across cities and campuses throughout the country. On July 4, 1965, thousands of young people, many of them college students, got carried away with their holiday celebrations in the resort towns of Russells Point and Geneva-on-the-Lake. Local police could not handle the rioters, and Governor Rhodes sent in the National Guard. Although the riots did not stem directly from political protests or complaints about the universities, the General Assembly's reaction foreshadowed future responses to campus unrest. On July 8, two members introduced a bill to increase the jail time for riot and unlawful assembly from a maximum of thirty days to a minimum of thirty days and a maximum of one year. The bill passed easily.[44]

The General Assembly had already adjourned when a year later a riot erupted in Cleveland's predominantly black Hough neighborhood. A grand jury investigating the causes of the riot recommended passage of a broader riot law that would, among other things, prohibit incitement to riot, enhance the penalty for rioting, and create a separate crime of assaulting police officers or firefighters who were acting in their official capacities. When the next General Assembly met in 1967, it duly passed the recommended legislation. The lawmakers were in recess later that year when hundreds of Ohio State students demonstrated in support of striking university employees. In the wee hours of the morning, the students dumped garbage into the street, set the trash on fire, and fought with police. As soon as the General Assembly came back into session, Senators Robert Stockdale and Oliver Ocasek introduced a bill to require the trustees of state universities to maintain order on campus and to adopt codes of conduct for students, faculty, and staff. The bill also authorized university administrators to call in police agencies to help enforce the regulations. It passed with broad bipartisan support.[45]

In May 1970, student demonstrations reached a dramatic and dreadful climax with the killing of four students by members of the Ohio National Guard during an antiwar protest on the Kent State University campus. Lawmakers quickly responded with a flurry of bills and resolutions, most of them aimed at punishing participants in commotions on university grounds. The General Assembly passed a law that prohibited disruptive conduct on campuses and provided for the suspension or dismissal of university students and employees who engaged in such conduct. At least nineteen other proposed measures, most of them punitive in nature, were referred to a new joint investigative committee on campus disturbances.[46]

After holding hearings around Ohio during the summer, the committee found in its first report in October that "[w]hile pollution, poverty, women's rights, racism, the Southeast Asian war, and other issues of national and international prominence are sources of deep and legitimate concern to students," issues "peculiar to academic communities" were more closely related to campus unrest. The committee maintained that the chief responsibility for addressing these problems rested with university authorities and not with the legislature, but, noting that the conduct of the State Highway Patrol in response to campus disturbances had received "almost universally favorable comment," the committee recommended that the patrol's size and jurisdiction be immediately expanded.[47]

Notwithstanding its initial reluctance to suggest legislative action, the committee, after revisiting state university campuses and hearing from administrators, professors, students, law enforcement agencies, judges, and others, issued another report with forty-nine recommendations, many of them calling for legislation dealing with everything from faculty teaching loads and the construction of dormitories to trespass and conspiracy. Many of the legislative proposals would have strengthened the supervision of the Ohio Board of Regents over state universities; however, few of the committee's suggestions concerning the board were introduced in the General Assembly, let alone enacted. Whether anyone heeded the committee's recommendations for modifications of the criminal law is hard to say. Other committees had been hard at work revising the criminal code for years. In March 1971, the technical committee to study Ohio's criminal laws issued its final report. The proposed criminal code included some ideas put forth by the committee on campus disturbances, such as a broader criminal trespass statute and a requirement that someone with knowledge that a felony had been or was about to be committed report it to the proper authorities. However, the technical committee had been considering some of these propositions since 1968 before the Kent State shootings. In 1971, the legislature passed a law allowing the Highway Patrol to assist county sheriffs and city police chiefs in controlling civil disorders off state property, but this idea had had strong support for years and might have become law even without the committee's urging. Although the General Assembly no doubt created the committee on campus disturbances in good faith and the members worked hard to gather information, analyze the issues, and make recommendations, the committee's main accomplishment may have been to mollify public opinion by giving the appearance that the legislature was doing something. Given the temper of the times, this may have been achievement enough.[48]

The large number of standing committees in the first half of the twentieth century caused scheduling headaches. In a typical year, the full House might convene at 1:30 P.M. on Tuesdays, Wednesdays, and Thursdays, at 9:00 A.M. on Fridays, and, beginning in 1931, on Monday evenings as well. Committees had to work around that schedule. Given the haphazard nature of committee hearings in those days, it is possible that no one established fixed meeting times for committees. Committees may simply have met at the call of the chair, as in the Senate, whenever and wherever the chair felt the need and could secure a room. The House eventually appointed a committee on room assignments to set a fixed time and place for each committee to meet. In 1931, it scheduled regular committee meetings for every evening Monday through Thursday and for Tuesday, Wednesday, and Thursday mornings. A few years later, it dropped Monday and Thursday evenings from the committee schedule, perhaps to save members the cost of two nights' lodging. (There were still those full Monday night sessions, but many members skipped them.) Some committees had only one regular time slot per week; most had two, in the morning one day and the evening another. Morning committees normally had an hour and a half to take care of business. The room assignment committee urged committees to stick to their schedules to avoid conflicts. Committee chairs sometimes added to the confusion by calling special meetings. The Senate had to admonish committee chairs to follow posted schedules "to the letter" and not to call special meetings without consulting first with the other chairs.[49]

At midcentury, the full House had regular daily sessions scheduled on Monday evenings, Tuesday and Wednesday afternoons, and Thursday and Friday mornings. Committees met around that schedule, from Tuesday mornings to Thursday mornings. To squeeze in the forty-five committees of 1911 would have been impossible; with about half that number in 1951, the House made do. In the 1970s, the General Assembly went to a three-day session week, with leaders adding or canceling session days as appropriate. Thereafter, most committees met around floor sessions Tuesdays through Thursdays, usually during the day. For a half century after 1943, when the Senate started publishing its committee schedule in the

A House committee meeting in the late 1960s. *Courtesy of the Ohio House of Representatives*

Senate roster, four committees typically scheduled regular evening meetings. In 1991, that number fell to one, and in 2001 to zero. Night meetings did not entirely disappear. Some committees met after session, so a long session could mean an evening committee. In the budget year of a biennium, the finance committees and subcommittees might meet at night for several weeks. And all committees were subject to the call of the chair, outside the normally scheduled time.[50]

Notwithstanding efforts to avoid conflicts, members often found two of their committees meeting simultaneously. A large number of witnesses or extended discussion might cause a hearing to run long or be recessed to an unscheduled hour and thereby bump into another committee's time. For most of the twentieth century, the rules required the members of a committee to be physically present to vote on a matter before the committee, but, by 1953, some chairmen were permitting committee members who had missed a meeting to vote up to two weeks later. In 1971, the House rules formally allowed chairs to keep the roll open for a time so that a member who had to leave the meeting temporarily could vote later on. The Senate adopted a similar rule in 1981. The practice of "checking in"—popping into the meeting room to let the chair know you weren't

The Second Century

A Senate committee meeting in 1985. *Courtesy of the* Columbus Dispatch *Archives*

AWOL and then attending to other business elsewhere—allowed committee members not only to vote on a bill when they had not been present for pertinent testimony but also to be counted in the committee quorum. As long as a quorum had checked in, the committee chair could conduct a hearing all by himself.[51]

There were always committees that met rarely and handled little business. The members of the Eighty-third General Assembly (1919–20) introduced more than one thousand bills and joint resolutions. Of the eighty-three standing committees in that legislature, thirty-seven considered five or fewer measures. In 1929, the Senate referred 115 bills to one committee, two to another. Of the 725 or so bills and resolutions referred to House committees in the 125th General Assembly (2003–4), about one-third went to just three committees. Even accounting for the fact that some committees do not deal primarily with the substance of legislation, and that many measures have little importance, the figures show that not all committees are created equal.[52]

For a good part of the twentieth century, the mere existence of a time slot for a committee did not mean that interested parties, including a bill's sponsor, would know exactly when a bill would be considered. The joint rules continued

The committee board outside the bill room on the second floor of the statehouse shows the House committee schedule for the week of November 11, 1984. *Courtesy of the Ohio Legislative Service Commission*

to require that the author of a bill be given notice of a time and place when he could be heard only in case of an objection or material amendment to the bill. By the 1930s, however, committee procedure had improved dramatically over its scandalous state at the beginning of the century. House rules prohibited voting by proxy or by a member who was not present while the committee was in session. A House committee member could not sign a committee report unless he or she was there when the reported action was taken. House committees had to post due notice of their hearings—by midcentury, committee schedules had to be "publicly announced on the House bulletin board and in the printed calendar"—and both the House and the Senate required that committees conduct their hearings openly and keep records of their proceedings. Despite the practice of checking in, a necessary evil that diluted some of the improvements, the committee process had taken great strides since the days of "snap" hearings held behind closed doors.[53]

Still, the committee system stood in need of improvement. Studies conducted between 1966 and 1971 observed that "[t]he work of the standing committees is the heart of the legislative process" and asserted that a "legislature . . . cannot function smoothly without an operative committee system." But the standing committees in many states performed poorly. They were too numerous; they were "strapped for space, time, and staff"; they couldn't get quorums; they did not record their proceedings. Ohio's standing committees suffered chiefly from inadequate staffing. As of 1966, they lacked even secretarial help; only the finance committees could count on technical assistance, and then only occasionally.[54]

The next year, the Legislative Service Commission started to assign staff members to standing committees, a development that legislators generally welcomed. Staff members were nonpartisan and not answerable to the committee chairs. Typically, they stayed out of committee debate and avoided any commitment to a position on the legislation under discussion. They prepared analyses of the bills and discussed potential problems with sponsors or committee chairs. For the most part, legislators expressed satisfaction with the new program. The chief objections came from professional lobbyists, who perhaps resented the intrusion of a rival, independent source of legislative expertise into the committee system.[55]

In 1971, the Citizens Conference on State Legislatures could report that Ohio's committee system was in fairly good shape, but the conference still found staffing to be short of ideal, particularly with regard to fiscal matters. In 1977, the General Assembly directed the Legislative Budget Office to provide standing committees with a fiscal analysis of every bill that seemed likely to affect the revenues or expenditures of any governmental entity, but the analysts themselves did not regularly attend the meetings of committees, other than the Finance Committee, until 1995.[56]

The dearth of official records and memoirs makes it impossible to know what actually went on during committee meetings in the first half of the twentieth century. Under the practice that has prevailed at least since the 1970s, a serious bill—one that the sponsor really wants and that is not ridiculous on its face— gets two, three, or more hearings if it is sponsored by a member of the majority party. In 1995, after regaining control of the House for the first time in twenty-two years, Republicans changed the rules to require that every bill introduced by May 15 of the second year of the biennium get at least one hearing. Bills lacking a majority-member sponsor often drift into oblivion thereafter. Even a majority-member bill may not get more than one hearing because the sponsor introduced it only to satisfy a constituent, or another bill addresses the same subject, or the party leaders are upset with the sponsor, or for any number of other reasons.[57]

MUPPET SHOW SONG

One of the hit movies of 1979 was the Muppet Movie. Some of the members of the General
Assembly are such ø Muppet fans that one committee/heard, just before one of its meetings
this year, singing a song to the tune of the familiar opening number from the Muppet Show.
Fortunately the LSC staffer was there to hear it and has persuaded the committee to come sing
it for us tonight.

(Verses are to the tune of "It's time to play the music,/ It's time to
light the lights"; "solos" are to the tune of "To introduce Miss Piggy,
that's what I'm here to do.")

verse 1. It's time to start the meeting,
          "   "   " settle down;
          "   "   " bang the gavel on the greatest show in town.

verse 2. It's time to light up stogies,
          And fill the room with smoke;
          We do a lot of talking, and fresh air hurts our throats.

solo 1.   Our LSC staff people
          Have little else to do,
          So we feel free to call on them to act as pages, too.

verse 3. It's time to make some speeches,
          It's time to use clichés;
          It's time for resolutions in support of Woody Hayes.

verse 4. It's time to find a quorum,
          We need five more to start;
          It's time to send some pages over to the Neil House bar.

solo 2.   We'd like to pose a question
          To our friend from LSC:
          Why do all your analyses start out ⎡pause⎤ "Would you believe ....?"

verse 5. It's time to stop this singing,
          It's time to call the roll;
          It's time to get things ø started on the most orational, informational,
                          legislational, no-taxational ... xxix welcome to
                          tonight's committee show!

Typically, at a first hearing, the sponsor describes the bill to the committee, explains its purpose, and fields some general, frequently innocuous questions. Subsequent hearings give proponents and opponents the chance to testify. The witnesses may include lobbyists, legislative liaisons from state agencies, representatives of business or nonprofit organizations, or other interested parties. Controversial bills may get further hearings, with proponents and opponents appearing again and perhaps facing tough but generally civil questioning. Along the way, committee members may offer amendments and the chair may direct the Legislative Service Commission employee who staffs the committee to draft a substitute bill. When the committee chair decides that it's time to close discussion and vote on the bill—chairs have been known to hold bills without putting them to a vote as a bargaining ploy or in a fit of pique—he or she places the bill on the committee's agenda with the notation that a vote will be had. If at that meeting a majority of the committee votes in favor of the bill, the bill is reported out—that is, the chair's office sends it to the House or Senate clerk with a report of the vote recommending passage.

What the committee members ordinarily do not do directly is write any portion of the bill. Before the rise of professional bill-drafting services, Ohio's committee practice may have been more like that of Vermont, which in the twenty-first century still has a citizen legislature, with little in the way of staff services. Ralph G. Wright, who entered the Vermont legislature in 1979, recalled that he "learned a ton about the nuts and bolts of the process" in his first year of committee work. "Marking up bills, referencing them to the present statute, amending them, totally rewriting them (called 'strike-alls'), became second nature." Committees in Ohio perhaps engaged in this type of work before the Legislative Service Commission assigned staff members to each committee. A representative in the 1950s later recalled that she had enjoyed serving on subcommittees because she "liked playing around with the phrasing of bills that weren't clear and trying to resolve differences," but for at least the last several decades, committees have generally left the drafting to the professional staff.[58]

Be It Resolved

The professional staff drafts resolutions too. The rules have never had much to say about them, but traditionally resolutions came in two forms, simple and joint. The House or Senate would use simple resolutions to address matters that concerned only itself, from the hiring of a page to the appointment of an investigating committee to the expression of its sentiments on international affairs. The General Assembly used joint resolutions when the joint action of the two houses was desired: to set a date for adjournment, to instruct Ohio's U.S. senators, to put a constitutional amendment on the ballot.

In the 1920s, a new type of resolution cropped up. In Congress, a distinction had long been recognized between joint resolutions, which went to the president for signature and had the force of law, and concurrent resolutions, which simply expressed congressional opinions or wishes. Ohio had no need for concurrent resolutions—there was nothing the General Assembly could accomplish with a concurrent resolution that it couldn't get done with the traditional joint resolution—but they began to appear anyway. For decades afterward, there was no rhyme or reason to the choice of a concurrent or joint resolution. Eventually, joint resolutions, which must be filed with the secretary of state, came to be used primarily for the proposal of amendments to the Ohio constitution and concurrent resolutions for just about everything else.

Also in the 1920s, members found a new use for simple resolutions and sometimes for joint and concurrent resolutions as well. Both the House and the Senate had customarily adopted resolutions mourning the death of a member, expressing hope for a recovery from illness, sympathizing with the family of a deceased public official, or thanking a member or legislative employee for a job well done. In 1925, if not sooner, some members got the idea of using resolutions to recognize individuals or organizations, usually constituents, for various accomplishments. In one early example, the House and Senate both commended the Gospel Trumpet Company of Indiana for making Sunday school literature available to the blind for free. Before long, the members were introducing resolutions to honor the winners of spelling bees and pie-baking contests and to commemorate village centennials and wedding anniversaries. In the first month of the 1951 session alone, the House adopted resolutions saluting the Miami University football team (for winning the Salad Bowl), the Cleveland Browns (for capturing the National Football League championship), the Ohio Mother of the Year, the state tomato-growing champion, high school football and basketball champions, the winner of a national get-out-the-vote contest, and the Sandusky County Fair. Members also took to recognizing constituents in letters signed by the Speaker of the House or president of the Senate. These letters served the same purpose as resolutions but did not require formal introduction and adoption. The number of commendatory resolutions grew so large that in 1977 the clerks stopped indexing them in the journals. In the late 1990s, when the volume of resolutions approached 4,000 one year and the number of letters neared 50,000 in another, the two houses established guidelines for their use. No longer would the runner-up in the Soap Box Derby or the new general manager of a radio station qualify for a congratulatory resolution. In 2006, members' requests for resolutions and letters totaled a mere 260 and 28,341, respectively.[59]

17

THE TRANSFORMATION

OF LEGISLATIVE LIFE

I N 1979, REPRESENTATIVE DONNA POPE wrote that being a member of
the General Assembly "takes my *full*-time. Because of the legislative schedule—session, committees, sub-committees, etc., etc., it is difficult for me to imag-
ine someone having time to spend at another job and still do a good 'legislative/
representative' job." Pope must have thought that anyone who put in so many
hours of work ought to be recognized as a full-timer and paid accordingly; in 1981,
she resigned to become the director of the U.S. Mint.[1]

From Part-Time to Full-Time

By Pope's day, state senators and representatives had gone from being part-time
citizen-legislators to full-time professional lawmakers. In the first half of the
twentieth century, the General Assembly met for regular sessions every other
year, although special sessions became common during the Great Depression and
remained so for another thirty years. Until the 1940s, regular sessions rarely lasted

past May, and the members generally took a break of a week or two before the last day. Even during the extended special sessions of the 1930s, there were long periods when committees and leaders may have been active but the General Assembly as a whole did not meet.

Before 1950, many members had little or no prior experience in the General Assembly. In 1900, two-thirds of the members had never been in the legislature and another quarter had served just one term. Forty years later, after a trend toward careerism had set in, three-fifths of the members still had no more than a single term behind them. A student of state legislatures commented in 1918 that most legislators were easily led, often by blind leaders. Many knew little of the issues they would confront, as the zealous reformer Frederic C. Howe learned to his dismay. Newly elected to the Ohio Senate, in 1906, Howe called together his fellow Democratic senators-elect for a presession caucus. He found that hardly anyone had read the party platform or cared about legislation. They were mostly older men—"insurance agents, real-estate men, farmers"—who had come to Columbus for a good time. "They did not want to be bothered about ideals," Howe recalled. "They would get their orders from the county committee, the court-house crowd, whom they did not wish to offend. What they wanted was their share in the patronage—an insignificant job as a stenographer, assistant clerk, or messenger for a relative or friend." Around the same time, the Speaker of the House felt compelled to remind his colleagues that "[w]e are not here for pleasure, neither should this hall be used to be the headquarters for pleasure trips throughout the state."[2]

Even at midcentury, the legislature was "often a playpen for members who had little interest in the job but looked forward to higher office or simply a frolic in Columbus at the expense of a lobby." For those who took their job seriously, however, being a legislator could be confusing and time-consuming. A political scientist and former legislative employee described the dilemmas of the neophyte legislator. Candidates have offered themselves for leadership positions. Rumors of deals are floated. With some patronage at his disposal, he secures the position of doorkeeper for a constituent, only to find that the fellow wanted to be sergeant at arms. He is importuned for legislation, and bills pour in—far more than he can read. Two weeks into the session, he is spending all his energy on the "inner-politics of the legislature" rather than on the measures he had naively hoped to advance. "Constituents, lobbyists, committee members of the House, committee members of the Senate, more lobbyists, a conference with the Governor, a matter of patronage, engross his attention." As the end of the long session approaches, the members are talking of limiting debate and of meeting on Monday mornings and Saturdays, and bills are jammed through in flawed form. Adjournment sine die comes as a great relief.[3]

In the 1940s, regular sessions started stretching into the summer. In 1963, the General Assembly sat until August and reconvened in the late fall. In 1967, the legislators stayed in session into September and then met again from January through March of 1968. That marked the end of the true biennial session. A statute in 1968 and a constitutional amendment in 1973 did away with the fiction of the biennial session and mandated instead two regular sessions. Before long, the General Assembly was formally staying in session until December of the second year.[4]

The actual number of session days probably did not increase with the duration of sessions. It may even have decreased as cancellation of scheduled session days and long breaks for holidays and campaigning became common. And frequently the House and Senate held "skeleton" sessions at which no one but the clerk, presiding officer, and a single other member appeared. Some business might take place at these skeleton sessions; the House and Senate adopted many congratulatory resolutions on the aye of the sole member present on the theory that no one would object. Skeleton session got the leaders of the two chambers around the constitutional rule that neither house could adjourn for more than five days (raised from two in 1973) without the consent of the other. But a cynic might say that the real reason for skeleton sessions was the federal law, enacted in 1976, that gave a valuable tax deduction for living expenses to state legislators who lived more than fifty miles from the capital, regardless of whether they were actually in the capital on a given "legislative" day (including days of skeleton sessions and up to four consecutive nonsession days).[5]

When regular sessions went deep into summer, special sessions—productive ones, anyway—virtually vanished. A long special session called in November 1964 by Governor Rhodes resulted in dozens of laws and three constitutional amendments. The five special sessions of the 1970s, including the first called by the presiding officers of the General Assembly under a constitutional amendment allowing them to convene special sessions, produced just one minor statute. The Speaker and Senate president called another special session in 1985, in the midst of the regular session, to deal with the imminent collapse of Ohio's savings and loans associations. The session featured Vern Riffe's first speech from the floor since becoming Speaker twelve years earlier, but it just failed to produce legislation to deal with the crisis after a senator asked to be excused from voting because of a possible conflict of interest. That was the last special session for nearly two decades.[6]

The lengthening of sessions helped turn the legislator's job into a full-time occupation. There had always been lawmakers who worked beyond the date of adjournment by campaigning, assisting constituents, or serving on interim committees. The amount of logrolling that went on between sessions astonished one fledgling representative in the 1880s. In 1925, Robert Taft, Speaker pro tempore of the House, spent most of the week in Columbus during session, working late into the evening and complaining that he couldn't keep up with his law practice. But most members in Taft's day had plenty of time for other jobs. A half century later almost everyone found that the business of legislating ate up enormous amounts of time. Donna Pope observed that the General Assembly had met for 188 days in 20 months during the preceding biennium and that much of her work, including committee meetings, took place in the evenings and on nonsession days.[7]

Constituent services could take up as much time as daily sessions and committee meetings. Legislators had to stay in touch with the folks back home, whether by letter, telegraph, telephone, or e-mail. In 1945, state representative and future U.S. senator Howard Metzenbaum produced the first member's "informational service," a mimeographed newsletter that he mailed to his constituents. But constituent work involved more than keeping the voters informed of goings-on in the capital. It meant listening and responding to ideas, opinions, and complaints about legislation, often at meetings in the member's district. It also meant handling individual cases. A member might help constituents track down information, frequently on matters unrelated to lawmaking, or "act as an intermediary or liaison between state agencies and constituents." For example, wrote one senator in his hometown newspaper, "[i]f . . . you are dealing with the Ohio Bureau of Workers' Compensation, we can do a number of things to help. We can find out the status of your appeal, find alternative programs you may qualify for, check on the status of a claim or rebate, report and attempt to resolve mistakes in rates and find out why you have been denied." These types of constituent services, possibly more important to reelection than votes on bills, drew heavily on a legislator's time, energy, and equanimity.[8]

In 1999, the *Cincinnati Post* still called the General Assembly a "part-time legislature," but even legislators who thought the job should be part-time were actually putting in full-time hours. As early as 1974, a graduate student in public administration concluded from interviews with members that "the conscientious Ohio legislator" was spending forty hours or more per week on legislative business, even if he or she held another full-time job. In 2003, a national survey asked state legislators how much time they devoted to their legislative labors, including constituent service, campaigns, and work between as well as during sessions. In Ohio and eight other states, the lawmakers reported spending the equivalent of 80–100 percent of a full-time job on their legislative duties. In another study, 39 percent of Ohio lawmakers described themselves as full-time legislators. Eighty-nine percent reported that during session they put in 40 or more hours per week and 25 percent reported more than 60 hours per week. Even when the legislature was not in session, 71 percent of the members spent at least 25 hours per week and 43 percent at least 35 hours per week on legislative and political matters. The demands of the job could put a strain on marriages as well as pocketbooks. One member's husband told a reporter, "I resent that emotionally, intellectually, physically she is exhausted when she gets home. I'll be at home, waiting for her, fixing dinner, and she'll come in the door and say, 'I'm too exhausted, don't talk,' and she'll go right upstairs."[9]

Compensation

Even though lawmaking had become a full-time occupation by the end of the twentieth century, term limits encouraged members to hold other jobs so they would not be scrambling for income when their legislative careers ended. In 2004, more than two-fifths of the legislators had outside work that produced income of $10,000 or more. One claimed that lawmakers practically needed a second job just to pay travel expenses. In truth, for most of the twentieth century the members' compensation remained more suitable for part-timers than for full-timers. In 1906, the lawmakers raised their annual pay from $600 to $1,000, but some griped that it still wasn't enough. When the 1911 session ran into May, Senator H. L. Yount declared, "If it keeps up much longer I shall be in the poorhouse. Every day I am here I am losing money." The legislator's salary, said Yount, just paid his living expenses, while, for many members, the cost of nomination and election was "no little sum of money." No wonder, then, that some members were tempted by bribes. A few years later, a representative introduced a poetic

The Second Century

resolution urging a committee to act quickly on an appropriations bill because the members were going broke.[10]

The members kept their annual salary at $1,000 for three decades until, at the trough of the Great Depression, they doubled their compensation. The increase came only after the members had cut their salaries, along with those of other state workers, and then found they couldn't afford to stay in Columbus for the protracted Depression-era sessions. They tried paying themselves four dollars per day for living expenses during a special session, but the supreme court struck down that plan as a violation of the constitutional requirement that members receive a "fixed" compensation. The people must have understood the legislators' dilemma, for the 100 percent salary increase that followed does not seem to have raised an outcry.[11]

The supreme court's ruling cast doubt on the legality of the mileage allowance too, but in a strained decision a few years later, an appellate court upheld it. When Columbus hotels raised their rates by as much as two dollars a day before the 1951 session, a representative predicted that the action would cost the taxpayers money because legislators could not afford such "exorbitant" rates on their salaries at the time. In fact, the General Assembly soon raised the members' pay to $3,200, a middling amount in comparison with legislative salaries in other states but probably not enough. One member called it "trifling." The members helped themselves somewhat by doubling their travel allowance to ten cents per mile for a weekly trip home during session, but, for members who paid eight or ten dollars a day just for lodging, the lack of a living allowance could be a serious burden and an inducement to befriend lobbyists who picked up hotel tabs. The lawmakers boosted their salary as of 1957 to a more respectable $5,000 per year, about the same as the average annual wages of manufacturing employees and miners, but less than federal civilian workers and much less than the typical doctor or lawyer.[12]

Not everyone agreed that the members deserved their compensation. In 1959, the *Columbus Citizen* grumbled that the members were "skimping their jobs. They get $5000 a year, or $10,000 for the two-year term, plus generous travel allowances. They meet once every two years, so their pay averages $400 to $500 for every week they're in session." And just what did their work week consist of? "They meet late Monday, hold session Tuesday and Wednesday, go home again Thursday noon. Two full days a week!"[13]

As in the past, the members hurt their case for increased pay by absenting themselves from work. Many skipped extraordinary Friday sessions. Some cut even the normal week short on both ends, getting to the capital on Tuesday and leaving Wednesday evening. The problem got so bad in the 1940s that legislative leaders threatened to dock the pay of absentees, but few took the threats seriously because that sanction had rarely if ever been imposed. Some absences in that decade were unavoidable. In 1944, seven representatives, including the Speaker, minority floor leader, and majority whip, were in military service at the same time. Few if any absentees in the 1960s and 1970s had that excuse. A Columbus paper noted in 1965 that both chambers were "liberally sprinkled with empty seats" during Monday night and Thursday morning sessions, with anywhere from seven to twenty-four of the 137 House members missing at those times. Republicans and Democrats seemed equally likely to be AWOL. (After the story appeared, a senator with a good attendance record who happened to be out the day the paper counted heads "expressed his unhappiness in an oratorical style best described as colorful.") But at least the General Assembly no longer suffered from lack of a quorum, as it often did in the late nineteenth century. By 1980, even members near the bottom of the attendance ranking showed up for more than 70 percent of the voting sessions.[14]

Slackers skipped committee meetings as well as sessions. In the 1950s, a senator griped that his colleagues' indifference to committee duties slowed down the legislative process, and the president pro tempore of the Senate, to ensure that the committee hearing one of his bills would have a quorum, had to dust off a little-used rule that made him a voting member of all committees. The large number of committees at that time didn't help; a senator could not be in two places at once. But absenteeism remained a problem even as the number of committees dwindled. In 1991, according to a study by the *Lancaster Eagle-Gazette*, committee attendance stood at 81.4 percent for senators and 86.1 percent for representatives. Those were not awful numbers overall, but members with the poorest records attended fewer than 60 percent of their committee meetings. The statistics overstated actual attendance because the rules allowed committee members to check in, be counted, and vote later, even though they were not physically present for part or all of the meeting. Members legitimately blamed scheduling conflicts and the burden of constituent work for their absences, but one disdainfully dismissed committee work as a waste of time. Some other legislators conceded that the important decisions were made in caucus or leadership meetings, but most regarded committee work as crucial. One member, E. J. Thomas, in response to another survey of committee absenteeism in 1991, pointed out that he had been

Marine reservist Josh Mandel on duty in Iraq's Anbar Province in 2004. After his election to the General Assembly in 2006, Mandel went back to Iraq for a second tour of duty. *Courtesy of Josh Mandel*

on military duty in the Persian Gulf for the first three months of the year. (At least four other sitting lawmakers, John Boccieri, Steve Stivers, Josh Mandel, and Danny Bubp, would serve in Iraq in the twenty-first century.) Thomas aside, the *Eagle-Gazette* decried committee absenteeism as an insult to citizens who took the time, trouble, and expense to travel to Columbus to testify and as a circumvention of the democratic process.[15]

Notwithstanding complaints about absenteeism and short work weeks, the legislators gave themselves frequent, sometimes hefty pay increases beginning in 1964. By the late 1970s, their annual salary, not counting the extra compensation given to leaders, was $22,500, supplemented by a travel allowance of twenty cents per mile. Ohio's salaries ranked among the highest in the country. (Again, though, the lack of an allowance for living expenses should be taken into account. By one estimate, a legislator's cost of living in Columbus for the 1972 session was $5,000, more than one-third of the yearly pay.) Another big boost in

1984 brought salaries to $30,152. Despite the high rate of inflation in those years, the raises increased the members' purchasing power. To keep up with inflation, the lawmakers gave themselves annual 5 percent raises from 1986 through 1992. In 2000, after eight years of flat salaries eroded the real value of their compensation, they set their base salary at $51,674 per year with annual increases based on the consumer price index, up to 3 percent per year, through 2008. Extra stipends for legislative leaders of both parties and for committee chairs, vice chairs, subcommittee chairs, and ranking minority members added anywhere from $5,000 to nearly $29,000 for many members.[16]

Statutes giving additional pay to leaders recognized the leadership structure that had developed since 1900. The evolution of leadership positions in Ohio probably followed the federal pattern. In the nineteenth-century U.S. House of Representatives, the chairman of a key committee, who might have been the Speaker's chief rival for presiding officer, often served as the majority party's floor leader, with responsibility for leading the debate on important bills, keeping in touch with committee chairmen, tracking the status of legislation, and making motions necessary to keep legislation on course and prevent parliamentary snafus. The minority party also chose a leader, who would usually be that party's defeated candidate for presiding officer. The minority leader tried to advance his party's policies in the same way as the majority leader, although, being in the minority, he generally had to play defense.[17]

The majority leader in the Ohio House or Senate was usually the Speaker or president pro tempore, but the minority leader had no official title. The term "minority leader" came into general currency in the early twentieth century. By 1922, "long established precedent" dictated that the defeated candidate for Speaker or president pro tem be recognized by his party as minority floor leader. In 1917, for instance, resolutions referred to Republicans Frank H. Reighard in the House and Otto Vollenweider in the Senate, both of them defeated candidates for presiding officer, as minority floor leaders. Both men also served on the vital Rules Committee, a regular assignment of both the majority and minority leaders.[18]

The position of party whip developed later. The term originated in the British House of Commons, where a "whipper-in" rounded up party members for votes. In 1925, commentators described the whip as "a functionary almost unknown" in America and referred to the majority whip in the U.S. Senate as an "obscure position," but the whip soon became a prominent figure in American legislatures.

The whip ensured that members attended for important votes, kept them informed of party policy, tried to induce members to act as the party desired, and let the party leaders know who was not toeing the line.[19]

Aside from the lieutenant governor, who until 1979 presided over the Senate, the Ohio constitution recognized only two legislative leaders, the Speaker of the House and the president pro tempore of the Senate. Both of these officers received compensation beyond the regular member's salary from 1955 on. Beginning in 1961, the rest of the leadership hierarchy started to get official recognition in the salary statutes. First came bonuses for the Senate minority leader, Speaker pro tempore of the House, and House minority leader. Other pay supplements followed until by 2003 the beneficiaries included the Senate president (who had replaced the lieutenant governor as presiding officer), president pro tem, assistant president pro tem, majority whip, minority leader, assistant minority leader, minority whip, and assistant minority whip, and the House Speaker, Speaker pro tem, majority floor leader, assistant majority floor leader, majority whip, assistant majority whip, minority leader, assistant minority leader, minority whip, and assistant minority whip. Nothing in law and very little in the legislative rules defined the roles of all these functionaries, and it was not always clear just what each one did. It seems unlikely that the Senate Democratic caucus of 2003 really needed four leaders to keep tabs on its eleven members.[20]

The successive salary increases reflected the full-time character of the legislator's job. The formal work week actually grew shorter after the *Columbus Citizen* complained about it in 1959 because leaders and committee chairs often canceled scheduled session or committee dates and the General Assembly eventually gave up altogether on Monday evening sessions. Still, in its study of absenteeism the *Lancaster Eagle-Gazette* estimated that lawmakers averaged 2.7 forty-hour workweeks per year of scheduled committee meetings. Moreover, as we have seen, sessions themselves grew longer. During what was then an unusually long session, drawn out because of the great fight over creating a state income tax, the *Columbus Citizen-Journal* reported that some members had "virtually abandoned their back-home jobs." The loss of income, said the paper, was "being felt by wives and families who are becoming critical."[21]

But it was the amount of time spent outside the statehouse that made the members full-time legislators. Caucus meetings, the rising cost of election campaigns and concomitant need to raise funds, responses to mail and other constituent work for constituencies that after 1966 were fixed in number but growing in size, frequent travel between the capital and home—all, when added to the more formal legislative work of consulting with professional staff and representatives of interest groups on the drafting of legislation and preparing for and attending committee meetings and sessions, could take up great chunks of time. Members found it harder and harder to maintain outside jobs in addition to their legislative careers. The number of members who identified themselves as full-time legislators rather than as farmers, physicians, or businessmen who happened to get elected to the House or Senate steadily increased.

Decorum

Donna Pope, who thought of herself as a full-time representative in 1979, was a new breed of legislator in more ways than one. Women first entered in the General Assembly in 1923. They cracked the House leadership in 1979, when both parties elected female whips. In 1992, Joanne Davidson became the first woman since Margaret Mahoney in 1949 to head a caucus by winning election as House minority leader. When Republicans took control of the House in 1995, she became Speaker. By then the presence of women in key positions was becoming routine. In 1996, women chaired three of the Senate's fourteen committees and two of the House Finance Committee's subcommittees.[22]

Davidson brought a new style of leadership to the House, more open and conciliatory, at least on the surface, than that of her long-serving predecessor Vern Riffe. (When Davidson became minority leader in 1992, she promised a "more aggressive leadership style," and no one ever accused her of being soft.) Although her methods could have been characterized as feminine, her style probably had more to do with a widespread desire for change, especially among Republicans who had chafed under Riffe's heavy-handed ways. Female lawmakers proved to be much like their male colleagues when it came to matters of policy. In the mid-1980s, when they still made up a small group, the women would meet informally, often at lunch, to discuss issues of special concern to them on which they largely agreed. When Priscilla Mead moved from the House to the Senate in 2001 to become the only female in the Republican Senate caucus, she found that she missed the "casual warmth of sharing experiences with another woman." Despite their affinity for one another, the women of the Ohio General Assembly, unlike female legislators in some other states, could not form a true bipartisan women's caucus because they held such divergent political views.[23]

Proponents of woman suffrage in the early twentieth century argued that females in the statehouse would have a salutary effect on the comportment of male lawmakers, but whether they smoothed the rough edges of masculine manners is debatable. An observer in the 1950s noticed that the men sprawled in their seats and swiveled them back and forth, while the women sat up straight and looked attentive. Decorum probably improved gradually for a number of reasons, including the presence of female employees and lawmakers, the long weekends when members broke camp and returned to refreshers in domesticity, and the professionalization of government. But the transformation took time. In the 1930s, the Senate, disturbed by the constant "confusion and noise" in the lobby and the back of the Senate chamber, directed the sergeant at arms to keep the space behind the rail clear and to confine visitors to seats along the side of the room or in the gallery. Reporters likened the scenes on the House and Senate floors to a high school corridor between classes or a schoolroom when the teacher was out. A student visiting the statehouse with her class in 1935 "did not enjoy it at all because I could not hear anything to enjoy." She was surprised to see "how inattentive the representatives were. Some ate apples, some smoked and some slept. Whenever they wanted to go out, they went out. . . . Disgusting."[24]

When Vern Riffe became Speaker in 1975, he insisted that no "hanky-panky" or "cutting up" take place on the House floor. Modeling himself on Roger Cloud, the Speaker when Riffe joined the House in 1959, he forbade the members to drink coffee or read newspapers at their desks and insisted that they keep the noise down. Riffe did not want his House to leave the kind of impression on students that the representatives had created forty years earlier. Senate leaders too found it necessary to crack down on disorder in the hall. Even in the twenty-first century, President Richard Finan, embarrassed by the animated exchanges taking place in the presence of high schoolers, had to lecture the senators on proper behavior during session.[25]

At least the young visitor of 1935 did not see any violence, which had disappeared almost entirely. In 1913, one representative threatened to thrash another "regardless of your gray hairs," a challenge that the grizzled lawmaker accepted, but tempers cooled and nothing happened. A Columbus newspaper headline in 1927 declared, "Rushing House Rules Brings Fistic Clash: Blows Supplant Words as Regulars and Insurgents Battle." The story, however, said nothing about fisticuffs, and an angry House forced the paper to apologize. When tempers flared, members sometimes resorted to less drastic but no less dramatic means of resolving their differences. In 1959, after "hours of bargaining, trading, dealing and bickering," the Senate finally convened at 9:25 P.M. to consider a tax bill favored by the Democratic majority. When a group of Democratic dissidents threatened to scuttle the bill, Lieutenant Governor John Donahey, as presiding officer, declared the session adjourned. "[A]mid shouts and yells from the floor," a Republican member tried to gavel the Senate to order, asserting that Donahey had "refused to preside over the Senate in violation of rules and the constitution." Then the chamber went dark. Longtime reporters could not recall another instance of the lights being turned off to end a session. A few days later, as the "torrent of angry words and charges" continued, House wits held that a local auto dealer was considering sponsoring the "Wednesday Night Fights From the Ohio Senate" on television. More typically, members vented their feelings with name calling or sarcastic resolutions, which, when not received good-naturedly by the targets, might be denounced for tarnishing the public image of the legislature.[26]

Sometimes strained relations between the House and Senate led to conduct that Representative Patrick Dunn described in 1951 as "ungentlemanly, unprofessional, uncouth and unpolitic." As noted in chapter 16, the two bodies had different traditions, and some senators regarded House members with condescension. Affronted by senatorial superciliousness, Dunn proposed that representatives tip their hats to senators in the hope "that such deference to the so-called upper house will cause the state senators to swallow their concepts of individual grandeur" or at least induce them to behave more courteously toward "lowly state representatives."[27]

For a long time, decorum suffered badly at the end of a session. The general laxity in the conduct of business as well as the anxiety of members to close up shop and go home no doubt accounted for the mischief. Commentators regularly deplored the chaos that accompanied the end of legislative sessions throughout the country. The "despicable" practice of logrolling reached its height on the final day, and lawmakers indiscriminately suspended the rules so that bills could go from introduction to passage in a matter of seconds. In Ohio, it was not uncommon for a bill to be reported out of committee, immediately engrossed at the clerk's desk, and promptly put to a final vote. By "gentlemen's agreement," the lawmakers passed dozens of bills so that each member would have something to show the folks back home. No one but the sponsor read or cared about these bills. In this manner, the General Assembly passed an astounding heap of legislation. At the 1912 constitutional convention, Edward W. Doty, former legislator and House clerk, reminded his fellow delegates, "You have been here on the last day of a session of the legislature, and you have seen fifty per cent. of the bills passed and sent to the governor, and then the legislature adjourned and the members went home." On the last day of the 1915 session, the General Assembly passed 43 separate measures and 347 amendments to appropriations bills.[28]

Last-day meetings ran late into the night. To conform to resolutions setting a date certain for adjournment sine die, legislators would cover the clock, as if that would prevent midnight from arriving. Legislators continued to cover the clock into the 1950s, pretending that the day chosen for the last regular working session hadn't really ended as they passed bills into the wee hours of the next morning or even later. (There might be a break to allow for the enrollment of bills, after which the members returned for a final session or two to handle formalities or to consider bills vetoed by the governor.) As late as 1966, a textbook on Ohio government asserted that covering the clock was "not a figure of speech; the sergeant-at-arms actually places a cover over the clock." According to the 1974 edition, though, the expression remained in use but the actual practice had been abandoned. The all-night sessions produced "legislation by exhaustion." Describing the "production line legislating" that occurred at the end of one session, the *Columbus Citizen* reported that "[m]embers were voting for bills without knowing what was in them, approving amendments they had never seen, accepting conference committee reports without apparently caring what they provided."[29]

Some observers blamed the last-minute frenzy on early-session indolence. One Ohio House Speaker decried the "needless and demoralizing" custom of "practically wasting the first month or six weeks of every session in formalities and dilatory practice." Complaints that the lawmakers did little in the opening weeks of a session persisted for decades. To deal with the resulting late-session crunch, the House and Senate created special steering committees to arrange the calendar so that more important bills had priority. The Speaker of the House and president pro tempore of the Senate, who chaired the Rules Committees, usually headed the steering committees as well. Eventually the Rules Committees took direct control of the calendars. The General Assembly also attempted to deal with the late rush of legislation by prohibiting the introduction of bills after a set date without the unanimous consent of the house, but the rule did not prevent the traditional all-night sessions. Instead, it simply added night sessions and a rush of introductions as the filing deadline approached. On April 13, 1971, for example, members of the House introduced more than three hundred

The House clock covered in 1951 to extend a legislative day late in the session.
Reproduced by permission of the Ohio Historical Society

bills; for the rest of the year they could introduce bills only on motion. Other deadlines—the constitutional due date for a budget act or, when second regular sessions became standard, scheduled spring and summer breaks in even-numbered years, when the legislators wanted to go home and campaign—could also produce tumults.[30]

To make matters worse, the childish antics that characterized the end of session in the late nineteenth century continued into the twentieth. Frederic C. Howe, who served in the Senate from 1906 to 1908, recalled that the "last hours were pandemonium. Many of the members were drunk. Nobody paid any attention to what was going on." On the last day of the 1911 session, dozens of representatives threw papers and wastebaskets at each other to the accompaniment of singing by some members and clucks of "shame" from others. In the Senate, reported the *Columbus Citizen*, "dignity was maintained to the last. They were too busy cluttering up the aisle in front of the president's stand trying to get pet bills called up for a vote to do much horse play." One year the reserved House majority leader Robert A. Taft suffered a wastebasket of trash being dumped over his head. Even the Great Depression failed to instill gravity into the proceedings of the last day, at least in the House. In 1935, representatives threw their wastebaskets, books, and rolls of toilet paper across the chamber to shouts of "Message from the Senate!" and "Message from the governor!"[31]

The frolicking eventually diminished in intensity, but late-session exhaustion still induced lapses in judgment. In the 1950s, overly giddy members celebrated the close of business with "firecrackers [set off in the House chamber], hooting, catcalls and singing." One year, in the supposedly more dignified Senate, Democratic leaders "cavorted about in railroad engineers' caps and red neckerchiefs" as the Republicans sang "Deep in the Heart of Taxes." Even as the General Assembly evolved into a professional legislature and sessions extended through the whole biennium, all-nighters and questionable legislative practices continued to characterize the end of session. But the season lost much of its color. When longtime legislator A. G. Lancione retired in 1978, he fondly recalled the hijinks of his early years. "We used to have fun," he said. "Now the job is full-time and more serious." Perhaps the worst that can be said of the twenty-first-century legislators' personal behavior at session's end is that some of them display a distinct lack of taste in speeches made upon the numerous retirements brought on by term limits.[32]

The press contributed to the general disorder on the floor, at least in the Senate. From their desks in front of the president's rostrum, they talked with the front-row senators and wandered around during session. In 1974, some senators thought of moving the newsmen to a platform off to the side of the rostrum to improve order and incidentally give themselves a bit more elbow room. The growth of the statehouse press corps necessitated the move anyway in the House as well as the Senate, and eventually the correspondents were repositioned to the sides of both halls.[33]

Rituals Old and New

Legislative foolishness and frolics occurred notwithstanding the fervent prayers of clergymen for divine guidance. For the first two decades of the twentieth century, the General Assembly continued the tradition of asking the local clergymen to send one of their number to open session with a prayer each day. At some point,

House members are sworn into office in 1947. *Reproduced by permission of the Ohio Historical Society*

the legislators starting paying the clerics; in 1915, a House member proposed that the representatives open each day by reciting the Lord's prayer in unison, both to settle a dispute over who should offer the prayer and to save money. The suggestion fell flat, and within a few years both houses started naming regular chaplains whose chief if not sole function seems to have been to deliver the daily invocation. In 1941, the House voted its chaplain a salary of $400 for his term of office. Fifty-three years later, at the end of his two-decade tenure, House chaplain Father Kenneth Grimes was receiving $6,600 annually. The House did away with the office of chaplain in 1995 and instead allowed the members to request that particular clergymen be invited to offer the prayer. When no minister was scheduled and no local clergyman could be reached to step in, a member might be tapped for the job. Guest clergymen received instructions to keep the prayers religiously and politically inoffensive, but some could not resist the temptation to display their sectarian or political preferences.[34]

The Second Century

With the patriotic fervor of World War II came a new ritual, the recitation of the pledge of allegiance following the prayer. Since World War I and the Russian Revolution, there had been a growing fear of foreign influences on American life. In 1919, the General Assembly banned the teaching of German in all schools, private as well as public, before the eighth grade, required that English be the language of instruction through seventh grade (a law that the U.S. Supreme Court struck down), ordered teachers to take loyalty oaths, and repealed a law providing for the publication of legal notices in German, Polish, and Bohemian. Declaring that large numbers of aliens were "associated together in movements deliberately designed to inspire class hatred, provoke racial antipathies and social prejudices, and to cause, by violence, the destruction of the American form of government, and the substitution of the condition commonly known as 'Bolshevism,'" the legislature urged Congress to provide for the immediate deportation of unnaturalized aliens who engaged in subversive activities and to make the naturalization of aliens revocable for "proper cause shown." It barred the advocacy of class revolution in print or speech, outlawed the organization of groups that taught or advocated such ideas, and prohibited the display of the red flag of socialism, the black flag of anarchism, and sacrilegious banners. In 1921, the General Assembly unanimously called upon Congress to bar the immigration of diseased and immoral Europeans, "anarchists, bolshevists, [and] enemies of all democratic government." For a time, the Ku Klux Klan used its influence in the General Assembly to push legislation aimed at weakening the Catholic Church, to which so many of the recent immigrants belonged.[35]

The Klan's sway quickly waned, but the approach of World War II once again heightened concerns about fifth columns in America. In 1941, the General Assembly barred "un-American" parties from the ballot and for the first time adopted a resolution that the pledge of allegiance follow the prayer at the first session of each week. The journals do not indicate whether the House continued the practice in every session after the war, but, from 1951 on, the pledge always followed the prayer at the week's first meeting. In 1954, as a way of distinguishing America's political faith from atheistic communism, Congress inserted "under God" into the pledge. The Ohio House soon embraced the new version. The senators do not appear to have contracted the pledging habit until 1961, but by the late 1980s they were reciting the pledge at every full session. The House soon followed suit. (Whatever the wording of the pledge resolutions, the members may actually have said the pledge at every nonskeleton session all along. In 2007, the House resolved to make the pledge "at the opening session of each week," but in fact the representatives had been doing it at every voting session for as long as anyone could remember.)[36]

About the time the recitation of the pledge became a House ritual, another custom, seat selection by lot, started to fade. In 1941, the seating resolution included a new wrinkle: if a county had three or more representatives, the first one from that county to draw for a seat could, with the consent of the other delegates from the county, choose the seats for them as well. The purpose may have been to ensure that members from large counties could, if they wished, sit together, although the provision set up a potential conflict with another that set aside the north side of the hall for members of the majority party and the south side for the minority. In 1943 and 1945, there were no seating resolutions. The Speaker or possibly the Rules Committee assigned seats. Gus Kasch, the fractious member from Akron, objected to being put far from his fellow Summit County delegates and caused an uproar by sitting in other members' seats. In 1947, swayed perhaps by Kasch's fit even though Kasch himself was gone, the House resurrected the lottery, but it didn't last. Over the years, more and more members had been given priority in selecting seats. In 1951, members with physical handicaps or prior service got to choose seats ahead of the drawing. With the lengthening of tenures, these groups made up two-thirds of the House. The resolution further diluted the drawing by allowing the first delegate from any multimember county to select seats for his or her fellows. The lottery finally met its demise in 1953, when the House authorized the Speaker to assign seats, taking into account the age, physical condition, and seniority of the members. Thereafter, the House did not even bother with seating resolutions, and the last remnant of the quaint old convention disappeared.[37]

The legislature's manner of dealing with the deaths of members also lost whatever remained of its old-fashioned flavor, continuing a trend that began in the nineteenth century. Before 1900, the House and Senate typically adopted resolutions eulogizing their departed fellows on or soon after the day of death, if that came during session; after 1900, a month or more might go by before passage of the resolution, and then it would be too late for mention of the funeral service or a display of mourning. Twentieth-century lawmakers usually adopted resolutions of regret by a rising vote (that is, by standing up to be counted), but the resolutions rarely did more than express sorrow at the member's passing and recite his or her accomplishments. The House of the Ninety-seventh General

Assembly (1947–48) lost the astonishing number of twelve members, but only one of the resolutions called for the Speaker to appoint a committee to attend the funeral. On a Tuesday in 1979, when Speaker Vern Riffe learned of Representative Irma Karmol's passing, he canceled all full sessions and committee meetings for the rest of the week, but even that was an extraordinary gesture.[38]

The Working Environment

The working environment for members generally improved over the years, but the members sometimes disagreed over what constituted an enhancement. The ban on smoking in the House and Senate chambers provides a prime example. The young girl who complained about the legislators' behavior in 1935 noted with disgust that some of them smoked during session. Both houses had banned smoking on the floor during session in the nineteenth century, but neither enforced the rule. A newspaper complained that rampant smoking in the Senate in flagrant violation of the rules fostered disrespect for the law. One reporter observed in 1947 that the Senate chamber had ashtrays, whereas House members dropped their ashes on the linoleum under their desks, to be swept up later by the custodians. Another correspondent noted in 1955 that the new General Assembly had opened "in an atmosphere softly scented by roses and good tobacco." The flowers were only for the opening of session. The tobacco was standard, at least for the members; spectators had to go outside to smoke.[39]

The Senate banned smoking in the chamber in 1985, "apparently," one newspaper remarked inaccurately, "for the first time in the Senate's 182-year history." Spittoons for tobacco chewers remained on the floor, at least for the time being. (C. Stanley Mechem, "a Hollywood casting director's ideal of a rustic, suspender-snapping, tobacco-chewing Midwestern state legislator" who often roamed far from his desk while debating, could launch a spitball toward his spittoon with great accuracy.) Minority leader Harry Meshel objected to singling out smoking for condemnation when members sometimes brought the whiff of alcohol and other offensive odors to the floor. "Maybe we ought to require all members to have bathed before arriving," he growled. "They would embarrass a rhinoceros and intimidate a camel."[40]

Notwithstanding their long disregard of the rules against smoking in the chambers, the members provided themselves with the proverbial smoke-filled backroom. In 1910, in what looks like a Progressive blow against lobbies, the House directed the sergeant at arms to keep unauthorized personnel out of the smoking room while the House was in session. Decades later, the House's "newly decked modernistic smoking room, quickly dubbed the 'cocktail room' by those who viewed its dusty rose walls and its leather chairs and davenports," generated considerable interest among the members arriving for the opening of the session. In 1976, the General Assembly by statute required that places of public assembly, including the statehouse, have designated nonsmoking areas. It gave to the House and Senate Rules Committees the job of designating the areas within those parts of the statehouse used by the legislature. The nonsmoking areas gradually expanded. In 1987, the Senate rules designated the floor inside the railing and the galleries on the north and south sides of the floor as nonsmoking. Ten years later, they prohibited smoking in the entire chamber. In 1999, Governor Bob Taft by executive order banned all smoking in state buildings, which covered both the statehouse and the members' office buildings. Some members disputed the governor's authority to issue a ban that applied to their space, but, as far as the statehouse was concerned, the dispute was academic. In 2005, the Senate rules prohibited smoking in the chamber, the members' lounge, and adjoining areas as well. Despite the executive order, members continued to smoke in a designated smoking room in the Riffe Center and in their offices until the voters adopted the Smoke-Free Workplace Law in 2006.[41]

If a ban on the noxious indulgence of smoking could cause such controversy, what would happen when lawmakers couldn't get their caffeine fixes? In 2007, the Senate not only formalized its prohibition of food and drink in the Senate chamber, it barred comestibles from committee rooms as well, chiefly in order to bring down carpet cleaning costs. The rule raised the thought that drowsy, grumpy, "caffeine-deprived" senators might have trouble following the proceedings. "We'll see," said a chairman whose committee met at 9 A.M., "whether the coffee Gestapo prevails."[42]

The conveniences with which the legislators supplied themselves in Ohio's second century ranged from drinking cups to laptop computers. Telephones proved popular at an early date, and their abuse became a constant concern. In 1906, the House Democratic caucus, prodded by such examples as the senator who called home every morning to hear his dog bark into the phone, demanded that members no longer be allowed to charge long-distance calls to the state. The House that year established a special committee to draw up regulations for the use of its phones. In 1917, a proposed Senate resolution described the abuse of long-distance phone service in the General Assembly as "intolerable." For many years, the two houses regularly adopted resolutions that instructed clerks or telephone attendants to refuse long-distance calls, directed that only the clerks could accept long-distance calls, or restricted long-distance calls to state business. But they also voted to give the telephone operator access to the House's loudspeaker system to page members who had incoming calls. By 1970, members had access to free (for them) telephones in the statehouse, but, according to one newspaper report, they racked up tens of thousands of dollars in questionable long-distance calls at public expense, including calls by married men to female friends.[43]

The members also sought more basic amenities. In 1913, the House instructed the sergeant at arms to furnish the washroom with individual towels for the members. A resolution to have him procure sanitary drinking cups never got to a vote. A few years later, a similar resolution, prefaced with the statement that the use of a common cup by all the members violated state health regulations, passed, but still over the opposition of seventeen members. The representatives learned to appreciate their individual cups; next time around the resolution passed unanimously. On the other hand, Representative George Lonz's proposal to purchase seat pads to prevent wear of the members' trousers failed to get out of committee, even though Lonz kept pressing the issue.[44]

The House and Senate recurrently authorized either the presiding officer or the sergeant at arms to appoint a "suitable person" to operate cigar or snack stands outside the chamber doors. The stands probably first appeared in the early twentieth century. Before then, vendors of refreshments and hawkers of wares catered to members on the chamber floors. In 1906, the House directed the sergeant at arms to bar from the floor "all canvassers and peddlers of every description whatsoever, excepting newsboys." The cigar stands were a more decorous means of addressing the members' wants. Lillian B. Levey proved to be an eminently suitable stand operator. In 1941, the House formally thanked her for more than twenty years of "efficiently tend[ing] to the physical needs of the members . . . in her stand just outside the entrance to the Hall." By the early 1950s, a more substantial lunchroom had opened in the basement. A House resolution praised its "excellent food and services," but in fact it was a "rathole" for years. But at least members and employees could get bacon and eggs, soup and sandwiches, and other light fare and could schmooze with the statehouse crowd. Legally blind Mary Wisnewski, who started dispensing refreshments at the statehouse in 1952, took over the snack bar when it was refurbished in 1960 and ran the place for nearly thirty years. Mary's became a staple of statehouse lore, a noisy, friendly eatery sometimes referred to as the "Ptomaine Palace." Everyone knew Mary's shout of "Chili, Willy!" directed at the hefty cook who literally sweated over the grill, to the disgust of some of the patrons. Mary retired when the governor and representatives moved the Riffe Center. Her successor had to shut down during the renovation of the statehouse, causing one lobbyist to wail, "They're destroying my base of operations." The base reopened, but it never recaptured the spirit of Mary's.[45]

Although House members saw to their towels, cups, and refreshments, they hesitated to provide themselves with an adequate sound system for the conduct of business. Newspapers printed conflicting reports on the subject of sound in the smaller Senate. One midcentury correspondent called the Senate "quiet, like a rich men's club," while another, visiting the Senate in the hectic last days of a session, wrote that "the insidious buzz of voices and the running to and fro" made it difficult to follow the proceedings. House members, though, definitely had trouble hearing their colleagues. In 1937, the Rules Committee recommended that the House install an amplifying system, only to have the full House reject the idea. The House did place a few microphones on the floor, but years later members still complained about the need for more so that all members would have access to them. In 1954, the House installed sixty-one microphones scattered around the floor but controlled by the clerk so that only members who had been recognized could use them. Eventually all members in both houses would have microphones at their desks.[46]

Of all the improvements in physical facilities over the years—drinking fountains, snack shops, sound systems, the underground parking garage, and so on, all befitting a full-time legislature—perhaps nothing outweighed individual offices for the rank and file. An LSC study noted in 1966 that to answer mail, examine legislative proposals, talk to constituents, and perform the other functions of their positions, "most legislators have only the corridors, the lounges, telephone booths, their desks on the floor of the chamber, or other public and crowded places." The House had to ban all visitors from the floor even when it was not in session because roaming lobbyists interfered with members' attempts to work at their desks. Only a handful of leaders and a minority of committee chairmen had their own offices, most of which were cramped. Some members might have found such conditions to be perfectly adequate, but it was no way to do business. Senators soon got their own offices, originally cubicles in the basement of the main building or the annex and later, after the supreme court and attorney general moved to the Rhodes Office Tower, refurbished rooms on the annex's upper floors. Representatives had to work at their desks in the House chamber until the early 1970s, when several rooms in the basement were furnished with desks and chairs. In these large rooms, some allocated to Democrats, others to Republicans, members sat at side-by-side desks and shared phones and pool secretaries. Over the next few years, the House got small spaces in the annex that could be occupied by one or two members. Jane Campbell, elected in 1984, recalled drawing straws with other freshmen for a choice of offices as well as for seats in the House chamber. She chose the only private room available, one with a large window, only to find a desk covered with snow because the window didn't close. Representatives would not have comfortable private offices until the Riffe Center opened in 1988.[47]

There were other indicia of the General Assembly's growing professionalism besides the improvement in physical facilities and conveniences. Recognizing the need for some kind of instruction for new legislators, the chairman of the House Reference Committee announced early in the 1927 session that he would "say a few words" on "the technique of legislation" for new members and for others who had "not had occasion to learn." In 1966, when the reapportionment revolution produced an unusually large crop of freshmen for that era, the Senate majority leader planned a special one-day presession meeting to acquaint new members with legislative procedures. Two years later the Legislative Service Commission took members to a retreat at a state park, but lobbyists "descended upon them like locusts" and ruined it. In 1973, leaders of both parties organized three days of seminars on major state issues at the Ohio State University, but at least half the members skipped the sessions. The LSC offered two-day orientation seminars for new members in Columbus at least sporadically beginning in 1972 and regularly in the 1990s, but they degenerated into rounds of dinners and cocktail parties given by lobbyists and state agencies. As the election of 2000 approached, with its certainty of mass turnover owing to term limits, legislative leaders called for more substantial orientation programs away from Columbus, with input from academics and with lobbyists kept under control. The LSC organized an intensive, five-day training program for all members, new and old, at an out-of-town lodge. Most of the forty-nine freshmen attended at least some of the sessions, as did twenty or so veterans. An agency information fair offered legislators a chance to meet high-level agency staff and learn about their operations. Caucus leaders held postelection meetings of their own to discuss policy,

In the 1960s, members who lacked private
offices could work in a fourth-floor library
in the statehouse and make calls from the
telephone room. *Courtesy of the Ohio House of*
Representatives

Representative Robert Netzley prepares to move from his office in the statehouse to the new Riffe Center in 1988. *Courtesy of the* Columbus Dispatch *Archives*

draw up an agenda for the legislative session, and conduct mock committee hearings. After the 2004 election, the LSC orientation program returned to Columbus. Lobbyists stayed on the schedule, but the program organizers provided the meals and kept the attendees busy with panels on lawmaking, ethics, media relations, and so on as well as tours, photo sessions, and other activities.[48]

In the transformation of the General Assembly into a professional legislature, nothing surpassed in significance the development of the legislature's own specialized services for research and bill drafting. In the first half of the nineteenth century, and probably well beyond, individual lawmakers carried the burden of drafting key legislation. Ephraim Cutler personally dug up information on taxes and schools and sat in his room writing out bills. Alfred Kelley, "entrusted with the care of many measures requiring laborious thought and investigation," put his energy and experience into crafting vital revenue and banking laws. But few members had the expertise in either the subject matter or the drafting of legislation, or the drive to acquire it, to be able to prepare bills. They had to depend on better-educated, more experienced colleagues or interested parties outside the General Assembly. By the twentieth century, the situation had grown even worse because of the growing complexity of the issues facing state legislatures and the ever-increasing volume of legislation. Lawmakers had to deal with "all sorts of ugly things," wrote one observer, things "that were abstract and much too far beyond the man of medium learning capacity." It was easy to berate the intelligence of the legislators, but "we seldom consider the utter helplessness of even the most erudite getting any acquaintance at all with the legislation that is ground through a session of a state legislature."[49]

For help in understanding an issue or writing a bill, an individual lawmaker could turn to "the lobby, hire his own secretary to gather material, or consult an attorney for opinions on legislative constitutionality or suitability. And about the only thing he did was the first of the three." In the early 1900s, organized interest groups such as the Anti-Saloon League, the Ohio Chamber of Commerce, the Ohio State Federation of Labor, and public utility lobbyists drew up much of the most important legislation. But so did special commissions authorized by the General Assembly and appointed by the governor to prepare tax legislation, overhaul the municipal code, and study agricultural credit, the leasing of canal lands, coal screening, fire insurance, flood prevention, judicial procedure, municipal finance, occupational diseases, highways, the public school system, and other issues. In some instances, the special commissions worked closely with legislative committees.[50]

Special commissions, however, did not provide lawmakers with everyday help. For this, beginning in 1910, the members could turn to the state library's Legislative Reference and Information Department and its successors. These organizations are discussed in detail in the next chapter. For now, it need only be noted that as the legislature's professional, nonpartisan research, bill-drafting, and fiscal services slowly grew from a tiny operation in the state library to a full-fledged legislative agency occupying three floors in a state office tower, so did the ability of the members to produce well-crafted legislation based on reliable information.

The Sources of Legislation

The advent of professional legislative services in 1910 did not immediately ensure the General Assembly's primacy over the executive branch or lobbies in shaping statutory law. From the early days of statehood the governor, in his annual address to the General Assembly, had suggested subjects for legislation and sometimes of-

James M. Cox. *Reproduced by permission of the Ohio Historical Society*

fered specific proposals. The General Assembly had responded by appointing committees to inquire into the issues raised. In the twentieth century, with experts and the veto at his disposal, the governor took a more energetic role in forming the legislature's agenda. Much depended on the governor's personality and the political situation, of course, but under the right circumstances, as James M. Cox demonstrated, the governor could be the legislative leader. After the election of 1912, Cox drew up a legislative program, assigned to selected legislators the task of carrying particular bills, dictated the caucus nominees for officers of the two houses, and threatened to withhold appointments if he did not get his way. Between 1902 and 1966, when the General Assembly met in regular session every other year, governors called numerous special sessions, for which, under the constitution, they could limit the purpose. Once, when the governor and legislature were at odds over tax legislation and the time of adjournment, the governor exercised his previously dormant constitutional power of proroguing the General Assembly.[51]

Bills emanating from the governor and his administration made up a large percentage of all legislation introduced and passed. In a series of studies conducted in the 1920s and 1930s, political scientist Harvey Walker and his students at the Ohio State University found that "public" bills, those originating with the governor or state, local, or federal governmental agencies, made up roughly a third of all bills introduced and 40 percent of all bills passed. Organized interest groups accounted for an even higher percentage of introductions and about the same number of enactments. Members of the General Assembly initiated the leftovers. Walker concluded that Ohio's legislators were more "law reviewers" than "law makers" and that the legislature needed professional assistance in reviewing proposed laws from both a technical and a policy perspective.[52]

Walker's findings highlighted the influence of lobbies. A Columbus newspaper observed in 1950 that while "[o]fficially, a proposed new law or proposed change in the existing law is introduced by a senator or representative in the form of a bill bearing his name," the bill was usually "the handiwork of some pressure group whose interests it will affect . . . Often a bill becomes the subject of a battle between opposing lobby groups—one striving to get it passed, the other to kill it. Committee hearings in such cases take the form of debates between clashing lobbyists." In the absence of a "well-staffed research agency," lawmakers depended on lobbyists for information. Some lobbyists, joked the *Columbus Citizen*, "threatened to tell the leadership of the Legislature that if they don't provide better accommodations for the lobbyists they, in turn, will stop telling the legislators what the bills are all about." But the knowledge that some lobbyists brought to their work was indispensible. By the 1920s, well-financed organizations such as the Ohio Chamber of Commerce and the Farm Bureau Federation had research departments that could produce expert studies on demand. "The better lobbyists," one member commented, "are very careful to present accurate, factual information."[53]

Sometimes the lobbyists just knew too much for the legislators. When prominent lobbyist Ed Schorr, representing the Ohio Reclamation Association, testified before a Senate committee on a strip-mining bill, he "had more information—either in his head or in his notebook—than anyone in the room," including the chief of the State Reclamation Division. After Schorr argued against amending the existing strip-mining statute, "[t]he committee sent the bill to a sub-committee, and probable slow death."[54]

In 1953, the year in which lobbyist Schorr killed the strip-mining bill, the General Assembly created the Legislative Service Commission, a small agency devoted mostly to research. The agency grew slowly for a decade, then suddenly

The Second Century

doubled in size at a time when legislatures around the country were attempting to modernize and to assert their independence from governors and lobbyists. The same period saw the births of three organizations dedicated to the improvement of state legislatures nationwide. In 1975, they united to form the National Conference of State Legislatures (NCSL). Ohio House Speaker Charles Kurfess, who played a leading role in the merger movement, called the union "the most important step we can take to convince the nation of the strength and the quality of state legislatures." Ohio legislators continued to draw upon the Council of State Governments, a source of valuable information and ideas since 1933, but that organization did not focus on the needs of legislatures. The NCSL quickly emerged as an advocate for state legislatures and a major resource for lawmakers, with national conferences, a large research staff, professional development programs, and a bimonthly magazine. In 1973, yet another national organization, the conservative American Legislative Exchange Council, arose to provide legislators with policy recommendations through publications and conferences.[55]

The steady growth of the LSC and NCSL and their expansion of services in the last quarter of the twentieth century did not mark the end of outside influence on the legislative process; nor should it have. Legislators and LSC staff members continued to consult extensively with representatives of executive agencies and private interest groups in drafting bills, and in cases involving highly technical matters "outsiders" often provided the bulk of legislative language. But however beholden to interest groups lawmakers may have been for campaign contributions, the existence of their own professional staff and national organization largely freed them from the dependence that characterized the typical part-time citizen legislator.

18

FROM PATRONAGE TO

PROFESSIONALISM

N O SOONER HAD Warren Harding been elected to the Ohio Senate in
1899 than the beseeching letters from office-seekers began to arrive: this
one wanted to be the Senate message clerk, that one the statehouse superintendent, another the second assistant sergeant at arms. After Harding's reelection
in 1901, an acquaintance asked him to secure the appointment of a poor working
girl from Logan County as a stenographer or typist. A candidate for doorkeeper
asked Harding to have a hundred ballots with his name on them printed for distribution to the senators before the vote. Dealing with such patronage requests
could be a nightmare. Louis XIV once complained that every time he filled a
vacant office he made a hundred malcontents and one ingrate.[1]

A century after Harding's time in the Senate, patronage remained an important path to employment with the General Assembly. But there were also other
avenues, and the nature of legislative employment had changed. In 1900, the le-
gion of workers included few professionals. In 2000, most members of the even
larger throng had an advanced education, many had professional degrees, and
scores were making a career out of serving the legislature.

The Patronage Roster

In 1900, the roster of legislative employees included the clerks and sergeants at arms and their assistants, along with a large number stenographers, pages, porters, custodians, and other personnel. The number continued to grow. In 1935, for example, right after the House appointed the usual complement of assistant clerks —a deputy clerk, journal clerk, message clerk, engrossing clerk, enrolling clerk, and recording clerk—the chief clerk asked for the appointment of additional help, to be chosen by him (no doubt after consultation with party leaders). The House assented to the appointment of an assistant clerk, a bill clerk, three assistant bill clerks, an index clerk, an assistant index clerk, an assistant journal clerk, an assistant message clerk, a mail clerk and a mailing clerk, a compiling clerk, a reading clerk, a reference clerk, a clerk for the Finance Committee, and a clerk for the Speaker.[2]

The sergeant at arms had under his direction another host of employees, including three assistant sergeants at arms. There were fewer porters than earlier in the century—just six, as opposed to the seventeen of 1900—but some porters apparently just had new titles. There were seven custodians of committee rooms, two cloak room attendants, six doorkeepers, an assistant postmaster, four telephone attendants, a matron, two maids, two guides, and twenty-three pages. Four pages and three other positions were part-time. The House steno pool now comprised eighteen stenographers, including four part-timers and two designated press stenographers. What the matron did is anyone's guess. Frances McGovern, writing of her tenure in the House in the 1950s with a handful of other female legislators, recalled, "We had our own sitting room at the back of the House chamber and a matron of the majority party whose only duty was to visit us."[3]

A similar expansion of the Senate staff had occurred by 1935. In fact, it was greater relative to the size of the body. With fourteen stenographers, the Senate had one for every 2.4 members. The Senate had seventeen full-time pages—one for every two members—and sixteen part-time pages, plus two telephone messengers (in addition to the two telephone attendants). Of course, there was the usual quota of porters, cloak room attendants, and other employees.[4]

The Senate also designated a head porter in 1935, at a monthly salary rather than the per diem compensation usually received by legislative workers. Patronage considerations perhaps played a role, but the appointment could have been justified by the growing staff size and the increasingly specialized division of labor.

The Senate had named a superintendent of stenographers in the past and would designate a head page in the future.[5]

The Senate and House adopted resolutions recognizing a couple of extraordinary employees in 1935. As the election of James A. Rhodes as House journal clerk illustrates, a position in the clerk's office could still be a station on the way to elective office. It could also be a station on the way from elective office, although not necessarily less political influence. In 1935, the Senate remembered Edward Doty, a member of the House in the 1890s and House clerk from 1904 to 1909. Doty had been active in public affairs in Cleveland for many years, had been a delegate to the 1912 constitutional convention, and had served on the Public Utilities Commission.[6]

The House took time in 1935 to congratulate another employee, Edward W. Hughes, on his seventieth birthday. Hughes was the only parliamentarian the House had ever had to that point, and he had served as the Senate parliamentarian as well. The son of Welsh immigrants, Hughes published a newspaper for fifteen years and served two years as the Wilmington city clerk before becoming interested in the workings of legislatures. In 1900, he took a job as a message clerk in the House. A decade later, the House set him to work revising its rules and preparing a parliamentary guide for the General Assembly. The guide evolved into the standard book on American parliamentary law, described by Ohio's legislative historian as "the most complete and valuable work of its kind ever published."[7]

The large number of pages allowed the legislators to provide jobs for their favorite young men. The average age of the pages probably crept upward as the school day and year increased. A representative introduced a resolution in 1906 to release all pages and other employees under the age of fourteen so that they could attend school as required by law. The depression of the 1930s gave the job added importance for college students. The growing professionalism of government may have reduced the appeal of urchins scampering underfoot, but the combination of hard times and football fever probably played a bigger part in turning college athletes into pages. In 1935, during a feud with the Ohio State University over its budget, Governor Martin Davey mordantly remarked that most of the football team was on the state payroll. The university's athletic department claimed that only fourteen of the team's fifty-four members had part-time jobs with the state, three as House pages and one as the House's assistant bill clerk. But football players weren't the only Ohio State athletes working for the House. In 1935, the pages also included track teammates Jesse Owens and David Albritton.

Representative Grant Ward, a former Ohio State football coach, induced a star-struck House to make Owens an honorary page and assistant to the House custodian between its May adjournment and September special session, with pay at the regular per diem rate.[8]

Owens's job as a page got him into trouble with the Amateur Athletic Union (AAU). His pay included a salary of three dollars per day and expenses for travel on official business. In 1935, the state paid for the track star's round trip to California. Then came the resolution to make Owens an honorary page. Because the rules of amateur athletics prohibited athletes from accepting pay for sham jobs, the AAU decided to investigate. In August, Owens admitted receiving pay for June and July even though he hadn't been in Columbus, but since the committee to which he had been assigned had not met, the AAU let him off the hook. His amateur status intact, Owens went on to win four gold medals in the 1936 Olympics.[9]

Another athlete-page who attracted attention was Howard "Hopalong" Cassady, Ohio State football star and winner of the Heisman Trophy in 1955. Folks who cared little about the legislature visited the House galleries just to get a look at him. The rest of the pages, recalled Representative Frances McGovern, "might as well have been wallpaper." They could, however, be useful sources of information. Over beer imbibed at the Ringside, "a little pub in an alley across from the statehouse," McGovern "learned far more about what was going on in the legislature from [the pages] than I could ever have learned on my own."[10]

By Cassady's day, the lengthening sessions extended beyond Ohio State's academic year. When part-time pages graduated, they quit to look for regular employment, leaving the legislature shorthanded. The House then had to authorize the clerk to hire replacements for the remainder of the session.[11]

No legislative employee held a more honored place in General Assembly lore than the legendary Fred Blankner. Born in Germany in 1836, Blankner had been brought to Ohio as an infant. He served briefly as House third assistant sergeant at arms before enlisting in the Union army during the Civil War. Upon his return, he resumed his post and, with one two-year hiatus, held it until 1917. He also served as sergeant at arms for the third and fourth constitutional conventions, held thirty-eight years apart. In 1878, the *Ohio State Journal* could already state that a "Legislature without Fred would not amount to much." The House chamber belonged to Blankner more than to any other individual. He built the cloakroom, replaced the furniture, and saw to the members' needs. As he

David Albritton as an Ohio State track star, 1937. *Reproduced by permission of the Ohio State University Photo Archives*

approached a half century of service, the House directed that his portrait, then hanging above his locker on the west wall of the chamber, be purchased and remain there "for all time." (No one now seems to know where the portrait is.) When poor health finally forced Blankner to retire, the House named him honorary third assistant sergeant at arms, without pay but with the privilege of the floor, for life.[12]

Blankner held on to his post through Republican and Democratic control of the legislature, a remarkable achievement. Other employees, even those low down on the totem pole, often owed their jobs to political connections. A 1957 House resolution paying tribute to a stenographer of the 1890s noted that her brother had been a representative at the time. In remembering Ann Makely, a former head of stenographers and assistant clerk during three sessions of the General Assembly, the House noted her service to the Democratic Party. In fact, Makely served during another session as well. The Democrats ran the House in

The Second Century

Howard "Hopalong" Cassady with his father, Pearl Cassady, and the 1955 Chic Harley Award, given to the college football player of the year by the Touchdown Club of Columbus. *Courtesy of the Columbus Citizen-Journal Collection, Scripps-Howard Newspapers/Grandview Heights Public Library/Photohio.org*

three of her four sessions; in the fourth, two disgruntled Republicans gave the Speakership to the Democrats, possibly allowing Makely to keep her job. Ella Scriven's forty-seven years as House recording clerk may be attributed to the Republicans' usual dominance of that chamber; whenever the Democrats took over, they threw her out. Tom Bateman worked for the Senate almost continuously from 1921 through 1971, most of the time as clerk. The only gaps occurred in the years 1935–38, 1949–50, and 1959–60 when the Democrats held a majority of the seats.[13]

Bateman may have been the most influential legislative employee in the history of the General Assembly. A critical Columbus newspaper called him the "undisputed boss" of the Senate. "I work for the representatives," the House clerk commented, "but the senators work for Tom." A lawyer with a thorough understanding of legislative matters, Bateman drafted bills, raised money, and served as secretary of the all-important Rules Committee. A friend and onetime journal clerk under

Officers of the House of Representatives of the Eighty-third General Assembly
(1919): (1) John Fielding, engrossing clerk; (2) Charles E. Harper, enrolling
clerk; (3) Holmes H. Kress, message clerk; (4) Ella M. Scriven, recording clerk;
(5) Edward W. Hughes, parliamentarian and deputy clerk; (6) John P. Maynard,
clerk; (7) C. E. Spring, journal clerk; (8) Frederick Blankner, honorary third assistant sergeant at arms; (9) James M. "Private" Dalzell, first assistant sergeant at
arms; (10) J. D. Thomas, third assistant sergeant at arms; (11) Alfred Robinson,
sergeant at arms; (12) Charles Berry, second assistant sergeant at arms. *Reproduced
from James K. Mercer, Ohio Legislative History (Columbus: F. J. Heer [1921?]), 3:450*

Clerk and staff of the Senate of the Eighty-fourth General Assembly (1921–22): (1) Lloyd D. Bower, journal clerk; (2) Joseph E. Cross, assistant clerk; (3) Thomas E. Bateman, message clerk; (4) Walter Dale, enrolling clerk; (5) William E. Halley, clerk; (6) Harry D. Knox, index clerk; (7) Elsie J. Jennings, stenographic clerk; (8) Helen P. Roads, engrossing clerk; (9) M. B. Copeland, recording clerk. *Reproduced from James K. Mercer, Ohio Legislative History (Columbus: F. J. Heer [1923?]), 4:326*

Senate clerk Tom Bateman late in his career. *Reproduced by permission of the Ohio Historical Society*

Bateman described him as "a one-stop shop." Bateman served the Senate longer, knew more about the legislative process, and knew more key people than just about any senator; his knowledge was the source of his power.[14]

The army of legislative employees brought forth scathing criticism from Lauren Glosser, an Ohio State graduate student working under the direction of political science professor Harvey Walker in 1932. Walker and his students were then engaged in ongoing studies of the General Assembly. Glosser reported how, before the opening session of a new legislature, the patronage committees of the majority party caucuses would dole out positions. Bateman described the process to Glosser as "a big fuss, taking usually a day of trading, bickering, and compromising." The Senate had more employees than members, so each senator had at least one position to dispose of. The larger House saw more intense politicking by members for jobs to give to their constituents. "Thrown into the selfish hands of the members," wrote Glosser, "the predominating motive in selection has been the desire of these members to use the positions as a means of reenforcing their political strength in their constituency."[15]

The Second Century

Selection by patronage produced predictable results. The demand for jobs led to an unnecessarily large and unqualified staff. Bateman remembered one session in which "there were 78 employees in and about the [Senate] chamber. They were almost falling over one another." Many employees had nothing to do, Glosser reported. Some members of the permanent staff, with little to occupy them during the off years of the biennium, sat in their offices twiddling their thumbs. Others engaged in party work and didn't bother to show up at all. Per diem employees got paid from the opening to the close of a session, weekends, holidays, and recesses included, and permanent employees never got docked for being absent. Hardly anyone got fired, regardless of how lazy or incompetent he or she might have been. Ironically, within the next few years Glosser himself would work in both the House and Senate clerks' offices and would later head the Legislative Service Commission.[16]

Thirty-five years later, William Parker Blair III, another of Walker's students, came to similar conclusions. Blair found that the Senate staff had grown and that all the employees now received salaries rather than per diem pay. Bateman, still firmly ensconced in office, told Blair that for decades he rather than a patronage committee determined who got hired and fired in his office. But Bateman still complained that there were too many employees, especially pages. The senators needed numerous page positions to pay off political debts back in their districts. Blair questioned the need for other employees as well. When session ended, he said, the assistant clerk went home to practice law, and one of the "girls" in Bateman's office spent her time doing crossword puzzles. What the Senate really needed, thought Blair, were more secretaries and more professional staff.[17]

A comparison of rosters at quarter-century intervals reveals the growth in the General Assembly's workforce in the second half of the twentieth century. The Senate roster for the General Assembly of 1951–52 lists the traditional officers: clerk; assistant, journal, message, engrossing, enrolling, and recording clerks; secretary to the clerk; sergeant at arms and three assistant sergeants at arms. The House officers were almost the same but included a reading clerk instead of an assistant clerk, a Speaker's clerk, and a parliamentarian. The lower-level employees of the Senate included a bill clerk and assistant bill clerk; postmaster and assistant postmaster; eleven stenographers; a press room clerk; two doorkeepers; four committee room attendants; two telephone attendants; two telephone messengers; two cloak room attendants; two elevator attendants; five pages; and six porters. The House employed a minority leader's clerk; assistant journal clerk; assistant message clerk, two postal clerks; a reference clerk; a supervisor of bill

Stenographers' room in the statehouse around 1959. *Courtesy of the Ohio House of Representatives*

room clerks and four bill room clerks; a press clerk; one secretary each to the Speaker, the minority leader, and the Finance Committee; a supervisor of stenographers and nine stenographers; a supervisor of telephones and two telephone attendants; three cloak room attendants; five doorkeepers; four committee room attendants; five House attendants; three elevator attendants; four matrons; and a supervisor of pages and thirty part-time pages.

Twenty-five years later, the message clerk and two assistant sergeants at arms had been dropped from the list of Senate officers in favor of an administrative assistant, a personnel officer, and a deputy sergeant at arms. The House staff had undergone a more significant change. In 1969, the House divided the duties of the clerk's office between a legislative clerk and an executive secretary. The executive secretary assumed responsibility for reproducing documents, maintaining furniture and equipment, distributing supplies and publications, and carrying out other functions not directly related to legislation. The legislative clerk saw to printing and enrolling bills, keeping the journal, publishing the calendar, and generally handling tasks that were part of the legislative process.[18]

The Senate followed suit, creating the post of executive secretary in 1983 and then replacing it with a chief executive officer in 1985. Since then, the size of the House and Senate staffs has grown and the division of labor has become more detailed. In 2005, the House clerk had the traditional cast of assistants (although some of the titles had been combined), along with a public information clerk and bill room supervisor. The House administrative office had a chief administrative officer, fiscal officer, payroll officer, page coordinator, purchasing officer, attendance officer, telecommunications officer, a staff of information technology employees to maintain the House computer network and Web site, and other individuals in the mail room, copy center, and House floor. The House majority and minority caucuses each boasted a chief of staff, legal counsel, policy researchers and assistants, communications officers, Legislative Service Commission interns, and other personnel. The Senate had a similar although naturally shorter list of workers.

The legislative staff available to individual members also changed in response to widespread study and criticism of state legislatures in the 1960s and 1970s. By 1977, the Senate's majority and minority leaders had acquired more secretarial and administrative assistants. Twenty secretaries served the rest of the senators, a dozen handled the committees, and two women made up the steno pool. In addition, each senator now had an aide. The expanding House leadership of each party had secretaries and receptionists, and each standing committee had a secretary. Other than the leaders, House members did not have personal secretaries or assistants. They relied on a pool of thirty-seven stenographers and more than five dozen pages. The House matrons and many of the attendants, doorkeepers, and other lower-level employees were gone. The legislative aides, secretaries, and pages that session included a future minority chief of staff and majority legislative director (Andy DiPalma), Senate clerk (Martha Butler), director of the state office of budget and management (Bill Shkurti), and congressman, presidential candidate, and television show host (John Kasich). By 1985, every senator had both a personal legislative assistant and a secretary. In the House, leaders and committee chairs had their own staffs. Other members shared secretaries and aides for a time, but the number of employees kept growing so that by the 1990s every representative had at least one personal assistant.[19]

The patronage system that had so disturbed Lauren Glosser in 1932 remained in existence but in modified form. In the 1980s, maintenance, custodial, and laborer jobs became union or civil service positions usually filled without regard to political considerations. Similarly, members could recommend students for employment as pages, but most pages came to be hired through an open application process not dependent on political connections. When the House changed hands in 1995, the sergeant at arms retired, but the new Republican majority retained all of his numerous assistants. Attrition soon reduced their ranks, but a few hung on until the Speaker discharged them in 2000 when the House required the sergeant at arms and his assistants to have training as peace officers. Even the clerks' positions became less partisan with the splitting up of caucus staffs into political and administrative divisions. In short, the trend toward professionalism in the General Assembly invaded even the stronghold of patronage.[20]

Professional and Nonpartisan

Among the ever-growing ranks of legislative employees, none better reflected the increasing professionalism of the General Assembly than the staffs of the legislative reference services. The legislative service movement began early in the Progressive era. Historian Charles McCarthy of Wisconsin believed, in good Progressive fashion, that government ought to have at its command the same expertise as private interests in the crafting of legislation. He talked the Wisconsin state library commission into creating the position of legislative librarian in the state library. The office evolved into the first modern legislative reference service. It had a research division to collect and catalogue all sorts of information that might be useful to the lawmakers and a bill-drafting division that prided itself on being technically proficient and completely nonpartisan.[21]

McCarthy's library spawned imitators in other states. Ohio joined the legislative service movement in 1910 with the creation of the Legislative Reference and Information Department, headed by a legislative reference librarian, in the state library. The librarian was to be a person "well fitted by training and experience" for the job, which involved collecting information and assisting members of the General Assembly "in the preparation and formulation of bills."

In the meantime, the University of Cincinnati, under president Charles W. Dabney, was becoming the "brains" of the Queen City, cooperating with "all the education, social, and industrial interests of Cincinnati" in an effort to make the city a progressive showcase. In 1913, the political science department established the Municipal Reference Bureau under the direction of Selden Gale Lowrie, a McCarthy protégé, to provide information to city councilmen, administrators, and the public.[22]

Dabney and Governor James M. Cox, a progressive Democrat, thought the state ought to have an agency like the Municipal Reference Bureau. In his first address to the General Assembly in 1912, Cox called for the creation of a "bureau of legislative research for the development of every subject vital to the state and the legislature," headed by a director "related to the department of political economy" at the Ohio State University (even though Dabney thought the Buckeye faculty consisted chiefly of partisan Republicans) and employing "an official draftsman during the session of the legislature for the use of its members." In 1913, the General Assembly replaced the Legislative Reference and Information Department with the Legislative Reference Department (LRD). The new department's functions were generally the same as those of the one it replaced but on a grander, or at least grander-sounding, scale. The statute spelled out the tasks in considerable detail, specified the kind of staff the department would employ, and provided for a much larger budget. Lowrie moved from Cincinnati to head the department.[23]

The LRD, which, according to a 1922 description, "collects information on public affairs useful to legislators, drafts bills on request, and compiles, edits and indexes laws and compilations on special subjects," was actually a very small operation. Lowrie departed after less than a year, leaving attorney George Edge in charge of one assistant. The department soon acquired a librarian and a stenographer, for a total staff of four, but that's as much as it grew in its first decade. Notwithstanding its title, the LRD was not controlled by the legislature. Cox rode into the governor's office on the high tide of Progressivism. A strong Democratic leader with big majorities in both houses of the General Assembly, Cox vigorously pressed his Progressive agenda. Unlike the governors of old, who had no veto, little patronage power, and few executive agencies under their control, Cox had both formal power and the will to use it. The LRD was one more instrument this forceful executive leader could use to implement his ambitious program. While the State Library Commission had general supervision of the department, the governor had to approve the appointment and salary of the director. The governor as well as the legislature could call upon the LRD to conduct research and draft bills. Lowrie worked closely with Cox in pursuit of the Progressive program. It was Lowrie who proposed the creation of a budget bureau at a "cabinet" meeting in 1913. Following the passage of key components of Cox's program, Lowrie and one of his employees wrote articles explaining and extolling them.[24]

The remarkable session of 1913 involved far more legislation than Lowrie and his small staff could handle, although, if they were anything like McCarthy, they worked all hours trying. Their job was not to draft every bill, a task that would have been impossible. It was, more likely, to gather and synopsize data on matters that seemed likely to come up during session, to respond to specific requests for information, and to assist in bill-drafting when asked. The assistance might come in the form of meetings between Lowrie or a member of his staff, out-side experts, perhaps from a university, and the committee responsible for the bill. Cox recalled in his memoirs that "[w]e employed an expert draftsman to be constantly at the call of members of the Assembly and to be used primarily in drawing up measures dealing with provincial conditions. This avoided any pos-sibility of conflict with existing laws or objections that might be raised in test cases before the courts." By "provincial conditions" Cox may have meant the circumstances of agriculture and rural schools; Lowrie drafted the agricultural commission law. Outside experts prepared other extensive and complicated bills. A special commission appointed before Cox's election drafted the children's code; a committee of the Ohio Municipal League wrote the municipal charter law; two members of the old Public Service Commission and two law professors from Ohio State prepared the bill creating the Public Utilities Commission of Ohio.[25]

In 1933, the General Assembly separated the Legislative Reference Depart-ment from the state library and renamed it the Legislative Reference Bureau (LRB). The bureau's governing board consisted of the governor and the House and Senate clerks. The state library's move out of the capitol and into a new state office building prompted the change, but the General Assembly may also have felt that the agency ought to be under the direct control of the governor and legislature rather than the Department of Education, where the state library had been placed years before.[26]

Over time, the LRD and then the LRB came to devote more attention to bill-drafting and less to research. George Edge personally drafted hundreds of bills each session. On April 24, 1921, a newspaper reported that he had prepared 376 of the Eighty-fourth General Assembly's 595 bills introduced so far that year. Many times a legislator had only the foggiest notion of the kind of bill he wanted. In those cases Edge had to study the issue, research Ohio law and the statutes of other states, write the bill, and risk getting blamed for any flaws. In 1923 the LRD drafted 600 bills, nearly two-thirds of the total introduced that year. In 1950 a senator estimated that the LRB drew up 75 percent of all bills, with the rest being prepared by "private attorneys, organizations, or the members them-selves," while the director of the LRB reported that his agency drafted 90 percent of the bills and virtually all of the resolutions. To make up for the loss of research capability, in the 1940s the General Assembly created first the Ohio Program Commission to produce special studies and make policy recommendations and then the Legislative Research Commission to provide financial information to the legislature. The former included executive officers and gubernatorial appointees, but the latter consisted solely of six legislators with the authority to hire a staff. The research commission represented a step toward legislative independence from the governor. Also in the 1940s, the General Assembly created the Bureau of Code Revision to reorganize the General Code and to keep it up-to-date by incorporating laws as they were enacted.[27]

In 1953, the General Assembly merged several of these functions in the Legislative Service Commission, although the LRB continued in existence until 1981. A legal scholar wrote at the time that the act creating the LSC was "the first successful effort by any state to consolidate legislative services previously provided by several independent agencies into one agency" and would be "watched with interest . . . throughout the country." At first, the LSC concentrated on research studies and fiscal analyses, but, as the demand for bill-drafting services increased, it took on more and more drafting assignments. Beginning with a staff of seven, the LSC grew slowly but steadily until, in the mid-1960s, computerization and the increasing demand for bill-drafting, fiscal analysis, and committee services led to a sudden doubling of professional and clerical staff from sixteen to thirty-three. In 1973, the LSC established the Legislative Budget Office to provide fiscal research and analyses of bills, but it abolished the office and folded it back into the LSC in 2000. All of these agencies had to be staffed with librarians, lawyers, economists, and other professionals. By 1979, the combined staff of the LSC and the Legislative Budget Office was over one hundred and still growing.[28]

Women's Work

The expansion of the legislative workforce opened new opportunities for African Americans and women. In 1899, a black job-seeker wrote to newly elected senator Warren G. Harding asking for his support. He noted that Republican Senates in Ohio had made it a practice "to award the position of Enrolling Clerk to a colored man." Photographs from the 1920s show that blacks continued to hold positions as engrossing or enrolling clerks, which they had been doing since the late nineteenth century. Their greatest progress, though, may have come in the last quarter of the twentieth century when lawmakers got personal aides. The reapportionment decisions of the 1960s brought more African American members to the General Assembly. Perhaps their very presence attracted black applicants for aide positions. In any case, by the end of the century, African Americans were filling slots in the expanding personal and caucus legislative staffs of both parties in both houses.[29]

The progress made by women in securing legislative employment, so evident in the late nineteenth century, screeched to a halt in the twentieth. Women did not regress; they just ceased to go forward. Women often served as assistant clerks. In 1935, for example, the House deputy clerk, engrossing clerk, and recording clerk and the Senate engrossing clerk, enrolling clerk, and secretary to the clerk were all women. Men made up all the other statutory officers of the legislature (except when Mrs. S. I. Gruner succeeded her deceased husband as the Senate's first assistant sergeant at arms for the special session of 1935–36) and almost all of the numerous assistant clerks authorized by resolution. The pages, porters, postmasters, custodians, doorkeepers, and cloakroom attendants were male. (In 1921, the Senate appointed Ruth LeFever, the daughter of Senator Errett LeFever of Athens County, a messenger, but she was probably one of a kind.) Stenography and typing, which had been women's entree into the white-collar world, had become routinized and lost their professional cachet, and it was in these now distinctly subordinate positions that women chiefly found work with the legislature. Of the thirty-two stenographers listed in the 1935 House and Senate rosters, only the two press stenographers were male. Women held a few other jobs, such as telephone attendant, guide, and House matron, but their main place of work was the steno pool.[30]

The expansion of legislative staff coincided with the high tide of the feminist movement in the 1970s. Not surprisingly, the female presence in and around the General Assembly grew. The ever-growing secretarial staff was exclusively female. More than half of the Senate aides in 1977 were women, as were about a fifth of the House pages. The arrival of female pages in 1971 brought the General Assembly into conflict with a 1913 statute that prohibited the employment of females under twenty-one years of age to deliver messages. Rooted in more general child-labor legislation, the law probably had been designed to keep girls and young women from walking city streets with telegrams and business messages late at night. In 1973, the General Assembly reduced to eighteen the age at which females could be employed to deliver messages, and a few years later it repealed the ban altogether. At first, some members thought that young women would not be able to haul members' luggage or handle some of the other chores a page might be called on to do, but the concern proved unfounded. "Anyway," the Senate clerk said, "I think the male pages like having the girls around."[31]

Members of the House clerk's staff around 1969. *Left to right:* Harriet R. Murphy, recording clerk; Julia M. English, fiscal clerk; Patricia R. Riffle, enrolling clerk; Ruth V. Pennell, enrolling clerk. *Courtesy of the Ohio House of Representatives*

Women also held about half of the assistant clerks' positions. They continued to advance in these positions until they dominated the offices. At the opening of the twenty-first century, the Senate chief of staff, Senate deputy chief of staff, House chief administrative officer, House clerk, and most of the assistant clerks in each house were females. Women also made up roughly 60 percent of the staff of the Legislative Service Commission. By the time women came to occupy the highest administrative positions in the General Assembly in the 1980s these offices no longer entailed the political clout of the Tom Bateman days, but by then women were moving up the party leadership ladders, and before long a woman would become Speaker of the House.

19

MILKERS, WILD WOMEN,

AND PANCAKES

THE OHIO GENERAL ASSEMBLY and other state legislatures entered the twentieth century with a well-earned reputation for sleaze. Progressive reformers and their successors attacked sordidness in the General Assembly with limited success. The big problem was the influence of lobbyists. Powerful lobbies provided much of the excitement of legislative life—the food, the drink, the entertainment—and thereby gained the friendly consideration of many members. In addition, lobbyists were the most important sources of information and expertise on many issues. Without an independent, impartial provider of information, legislators depended too much on these highly useful, often intelligent and well-informed, but hardly unbiased sources.

Lobbies, like legislatures, had a terrible reputation in the early twentieth century. Given the mass of bills introduced and the "snap" nature of committee business, interest groups could hardly do without paid agents in the capital, if only to keep track of legislation. Nevertheless, legislative leaders joined in the antilobby outcry. To reduce the lobbies' clout the General Assembly outlawed free railroad passes—a measure of little significance because eastern railroads had already agreed among themselves to stop issuing the much-abused passes—stiffened the penalties for offering, soliciting, and accepting bribes, and began to regulate legislative agents. A lobby registration bill made it through the House in 1910 after a committee investigation turned up evidence that a telephone company had tried to bribe two representatives, but the Senate killed it. Reformers had more success in the Progressive-leaning legislature of 1913. The new law required all paid lobbyists to register with the secretary of state, listing the names of their employers and the bills in which they were interested. Without a certificate of registration, they could not appear before any House or Senate committee. The law also obligated lobbyists to file itemized statements of receipts and expenditures after a General Assembly's final adjournment. The bill passed handily over objections that it infringed on the constitutional rights of citizens to petition the legislature and to instruct their representatives.[1]

Bribery

For all the clamor over the corrupting influence of lobbies, however, the fault for the greatest bribery scandal in the General Assembly's history lay with legislators, not corporations or interest groups. Greedy lawmakers and lobbyists knew how to milk money from businesses by threatening them with burdensome regulatory laws. In 1906, Governor Myron T. Herrick denounced the sponsors of "milking bills" as more reprehensible than lobbyists because they gave lobbies the excuse of self-defense for coming to the legislature. Some lobbyists collaborated in the introduction of "milkers." Early in the session, wrote reporters George Creel and Sloane Gordon,

> swarms of lobbyists, many of them ex-members, have appeared in Columbus laden with carefully drawn measures, the passage of any one of which would mean much financial loss to some "interest." The lobbyist would establish friendly relations with a member of the House or Senate and prevail upon him to introduce the bill. The next move on the part of the lobbyist would be to arrange with the threatened "interest" to prevent the passage of the measure, the legislator introducing it being, as a rule, a party to the game.[2]

In 1911, legislators reportedly introduced 118 "milkers." Senate sergeant at arms Rodney Diegle, who first got to know members through his hotel at Put-in-Bay, where the lawmakers held their annual reunions, acted as the middleman between the "interests" and the buyable senators. Diegle handled the negotiations; when the parties agreed on a price, Senator Isaac E. Huffman, chairman of the Judiciary Committee and member of the Finance Committee, would steer the bill to the appropriate committee for pigeonholing. A crooked crowd in the House operated in similar fashion.[3]

The cost of buying protection eventually got too high for members of the Ohio Manufacturers Association. In cooperation with the Franklin County prosecutor, they hired detectives to pose as lobbyists and lured the offending lawmakers into a trap. The ensuing investigation, wrote Creel and Sloane, proved beyond doubt "that the present Legislature is the most hopelessly corrupt body of public looters that ever disgraced Ohio or any other state." The chief detective declared, "You could not pass a bill in Ohio to stop the plague without bribing the legislature." The grand jury indicted nine members from both houses and both parties, along with Diegle, one of Diegle's assistants, and several lobbyists, on bribery-related charges. The Senate tried to thwart the prosecutions by launching its own investigation and granting immunity to witnesses, but a storm of public indignation and the House's refusal to appropriate money for the committee frustrated the gambit. Eventually, six of the accused either confessed or were convicted after trial; four went to prison.[4]

Rumors of bribery continued to plague the General Assembly long after the scandal of 1911 faded away. In 1919, a joint investigative committee rejected allegations of widespread corruption made in a newspaper editorial, but it did find that one representative had sought "some consideration" for his vote on a bill. The committee recommended that the offender be censured or expelled, but the House took no action. In 1923, newspapers reported scuttlebutt that two senators had been offered bribes in connection with a bill to limit the liability of hotel keepers for the property of their guests. Republicans controlled the Senate and could determine the scope of any investigation, but "regular" and "progressive" senators bickered over the composition of the investigating committee. Most senators sought to keep the probe in the hands of three named members, but a small group of Republicans and Democrats wanted the Democratic lieutenant governor to select the committee. A "'hand-picked' committee lays us all open to suspicion," declared one Republican. "If the lieutenant governor, who is of the opposite political faith, appoints this committee, and it brings out a report vindicating those under suspicion in these rumors, it will be a vindication that will be accepted as impartial and above suspicion." The Senate ignored this advice and adopted the "regular" resolution. The committee of investigation cleared the implicated lawmakers, finding the source of the rumors in a rivalry among lobbyists for the hotel industry.[5]

In 1933, Representative Forest W. Hall of Guernsey County told reporters and then the House that a lobbyist had offered him a $1,000 bribe to "forget" a bill he had introduced. Hall refused to provide the prosecutor with an affidavit, without which the county prosecutor would not present the case to the grand jury. But the House, affronted by the widespread adverse reflections on its integrity, conducted its own investigation. The committee found Hall's testimony questionable but still recommended a grand jury investigation, with or without Hall's affidavit. The prosecutor, who, according to Hall, "didn't seem overly zealous about the matter," seems to have let the issue drop without an inquest.[6]

On the other hand, an overly zealous Franklin County prosecutor that same year obtained an indictment of Senator William H. Herner on a charge of soliciting a $1,500 bribe from a lobbyist. It was the first indictment stemming from a grand jury investigation of lobbying activities; however, as a Columbus newspaper noted, "to pin conviction for bribery, or for the offering or soliciting of bribes, on the guilty, is a difficult matter, likely to tax the abilities and the energies of any prosecutor to the utmost." The chief witness for the prosecution denied that Herner had solicited money, and the judge directed a verdict for the senator.[7]

The Swarm of Lobbyists

The crude offering and solicitation of cash bribes probably did not disappear completely after 1933, but they seem to have gone out of style. Bribery had always been illegal and immoral, and after the 1911 scandal especially unpopular. A bigger problem was that lobbying had become a profession, and the lobbyists were ubiquitous. Critics likened them to a swarm or to worms "crawling out of the woodwork." "Ever since Governor White asked the Legislature to put a tax on soft drinks, malt, tobacco and amusements," wrote the *Ohio State Journal* in 1933, "members of the House and Senate have been buttonholed many times by opponents of the taxes. They have been called on the phone, they have received letters, and they have been personally waylaid." Lobbyists crowded the "duck pond" at the rear of the House chamber, to the irritation of a growing number of representatives. Notwithstanding rules that barred lobbyists from the floor during session, many of them, especially former legislators with friends among the doormen and lawmakers, boldly ignored the rules. It was the pressure of their constant presence and their chumminess with the members, rather than outright bribery, that most seriously distorted the legislative process.[8]

In 1930, muckraking journalist Walter W. Liggett, in one of a series of exposés on the evils of Prohibition, painted a lurid picture of corruption in Columbus: "public utility lobbyists wining and dining staunch Anti-Saloon League followers and throwing mixed [interracial] parties where 'wild women' do their stuff"; "liquor consumed in the Capitol building itself to celebrate the passage of a measure drafted by Anti-Saloon League leaders"; "Babylonian revels" featuring abundant booze, crap-shooting, and as many as a dozen female "entertainers" dancing in the nude.[9]

Neither the lobby registration law, which was not enforced, nor Liggett's revelations had much impact on the activities of lobbyists. Complaints persisted from within and without the legislature. Irate members introduced resolutions demanding investigations—of a dinner and entertainment given by personal finance companies for Banking Committee members, of judges who allegedly used their influence and provided entertainment to affect a judges' pension bill, of industry lobbyists who spent many thousands of dollars to influence legislation, gave free food and liquor to members, and threatened bodily harm to a senator —but the resolutions were tabled or died in committee. In the 1950s, Representative Guy C. Hiner, who had been suspicious of lobbyists ever since one offered him a $500 bribe in 1939, griped about the General Assembly's failure to take lobbying abuses seriously. Nearly thirty years after Liggett's exposé, lobbyists appeared to be securing votes with contributions to "financially-starved county chairmen" and entertainment described in rumors "too ugly to repeat."[10]

The enactment of federal lobbying legislation in 1946 and subsequent enforcement and investigative activities by the Department of Justice and by a congressional committee stimulated interest in lobby regulation among state legislatures. In 1953, following a "hue and cry" about the activities of lobbyists, the House directed the Legislative Service Commission to study lobbying and recommend changes to the lobby law. It was "common knowledge," said the House resolution, that some lobbyists "have become, by their flagrant disregard of good taste, propriety, and morality, a reproach to the integrity, motivations, and intelligence of the members of the General Assembly." As the prime example, the resolution pointed to lobbyists' renting of suites at Columbus hotels, where they dispensed free food and drink to legislators. The prevalence of such nefarious activities indicated the laxity of both the law and law enforcement.[11]

The commission got off to an inauspicious start. The dozen legislators who made up the commission did not appoint a committee of colleagues to conduct the investigation for seven months. Two months after the appointments, committee chairman Senator Raymond Hildebrand said that he had not heard from any of the other committee members or from the sponsors of the 1953 resolution expressing any interest in the investigation. "Maybe," he said, "we'd better ask the members of the committee if any of them ever accepted a sandwich or a meal from lobbyists and if they did, disqualify them and disband the committee."[12]

The committee finally conducted a series of public hearings between April 14 and December 17, 1954, and, in 1955, the LSC research staff produced a report reaffirming what everyone already knew: that lobbyists and their employers often failed to file the required financial forms, that the forms they did file frequently lacked enough detail to be useful, and that nobody seemed to be in charge of enforcing the lobbying law. The report recommended some changes to strengthen the law but concluded that the "basic safeguard against improper lobbying practices" was the election of legislators with the "courage and integrity" to resist "improper influences." With such a lukewarm endorsement of legislative action, the legislature did nothing for the next twenty years.[13]

During the long and, for the legislators, expensive session of 1959, the Franklin County grand jury looked into charges that lobbyists had picked up hotel tabs for legislators. This was not a new practice. In the 1940s, some members bragged about not having to pay for their meals during session and expected lobbies to pick up their hotel bills. In 1959, the Columbus Citizen reported that members "allowed their hotel bills to pile up for the entire seven-month session. They expected some friendly lobbyist to discreetly take care of the bills after sine die adjournment scheduled for Aug. 14. Some of the bills range around $2000." Both lobbyists and lawmakers faced the prospect of embarrassing publicity and criminal prosecution, the former for failing to file accurate financial statements and both for violating the bribery statute. Lobbyists had not been in the habit of filing detailed financial reports; not surprisingly, the grand jury found the ones they examined to be out of compliance with the law. The investigation resulted in a rare conviction of a lobbyist.[14]

While the legislators involved in the hotel case might have gotten into trouble for soliciting or accepting bribes, they, unlike the lobbyists, could not have been charged with failing to file honest financial statements. Legislators had no legal obligation to report gifts or other income received in their capacity as members of the General Assembly. In the 1940s, recalled William Saxbe, "[e]thical control was unknown, and financial reporting on contributions of gifts, trips, meals, etc. was scant to none."[15]

How much difference all the free dinners and entertainment made in the lawmakers' votes, as opposed to their social lives, is hard to say. A midcentury legislator doubted "that free meals and entertainment, . . . organized floods of mail . . . suggestions of political support or political reprisal, have any great influence on most legislators . . . The most subtle and . . . powerful lobbying technique is that of 'cronyism,' based on friendships between veteran legislators and veteran lobbyists." Decades later, after legislative salaries had become respectable, a member derided the idea that lobbyists could buy votes with dinners. "I've gone out plenty of times to dinner with lobbyists and voted against them the next day," he said. But the very presence of a crowd of lobbyists in and around the statehouse seemed wrong, especially when the public regarded lobbyists as practically a "criminal class." It was bad enough that registered lobbyists far outnumbered the legislators; much worse was the spectacle of unregistered lobbyists "swarming over the halls of the Senate and House of Representatives." The "brazen disregard" of the registration requirement, warned Governor Michael DiSalle, fostered "the suspicion that a privileged few can always manipulate for the benefit of a few to the detriment of the whole."[16]

The infestation of lobbyists, registered and unregistered, disrupted the business of the legislature. Notwithstanding rules that prohibited anyone but members, legislative employees, reporters, and specially invited guests from being on the floor of the House or Senate while the body was in session, lobbyists crowded the floor, creating noise and confusion. In the 1930s and early 1940s, resolutions directing the sergeant at arms or adjutant general to keep lobbyists off the floor, out of the halls, or even off statehouse grounds entirely, especially during the end-of-session lunacy, went nowhere. The House got serious about enforcing its rules sooner than the Senate. On June 27, 1945, the House, noting its prior decision to finish business by the next day, instructed the sergeant at arms to keep the House free of lobbyists. In the 1950s, Speakers insisted that lobbyists fill out papers stating their purpose and whether they were being paid, and they made more determined efforts to keep lobbyists off the floor during session. With its roomy galleries, the House could banish spectators to the upstairs seats. The Senate, however, continued to give "free rein" to lobbyists. In 1957, the Senate resolved to keep unauthorized persons outside the railing, a stricture it felt necessary to repeat as late as 1965, but, even after that, the president often had to gavel down noisy lobbyists in the back of the hall.[17]

The General Assembly's attempts to curb the influence of lobbyists, at least on the floor of the House and Senate, came at a time of general public trust in government, which peaked in the 1950s and early 1960s. While the reasons for the favorable view of government in those years are in dispute, there is no doubt that confidence in government began a long downward slide in the 1960s and has never really recovered. It is surely no coincidence that the idea of a formal code of ethics for state legislatures, floated in the early 1950s, gained strength only after faith in government began to erode. In 1961, Ohio governor Michael DiSalle chided the General Assembly for refusing to pass ethics legislation, forc-ing him to promulgate a code of ethics for the executive branch alone. DiSalle called upon the lawmakers to "establish an equality of responsibility for both the appointed and the elected pubic official." But the General Assembly did not act.[18]

In 1967, the Council of State Governments published a model act relating to legislative ethics, and the next year the National Legislative Conference staff drafted a Model Code of Legislative Conduct for state legislators. Only eight states had legislative ethics statutes at the time. In 1972, the General Assembly established a joint House-Senate ethics committee to adopt a legislative code of ethics, recommend measures to be taken when individual members breached ethical standards, and advise both the General Assembly and individual mem-bers on ethical questions.[19]

All the fuss over ethics bewildered some people, including lobbyists. In 1972, the Ohio Trucking Association contributed handsomely to the attendance of key legislators and their wives at a five-day convention in the Bahamas. It was, said a newspaper, the "best junket of any week." When questioned about his associa-tion's generosity, a spokesman pointed out that legislators always participated in conventions held in Columbus hotels. "He seemed puzzled," the paper reported, "that more questions were asked about a five-day junket to a plush resort than were asked about taking part in a panel that requires a five-minute walk from the State House."[20]

Lobbyists continued to buzz around the statehouse, far outnumbering the leg-islators. In 1973, the Ohio Manufacturers' Association and the Ohio AFL-CIO had ten and eight agents, respectively, working the legislature. Ex-legislators lobbied their former colleagues. The amount spent by lobbyists per member over the course of a biennium exceeded four thousand dollars. Trade associations gave dinners and parties for the lawmakers and treated them at their conventions. Groups that previously had shunned entertainment as a means of promoting their interests gave in. Four retirement systems representing teachers and public employees gave a reception for legislators at the Sheraton Hotel featuring "striking hostesses in bright dresses" and "free booze and hors d'oeuvres (jumbo shrimp and liver wrapped in bacon)."[21]

Ethics and Lobbying Reform

It took the Watergate scandal to produce major ethics reform. The episode sparked a rash of legislation dealing with ethics in government. In 1974, the General Assembly passed an ethics law that dealt with every branch of state government and regulated local elected officials as well. It targeted conflicts of interest, gifts, nepotism, and the activities of ex-legislators and other former public employees who became lobbyists and sought to influence their old colleagues and employers. Violations of the law were made criminal offenses. Furthermore, the law subjected many public officials, including members of the General Assembly, to more stringent financial disclosure requirements. It also abolished the joint ethics committee in favor of a separate committee for each house and gave the committees all the powers of the joint committee plus the authority to hear complaints, subpoena witnesses, and recommend sanctions.[22]

In 1976, the General Assembly rewrote the lobby law. The new statute required paid lobbyists (or "legislative agents") and their employers to register with the Senate clerk. Registrations expired on the last day of the legislative biennium. Registrants had to file statements of expenditures with the Senate clerk every six months, and a statement had to show considerable detail about expenditures for any one member that exceeded $150 during the reporting period. Registrants also had to report any financial transactions with members, including any purchase, sale, or gift of more than $25. The law actually reduced the criminal penalties for violations, but, given the previous lack of enforcement, that hardly mattered.[23]

The new ethics and lobbying laws failed to rid state government of its bad odor, but legislators were not the worst offenders. Governor Richard Celeste and

Lieutenant Governor Myrl Shoemaker paid themselves handsome political consulting fees from campaign funds, and scandals involving state contracts and political tests for state employment added to the poisoned atmosphere. The "sleaze factor" prompted the passage of another ethics law in 1986 that attempted to reduce improper influences on public officials in all branches of government.[24]

But legislators shared in the tawdriness. During the 1980s, they turned "pancaking" into a fine art. The 1974 ethics law required lawmakers to report the source of each gift of more than $500 and every source of income over $500 in the preceding calendar year, but nothing limited the amount a lobbyist could spend on wining, dining, and entertaining a lawmaker. Some influential members found they could fatten their wallets substantially by charging speaking fees of $500—just short of the reportable amount. Better yet, they sometimes collected multiple $500 checks for attending a single event, a practice known as pancaking. Democratic representative Paul Jones's proficiency at pancaking led to his downfall. In 1993, a newspaper reported that Jones, the chairman of the House Health and Retirement Committee, had collected speaking fees of $500 apiece from five different health care groups for attending one event. To make matters worse, when another Democratic representative asked Jones to speak at the annual meeting of a nonprofit health care organization, he insisted on his $500 fee.[25]

A number of Democrats, upset by the bad publicity, the prevalence of pancaking, and Jones's "shakedown" of a fellow Democrat, called on Speaker Vern Riffe to relieve Jones of his chairmanship, and they joined Republicans in urging remedial legislation. Such impudence did not sit well with the autocratic Riffe, who insisted that intraparty squabbles be settled in the privacy of the caucus room. Riffe defended Jones, a protégé who was married to the college roommate of Riffe's daughter. Riffe had another reason for wanting to resolve the matter behind closed doors: he was a champion pancaker himself.[26]

Republicans, it turned out, also had a fondness for pancakes. In 1991, Stanley Aronoff, the Republican president of the Senate, joined Riffe at an affair where each of them collected six $500 checks. In 1993, fourteen legislators, Republicans and Democrats, each received and failed to report multiple $500 checks for attending either a seminar at the Columbus office of a securities firm or a dinner at the home of a prominent Columbus lobbyist. A special prosecutor cleared members who accepted but did not report only one check for either event, but the executive director of a public interest group condemned even this legal activity as a "sham." "Lawmakers can walk into a party sponsored by a firm that could have interest in legislation, eat cookies, drink soft drinks and be handed a check for their personal account," she observed in disgust. "[F]or that to be found acceptable is insulting."[27]

To determine the extent to which lawmakers collected such honoraria, the *Columbus Dispatch* sent a questionnaire to every member of the General Assembly asking how much money the member had received in speaking fees since January 1, 1992. Seventy-five reported no income from honoraria; twenty-three others reported less than $500. Twenty members, many of them in leadership positions, reported amounts over $500, the highest being $4,400. Some noted that they received fees for only a small percentage of their speaking engagements. Representative Daniel Troy, for example, said he spoke at ninety-eight functions but received only seven honoraria averaging $350 each, and some of that money was used to cover travel costs. Fourteen members, including Riffe and Aronoff, declined to answer the survey, although both insisted that they accepted fees for a relatively small number of their numerous speaking engagements.[28]

It was not illegal for legislators to charge speaking fees or accept honoraria for attending breakfasts or addressing interest groups, but it smelled rotten. Pancaking itself was a dubious practice, and other payments came to light that had not been properly reported by legislators or lobbyists. The outcry over the growing scandal caused "rampant paranoia" at the statehouse. The House quickly passed a bill intended by the sponsors "to get rid of the public perception that politicians, including legislators, are crooks—bought for a few drinks, a game of golf at a swank country club or a trip to a conference at a resort." In its final form, the bill did away with the separate House and Senate ethics committees in favor of the Joint Legislative Ethics Committee; authorized the joint committee to hire a Legislative Inspector General and a staff; required more detailed reporting by legislators of their sources of income and of expenditures by lobbyists for the care and feeding of legislators; required lawmakers to report all gifts worth more than $75 ($25 if from a lobbyist); barred former members from lobbying for one year after leaving the General Assembly; and prohibited members from accepting appearance or speaking fees except for legitimate business or other purposes unrelated to their jobs as legislators.[29]

As the legislation worked its way through the General Assembly, the investigations began. The ethics committees, a special prosecutor, and the Franklin County prosecutor all got into the act. Representative Jones, whose activities started the scandal, never faced criminal charges. He resigned his chairmanship under pressure, was reinstated by Riffe after being cleared by the House Ethics Committee, resigned again, and lost his bid for reelection in 1994, scapegoated, he claimed, for doing nothing more than what others were doing. In 1996, the Franklin County grand jury indicted Riffe, Aronoff, Senator Gene Watts, and a couple of lobbying firms. Aronoff pleaded guilty and Watts no contest to misdemeanor charges for not properly filing financial disclosure statements. Riffe fought similar charges, but, worn down by the legal battle and poor health, he eventually pled guilty to nondisclosure of honoraria "and/or" interest income from an inheritance. All three received fines and community service in the form of speaking to students about ethics.[30]

The convictions did not affect the defendants' political careers. Riffe had already retired and Aronoff had announced his retirement; Watts frankly admitted his mistake, won reelection, and retained his leadership position. Nor did the guilty pleas seriously mar the reputations of Riffe and Aronoff, both of whom had had long, productive political careers otherwise unsullied by legal irregularities. The leaders' actual transgressions were trifling matters. The real significance of the convictions lay in their suggestion that Ohio had entered a new era of ethical fastidiousness.[31]

For all the complaints about lobbying over the course of the twentieth century, the brouhaha over honoraria was a rare legal occurrence. By one account, no lobbyist had been charged with a criminal violation since 1959, when a court fined a representative of coal mining interests for improprieties in reporting the payment of restaurant and hotel bills for five legislators; and that was said to have been the first such prosecution in forty years. The last previous indictments of legislators for lobby-related offenses had come in 1911. In 2006, the legislative inspector general complained that he had almost no administrative power to enforce the lobbying laws.[32]

Other Ethics Issues

Not all of the ethical controversies in the twentieth century involved lobbying. Some stemmed from dual officeholding. The constitution prohibited any person who held any "lucrative office" (amended in 1973 to "public office") under the authority of the state from sitting in the General Assembly. In 1890, the General Assembly passed a law declaring vacant the seat of any member who took a position as a trustee of any state institution. Neither the constitution nor the statute deterred all members from accepting paid positions in the executive branch of government. A House resolution of 1914 charged that four representatives illegally held lucrative jobs in administrative agencies. Looking back twenty years, an investigating committee found that many members had simultaneously been employed in other branches of government, as automobile inspectors for the registrar of automobiles, attorneys for the Banking Department, agents for the Bureau of Labor Statistics, inspectors for the Department of Agriculture, and in a variety of capacities for state and local government. The committee concluded that the practice was not necessarily illegal because not every job was an "office," but it denounced the practice as a bad idea that gave members the opportunity to influence legislation unduly. In 1914, the General Assembly amended the 1890 statute to prohibit members from serving on or accepting paid employment from any committee or commission created by the legislature. In 1915, the lawmakers extended the ban to executive departments and administrative agencies.[33]

Just as the lobbying scandal of 1911 had a counterpart in the late twentieth century, so did the hubbub over dual officeholding. In 1992, the House Ethics Committee ruled that Representative Ray Miller could not serve as Vice President for Minority Affairs at Columbus State Community College while holding a seat in the House. The vice president's job, said the committee, was a managerial position and could not be held consistently with the then-current version of the 1890 law. Miller resigned as vice president and promptly accepted the post of Special Assistant to the President for Minority Affairs. Tinkering with the job title and description did not help. The Ethics Committee again ruled against Miller, and he had to give up his paid connection to the college.[34]

In 2005, the legislative inspector general, for the first time since the creation of the office in the wake of the speaking-fee scandal, referred a case to a prosecutor. The alleged offense involved the use of state employees and equipment for private purposes. The prosecutor declined to pursue criminal sanctions and the case ended with the member's apology and the payment of restitution. At the same time, the Joint Legislative Ethics Committee reproved three other legislators for failing to report that they had accepted dinner and football tickets from a lobbyist.[35]

Occasionally, other types of ethics cases arose. A proposed House resolution of 1941 complained of a numbers racket being run openly in the statehouse. One member was accused of molesting a female police officer. Another lost a sexual-harassment lawsuit brought by a former aide, although the legislator maintained his innocence throughout. A third survived a similar suit unscathed when the plaintiff, his onetime secretary, failed to turn over medical records. Members racked up tens of thousands of dollars in questionable long-distance telephone calls at public expense. The House majority leader got into hot water for raising money for his own personal benefit by selling mock stock certificates to lobbyists. A representative received the first censure by the House under the 1994 ethics law and loss of a committee chairmanship for accepting plane fare and lodging from a lobbyist, although most members, according to one, thought he was guilty only of "sloppy bookkeeping." Senator Jeffrey Johnson, the head of the Legislative Black Caucus, was convicted under federal law of extorting campaign contributions and loans from businesses. (Within ten years he was back as the Black Caucus's executive director.)[36]

The biggest ethical controversy of the early twenty-first century, like the pancaking fuss of the 1990s, did not involve a violation of the ethics laws. The Republican Speaker of the House, Larry Householder, stirred up a commotion by allegedly raising money for a nonprofit organization and then having the organization use the money to promote Republican legislative candidates. Householder also directed money into state candidate funds, to which individuals could contribute far more than they could to individual candidates, allegedly for the purpose of funding his planned campaign for governor. The Speaker, his former chief of staff, and his leading fund-raiser became the targets of a federal investigation because of their strong-arm tactics. No charges resulted from the investigation, but the episode tarnished Householder's reputation and thwarted his political ambitions.[37]

20

THE RISE AND FALL OF

THE CORNSTALK BRIGADE

I N 2001, A COLUMNIST for the *Cleveland Plain Dealer* lambasted the Ohio
House of Representatives for passing a bill that declared same-sex marriage
to be against the public policy of the state. Republicans voted nearly unanimously
for the bill, Democrats mostly against it. But eleven Democrats, including "bumpkins" and a corn-belter, supported the measure. That Republicans had enough
votes to pass the bill without Democratic help was no surprise; Republicans had
dominated the General Assembly for most of the preceding century. That most
Democrats lined up against the Republicans was also to be expected; controversial issues had often produced partisan votes. And even though the columnist put
quotes around the word "Democrat" when referring to the eleven dissidents, the
decision of "bumpkins" to break party ranks could not have come as a shock. Since
the explosive growth of the cities in the late nineteenth century, there had been
a strong undercurrent of Ohio's legislative politics: a divergence between urban
and rural legislators that sometimes overrode party loyalty and discipline.[1]

Ohio saw far less turmoil in the partisan competition for power after 1900 than
it had before. The Republican and Democratic parties functioned continuously
throughout the twentieth century, and no third party challenged their domi-

nance. Some areas of the state remained loyal to one party or the other for a very long time, but that steadfastness may have been more habitual than heart-felt. When Wayne Wheeler of the Anti-Saloon League stumped among Ohio's Republicans for the dry Democratic candidate for governor forty years after the Civil War, he "had a hard job making the people see that they were not giving up their religion when they voted Democratic. That was especially true in the rural sections, where they always voted a straight Republican ticket in honour of Lincoln. I used to tell them that he wasn't running this year." But loyalty to a long-dead president is not the same as enthusiasm for the president's party. The passion that had once characterized both devotion to and divorce from one's party and fostered the rise of new political movements had melted away.[2]

Twentieth-century studies of voting behavior in the General Assembly showed that, notwithstanding the weakening of party fervor among the electorate, party affiliation proved more significant than any other factor in determining how leg-islators voted on contested issues. It is therefore a crucial fact of legislative politics that Republicans dominated the General Assembly for most of Ohio's second century. After the Civil War, control of the legislature alternated between the parties until the Republican victory of 1891. Without the depression that began under a Democratic administration in Washington in 1893 or the controversial presidential candidacy of Democrat William Jennings Bryan in 1896, the pen-dulum might have swung back toward the Democrats, as it had in the past. But that is speculation. The fact is that the election of 1891 ushered in a long era of Republican dominance.

Of the twenty General Assemblies elected between 1891 and 1930, the Demo-crats held both houses just three times, all between 1911 and 1918. In two other sessions, they had a slight edge or a tie only in the Senate. The rest of the time, the Republicans held sway in both houses, often by stupendous margins. Firm control of a chamber was not unusual, regardless of which party dominated; more often than not, the majority party had more than 60 percent of the membership of the House, the Senate, or both. But the Republican majorities often went far beyond that. In eight General Assemblies between 1892 and 1932, the majority members made up more than 75 percent of the House, and in ten they comprised more than 75 percent of the Senate. All of these lopsided House majorities and eight of the ten huge Senate majorities were Republican. From 1921 to 1930, Republicans made up an average of 84 percent of the House and 95 percent of the Senate. Even during the decade of the Depression, the Democrats controlled both houses only once; in another session, they had a majority in the House and a tie in the Senate. Of the eighteen legislatures that sat from 1939 through 1974, the Republicans controlled both houses fourteen times—fifteen if we count the 106th General Assembly, in which the Republican lieutenant governor had the tie-breaking vote in the Senate. The Democrats held both houses only twice during that period. Even after the Democratic breakthrough in the 1974 election, which inaugurated a long stretch of Democratic rule in the House, the Democrats could retain both chambers for only three sessions before temporarily losing control of the Senate in 1980. Republicans took the Senate again in 1984 and from 1994 through 2006 won both houses in every contest.[3]

The Underrepresented Cities

Republican dominance bore a complex relationship to the rise of cities and suburbs, the development of distinct urban and suburban political interests, and the apportionment of seats in the General Assembly. The astounding growth of the cities that began in the nineteenth century continued into the twentieth. Immigrants from southern and eastern Europe, whites from rural Ohio and West Virginia, and blacks from the South flocked to Ohio's industrial centers in the early twentieth century. Between 1900 and 1920, Cleveland's population more than doubled to nearly 800,000. Immigrants from central, southern, and eastern Europe and their children made up a majority of the inhabitants. Akron's population nearly quintupled, from 42,728 to 208,435. All of Ohio's major cities grew phenomenally.[4]

Immigration restrictions cut off the flow from Eastern Europe after 1921, but cities continued to expand for several more decades. African Americans accounted for much of the growth. From 1920 to 1950, the black population of Cleveland leaped from 34,815 to 147,847, of Cincinnati from 30,150 to 78,196, and of Columbus from 22,310 to 46,692. After 1950, the black urban population kept going up, but the total population of Ohio's great cities declined. As more affluent families moved out to the suburbs, Cleveland and Cincinnati shrank; Columbus avoided that fate by annexing surrounding territory. By 1963, more people lived in the suburbs and adjacent areas of Ohio's thirteen major metropolitan areas than in the cities themselves.[5]

Street railroads and then the automobile enabled the boom of suburbia. Between 1920 and 1930, the population of Cleveland grew by 13.5 percent; the suburbs of Garfield Heights and Shaker Heights increased respectively 500 percent and 1,000 percent. Even after the cities got smaller, their metropolitan areas continued to grow. The definition of a metropolitan area used by the U.S. Bureau of the Census has changed over the years, but in general it has meant a county having a city of at least fifty thousand people together with adjacent counties that are socially and economically integrated with the central county. Under this definition, many rural residents are included in metropolitan areas, but as urban sprawl and longer commuting distances brought formerly outlying areas into the orbit of the metropolis, the logic of defining metropolitan areas by county boundaries grew stronger. The Cincinnati metropolitan area now includes Brown, Butler, Clermont, Hamilton, and Warren counties as well as counties in Kentucky and Indiana. Cincinnati's population has been contracting steadily since the 1960s, and Hamilton County has been shrinking for almost as long, but the total population of the Ohio counties within Cincinnati's current metropolitan area grew by almost 30 percent between 1960 and 2005. Cleveland is now about half the size it was in 1950, but its five-county metropolitan area is larger. The Cleveland suburb of Parma had more than 100,000 inhabitants in 1970, and, although it has lost population since then, it is still the eighth largest city in Ohio. The entire Cleveland metropolitan area has also gotten smaller in recent years, but all the shrinkage has been in Cuyahoga County.[6]

The increasing importance of Ohio's metropolitan areas and of the suburbs can be seen in the percentages of the state's population living in the biggest counties and cities. In 1920, the population of each of the eight largest counties —Cuyahoga, Franklin, Hamilton, Lucas, Mahoning, Montgomery, Stark, and Summit—exceeded 100,000 and seven of the eight contained a city of 100,000 or more. Let's call these counties the Big Eight, even though by 2000 two others had passed Mahoning in population. In 1920, half of all Ohioans lived in the Big Eight, 39 percent in the eight largest cities. Forty years later, the Big Eight had 55 percent of the state's people, but the eight biggest cities only 31 percent. In 2000, three-quarters of all Buckeyes lived in the Big Eight, but only 21 percent in their largest cities. More than half the state's residents lived in the "suburbs" (that is, outside the borders of the biggest cities) in just eight counties. As we will see, the rise of the metropolitan areas and the shift of population to the suburbs had important implications for legislative politics.

The growth of the cities after 1900 aggravated problems of public health, pollution, labor relations, urban governance and finance, and other matters that had already appeared in the nineteenth century. Many of these issues held little interest for rural legislators or presented conflicts with rural traditions. There developed an urban political consciousness that sometimes set metropolitan lawmakers against their parties. In the early twentieth century, for example, the Republican representatives of Hamilton County (Cincinnati) often voted with the Democrats against measures advocated by the Anti-Saloon League. In the late twentieth century, urban and rural Democratic members frequently found themselves at odds over social issues such as gun control and same-sex marriage.

The impact of distinctive urban political interests on partisan legislative politics cannot be understood apart from the issue of apportionment, especially in the House. The constitution as adopted in 1851 allotted one representative to every county that had a population of one-half or more of the "ratio of representation" (the state population divided by one hundred). Back then, twelve counties lacked the requisite population and had to be joined to other counties to form House districts. Seeing how Ohio's population had grown, the framers of the constitution anticipated that, before long, no county would be without its own representative. Indeed, by 1870, only one county failed to qualify for separate representation in the House. But then the cities began to outpace the countryside in population growth, and the number of counties with less than half the ratio of representation increased. There were ten such counties in 1900; forty-six others had less than the full ratio.[7]

Still committed to the traditional idea of representation by geopolitical units, the General Assembly in 1902 sought to retain representation by county with a constitutional amendment giving every county at least one representative in the House. The amendment was known as the Hanna amendment because Mark Hanna allegedly secured its passage to ensure enough favorable votes for his reelection to the U.S. Senate. However, the idea had had strong support as far back as the 1850–51 constitutional convention, and, in 1893, a similar amendment had received a large majority of the votes cast on the issue, although not a majority of all votes cast at the election. Only four members of the General Assembly voted against the Hanna amendment. The Republican state convention unanimously endorsed it, while a divided Democratic convention ultimately gave it halfhearted support. With the new procedure by which a straight-ticket vote automatically included a vote in accord with the party's position on proposed constitutional changes, the voters ratified the amendment by a margin of nearly 29 to 1.[8]

At the time the Hanna amendment passed, only particularly prescient observers could have described it as a pro-Republican measure. The amendment diluted the power of the great urban centers in the legislature, but they were not reliable Democratic strongholds. In 1905, Cuyahoga, Lucas, and burgeoning Summit counties all moved into the Democratic column, and, in 1908, 1910, and 1912, the Big Eight counties all voted Democratic. But in the 1920s, Republicans rolled up huge victories in the cities as well as the countryside. Every large urban county sent Republican delegations to the General Assembly throughout the decade. In the five General Assemblies of the 1920s, the Republicans had an average of 43 members to the Democrats' twenty-two; few of the minority members came from big cities. As long as Republicans carried both the large and small counties, the overrepresentation of rural counties in the legislature made little difference to the partisan complexion of that body.

As the population growth of the cities continued to outpace that of the countryside, the malapportionment of the House grew more pronounced. In the 1920s, seventeen rural counties, having a combined population less than one-third the size of Cuyahoga County's, sent about the same number of representatives as Cuyahoga to the House. In the 1930s, the five small counties of Morgan, Morrow, Noble, Pike, and Vinton, with a total population of 67,282, had five seats in the House. Muskingum County, with almost the identical population, had one, while Franklin, Lucas, and Summit counties together had fifteen times the population but only three times the number of seats. Sixty-four counties with 1,781,282 total residents could outvote the eleven biggest counties, with an aggregate population of 3,921,726, 64 to 28. In 1929, Republican senator George Bender of Cleveland tried to organize a petition campaign for a constitutional amendment that would have based apportionment on population, but he dropped the idea in the face of rural opposition that might have jeopardized a taxation amendment that he also favored.[9]

The Reapportionment Revolution

The U.S. Supreme Court finally destroyed the time-honored scheme of representation by political subdivision in the 1960s. "State legislatures," said the Court, "are the fountainhead of representative government in this country. . . . But representative government is in essence self-government through the medium of

elected representatives of the people, and each and every citizen has an inalien
able right to full and effective participation in the political processes of his State"
legislative bodies. . . . Full and effective participation by all citizens in state gov
ernment requires, therefore, that each citizen have an equally effective voice in
the election of members of his state legislature." Political equality, the Court de
clared, "can mean only one thing—one person, one vote." Lest anyone harbo
the illusion that the venerable system of representation by county could withstand
this constitutional assault, the Court observed that "a scheme of giving at leas
one seat in one house to each political subdivision (for example, to each county
could easily result, in many States, in a total subversion of the equal-population
principle in that legislative body."[10]

In 1964, the Supreme Court struck down Ohio's apportionment scheme. In re
sponse, the General Assembly, meeting in special session, proposed a population
based apportionment of the House, which was far more grossly malapportioned
than the Senate. In May 1965, the voters defeated the amendment. In its regular
session that year, the General Assembly could not muster the necessary three
fifths majority of each house to put another amendment on the ballot—mos
Republicans, one columnist noted, thought they would get a "fairer shake from
a federal court than from the bloc of 16 Senate Democrats"—and it adjourned
leaving the matter in the hands of the federal district court. After finding the ap
portionment of the Senate also unconstitutional, the court approved a temporary
plan submitted by the Ohio Apportionment Board for the 1966 elections. This
plan provided for ninety-nine single-member House districts of approximately
equal population and thirty-three Senate districts (the same number established
by the constitution back in 1851) each made up of three House districts. The
plan allowed for a deviation of 15 percent from the ideal population of a district
In 1967, the General Assembly put this arrangement before the voters as a constitutional amendment, but with an allowable deviation of only 5 percent. This
time the voters approved. The amendment also made the apportionment board
a constitutional body and increased its membership by two persons, to be appointed by the legislative leaders of the two major parties. The amendment
paid homage to the venerable concept of representation by geopolitical unit
by requiring that legislative district lines be drawn along political boundaries
where feasible, but population now trumped territory as the primary principle
of representation.[11]

The constitutional change ended the anomalies of "fractional" representation
the fluctuating sizes of the two chambers, and different terms of office for sena-

tors. As we saw in chapter 2, the constitution adopted in 1851 had a complex formula for determining the size of a district's legislative delegation. The number of senators or representatives sent to the General Assembly by a district or county might change not only from census to census but even within the ten-year period between censuses. Moreover, from 1956 through 1967, not all senators had the same term of office. A constitutional amendment in 1956 extended the senatorial term to four years for most senators (and staggered the terms so that half of the four-year senators would be elected every other year), but because some districts got additional senators in the middle of a decennial period, at the end of which the size of the district's delegation would have to be recalculated, the additional senators had terms of only two years. The constitutional changes of 1967 settled the number of House districts, fixed the total number of representatives and senators, and gave all senators except those who filled vacancies terms of four years.[12]

The apportionment revolution urbanized and suburbanized the General Assembly. Cuyahoga County's share of House seats rose from 12 percent to 17 percent. The combined share of the six biggest counties, including two districts that covered parts of Stark as well as Summit County, just exceeded 50 percent. The representatives of urban and suburban districts within these counties might sometimes find themselves at odds, but the new makeup of the House meant that the diminished Cornstalk Brigade could no longer run roughshod over the metropolitan areas of the state.

The single-member districts introduced as part of the new method of apportionment had the incidental effect of improving the quality of the Cuyahoga County delegation. The at-large election of as many as seventeen representatives on the county's infamous "bedsheet ballot" had given a great advantage to party hacks. According to Richard G. Zimmerman, who covered the legislature for the *Cleveland Plain Dealer* in the 1960s, "Any candidate bearing a recognizable ethnic surname (Irish, Italian, Slovakian, Slovenian, Polish, etc.) and who had the backing of the influential county Democratic machine stood a good chance of being nominated and a better chance of being elected." After reapportionment, the hacks could no longer hide in the crowd and the voters could more easily learn about the candidates.[13]

Contemporary observers generally assumed that reapportionment along the lines mandated by the Supreme Court would benefit Democrats by increasing the political clout of cities nationwide. When the elections immediately following the reapportionment revolution disappointed Democrats' expectations of major gains, commentators began to note that the biggest winners from reapportion-ment were not the cities but the suburbs. The population of every major city in Ohio except Columbus peaked before the apportionment decisions. Between 1950 and 1965, the population of Cleveland declined by 4.2 percent as its suburbs grew by 67.2 percent. Cincinnati lost just .3 percent of its population, but its Ohio suburbs grew by 64.4 percent. The creation of single-member districts of equal population empowered the suburbs. A few years after reapportionment, an offi-cial of the Citizens League of Greater Cleveland said, "The suburbs are now the most powerful bloc, dealing with either the center cities or the cornstalk brigade from the rural areas to form a majority on specific issues."[14]

A 1971 study found that in the northern states east of the Mississippi, where Republicans often ruled the rural areas and Democrats dominated the cities, the Democrats did in fact get a slight boost from reapportionment. In Ohio, the new method of apportionment gave them no immediate noticeable advantage. In the 1964 election, the last before "one man one vote" took effect, Republicans won 55 percent of the House seats and 50 percent of the Senate seats. In 1966, after reapportionment, Republicans won 63 percent of the House and 70 percent of the Senate. The Democrats did not take control of the House until 1972 or the Senate until 1974.[15]

Republicans fared well in the large counties in 1966. In 1964, Hamilton and Franklin were already strongly Republican, while Lucas leaned heavily Democratic. That year, those three counties sent thirteen Republicans and eight Democrats to the House. In 1966, Republicans picked up one seat each in Hamilton and Lucas, electing fifteen of the twenty-one members from the three counties. In the Democratic stronghold of Cuyahoga, there had long been complaints that city candidates dominated the at-large elections, leaving suburban and rural areas vir-tually unrepresented. In 1964, Cuyahoga elected sixteen Democrats and no Repub-licans to the House. After the creation of single-member districts, Cuyahoga elected twelve Democrats and five Republicans. Of the nine winners who listed Cleveland as their homes in the General Assembly roster, eight were Democrats. In Cuyahoga County outside of Cleveland, Republicans and Democrats elected equal numbers of representatives. Democrats might have hoped that the separation of the city from the suburbs would cut into Republican strength in Hamilton and Franklin counties, but Cincinnati and Columbus remained Republican.[16]

In the short run, then, single-member districts seemed to benefit the Repub-licans; however, the Republicans' success in 1966 had other causes, including the popularity of their gubernatorial candidate James A. Rhodes, better party organization in key counties, and the fact the Republican-controlled Apportionment Board had drawn the district lines. Furthermore, single-member districts cut both ways. The consolidation of rural counties into large, single-member districts cost Republicans many more seats than it cost Democrats.[17]

In the longer term, reapportionment (or, more properly, redistricting, since the size of each house was now fixed) contributed to the establishment of Democratic rule. In many states, the effects of the one-man, one-vote principle took a few years to kick in as the party in power at the time protected key incumbents. In the 1970 Ohio elections, Democrats won all but one of the statewide executive branch races, aided by a campaign finance scandal in which top Republicans received contributions from a loan-finding company that had induced the state treasurer to make large, legally dubious loans to out-of-state businesses that soon went bankrupt. Republicans kept control of the General Assembly despite Demo-cratic gains, but the Democrats got control of the Apportionment Board. In 1972, the Democrats won the House and cut the Republican lead in the Senate to one seat. In 1974, they took over both chambers for the first time in a generation.[18]

Control of the redistricting process aided the Democratic resurgence, but it was not the whole story. The popular notion that whoever controls redistricting can dictate the partisan composition of the General Assembly is overly simplistic. It does not account for such unrelated political factors as long-term partisan shifts in the electorate, changes in the relative organizational strengths of the parties, or unique events (for example, the big turnout of Democratic voters in 1972 in response to a proposed constitutional amendment to repeal the recently enacted income tax). Nor does it explain the success that the opposing party sometimes achieves in spite of unfavorable district boundaries. Republicans won control of the Senate in 1984 and increased their lead in 1988 even though a majority-Democrat Apportionment Board had drawn the district lines. For Republicans to take over the board, they first had to win two of the three state-wide seats on the board, which they did by electing the governor and secretary of state in 1990. In 1992, notwithstanding redistricting by the Republican-controlled board, the Democrats picked up a seat in the Senate and retained control of the House, though with a diminished majority. Not until 1994 did the Republicans again win both houses of the legislature for the first time in nearly a quarter century.[19]

Nevertheless, there is a widespread popular feeling that redistricting should not be a partisan process. In 1981, Republicans backed a constitutional amendment to create a nonpartisan commission to draw district lines in accordance with a fixed formula. Democrats, happy with their legislative majority, saw to its defeat at the polls. In 2005, an initiative drive organized by the liberal organization Reform Ohio Now succeeded in putting a similar amendment on the ballot, again with the professed aim of ending gerrymandering by taking politics out of the process. This time the Republicans, in control of both houses, generally opposed the measure while Democrats leaned in favor. Under the proposal, a redistricting commission consisting of two members selected by senior appellate judges of different parties and three members chosen by the judicially selected members would have been charged with establishing competitive districts using criteria set forth in the constitution.[20]

Critics of the proposed amendment focused on the weird district lines the commission would have had to draw to ensure competition in many areas of the state. What proponents failed to see and what no one would publicly admit was that many areas of the state were inherently uncompetitive. In 2004, more than one-fifth of the House races were uncontested and most of the rest were one-sided, facts attributed by critics of the apportionment system to gerrymandering and the power of incumbency. But studies had shown that many counties stubbornly adhered to one party or the other for generations, dating back to a time when few people made a career out of legislative service. Before 1966, when the county was the unit of representation in the House and the Apportionment Board had no power to draw district lines, many legislative races were lopsided and some uncontested altogether. In 1944, for example, twenty small-county Republicans ran unopposed. Eight years later, twenty-three counties sent Republicans to the House by default. Ten of the twenty one-candidate counties of 1944 were one-candidate counties again in 1952. Seventeen went Republican in every election from 1944 through 1952, while two others elected a Democrat only in 1948. Of the thirteen counties that had contested elections in 1944 but not in 1952, only one elected a Democrat in those years, and only once. From 1948 through 1968, one party, usually the Republican, won every election in thirty-six counties and every election but one in another sixteen counties. Gerrymandering had nothing to do with Republican dominance in these counties.[21]

Incumbency has its advantages, but it too probably had little to do with the longstanding Republican control of so many rural counties. It is true that nineteen of the twenty representatives who ran unopposed in 1944 and twenty-two of the twenty-three in 1952 were incumbents. However, only three of the 1952 incumbents had also been elected in 1944. Unless any of the unopposed candidates of 1952 had been appointed to fill vacancies, twenty of the twenty-three ran as nonincumbents at some point between 1946 and 1952. The lack of competition in many rural races probably had far more to do with voting habits than with either gerrymandering or incumbency.

Studies of presidential and gubernatorial election returns confirm the durability of party attachments in Ohio, based largely on traditions inherited from long-ago settlers. Areas settled by New Englanders or Kentucky Whigs decades before the Civil War tended to stay Whig-Republican, while regions settled by migrants from Pennsylvania and immigrants from Germany continued to lean strongly Democratic. The disruptions caused by the Whig collapse of 1853, the Civil War, and the Panic of 1893 proved temporary; old party loyalties quickly reasserted themselves. Major shifts occurred during World War I, when traditionally Democratic Germans moved into the Republican column because of their opposition to the war, and during the Great Depression, when Democrats gained in heavily industrialized areas with large immigrant populations. Nevertheless, many counties that were strongly Republican or Democratic in the 1960s, when the voting studies were conducted, could trace their political pedigrees back to the pre–Civil War era.[22]

Analyses of roll-call votes in the General Assembly found strong party solidarity among the legislators as well. John M. Wegner, upon examining roll-call votes in the House from 1900 through 1911, found a significant degree of party difference on taxation, government personnel matters, and alcohol-related issues. Political scientist Thomas A. Flinn studied votes in the House and Senate for the years 1935, 1949, 1955, and 1957. Eliminating from consideration the great number of unanimous and near-unanimous votes, Flinn considered not only the degree of party cohesion but also the degree of similarity between urban and rural members within each party. He concluded that "party conflict is frequent in the Ohio legislature and that the parties attain high levels of internal unity often enough when in opposition to each other to provide definite alternatives to the voters of the state." He also found that "[u]rban-rural factionalism is unimportant." An examination of the 1967 House by Charles W. Chance produced similar results, although Chance noted the existence within each party of urban and rural blocs that sometimes voted differently on measures of lesser partisan importance.[23]

City versus Country

Participants in and nonacademic observers of Ohio legislative politics, however, often noted the conflicts between urban and rural lawmakers. Republican representative Robert Taft of Cincinnati struggled to revise a tax system that left Ohio's large cities "crippled financially." Taft wrote in 1924 that "[t]he difficulty lies rather with the rural Legislators, and with the lack of understanding in the cities themselves of the necessity for some action." Taft complained of rural Republicans' opposition to spending for the cities and their "niggardliness" toward state government, and he described tightfisted Democratic governor Vic Donahey of bucolic Tuscarawas County as the "smallest kind of rural politician." A student of Taft's state legislative career repeatedly noted the difficulties Taft had with rural members of his party. In 1930, investigative journalist Walter Liggett blamed "penurious rural legislators" for the dreadful state of the penitentiary and for the crime and corruption associated with Prohibition.[24]

In the 1940s, prominent newspaperman and future presidential assistant Clayton Fritchey blamed Depression-era relief problems in Ohio's cities on rural legislators who controlled the General Assembly and could not or would not comprehend the extent of suffering in the cities. Journalist Richard L. Maher, a severe critic of the legislature, observed that the Cornstalk Brigade grabbed gasoline tax revenue to build rural feeder roads, that desperate urban school districts never qualified for cigarette tax money earmarked for needy school districts, and that when sales tax revenue jumped dramatically after the Depression, the General Assembly reduced the percentage destined for local governments. Maher described government in Ohio as "oxcart government." At the same time, travel writer John Gunther observed that the Cornstalk Brigade was still "the biggest single force in the legislature." Two Cleveland representatives, fed up with rural rule, introduced a bill to allow Cuyahoga County to secede from Ohio and become a separate state. In 1957, both senators and representatives, when presented with a list of six types of conflict, including that between the parties, ranked the urban-rural clash as the most important.[25]

The seeming contradiction between the roll-call analyses and the comments of Taft, Liggett, Fritchey, Maher, and Gunther can be explained, in part at least, by the limitations of roll-call studies. First, they tend to focus on broad voting patterns without distinguishing between major and minor issues. Second, they don't account for the reasons for votes. Roll-call votes on final passage do not reflect the compromises that often precede action on the floor. For example, when Taft sought to raise the ceiling on the property tax rate from ten mills to seventeen mills so that cities would have adequate revenues to finance their mushrooming expenses, he limited the rate to fourteen mills outside the cities to mollify parsimonious rural representatives. In 1959, House Democrats engaged in a bruising intraparty battle over a workers' compensation bill. The final vote of 126 to 1 "gave no indication of the lasting schisms the debate had begotten." A twenty-first-century liberal Democrat voted for a bill he thought highly objectionable because, he said, "I'm operating in such a right-wing environment that sometimes compromise is the only way out."[26]

A study of roll-call votes in the House from 1957 through 1964 concluded that an urban-rural conflict "exists, but only with a moderate degree of intensity and only on a few specific issues." But questionnaires filled out by legislators suggested that the conflict was significant in party caucuses even though it did not always show up in voting on the floor. David A. Johnston, director of the Legislative Service Commission, pointed out in 1972 that "some of Ohio's most controversial bills have passed both houses unanimously without any substantive disagreement or floor amendments" because of bargaining that took place "outside of the vote-counting part of the process." Even when roll-call studies account for votes on motions or amendments, they don't reveal the underlying strategies of the members and party leaders.[27]

For all their limitations, though, roll-call votes on some major issues suggest that in Ohio's second century, the urban-rural conflict in the General Assembly was real and important, even if only as a subtext to partisan divisions. The votes on important liquor bills in the House, where each county had at least one representative, show a distinct split between urban and rural areas in the early decades. (Using a crude but serviceable categorization, we may regard the Big Eight counties as "urban" and the rest as "rural.") The most significant liquor law before the enactment of prohibition was the Rose local-option law of 1908, a pivotal measure in the Anti-Saloon League's incremental construction of prohibition. Since 1888, a series of laws had gradually extended the territory subject to local-option elections. The Rose bill provided for countywide elections, so that whole counties could vote themselves dry over the objections of city dwellers within their borders. The House passed the bill by a 3-to-1 margin. Of the fifty-eight Republicans who voted, 93 percent voted aye. The Democratic vote was more revealing. Democrats made up the entire delegations from the counties with the two largest cities in the state, Cuyahoga and Hamilton counties. Those delegations opposed the bill 19 to 1, while two-thirds of the rural Democrats voted for it. The same thing happened in the Senate: most Republicans and rural Democrats backed the bill, and the eight senators from Cuyahoga and Hamilton counties, Democrats all, voted no. Not coincidentally, Hamilton County had nearly 120,000 Catholic residents, mostly immigrants or descendants of immigrants from Germany and Ireland, while Cuyahoga County's population of Catholic immigrants from southern and eastern Europe was growing by leaps and bounds. Immigrants, especially Catholics, had long been attracted to the Democratic Party, and they had long opposed the temperance movement.[28]

The matter of Catholic and immigrant constituencies is worth a brief digression. We saw at the end of chapter 10 how the ethnocultural issue of prohibition and the nonpartisan tactics of the Anti-Saloon League disrupted party loyalties in the late nineteenth century. The Bryan presidential candidacy and the economic depression of the 1890s aggravated the confusion. So did election law reforms, new methods of campaigning, and the decline in voter turnout. Ethnocultural conflict continued to enliven the political scene after the turn of the century, and there were times when particular issues or candidates could revive old party alignments. In general, though, its influence in determining party identification gradually diminished. Divisions over prohibition and other cultural issues in the early twentieth century seem to have been as much along urban-rural as along ethnoreligious lines. Catholic immigrants and their descendants who congregated in big cities helped shape urban culture, but as the metropolitan areas grew, urban-rural differences may have outweighed ethnocultural ones. Catholics never made up a majority of the electorate in any small or medium-sized county and may never have controlled the choice of state representative. Still, more than a dozen such counties had significant Catholic populations in 1908. Most of the representatives from those counties, Democrats and Republicans, voted for the Rose local-option law.[29]

Republicans were usually associated with the dry cause, but those who won election to Hamilton County's seats in the legislature voted wet. In 1915, a Republican General Assembly undid the Democrats' creation of a state liquor licensing authority and returned licensing to local control in the form of thirty-four licensing districts. (This dry victory didn't last; the voters rejected the act in a referendum.) Democrats in the House and Senate voted unanimously against the bill, Republicans overwhelmingly for it. The only Republicans to break ranks

"There is no inherent right in a citizen to sell intoxicating liquors by retail."—United States Supreme Court.

Anti-Saloon Campaign Manual For Ohio

MAY 1914

FIRST EDITION

"The liquor traffic is the acknowledged source of much of the crime and pauperism of the state."—Ohio Supreme Court.

hailed from Hamilton County, home to a largely German and Irish, urban, anti-Prohibition constituency (and a wet Republican machine).[30]

The vote on ratification of the Prohibition amendment to the U.S. Constitution in 1919 tells the same story. Republican legislators supported the amendment 82 to 11. Ten of the eleven no votes came from Hamilton County, the other from Montgomery County. House Democrats divided evenly, but those from large urban counties voted 16 to 4 against ratification. Members from Cuyahoga, Hamilton, and Lucas counties—twenty Democrats and ten Republicans—provided twenty-one of the twenty-nine House votes and nine of the twelve Senate votes against ratification and none in favor.[31]

The urban-rural split affected other issues besides liquor. For example, in 1925, during the brief heyday of the Ku Klux Klan in Ohio, the General Assembly passed an act, later vetoed by the governor, requiring the reading of the Bible in public schools. In the House, twice as many members of each party supported the bill as opposed it. Rural representatives voted overwhelmingly for the bill. Urban

The Rise and Fall of the Cornstalk Brigade   433

delegates divided slightly against it, but twenty of the twenty-four no votes came from the biggest counties, Cuyahoga and Hamilton. In the same year, Representative John T. Brown, a farmer, introduced legislation to create a gasoline tax to help pay for highways, the costs of which were being disproportionately borne by rural landowners. The bill sparked "a resounding urban-rural battle." After much legislative maneuvering, the House passed the bill handily. Some support but almost all the opposition came from big-city representatives. In the Senate, following further amendment, urban and rural members could be found on both sides, but more than half the opposition came from the six Cuyahoga County senators. Governor Vic Donahey vetoed the act, noting that there had been "much misleading propaganda to convince the farmers of Ohio that this bill was enacted for their especial benefit," but the lawmakers, strongly encouraged by Farmer Brown, overrode the veto.[32]

Troublesome cultural issues or tax matters did not necessarily cause members to line up across the urban-rural divide. Sometimes, as in the case of the Bible-reading bill, either the urban or the rural members differed among themselves. On other occasions, legislation dealing with otherwise controversial subjects such as liquor and taxation passed almost unanimously. Nevertheless, it seems clear that urban and rural legislators brought to the statehouse contrasting outlooks on key policy issues. Even when urban lawmakers disagreed with each other, urban-rural differences could account for the discord. More than half the population of Akron, for example, consisted of rural Buckeyes and West Virginians who had flocked to the city to work in its factories. Akron's delegates voted unanimously for the Klan-backed Bible-reading bill. The members from Cuyahoga County, dominated by a city of European immigrants, voted 20 to 1 against it.[33]

Prohibition lost much of its disruptive power in the late 1920s as the crusading fervor dissipated and the repression and corruption associated with enforcement, particularly in the large cities, made a mockery of the law. The Great Depression brought economic issues to the fore. Indeed, many proponents of repeal saw liquor taxes as a source of desperately needed revenue for the financially strapped states. In 1933, as the Twenty-first Amendment repealing national prohibition worked its way through the ratification process, the General Assembly voted to put on the ballot a constitutional amendment to rescind state prohibition as well. Rural members divided almost evenly over the measure, but the great majority of legislators from the Big Eight counties, from both parties and in both houses, supported it.[34]

The demise of Prohibition did not bring to an end the sharp division between urban and rural legislators. During the Great Depression, rural lawmakers tended to view welfare as a chiefly urban problem and thwarted the efforts of urban members to raise taxes for relief, although the availability of federal funds for struggling cities eased urban-rural tensions somewhat. In the 1940s, municipal demands on the General Assembly rose again as growing suburbs required more services and inner cities deteriorated. The legislature did not respond to the cities' satisfaction. "The small-county legislators who dominate the House," observed a columnist for an urban newspaper, "tend to look with suspicion on big-city calls for help. Their resistance is always hard to overcome." Political scientist Gordon E. Baker noted in 1955 that small-town legislators often thwarted the attempts of cities to deal with serious problems. "Among states where this situation has been especially acute is Ohio," Baker wrote. "There urban redevelopment legislation, aimed at eliminating blighted slum areas, has in the past met a quick death in the lower house, where rural counties are heavily overrepresented." Baker further observed that rural legislators had secured a minimum distribution of sales tax revenue for each county, which cut deeply into the amount going to the cities. Around the same time, the *Columbus Citizen* reported on another "[b]ig battle between rural and urban legislators," this one over the allocation of money for highway construction. A recent constitutional amendment had authorized the sale of state bonds to raise $500 million for the construction of "major thoroughfares of state highway system and urban extensions thereof"; however, mileage could be added to or subtracted from the state highway system by a construction council. Urban lawmakers complained that the council was diverting too much money from city expressways to rural roads. "On the other hand," noted the *Citizen*, "rural legislators who know they can have anything they want in Ohio Legislature if they stick together, and they always do, want to add some more rural mileage to the system and spread that $500 million fund around a little more."[35]

The urbanization and suburbanization of the legislature brought about by reapportionment altered the allocation of state funds. Reapportionment led to a shift in dollars from formerly overrepresented to formerly underrepresented counties. The amount of intergovernmental revenue per capita that counties of every size received from the state more than tripled from 1962 to 1976. The increase for Cuyahoga County was 557 percent and for counties having between 250,000 and 1,000,000 inhabitants just under 400 percent or more, while the 43 counties with fewer than 50,000 residents experienced a per capita increase of just 213 percent.[36]

Aside from the redirection of state money to metropolitan areas—a development of less importance after 1965 than it would have been earlier because of the dramatic rise in federal aid going directly to cities—the effect of reapportionment on legislative policy was not nearly as noteworthy as proponents of reapportionment had predicted. Ohio's parties lacked the ideological vision that had once defined them. One political scientist famously claimed in 1966 that Ohio had "issueless politics." Surveys conducted in 1957, 1969, and 1988 showed a steep decline in the number of legislators who agreed with the statement that a member should vote with his or her party on a bill that was important for the party's record, even if the vote would cost some support in the member's district. In 1957, 63 percent of those surveyed agreed with the statement; in 1969, 53 percent; and in 1988, 37 percent. The state's most powerful politicians of the postreapportionment decades, Vern Riffe and Jim Rhodes, were quintessential pragmatists. Democrat Riffe ruled the House as Speaker from 1975 until 1994. Republican Rhodes served as governor for sixteen years (1963–71 and 1975–83). These two hard-nosed, nonideological leaders understood each other, got along famously, and worked together toward shared goals.[37]

At the same time, metropolitan sprawl and the growth of smaller cities eroded the distinction between Ohio's original Big Eight counties and other parts of the state. In 1950, twelve counties had more than 100,000 inhabitants apiece. In 2000, Ohio included twenty-seven such counties and eighteen cities each having a population of 50,000 or more. In addition, a shared culture seemed to be bridging the gap between even the most rural and urban lawmakers. Historian Richard Hofstadter observed that the "hayseed" had begun to vanish even before the twentieth century, and by 1940 scholars noted a significant diminution of differences between the city and the country across America. Better roads and automobiles, radio, and the movies broke down rural isolation, farming became more mechanized, and cities developed an appreciation of fresh air and green space with parks and residential suburbs. In 1955, political scientist Gordon Baker observed that "representatives from rural constituencies are often not farmers, but small-town lawyers and business men. On many issues they share a natural community of interests with city groups representing a similar social and economic outlook." Although urban and rural lawmakers might form opposing blocs on particular issues, they were all subjected to numerous and sometimes conflicting pressures.[38]

Some big-city legislators found to their surprise that they liked and respected their country colleagues. Frances McGovern of Akron, who served in the 1950s, discovered that the members of the Cornstalk Brigade "were no bumpkins. They were smart, they were wise, and one in particular had a great sense of humor." Carl Stokes of Cleveland recalled that his fellow Cuyahoga County delegates in the 1960s "refer[red] to the legislators from the downstate areas almost contemptuously as the hayseed members of the 'cornstalk brigade'" but that during budget debates "it was the down-state, small-city legislators who were best informed."[39]

Yet some issues always seemed to produce party-line votes and others split the legislators into urban and rural camps. McGovern remembered that while there were not many partisan questions in her day, "[l]abor issues were the exception—always partisan." They remained partisan after McGovern left the legislature. In 1963, for example, the General Assembly tightened eligibility requirements for unemployment benefits and reduced the amount of the benefits available. The bill passed on an almost straight party-line vote. That same year, Republican legislators supported a workers' compensation bill by a combined vote of 91 to 13, while Democrats opposed it 53 to 2. At times, business and labor organizations could work out their differences, as they did in 1971 with regard to workers' compensation and unemployment compensation benefits, and then the General Assembly passed agreed-upon legislation with little or no dissent. On other occasions, the same issues produced strict partisan divisions. When the House passed an unemployment benefits law in 1975, only two members in either house strayed from the party line. In 1993, the Democratic House and Republican Senate passed two different versions of a workers' compensation bill on straight party-line votes. Not a single member of either party in either chamber broke ranks. A conference committee produced a compromise that both houses accepted, but still with party-flavored votes. Of the twenty representatives who opposed the conference committee report, eighteen were Democrats. The Senate vote hewed closely to its original partisan split.[40]

The history of collective bargaining bills tells a like tale. For a decade, Democrats failed to push through either house a bill granting collective bargaining rights to public employees. After getting control of the General Assembly, they passed a collective bargaining bill in 1975 on a party-line vote, only to see Republican governor Rhodes veto it. They lacked the strength for an override, prompting unions to campaign for a veto-proof legislature. In 1977, a more strongly Democratic General Assembly passed a similar bill, which Rhodes vetoed. The Senate voted along party lines to override the veto; a Democratic senator got caught in a blizzard and missed the vote, but one Republican dissenter provided the margin of victory. The House leadership refused to put the veto to a test, even though the bill had originally passed on a nearly strict party-line vote with just enough support to override. Not until 1983 did a Democratic governor sign a public employee collective bargaining bill, passed by a Democratic legislature on a party-line vote. Nothing in any of these votes suggests a split between urban and rural members.[41]

Economic issues not directly related to labor relations also led to sharp partisan divisions. The comprehensive tort-reform bill of 1996, later invalidated by the supreme court, passed the House 54 to 44. Republicans backed the bill 48 to 8; Democrats opposed it 36 to 6. Seven of the eight Republicans who voted no were attorneys who may have had professional scruples about the bill. Leaving attorneys out of the count, Republicans voted for the bill 45 to 1. In the Senate, only one member deviated from the party position. The General Assembly passed another tort-reform law in 2004. Except for two Republicans who opposed the bill, the Senate passed it on a party-line vote. The House passed an amended version 65 to 32, with Democrats casting all but one of the negative votes. When the bill came back to the Senate for concurrence in the House amendments, the two previously dissident Republicans voted for passage and the Senate concurred with a straight partisan split.[42]

Toward the end of the twentieth century a conservative renascence—and the end of the Riffe era, when a powerful, pragmatic Speaker controlled the House— brought ideologically contentious social and moral issues to center stage in the General Assembly. Political analyst Lee Leonard blamed term limits for the divisiveness: hot-button, black-and-white issues were easier for short-termers to deal with than complex matters such as schools, jobs, and health. Why was the legislature divided "when Republicans control it all"? Because, wrote Leonard, "[i]t's hard to come together on extreme views."[43]

Leonard was right about the difficulties of developing expertise on complicated subjects under term limits, but Republicans usually managed to get together on the hot-button issues. What prevented a neat Republicans-versus-Democrats alignment were differences between Democratic rural and urban representatives reminiscent of the split among Republican legislators over liquor laws early in the century. Consider the votes on the following bills, all passed between 1995 and 2004. House Republicans supported a bill banning partial-birth abortions 56 to 0; House Democrats supported it 26 to 15. After a court struck down the law, House Republicans voted unanimously for another bill penalizing partial-birth abortions and creating a civil cause of action against persons who performed them; House Democrats voted for it 20 to 15. A bill to name a highway passed the Senate unanimously, but then the House Transportation Committee added an authorization of "choose life" license plates. Republicans voted for the bill 61 to 1; Democrats voted for it 21 to 14. When the bill went back to the previously unanimous Senate for concurrence, Republicans supported it 17 to 1, Democrats opposed it 8 to 3. House Republicans supported a bill banning same-sex marriages 60 to 1; Democrats opposed it 22 to 14. When the House passed a bill allowing individuals to get a permit to carry concealed handguns, Republicans voted 58 to 3 for the bill, Democrats 25 to 11 against. The votes reflect a Republican Party solidly united on key social issues and a Democratic Party seriously divided, with no Vern Riffe to hold the two wings together. (Republican solidarity on floor votes may have masked urban-rural tensions within the party. When Republican Priscilla Mead resigned from the Senate in 2003, she suggested that most of her caucus didn't understand the problems of urban-suburban districts.)[44]

At the core of the Democratic opposition on all these bills stood a bloc of urban members, mostly from northeastern Ohio. Small-town Democrats tended to side with the Republicans. In 2004, Representative Derrick Seaver of rural Auglaize County, who had voted with the Republicans on gun rights, gay rights, and abortion, switched parties, claiming that "Democrats weren't very willing to accept Democrats like myself anymore." And the Democratic Party, while still hoping to win back rural waverers by stressing economic issues, contemplated the conversion of suburban Republicans who leaned liberal on social issues. Suburbanization, reapportionment, and cultural convergence had wrought big changes over the course of a century, but, in some ways, legislative politics at the time of Ohio's centennial and at the bicentennial looked a lot alike.[45]

21

THE FEDS, THE BUREAUCRATS, AND THE SCOPE OF LEGISLATION

I N 1912, THE CUYAHOGA RIVER caught fire, something it had been doing sporadically since 1868. Sparks from a tugboat ignited an oil slick, causing explosions, a furious conflagration, and the deaths of five men. Clevelanders called for the enforcement of a city ordinance that prohibited refineries from releasing oil into the river, but there was no reaction from the federal government. In 1969, the Cuyahoga caught fire again. Despite the blaze's dramatic appearance, it caused little damage and was quickly contained. Yet the fire became a "seminal event" in the modern environmental movement. It helped spur Congress to pass the Clean Water Act, which gave to the federal Environmental Protection Agency (EPA) the job of regulating the discharge of pollutants into navigable rivers. One of the major functions of the Ohio Environmental Protection Agency, created in 1970, would be to enforce compliance with the Clean Water Act and the federal EPA's regulations.[1]

Besides reflecting the growing importance of environmental concerns in the American public consciousness, the strong response to the 1969 fire exemplified two twentieth-century legal trends that altered the character of state legislative activity: the enormous expansion of federal authority and the growth of administrative government. Congress encroached upon policy areas that previously had been left to the states, and the U.S. Supreme Court upheld the advances. The Supreme Court further restrained the states by expanding the reach of federal constitutional provisions over state policy. Because acts of Congress and the U.S. Constitution were the supreme law of the land, there was nothing a state legislature could do about these restrictions on their ability to shape public policy.[2]

The increasing need for administrative agencies with the power to carry out policies established by the legislature was evident by the opening of the twentieth century. The necessity stemmed from the changing nature of society. Ohio had become a big state, with big cities, big industries, big government, and big problems. But the General Assembly remained small, not so much in the number of its members, which was greater than it is today, but in the scope of its operations and the responsibilities it bore for the administration of the law. The legislature met once every two years, except when called into special session. Turnover in the membership remained high, with many newcomers entering the ranks every session. Members had no offices and almost no staff support. The apportionment amendment of 1903 ensured that small-town representatives, many of them unfamiliar with the needs of big cities, would make up a disproportionately large percentage of the House. In an earlier time, when Ohioans lived life on a smaller scale, citizen-legislators could rely on a handful of members to analyze issues and draft appropriate legislation and could adjourn with the feeling that they had addressed the people's needs. By the start of the twentieth century that time had passed. Unable to deal directly with the great problems of an urban, industrial society, the General Assembly took giant steps toward the creation of an administrative state. Legislators increasingly delegated their work to administrative agencies that made rules, issued licenses, and conducted hearings.[3]

Of course, the General Assembly passed thousands of laws, some of them of great importance, that embodied policy decisions unrelated to either federal law or administrative development. For example, the legislature twice made sweeping changes in the state's criminal sentencing laws. Effective 1974, it made all prison sentences indefinite. Ohio had been a pioneer in the field of indefinite sentencing, with its "good time" statute of 1856 and indeterminate sentencing and parole statutes in the 1880s. Under the new law, judges could select from a range of minimum sentences, but the actual time a defendant served depended largely on prison officials and parole boards, whose expertise supposedly allowed them to determine when a prisoner had been rehabilitated.[4]

In the 1980s and 1990s, rising public concern about violent crime and the costs of incarceration led policymakers to rethink of the concept of indeterminate sentencing. In 1982, the General Assembly reestablished determinate sentencing for felons for the first time in sixty years, giving judges the authority to set definite terms for low-level felonies. The statute also created new tiers of "aggravated felonies." In 1993, the Ohio Criminal Sentencing Commission recommended that indeterminate sentencing be scrapped in favor of "truth in sentencing." The commission insisted that "the overriding purposes of criminal sentencing should be to protect the public and to punish offenders."[5]

Rehabilitation, the goal behind indeterminate sentencing and the parole system, played a distinctly secondary role in the commission's thinking. If the General Assembly had any thoughts of reversing the order of importance of these goals, the Lucasville prison riot of 1993 probably dispelled them. The riot, which took place during the biennial budget hearings, induced the lawmakers to take nine million dollars that been slated for residential facilities designed to integrate offenders into the community and to use the money for prison staff. In 1995, following the commission's recommendations, the General Assembly revamped the sentencing laws. Judges could now choose from a wide range of sanctions, including incarceration, fines, community service, day reporting, and so on, but they had to impose definite sentences. For instance, the term of imprisonment for a first-degree felony might be anywhere from three to ten years, but it had to be a specific number of years. The reform abolished parole except for certain offenses that carried the possibility of life in prison, but parole boards still supervised released felons during a period of "post-release control." The statute also simplified the confusing classification of felonies that had grown up, rearranged and reduced the nearly 1,900 offenses that the commission had found scattered throughout the Revised Code, and established victims' rights (such as allowing crime victims to address the court at sentencing). The availability of alternative sanctions, particularly for theft offenses, was expected to reduce prison overcrowding and the costs of supervising offenders.[6]

The General Assembly made many other important policy decisions that were dictated neither by federal law nor by dependence on an administrative style of government. In 1974, it added to the grounds for divorce for the first time in over a century by providing for no-fault divorce, and it created the dissolution of marriage, a relatively quick and easy alternative to divorce. The Divorce Reform Act also abolished some antiquated defenses to divorce actions, made the best interests of the child the sole criterion for awarding child custody, and modified the statutes governing alimony and child support. In the realm of state finance, the General Assembly first authorized the use of revenue bonds to fund public works projects in 1919. In the 1960s, prompted by Governor James Rhodes, it proposed a half dozen constitutional amendments allowing the issuance of bonds for capital construction and job creation, all of which the voters approved. During the Great Depression, the legislature adopted a retail sales tax over stiff resistance. The sales tax passed only after a constitutional amendment, put on the ballot through the initiative process, limited property taxes and helped put the public schools in desperate straits. The sales tax became the state's biggest source of revenue until the income tax surpassed it. The General Assembly passed the income tax law in 1971 when the state's financial needs threatened to exceed its resources. The income tax also provoked a fierce battle. Pressed upon a Republican legislature by Democratic governor John Gilligan, it became law only because a significant minority of Republican lawmakers, most notably House Speaker Charles Kurfess, defied their caucuses and voted with a solid phalanx of Democrats. The anger of conservative Republicans with the defectors caused a split in the House caucus and a suspicion of the party's legislative leadership that lasted into the 1990s.[7]

The General Assembly greatly expanded Ohio's system of public higher education in the second half of the century. In 1947, John Gunther described the Ohio State University as a "colossus," with more than seventy buildings, 14,000 students, and a 74,000-seat stadium. Thirty years later, the university had more than 50,000 students. During that period, the system of state-supported institutions of higher education grew from a handful of four-year schools to a dozen universities, two independent medical colleges, an agricultural research center, eight community colleges, and seventeen technical colleges, plus more than two dozen branch campuses. The General Assembly also adopted many uniform laws recommended by legal experts to standardize the law among the states. Some, such as the Uniform Partnership Act (1949) and Uniform Commercial Code (1961), involved business affairs. Others—for example, the Reciprocal Act for Support of Dependents (1951) and the Uniform Child Custody Jurisdiction and Enforcement Act (1977)—sought to reduce conflicts relating to child and spousal support and child custody among the courts of different states and to improve the enforcement of court orders on these subjects.[8]

In short, the General Assembly had great leeway to enact policy in many areas, unpressured by federal law or administrative needs. Yet those federal and administrative influences largely distinguish nineteenth- from twentieth-century statutory law. Neither existed to a significant degree in the nineteenth century. Both, became powerful after 1900.

The Federal Impact on State Law

The federal influence on state law began to grow in the early twentieth century. In the Army Reorganization Act of 1900, Congress started to standardize the training and equipment of the National Guard and to integrate the guard into the regular military service of the United States. In 1902, the General Assembly authorized the governor, as commander in chief, to change the organization of the Ohio National Guard to correspond with the organization of the U.S. Army, and, in 1917, it conformed Ohio's military law to federal law by a wholesale revision of the state statutes. Also in 1917, the General Assembly accepted the terms of the national Vocational Education Act, which required every state that wished to receive federal money for vocational education to create a separate state board to administer the funds in accordance with federal standards and to appropriate matching funds. That same year, the lawmakers authorized domestic insurance companies to invest in bonds issued by federal land banks under the Federal Farm Loan Act of 1916.[9]

The federal impact on state legislation intensified during the Great Depression as Ohio's legislators reached out for federal aid offered under the New Deal. Relief for the poor had traditionally been provided by local governments, but these entities could not meet the rapidly growing demand for assistance during the 1930s. The General Assembly created the State Relief Commission to coordinate federal, state, and local relief efforts, but the lawmakers proved reluctant to provide funding. Instead, they augmented the authority of local governments to issue bonds and relied heavily on federal agencies to provide relief and jobs. In 1933, the voters took some matters into their own hands. Using the initiative process, they amended the state constitution to reduce the ceiling on real property taxes that could be imposed without popular approval at the polls and they adopted a law providing for old-age pensions. The need to fund the pensions, to aid desperate school districts, and to boost local relief efforts finally induced the legislators to go beyond cigarette, cosmetic, and other nuisance taxes and adopt a sales tax. Still, the General Assembly refused to pass comprehensive legislation to meet the crisis. It didn't help that Martin Davey, elected governor in 1934, fought so much with President Roosevelt and his relief administrator, Harry Hopkins, that the federal government refused to work through state agencies and took over the administration of federal relief in Ohio. Even after Davey's term ended, the General Assembly continued to place the main burden of relief on local governments and on the Works Progress Administration and other federal agencies.[10]

During the Depression, the General Assembly amended Ohio's bond law so that political subdivisions could partake of federal aid offered under the National Industrial Recovery Act. It agreed to comply with federal regulations in order to accept funds made available for public works projects under the Emergency Relief Appropriation Act of 1935. It conformed state law to federal law so that banks could participate in the federal deposit insurance program created by the Banking Act of 1933. It altered state laws dealing with old age assistance, aid to dependent children, and blind relief so that the state could receive federal funds under the Social Security Act. Given Ohio's desperate need for help in dealing with the Depression, the General Assembly may have readily allowed the federal government to shape state law in these and many other ways. Still, the state's Depression-era legislation represented a surrender of major power to the federal government.[11]

The enticement of federal money continued to shape state law after World War II. The elaboration of the interstate highway system, with the federal government providing 90 percent of the funding for highway projects, drew states into the federal orbit. Before 1956, the federal government made highway money available to the states in relatively small amounts and with little oversight. Funding dramatically increased under the Federal-Aid Highway Act of 1956, which created the modern interstate highway system. Federal regulation, relatively light at first, increased as new social and environmental concerns came to the fore in the 1960s and Congress "chose to superimpose upon [the interstate highway program] a patchwork of strings and conditions." Once committed, the states had little practical choice but to adhere to federal standards, and not just in relation to highway construction and maintenance. When Congress directed the secretary of transportation to reduce federal highway funds to states that did not prohibit the sale or public possession of alcoholic beverages to persons under twenty-one years of age, it effectively established a national minimum drinking age. Indeed, commentators commonly referred to the law as the National Minimum Drinking Age Act. In 1987, in response to the law, the General Assembly raised the drinking age in Ohio from nineteen to twenty-one.[12]

Congress began to shape state health care policy in a significant way with the establishment of the Medicaid program in 1965. Intended to help states make health care available to the poor, this theoretically optional program created powerful financial pressure on the states to participate. The federal government would bear more than half of each state's cost of participation and would cut off federal matching funds under preexisting programs to states that refused to take part. Within five years, Ohio and forty-seven other states signed up. Previous federal health care programs had made money available to the states without much supervision. The Medicaid program required adherence to federal criteria. Federal control, light at first, soon tightened. As federal regulation increased, so did the length of Ohio's Medicaid laws, which grew from a single, short section to a whole chapter of the Revised Code, replete with references to federal law. Ohio's Medicaid bureaucracy became "an increasingly complex maze," and the state's share of Medicaid costs "swamp[ed] the state budget."[13]

A House select committee studied the Medicaid problem in 2002, holding numerous public hearings, but Medicaid apparently swamped the committee, too, for it never issued a report. In 2003, the General Assembly created the Ohio Commission to Reform Medicaid, authorized it to hire a staff, and directed it to conduct a complete review of the program and make recommendations. Among other things, the commission urged the creation of a new, cabinet-level department just to deal with Medicaid. Unwilling to go quite that far on short notice, the General Assembly, in its main appropriations bill for 2005–6, declared its intent to get the new department going by 2007 and established a council to investigate the administration of the program and make recommendations regarding the department. The General Assembly also created a statutory joint legislative committee on Medicaid technology and reform, with authority to hire an executive director, and directed the Legislative Service Commission to employ a person to focus on Medicaid and other "federally-funded, caseload driven programs." All of this state spending and bureaucracy is subject to federal statutes and over a thousand pages of federal regulations administered by the Center for Medicaid and State Operations in the federal Department of Health and Human Services.[14]

The Second Century

Although the interstate highway and Medicaid programs use money taken from the states as inducements, they may still be viewed as carrots rather than sticks; for the most part, the states do not, theoretically, have to participate. In the 1960s, federal courts began wielding the constitutional stick in earnest, forcing the states to adhere to policies established in Washington on issues that had long been left to the states. Consider, for example, legislation governing sexual behavior. The Ohio Revised Code of 1953, the fruit of years of work on a recodification and modernization of Ohio's statutes, included a chapter entitled "Offenses Against Chastity." The chapter retained old prohibitions on adultery, fornication, bestiality, sodomy, seduction of a female under a promise of marriage, giving liquor to a female with the aim of rendering her amenable to sex, uttering obscene language in the presence of a female, selling or publishing obscene material, advertising or providing drugs that induced abortion, performing abortions, and other acts regarded as offenses against moral purity. By the late 1960s, a committee established by the General Assembly to rewrite the criminal code considered many of these prohibitions to be antiquated, dead letters in practice or unwarranted interferences in the private lives of consenting adults. The new criminal code, adopted in 1972, omitted many of them.[15]

Still, the General Assembly saw fit to keep some of the old prohibitions in the interests of morality, public health, or the protection of children. U.S. Supreme Court decisions helped shape the statutes. A state court criticized the General Assembly's failure to define obscenity as an abdication of legislative responsibility, but when the lawmakers supplied a definition in 1970, they had to stay within free-speech parameters set by the Supreme Court in the 1950s and 1960s. Similarly, the drafters of the new criminal code's prohibition against pandering obscenity worked with a 1966 Supreme Court decision in mind. Cognizant of judicial wariness of legislatively imposed limitations on freedom of expression, in 2005, the House included a declaration of legislative intent in a bill to regulate adult entertainment establishments, citing six Supreme Court and nineteen lower federal court decisions dealing with public health and safety justifications for limiting freedom of expression. *Roe v. Wade*, handed down between the passage and the effective date of the 1974 criminal code, required a wholesale revision of Ohio's abortion statutes. In 1997, a federal appeals court struck down the General Assembly's first attempt to ban partial-birth abortions, forcing the General Assembly to rewrite the statute.[16]

Capital punishment offers another illustration of how federal judicial decisions forced changes in state laws that for nearly two centuries had been unaffected by federal power. After the crusade against capital punishment fizzled in the middle of the nineteenth century, opponents continued to press for abolition with limited success. In Ohio, public executions disappeared and the electric chair, thought to be more humane than hanging, became the method of dispatching the condemned. (The man who installed Ohio's electric chair got to test the theory when he was sentenced to death for murder.) The last electrocution took place in 1963. For the next thirty-six years, largely because of decisions of the U.S. Supreme Court, Ohio did not execute anyone.

In 1972, the Supreme Court ruled the Georgia and Texas death penalty statutes unconstitutional because they gave too much discretion to the judge or jury in deciding upon a death sentence. Ohio's statute sufficiently resembled the Georgia and Texas laws that the Ohio Supreme Court declared it unconstitutional as well. The General Assembly quickly responded to these decisions with a law that set forth aggravating and mitigating circumstances to be considered by the judge or jury when deciding whether or not to impose the death penalty. In 1978, the U.S. Supreme Court struck down the new statute because it did not allow for the consideration of every conceivable mitigating factor in a case. As a result, 110 individuals on Ohio's death row had their sentences commuted to life in prison. In 1981, the General Assembly amended the statute to conform to the Supreme Court's latest pronouncement. Still, no executions occurred, in part because of Governor Richard Celeste's controversial commutations as his term expired in 1991.

By 1993, electrocution had lost its reputation as a humane manner of execution. The General Assembly therefore allowed a person about to be executed to choose between the electric chair and a lethal injection. Under this law, executions resumed in 1999. In 2001, a death row inmate demanded to be dispatched by electrocution as a protest against capital punishment. Electrocution had by this time been eliminated almost everywhere in the United States. Concerned about Ohio's image, the legislature passed an emergency law making lethal injection the sole method of execution.[17]

The Regulatory State

The growing complexity and interconnectedness of modern society were as important as the increase of federal authority in shaping twentieth-century state laws. We noted in an earlier chapter the movement toward "centralization of administration" and the expansion of administrative agencies and administrative law to deal with matters that overtaxed the legislature's capacity. In creating the administrative state,, the General Assembly became like the board of directors of a corporation, establishing broad policy guidelines and leaving implementation and problem solving to the managerial employees. The General Assembly voluntarily handed over much of its power to agencies better able to deal with the intricacies of social issues on a day-to-day basis.

The movement typified many areas of public law. For example, the creation of a state system of public education began with the centralization of township schools. In 1900 the General Assembly authorized and, on petition of one-quarter of a township school district's electors, required the township trustees to submit to a referendum the question of abolishing subdistricts and providing for one or more central schools. Additional legislation in 1904 and 1914 essentially did away with subdistricts and made the county the chief unit of school administration. The advance of centralization and uniformity did not occur without opposition. At an educational congress held in Columbus in 1913, one rural delegate declared his distaste for "these newfangled notions. The little red brick schoolhouse was good enough for Pap, it was good enough for me and it is good enough for my children." Yet the movement continued apace. The office of state commissioner of common schools, renamed superintendent of public instruction and then director of education, steadily grew in size and responsibility. Before it lost some functions during the Depression, the Department of Education, created in 1921, had expanded to twenty-three divisions with authority over teacher certification, the state library, occupational licensing, film censorship, parental education, and other matters more or less related to education.[18]

The educational bureaucracy underwent major changes in the second half of the twentieth century, but it remained large and influential. Occupational licensing boards became independent entities, and film censorship ended as a result of U.S. and Ohio Supreme Court decisions. But the General Assembly formally gave up some authority when it set up a state board of education in 1955 to establish educational standards and curricular guidelines for schools, leaving to the Department of Education the job of implementing the board's policies. The legislature stayed out of the great debates over the teaching of evolution, creationism, and intelligent design. It authorized charter schools, called community schools in Ohio, and required standardized proficiency and achievement testing at different grade levels, but it left the oversight of both in the department's hands.[19]

The centralizing tendency and new transportation technology joined to pro-duce new state bureaucracies and to expand state activities. In changing the physical and social landscape of twentieth-century America, the automobile gen-erated a lot of legislation relating to the construction and improvement of high-ways, licensing of drivers, administration of highway and motor vehicle laws, and a host of related concerns. In 1908, its first full year of operation, the auto-mobile division of the secretary of state's office recorded 10,649 registrations. In 1914, the number topped 100,000 and in 1923, one million. Roads designed for horses and wagons could not accommodate millions of cars and trucks. The Gen-eral Assembly first addressed the need for new and improved roads in 1904 when it created a state highway department. The law still left most of the responsibility for road building and maintenance to the counties and townships. In 1911, the legislature expanded the department and its responsibilities. The department would now have separate bureaus for construction, maintenance and repair, and bridges. It would be responsible for creating maps and collecting statistics, nam-ing and numbering state highways, and administering an active program of state aid to counties and townships for the construction and repair of highways. Through its administrative merger with and then separation from the Public Works Department in the 1920s and its subsequent enlargement, the Highway Department retained its old functions and added new ones, such as long-range planning and research.[20]

Between 1920 and 1935, the state highway system grew from 3,000 to more than 12,000 miles, and many more miles of county and township roads were built or paved. To pay for all the road construction and maintenance, the Gen-eral Assembly first levied a state property tax for highway purposes in 1913 and later authorized county levies beyond the normal limits. In 1925, the legislature adopted the first motor fuel tax, intended to provide money for the upkeep and repair of highways. After World War II, those who relied on highways the most—"[g]asoline, road material, and automobile interests," according to one observer—insisted on getting all the benefit from the fuel taxes. Using the initiative pro-cedure, they secured a constitutional amendment that dedicated gas tax revenues to highway purposes. In the 1950s, a new agency, the Ohio Turnpike Commis-sion, spent hundreds of millions of dollars building a superhighway through northern Ohio from the Pennsylvania border to Indiana.[21]

While all this taxing and spending for roads was going on, air travel evolved from the dream of a couple of bicycle shop owners in Dayton into a huge segment of the transportation industry. Naturally, new regulatory agencies evolved along with it. In 1929, the General Assembly created an aviation board, which turned into the Office of Aviation in the Department of Transportation, with the power to establish safety rules for air traffic and airports.[22]

The administrative state reached into dozens of occupations. As noted in chapter 13, by the opening of the twentieth century, Ohio had agencies to oversee the enforcement of health and safety laws and in some cases to regulate the business side of industries. The legislature also created numerous boards and commissions to ensure the fitness of individuals to practice various professions. Many of these entities had the authority to set standards for admission to the profession, examine applicants, issue licenses, regulate the conduct of practitioners, and conduct disciplinary hearings. The General Code of 1910 provided for state governing boards for physicians, pharmacists, dentists, embalmers, steam engineers, veterinarians, and certified public accountants. The Code left the oversight of the legal profession to the supreme court and provided for shared state and local control of teachers. By the time the Revised Code replaced the General Code in 1953, the list of licensed professions had grown to include architects, barbers, cosmetologists, nurses, optometrists, engineers, and real estate brokers, and it continued to grow. Covered professions included many in allied health fields—physician's assistants, physical therapists, respiratory case professionals, and so on—as well as such disparate occupations as psychologists, private investigators, social workers, and real estate appraisers. The General Assembly could not constitutionally place all these occupations under the aegis of regulatory bodies without some legislative direction, but in practice it turned the supervision of ever-growing numbers of workers over to unelected boards and commissions.

The Shaping of Environmental Law

Perhaps in no area of public policy can the combined effect of growing federal control over state policy and the rising importance of administrative government be seen more clearly than in environmental policy. Preindustrial Americans took a cavalier attitude toward the environment. Before the Civil War, the General Assembly adopted hunting restrictions to protect certain game animals and prohibited people from contaminating streams with animal carcasses, but for the most part it left environmental protection to local ordinances and to private

lawsuits based on the common law of nuisance, negligence, or riparian rights. Eve
the environmental damage wrought by the industrialization and urbanization c
the postbellum period failed to bring about much governmental action. John D
Rockefeller recalled how his Cleveland oil refinery frequently dumped wast
crude in the Cuyahoga River. "We used to burn it for fuel in distilling the oil
he said, "and thousands and hundreds of thousands of barrels of it floated dow
the creeks and rivers, and the ground was saturated with it, in the constant effoi
to get rid of it." In 1881, Cleveland's mayor described the Cuyahoga as "an ope
sewer through the center of the city." The city itself behaved no better than th
industrialists. Cleveland added to the pollution by sending untreated wastewate
from its sewer system into Lake Erie. In his contribution to the series "Thes
United States" published in the *Nation* in the 1920s, Sherwood Anderson calle
Ohio's industrial cities "as ugly, as noisy, as dirty" as any in the country. Not ex
culpating himself entirely for the sorry state of the environment, Anderson re
called how, during his own days as a manufacturer, he dumped factory waste int
a stream "and killed the fish in it and spoiled it just splendid for a while."[23]

In the late nineteenth and early twentieth centuries, the General Assembl
took some measures to slow down the ravages of pollution and expanding huma
habitation. It created a State Game Commission (later the Fish and Game Com
mission), regulated hunting and fishing through licensing, prohibited coal min
operators from dumping mine refuse into rivers or other bodies of water, an
gave the State Board of Health the power to limit stream pollution. The Genera
Assembly also created the first state parks in the 1890s by designating reservoir:
originally built to feed the canals, as public recreation areas.[24]

But these were small steps that barely addressed a big problem. Serious con
servation efforts at the state level really began in the 1940s with the enactmen
of a soil conservation statute that created a soil conservation commission in th
Ohio State University Department of Agriculture and authorized landowners t
create soil conservation districts. The voluntary program encouraged soil re
search and the development and implementation of soil conservation plan:
Other laws took on the devastation caused by the strip mining of coal. The
prohibited strip mining without a permit from the Division of Mines, created
Division of Reclamation in the Department of Agriculture, and required stri
mine operators to take safety measures and to reclaim strip-mined land in ac
cordance with approved plans. In 1949, the legislature consolidated many envi
ronmental functions that were scattered among various state offices into a nev

Department of Natural Resources that included divisions of lands and soil, water, forestry, wildlife, geological survey, parks, and beach erosion.[25]

During the 1950s, the General Assembly slowly added to the administrative apparatus of environmental protection. First came the water pollution control board, with regulatory and adjudicatory authority, in the Department of Health. The law that created the board prohibited the pollution of state waters without a permit. However, it did not apply to industrial wastes or acid mine drainage until the board determined, after a hearing, "that practical means for the removal of the polluting properties of such wastes or drainage are known." In other words, as long as no one knew how to make the wastes environmentally safe, they could be discharged into lakes and streams. Nor did the act prohibit farmers from dumping animal excrement into state waters or ban the discharge of industrial or other wastes into publicly maintained sewage systems. The gaps in the law were only partially filled by a statute that prohibited the maintenance of sewers through which harmful, untreated sewage or industrial wastes generated by non-residential users could be discharged into public waters. In 1957, the General Assembly established a water survey committee consisting of gubernatorial appointees to study water conservation and management in Ohio and to report to the legislature. It also directed the Department of Health to maintain a laboratory for the study of air pollution.[26]

The environmental legislation of the 1940s and 1950s lacked drama and teeth, but it laid the groundwork for the far more substantial legislation of the 1960s. Academics as well as activists have often asserted that the states did little to protect the environment before the federal government forced them to act in the 1970s, but that is a myth. During the late 1950s and the 1960s, the General Assembly moved to ameliorate the deplorable condition of Lake Erie by tightening the permitting process for mining in the lake's bed and along its shores and by ratifying the Great Lakes Basin Compact, an agreement among Great Lakes states and Canadian provinces to cooperate in the development and conservation of the water resources of the basin. The legislature also sought to protect the state's waters by outlawing dumping in lakes and streams; prohibiting farmers from polluting streams with animal waste; authorizing the Division of Oil and Gas to regulate the disposal of brine and other oil field wastes that caused water pollution; and empowering the Department of Natural Resources to create scenic river areas. The General Assembly moved the Division of Reclamation, which regulated strip mining, from the Department of Agriculture to the

Department of Natural Resources, created an air pollution control board with broad regulatory powers, and, as the 1970s dawned, regulated the use of pesticides and provided funding for the construction of solid waste treatment facilities.[27]

In 1969, the Cuyahoga River caught fire, and the great Santa Barbara oil spill occurred off the coast of California. These marvelously newsworthy occurrences —the media turned the rather mild Cuyahoga fire into a spectacular event— together with the preexisting national trend toward increased regulation of the environment, goaded the federal government, academics, and the public into crucial action. In the landmark year of 1970, "the nation witnessed the signing of the National Environmental Policy Act, the creation of the President's Council on Environmental Quality, the first nationwide celebration of Earth Day, the creation of the U.S. Environmental Protection Agency, and the passage of the federal Clean Air Act's demanding and uncompromising air pollution control program." Governor Ronald Reagan of California declared war on the degradation of the environment, state governments put environmental action at the top of their agendas, and the first environmental law journal was published.[28]

Ohio's governor that year, Republican James Rhodes, worried that too much environmental regulation would hamper economic development, but his Democratic successor, John Gilligan, looked more favorably on state action. In 1972, the most important environmental law in Ohio's history created the Ohio Environmental Protection Agency (EPA). The EPA had responsibility to "administer the laws and regulations pertaining to the prevention, control, and abatement of air and water pollution, public water supply, comprehensive water resource management planning, and the disposal and treatment of solid wastes, sewage, industrial waste, and other wastes." The statute authorized the EPA director, first and foremost, to "provide such methods of administration, appoint such personnel, make such reports, and take such other action as may be necessary to comply with the requirements of the federal laws and regulations pertaining to air and water pollution control, public water supply, water resource planning, and waste disposal and treatment." A major new agency had been brought into being for the primary purpose of administering federal law.[29]

The federal impact on state environmental law has grown steadily since then. One scholar's list of just the major federal environmental protection laws enacted during the 1970s included eighteen statutes. It is hard now to find any area of state environmental or natural resources law that is not shaped to some degree by an act of Congress. For example, the section of the Ohio Revised Code that enumerates the power of the Division of Real Estate and Land Management in the Ohio Department of Natural Resources refers explicitly to four distinct federal laws, and these do not exhaust the list of references in the section to federal agencies or federally funded programs.[30]

To comply with federal law or to make Ohio agencies eligible for federal grants, the General Assembly has passed wide-ranging regulatory acts varying in subject from recycling to hazardous waste disposal, from Lake Erie coastal management to reclamation of land marred by surface mining. On occasion, the General Assembly has enacted environmental legislation not required by and only peripherally related to federal law. In 1988, for example, the General Assembly passed a comprehensive solid waste management law, and, in 1994, it created a voluntary program that gave to owners of land that had been contaminated by petroleum or hazardous substances tax abatements and partial protection from liability for cleaning up the land in accordance with state standards. In neither case did the legislature act in response to federal mandates or incentives. But, for the most part, the evolution of Ohio's environmental statutes illustrates the extent to which both federal law and the practical need for government by administrative agencies have directed the exercise of legislative authority by the modern General Assembly.[31]

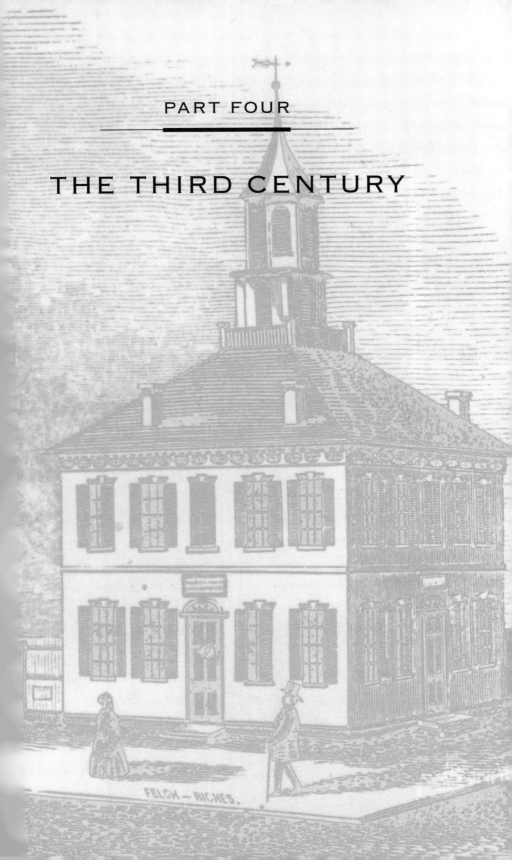

PART FOUR

THE THIRD CENTURY

22

THE FORESEEABLE FUTURE

I n 1972, the Ohio Citizens' Committee on the State Legislature, a study group created by statute to consider ways to strengthen the General Assembly, issued its final report. The committee recommended that the General Assembly meet in regular annual sessions so that it could better deal with the increased demands being made upon state government. It urged that time be set aside before each new General Assembly convened for member orientation and for presession drafting, filing, referral, and even initial committee consideration of bills. It proposed that the time between sessions be devoted to research and investigation by individual legislators and standing committees. Without explicitly recommending higher pay, the Citizens' Committee noted that the salaries received by Ohio's lawmakers, while tenth-highest in the nation, were relatively low for such a populous and developed state, and it openly recommended that the members be allowed to receive reimbursement for expenses related to their work. The committee urged that legislative leaders and the finance committees have more staff support and that each house have a permanent Republican and Democratic fiscal officer. It suggested that the legislative internship program be expanded to provide more assistance to individual members and that the Legislative Service Commission and Legislative Reference Bureau be merged into a single, stronger drafting and research agency. The committee advised the General Assembly to develop a master plan for the use of space in the statehouse once the new state office tower then under construction was completed and to consider the increased use of computers to produce legislative documents and track legislation.[1]

These were precisely the sorts of measures that would transform the General Assembly into a professional legislature. Yet the Citizens' Committee directly disavowed such a goal. The committee knew there was "considerable doubt" that a legislator who did not devote most of his attention to state business or enjoy the support of a "qualified staff" could "possibly master the array of problems upon which the legislature must act." But it clung to the ideal of the citizen-legislator, the part-time lawmaker who made his living doing something else, who did not spend all his time on state business but was "a part of his community, subject to the same economic, political and social problems and pressures as his constituents." It was the citizen-legislator that made the General Assembly the "people's branch" of government.[2]

But the transformation was already under way and would not be halted. By the end of the twentieth century, the General Assembly had become a full-time professional legislature. Recall the "five S's" mentioned in the preface: space, sessions, structure, staffing, and salaries. By these measures, the professionalism of the General Assembly was beyond dispute. The members worked in a beautifully renovated statehouse. Senators had private, nicely appointed offices in the statehouse annex, refurbished and restored as part of the renovation project. Representatives occupied several floors of a modern office tower across the street, where each member of the House had a private office. The statehouse had more than enough committee rooms to meet the needs of the legislature, and both the annex and the office tower had conference rooms as well.

Both the House and Senate had a reasonable number of committees (although the numbers were creeping toward the unreasonable range), each staffed by nonpartisan professionals of the Legislative Service Commission. Every member of the General Assembly had at least one personal assistant; many had two. Both parties had caucus staffs consisting of policy advisers, legal counsel, fiscal experts, and other personnel. The House and Senate administrative offices employed well-educated, competent individuals. The Legislative Service Commission, 160 strong, provided independent, nonpartisan bill-drafting and legal and fiscal research services.

Computers provided instant, up-to-date access to laws, bills, and resolutions, analyses, rules, and information for and about the members, as well as live online broadcasts of floor sessions and archived video recordings of floor sessions going back to 1997. Every member had a computer in his or her office and would soon have one on his or her desk on the floor of the House or Senate. Naturally, the legislature employed information technology people—Web managers, systems engineers, telecommunications personnel—to keep all the computers and communications equipment in operation.

No one was going to get rich on a member's salary, but the compensation was adequate, particularly when health and retirement benefits were considered. Citizens who failed to account for all the time put in outside of floor sessions and committee meetings might think the members only worked part-time, but they could no longer accuse lawmakers of collecting two years' pay for a few months' work every other year. The General Assembly met annually. In the first year of a biennium, it stayed in session into the summer, took a break, and came back in the fall. In the second year, it usually left town a bit earlier, perhaps returned for a few preelection sessions, and came back after elections to wrap up business. But the House and Senate leaders could call the members back into session at any time. The members clearly regarded themselves as full-time legislators. On twenty-first-century rosters, between 40 and 50 percent either listed legislator as their sole occupation or gave no other current occupation.

Ironically, the movement to professionalize the legislature collided with another reform with a directly contrary tendency: term limits. This was a change not contemplated by the Citizens' Committee in 1972. According to one scholar, term limits have "dismantled" legislative professionalism. "Limits appear to have the power to turn back the clock on some of the nation's most professional bodies," writes political scientist Thad Kousser, "bringing changes that narrow the broad gap between citizen legislatures and houses with long sessions, high salaries, and large staff." In particular, Kousser believes that terms limits destabilize and weaken leadership, aggravate partisanship, diminish the effectiveness of committees, reduce policy innovation, and impair the legislature's resistance to the executive.[3]

As the full effects of Ohio's term-limits initiative began to be felt, legislators foresaw seriously detrimental consequences. A common lament was the "loss of institutional memory" with the departure of seasoned members. When crises arose, who would know from experience how to deal with them? Senator Rhine McLin recalled how in 1997 the Ohio Supreme Court had given the General Assembly one year to revamp the system of funding the public schools. "It was during this time," she wrote, "that Republicans turned to Senator Robert R. Cupp. As a veteran member of the Senate, Cupp was familiar with the intricate details of the old formula of funding and was able to both explain it and suggest a plan for improvement." What, McLin wondered, would the legislature have done without such experience?[4]

Legislators typically report that it takes one or two sessions for a member to learn the ropes. From the time when long tenures became common in the 1930s through the end of the twentieth century, the General Assembly never lacked a large group of individuals who knew how to play the game and could mentor new members. Term limits made it likely that inexperienced members who needed to learn the legislator's craft would soon dominate. Senate President Richard Finan predicted in 2001 that "[t]his learning curve will be most apparent as new members seek an understanding of the budget process. Since the budget process occurs every two years, by the time a legislator learns the process fairly well, he or she will be forced out of office due to term limits."[5]

Observers foresaw other negative consequences of term limits. They predicted a decline in the quality of leadership because would-be leaders would no longer have the time to develop a style and a vision, a deep knowledge of the institution, and a network of personal relationships on which to build authority. New members with short official life spans would make life difficult for leadership. Anxious to build their records fast, the newcomers would express themselves more openly and would be less deferential to and less reliant on their leaders. Political commentators predicted a shift in power from a weakened legislature to the executive branch. They thought that the role of lobbyists in educating members, especially with regard to complex issues, would become more difficult because the teachers would constantly be starting over. Moreover, big lobbying firms with the manpower and sophistication to handle their expanded educational role would swallow up small ones, and interest groups that lacked professional lobbyists would be left out in the cold. More members would resign before the end of their terms to take other jobs. The legislature would become a stopping point for people on the way to somewhere else, so that for many members the effective term limit would be seven years. With such a short time to make an impact, legislators would be more interested in getting "quick returns" than in pursuing long-term legislative agendas, making consensus harder to reach.[6]

Besides all that, term limits threatened to destroy the less measurable aspects of legislative life that made progress possible. Legislatures had come to rely on the personal relationships built over time that allowed for compromise. The legislator's belief in the trustworthiness of other members—that they meant what they said, would vote the way they promised, and presented factual matters truthfully—undergirded the "civility, courtesy, understanding and respect" that made legislative work enjoyable and productive. Even in the days of Vern Riffe, whose breathtaking power contributed to the success of the term-limits movement in Ohio, members relied on personal relationships built up over not just years but decades. Riffe himself spent a long time as a backbencher before rising to the Speakership. The members, including those who disliked his authoritarian methods, knew and trusted him. He was as good as his word. He developed close friendships with Republican legislative leaders and did not always stifle minority amendments or bills simply because they came from the opposing party. Term limits, it seemed, would not allow enough time for ideological hard edges to soften, or to let members get to know and trust one another so that the legislative process could work itself out without rancor.[7]

The term-limits clock started running in 1992, even for incumbents who had been in the General Assembly for decades. As a result, the amendment did not have its full impact until the 2000 elections. It is too soon to tell for sure whether term limits have produced the dire results predicted by its critics, but anecdotal evidence, much of it unpublished and not given for attribution, suggests that the criticisms had some merit. Resignations have in fact increased. The budget process has become more chaotic (although passage of the main operating budget bill in 2007 went remarkably smoothly). The lack of experience and mentoring has been apparent, relations between the parties have been acrimonious, and leadership has at times been clumsy. According to one critic, the prevalence of "novice legislators" helped produce a badly drawn tort-reform law in 2004 written mostly by big lobbies. On the other hand, power does not seem to have shifted appreciably to the executive branch. An academic report issued in 2004 found that Ohio differed from other states with term limits in that power had moved away from the governor toward "parties in the legislature (partisan staff members, party leaders and party caucuses)." Perhaps Ohio's abnormality was due to the political weakness of Governor Bob Taft, who held office from the time term limits went into effect through 2006, or to the possibility that, as a former legislator, Taft had greater respect for the General Assembly than some of his predecessors who lacked legislative experience.[8]

Some of these situations may be temporary. There is a growing tendency for members to move back and forth between the houses or to return to the General Assembly after a four-year hiatus. Throughout the period of term limits, most senators have been former representatives. If the trend continues, there will be an increase in experience and a restoration of at least some of the personal relationships upon which practical achievements as well as civility are built. Improved training for new members may enhance their performance in the early years. In 2000, when term limits had their first big impact on the General Assembly, the Legislative Service Commission expanded its orientation program for new members from one and a half to four and a half days. Longtime staff also help keep the institutional memory alive. In the House in 2006, for example, the minority chief of staff, director of administration, and director of policy collectively had nearly ninety years of experience at the statehouse, and the Legislative Service Commission had over twenty staff members with more than twenty years of service apiece. Video archives of legislative proceedings, should anyone care to use them, may also help preserve institutional memory.

Stronger governors may ultimately succeed in siphoning power away from the legislature, but that will depend more on personalities and politics than on the nature of term limits. Term limits have rid legislatures of old chaff as well as ripe wheat and have brought in well-educated, assertive new members. As leaders adapt to the new circumstances, they may find more than enough strength to maintain legislative independence. Indeed, one professional student of state legislatures speculated in 2005 that term limits had actually strengthened the General Assembly vis-à-vis the governor by bringing a particularly strong Speaker to the fore.[9]

Political scientist Alan Rosenthal has stated unequivocally that term limits will make legislatures worse. Two other scholars, after examining the effects of term limits in Ohio, acknowledged that term limits made the legislative process "chaotic and unpredictable" but concluded that "the Ohio legislature is functioning and functioning rather well. Perhaps it is in spite of term limits. Perhaps it is because of term limits. Our guess is that it is a little of both." Term limits have been in effect in Ohio for only a few years. It will take longer than that to see how successfully the General Assembly adapts to the change. In the meantime, the limits themselves may be modified. In 2007, the leaders of both parties and the newly elected governor came out in favor of extending term limits to twelve years, three ex-governors called term limits a failure, and several major newspapers editorialized in favor of an extension or abolition of term limits. On the other hand, a Rasmussen poll found that a large majority of Ohioans not only supported term limits but thought that eight years was just about right.[10]

The importance of term limits cannot be denied, but some of the changes that term limits are thought to have wrought, or at least threatened, have other roots. The decline of trust and interpersonal relationships could be seen before term limits. In some cases, the causes lay in the reform movement that was meant to strengthen and improve the legislature. For example, the advent of private offices for members affected personal interactions among them. When members had no private offices to retreat to, they saw each other constantly in the corridors, at their desks on the floor or, for a time, in large rooms shared by many legislators. In the 1970s and 1980s, senators and representatives literally went their separate ways, the former to their renovated annex east of the statehouse, the latter to the Riffe Center across High Street to the west. In both buildings, the members had individual spaces, spread over multiple floors. In the Riffe Center, offices were grouped by party, and visitors, rather than roaming around at will, had to check in with a receptionist on each floor and have a member or aide come out to escort them to their destination. Isolation became natural; mingling required seeking out others.

Some commentators blamed ethics laws for at least part of the decline of the old camaraderie. Before term limits had any effect on the composition of the General Assembly, financial disclosure requirements and limitations on the amount that lobbyists could spend on drinks and dinners for legislators boosted the popularity of party fundraisers as social events. Members received free tickets and no one had to fuss with disclosure reports. But these were partisan affairs. Republicans and Democrats did not mingle at fund-raisers the way they had at bars and restaurants. In 1995, a Democratic legislator doubted that a major health care bill would have been passed a few years earlier had it not been for the personal bond forged with a Republican colleague over dinners. "I learned more about him as a person and his district," he said. "We wouldn't get into those things if you didn't have a more relaxed setting." Of course, ethics laws did not prevent members from hanging out together after hours, but there were only so many dinners a member could afford in places conducive to low-key yet informative exchanges.[11]

Living arrangements and the decline of night work also affected collegiality. When most members stayed at hotels close to the statehouse, they would eat together and walk to and from work together. And in the days when evening sessions and committee meetings were common, many members would repair afterwards to the Red Lion bar in the Neil House or other downtown bars or restaurants to unwind. But then members scattered to apartments, the Neil House closed, night worked waned, and the opportunities for members to become intimately acquainted with one another dwindled.

Diminished collegiality has been associated with a rise in partisanship and decline in civility. As already suggested, it is harder for members to reach across party lines when they don't know each other. Beyond that, the way of dealing with partisan issues seems to have changed. One member who served in the 1970s and 1980s claimed that there used to be partisanship without malice. Legislators could handle partisan issues with humor and mutual respect. In recent years, the tone of partisan debates has become harsher, and ideological line drawing seems to have left less room for compromise. But the extent to which heightened partisanship can be attributed to term limits or any of the other phenomena that have contributed to the loss of collegiality is difficult to assess. Partisan bitterness has grown everywhere, including Congress, whose members have long had private offices and are not subject to term limits.[12]

Even less predictable than the long-range effects of term limits is the impact of technological change. That changes will continue to come rapidly and dramatically seems certain. Both legislators and the public now receive much of their information over the Internet. Lawmakers are in constant contact with lobbyists, constituents, and each other by cell phone and e-mail. Fund-raising and campaigning through the Internet will surely spread. Internet voting, permitted in Oregon, has been proposed for Ohio. It may be that the use of the initiative process, which has proliferated in recent years, will become even more popular through the circulation of petitions online. Perhaps legislators will be able to telecommute, attending committee meetings and floor sessions through teleconferencing or the Internet. Legislative proceedings will become easier to record, store, and search and will be accessible to a wide public, with vast implications for politics, obviously, but also perhaps for courts looking for the legislative intent behind statutes. Information technology specialists make up an important part of the legislative staff, and the members themselves need to be practiced in the use, if not necessarily versed in the science, of computers and digital equipment. New technology will also form an increasingly important part of the legislative agenda as the General Assembly confronts issues related to electronic voting, computer crimes, regulation of telecommunications, and a host of other issues related to technology. But the pace of change is so fast that any attempt to predict its nature and consequences for the General Assembly more than a few years into the future would be dicier than forecasting Columbus' notoriously changeable weather.

Some things never change. One is the split, or at least the perception of a split, among urban, suburban, and rural lawmakers. In 2007, a spokesman for the mayor of Columbus, grousing about a new law that overrode local gun-control ordinances, declared, "We have a bunch of legislators who don't live in urban areas setting policy for urban communities." The future, though, may feature a new twist on that theme as exurbs (areas beyond the suburbs) grow in population and political influence. Another seemingly permanent feature of the General Assembly is the chaos that accompanies the end of a session or some other deadline. In 2006, the 126th General Assembly ended with a frenetic "blur of legislative activity." The Senate finally wrapped up business on its final, contentious day of work at 4:15 A.M. After vetoing a bill passed in those last frantic hours that his predecessor would neither veto nor sign, the new governor alleged that the bill represented "hasty action during a lame-duck session, where there is not sufficient discussion, input or deliberation." Six months later, notwithstanding a degree of bipartisanship on the budget that hadn't been seen in half a century, the lawmakers behaved as if the June 30 budget deadline were the last day of the biennium. The whirl of activity included the last-minute substitution of bills or introduction of amendments that few members had even seen. In one case, the House modified an important and controversial Senate bill by adopting an amendment requested by municipal officials at "the eleventh and a half hour," even though the provision that so upset the cities had been in the bill from the start. It seems unlikely that more than a handful of members had any idea of what they were voting on. In 1910, the Speaker of the House blamed the late-session tumult on time-wasting during the first four to six weeks. In 2007, the Speaker did not appoint standing committees until the middle of February, and the legislature passed exactly one bill before May 1.[13]

Popular disenchantment with the legislature also persists. Notwithstanding all the squeals about too-short tenures from lawmakers and close observers of the legislative process, a large majority of Ohioans want to retain the eight-year term limits for legislators. The people still want government to do big things, but their faith in government remains low.[14]

Alan Rosenthal believes that the American people do not appreciate their legislatures because the assemblies are not pleasing to look at. They are "burdensome and contentious" and do "not always give us what we want." But Rosenthal is a big fan of state legislatures. Despite their imperfections, he writes, they are better than "any conceivable alternatives. Not only that, they actually work, albeit in rather messy and somewhat mysterious ways—representing, lawmaking, and balancing the power of the executive. They deserve more understanding and greater support than they have been given. Without that, the public might not

In an inspiring display of bipartisanship, Republican senator Gene Watts and Democratic representative Mike Stinziano, accompanied by the Ohio State University Pep Band, sing "Hang On, Sloopy" on the Senate floor following the adoption of a resolution naming the tune Ohio's official rock song. *Courtesy of the* Columbus Citizen-Journal *Collection, Scripps-Howard Newspapers/Grandview Heights Public Library/Photohio.org*

be able to continue counting on them to do the job that they have been doing—and doing well."[15]

It need only be added that, for all the fractiousness that sometimes characterizes legislative proceedings, for all the campaign fund-raising, end-of-session bedlam, and occasional nuttiness that engender public distrust, the Ohio General Assembly does its job better now than it ever has in the past. That does not mean that the General Assembly of 2008 was better than that of 2006 or 1996. A legislature has its ups and downs from year to year, and the path to the future is not smooth. By historical standards, though, the modern General Assembly is elected cleanly, operates openly, handles complex issues competently, and represents a large, diverse, and contentious people about as well as can be expected in a messy democracy.

APPENDIX A

NOTE ON OHIO LEGISLATIVE

PUBLICATIONS

LEGISLATIVE PUBLICATIONS, particularly the House and Senate journals and the session laws, both discussed in appendix B, "Notes on the Notes," are the indispensable primary materials for the history of a legislature. Ohio's constitutions have always required each house to keep a journal of its proceedings, but they have not specified with much detail what the journals must contain. The contents have varied widely with time and the inclinations of the clerks. Early journals included executive materials, such as governors' addresses to the legislature and reports of state officials. Most of this was eliminated in the 1830s and published thereafter in separate volumes of executive documents. But the nineteenth-century journals continued to include much fascinating material, especially committee reports. Today in Ohio, the term "committee report" refers to the version of a bill reported by a committee, but in the nineteenth century, it often meant a narrative report on the merits of a bill, on an issue of major public concern, or on the results of an investigation. Some of the earliest journals also carried the records of impeachment proceedings. In the 1830s, committee reports began to appear in appendices, usually bound with the daily proceedings of the legislature but sometimes in a separate volume. The appendices frequently included other interesting and sometimes frivolous matter, even doggerel. In the twentieth century, most of these good things disappeared, leaving a dry-as-dust chronicle of roll-call votes and other dreary stuff. The House and Senate clerks publish a journal after each legislative day, with bound volumes appearing annually. The current journals and those for the last few years may be found at the General Assembly's Web site (http://www.legislature.state.oh.us).

The journals have never included the text of bills. Bound volumes of the different versions of bills as they were introduced, reported, and passed, at least for some twentieth-century sessions, can be found in a few libraries. Nor have the journals ever contained speeches and debates, a fact lamented in 1888 by former senator

469

James Monroe, who wondered how historians would be able to construct a history of the legislature.[1] The General Assembly now posts on its Web site all versions of bills on which official action has been taken. The Ohio Channel (www.ohiochannel.org) broadcasts House and Senate floor sessions live online. Through the Ohio Channel, viewers can access archived broadcasts going back to 1997.

The Ohio session laws (the laws passed during each session of the legislature) beginning with the First General Assembly in 1803 are available in many libraries. The Legislative Service Commission (LSC) publishes a *Digest of Enactments* (formerly called *Summary of Enactments*) that synopsizes the laws of every session. The *Digests* and a variety of other legislative materials going back several sessions can be accessed at the LSC Web site (http://www.lsc.state.oh.us). For the laws of the Northwest Territory, see Theodore Calvin Pease, ed., *The Laws of the Northwest Territory, 1788–1800* (Springfield: Trustees of the Illinois State Historical Library, 1925), and Salmon P. Chase, ed., *The Statutes of Ohio and of the North Western Territory, Adopted or Enacted From 1788 to 1833, Inclusive,* 3 vols. (Cincinnati: Corey and Fairbank, 1833–35).

Ohio had no official code of laws until 1880. Early General Assemblies occasionally ordered that some or all of the laws in force as of the end of a session be reprinted in the session laws, and sometimes related laws were grouped together by subject matter. The first serious attempt at an organized code came with Judge Joseph R. Swan's *Statutes of the State of Ohio* (Columbus: Samuel S. Medary, 1841), a collection of laws arranged alphabetically by subject matter. In 1879, the General Assembly adopted Ohio's first official code of laws, the Revised Statutes, effective January 1, 1880. New codifications followed in 1910 (the General Code) and 1953 (the Revised Code). The LSC keeps the Revised Code up to date. Since Swan's day, private publishers have put out their own editions of Ohio's statutes, usually with case annotations and other information useful to lawyers. Except for the act that adopted the Revised Code in 1953, the state has never published an official version of the Revised Code. An unofficial, unannotated version from Lawriter LLC is available at the state's Web site (http://codes.ohio.gov/orc). For a history of codification in Ohio up to the eve of the Revised Code's adoption, see Ervin H. Pollack and Charles F. O'Brien, "The History of Legislative Publications in Ohio," *Ohio State Law Journal* 13 (Summer 1952): 307–49.

In 1917, if not before, the General Assembly started publishing weekly bulletins during legislative sessions to keep members and the public informed of the status of bills that had been introduced. At the end of each session, a final *Bulletin* for the session was published. Today the progress of legislation as it moves through the General Assembly can be tracked through the LSC's Status Report (available at the LSC Web site). The Senate clerk still publishes the final *Bulletin*. The content of the final *Bulletins* has varied over the years. At one time, the *Bulletins* included figures on the number of bills referred to each standing committee. They have always contained information on vetoes. After 1974, the journals no longer included more or less complete indexes; the *Bulletins* became the indexes and the only printed sources that track legislative history.

Beginning in the 1850s, rosters of members sporadically appeared in the House and Senate journals. Near the end of the nineteenth century, rosters of members and employees became a regular feature of the journals. These later rosters listed not only the names and addresses of legislators but also their party affiliations and prior experience in the General Assembly. Perhaps as early as 1894 and definitely by 1910, the General Assembly was publishing the rosters as separate booklets, and eventually the journals dropped the rosters. The content of the roster booklets varied, although some features such as committee assignments remained pretty much constant. Unfortunately, around 1980, the House roster stopped listing all the employees; a few years later the Senate roster followed suit; and, after the 124th General Assembly (2003–4), the Senate ceased publishing its roster altogether. Much of the information formerly available in the rosters may be found at the General Assembly's Web site (www.legislature. state.oh.us), but not conveniently in one place. For an unofficial roster, see the *Ohio Government Directory* published biennially by the Ohio Trucking Association.

As discussed in chapter 4, in 1891, Senate clerk W. A. Taylor published a historical roster, the *Hundred-Year Book and Official Register of the State of Ohio, from 1789 to 1891, Inclusive* (Columbus: Westbote, 1891), as an appendix to the Senate journal. The General Assembly authorized the publication of several updates under the names of *Hundred-Year Book* or *The Biographical Annals of Ohio* in the early twentieth century. These books are replete with errors and must be used with caution. In 1966, House clerk Carl Guess, pursuant to a resolution, published the *Ohio House of Representatives Membership Directory 1803—1965–66* (Columbus: Blank Book, 1966).

In 1913, the General Assembly authorized the preparation, printing, and distribution of "a history of legislation in Ohio for the years 1909–1913, inclusive, in connection with the official history of the state administration for the years 1909–1912."[2] The result, along with subsequently authorized "histories," was a series of six volumes under the general title *Ohio Legislative History* prepared under the editorial supervision of James K. Mercer and covering the period from 1909 through 1926. Although these books are not really histories of anything, they do contain some useful data, including governors' addresses to the legislature, lists of bills passed, photos and saccharine biographies of members and some employees, information on state agencies, and legislative miscellanea.

The House, Senate, and joint rules have always been published in the journals, often in appendices. The General Assembly began putting out separate rules booklets around 1950 and continues to do so. The current rules may also be found at the General Assembly's Web site. In the late nineteenth and early twentieth centuries, the

General Assembly issued "manuals of legislative practice" that included the rules, rosters, brief biographies of members, and related information. Notwithstanding their titles, these manuals had little to say on parliamentary practice beyond the rules. In 1912, House parliamentarian Edward Wakefield Hughes published a *Guide to Parliamentary Practice in the Ohio House of Representatives* (Columbus: State of Ohio, 1912). The book grew into a comprehensive treatise on American parliamentary practice, culminating with *Hughes' American Parliamentary Guide: Mechanics of Lawmaking*, rev. new ed. (Columbus: Heer, 1932). "Ohio" dropped out of the title, but the book continued to discuss Ohio as well as general parliamentary practice.

The LSC published its first *Guidebook for Ohio Legislators* in 1970. Now in its eleventh edition and updated for each new General Assembly, the *Guidebook* is a reference source for legislators and their staffs. It contains a great deal of useful information on subjects ranging from the history of the statehouse to legislative procedure to the salaries and benefits of members. The appendices include charts that provide demographic data on the members and statistics on legislation. Insights into the modern history of the General Assembly can be gleaned from comparisons of different editions of the *Guidebook*. The current *Guidebook* is available at the LSC Web site.

Although not official publications of the General Assembly, the memoirs and collected correspondence of lawmakers perhaps ought to count as quasi-legislative publications. Jacob Burnet, one of the most influential and productive members of the territorial legislature, covers the work of that body in *Notes on the Early Settlement of the North-Western Territory* (Cincinnati: Derby, Bradley, 1847). The only book-length account for the statehood period is Vernal G. Riffe Jr. with Cliff Treyens, *Whatever's Fair: The Political Autobiography of Ohio House Speaker Vern Riffe* (Kent, Ohio: Kent State University Press, 2007). Shorter first-person reports may be found in the autobiographies, and scattered insights in the letters, of political figures who did not make a career of serving in the General Assembly. A good source for the early nineteenth century is Julia Perkins Cutler, ed., *Life and Times of Ephraim Cutler Prepared from His Journals and Correspondence* (1890; repr., New York: Arno, 1971). For the mid-nineteenth century see "The Autobiography of Alexander Long," ed. Louis R. Harlan, *Bulletin of the Historical and Philosophical Society of Ohio* 19 (April 1961): 98–127, and Charles Reemelin, *Life of Charles Reemelin, In German: Carl Gustav Rümelin, From 1814–1892* (Cincinnati, Weier and Daiker, 1892). In *Oberlin Thursday Lectures, Addresses and Essays* (Oberlin, Ohio: E. J. Goodrich, 1897), scholar James Monroe reminisces on his service in the Ohio Senate during the 1850s. Letters by and to James A. Garfield shed a bit of light on the doings of the legislators around 1860, when Garfield was in the Ohio Senate, and 1880, when the General Assembly elected Garfield to the United States Senate. See, for example, John Shaw, ed., *Crete and James: Personal*

Letters of Lucretia and James Garfield (East Lansing: Michigan State University Press, 1994), and James D. Norris and Arthur H. Shaffer, *Politics and Patronage in the Gilded Age: The Correspondence of James A. Garfield and Charles E. Henry* (Madison: State Historical Society of Wisconsin, 1970). On the political life of Ohio's second African American legislator, who served in both the House and Senate in the 1880s and 1890s, see John P. Green, *Fact Stranger Than Fiction: Seventy-five Years of a Busy Life, with Reminiscences of Many Great and Good Men and Women* (Cleveland: Riehl Printing, 1920). Allen O. Myers, *Bosses and Boodle in Ohio Politics: Some Plain Truths for Honest People* (Cincinnati: Lyceum Publishing, 1895) is not autobiographical, but, as a fevered rant on Gilded Age venality by a former member and close observer of the General Assembly, it offers an interesting interpretation of how that body functioned.

Frederic C. Howe, *The Confessions of a Reformer* (New York: Charles Scribner's Sons, 1925), and William B. Saxbe with Peter D. Franklin, *I've Seen the Elephant: An Autobiography* (Kent, Ohio: Kent State University Press, 2000), devote a few enlightening pages apiece to the authors' short state legislative careers in the early and mid-twentieth century, respectively. Several informative letters from the 1920s can be found in *The Papers of Robert A. Taft: Volume 1, 1889–1939*, ed. Clarence E. Wunderlin Jr. (Kent, Ohio: Kent State University Press, 1997). Frances McGovern, who served several terms in the House, provides a wonderful portrait of legislative life in the 1950s in *Fun, Cheap, and Easy: My Life in Ohio Politics, 1949–1964* (Akron: University of Akron Press, 2002). For the reflections of the first Democratic African American to be elected to the General Assembly, see Carl B. Stokes, *Promises of Power: A Political Autobiography* (New York: Simon and Schuster, 1973). C. J. McLin Jr., the long-serving (1967–88) founder of the Black Caucus, offers his recollections in *Dad, I Served: The Autobiography of C. J. McLin, Jr.*, ed. Lillie P. Howard and Sarah Byrn Rickman (Dayton: Wright State University Office of Public Relations, 1998). Richard G. Zimmerman, a statehouse correspondent for a leading newspaper, devotes a colorful chapter to legislators and lobbyists in the 1960s in *Plain Dealing: Ohio Politics and Journalism Viewed from the Press Gallery* (Kent, Ohio: Kent State University Press, 2006).

Finally, for readers interested in the more general history of American state legislatures, a good place to start is Joel H. Silbey, ed., *Encyclopedia of the American Legislative System: Studies of the Principal Structures, Processes, and Policies of Congress and the State Legislatures Since the Colonial Era*, 3 vols. (New York: Scribner, 1994). Another recent, valuable introduction, with an extensive bibliography and commentary on the historiography of the field, is Peverill Squire, "Historical Evolution of Legislatures in the United States," *Annual Review of Political Science* 9 (2006): 19–44. Robert Luce, *Science of Legislation*, 4 vols. (Boston: Houghton Mifflin, 1922–35), is a much older but still important history and analysis of American legislatures. The individual volumes are *Legislative Procedure*, *Legislative Assemblies*, *Legislative Principles*, and *Legislative Problems*. Of the handful of histories of individual state legislatures, most focus on public policy as reflected in the laws passed and say little about the institutions themselves. Two of the better, more comprehensive studies are Justin E. Walsh, *The Centennial History of the Indiana General Assembly, 1816–1978* (Indianapolis: Select Committee on the Centennial History of the Indiana General Assembly in cooperation with the Indiana Historical Bureau, 1987) and Carl N. Everstine, *The General Assembly of Maryland*, 3 vols. (Charlottesville, Va.: Michie, 1980–84) (covering the period from 1634 to 1920). Instructive and readable accounts of legislative life by state legislators outside of Ohio include Willie Brown, *Basic Brown: My Life and Our Times* (New York: Simon and Schuster, 2008) (California); Harriet Keyserling, *Against the Tide: One Woman's Political Struggle* (Columbia: University of South Carolina Press, 1998) (South Carolina); Tom Loftus, *The Art of Legislative Politics* (Washington, D.C.: Congressional Quarterly Press, 1994) (Wisconsin); H. L. "Bill" Richardson, *What Makes You Think We Read the Bills?* (Ottawa, Ill.: Caroline House Books, 1978) (California); Frank Smallwood, *Free and Independent* (Brattleboro, Vt.: S. Green Press, 1976) (Vermont); and Ralph G. Wright, *Inside the Statehouse: Lessons from the Speaker* (Washington, D.C.: CQ Press, 2005) (Vermont).

Notwithstanding Squire's reservations about the value of Congress as a model for understanding the evolution of state legislatures, the history of Congress does give one a feel for the growth of American assemblies. Developments in Congress often served as examples for or paralleled developments in the states. George B. Galloway, *History of the House of Representatives*, 2d ed., rev. by Sidney Wise (New York: Thomas Y. Crowell, 1976), and Robert V. Remini, *The House: The History of the House of Representatives* (New York: Smithsonian Books in association with Harper-Collins, 2006), together cover the House very well. The Congressional Research Service published an updated and somewhat different version of Galloway's book, *History of the United States House of Representatives, 1789–1994* (Washington, D.C.: GPO, 1994), without listing Galloway as the author. There is no comparable comprehensive history of the Senate, but see Robert C. Byrd, *The Senate, 1789–1989: Addresses on the History of the United States Senate*, ed. Mary Sharon Hall, 4 vols. (Washington, D.C.: GPO, 1988–94).

NOTES ON THE NOTES

General Assemblies and Sessions

THE GENERAL ASSEMBLY is the legislature of the State of Ohio. A General Assembly is the legislature that is elected for a particular period of time. The 126th General Assembly, for example, is the legislature that convened on January 3, 2005, for the 2005–6 biennium. Its authority to act expired at the end of the day on December 31, 2006. Under the present state constitution, a new General Assembly meets for the first time on the first Monday in January, or on Tuesday if the first Monday is New Year's Day, of each odd-numbered year. This is the beginning of the legislature's first regular session. The second regular session meets in January of second year of the biennium. Until 1973, there was technically only one regular session, but the lawmakers often adjourned in the middle of the first year to January of the second year. When a General Assembly winds up business, it adjourns sine die (without day). That is, the members go home and can only be called back by someone having the constitutional authority to call a special session.

The term *session* is also used to refer to the actual meeting of a legislative chamber. To say that the House or Senate is in session is to indicate that the members are at that moment meeting to conduct business, unless they are taking a recess. The House and Senate rules state that, except during a recess, a committee may not meet, without special permission, while the full body is in session.

Senate and House Journals

The notes contain many citations to the journals of the Ohio Senate and House of Representatives. The general citation format used in this book includes the volume number, the abbreviation S.J. or H.J., the page on which the referenced material appears, and the year in which the vote or other action occurred. For example, "1 H.J. 50 (1803)" refers to volume 1 of the House journal, page 50, and indicates that the vote or other action occurred in 1803. This simple format belies the complications involved in referencing the journals. The First General Assembly met in March and April of 1803. Thereafter, through 1851, every General Assembly convened in December and adjourned in the following calendar year. From 1852 on, every General Assembly first met in January following the election every other year for a session that could last anywhere from a few months to two calendar years. The exception occurred in 1906–8 because of a constitutional amendment that moved the elections for the legislature from odd-numbered to even-numbered years. Sometimes the General Assembly met in a special session called by the governor or, after 1973, by the presiding officers of the House and Senate.

Whoever numbered the volumes of the journals, presumably either the clerks of the two chambers or the state printer, did not follow a consistent pattern. At first, the title page of each volume included a volume number. After a few years, the volume number disappeared; it did not show up again until the 1843–44 session; however, since there was only one volume of each journal for each of the intervening legislatures, there is no problem assigning volume numbers to them.

Beginning with the Fiftieth General Assembly in 1852, the first under the new constitution, a new legislature convened every other year. The volumes for the 1852 journals are appropriately numbered 50. But instead of adjourning sine die and going home for good after a few months as anticipated, the General Assembly adjourned until November and then stayed in session into 1853. The journals for the adjourned session are numbered volume 50, part 2, with new pagination. For the rest of the nineteenth century, there was a new volume for each initial and adjourned session of any given General Assembly. Adjourned sessions usually began in January of the second year of the biennium. Until 1894, when the legislature decided to meet every other year, that usually meant one volume per calendar year and therefore two volume numbers for each General Assembly. From 1895 through 1966, there were seventeen calendar years in which the General Assembly did not meet at all, even for special sessions. (The only time that had happened before 1895 was in 1855.) The Sixty-ninth General Assembly (1890–91) and Eightieth General Assembly (1913–14) each had three volume numbers because of separately numbered journals issued for special sessions. Beginning in 1915, one volume number was assigned to each General Assembly, regardless of how many special sessions it held or how many bound volumes were issued. (The only exception was for the House journals of 1933–35, discussed below.)

The volume number for a special session is usually, but not always, the same as for the regular session. During the period in which the title pages of the journals did not bear a volume number, the same number can be assumed for the regular and special sessions. For example, the regular session of the Twentieth General Assembly ran from December 3, 1821, through February 4, 1822. A special session was held in May 1822. In the set of journals I used for this book, the separately paginated House and Senate journals of the special session are bound with the journals for the regular sessions of both the Twentieth and Twenty-first General Assemblies. Regardless of where the special-session journals are bound, though, they should bear the same volume number as the journals for the regular session of the Twentieth General Assembly. Thus, a citation to one of the special-session journals should include the volume number 20 along with a reference to the special session to indicate that the page number is not that of the journal for the regular session: 20 H.J., spec. sess., 1 (1822).

Sometimes special sessions produced individually numbered volumes. The Sixty-ninth General Assembly met in special session in 1890, between its first session and its 1891 adjourned session. The Senate and House clerks each published a separate journal with its own volume number for the special session, so there are three numbered volumes of each journal for the Sixty-ninth General Assembly. That's different from the 1822 special session but easy enough to follow. However, the special session of 1902 thoroughly bollixed up the numbering. The journals for the regular session of 1902 bear volume number 95. The Senate journal for the special session is volume 96; the House journal is not numbered. The Senate journals for 1904, 1906, and 1908 logically should have been numbered, respectively, 97, 98, and 99. Instead, they are numbered 96, 97, and 98. The House journals for those years are not numbered at all. The numbering got back on track with the journals for the special session of 1909, both of which are volume 100. I have filled in and corrected the volume numbers for 1902 through 1908 in accordance with the chart below. I have also corrected the volume numbers for the Eighty-fourth General Assembly (1921–22). The House journal for the regular session is numbered 109, but the Senate journal for the regular session and both journals for the special session are numbered 108. All journals for the Eighty-fourth General Assembly should be numbered 109.

Special sessions during the Great Depression also caused numbering problems. The Senate journal for the regular session and all three special sessions of 1931–32 are all in volumes numbered 114, but the House journal for the third special session is in a separate volume numbered 115. The Senate journal for the regular session of 1933 is numbered 115, while the House journal for that year is 116. For the three special sessions of 1933–34, the Senate journal is still in volume 115 and the House journal reverts to 115. The House and Senate journals for 1935–36 are both numbered 116, and, from then on, there are no more discrepancies. Since the numbering of the Senate journals is more logical than that for the House journals for 1933–35, I have used the Senate volume numbers for the journals of both chambers for those years.

To deal with special sessions, the clerks sometimes used part numbers, with each part of a journal being individually paginated; however, because they used part numbers inconsistently, I have ignored them in my citations and referred instead to the special session where necessary: 115 H.J., 2d spec. sess. 346–50 (1934). Part numbers also appear on the bindings of the multiple journal tomes for recent legislatures. These numbers are meaningless because the multipart volumes are continuously paginated. The only time I have used a part number in a citation to a journal is in referring to the adjourned (not special) session of the Fiftieth General Assembly (1852–53), the first to meet under the 1851 constitution.

The clerks also dealt with journal appendices in varying ways. If a citation is to an appendix that is not separately paginated, I have used the standard journal citation form. If the appendix is separately paginated, the note indicates that the referenced source is an appendix: 43 S.J., app., 12–17 (1844). If a volume of the journal has multiple appendices, each of which is separately paginated, the note also includes the appendix number: 43 H.J., app. no. 6, 9–11 (1845).

Session Laws

Session laws are the statutes passed by a particular General Assembly. There is a volume of session laws for each legislature, and the volumes are numbered sequentially. For example, the laws enacted by the First General Assembly are in volume 1 of the session laws. Special sessions occasionally led to quirks of numbering and pagination. The session laws passed at the regular session of the Twentieth General Assembly are in volume 20, but those passed at the special session are in volume 21. The laws of the Twenty-first General Assembly are in another volume also numbered 21. The session laws for the regular session of the Eighty-ninth General Assembly are in volume 114, while those for all three special sessions are in volume 114, part 2, which is paginated separately from the first part but continuously for all the special sessions. The same pattern holds for the Ninetieth General Assembly.

The title as printed on the title page has changed over the years, but in standard legal form, the session laws are referred to as Ohio Laws. I cite them by the abbreviation O.L. In recent decades, the volumes have grown so large that they cannot fit within one binding and have been published in multiple, separately bound parts. The pagination is usually continuous, so there is rarely a need to refer to the parts (which in any case are indicated only on the bindings). I have cited the session laws by volume, O.L., page on which the act begins, and year of enactment. From 1822–23 (Twenty-first General Assembly) through 1852 (Fiftieth General Assembly, first session), the printers typically divided the session laws into two categories, general laws and local/special laws, and put them into separately paginated sections of the statutes. Local laws were laws that affected individual localities. Special laws applied to individual persons or organizations—for example, laws that granted divorces or corporate charters. Joint resolutions of the House and Senate followed and were paginated with the local laws. In citations to volumes of session laws that have separately paginated sections, all page references are to the general-law section except where "local laws" is specified in the citation.

Absence of Citations

For some information in the text, there are no supporting citations. This is true, for example, of breakdowns of votes in the House and Senate by party or type of district (urban or rural), and of data about members (age, occupation, and so on). The information in these cases had to be compiled from House and Senate journals and other legislative documents, newspapers, county histories, and other sources, not all of them published. To calculate rates of absenteeism (chapter 7) and the percentage of bills vetoed (chapter 13), I had to resort to the journals and bulletins. In writing about the period since 1950, I have sometimes drawn on formal interviews but more often on conversations and e-mail correspondence with colleagues at the Legislative Service Commission, other legislative employees, current and former members, and other people associated in one way or another with the General Assembly. There is no convenient way to provide references to these sources.

Journal Volume Chart

For reasons explained above, citations to the Ohio House and Senate journals can be confusing. The following chart relates the volume numbers used in the endnotes to the General Assembly and years associated with each journal. The journals for the 126th (2005–6) and 127th (2007–8) had not yet been published in hard copy when this book went to press, but they are available online at the General Assembly's Web site, http://www.legislature.state.oh.us/search.cfm.

Table of Correspondences for Journal Volume Numbers and General Assemblies

Volume	General Assembly	Year(s)
1	1st	1803
2	2nd	1803–4
3	3rd	1804–5
4	4th	1804–5
5	5th	1805–6
6	6th	1806–7
7	7th	1808–9
8	8th	1809–10
9	9th	1810–11
10	10th	1811–12
11	11th	1812–13
12	12th	1813–14
13	13th	1814–15
14	14th	1815–16
15	15th	1816–17
16	16th	1817–18
17	17th	1818–19
18	18th	1819–20
19	19th	1820–21
20	20th	1821–22
21	21st	1822–23
22	22nd	1823–24
23	23rd	1824–25
24	24th	1825–26
25	25th	1826–27
26	26th	1827–28
27	27th	1828–29
28	28th	1829–30
29	29th	1830–31
30	30th	1831–32
31	31st	1832–33
32	32nd	1833–34
33	33rd	1834–35
34	34th	1835–36

Table of Correspondences (cont.)		
Volume	General Assembly	Year(s)
35	35th	1836–37
36	36th	1837–38
37	37th	1838–39
38	38th	1839–40
39	39th	1840–41
40	40th	1841–42
41	41st	1842–43
42	42nd	1843–44
43	43rd	1844–45
44	44th	1845–46
45	45th	1846–47
46	46th	1847–48
47	47th	1848–49
48	48th	1849–50
49	49th	1850–51
50	50th	1852
50 pt 2		1852–53
51	51st	1854
52	52nd	1856
53		1857
54	53rd	1858
55		1859
56	54th	1860
57		1861
58	55th	1862
59		1863
60	56th	1864
61		1865
62	57th	1866
63		1867
64	58th	1868
65		1868–69
66	59th	1870
67		1871

Table of Correspondences (cont.)		
Volume	General Assembly	Year(s)
68	60th	1872
69		1873
70	61st	1874
71		1874–75
72	62nd	1876
73		1877
74	63rd	1878
75		1879
76	64th	1880
77		1881
78	65th	1882
79		1883
80	66th	1884
81		1885
82	67th	1886
83		1887
84	68th	1888
85		1889
86	69th	1890
87		1890
88		1891
89	70th	1892
90		1893
91	71st	1894
92	72nd	1896
93	73rd	1898
94	74th	1900
95	75th	1902
96		1902
97	76th	1904
98	77th	1906
99		1908
100	78th	1909
101		1910

	Table of Correspondences (cont.)	
Volume	*General Assembly*	*Year(s)*
102	79th	1911
103	80th	1913
104		1914
105		1914
106	81st	1915
107	82nd	1917
108	83rd	1919–20
109	84th	1921–22
110	85th	1923
111	86th	1925–26
112	87th	1927
113	88th	1929
114	89th	1931–32
115	90th	1933–34
116	91st	1935–36
117	92nd	1937–38
118	93rd	1939–40
119	94th	1941
120	95th	1943–44
121	96th	1945–46
122	97th	1947–48
123	98th	1949
124	99th	1951
125	100th	1953–54
126	101st	1955–56
127	102d	1957–58
128	103d	1959–60
129	104th	1961
130	105th	1963–64
131	106th	1965
132	107th	1967–68
133	108th	1969–70
134	109th	1971–72
135	110th	1973–74

Table of Correspondences (cont.)		
Volume	General Assembly	Year(s)
136	111th	1975–76
137	112th	1977–78
138	113th	1979–80
139	114th	1981–82
140	115th	1983–84
141	116th	1985–86
142	117th	1987–88
143	118th	1989–90
144	119th	1991–92
145	120th	1993–94
146	121st	1995–96
147	122d	1997–98
148	123d	1999–2000
149	124th	2001–2
150	125th	2003–4
151	126th	2005–6
152	127th	2007–8

NOTES

Preface

1. 2 S.J. 70–72, 74 (1804); 2 H.J. 82, 86 (1804); 2 O.L. 67 (1804).

2. 2 O.L. 71 (1804).

3. 97 S.J. 134, 137, 253–54 (1904); ibid., app., 72; 97 H.J. 331, 350, 391, 492 (1904); 97 O.L. 83 (1904).

4. Legislative documents relating to Seitz's bill, Sub. H.B. 272 of the 125th General Assembly, can be found at http://www.legislature.state.oh.us.

5. Alan Rosenthal, *Legislative Life: People, Process, and Performance in the States* (New York: Harper and Row, 1981), xi; Peverill Squire, "Historical Evolution of Legislatures in the United States," *Annual Review of Political Science* 9 (2006): 19–44.

6. Raymond W. Smock, "The Institutional Development of the House of Representatives, 1791–1801," in *The House and Senate in the 1790s: Petitioning, Lobbying, and Institutional Development*, ed. Kenneth R. Bowling and Donald R. Kennon (Athens: Ohio University Press, 2002), 324.

7. George B. Galloway, *History of the House of Representatives* (New York: Thomas Y. Crowell, 1962); George B. Galloway, *History of the House of Representatives*, 2d ed., rev. by Sidney Wise (New York: Thomas Y. Crowell, 1976); Congressional Research Service, *History of the United States House of Representatives, 1789–1994* (Washington, D.C.: GPO, 1994); Joel H. Silbey, *The American Political Nation, 1838–1893* (Stanford, Calif.: Stanford University Press, 1991), 8–9, 238.

8. Alan Rosenthal, *The Decline of Representative Democracy: Process, Participation, and Power in State Legislatures* (Washington, D.C.: CQ Press, 1998), 49–84; Christopher Z. Mooney, "Measuring U.S. State Legislative Professionalism: An Evaluation of Five Indices," *State and Local Government Review* 26 (Spring 1994): 70–78.

9. Thomas A. Flinn, "The Ohio General Assembly: A Developmental Analysis," in *State Legislative Innovation: Case Studies of Washington, Ohio, Florida, Illinois, Wisconsin, and California*, ed. James A. Robinson (New York: Praeger, 1973), 226–78; Edward Ivan Sidlow, "Professionalism in a State Legislature: The Case of Ohio" (Ph.D. diss., Ohio State University, 1979); Samuel C. Patterson, "Legislative Politics in Ohio," in *Ohio Politics*, ed. Alexander P. Lamis (Kent, Ohio: Kent State University Press, 1994), 236; Alan Rosenthal and Rich Jones, "Trends in State Legislatures," in *The Book of the States* 36 (Lexington, Ky.: Council of State Governments, 2004), 71.

Chapter 1: The Nabob and the Ignorant Multitude

1. An Ordinance for the Government of the Territory of the United States northwest of the river Ohio, 1 Stat. 51n1 (1789), §§ 3–8.

2. Ibid., §§ 9, 11.

3. William F. Swindler, *Sources and Documents of United States Constitutions* (Dobbs Ferry, N.Y.: Oceana, 1979), 10:40, 46–47.

4. William Henry Smith, ed., *The St. Clair Papers. The Life and Public Services of Arthur St. Clair . . .* (Cincinnati: Robert Clarke, 1882), 2:68–76, 334, 356–57, 363–66; Clarence Edwin Carter, ed., *The Territorial Papers of the United States* (Washington, D.C.: GPO, 1934), 2:246, 430–31, 457; ibid., 3:399–400, 407, 412–13.

5. *Centinel of the North-Western Territory*, 30 November 1793, 20 September 1794, 27 September 1794; Donald J. Ratcliffe, *Party Spirit in a Frontier Republic: Democratic Politics in Ohio, 1793–1821* (Columbus: Ohio State University Press, 1998), 18.

6. Carter, *Territorial Papers*, 3:514–15; Chilton Williamson, *American Suffrage from Property to Democracy, 1760–1860* (Princeton, N.J.: Princeton University Press, 1960), 117; Alexander Keyssar, *The Right to Vote: The Contested History of Democracy in America* (New York: Basic Books, 2000), app., table A.2.

7. Daniel J. Ryan, *History of Ohio: The Rise and Progress of an American State* (New York: Century History Company, 1912), 3:37–38.

8. Ibid., 3:37–41; Carter, *Territorial Papers*, 2:578; Jacob Burnet, *Notes on the Early Settlement of the North-Western Territory* (Cincinnati: Derby, Bradley, 1847), 31–37, 288–97; Andrew R. L. Cayton, *The Frontier Republic: Ideology and Politics in the Ohio Country, 1780–1825* (Kent, Ohio: Kent State University Press, 1986), 71; Alfred Byron Sears, *Thomas Worthington: Father of Ohio Statehood* (Columbus: Ohio State University Press, 1958), 54–55.

9. Henry Halcomb Bennett, ed., *The County of Ross: A History of Ross County . . .* (Madison, Wisc.: Selwyn A. Brant, 1902), 62; Samuel Williams, "Governor Tiffin," in James B. Finley, *Sketches of Western Methodism: Biographical, Historical, and Miscellaneous; Illustrative of Pioneer Life* (Cincinnati: privately printed, 1855), 273; Henry Howe, *Historical Collections of Ohio . . .*, Ohio centennial ed. (Cincinnati: State of Ohio, 1904), 2:496.

10. *American National Biography*, s.v. "Tiffin, Edward"; Andrew R. L. Cayton, "'Language Gives Way to Feelings': Rhetoric, Republicanism, and Religion in Jeffersonian Ohio," in *The Pursuit of Public Power: Political Culture in Ohio, 1787–1861*, ed. Jeffrey P. Brown and Andrew R. L. Cayton (Kent, Ohio: Kent State University Press, 1994), 34–35; Williams, "Governor Tiffin," 264.

11. *American National Biography*, s.v. "Burnet, Jacob"; Burnet, *Notes*, 310–11; Beverley W. Bond Jr., *The Foundations of Ohio*, vol. 1, *The History of the State of Ohio*, ed. Carl Wittke (Columbus: Ohio State Archaeological and Historical Society, 1941), 439.

12. Linda K. Kerber, "The Federalist Party," in *History of U.S. Political Parties*, ed. Arthur M. Schlesinger Jr. (1973; rpt., Philadelphia: Chelsea House, 2002), 1:3–29; Noble E. Cunningham Jr., "The Jeffersonian Republican Party," ibid., 1:239–72.

13. Ratcliffe, *Party Spirit*, 15–17, 24–25, 35–37.

14. Burnet, *Notes*, 289; Bond, *Foundations*, 446; Ratcliffe, *Party Spirit*, 31–33; Carter, *Territorial Papers*, 3:198–99.

15. Burnet, *Notes*, 374–80; Ratcliffe, *Party Spirit*, 33; Bond, *Foundations*, 447–48; Smith, *St. Clair Papers*, 2:474–80; Sears, *Worthington*, 51–52.

16. Sears, *Worthington*, 52–55; Ratcliffe, *Party Spirit*, 32–33, 40–41; Cayton, *Frontier Republic*, 69, 71; Smith, *St. Clair Papers*, 2:482.

17. Ratcliffe, *Party Spirit*, 33–37; Cayton, *Frontier Republic*, 71.

18. Burnet, *Notes*, 300–301; Bond, *Foundations*, 438–40, 446–47; Ratcliffe, *Party Spirit*, 32.

19. Theodore Calvin Pease, ed., *The Laws of the Northwest Territory, 1788–1800* (Springfield: Trustees of the Illinois State Historical Library, 1925), 337–47, 389–401, 418–43, 467–94.

20. Ibid., 347–50, 368–76, 452–67, 503–5.

21. Ibid., 352–54, 357–60, 366–68; Bond, *Foundations*, 466–67; Salmon P. Chase, ed., *The Statutes of Ohio and of the North Western Territory, Adopted or Enacted From 1788 to 1833, Inclusive . . .* (Cincinnati: Corey and Fairbank, 1833), 1:306–8; An Act authorizing Zaccheus Biggs and Zaccheus A. Beatty to erect a bridge over Mills' creek, 9 January 1802, Northwest Territory Collection, box, 2, folder 3, Ohio Historical Society; An Act authorizing Jonathan Lane and others to erect a toll bridge over the Muskingum river, 23 January 1802, ibid., folder 4.

22. Pease, *Laws*, 377–83.

23. Ibid., 384–88; *History of Washington County, Ohio, with Illustrations and Biographical Sketches* (Cleveland: H. Z. Williams and Bro., 1881), 435; Bond, *Foundations*, 459, 466.

24. Burnet, *Notes*, 306–7; Bond, *Foundations*, 445–46.

25. Peter S. Onuf, "From Constitution to Higher Law: The Reinterpretation of the Northwest Ordinance," *Ohio History* 94 (Winter–Spring 1985): 12–13; Cayton, *Frontier Republic*, 74–76; Sears, *Worthington*, 65–66, 73–85.

26. Daniel J. Ryan, "From Charter to Constitution," *Ohio Archaeological and Historical Publications* 5 (August 1897): 74–78.

27. Ratcliffe, *Party Spirit*, 50, 54–57; Sears, *Worthington*, 89–93; Smith, *St. Clair Papers*, 2:482–83; Carter, *Territorial Papers*, 3:254–55, 257–58.

28. Ratcliffe, *Party Spirit*, 66–74; Julia Perkins Cutler, ed., *Life and Times of Ephraim Cutler Prepared from His Journals and Correspondence* (1890; rpt., New York: Arno, 1971), 70; Burnet, *Notes*, 351.

Chapter 2: Republicanism and Representation

1. Donald J. Ratcliffe, *Party Spirit in a Frontier Republic: Democratic Politics in Ohio, 1793–1821* (Columbus: Ohio State University Press, 1998), 70–71; Alfred Byron Sears, *Thomas Worthington: Father of Ohio Statehood* (Columbus: Ohio State University Press for

the Ohio Historical Society, 1958), 101–2; Helen M. Thurston, "The 1802 Constitutional Convention and the Status of the Negro," *Ohio History* 81 (Winter 1972): 21–29; *Journal of the Convention, of the Territory of the United States North West of the Ohio. . . .* , rpt. in Daniel J. Ryan, "From Charter to Constitution. . . . ," *Ohio Archaeological and Historical Publications* 5 (August 1897): 114–16, 122; Jacob Burnet, *Notes on the Early Settlement of the North-Western Territory* (Cincinnati: Derby, Bradley, 1847), 354–56.

2. Ratcliffe, *Party Spirit,* 71–72; *Journal,* in Ryan, "From Charter to Constitution," 113; Ohio const. of 1802, art. 4, § 5; Salmon P. Chase, ed., *The Statutes of Ohio and of the North Western Territory, Adopted or Enacted From 1788 to 1833, Inclusive . . .* (Cincinnati: Corey and Fairbank, 1833), 1:262, 338.

3. J. V. Smith, rptr., *Report of the Debates and Proceedings of the Convention for the Revision of the Constitution of the State of Ohio* (Columbus: S. Medary, 1851), 2:550–51.

4. Ibid., 2:552–54.

5. Robert W. Audretsch, ed., *The Salem, Ohio 1850 Women's Rights Convention Proceedings* (Salem, Ohio: Salem Area Bicentennial Committee, 1976), 32, 58; Smith, *Report,* 2:555–56.

6. Smith, *Report,* 635, 640.

7. 53 S.J., app., 518–27 (1857); 55 H.J., app., 88–93 (1859).

8. J. G. Adel, rptr., *Official Report of the Debates and Proceedings of the Third Constitutional Convention of Ohio* (Cleveland: W. S. Robison, 1873–74), 2:1872, 2800, 2808.

9. 85 H.J. 355 (1889); 85 S.J. 864 (1889); *Ohio State Journal,* 25 February 1889; 91 O.L. 182 (1894); A. P. Peabody, "The Voting of Women in School Elections," *Journal of Social Science,* no. 10 (October 1, 1879): 42–54; Mary A. Greene, "Results of the Woman-Suffrage Movement," *Forum* 17 (June 1894): 422; Alexander Keyssar, *The Right to Vote: The Contested History of Democracy in America* (New York: Basic Books, 2000), 186; Elizabeth Cady Stanton, Susan B. Anthony, and Matilda Joslyn Gage, eds., *History of Woman Suffrage* (Rochester, N.Y.: National American Woman Suffrage Association, 1887), 4:1880–81.

10. Ohio const. of 1802, art. 4, § 1; Ratcliffe, *Party Spirit,* 119–20; Donald J. Ratcliffe, *The Politics of Long Division: The Birth of the Second Party System in Ohio, 1818–1828* (Columbus: Ohio State University Press, 2000), 121, 249–50; 25 H.J. 327 (1827); 35 H.J. 371 (1837).

11. Kenneth J. Winkle, *The Politics of Community: Migration and Politics in Antebellum Ohio* (New York: Cambridge University Press, 1988), 161–64; 39 O.L. 13 (1841); Smith, *Report,* 2:9.

12. Philip D. Jordan, *Ohio Comes of Age, 1873–1900,* vol. 5, *The History of the State of Ohio,* ed. Carl Wittke (Columbus: Ohio State Archaeological and Historical Society, 1943), 255; Adel, *Official Report,* 1:1192; ibid., 2:1802, 1839–40, 1916; Keyssar, *Right to Vote,* 136–38.

13. John Phillip Reid, *The Concept of Representation in the Age of the American Revolution* (Chicago: University of Chicago Press, 1989), 131–34; Rosemarie Zagarri, *The Politics of Size: Representation in the United States, 1776–1850* (Ithaca, N.Y.: Cornell University Press, 1987), 36–39; Gordon S. Wood, *The Creation of the American Republic, 1776–1787*

(Chapel Hill: University of North Carolina Press, 1969), 162–81; Marc W. Kruman, *Between Authority and Liberty: State Constitution Making in Revolutionary America* (Chapel Hill: University of North Carolina Press, 1997), 65–76.

14. Zagarri, *Politics of Size*, 36–60.

15. Ohio const. of 1802, art. 1, §§ 2, 6.

16. Smith, *Report*, 1:99–100, 134–35, 145, 153.

17. Ibid., 1:102, 132, 134, 140, 145, 151.

18. Ibid., 1:99, 103, 133, 141.

19. Ibid., 1:101, 131, 133, 151, 152, 271.

20. Ibid., 1:142. 150, 146; State ex rel. Evans v. Dudley, 1 Ohio St. 437, 443 (1853).

21. Ohio const. of 1851, art. 11.

22. Reid, *Representation*, 98–102, 105–6; Edmund S. Morgan, *Inventing the People: The Rise of Popular Sovereignty in England and America* (New York: Norton, 1988), 212–13, 218; Ratcliffe, *Party Spirit*, 47–50, 191; Ohio const. of 1802, art. 8, § 19.

23. Margaret E. Monsell, "Stars in the Constellation of the Commonwealth: Massachusetts Towns and the Constitutional Right of Instruction," *New England Law Review* 29 (Winter 1995): 301–2; Ratcliffe, *Party Spirit*, 226, 232; *Niles' Weekly Register*, 24 October 1818; Reid, *Representation*, 98; Stephen C. Fox, "The Bank Wars, the Idea of 'Party,' and the Division of the Electorate in Jacksonian Ohio," *Ohio History* 88 (Summer 1979): 263–64; Reginald C. McGrane, "Orator Bob and the Right of Instruction," *Bulletin of the Historical and Philosophical Society of Ohio* 11 (October 1953): 266.

24. Julia Perkins Cutler, ed., *Life and Times of Ephraim Cutler Prepared from His Journals and Correspondence* (1890; rpt., New York: Arno, 1971), 119; 27 O.L. (local laws) 172 (1829).

25. 32 S.J. 252 (1833); 32 H.J. 251–53 (1833).

26. 33 H.J. 134, 716 (1834–35); 33 O.L. (local laws) 443–44 (1835).

27. 34 O.L. (local laws) 633 (1836); C. Edward Skeen, "An Uncertain 'Right': State Legislatures and the Doctrine of Instruction," *Mid-America* 73 (January 1991), 40–42.

28. 36 O.L. 405–7 (1838).

29. Skeen, "Uncertain 'Right,'" 43–45; 43 O.L. (local laws) 429–41 (1844–45); Robert Luce, *Legislative Principles: The History and Theory of Lawmaking by Representative Government* (Boston: Houghton Mifflin, 1930), 474–77; Clement Eaton, "Southern Senators and the Right of Instruction, 1789–1860," *Journal of Southern History* 18 (August 1952): 318–19.

Chapter 3: Democracy and Distrust

1. James J. Hitchman, ed., "John Jay Janney and His 'Recollections of Thomas Corwin,'" *Ohio History* 73 (Spring 1964): 109; Gordon S. Wood, *The Creation of the American Republic, 1776–1787* (Chapel Hill: University of North Carolina Press, 1969); Allen Nevins, *The American States during and after the Revolution, 1775–1789* (1924; rpt., New York:

Augustus M. Kelley, 1969), 139–205; Donald S. Lutz, "The Theory of Consent in the Early State Constitutions," *Publius* 9, no. 2 (1979): 11–42; Jackson Turner Main, *The Sovereign States, 1775–1783* (New York: New Viewpoints, 1973), 143–221; Richard B. Morris, *The Forging of the Union, 1781–1789* (New York: Harper and Row, 1987), 111–29.

2. Julia Perkins Cutler, ed., *Life and Times of Ephraim Cutler Prepared from His Journals and Correspondence* (1890; rpt., New York: Arno, 1971), 69; William F. Swindler, ed., *Sources and Documents of United States Constitutions*, 12 vols. (Dobbs Ferry, N.Y.: Oceana, 1973–88) (Ohio const. of 1802: 7:547–56; Tennessee const. of 1796: 9:141–50; Kentucky const. of 1799: 4:153–64); Ohio const. of 1802, art. 2, §§ 12, 5, 7, 8, 9.

3. Lutz, "Theory of Consent," 37–39; Ohio const. of 1802, art. 8.

4. Ohio const. of 1802, art. 1, §§ 1, 24; ibid., art. 2, § 16; ibid., art. 6, § 2; ibid., art. 3, § 8; ibid., art. 5, § 5; *Journal of the Convention, of the Territory of the United States North West of the Ohio. . . .*, rpt. in Daniel J. Ryan, "From Charter to Constitution. . . .," *Ohio Archaeological and Historical Publications* 5 (August 1897): 105–10, 120–21.

5. Cutler, *Life and Times*, 70–73; Jacob Burnet, *Notes on the Early Settlement of the North-western Territory* (Cincinnati: Derby, Bradley, 1847), 356; Ohio const. of 1802, art. 3, §§ 1, 2–5, 8; ibid., art. 1, § 19.

6. Larry D. Kramer, *The People Themselves: Popular Constitutionalism and Judicial Review* (New York: Oxford University Press, 2004); Donald F. Melhorn Jr., *"Lest We Be Marshall'd"*: *Judicial Power and Politics in Ohio, 1806–1812* (Akron, Ohio: University of Akron Press, 2003), 7–18.

7. 3 O.L. 14 (1805); Melhorn, *"Lest We Be Marshall'd,"* 193–96; 5 H.J. 66, 78–81 (1806–7).

8. Ervin H. Pollack, ed., *Ohio Unreported Judicial Decisions Prior to 1823* (Indianapolis: Allen Smith, 1952), 72–94.

9. William T. Utter, *The Frontier State, 1803–1825*, vol. 2, *The History of the State of Ohio*, ed. Carl Wittke (Columbus: Ohio State Archaeological and Historical Society, 1942), 46; 6 H.J. 44, 61, 62 (1807–8); 7 H.J. 47, 72–76, 79–81 (1808).

10. *Journal of the Senate, of the State of Ohio, in Cases of Impeachment* (Chillicothe, Ohio, 1809) (bound with 7 S.J.), 14–16, 26 38, 52–54, 59–74, 78–93.

11. Ibid., 47, 100; 7 O.L. 43, 49 (1809), § 5; 29 O.L. 170, 171 (1831), § 1(2); Melhorn, *"Lest We Be Marshall'd,"* 129–33.

12. 14 H.J. 362, 423 (1816); Utter, *Frontier State*, 55; McCormick v. Alexander, 2 Ohio 65 (1825); Lessee of Good v. Zercher, 12 Ohio 364 (1843); Way v. Hillier, 16 Ohio 105 (1847).

13. Edward Tiffin to Thomas Worthington, 7 December 1803, 8 December 1803, 13 January 1804, 19 January 1804, G. Hoffman to Worthington, 30 December 1803, Duncan McArthur to Worthington, 2 February 1804, Thomas Worthington Papers, Ohio Historical Society; Andrew R. L. Cayton, *The Frontier Republic: Ideology and Politics in the Ohio Country, 1780–1825* (Kent, Ohio: Kent State University Press, 1986), 86; Donald J. Ratcliffe, *Party Spirit in a Frontier Republic: Democratic Politics in Ohio, 1793–1821* (Columbus: Ohio State University Press, 1998), 194–95.

14. David M. Gold, "The General Assembly and Ohio's Constitutional Culture," in *The History of Ohio Law*, ed. Michael Les Benedict and John F. Winkler (Athens: Ohio University Press, 2004), 1:97–98; 17 O.L. 14 (1819).

15. 17 S.J. 84 (1818); John S. Still, "Ethan Allen Brown and Ohio's Canal System," *Ohio Historical Quarterly* 66 (January 1957): 22–56; Harry N. Scheiber, *Ohio Canal Era: A Case Study of Government and the Economy, 1820–1861* (1968; rpt., Athens: Ohio University Press, 1987), 14–30; Salmon P. Chase, ed., *The Statutes of Ohio and of the North Western Territory, Adopted or Enacted From 1788 to 1833, Inclusive . . .* (Cincinnati: Corey and Fairbank, 1833), 1:46.

16. Scheiber, *Canal Era*, 94–112; 35 O.L. 76 (1837).

17. Michael F. Holt, *Political Parties and American Political Development from the Age of Jackson to the Age of Lincoln* (Baton Rouge: Louisiana State University Press, 1992), 52; James D. Richardson, *A Compilation of Messages and Papers of the Presidents, 1787–1897* (Washington, D.C.: GPO, 1896), 3:344.

18. 35 S.J. 518 (1837); 35 H.J. 679 (1837); 35 O.L. 76 (1837); Scheiber, *Canal Era*, 67, 133, 157–58; Ernest Ludlow Bogart, *Internal Improvements and State Debt in Ohio: An Essay in Economic History* (New York: Longmans, Green, 1924), 242; 38 O.L. 55 (1840); 40 O.L. 63 (1842).

19. Scheiber, *Canal Era*, 156–58.

20. Ibid., 284–87, 297–98; David M. Gold, "Public Aid to Private Enterprise under the Ohio Constitution: Sections 4, 6, and 13 of Article VIII in Historical Perspective," *University of Toledo Law Review* 16 (Winter 1985): 408–11.

21. 25 H.J. 325–28 (1827); 33 H.J. 504, 648 (1835); 36 H.J. 48–49 (1837); 40 S.J. 565 (1842); 42 H.J. 227, 275–76 (1844); 43 H.J. 53, 66–67, 104 (1844); 44 H.J. 27 (1845); 44 S.J. 302, 725 (1846); 45 H.J. 443–44 (1847); 46 H.J. 639–40, 657–59 (1848); 46 H.J., index, 84n (1848); 47 H.J., app., 1–8 (1849); 47 S.J. 236–37 (1849).

22. 47 H.J. 114, 504, 573, 768, 774 (1849); 47 S.J. 648, 660, 669–70 (1849); J. V. Smith, rptr., *Report of the Debates and Proceedings of the Convention for the Revision of the Constitution of the State of Ohio* (Columbus: S. Medary, 1851), 2:432–33; *Cincinnati Enquirer*, 22 March 1849; John F. Morse to Salmon P. Chase, 9 April 1849, Salmon P. Chase Papers, Historical Society of Pennsylvania; 48 O.L. 68 (1850).

23. *New Constitution* (Columbus), 5 May 1849.

24. Smith, *Report*, 1:174.

25. Ibid., 1:124.

26. Ibid., 1:174–77, 182–84; Nicole Etcheson, "Private Interest and Public Good: Upland Southerners and Antebellum Midwestern Political Culture," in *The Pursuit of Public Power: Political Culture in Ohio, 1787–1861*, ed. Jeffrey P. Brown and Andrew R. L. Clayton (Kent, Ohio: Kent State University Press, 1994), 88–89.

27. Smith, *Report*, 1:177–81.

28. Ibid., 1:340–63.

29. Ibid., 1:353.

30. Ohio const. of 1851, art. 12, § 3; ibid., art. 13, §§ 1, 2, 4, 7.

31. Smith, *Report*, 1:469, 523.

32. Ibid., 1:513; 2:123; 472.

33. John J. Kulewicz, "Reinventing the Governor: A History of Executive Power under Ohio Law," in *The History of Ohio Law*, ed. Michael Les Benedict and John F. Winkler (Athens: Ohio University Press, 2004), 1:147–49; Smith, *Report*, 1:310–13.

34. Ohio const. of 1851, art. 4, §§ 1–10.

35. Ohio const. of 1851, art. 2, §§ 1, 28, 30; ibid., art. 14; ibid., art. 12, § 2.

36. Ohio const. of 1802, art. 7, § 5; Ohio const. of 1851, art. 16, §§ 1–3.

37. Smith, *Report*, 2:16, 703; Ohio const. of 1851, art. 6, § 2.

38. Smith, *Report*, 2:712–23; Ohio const. of 1851, schedule, § 18.

39. Smith, *Report*, 2:474; Charles Richard Williams, ed., *Diary and Letters of Rutherford Birchard Hayes, Nineteenth President of the United States* (Columbus: Ohio Archaeological and Historical Society, 1922), 1:422.

40. 53 O.L. 252 (1856); 52 S.J., app., 33–36 (1856); 52 H.J., app., 81–84 (1856); Isaac Franklin Patterson, *The Constitutions of Ohio. . . .* (Cleveland: Arthur H. Clark, 1912), 161–68; Steven H. Steinglass and Gino J. Scarselli, *The Ohio State Constitution: A Reference Guide* (Westport, Conn.: Praeger, 2004), 354.

41. Philip D. Jordan, *Ohio Comes of Age, 1873–1900*, vol. 5, *The History of the State of Ohio*, ed. Carl Wittke (Columbus: Ohio State Archaeological and Historical Society, 1943), 16–17; Daniel J. Ryan, *History of Ohio: The Rise and Progress of an American State* (New York: Century History Company, 1912), 4:317–26; Morton Keller, *Affairs of State: Public Life in Late Nineteenth Century America* (Cambridge, Mass.: Harvard University Press, Belknap Press, 1977), 165–68, 185–87; J. G. Adel, rptr., *Official Report of the Proceedings and Debates of the Third Constitutional Convention of Ohio* (Cleveland: W. S. Robison, 1873–74), 2:2522–23, 2528.

42. Exchange Bank of Columbus v. Hines, 3 Ohio St. 1 (1853); Work v. State, 2 Ohio St. 296 (1853); McCoy v. Grandy, 3 Ohio St. 463 (1854); State v. Comm'rs of Perry County, 5 Ohio St. 497 (1856); Matheny v. Golden, 5 Ohio St. 361 (1856); State v. Medbery, 7 Ohio St. 522 (1857); State v. Kennon, 7 Ohio St. 546 (1857); Reeves v. Treasurer of Wood Co., 8 Ohio St. 333 (1858); Adel, *Official Report*, 1:699, 701, 702, 703; F. R. Aumann, "The Course of Judicial Review in the State of Ohio," Judicial Organization and Procedure, *American Political Science Review* 25 (May 1931): 371–72.

43. Kulewicz, "Reinventing the Governor," 159–62; Adel, *Official Report*, 2:296–308.

44. Steinglass and Scarselli, *Ohio State Constitution*, 354–56; John T. Kenny, "The Legislature That Elected Mr. Hanna," *Arena* 21 (March 1899): 311–12.

Chapter 4: Delegates Fresh from the People

1. J. V. Smith, rptr., *Report of the Debates and Proceedings of the Convention for the Revision of the Constitution of the State of Ohio* (Columbus: S. Medary, 1851), 1:220; Samuel S. Cox, *Eight Years in Congress, from 1857–1865: Memoirs and Speeches* (New York: D. Appleton, 1865), 306.

2. W. A. Taylor, *Hundred-Year Book and Official Register of the State of Ohio, from 1789 to 1891, Inclusive* (Columbus: Westbote, 1891), in 88 S.J., app., 44–121 (1891).

3. A. P. Sandles and E. W. Doty, *The Biographical Annals of Ohio, 1906–1907–1908: A Handbook of the Government and Institutions of the State of Ohio* (Springfield, Ohio: Allied Printing, [1908?]), 165–341.

4. Justin E. Walsh, *The Centennial History of the Indiana General Assembly, 1816–1978* (Indianapolis: Select Committee on the Centennial History of the Indiana General Assembly in cooperation with the Indiana Historical Society, 1987), 702; J. D. B. DeBow, *The Seventh Census of the United States: 1850* (Washington, D.C.: Robert Armstrong, 1853), 851, table 3; U.S. Bureau of the Census, *Thirteenth Census of the United States Taken in the Year 1910*, vol. 1, *General Report and Analysis* (Washington, D.C.: GPO, 1913), 756, table 40.

5. U.S. Bureau of the Census, *Historical Statistics of the United States, Colonial Times to 1970*, bicentennial ed., pt. 1 (Washington, D.C.: U.S. Department of Commerce, Bureau of the Census, 1975), 56.

6. Judge [Alfred G. W.] Carter, *The Old Court House: Reminiscences and Anecdotes of the Courts and Bar of Cincinnati* (Cincinnati: Peter G. Thomson, 1880), 245–46; *The Biography of Elder David Purviance . . . Written by Himself* (Dayton, Ohio: privately printed, 1848), 93–94.

7. Capitol Square Review and Advisory Board, "African-American Legislators," *George Washington Williams*, http://www.georgewashingtonwilliams.com; John P. Green, *Fact Stranger Than Fiction: Seventy-five Years of a Busy Life, with Reminiscences of Many Great and Good Men and Women* (Cleveland: Riehl Printing, 1920), 191–94.

8. Linda Elise Kalette, *The Papers of Thirteen Early Ohio Political Leaders: An Inventory to the 1976–77 Microfilm Editions* (Columbus: Ohio Historical Society, 1977), 13.

9. James L. Bates, *Alfred Kelley: His Life and Work* (Columbus: Robert Clarke, 1888); Harry N. Scheiber, "Alfred Kelley and the Ohio Business Elite, 1822–1859," *Ohio History* 87 (Autumn 1978): 365–92; J. H. Kennedy, "Alfred Kelley," *Magazine of Western History* 3 (March 1886): 550–57; *American National Biography*, s.v. "Kelley, Alfred N."; *Columbus Tax-Killer*, 13 June 1846; Francis P. Weisenburger, *The Passing of the Frontier, 1825–1850*, vol. 3, *The History of the State of Ohio*, ed. Carl Wittke (Columbus: Ohio State Archaeological and Historical Society, 1941), 444.

10. Fred J. Milligan, *Ohio's Founding Fathers* (New York: iUniverse, 2003), 128–31; S. Winifred Smith, "Thomas Kirker," in *The Governors of Ohio*, 2d ed. (Columbus: Ohio Historical Society, 1969), 4–6; Donald J. Ratcliffe, *Party Spirit in a Frontier Republic: Democratic Politics in Ohio, 1793–1821* (Columbus: Ohio State University Press, 1998), 144–45; Allen Trimble, *Autobiography and Correspondence of Allen Trimble, Governor of Ohio, with Genealogy of the Family*, ed. Mary McA. T. Tuttle and Henry P. Thompson (Columbus: n.p., 1909), 122.

11. *History of Geauga and Lake Counties, Ohio, with Illustrations and Biographical Sketches of Its Pioneers and Most Prominent Men* (1878; rpt., Evansville, Ind.: Unigraphic, 1973), 60.

12. 42 H.J. 740–45 (1844); 43 H.J., app., 25–35 (1845); 46 S.J., app., 74–86, 115–22, 171–84 (1848); Theresa A. Maienknecht and Stanley B. Maienknecht, *Monroe County, Ohio: A History* (Mt. Vernon, Ind.: Windmill, 1989), 127, 140, 147, 212.

13. Lyle S. Evans, ed., *A Standard History of Ross County, Ohio* (1917; rpt., Baltimore: Gateway, 1987), 2:649; 37 H.J. 20, 22, 318, 322, 527, 533, 662, 728, 800 (1837–38).

14. Jack M. Thompson, "James R. Garfield: The Making of a Progressive," *Ohio History* 74 (Spring 1965): 84; Frederic C. Howe, *The Confessions of a Reformer* (New York: Scribner's, 1924), 161.

15. Ohio const. of 1802, art. 1, §§ 4, 7; Ohio const. of 1851, art. 2, §3; ibid., art. 15, § 4; ibid., art. 5, § 1; Jeffries v. Ankeny, 11 Ohio 372 (1842); Anderson v. Millikin, 9 Ohio St. 568 (1859).

16. Emil Pocock, "'A Candidate I'll Surely Be': Election Practices in Early Ohio, 1798–1825," in *The Pursuit of Public Power: Political Culture in Ohio, 1787–1861*, ed. Jeffrey P. Brown and Andrew R. L. Cayton (Kent, Ohio: Kent State University Press, 1994), 49, 56–57; Calvin Fletcher to Jesse Fletcher, 21 November 1818, Calvin Fletcher Papers, Indiana Historical Society.

17. Pocock, "Candidate," 58–61.

18. Ibid., 60; Ratcliffe, *Party Spirit*, 130–34.

19. Ratcliffe, *Party Spirit*, 192–93, 196, 213–14, 244–45; Donald J. Ratcliffe, *The Politics of Long Division: The Birth of the Second Party System in Ohio, 1818–1828* (Columbus: Ohio State University Press, 2000), 290; Pocock, "Candidate," 61–62.

20. Ratcliffe, *Party Spirit*, 210; Ratcliffe, *Long Division*, 45–46.

21. Ratcliffe, *Long Division*, 297–98; Homer J. Webster, "History of the Democratic Party Organization in the Northwest, 1824–1840," *Ohio Archaeological and Historical Publications* 24 (January 1915): 52; James Monroe, *Oberlin Thursday Lectures, Addresses and Essays* (Oberlin, Ohio: E. J. Goodrich, 1897), 100.

22. *Commemorative Historical and Biographical Record of Wood County, Ohio* (Chicago: Beers, 1897), 967; Alan Peskin, *Garfield: A Biography* (Kent, Ohio: Kent State University Press, 1978), 61; 26 O.L. 66 (1828).

23. Alan Ware, *The American Direct Primary: Party Institutionalization and Transformation in the North* (Cambridge: Cambridge University Press, 2002), 57–61; Frederick W. Dallinger, *Nominations for Elective Office in the United States* (New York: Longmans, Green 1897), 51–72; Francis Russell, *The Shadow of Blooming Grove: Warren G. Harding in His Times* (New York: McGraw-Hill, 1968), 105–7.

24. Dallinger, *Nominations*, 56–58; John Hope Franklin, *George Washington Williams: A Biography* (Durham, N.C.: Duke University Press, 1998), 29.

25. Dallinger, *Nominations*, 55–56, 128; *Ohio State Journal*, 18 April 1892; Albert Watkins, "The Primary Election Movement," *Forum* 33 (March 1902): 94; *Portage Sentinel* (Ravenna, Ohio), 6 September 1848; Edward Insley, "How to Reform the Primary-Election System (with Particular Reference to Reforms in Operation or Proposed)," *Arena* 17 (June 1897): 1013–14, 1018; Ware, *American Direct Primary*, 98.

26. 68 O.L. 27 (1871); Watkins, "Primary Election Movement," 95; Insley, "Reform," 1013–23.

27. 88 O.L. 449 (1891); 89 O.L. 432 (1892); John H. Wigmore, "Ballot Reform: Its Constitutionality," *American Law Review* 23 (September–October 1889): 731; State ex rel. Lewis v. Kinney, 57 Ohio St. 221 (1897).

28. Michael Schudson, *The Good Citizen: A History of American Civil Life* (Cambridge, Mass.: Harvard University Press, 1998), 136; Ratcliffe, *Party Spirit*, 210, 237; Pocock, "Candidate," 62–65.

29. Harry R. Stevens, *The Early Jackson Party in Ohio* (Durham, N.C.: Duke University Press, 1957), 15; James Thurber, *The Thurber Album: A New Collection of Pieces about People* (New York: Simon and Schuster, 1952), 7–8.

30. Robert Gray Gunderson, "The Dayton Log-Cabin Convention of 1840," *Bulletin of the Historical and Philosophical Society of Ohio* 7 (October 1949): 202–10; Delmer J. Trester, "David Tod and the Gubernatorial Campaign of 1844," *Ohio State Archaeological and Historical Quarterly* 62 (April 1953), 169–70, 177; Kenneth J. Winkle, *The Politics of Community: Migration and Politics in Antebellum Ohio* (New York: Cambridge University Press, 1988), 141–42.

31. Joseph Benson Foraker, *Notes of a Busy Life* (Cincinnati: Stewart and Kidd, 1916), 1:115–16; Peskin, *Garfield*, 77–79; Franklin, *Williams*, 72–73; James D. Norris and Arthur H. Shaffer, *Politics and Patronage in the Gilded Age: The Correspondence of James A. Garfield and Charles E. Henry* (Madison: State Historical Society of Wisconsin, 1970), 246; Michael E. McGerr, *The Decline of Popular Politics: The American North, 1865–1928* (New York: Oxford University Press, 1986), 107–37.

32. Richard Jensen, *The Winning of the Midwest: Social and Political Conflict, 1888–1896* (Chicago: University of Chicago Press, 1971), 165–77; McGerr, *Decline*, 69–106; B. J. Wade to Grover Cleveland, 21 September 1892, Grover Cleveland Papers, microfilm, Ohio Historical Society; McGerr, *Decline*, 159–60.

33. 92 O.L. 123 (1896); Thompson, "Garfield," 81; Dalton v. State, 43 Ohio St. 653 (1885); 95 O.L. 77 (1902); Perry Belmont, "Publicity of Election Expenditures," *North American Review* 180 (February 1905): 175–76.

34. Ratcliffe, *Party Spirit*, 83–85, 188; Ratcliffe, *Long Division*, 173; Marie Dickoré, *General Joseph Kerr of Chillicothe, Ohio, "Ohio's Lost Senator," from the Carrel Manuscript Collection* (Oxford, Ohio: Oxford, 1941), 39–40; Winkle, *Politics*, 140.

35. 1 O.L. 76 (1803).

36. 4 O.L. 39 (1806); 7 O.L. 112 (1809); 29 O.L. 44 (1831); 39 O.L. 13 (1841); 43 O.L. 116 (1845); Winkle, *Politics*, 77–79.

37. Kenneth J. Winkle, "Ohio's Informal Polling Place: Nineteenth-Century Suffrage in Theory and Practice," in Brown and Cayton, *Pursuit*, 169–70; 45 S.J., app., 48–49, 124 (1846); Gilbert H. Stewart, "Politics and Politicians," *Ohio Illustrated Magazine* 2 (April 1907): 347–48; 43 H.J. 29, 45 (1844).

38. Winkle, *Politics*, 161–64, 149–61; Winkle, "Informal," 176–81; 35 H.J. 374 (1837); William Cheek and Aimee Lee Cheek, *John Mercer Langston and the Fight for Black Freedom, 1829–65* (Urbana: University of Illinois Press, 1989), 283; 39 O.L. 13 (1841).

39. Winkle, "Informal," 172–77; Pocock, "Candidate," 65–66; Ratcliffe, *Party Spirit*, 106; William A. Taylor, *Ohio Statesmen and Annals of Progress, from the Year 1788 to the Year 1900*, 2 vols. (Columbus: Westbote, 1899).

40. 60 O.L. 80 (1863); Lehman v. McBride, 15 Ohio St. 573 (1863).

41. Frances Fox Piven and Richard A. Cloward, *Why Americans Still Don't Vote and Why Politicians Want It That Way* (Boston: Beacon, 2000), 32–33; *Cleveland Plain Dealer*, 14 April 1881; *Ohio State Journal*, 18 January 1870; 66 H.J. 23 (1870); 82 O.L. 232 (1885); 81 S.J. 578 (1885); 81 H.J. 906–7 (1885); Daggett v. Hudson, 43 Ohio St. 548 (1885); 83 O.L. 209 (1886).

42. 82 S.J. app., 6, 25 (1886); *Weekly Law Bulletin* 14 (2 November 1885): 275.

43. Jenson, *Winning of the Midwest*, 38–39; Genevieve B. Gist, "Progressive Reform in a Rural Community: The Adams County Vote-Fraud Case," *Mississippi Valley Historical Review* 48 (June 1961): 60–78; Joseph P. Harris, *Registration of Voters in the United States* (Washington, D.C.: Brookings Institution, 1929), 99–100, 108–9; 84 O.L. 19 (1887); *Ohio State Journal*, 9 November 1887; *Weekly Ohio State Journal*, 3 October 1889, 31 October 1889.

44. 58 O.L. 65 (1861); 65 O.L. 138 (1868); 71 O.L. 31 (1874); M. A. Daugherty, John S. Brasee, and George B. Okey, eds., *The Revised Statutes and Other Acts of a General Nature of the State of Ohio, in Force January 1, 1880* (Columbus: H. W. Derby, 1879), 1:771, § 2948; Elden Cobb Evans, *A History of the Australian Ballot System in the United States* (Chicago: University of Chicago Press, 1917), 7–8; Beresford v. Hawkins, 9 Ohio Dec. Rep. 100 (Dist. Ct. Ham. Cty. 1883).

45. 88 O.L. 449 (1891); George Hoadly, "Methods of Ballot Reform," *Forum* 7 (August 1889): 623–33; Henry T. Blake, "The Official Ballot in Elections," *New Englander and Yale Review* (December 1891), 516–17; Alan Ware, *American Direct Primary*, 38–39, 79–80.

46. 88 O.L. 449, 460 (1891); "The Rights of a Voter, Given by the Constitution, Cannot Be Abridged," *Weekly Law Bulletin and the Ohio State Law Journal* 36 (7 September 1896): 110–11; Wickham v. Coyner, 12 Ohio C.C. (n.s.) 433 (1902); 87 Ohio St. 12 (1912).

47. Calvin Fletcher to Jesse Fletcher, 21 November 1818; Pocock, "Candidate," 65; Stevens, *Early Jackson Party*, 72; 82 S.J. app., 6 (1886).

48. John Melish, *Travels through the United States of America, in the Years 1806 & 1807, 1810, & 1811; Including an Account of Passages Betwixt America and Britain, and Travels through Various Parts of Britain, Ireland, & Canada* (Philadelphia: printed for the author; London: rpt. for George Cowie, 1818), 435; Sándor Bölöni Farkas, *Journey in North America, 1831*, trans. and ed. by Arpad Kadarkay (Santa Barbara, Calif.: ABC-Clio, 1978), 163.

49. Carlos B. Shedd, *Tales of Old Columbus* (Columbus: n.p., 1951), 12–13; 86 H.J. app. 34 (1890); 67 H.J., app., 28, 56–59, 123 (1871); 72 H.J. 909–19 (1876); 58 H.J., app., 49 (1862).

50. Shedd, *Tales*, 13; *Ohio State Journal*, 12 October 1881, 9 November 1887.

51. *Ohio State Journal*, 12 October 1881, 9 November 1887, 6 November 1895; 83 O.L. 209, 213–14 (1886); 102 H.J. 1279–81 (1911).

52. 1 H.J. 6, 14, 16–17 (1803); 1 S.J. 6–8, 11, 18–19 (1803).

53. 39 S.J., app. nos. 1 and 5 (1841).

54. Winkle, *Politics*, 167–68, 216n78; 45 S.J., app., 1–272 (1846) and 321–28 (1847).

Chapter 5: A Delightful Capital

1. James Loudon to Elizabeth Loudon, 25 December 1834, DeWitt Clinton Loudon Papers, Ohio Historical Society.

2. B. F. Morris, ed., *The Life of Thomas Morris: Pioneer and Long a Legislator of Ohio, and United States Senator from 1833 to 1839* (Cincinnati: Moore, Wistach, Keys, and Overend, 1856), 41.

3. Charles C. Cole Jr., *A Fragile Capital: Identity and the Early Years of Columbus, Ohio* (Columbus: Ohio State University Press, 2001), 49–54; William T. Utter, *The Frontier State, 1803–1825*, vol. 2, *The History of the State of Ohio*, ed. Carl Wittke (Columbus: Ohio State Archaeological and Historical Society, 1942), 207, 217; H. Roger Grant, *Ohio on the Move: Transportation in the Buckeye State* (Athens: Ohio University Press, 2000), 72–74; George White Dial, "The Construction of the Ohio Canals," *Ohio Archaeological and Historical Society Publications* 13 (October 1904): 478–79; R. S. Kaylor, "Ohio Railroads," *Ohio Archaeological and Historical Society Publications* 9 (October 1900): 190–91.

4. Charles Dickens, *American Notes, & Pictures from Italy* (Philadelphia: George W. Jacobs, 1868), 185–86, 189, 191; John Armstrong Smith to Jane McDowell Smith, 7 December 1842, John Armstrong Smith Papers, Ohio Historical Society; James Loudon to Elizabeth Loudon, 5 March 1843, Loudon Papers.

5. Julia Perkins Cutler, ed., *Life and Times of Ephraim Cutler Prepared from His Journals and Correspondence* (Cincinnati: Robert Clarke, 1890; rpt., New York: Arno, 1971), 281–82.

6. Eugene H. Roseboom, *The Civil War Era, 1850–1873*, vol. 4, *The History of the State of Ohio*, ed. Carl Wittke (Columbus: Ohio State Archaeological and Historical Society, 1944), 109; Philip D. Jordan, *Ohio Comes of Age, 1873–1900*, vol. 5, *The History of the State of Ohio*, ed. Carl Wittke (Columbus: Ohio State Archaeological and Historical Society, 1943), 112–15, 126–31; 50 S.J. pt. 2, 16 (1852); *Ohio State Journal*, 15 November 1852; 61 S.J. 103–4 (1865); ibid., app., 28.

7. Henry Howe, *Historical Collections of Ohio. . . .*, Ohio centennial edition (Cincinnati: State of Ohio, 1904), 2:496; Ohio const. of 1802, art. 7, § 4.

8. 8 O.L. 220 (1810); Donald J. Ratcliffe, *Party Spirit in a Frontier Republic: Democratic Politics in Ohio, 1793–1821* (Columbus: Ohio State University Press, 1998), 155–56; Utter, *Frontier State*, 53–54; Cole, *Fragile Capital*, 1–2, 4; Alfred Byron Sears, *Thomas Worthington: Father of Ohio Statehood* (Columbus: Ohio State University Press, 1958), 149; Ethel Conrad, ed., "Touring Ohio in 1811: The Journal of Charity Rotch," *Ohio History* 99 (Summer–Autumn 1990): 144; Norris F. Schneider, *Y Bridge City: The Story of Zanesville and Muskingum County, Ohio* (Cleveland: World, 1950), 60–66.

9. 10 O.L. 92, 204 (1812); Cole, *Fragile Capital*, 4–8.

10. John Cotton, "From Rhode Island to Ohio in 1815," *Journal of American History* 16 (July–September 1922): 254; Cole, *Fragile Capital*, 10–11, 20–21.

11. Cole, *Fragile Capital*, 37, 44–45; James H. Rodabaugh, ed., "From England to Ohio, 1830–1832: The Journal of Thomas K. Wharton," pt. 2, *Ohio Historical Quarterly* 65 (April 1956): 134; James Taylor Dunn, ed., "'Cincinnati Is a Delightful Place': Letters

of a Law Clerk," *Bulletin of the Historical and Philosophical Society of Ohio* 10 (October 1952): 264.

12. Cutler, *Life and Times*, 118, 139.

13. Dickens, *American Notes*, 190; Abraham Hegler to friends, 6 December 1838, Abraham Hegler Papers, Ohio Historical Society; Hegler to Dolly Hegler, 17 February 1839, ibid.; Cole, *Fragile Capital*, 85.

14. Lida Rose McCabe, *Don't You Remember?* (Columbus: A. H. Smythe, 1884), 96.

15. Cole, *Fragile Capital*, 85; A. E. Lee, *History of the City of Columbus* (New York: Munsell, 1892), 1:287; A. G. Riddle, "B. F. Wade, The Politician," pt. 5, *Magazine of Western History* 3 (March 1886): 480; 35 H.J. 20–21 (1836); 37 H.J. 284 (1839).

16. Isaac Appleton Jewett to Samuel Appleton, 22 February 1833, quoted in Lee, *History of Columbus*, 1:731–32.

17. Dickens, *American Notes*, 188; 33 H.J. 836–37, 965 (1835); 33 S.J. 776–77 (1835); 38 H.J., app. no. 15 (1840); Dunn, "Cincinnati," 273.

18. Joshua Giddings to Laura Giddings, 26 January 1837, Joshua R. Giddings Papers, Ohio Historical Society; John Melish, *Travels through the United States of America, in the Years 1806 & 1807, 1810, & 1811; Including an Account of Passages betwixt America and Britain, and Travels through Various Parts of Britain, Ireland, & Canada* (Philadelphia: printed for the author; London: rpt. for George Cowie, 1818), 479; 50 S.J., pt. 2, 139 (1853).

19. Cole, *Fragile Capital*, 162–71; "Early Attempts to Entertain Columbus," *Ohio State Journal*, 24 April 1921; W. D. Howells, "In an Old-Time State Capital," *Harper's Monthly Magazine* 129 (September 1914): 601–2; Muriel Kinney, "John Cary, An Ohio Pioneer," *Ohio Archaeological and Historical Publications* 46 (April 1937): 175; John Armstrong Smith to Jane McDowell Smith, 3 August 1842, Smith Papers.

20. Howells, "Old-Time State Capital," 598; McCabe, *Don't You Remember?* 186–87; Abraham Hegler to Dolly Hegler, 17 February 1839, Hegler Papers; John Armstrong Smith to Jane McDowell Smith, 5 January 1842, Smith Papers.

21. Cutler, *Life and Times*, 118–19, 139.

22. J. G. Adel, rptr., *Official Report of the Proceedings and Debates of the Third Constitutional Convention of Ohio* (Cleveland: W. S. Robison, 1873–74), 2:1830.

23. John Armstrong Smith to Jane McDowell Smith, 5 January 1842, 3 August 1842, Smith Papers; Abraham Hegler to friends, 18 December 1838, Hegler Papers; James Loudon to Elizabeth Loudon, 27 December 1843, Loudon Papers.

24. Michael Les Benedict, "The Party Going Strong," *Congress and the Presidency* 9 (Winter 1981–82): 46–48; Abraham Hegler to Dolly Hegler, 7 January 1839; Hegler to family, 6 March 1839, Hegler Papers.

25. John Armstrong Smith to Jane McDowell Smith, 3 August 1842, Smith Papers; *Biographical Directory of the United States Congress, 1774–Present*, s.v. "Smith, John Armstrong," http://bioguide.congress.gov.

26. Abbott Lowell Cummings, *The Alfred Kelley House of Columbus, Ohio: The Home of a Pioneer Statesman; With Mrs. Kelley's Recollections and Some Family Letters* (Columbus: Franklin County Historical Society, 1953), 42, 39–40.

27. Seabury Ford to Peter Hitchock, 10 February 1836, Charles Elmer Rice Papers, Ohio Historical Society.

28. 10 O.L. 199 (1812); William T. Martin, *History of Franklin County: A Collection of Reminiscences of the Early Settlement of the County; with Biographical Sketches and a Complete History of the County to the Present Time* (1858; rpt., Columbus: Linden Heights Kiwanis Club, 1969), 334–35; A. A. Graham, "The Beginnings of the Buckeye Capital," *Magazine of Western History* 1 (March 1885): 425; 48 S.J. 348 (1850).

29. Allen Trimble, *Autobiography and Correspondence of Allen Trimble, Governor of Ohio, with Genealogy of the Family*, ed. Mary McA. T. Tuttle and Henry P. Thompson (Columbus: n.p., 1909), 119.

30. Cyrus P. Bradley, "Journal of Cyrus P. Bradley," *Ohio Archaeological and Historical Publications* 15 (April 1906), 238–39; 10 O.L. 199 (1812); Martin, *Franklin County*, 340–41.

31. Martin, *Franklin County*, 343–45; Abbott Lowell Cummings, "Ohio's Capitols at Columbus, 1810–1861," typescript, Columbus Metropolitan Library, 1948, 1–21; Bradley, "Journal," 239.

32. A. G. Riddle, "Recollections of the Forty-seventh General Assembly of Ohio, 1847–48 [sic]," *Magazine of Western History* 6 (August 1887): 341, 344–45.

33. 36 S.J. 81–82 (1837), 147 (1838); 36 O.L. 13 (1838); Lee, *History of Columbus*, 2:568; Cole, *Fragile Capital*, 66–67; 43 H.J., app. no. 6, 9–11 (1845); Carl A. Saladino, "The Ohio Statehouse: Its Design Sources and Architectural History," computer printout, Ohio Legislative Service Commission library, Columbus, 4.

34. 50 S.J. 138–39 (1852); 50 H.J. 176 (1852); Lee, *History of Columbus*, 1:723; ibid., 2:570; Cummings, "Ohio's Capitols," 58–59, 66.

35. 50 S.J. 139–43 (1852); 50 H.J. 175, 178 (1852); 50 S.J. 592 (1852); 51 O.L. 356, 454 (1853); 50 S.J., pt. 2, 32–34 (1852); 52 O.L. 144 (1854); 53 O.L. 206, 209 (1856).

36. 50 H.J., pt 2, 75–76 (1852); Lee, *History of Columbus*, 2:571–74; Saladino, "Ohio Statehouse," 7–9.

37. Lee, *History of Columbus*, 2:574–77; William M. Awl, "Annual Report of the Superintendent of State House, to the Governor of the State of Ohio, for the Year 1863," in *Annual Reports Made to the Governor of the State of Ohio, for the Year 1863*, pt. 2 (Columbus: Richard Nevins, 1864), 651–52.

38. Awl, "Annual Report," 639–40.

39. 66 S.J. 57–58 (1870); 67 O.L. 163 (1870); 66 H.J., app., 43–44 (1870); Lee, *History of Columbus*, 2:576.

40. 67 H.J., app., 196 (1871).

41. 74 H.J. 1178–79 (1878); 67 O.L. 160, 162 (1870); 75 O.L. 1182 (1878); 89 H.J., app., 92 (1892); 76 H.J. 111 (1880); 73 S.J. 397 (1877); 72 S.J. 546 (1876); W. T. Wilson, "Report of the Comptroller of the Treasury," in *Executive Documents. Message and Annual Reports for 1876, Made to the Sixty-second General Assembly of the State of Ohio, at the Adjourned Session, Commencing January 2, 1877*, pt. 1 (Columbus: Nevins and Myers, 1877), 348; 88 O.L. 401 (1891); 77 H.J. 168, 219 (1881); 91 S.J., app., 37 (1894).

42. *Ohio State Journal*, 3 February 1882; *Cincinnati Enquirer*, 10 October 1890.

43. Samuel B. Smith, "Annual Report of the Adjutant General to the Governor of the State of Ohio, for the Year 1883," in *Executive Documents. Annual Reports for 1883, Made to the Sixty-sixth General Assembly of the State of Ohio, at the Regular Session, Commencing January 7th, 1884*, pt. 1 (Columbus: G. J. Brand, 1884), 246–47; 82 S.J. 476–78 (1886); 94 O.L. 763 (1900).

44. Bradley, "Journal," 243; Betty Garrett, *Columbus: America's Crossroads* (Tulsa, Okla.: Continental Heritage, 1980), 55–59.

45. Garrett, *Columbus*, 77–97, 223.

46. 78 H.J., app., 127, 134 (1882); Allan Peskin, *Garfield: A Biography* (Kent, Ohio: Kent State University Press, 1978), 67, 75; John Hope Franklin, *George Washington Williams: A Biography* (Durham, N.C.: Duke University Press, 1998), 80; L. Ada Judkins Burtoft and Clyde Hollingsworth Judkins, *Biographical Sketch of Hon. David A. Hollingsworth, Cadiz, Ohio* ([Cleveland?]: privately printed, 1920), 13.

47. *Daily Dispatch and Daily Ohio Statesmen*, 21 December 1874, 30 March 1875; *Ohio State Journal*, 5 February 1879.

48. *Ohio State Journal*, 7 January 1881, 4 March 1887, 18 February 1876, 6 February 1889; *Daily Ohio Statesman*, 28 March 1877.

49. Allen O. Myers, *Bosses and Boodle in Ohio Politics: Some Plain Truths for Honest People* (Cincinnati: Lyceum, 1895), 197–98; *Ohio State Journal*, 4 January 1881.

Chapter 6: The Rules of Play

1. David M. Gold, "Rites of Passage: The Evolution of the Legislative Process, 1799–1937," *Capital University Law Review* 30, no. 4 (2002): 635–38.

2. Thomas Jefferson, *A Manual of Parliamentary Practice: For the Use of the Senate of the United States*, 2d ed. (Georgetown, D.C.: Joseph Milligan; Washington, D.C.: William Cooper), in *Jefferson's Parliamentary Writings: "Parliamentary Pocket-Book" and A Manual of Parliamentary Practice*, ed. Wilbur Samuel Howell, Papers of Thomas Jefferson, second series (Princeton, N.J.: Princeton University Press, 1988), 357; Francis Lieber, *On Civil Liberty and Self-Government*, 2d ed. (Philadelphia: J. B. Lippincott, 1859), 192, 196.

3. Donald S. Lutz, "The Colonial and Early State Legislative Process," in *Inventing Congress: Origins and Establishment of the First Federal Congress*, ed. Kenneth R. Bowling and Donald R. Kennon (Athens: Ohio University Press, 1999), 49–75; Ralph Volney Harlow, *The History of Legislative Methods in the Period before 1825* (New Haven, Conn.: Yale University Press, 1917); Gold, "Rites," 631–35.

4. Ohio const. of 1802, art. 1, §§ 16–17.

5. Luther Stearns Cushing, *Elements of the Law and Practice of Legislative Assemblies in the United States of America* (1856; rpt., South Hackensack, N.J.: Rothman Reprints, 1971), 802, 828–29; Jefferson, *Parliamentary Writings*, 381.

6. 20 H.J. 155 (1820); 24 H.J. 42–53, 190–91 (1825–26); 26 S.J. 40 (1827); *Ohio State Journal and Columbus Gazette*, 8 December 1827.

7. 66 H.J. 383, 390 (1870); Cushing, *Elements*, 831, 842.

8. Cushing, *Elements*, 842; Herman R. Postle, *The Government of Ohio and an Outline of the Government of the United States* (Columbus: published by the author, 1901), 93; 64 H.J. 74–79, 86–88 (1868); Edward Wakefield Hughes, *Guide to Parliamentary Practice in the Ohio House of Representatives* (Columbus: State of Ohio, 1912), 16–17.

9. Cushing, *Elements*, 859; 1 H.J. 22 (1803); 1 S.J. 6 (1803); 44 H.J 463 (1846); ibid., app., 70 (1846); 46 H.J., app., 54 (1847).

10. Jefferson, *Parliamentary Writings*, 403–4; Cushing, *Elements*, 861–62; 64 H.J., app., 75 (1868).

11. Robert Luce, *Legislative Procedure: Parliamentary Practices and the Course of Business in the Framing of Statutes* (Boston: Houghton Mifflin, 1922), 211–12; Cushing, *Elements*, 831n.; Edward Wakefield Hughes, *Hughes' American Parliamentary Guide: Mechanics of Lawmaking*, rev. new ed. (Columbus: Heer, 1932), 754–55; Norman J. Singer, *Statutes and Statutory Construction*, 5th ed. (St. Paul, Minn.: West Group, 1994), vol. 1, § 10.04; Gold, "Rites," 634.

12. 2 O.L. 5 (1804); 1 H.J. 22 (1803); 40 S.J. 36 (1841); 40 H.J. 105 (1841).

13. Ohio const. of 1851, art. 2, § 16 (repealed 1973); 92 H.J., app., 51 (1896); Harvey Walker, *The Legislative Process: Law Making in the United States* (New York: Ronald, 1948), 231; Luce, *Legislative Procedure*, 217; Gold, "Rites," 647–48.

14. J. G. Adel, rptr., *Official Report of the Debates and Proceedings of the Third Constitutional Convention of Ohio* (Cleveland: W. S. Robison, 1873–74), 2:285, 293–94; *Cincinnati Enquirer*, 22 May 1878; Postle, *Government of Ohio*, 94.

15. Ohio const. of 1851, art. 2, § 16 (moved to § 15 in 1973); Millard H. Ruud, "No Law Shall Embrace More Than One Subject," *Minnesota Law Review* 42 (January 1958): 389–92; Brannon P. Denning and Brooks R. Smith, "Uneasy Riders: The Case for a Truth-in-Legislation Amendment," *Utah Law Review*, 1999, no. 4:957, 966 and n. 41; J. V. Smith, rptr., *Report of the Debates and Proceedings of the Convention for the Revision of the Constitution of the State of Ohio* (Columbus: S. Medary, 1851), 1:233.

16. Miller v. State, 3 Ohio St. 475 (1855); Pim v. Nichols, 6 Ohio St. 176 (1857).

17. 5 H.J. 23 (1806); 32 H.J. 150 (1833).

18. 37 H.J., app., 125–27 (1839).

19. 80 H.J. 46 (1884).

20. *Ohio State Journal*, 5 January 1880; 1 H.J. 5–6, 18, 20–21, 25 (1803); 1 S.J. 5–6, 18 (1803).

21. Gold, "Rites," 639–40.

22. Ibid., 640–41.

23. 34 H.J. 200–202 (1835); 42 S.J. 383–84 (1844); 43 S.J. 30, 107, 172–73 (1844–45); 43 H.J. 395 (1845).

24. Gold, "Rites," 642–46; Hughes, *Guide to Parliamentary Practice*, 23.

25. 65 H.J. 789–93 (1869); 46 S.J., app., 248 (1847); Luce, *Legislative Procedure*, 232.

26. 46 S.J., app., 19–22, 115–31, 171–98 (1848); Gold, "Rites," 649–51.

27. 49 S.J. 12–13 (1850); 49 H.J. 17–18 (1850); 94 S.J., app., 6–15 (1900); 94 H.J., app. 7–18 (1900).

28. *Weekly Ohio State Journal*, 27 January 1847.

29. Henry L. Dawes, "Has Oratory Declined?" *Forum* 18 (October 1894): 153; James Monroe, *Oberlin Thursday Lectures, Addresses and Essays* (Oberlin, Ohio: E. J. Goodrich, 1897), 125; *Western Reserve Chronicle*, 25 January 1860; John A. Lapp, "Actual State Legislation," *Annals of the American Academy of Political and Social Science* 43 (September 1912): 55–56; "One Means of Regulating the Lobby," *Century Illustrated Magazine* 41 (February 1891): 628–29; Samuel Maxwell, "The Evils of Lobbying, and Proposed Remedy," *American Law Review* 30 (May–June 1896): 403.

30. 36 H.J. 139 (1837); 82 S.J. 477 (1886); 98 S.J. 673–75 (1904); 99 S.J., app., 727–29 (1908).

31. Luce, *Legislative Procedure*, 133; *Ohio State Journal*, 18 February 1892, 17 March 1880, 3 February 1881, 22 February 1882, 28 January 1896.

32. 68 S.J. 78 (1872); 68 H.J. 119 (1872); 69 O.L. 300 (1872); 80 H.J. 879 (1884).

33. Paul S. Reinsch, *American Legislatures and Legislative Methods* (New York: Century, 1907), 159–62; *Ohio State Journal*, 20 May 1886; 48 S.J., app., 52–54 (1849); 93 S.J., app., 95–104 (1898).

34. *Manual of Legislative Practice, in the General Assembly of Ohio, Containing the Rules, the Statutes, and that Portion of the Constitution Relating to the Duties and Rights of Members of the Legislature* (Columbus: G. J. Brand, 1882); 94 S.J. 736 (1900); ibid., app., 77–102; 94 H.J., app., 77–102 (1900).

35. 56 H.J. 117 (1860).

Chapter 7: The Working Life

1. 38 H.J. 11 (1839); Joshua Giddings to Laura Giddings, 26 January 1837, Joshua R. Giddings Papers, Ohio Historical Society, Columbus; 1 S.J. 115 (1803); Julia Perkins Cutler, ed., *Life and Times of Ephraim Cutler Prepared from His Journals and Correspondence* (1890; rpt., New York: Arno, 1971), 142; Abbott Lowell Cummings, *The Alfred Kelley House of Columbus, Ohio: The Home of a Pioneer Statesman; With Mrs. Kelley's Recollections and Some Family Letters* (Columbus: Franklin County Historical Society, 1953), 41; *Weekly Ohio State Journal*, 27 January 1847.

2. *Ohio State Journal*, 11 January 1884.

3. J. G. Adel, rptr., *Official Report of the Proceedings and Debates of the Third Constitutional Convention of Ohio* (Cleveland: W. S. Robison, 1873–74), 2:1025–26, 1028, 1031, 1034, 1036, 1045.

4. Ibid., 2:1026, 1029, 1038, 1032, 1036, 3546, 3548.

5. John T. Kenny, "The Legislature That Elected Mr. Hanna," *Arena* 21 (March 1899): 311–12; Paul S. Reinsch, *American Legislatures and Legislative Methods* (New York: Century, 1907), 299–306; 91 O.L. 874 (1894); 91 H.J. 1249 (1894).

6. David B. Hill, "We Are Too Much Governed," *North American Review* 170 (March 1900): 367–73; James H. Eckels, "The Menace of Legislation," *North American Review* 165 (August 1897): 240–46; 75 H.J. 1230–31, 1354, 1346, 1422 (1879); 75 S.J. 917, 920 (1879); 83 H.J. 759–60 (1887); 86 H.J. 1190–1268 (1890); 86 S.J. 1329–94 (1890); 87

H.J. 46–47 (1890); 87 S.J. 41–43 (1890); 88 H.J. 1080–89 (1891); 88 S.J. 906–24 (1891); 89 H.J., index, 124–264 (1892); 89 S.J., index, 118–83 (1892); 90 H.J., index, 80–231 (1893); 90 S.J., index 14–69 (1893); 91 H.J., index, 70–231 (1894); 91 S.J., index, 66–149 (1894); 92 H.J., index, 84–235 (1896); 92 S.J., index, 68–137 (1896).

7. 33 O.L., 2d sess., 5, 7 (1835); Francis P. Weisenburger, *The Passing of the Frontier, 1825–1850*, vol. 3, *The History of the State of Ohio*, ed. Carl Wittke (Columbus: Ohio State Archaeological and Historical Society, 1941), 297–307; Daniel J. Ryan, *History of Ohio: The Rise and Progress of an American State* (New York: Century History, 1912), 4:395–97.

8. A. G. Riddle, "Recollections of the Forty-seventh General Assembly of Ohio, 1847–48 [sic]," *Magazine of Western History* 6 (August 1887): 346n.

9. Ohio const. of 1802, art. 1, § 15; Ohio const. of 1851, art. 2, § 13.; 5 S.J. 12, 17, 18, 24 (1806); 5 H.J. 11, 13, 20 and supplemental journal (bound with journal), 1–2 (1806); William T. Utter, *The Frontier State, 1803–1825*, vol. 2, *The History of the State of Ohio*, ed. Carl Wittke (Columbus: Ohio State Archaeological and Historical Society, 1942), 69–75; Edward Tiffin to Thomas Worthington, 18 December 1806, Thomas Worthington Papers, Ohio Historical Society; 5 O.L. 45 (1806).

10. M. Avis Pitcher, "John Smith, First Senator from Ohio and His Connections with Aaron Burr," *Ohio State Archaeological and Historical Quarterly* 45 (January 1936): 79–86; 5 O.L. 141 (1806); Robert W. Wilhelmy, "Senator John Smith and the Aaron Burr Conspiracy," *Cincinnati Historical Society Bulletin* 28 (Spring 1970): 38–60.

11. 13 S.J. 457–67 (1814); 13 H.J. 405–15 (1814); 57 H.J. 553–54 (1861); 57 S.J. 63 (1861); 60 S.J. 429–40 (Senate Executive Journal) (1864); 66 S.J. 561, 601, 603–4 (1870).

12. Charles William Chance, "Analysis of Legislative Agreements: The Case of Ohio" (Ph.D. diss., Ohio State University, 1970), 59–61, 304–9; Linda D. Taylor, "The Ohio Legislator: Part-Time or Full-Time?" policy paper, Ohio State University, 1974, 40–41; 53 H.J. 6–7 (1857); 91 H.J. 12 (1894); *Cleveland Gazette*, 6 January 1894; George B. Galloway, *History of the House of Representatives*, 2d ed., rev. Sidney Wise (New York: Crowell, 1976), 50; *Workingman's Advocate*, 9 January 1830; *Atkinson's Saturday Evening Post*, 8 February 1835, 3; Edmund Alton, *Among the Law-Makers* (New York: Charles Scribner's Sons, 1886), 132; 78 H.J. 39 (1882); 74 H.J. 368 (1878); 56 S.J. 7 (1860); Catherine M. Rokicky, *James Monroe: Oberlin's Christian Statesman and Reformer, 1821–1898* (Kent, Ohio: Kent State University Press, 2002), 56.

13. Broadside of seating plan of the Ohio House for the 47th General Assembly, Collection # OVS 1212, Ohio Historical Society; Riddle, "Recollections," 345; 91 H.J. 1250 (1894).

14. 40 H.J. 4 (1841); 41 H.J. 4 (1842); "Ohio Legislature," *Philanthropist*, 21 December 1842, 3; 42 H.J. 4 (1843); J. V. Smith, rptr., *Report of the Debates and Proceedings of the Convention for the Revision of the Constitution of the State of Ohio* (Columbus: S. Medary, 1851), 2:590.

15. 26 H.J. 329–30 (1828); 26 S.J. 334–35 (1828); 48 H.J. 900–901, 912, 939 (1850); 48 S.J. 960, 963–64 (1850); 50 H.J., pt. 2, 5, 16–19 (1852); 50 S.J., pt. 2, 3, 17 (1852); 78 H.J. 72–73 (1882); 78 S.J. 46 (1882); 83 S.J. 3, 26–27 (1887); 86 H.J. 32, 67 (1890);

86 S.J. 63–64, 115–16 (1890); 95 H.J. 844, 892–93 (1902); 95 S.J. 553–54 (1902); *Ohio State Journal*, 13 January 1882; *Cincinnati Enquirer*, 22 January 1890.

16. Marsh v. Chambers, 463 U.S. 783 (1983); *Workingman's Advocate*, 24 March 1832, 22 June 1833; *Niles' National Register*, 14 September 1839; 43 H.J. 32, 37–38 (1844); Charles Reemelin, *Life of Charles Reemelin, In German: Carl Gustav Rümelin, From 1814–1892* (Cincinnati: Weier and Daiker, 1892), 82; *Ohio Statesman*, 7 December 1846, 10 December 1846.

17. 43 S.J. 99–113 (1844).

18. 44 S.J. 7–8 (1845); 44 H.J. 8 (1845); *Ohio Statesman*, 9 December 1846; "Served Them Right," *Evangelical Magazine and Gospel Advocate*, 5 March 1847, 78; 45 H.J. 7 (1846); 45 S.J. 9 (1846); ibid., 175 (1847); 48 H.J. 13 (1849); 49 S.J. 10 (1850); 50 S.J., pt. 1, 6–7 (1852).

19. 73 O.L. 7 (1876); *Columbus Daily Dispatch*, 11 February 1876.

20. 41 H.J. 588–95, 609–15 (1843).

21. *Ohio State Journal*, 24 January 1884.

22. Barnas Sears, B. B. Edwards, and C. C. Felton, *Essays on Ancient Literature and Art: With the Biography and Correspondence and Eminent Philologists* (1843; Boston: Gould, Kendall and Lincoln, 1849), iv, xvii.

23. Samuel Williams, "Governor Tiffin," in James B. Finley, *Sketches of Western Methodism: Biographical, Historical, and Miscellaneous; Illustrative of Pioneer Life* (Cincinnati: privately printed, 1855), 267; Cutler, *Life and Times*, 122.

24. I. A. Jewett to Joseph Willard, 22 February 1833, Isaac Appleton Jewett Papers, Cincinnati Museum Center; James Taylor Dunn, ed., "'Cincinnati Is a Delightful Place': Letters of a Law Clerk," *Bulletin of the Historical and Philosophical Society of Ohio* 10 (October 1952): 267; Cyrus P. Bradley, "Journal of Cyrus P. Bradley," *Ohio Archaeological and Historical Publications* 15 (April 1906): 240, 242; Robert Luce, *Legislative Assemblies: Their Framework, Make-Up, Character, Characteristics, Habits, and Manners* (Boston: Houghton Mifflin, 1924), 631–59; Charles Dickens, *American Notes, & Pictures from Italy* (Philadelphia: George W. Jacobs, 1868), 118–21; George W. Julian, *Political Recollections 1840 to 1872* (Chicago: Jansen, McClurg, 1884), 105–6; Robert V. Remini, *The House: The History of the House of Representatives* (New York: Smithsonian Books, 2006), 240.

25. *Ohio State Journal*, 18 January 1884; 53 H.J. 95–96 (1857); 66 S.J. app., 9 (1870); 88 H.J. 1046 (1891); 70 S.J. 87 (1874).

26. *Ohio State Journal*, 27 February 1845, 1 March 1845; 44 H.J. 771–82, 785 (1846); 50 H.J., pt. 2, 543, 568–86 (1853).

27. 53 H.J. 31, 42–43, 58–9, 70, 97–99, and app., 77–84 (1857); 60 H.J. 501, 578–79, and app., 54–55 (1864).

28. *New York Times*, 1 May 1878; 74 H.J. 43, 179, 316–17, app., 1187–90 (1878); "The Diary of John Beatty, January–June 1884," ed. Harvey S. Ford, pt. 3, *Ohio State Archaeological and Historical Quarterly* 59 (January 1950): 73–74n50.

29. 74 H.J. 811–12, 822–23, 1116–17, 1137–38 (1878); *National Police Gazette*, 23 November 1878; *New York Times*, 28 April 1878, 12 May 1878, 18 June 1878, 11 December 1878.

30. 74 S.J. 684 (1878); *Columbus Daily Dispatch*, 2 April 1873; *Ohio State Journal*, 20 March 1875; *Columbus Daily Dispatch*, 11 December 1874; *Ohio State Journal*, 27 January 1883; *Ohio Statesman*, 19 January 1874.

31. *Ohio State Journal*, 16 February 1880, 13 April 1876; *Cincinnati Weekly Enquirer*, 27 April 1870; Brand Whitlock, *Forty Years of It* (New York: D. Appleton, 1914), 238.

32. *Ohio State Journal*, 26 February 1885.

33. Clement L. Vallandigham, *Speeches, Arguments, Addresses, and Letters of Clement L. Vallandigham* (New York: J. Walter, 1864), 13–15.

34. *American National Biography*, s.v. "Williams, George Washington."

35. 76 H.J. 47, 70–71, and app., 982–84 (1880); *Ohio State Journal*, 22 February 1882; John P. Green, *Fact Stranger Than Fiction: Seventy-five Years of a Busy Life, with Reminiscences of Many Great and Good Men and Women* (Cleveland: Riehl, 1920), 171, 178–80; Frederick M. Gittes, "Paper Promises: Race and Ohio Law after 1860," in *The History of Ohio Law*, ed. Michael Les Benedict and John F. Winkler (Athens: Ohio University Press, 2004), 2:791–97.

36. Cutler, *Life and Times*, 120, 123, 141.

37. "The Autobiography of Alexander Long," ed. Louis R. Harlan, *Bulletin of the Historical and Philosophical Society of Ohio* 19 (April 1961): 118, 120; John Shaw, ed., *Crete and James: Personal Letters of Lucretia and James Garfield* (East Lansing: Michigan State University Press, 1994), 103; *History of Geauga and Lake Counties, Ohio, with Illustrations and Biographical Sketches of Its Pioneers and Most Prominent Men* (Philadelphia: Williams Bros., 1878; rpt. Evansville, Ind.: Unigraphic, 1973), 60; Seabury Ford to Harriet E. Ford, 19 January 1836, Charles Elmer Rice Papers, Ohio Historical Society.

38. Ohio const. of 1802, art. 1, § 19; 14 O.L. 118 (1816); 20 O.L. 4 (1821); Salmon P. Chase, ed., *The Statutes of Ohio and of the North Western Territory, Adopted or Enacted from 1788 to 1833, Inclusive . . .* (Cincinnati: Corey and Fairbank, 1835), 3:1956; Donald J. Ratcliffe, *Party Spirit in a Frontier Republic: Democratic Politics in Ohio, 1793–1821* (Columbus: Ohio State University Press, 1998), 194; Donald J. Ratcliffe, *The Politics of Long Division: The Birth of the Second Party System in Ohio, 1818–1828* (Columbus: Ohio State University Press, 2000), 40–41, 245–48; C. Edward Skeen, "Vox Populi, Vox Dei: The Compensation Act of 1816 and the Rise of Popular Politics," *Journal of the Early Republic* 6 (Fall 1986): 253–74, reprinted in *The United States Congress in a Transitional Era, 1800–1841*, ed. Joel H. Silby (Brooklyn: Carlson, 1991), 2:387–408.

39. 44 H.J. 33 (1845), 44 S.J. app., 116 (1845); 42 S.J. 253 (1844).

40. 42 S.J. 253, 87–94 (1843).

41. Reginald C. McGrane, "Orator Bob and the Right of Instruction," *Bulletin of the Historical and Philosophical Society of Ohio* 11 (October 1953): 253; Monroe, *Oberlin Thursday Lectures*, 110; 42 O.L. 21 (1844); 45 O.L. 19 (1847).

42. Private [James M.] Dalzell, *Private Dalzell, His Autobiography, Poems and Comic War Papers; Sketch of John Gray, Washington's Last Soldier, Etc.* (Cincinnati: Robert Clarke, 1888), 38–40, 47–48.

43. 58 H.J. 62, 94–95 (1862); 50 H.J., pt. 2, 77 (1852).

44. *Ohio State Journal*, 6 February 1871, 30 April 1872, 28 January 1879; *Ohio States-man*, 2 March 1873; *Weekly Ohio State Journal*, 10 July 1875.

45. 50 O.L. 117 (1852); 59 O.L. 14 (1862); 63 O.L. 65 (1866); 77 O.L. 85 (1880).

46. *Ohio State Journal*, 8 January 1881, 18 February 1881, 18 February 1885, 8 April 1886, 19 March 1889, 28 March 1889.

47. *Ohio State Journal*, 6 May 1886, 7 May 1886, 11 May 1886, 5 January 1887; *Cleveland Plain Dealer*, 15 May 1886, 18 May 1886.

48. 16 H.J. 14, 37–42 (1817); 43 O.L. 58, 459 (1845); Daniel J. Ryan, "The State Library and Its Founder," *Ohio Archaeological and Historical Quarterly* 28 (January 1919): 100–102.

49. 80 H.J. 28 (1884); 93 H.J. 19 (1898); *Ohio State Journal*, 22 January 1894.

50. 63 H.J. 37 (1867); 80 H.J. 404 (1884); 56 H.J. 18 (1860); 93 H.J. 150 (1898); "The Columbus Orange Girl—A Real Life Romance," *Saturday Evening Post*, 26 May 1860, 7.

Chapter 8: Well-Fed Politicians, Little Boys, and Other Employees

1. 1 O.L. 5 (1803); 14 O.L. 119 (1816); Donald J. Ratcliffe, *Party Spirit in a Frontier Republic: Democratic Politics in Ohio, 1793–1821* (Columbus: Ohio State University Press, 1998), 194, 220; 50 O.L. 214 (1852); 59 O.L. 114 (1862); 63 O.L. 65 (1866).

2. Theodore Calvin Pease, ed., *The Laws of the Northwest Territory, 1788–1800* (Springfield: Trustees of the Illinois State Historical Library, 1925), 444; 1 H.J. 21 (1803); 19 S.J. 4 (1820); 1 Terr. H.J. 15 (1799); 48 H.J., app., 96–98, 190–91 (1849).

3. Pease, *Laws*, 43–44; 14 O.L. 119 (1816); 2 O.L. 293 (1804); 35 O.L. 3 (1836).

4. 2 O.L. 71 (1804); 31 O.L. 265 (1833); 32 O.L. (local laws) 434 (1834); 35 O.L. 3 (1836); 36 O.L. 3 (1837).

5. 48 H.J., app., 96–97 (1849).

6. 48 H.J., app., 105, 133–34, 138, 168 (1849).

7. 69 H.J., app., 21 (1873).

8. 50 H.J., pt. 2, 75, 80–81 (1852).

9. Ibid., 82.

10. 51 S.J., app., 8–11 (1853).

11. Ibid., 12–13.

12. Ibid., 16–17, 22.

13. Ibid., 17, 21.

14. 50 H.J., pt. 2, app., 250, 259–60 (1853).

15. 52 H.J., app., 101 (1856).

16. 59 H.J. 218, 259–60, 564–68 (1863).

17. Joseph R. Swan, ed., *Statutes of the State of Ohio, of a General Nature, In Force August, 1854: With References to Prior Repealed Laws* (Cincinnati: H. W. Derby, 1854), 442–43;

Clement Bates, ed., *The Annotated Revised Statutes of the State of Ohio, Including All Laws of a General Nature in Force January 1, 1898*, 3 vols. (Cincinnati: W. H. Anderson, 1897), 1:63–64.

18. 93 H.J. 26–27 (1898); 94 H.J., app., 6 (1900); 94 S.J., app., 4–5 (1900).

19. *Ohio State Journal*, 3 January 1878; William Larwill to John Larwill, 13 December 1829, Larwill Family Papers, Ohio Historical Society.

20. William Dean Howells, *Selected Letters, Vol. 1: 1852–1872*, ed. George Arms et al. (Boston: Twayne, 1979), 47–48; 56 H.J. 96, 101 (1860); 52 S.J. 151–54 (1856); 53 S.J. 25, 40–41 (1857); 72 S.J. 110 (1876).

21. 74 S.J. 11 (1878); 89 H.J. 16, 25–26 (1892).

22. *Columbus Democratic Call*, 16 January 1896; 89 H.J. 25–26 (1892); Robert Luce, *Legislative Assemblies* (New York: Houghton Mifflin, 1924), 578–88.

23. Jacob H. Studer, comp., *Directory of the 58th General Assembly, Including State Officers, of the State of Ohio, 1868* (Columbus: Columbus Printing, 1868), 5, 7; Robert C. Byrd, *The Senate, 1789–1989: Addresses on the History of the United States Senate*, bicentennial ed. (Washington, D.C.: Government Printing Office, 1991), 2:375–90; Edmund Alton, *Among the Law-Makers* (New York: Charles Scribner's Sons, 1886), 19, 31–32, 81–87, 174–81. My notes indicate that the expression of thanks to the "little boys" was made by the Speaker at the end of the Sixty-fifth General Assembly, but I have been unable to confirm the source.

24. 76 H.J. 671–72 (1880); *Ohio State Journal*, 30 March 1880.

25. 75 O.L. 1179 (1878); 92 H.J. 157 (1896).

26. 92 H.J. 25 (1896); 93 H.J. 32, 45 (1898); Bates, *Revised Statutes*, 1:65.

27. Bruce Bliven Jr., *The Wonderful Writing Machine* (New York: Random House, 1954), 58–70, 117; Elyce J. Rotella, *From Home to Office: U.S. Women at Work, 1870–1930* (Ann Arbor: UMI Research Press, University Microfilms International, 1981), 68; 93 S.J. 23 (1898).

28. Margery W. Davies, *Woman's Place Is at the Typewriter: Office Work and Office Workers, 1870–1930* (Philadelphia: Temple University Press, 1982), 55–56; W. L. Mason, "Women's Chances as Bread Winners: II—Women as Stenographers," *Ladies' Home Journal* 8 (February 1891): 8; "The Girl at the Typewriter," *Ladies' Home Journal* 21 (February 1904): 24; 94 H.J., app., 6 (1900); 94 S.J., app., 4 (1900); Bliven, *Writing Machine*, 71–79; Carole Srole, "'A Blessing to Mankind, and Especially to Womankind': The Typewriter and the Feminization of Clerical Work, Boston, 1860–1920," in *Women, Work, and Technology: Transformations*, ed. Barbara Drygulski Wright et al. (Ann Arbor: University of Michigan Press, 1987), 84–100.

29. *Ohio State Journal*, 12 April 1883; 79 S.J. 695–97 (1883); John F. Oglevee, "Annual Report of the Auditor of State, to the Governor of the State of Ohio, for the Fiscal Year ending November 15, 1883," in *Executive Documents. Annual Reports for 1883, Made to the Sixty-sixth General Assembly of the State of Ohio, at the Regular Session, Commencing January 7th, 1884*, pt. 2 (Columbus: G. J. Brand, 1884), 318; 93 H.J. 9 (1898); 94 H.J. 10 (1900); 94 S.J. 6 (1900); 95 H.J. 7–10 (1902); 95 S.J. 4–5 (1902).

30. 72 H.J. 90 (1876); 72 S.J. 47 (1876); *Biographical Directory of the United States Congress*, s.v. "Norton, James Albert," http://bioguide.congress.gov; *Cleveland Gazette*, 19 January 1884, 6 January 1894, 9 January 1886, 26 January 1886.
31. *Cleveland Gazette*, 9 January 1886.

Chapter 9: Statehouse Scandals

1. 35 H.J. 87–90, 97–99 (1836).
2. 35 H.J. 150, 155–57 (1837).
3. Bernard Bailyn, *The Ideological Origins of the American Revolution* (Cambridge, Mass.: Harvard University Press, Belknap Press, 1967), 86–93, 122–35; C. Peter Magrath, *Yazoo: Law and Politics in the New Republic: The Case of* Fletcher v. Peck (Providence, R.I.: Brown University Press, 1966), 1–19; Robert V. Remini, *Andrew Jackson and the Course of American Freedom, 1822–1832* (New York: Harper and Row, 1981), 16; Douglas E. Bowers, "The Pennsylvania Legislature, 1815–1869: A Study of Democracy at Work" (Ph.D. diss., University of Chicago, 1974), 183–224.
4. Jeffrey L. Pasley, "Private Access and Public Power: Gentility and Lobbying in the Early Congress," in *The House and Senate in the 1790s: Petitioning, Lobbying, and Institutional Development*, ed. Kenneth R. Bowling and Donald R. Kennon (Athens: Ohio University Press, 2002), 59.
5. Charles C. Cole Jr., *A Fragile Capital: Identity and the Early Years of Columbus, Ohio* (Columbus: Ohio State University Press, 2001), 4–7, 66–67; W. W. Williams, *History of the Fire Lands, Comprising Huron and Erie Counties, Ohio, with Illustrations and Biographical Sketches of Some of the Prominent Men and Pioneers* (1879; rpt., Evansville, Ind.: Whippoorwill, 1985), 134; Donald J. Ratcliffe, *Party Spirit in a Frontier Republic: Democratic Politics in Ohio, 1793–1821* (Columbus: Ohio State University Press, 1998), 209; Pasley, "Private Access," 60; *Ohio State Journal*, 15 February 1842.
6. 38 H.J. 188, 411–12, app. no.1, app. no. 2 (1840).
7. 38 H.J. 115, 137, 149, 765–74 (1840); 50 O.L. 174 (1852).
8. 38 H.J. 189, 195–97 (1840).
9. Seabury Ford to Peter Hitchcock, 20 February 1840, Charles Elmer Rice Papers, Ohio Historical Society; John Armstrong Smith to Jane McDowell Smith, 27 December 1842, John Armstrong Smith Papers, Ohio Historical Society.
10. Robert Luce, *Legislative Assemblies: Their Framework, Make-Up, Character, Characteristics, Habits, and Manners* (Boston: Houghton Mifflin, 1924), 419; 69 S.J. 350–51, 778–79 (1873).
11. 84 S.J., app., 5–45 (1888); 89 H.J., app., 16–71 (1892).
12. 78 H.J., app., 15–17 (1882); 78 H.J. 871 (1882); Watson v. State, 39 Ohio St. 123 (1883); Allen O. Myers, *Bosses and Boodle in Ohio Politics: Some Plain Truths for Honest People* (Cincinnati: Lyceum, 1895), 18, 198; 92 H.J., app., 33–45 (1896); *Ohio State Journal*, 23 January 1896, 28 January 1896, 2 February 1896; *Weekly Ohio State Journal*,

6 March 1896, 13 March 1896, 8 May 1896, 15 May 1896, 26 June 1896, 11 December 1896; "Bribery Cases," *Ohio Legal News* 4 (17 October 1896): 3; "Five Senators Indicted Then," *Ohio State Journal*, 7 May 1911.

13. James D. Norris and Arther H. Shaffer, *Politics and Patronage in the Gilded Age: The Correspondence of James A. Garfield and Charles E. Henry* (Madison: State Historical Society of Wisconsin, 1970), 201–2, 255.

14. Myers, *Bosses and Boodle*, 231–37.

15. 80 H.J. 45, 47–48 (1884); Myers, *Bosses and Boodle*, 245–47.

16. Myers, *Bosses and Boodle*, 260–62; 82 H.J. 914, 932–33 (1886); 82 S.J. 592, 599–600 (1886); Donald Walter Curl, "The Long Memory of the United States Senate," *Ohio History* 76 (Summer 1967): 103–13; *Compilation of Senate Election Cases from 1789 to 1913*, 62d Cong., 3d sess., S. Doc. 1036 (Washington: Government Printing Office, 1913), 700–718.

17. Myers, *Bosses and Boodle*, 279, 285, 288, 291.

18. P. T., "Reform in Senatorial Elections," Under the Rose, *Arena* 21 (March 1899): 391–93; Herbert Croly, *Marcus Alonzo Hanna: His Life and Work* (New York: Macmillan 1923), 248–59; Thomas Beer, *Hanna* (New York: Knopf, 1929), 175, 183–87; John T. Kenny, "The Legislature That Elected Mr. Hanna," *Arena* 21 (March 1899): 314–18; 93 H.J. 40–41 (1898).

19. 93 S.J. 35 (1898); P. T., Under the Rose, 391–93; Croly, *Hanna*, 259–64; 93 S.J., app., 83–94; *Compilation of Senate Election Cases*, 878–87.

20. 49 H.J., app., 33–39 (1851); 93 H.J., app., 53–128 (1898); 93 S.J., app. 83–94 (1898); Luce, *Legislative Assemblies*, 417–20, 426–31; Paul S. Reinsch, *American Legislatures and Legislative Methods* (New York: Century, 1907), 234; 93 H.J., app., 88 (1898).

21. Hoyt Landon Warner, *Progressivism in Ohio, 1897–1917* (Columbus: Ohio State University Press, 1964), 204n17; 93 H.J., app., 61 (1898); Myers, *Bosses and Boodle*, 52–54; 49 H.J., app., 37 (1851).

22. 78 H.J., app., 41 (1882); Margaret A. Schaffner, *Lobbying*, Comparative Legislation Bulletin No. 2 (Madison: Wisconsin Free Library Commission, Legislative Reference Department, 1906), 30–31; Reinsch, *American Legislatures*, 295–97.

Chapter 10: Banks, Race, and Demon Rum

1. Frances Trollope, *Domestic Manners of the Americans*, ed. Donald Smalley (1832; rpt., New York: Knopf, 1949), 102; Isabella Lucy Bird, *The Englishwoman in America* (1856; rpt., Madison: University of Wisconsin Press, 1966), 422–23.

2. Bird, *Englishwoman*, 413–15.

3. Donald J. Ratcliffe, *Party Spirit in a Frontier Republic: Democratic Politics in Ohio, 1793–1821* (Columbus: Ohio State University Press, 1998), 5; Andrew R. L. Cayton, "'A Quiet Independence': The Western Vision of the Ohio Company," *Ohio History* 90 (1981): 16; Andrew R. L. Cayton, *The Frontier Republic: Ideology and Politics in the Ohio Country, 1780–1825* (Kent, Ohio: Kent State University Press, 1986), 69–70.

4. Ratcliffe, *Party Spirit*, 204–7, 218–23, 234–39; William R. Utter, *The Frontier State, 1803–1825*, vol. 2, *The History of the State of Ohio*, ed. Carl Wittke (Columbus: Ohio Archaeological and Historical Society, 1942), 297.

5. Francis P. Weisenburger, *The Passing of the Frontier, 1825–1850*, vol. 3, *The History of the State of Ohio*, ed. Carl Wittke (Columbus: Ohio Archaeological and Historical Society, 1941), 215, 224, 249–50.

6. Weisenburger, *Passing of the Frontier*, 378; Daniel Feller, "Benjamin Tappan: The Making of a Democrat," in *The Pursuit of Public Power: Political Culture in Ohio, 1787–1861*, ed. Jeffrey P. Brown and Andrew R. L. Cayton (Kent, Ohio: Kent State University Press, 1994), 78–79; Michael F. Holt, *The Rise and Fall of the American Whig Party: Jacksonian Politics and the Onset of the Civil War* (New York: Oxford University Press, 1999), 399–402.

7. Herbert Ershkowitz and William T. Shade, "Consensus or Conflict? Political Behavior in the State Legislatures during the Jacksonian Era," *Journal of American History* 58 (December 1971): 591–621; Kurt P. Shadle, "Consensus and the Decline of the Second Party System: Ohio 1848–1854" (seminar paper, University of Virginia, 1978); Cayton, *Frontier Republic*, 115–26; Ratcliffe, *Party Spirit*, 193–94, 221–24; C. C. Huntington, "A History of Banking and Currency in Ohio before the Civil War," *Ohio Archaeological and Historical Society Quarterly* 24 (July 1915): 314–16 [reprinted in *A History of Banking and Currency in Ohio before the Civil War* (Columbus: Heer, 1915)]; Sean Wilentz, *The Rise of American Democracy: Jefferson to Lincoln* (New York: Norton, 2005), 205–7.

8. Ernest L. Bogart, "Taxation of the Second Bank of the United States by Ohio," *American Historical Review* 17 (January 1912): 315–29; Cayton, *Frontier Republic*, 125–32; Ratcliffe, *Party Spirit*, 225–29; Francis P. Weisenburger, "A Life of Charles Hammond: The First Great Journalist of the Old Northwest," *Ohio Archaeological and Historical Quarterly* 43 (October 1934): 352–62.

9. Bogart, "Taxation," 330–31; James D. Richardson, *A Compilation of Messages and Papers of the Presidents, 1787–1897* (Washington, D.C.: GPO, 1896), 2:1139; Robert V. Remini, *Henry Clay: Statesman for the Union* (New York: Norton, 1991), 449–50.

10. Weisenburger, *Passing of the Frontier*, 311–12; Marion A. Brown, *The Second Bank of the United States and Ohio (1803–1860)* (Lewiston, N.Y.: Edward Mellen, 1998), 181–82; Michael F. Holt, *Political Parties and American Political Development from the Age of Jackson to the Age of Lincoln* (Baton Rouge: Louisiana State University Press, 1992), 52.

11. James Roger Sharp, *The Jacksonians versus the Banks: Politics in the States after the Panic of 1837* (New York: Columbia University Press, 1970), 123–52; William Gerald Shade, *Banks or No Banks: The Money Issue in Western Politics, 1832–1865* (Detroit: Wayne State University Press, 1972), 86–87, 102–6; Kenneth J. Winkle, *The Politics of Community: Migration and Politics in Antebellum Ohio* (Cambridge: Cambridge University Press, 1988), 136–40; Huntington, "Banking," 405–8.

12. Huntington, "Banking," 437–38; Sharp, *Jacksonians*, 149, 152–59; Shade, *Banks*, 106–10; Citizens' Bank of Steubenville v. Wright, 6 Ohio St. 318 (1856).

13. Sharp, *Jacksonians*, 158; Shade, *Banks*, 178–83, 187–90, 210–11, 216–17.

14. Ratcliffe, *Party Spirit*, 231; Donald J. Ratcliffe, *The Politics of Long Division: The Birth of the Second Party System in Ohio, 1818–1828* (Columbus: Ohio State University Press, 2000), 143; Paul Finkelman, "Race, Slavery, and Law in Antebellum Ohio," in *The History of Ohio Law*, ed. Michael Les Benedict and John F. Winkler (Athens: Ohio University Press, 2004), 2:754–60; Frank U. Quillin, *The Color Line in Ohio: A History of Race Prejudice in a Typical Northern State* (1913; rpt., New York: Negro Universities Press, 1969), 31–32; Stephen Middleton, *The Black Laws: Race and the Legal Process in Early Ohio* (Athens: Ohio University Press, 2005), 47–55; 14 O.L. 387 (1816).

15. 17 O.L. 56 (1819); 22 H.J. 80–81, 170–71, 213 (1823–24); 22 S.J. 156–57 (1824); 26 H.J. 389 (1828); 26 S.J. 403 (1828); Finkelman, "Race," 760–64.

16. Ratcliffe, *Party Spirit*, 232–33; 18 S.J. 136–38, 146–47, 169 (1820); 18 H.J. 162–63, 176, 198–99 (1820).

17. Charles S. Sydnor, *The Development of Southern Sectionalism, 1819–1848* (Baton Rouge: Louisiana State University Press, 1948), 151–52; Merton L. Dillon, *Benjamin Lundy and the Struggle for Negro Freedom* (Urbana: University of Illinois Press, 1966), 104–6; Ratcliffe, *Party Spirit*, 223–29; 26 O.L. (local laws) 187–88 (1828); 31 O.L. 271, 274 (local laws) (1833); 29 O.L. (local laws) 237 (1831).

18. Weisenburger, *Passing of the Frontier*, 380–82; Thomas D. Morris, *Free Men All: The Personal Liberty Laws of the North, 1780–1861* (Baltimore: Johns Hopkins University Press, 1974), 88–92; H. L. Trefousse, *Benjamin Franklin Wade: Radical Republican from Ohio* (New York: Twayne, 1963), 34–37; 37 S.J. 385–90 (1839); 37 O.L. 38 (1839); 41 O.L. 13 (1843).

19. 37 H.J. 423 (1839); 37 S.J. 394 (1839); 37 H.J. 230–37 (1839); 37 S.J. 174 (1839); Michael Les Benedict, "Civil Liberty in Ohio," in Benedict and Winkler, *History of Ohio Law*, 686; 39 H.J., app. C (1841).

20. 36 S.J. 166–71, 288–91, 560 (1838); 36 S.J. 288–91 (1838); 36 H.J. 523–25 (1838); Trefousse, *Wade*, 31–32.

21. 43 S.J., app., 12–17 (1844); 43 O.L. (local laws) 437 (1845).

22. Vernon L. Volpe, *Forlorn Hope of Freedom: The Liberty Party in the Old Northwest, 1838–1848* (Kent, Ohio: Kent State University Press, 1990); Edgar Allan Holt, *Party Politics in Ohio, 1840–1850* (Columbus: F. J. Heer, 1931), 196–97 [previously published in *Ohio Archaeological and Historical Quarterly*, 37 (July 1928): 438–591, 38 (January 1929): 47–182), and 38 (April 1929): 260–402]; V. W. Smith to Oran Follett, 22 July 1843, in "Selections from the Follett Papers, III," *Quarterly Publication of the Historical and Philosophical Society of Ohio*, 10 (January–March, 1915): 7; Eric Foner, *Free Soil, Free Labor, Free Men: The Ideology of the Republican Party before the Civil War* (New York: Oxford University Press, 1970), 60, 93.

23. Leonard Erickson, "Politics and Repeal of Ohio's Black Laws, 1837–1849," *Ohio History* 82 (Summer–Autumn 1973): 154–75; 45 H.J. 123–27 (1847); 41 O.L. (local laws) 263 (1843); 42 O.L. 277 (1844); 43 O.L. (local laws) 434 (1845); 45 O.L. (local laws) 214 (1847); 45 S.J. 599 (1847), 45 H.J. 295 (1847); 46 O.L. 81 (1848), 47 O.L. 17 (1849); 47 O.L. (local laws) 395–96 (1849).

24. Stephen E. Maizlisch, *The Triumph of Sectionalism: The Transformation of Ohio Politics, 1844–1856* (Kent, Ohio: Kent State University Press, 1983), 64–66; Holt, *Party Politics*, 250–60; 45 H.J. 41, 575–76, 578, 582–83 (1846–47); 45 O.L. (local laws) 221 (1847).

25. Weisenburger, *Passing of the Frontier*, 313–14, 328–29; 35 H.J. 20–23, 41, 228–46 (1836–37); 35 S.J. 182 (1837); *Western Hemisphere and Ohio Monitor*, 18 January 1837.

26. 40 H.J., spec. sess., 15 (1842); John Armstrong Smith to Jane McDowell Smith, July 25, 1842, John Armstrong Smith Papers, Ohio Historical Society.

27. *Daily Ohio State Journal*, 10 August 1842; *Niles' National Register*, August 20 and 27, 1842; 40 H.J., spec. sess., 144–47 (1842); 40 S.J., spec. sess. 419 (1842).

28. 41 H.J. 270, 359–62, 673–74 (1843); 41 S.J. 695–96, 699, 708 (1843); 41 O.L. 61 (1843).

29. Holt, *Party Politics*, 352–58; Holt, *Rise and Fall*, 398–99.

30. 46 S.J. 205–9 (1848); 46 S.J. 51–60 (1847).

31. Holt, *Rise and Fall*, 399.

32. Louis R. Harlan, ed., "The Autobiography of Alexander Long, 1858," *Bulletin of the Historical and Philosophical Society of Ohio* 31 (April 1961): 118.

33. Holt, *Rise and Fall*, 399–402; B. H. Pershing, "Membership in the Ohio General Assembly," *Ohio Archaeological and Historical Quarterly* 40 (April 1931): 232–42; Quillin, *Color Line*, 36–43.

34. 47 S.J. 4–6, 29–41 (1848); Harvey S. Ford, "Seabury Ford," in *Governors of Ohio* (Columbus: Ohio Historical Society, 1969), 63; *Niles' National Register*, 17 January 1849; *Semi-Weekly Eagle* (Brattleboro, Vt.), 22 January 1849; 47 H.J. 51–146 (1849); A. G. Riddle, "Recollections of the Forty-seventh General Assembly of Ohio, 1847–1848 [sic]," *Magazine of Western History* 6 (August 1887): 348n.

35. Holt, *Party Politics*, 379–85.

36. Finkelman, "Race," 767–75; 49 O.L. (local laws) 811, 814 (1851); 49 H.J. 575–76 (1851); 48 O.L. (local laws) 713–14 (1850).

37. Eugene H. Roseboom, *The Civil War Era, 1850–1873*, vol. 4, *The History of the State of Ohio*, ed. Carl Wittke (Columbus: Ohio Archaeological and Historical Society, 1944), 265; *Cincinnati Gazette*, 17 December 1851.

38. Wilentz, *Rise of American Democracy*, 664–75; Holt, *Political Parties*, 237–38; Maizlish, *Triumph*, 91–98, 120; Roseboom, *Civil War Era*, 126.

39. Holt, *Political Parties*, 251, 295–96; William E. Gienapp, *The Origins of the Republican Party, 1852–1856* (New York: Oxford University Press, 1987), 56–60.

40. Holt, *Rise and Fall*, 782–83; Roseboom, *Civil War Era*, 223–24; Maizlish, *Triumph*, 181–84.

41. Maizlish, *Triumph*, 180, 182; Andrew R. L. Cayton and Paula R. Riggs, *City into Town: The City of Marietta, Ohio, 1788–1988* (Marietta, Ohio: Marietta College Dawes Memorial Library, 1991), 141; Carl Wittke, "Ohio's Germans, 1840–1875," *Ohio Historical Quarterly* 66 (October 1957): 342, 348–49; Jed Dannenbaum, "Immigrants and Temperance: Ethnocultural Conflict in Cincinnati, 1845–1860," *Ohio History* 87 (Spring 1978): 125–39.

42. Holt, *Political Parties*, 116–17, 122–27; Maizlisch, *Triumph*, 205; James A. Garfield, *The Diary of James A. Garfield*, vol. 1, *1848–1871*, ed. Harry James Brown and Frederick D. Williams (East Lansing: Michigan State University Press, 1967), 150.

43. Gienapp, *Origins*, 196–97; Maizlisch, *Triumph*, 202–24.

44. Gienapp, *Origins*, 113–21; Roseboom, *Civil War Era*, 284, 295.

45. Roseboom, *Civil War Era*, 306–7; Gienapp, *Origins*, 192–203.

46. Roseboom, *Civil War Era*, 328–29, 343–45; Morris, *Free Men All*, 180–82; 56 O.L. 120 (1859); Finkelman, "Race," 770; Quillin, *Color Line*, 24–25.

47. Ex parte Bushnell, 9 Ohio St. 77 (1859); George H. Porter, *Ohio Politics during the Civil War Period* (1911; rpt., New York: AMS, 1968), 30–42, 70.

48. Rokicky, *Monroe*, 56–67; Robert I. Cottom, "To Be among the First: The Early Career of James A. Garfield, 1831–1868" (Ph.D. diss., Johns Hopkins University, 1975), 113–29.

49. Porter, *Ohio Politics*, 58–60; 57 S.J. 19–20 (1861); 57 H.J. 38–43 (1861); 57 S.J. 66 (1861); 57 H.J. 81 (1861); 58 O.L. 6 (1861); David A. Gerber, *Black Ohio and the Color Line, 1860–1915* (Urbana: University of Illinois Press, 1976), 27–28.

50. 58 O.L. 89 (1861); 57 S.J. 284, 294, 301–2 (1861); 57 H.J. 509–10 (1861); 58 O.L. 110 (1861); 57 S.J. 291 (1861); 57 H.J. 546 (1861).

51. *Ohio State Journal*, 26 March 1863; 59 H.J. 267–68 (1863).

52. Frank Klement, *The Limits of Dissent: Clement L. Vallandigham and the Civil War* (Lexington: University Press of Kentucky, 1970), 118–19; John A. Marshall, *American Bastile: A History of the Arbitrary Arrests and Imprisonment of American Citizens in the Northern and Border States. . . .* (Philadelphia: Thomas W. Hartley, 1885), 586–605.

53. 59 H.J. 145–46 (1863); 59 H.J., app., 29 (1863).

54. 59 H.J. 363–64 (1863).

55. 59 H.J. 364–65, 381, 398–404, 412 (1863).

56. Porter, *Ohio Politics*, 183–84, 201–2, 208–10; *Crisis* (Columbus), 4 October 1865.

57. Porter, *Ohio Politics*, 219–20, 235–40, 247–48; Gerber, *Black Ohio*, 35–40; *Cincinnati Commercial*, 22 April 1867.

58. 65 O.L. 280 (1868); 64 S.J. 275–76 (1868); 64 S.J., app., 18; 65 O.L. 97 (1868); Monroe v. Collins, 17 Ohio St. 665 (1868); 65 H.J. 628 (1869), 65 S.J. 670–71 (1869); 66 S.J. 44 (1870); 66 H.J. 89 (1870); Frederick M. Gittes, "Paper Promises: Race and Ohio Law after 1860," in Benedict and Winkler, *History of Ohio Law*, 2:790–91.

59. Klement, *Vallandigham*, 438–39; 82 H.J. 342 (1886); 83 S.J. 255 (1887), 84 O.L. 34 (1887); 85 H.J. 495 (1889), 85 S.J. 548 (1889), 86 O.L. 169 (1889); 85 S.J. 78 (1889), 85 H.J. 780 (1889), 86 O.L. 220 (1889); David A. Gerber, "Lynching and Law and Order: Origins and Passage of the Ohio Anti-Lynching Law of 1896," *Ohio History* 83 (Winter 1974): 33–50; Middleton, *Black Laws*, 254–60.

60. Harry L. Watson, *Liberty and Power: The Politics of Jacksonian America* (New York: Hill and Wang, 1990), 186; Richard Jensen, *The Winning of the Midwest: Social and Political Conflict, 1888–1896* (Chicago: University of Chicago Press, 1971), 309–15.

61. 71 H.J. 422 (1875); Forrest William Clonts, "The Political Campaign of 1875 in Ohio," *Ohio Archaeological and Historical Quarterly* 31 (January 1922): 67–68.

62. *Columbus Dispatch and Statesman*, 16 March 1875, and 29 April 1875; *Ohio State Journal*, 28 August 1875; 72 H.J. 12 (1876); 73 S.J. 84–85 (1876).

63. Ballard C. Calhoun, "Public Policy and State Government," in Charles W. Calhoun, ed., *The Gilded Age: Essays on the Origins of Modern America* (Wilmington, Del.: Scholarly Resources, 1996), 317–18; 85 O.L. 169 (1888), 84 H.J. 736 (1888), 84 S.J. 742 (1888); 82 O.L. 49 (1885), 81 H.J. 130 (1885), 81 S.J. 162 (1885); 69 O.L. 174 (1872), 68 H.J. 145–46 (1872), 68 S.J. 713 (1872), 82 O.L. 184 (1885), 81 H.J. 739 (1885), 81 S.J. 587 (1885); 78 O.L. 126 (1881), 77 H.J. 114 (1881), 77 S.J. 331 (1881); 89 O.L. 252 (1892), 89 H.J. 285 (1892), 89 S.J. 441, 476 (1892).

64. 84 H.J. 27–31, 35–36 (1888); 84 S.J. 35–36, 108–9 (1888); Michael Cain Pierce, "The Plow and Hammer: Farmers, Organized Labor and the People's Party in Ohio" (Ph.D. diss., Ohio State University, 1999), 69–70, 86–87, 90–91.

65. Lloyd Sponholtz, "The Politics of Temperance in Ohio, 1880–1912," *Ohio History* 85 (Winter 1976): 5–9; 80 O.L. 384 (1883); F. M. Whitaker, "Ohio WCTU and the Prohibition Campaign of 1883," *Ohio History* 83 (Spring 1974): 94–98; Daniel J. Ryan, *History of Ohio: The Rise and Progress of an American State* (New York: Century History, 1912), 4:521.

66. 78 S.J. 274 (1882); 78 H.J. 633 (1882); 79 S.J. 623 (1883); 79 H.J. 786–87 (1883); 82 S.J. 551 (1886); 82 H.J. 853 (1886).

67. *Ohio State Journal*, 25 February 1884; 85 O.L. 116 (1888); 84 S.J. 560 (1888); 84 H.J. 516 (1888); 85 O.L. 55 (1888); 84 H.J. 236 (1888); 84 S.J. 345 (1888).

68. K. Austin Kerr, *Organized for Prohibition: A New History of the Anti-Saloon League* (New Haven, Conn.: Yale University Press, 1985), 68; Paul Kleppner, *The Cross of Culture: A Social Analysis of Midwestern Politics, 1850–1900* (New York: Free Press, 1970), 73–74, 121–24; Jensen, *Winning of the Midwest*, 63–68, 115–18.

69. Kerr, *Organized for Prohibition*, 38–39n4.

70. Thomas R. Pegram, *Battling Demon Rum: The Struggle for a Dry America, 1800–1933* (Chicago: Ivan R. Dee, 1998), 76; Michael E. McGerr, *The Decline of Popular Politics: The American North, 1865–1928* (New York: Oxford University Press, 1986), 205–9, 191–92, 211–13; Ann-Marie E. Szymanski, *Pathways to Prohibition: Radicals, Moderates, and Social Movement Outcomes* (Durham, N.C.: Duke University Press, 2003) 134; Gail Hamilton [Mary Abigail Dodge], "Prohibition in Politics," *North American Review* 140 (June 1885): 509–20.

Chapter 11: Legislation and the Public Good

1. 48 O.L. (general laws) 3–98 (1850); 48 O.L. (local laws) 3–709 (1850).

2. 97 O.L. 3–625 (1904).

3. Salmon P. Chase, ed., *The Statutes of Ohio and of the North Western Territory, Adopted or Enacted From 1788 to 1833, Inclusive* . . . (Cincinnati: Corey and Fairbank, 1833), 1:35–37.

4. Francis J. Amer, "The Growth and Development of the Ohio Judicial System," in *A History of the Courts and Lawyers of Ohio*, ed. Carrington T. Marshall (New York: American Historical Society, 1934), 1:186–98; Mark Pitcavage, "'Burthened in Defence of Our Rights': Opposition to Military Service in Ohio during the War of 1812," *Ohio History* 104 (Summer–Autumn 1995): 142–62; Matthew Oyos, "The Mobilization of the Ohio Militia in the Civil War," *Ohio History* (Summer–Autumn 1989): 147–74; 42 H.J. 352–53 (1844); William T. Utter, *The Frontier State, 1803–1825*, vol. 2, *The History of the State of Ohio*, ed. Carl Wittke (Columbus: Ohio Historical Society, 1942), 314–19, 324–25; Daniel J. Ryan, *History of Ohio: The Rise and Progress of an American State* (New York: Century History, 1912), 3:368–72; Harry N. Scheiber, *Ohio Canal Era: A Case Study of Government and the Economy, 1820–1861* (1968; rpt., Athens: Ohio University Press, 1987), 3–11; John S. Still, "Ethan Allen Brown and Ohio's Canal System," *Ohio Historical Quarterly* 66 (January 1957): 23–30.

5. Scheiber, *Canal Era*, 26, 28; Ryan, *History*, 3:372; Utter, *Frontier State*, 319–20; Julia Perkins Cutler, ed., *Life and Times of Ephraim Cutler Prepared from His Journals and Correspondence* (1890; rpt., New York: Arno, 1971), 148; 23 H.J. 229–31 (1825); 23 S.J. 223, 225 (1825).

6. Still, "Brown," 35; Scheiber, *Canal Era*, 27–30; Cutler, *Life and Times*, 116–17, 159–61; Donald J. Ratcliffe, *The Politics of Long Division: The Birth of the Second Party System in Ohio, 1818–1828* (Columbus: Ohio State University Press, 2000), 67–69; Ernest Ludlow Bogart, *Financial History of Ohio* (Urbana-Champaign: University of Illinois Press, 1912), 202; Nelson W. Evans, *A History of Taxation in Ohio* (Cincinnati: Robert Clarke, 1906), 18–25.

7. Edward Alanson Miller, *The History of Educational Legislation in Ohio From 1803 to 1850* (Chicago: University of Chicago, 1920), 11, 21 [previously published in *Ohio Archaeological and Historical Quarterly* 27 (January–April 1918): 1–271 and 27 (October 1918): 558–79]; Cutler, *Life and Times*, 172.

8. Ryan, *History*, 3:379.

9. Bernard Bailyn, *The Ideological Origins of the American Revolution* (Cambridge, Mass.: Harvard University Press, Belknap Press, 1992), 50, 122–25; Gordon S. Wood, *The Radicalism of the American Revolution* (New York: Knopf, 1991), 187–88.

10. Stephen A. Higginson, "Note: A Short History of the Right to Petition Government for the Redress of Grievances," *Yale Law Journal* 92 (November 1986): 142; Gregory A. Mark, "The Vestigial Constitution: The History and Significance of the Right to Petition," *Fordham Law Review* 66 (May 1998): 2153; Carl N. Everstine, *The General Assembly of Maryland, 1776–1850* (Charlottesville, Va.: Michie, 1982), 174; Paul Finkelman, "Exploring Southern Legal History," *North Carolina Law Review* 64 (November 1985): 110–11; Chase, *Statutes*, 1:107, 120; Gordon S. Wood, *The Creation of the American Republic* (Chapel Hill: University of North Carolina Press, 1969), 154–55; Carol Rice Andrews, "A Right of Access to Court under the Petition Clause of the First Amendment: Defining the Right," *Ohio State Law Journal* 60, no. 2 (1999): 596–611.

11. Joseph Stancliffe Davis, *Essays in the Earlier History of American Corporations* (1917; rpt. New York: Russell and Russell, 1965), 1:3–29, 104–7; ibid., 2:8–9; Lawrence M.

Friedman, *A History of American Law*, 3d ed. (New York: Simon and Schuster, 2005), 129n42; Everstine, *General Assembly of Maryland*, 176–78.

12. Wood, *Creation*, 401–2.

13. Victor S. Clark, *History of Manufactures in the United States* (New York: McGraw-Hill, 1929), 1:31–72; Stuart Bruchey, *Enterprise: The Dynamic Economy of a Free People* (Cambridge, Mass.: Harvard University Press, 1990), 199–206.

14. Kenneth J. Winkle, *The Politics of Community: Migration and Politics in Antebellum Ohio* (Cambridge: Cambridge University Press, 1988), 11–16.

15. Theodore Calvin Pease, ed., *The Laws of the Northwest Territory, 1788–1800* (Springfield: Trustees of the Illinois State Historical Library, 1925), 258; 3 O.L. 177 (1805); 20 O.L. 10 (1812); 32 O.L. 37 (1834).

16. 33 S.J. 223 (1835).

17. 29 S.J. 215–16 (1831); Martin Schultz, "Divorce in Early America: Origins and Patterns in Three North Central States," *Sociological Quarterly* 25 (Autumn 1984): 520, 517; 33 S.J. 223 (1835); 35 H.J. 59–60 (1836).

18. 12 S.J. 294 (1814); 12 O.L. 84 (1814); 46 H.J., app. 1–5, 33 -37 (1847–48); 46 H.J. 240 (1848); 46 S.J. 456 (1848).

19. Jamil S. Zainaldin, "The Emergence of a Modern American Family Law: Child Custody, Adoption, and the Courts, 1776–1851," *Northwestern University Law Review* 73 (February 1979): 1075–84; Stephen B. Presser, "The Historical Background of the American Law of Adoption," *Journal of Family Law* 11, no. 3 (1972): 515–16; David Ray Papke, "Pondering Past Purposes: A Critical History of American Adoption Law," *West Virginia Law Review* 102 (Winter 1999): 462–63; Michael Grossberg, *Governing the Hearth: Law and the Family in Nineteenth-Century America* (Chapel Hill: University of North Carolina Press, 1985), 268–73; Marian J. Morton, "Homes for Poverty's Children: Cleveland's Orphanages, 1851–1933," *Ohio History* 98 (Winter–Spring 1989): 6–12; 42 O.L. (local) 136 (1844); 31 O.L. (local) 52 (1833); 29 O.L. 436 (1831); 51 H.J. 169, 532–33, 558 (1854); 52 O.L. 78 (1854); Brower v. Hunt, 18 Ohio St. 311, 341–42 (1868); 56 O.L. 82 (1859).

20. Ohio const. of 1851, art. 13, §§ 1, 2; ibid., art. 2, § 26; 40 O.L. 28 (1842); 75 O.L. 1184, 1190 (1878); 92 O.L. 854 (1896); 66 H.J. 987–89, 991–1002, 1004–5 (1870).

21. 95 H.J. 1566 (1902).

22. S. P. Orth, "The Cleveland Plan of School Administration," *Political Science Quarterly* 19 (September 1904): 404; Nelson L. Bossing, *The History of Educational Legislation in Ohio from 1851 to 1925* (Columbus: F. J. Heer, 1931), 39–44 [previously published in *Ohio Archaeological and Historical Quarterly* 39 (January 1930): 78–291 and 39 (April): 223–399]; State ex rel. Wirsch v. Spellmire, 67 Ohio St. 77 (1902).

23. Bossing, *Educational Legislation*, 45–54.

24. Harvey Walker, "Municipal Government in Ohio before 1912," *Ohio State Law Journal* 9, no. 1 (1948): 2–10; Ohio const. of 1851, art. 13, §§ 1, 6.

25. 50 O.L. 223 (1852)

26. 66 O.L. 337 (1869); 87 O.L. 81, 255, 330 (1890); Delos F. Wilcox, *Municipal Government in Michigan and Ohio: A Study in the Relations of City and Commonwealth* (New York: Columbia University Press, 1896), 78–80.

27. Clement Bates, ed., *The Annotated Revised Statutes of Ohio* (Cincinnati: W. H. Anderson, 1897), 3:743–45; Samuel P. Orth, *The Centralization of Administration in Ohio* (New York: Columbia University Press, 1903), 15–16; Wade H. Ellis, *The Municipal Code of Ohio*, 3d ed., rev. Challen B. Ellis (Cincinnati: W. H. Anderson, 1907), xii.

28. Ellis, *Municipal Code*, xiii–xiv.

29. Ernest S. Griffith, *A History of American City Government: The Conspicuous Failure, 1870–1900* (New York: Praeger, 1974), 217.

30. Costello v. Wyoming, 49 Ohio St. 202 (1892); City of Cincinnati v. Steinkamp, 54 Ohio St. 284 (1896); State ex rel. Sheets v. Cowles, 64 Ohio St. 162 (1901).

31. Ellis, *Municipal Code*, xvi–xxi.

32. Ibid., xxx–xxxi; Ohio const. of 1851, am. 1912, art. 18; 145 O.L. 6790 (1994); Sub. H.B. 24, 125th Gen. Ass'y (2003); Tom Breckinridge, "Aw, Shut Your Speed Trap," *Cleveland Plain Dealer*, 30 September 1994; "Mayor's Courts Go Unchecked," *Akron Beacon Journal*, 21 July 2003; Michael Sangiacomo, "Ticket Town; New Rome Mayor Wants to Pull the Plug on Citation-Writing Police Department," *Cleveland Plain Dealer*, 3 May 2002; Vill. of Linndale v. State, 85 Ohio St.3d 52 (1999); editorial, "Welcome to New Rome," *Columbus Dispatch*, 21 July 2002; editorial, "New Rome Needs to Be Put Out of Our Misery," *Columbus Dispatch*, 6 February 2003; editorial, "No More New Rome?" *Columbus Dispatch*, 10 December 2003.

33. Harry L. Watson, *Liberty and Power: The Politics of Jacksonian America* (New York: Hill and Wang, 1990), 238–41; *Cleveland Plain Dealer*, September 8, 1845; Nicole Etcheson, *The Emerging Midwest: Upland Southerners and the Political Culture of the Old Northwest, 1787–1861* (Bloomington: Indiana University Press, 1996), 78–80; Stephen E. Maizlish, *The Triumph of Sectionalism: The Transformation of Ohio Politics, 1844–1856* (Kent, Ohio: Kent State University Press, 1983), 182.

34. William J. Novak, *The People's Welfare: Law and Regulation in Nineteenth-Century America* (Chapel Hill: University of North Carolina Press, 1996), 84, 86, 239–40.

35. Donna I. Dennis, "Obscenity Law and the Conditions of Freedom in the Nineteenth-Century United States," *Law and Social Inquiry* 27 (Spring 2002): 369–99.

36. 9 O.L. 19 (1811); Robert G. Paterson. "The Role of the 'District' as a Unit in Organized Medicine in Ohio," *Ohio State Archaeological and Historical Quarterly* 49 (October 1940): 367–71; Ratcliffe, *Long Division*, 242–44; 31 O.L. 27 (1833).

37. 32 O.L. 20 (1834); James C. Mohr, *Abortion in America: The Origins and Evolution of National Policy, 1800–1900* (New York: Oxford University Press, 1978), 39–40, 90–91.

38. 51 H.J. 562, 737 (1854); 51 H.J., app., 367–68 (1854); 53 H.J., app., 141–48 (1857); 52 H.J. 411 (1856).

39. 59 S.J. 406 (1862); 59 H.J. 539 (1862); 59 O.L. 63 (1862); 64 O.L. 202 (1867).

40. 59 O.L. 32 (1862); 69 O.L. 174 (1872); 73 O.L. 158 (1876); 75 O.L. 142 (1878); 65 O.L. 204 (1868); 75 O.L. 45 (1878).

41. 69 H.J. 673 (1872); 82 O.L. 209 (1885); 86 O.L. 320 (1889).

42. 59 H.J. 846 (1872); 73 H.J. 447 (1876); 73 H.J. 770 (1876); 59 H.J. 279 (1862); 59 S.J. 223 (1863); 75 S.J. 297 (1878); 75 H.J. 174 (1878); 81 H.J. 952 (1885); 81 S.J. 611 (1885).

43. Robert Luce, *Legislative Principles: The History and Theory of Lawmaking by Representative Government* (Boston: Houghton Mifflin, 1930), 530–31.

Chapter 12: Direct Democracy

1. Moorfield Storey, "The American Legislature," *American Law Review* 28 (September–October 1894): 686; Emmet O'Neal, "Distrust of State Legislatures," *North American Review* 199 (May 1914): 684–85; B. O. Flower, "Is the Republic Passing?" *Arena* 30 (November 1903): 3–21.

2. Frederic C. Howe, *The Confessions of a Reformer* (New York: Scribner's, 1926), 158; Clarence E. Walker, rptr., *Proceedings and Debates of the Constitutional Convention of the State of Ohio. . . .* (Columbus: F. J. Heer, 1912–13), 2:1246; H. S. Bigelow, "From Pulpit to Stump," *Independent* 61 (November 1, 1906), 1036.

3. Howe, *Confessions*, 171–73.

4. Morton Keller, *Affairs of State: Public Life in Late Nineteenth Century America* (Cambridge, Mass.: Harvard University Press, Belknap Press, 1977), 319.

5. Michael F. Curtin in collaboration with Julia Barry Bell, *The Ohio Politics Almanac*, 2d ed. (Kent, Ohio: Kent State University Press, 2006), 183, 194–95; Philip D. Jordan, *Ohio Comes of Age, 1873–1900*, vol. 5, *The History of the State of Ohio*, ed. Carl Wittke (Columbus: Ohio State Archaeological and Historical Society, 1943), 189–292.

6. Howe, *Confessions*, 177–78.

7. Hoyt Landon Warner, *Progressivism in Ohio, 1897–1917* (Columbus: Ohio State University Press, 1964), 295; Daniel J. Ryan, "The Influence of Socialism on the Ohio Constitution," *North American Review* 196 (November 1912): 665; George Kennan, "The Direct Rule of the People," *North American Review* 198 (August 1913): 150, 154–55; Charles Sawyer, letter to the editor, *North American Review* 197 (February 1913): 275–79; Daniel J. Ryan, letter to the editor, *North American Review* 197 (February 1913): 279–80; Robert E. Cushman, "Voting Organic Law: The Action of the Ohio Electorate in the Revision of the State Constitution in 1912," *Political Science Quarterly* 28 (June 1913): 208–9; C. L. Martzolff, "Ohio: Changes in the Constitution," Notes on Current Legislation, *American Political Science Review* 6 (November 1912): 573.

8. Walker, *Proceedings*, 2:1239.

9. 90 H.J. 937 (1893); 91 H.J. 106 (1894); 98 S.J. 271–72 (1906); 99 H.J. 497–97 (1908); 99 S.J. 184–85, 615–16 (1908); Warner, *Progressivism*, 195–96; Steven L. Piott, *Giving Voters a Choice: The Origins of the Initiative and Referendum in America* (Columbia: University of Missouri Press, 2003), 170–72, 259–99.

10. John S. Sheppard Jr., "Concerning the Decline of the Principle of Representation in Popular Government," *Forum* 44 (June 1910): 642–50; John W. Griggs, "Lawmaking," *American Law Review* 31 (September–October 1897): 705–10, 714; Walker, *Proceedings*, 1:933, 726, 683, 687–88; Ryan, letter, 280; Ryan, "Influence of Socialism," 668.

11. Thomas Goebel, *A Government by the People: Direct Democracy in American, 1890–1940* (Chapel Hill: University of North Carolina Press, 2002), 53–57; "Popular vs.

Delegated Government," *Independent* 69 (August 25, 1910): 430; Walker, *Proceedings*, 1:664, 383.

12. Warner, *Progressivism*, 320–23; Piott, *Giving Voters a Voice*, 180–82; Steven H. Steinglass and Gino J. Scarselli, *The Ohio State Constitution: A Reference Guide* (Westport, Conn.: Praeger, 2004), 358; Ohio const. of 1851, am. 1912, art. 2, §§ 1a, 1b.

13. George H. Shibley, "The Progress of the Campaign for Majority Rule," *Arena* 29 (June 1903): 625–37; Robert L. Owen, "The Restoration of Popular Rule: The Greatest of All Non-Partisan Issues," *Arena* 39 (June 1908): 643–50; Goebel, *Government by the People*, 122.

14. 89 O.L. 695 (1892); 88 O.L. 921 (1891), 89 O.L. 696 (1892), 92 O.L. 770 (1896), 93 O.L. 734 (1898), 98 O.L. 406 (1906), 99 O.L. 641 (1908), 102 O.L. 741 (1911); Allen O. Myers, *Bosses and Boodle in Ohio Politics: Some Plain Truths for Honest People* (Cincinnati: Lyceum, 1895), 291–93.

15. Howe, *Confessions*, 177; Alan Ware, *The American Direct Primary: Party Institutionalization and Transformation in the North* (Cambridge: Cambridge University Press, 2002), 105–8; C. B. S., "The Reform of Primaries," *Current Literature* 37 (July–December 1904): 23; Ira Cross, "Direct Primaries," *Arena* 35 (June 1906): 587–88; Edward Insley, "How to Reform the Primary-Election System (With Particular Reference to Reforms in Operation or Proposed)," *Arena* 17 (June 1897): 1013–23; Charles B. Spahr, "Direct Primaries," in *Proceedings of the Rochester Conference for Good City Government and Seventh Annual Meeting of the National Municipal League*, ed. Clinton Rogers Woodruff (Philadelphia: National Municipal League, 1901), 191.

16. 68 O.L. 27 (1871); 91 O.L. 769 (1894); 93 O.L. 652 (1898); Cincinnati v. Ehrman, 6 N.P. 169, 9 Ohio Dec. 1 (1899); A. H. Tuttle, "The Bronson Primary Law in Ohio," *Publications of the Michigan Political Science Association* 6 (March 1905): 111.

17. Tuttle, "Bronson Primary Law," 113–14; 97 O.L. 439 (1904); 97 H.J. 537, 670, 832 (1904); 97 S.J. 732 (1904).

18. 99 O.L. 214 (1908); Warner, *Progressivism*, 196–97, 324–25; Walker, *Proceedings*, 2:1243.

19. Walker, *Proceedings*, 2:1925–27; Steinglass and Scarselli, *Ohio State Constitution*, 357.

20. Warner, *Progressivism*, 392–94, 415n23; 104 O.L. 119 (1914); "Referendum Frauds Hearing Is Started," *Ohio State Journal*, 21 August 1913; "Equity People Leave Hearing before Graves," ibid., 22 August 1913; "Martin's Testimony Hits Kibler Harder," ibid., 23 August 1913; "Referendum Fraud Turns up Pay Dirt," ibid., 31 August 1913.

21. Goebel, *Government by the People*, 101; Ryan, "Influence of Socialism," 668.

22. Ryan, letter, 80; Arthur A. Schwartz, comp., *Amendment and Legislation: Proposed Constitutional Amendments, Initiated Legislation, and Laws Challenged by Referendum, Submitted to the Electors*, updated through 2006 by Jennifer Brunner (Columbus: Ohio Secretary of State, 2007) (http://www.sos.state.oh.us/sos/upload/elections/historical/issuehist.pdf); 115 H.J. 9 (1933) (H.B. 2); 115 O.L., pt. 2, 118 (1933); Mark Niquette, "Strip Club Bill Makes It into Law," *Columbus Dispatch*, 23 May 2007.

23. Schwartz, *Amendment*; Laura Johnston, "Voters Keep the Cap on Short-Term Loans at 28 Percent Mark," *Cleveland Plain Dealer*, 5 November 2008.

24. Ibid.; Steinglass and Scarselli, *Ohio State Constitution*, 360–75; State ex rel. Green-lund v. Fulton, 99 Ohio St. 168 (1919).

25. Ohio const. of 1851, am. 1954, art. 3, § 2; ibid., am. 1992, art. 5, § 8; U.S. Term Limits, Inc. v. Thornton, 514 U.S. 779 (1995)

26. Goebel, *Government by the People*, 121–24, 198; Ben A. Arneson, "Do Representatives Represent?" *National Municipal Review* 16 (December 1927): 753–54.

27. George Kennan, "The Direct Rule of the People," *North American Review* 198 (August 1913): 150–52.

28. Ware, *American Direct Primary*, 227–31; Oscar K. Davis, "Can You Trust the Primaries?" *Collier's Weekly* 73 (29 March 1924): 8–9, rpt. in *The Direct Primary*, comp. Lamar T. Beman (New York: H. W. Wilson, 1926), 157, 160–61; Henry M. Hyde, "Has the Direct Primary Made Good?" *McClure's Magazine*, August 1920, 15; Warner, *Progressivism*, 484.

29. Walker, *Proceedings*, 2:1926; Hyde, "Direct Primary," 16; Peter H. Odegard, *Pressure Politics: The Story of the Anti-Saloon League* (New York: Columbia University Press, 1928), 89–103.

30. Hyde, "Direct Primary," 16, 68; Richard Hofstadter, *The Age of Reform: From Bryan to F. D. R.* (New York: Vintage Books, 1955), 268; Robert A. Taft, *The Papers of Robert A. Taft: Volume 1, 1889–1939*, ed. Clarence E. Wunderlin Jr. (Kent, Ohio: Kent State University Press, 1997), 319.

31. Karl F. Geiser, "Defects in the Direct Primary," *Annals of the American Academy of Political and Society Science* 106 (March 1923): 31–39, rpt. in Beman, *Direct Primary*, 140–41; "Organize for Short Ballot Campaign," Citizen Action, *National Civic Review* 51 (September 1962): 463; "The Longest Ballot?" editorial comment, ibid., 52 (January 1963): 5.

32. Taft, *Papers*, 1:319, 302.

33. V. O. Key Jr., *American State Politics: An Introduction* (New York: Knopf, 1967), 177–78, 181–93.

34. Ware, *American Direct Primary*, 244–46, 254; Stanley Aronoff, interview by author, 1 May 2006.

35. Ohio Secretary of State, Elections Results (http://www.sos.state.oh.us/Index.aspx); Ohio Secretary of State, *Ohio Election Statistics*, 1989–1990, 145.

36. Ohio Secretary of State, *Ohio Election Statistics*, 1959–1960, 43–49, 108–14; Ohio Secretary of State, *Ohio Election Statistics*, 1979–1980, 51–65, 112–27.

Chapter 13: The Balance of Power

1. William J. Keefe, "The Functions and Powers of the State Legislatures," in *State Legislatures in American Politics*, ed. Alexander Heard (Englewood Cliffs, N.J.: Prentice Hall, 1966), 59–60.

2. *Columbus Dispatch*, 1 November 1903, 7; Clarence E. Walker, rptr., *Proceedings and Debates of the Constitutional Convention of the State of Ohio . . .* (Columbus: F. J. Heer, 1912–13), 1:566–67; 95 O.L. 352 (1902); Reginald Charles McGrane, "The Veto Power

in Ohio," in "Proceedings of the Mississippi Valley Historical Association, 1915–1916," special issue, *Mississippi Valley Historical Review* 9, extra number (April 1917): 185–86.

3. Ohio const. of 1851, am. 1903, art. 2, § 16; *Cincinnati Enquirer*, 16 May 1903; 98 O.L. 412 (1906); 99 O.L. 120 (1908); Alonzo H. Tuttle, "History of the Executive Veto in the Ohio Constitution," *Ohio State Law Journal* 2 (March 1936): 107–9.

4. Walker, *Proceedings*, 1:218–19, 224, 566–70; John J. Kulewicz, "Reinventing the Governor: A History of Executive Power Under Ohio Law," in *The History of Ohio Law*, ed. Michael Les Benedict and John F. Winkler (Athens: Ohio University Press, 2004), 1:171–72.

5. Henry L. Stimson and McGeorge Bundy, *On Active Service in Peace and War* (New York: Harper and Bros., 1948), 59–62; McGrane, "Veto Power," 185–88; Kulewicz, "Reinventing the Governor," 169; Walker, *Proceedings*, 1:570–71, 2:1201; *Cincinnati Enquirer*, 16 May 1903; K. Austin Kerr, *Organized for Prohibition: A New History of the Anti-Saloon League* (New Haven, Conn.: Yale University Press, 1985), 106–10; James K. Mercer, *Ohio Legislative History*, vol. 1 (Columbus: Edward T. Miller, [1913?]), 149; J. A. Meckstroth, "A. Victor Donahey," in *The Governors of Ohio*, 2d ed. (Columbus: Ohio Historical Society, 1969), 168; *Bulletin of the Eighty-sixth General Assembly of Ohio* (Columbus: F. J. Heer, 1925), 281.

6. Warren Van Tine et al., *In the Workers' Interest: A History of the Ohio AFL-CIO, 1958–1998* (Columbus: Center for Labor Research, Ohio State University, 1998), 134–35.

7. *Cleveland Plain Dealer*, 6 January 1857; Eugene H. Roseboom, *The Civil War Era, 1850–1873*, vol. 4, *The History of the State of Ohio*, ed. Carl Wittke (Columbus: Ohio Archaeological and Historical Society, 1944), 119; 64 O.L. 111 (1867); 83 O.L. 206 (1886); 86 O.L. 367 (1889); 92 O.L. 315 (1896).

8. Clement Bates, ed., *The Annotated Revised Statutes of the State of Ohio, Including All Laws of a General Nature in Force January 1, 1898* (Cincinnati: Anderson, 1897), 1:122–271; 93 O.L. 245, 387 (1898); Samuel P. Orth, *The Centralization of Administration in Ohio* (New York: Columbia University Press, 1903), 173–74.

9. Orth, *Centralization*, 20–21, 174–77.

10. 98 O.L. 342 (1906); Hoyt Landon Warner, *Progressivism in Ohio, 1897–1917* (Columbus: Ohio State University Press, 1964), 179, 233–37, 271–80, 400; James E. Meeks, "The Evolution of the Public Utility Commission of Ohio (PUCO): (Almost) One Hundred Years of Service to the People of Ohio," in Benedict and Winkler, *History*, 2:642–43.

11. Nelson L. Bossing, *The History of Educational Legislation in Ohio from 1851 to 1925* (Columbus: F. J. Heer, 1931), 319–21 [previously published in *Ohio Archaeological and Historical Quarterly* 39 (January 1930): 78–291 and 39 (April 1930): 223–399].

12. Kulewicz, "Reinventing the Governor," 163, 175.

13. Irene S. Rubin, "Who Invented Budgeting in the United States?" *Public Administration Review* 53 (September–October 1993): 438–44; W. O. Heffernan, "State Budget Making in Ohio," *Annals of the American Academy of Political and Social Science* 62 (November 1915): 93–96; 103 O.L. 658 (1913); 104 O.L. 64 (1914); Jonathan Kahn, *Budgeting Democracy: State Building and Citizenship in America, 1890–1928* (Ithaca, N.Y.:

Cornell University Press, 1997), 4; Richard G. Sheridan, *Follow the Money: Ohio State Budgeting* (Cleveland: Federation for Community Planning, 2000), 40.

14. Warner, *Progressivism*, 425; 109 O.L. 105 (1921); Heffernan, "State Budget Making" 98–99; "Sign 'Ripper' Monday," *Columbus Citizen*, 22 April 1921.

15. 107 O.L. 522 (1917); Cincinnati, Wilmington & Zanesville R.R. Co. v. Comm's of Clinton County, 1 Ohio St. 77, 88–89 (1852); Ex Parte Company, 106 Ohio St. 50 (1922).

16. William Herbert Page, ed., *Page's Desk Edition of the Ohio General Code Containing All Ohio Statutes of a General Nature in Force January 1, 1931* (Cincinnati: W. H. Anderson, 1930), §§ 871-1-871–45, 8624-23, 8624-28, 1295-24, 154-57, 1085-1169-1; Matz v. J. L. Curtis Cartage Co., 132 Ohio St. 271, 282 (1937).

17. Karl B. Pauly, *Bricker of Ohio: The Man and His Record* (New York: G. P. Putnam's Sons, 1944), 201–3; 120 O.L. 358 (1943); 121 O.L. 578 (1945).

18. Michael Burns, "The Legislative Reference Movement in Ohio: From Progressive Ideal to Session Satisfying," *University of Toledo Law Review* 32 (Summer 2001): 498; *Youngstown Vindicator*, 2 January 1957; David A. Johnston, "The Ohio Legislative Service Commission: A Nonpolitical Political Institution," memorandum P-116-8511, 31 January 1986, Legislative Service Commission library, 24–29.

19. Charles F. Kurfess, "From the Leader's Position . . . ," in *Strengthening the States: Essays on Legislative Reform*, ed. Donald G. Hertzberg and Alan Rosenthal (Garden City, N.Y.: Anchor, 1972), 137–46; Lee Leonard, "Vernal G. Riffe Jr.: The Definitive House Speaker," *Columbus Dispatch*, 25 December 1994.

20. Lee Leonard, "Rhodes's Second Eight Years, 1975–1983," in *Ohio Politics*, ed. Alexander P. Lamis (Kent, Ohio: Kent State University Press, 1994), 111; William J. Pohlman, comment, "The Continued Viability of Ohio's Procedure for Legislative Review of Agency Rules in the Post-*Chadha* Era," *Ohio State Law Journal* 49, no. 1 (1988): 266–67; 136 H.J. 2042–46 (1975); 136 S.J. 1160, 2372 (1976); 137 O.L. 2230 (1977).

21. Leonard, "Rhodes's Second Eight Years," 109–14; Thomas Suddes, "Panorama of Ohio Politics in the Voinovich Era, 1991–," in Lamis, *Ohio Politics*, 163–65; Brian Usher, "The Lausche Era, 1945–1957," in Lamis, *Ohio Politics*, 19–20.

22. Charles B. Nuckolls Jr., "The Governorship of Martin L. Davey of Ohio" (master's thesis, Ohio State University, 1952), 73–75.

23. "Davey Promises 'Bombshell' in Special Message," *Columbus Dispatch*, 30 December 1937; John P. Biehn, "Governor's Attack via Radio Fails to Halt Graft Probers," ibid., 4 January 1938; 117 H.J., 2d spec. sess., 166–74 (1938); 117 S.J. 2d spec. sess. 250–54 (1938).

24. 117 H.J. 2d spec. sess. 373–77 (1938); Nuckolls, "Governorship," 86–94.

25. State ex rel. Knisely v. Jones, 66 Ohio St. 453 (1902); Warner, *Progressivism*, 107–8; 84 O.L. 214 (1887); 83 H.J. 641 (1887); 83 S.J. 627 (1887); 86 O.L. 145 (1889); 85 H.J. 479, 568–69 (1889); 85 S.J. 454 (1889); 87 O.L. 78 (1890); 86 H.J. 444–45 (1890); 86 S.J. 519 (1890); State v. Lake Erie Iron Co., 33 Wkly. L. Bull. & Ohio L.J. 6 (1895), 51 Ohio St. 632 (1894); 87 O.L. 112 (1890); 86 H.J. 319, 597–98 (1890); 86 S.J. 579 (1890); State v. Wheeling Bridge & Terminal Ry. Co. v. Gilmore, 8 Ohio C.C. 658 (1894); Marsh

Bros. v. C. L. Poston and Co., 35 Wkly. L. Bull. & Ohio L.J. 327 (1896), 54 Ohio St. 681 (1896); City of Cleveland v. Clement Bros. Constr. Co., 67 Ohio St. 197 (1902); State v. Bateman, 10 Ohio Dec. 68, 7 Ohio N.P. 487 (1900); Palmer v. Tingle, 55 Ohio St. 423 (1896); Alter v. City of Cincinnati, 56 Ohio St. 47 (1897); State ex rel. Schwartz v. Ferris, 53 Ohio St. 314 (1895).

26. Steven H. Steinglass and Gino J. Scarselli, *The Ohio State Constitution: A Reference Guide* (Westport, Conn.: Praeger, 2004), 357–59.

27. Walker, *Proceedings*, 2:1409; Warner, *Progressivism*, 328–29; Jonathan L. Entin, "Judicial Supermajorities and the Validity of Statutes: How *Mapp* Became a Fourth Amendment Landmark Instead of a First Amendment Footnote," *Case Western Reserve Law Review* 52 (Winter 2001): 443–53.

28. Bd. of Educ. of the City Sch. Dist. of Columbus v. Columbus, 118 Ohio St. 295, 299 (1928); William M. Milligan and Joseph E. Pohlman, "The 1968 Modern Courts Amendment to the Ohio Constitution," *Ohio State Law Journal* 29 (Fall 1968): 845–46; Entin, "Judicial Supermajorities," 453–67.

29. City of Euclid v. Heaton, 15 Ohio St. 2d 65 (1968); DeRolph v. State, 78 Ohio St. 3d 193 (1997); Larry J. Obhof, "*DeRolph v. State* and Ohio's Long Road to an Adequate Education," *Brigham Young University Education and Law Journal* 2005, no. 1:83–149.

30. Ohio const. of 1851, am. 1968, art. 4, § 5(B); Milligan and Pohlman, "Modern Courts Amendment," 828–29; Josiah H. Blackmore II, "Not From Zeus's Head Full-Blown: The Story of Civil Procedure in Ohio," in Benedict and Winkler, *History*, 1:457; Cleveland Ry. Co. v. Halliday, 127 Ohio St. 278 (1933); Judd v. City Trust and Savings Bank, 133 Ohio St. 81 (1937); In re Thatcher, 80 Ohio St. 492 (1909); Eastman v. State, 131 Ohio St. 1 (1936), appeal dismissed, 299 U.S. 505 (1936); Smith v. Kates, 46 Ohio St. 2d 263 (1976).

31. State ex rel. Am. Acad. of Trial Lawyers v. Sheward, 86 Ohio St. 3d 451, 492, 478 (1999); Johnson v. BP Chems., Inc., 85 Ohio St. 3d 298, 309 (1999) (Cook, J., dissenting); DeRolph v. State, 89 Ohio St. 3d 1, 49 (2000) (Moyer, C.J., dissenting); David N. Mayer, "Legislature Should Oust 4 Judges," *Columbus Dispatch*, 6 June 2001; J. V. Smith, rptr., *Report of the Debates and Proceedings of the Convention for the Revision of the Constitution of the State of Ohio* (Columbus: S. Medary, 1851), 2:398.

32. Denison Univ. v. Bd. of Tax Appeals, 2 Ohio St. 2d 17 (1965); Exchange Bank of Columbus v. Hines, 3 Ohio St. 1 (1853); Theodore O. Finnarn, "Property Taxes and Farmers in Ohio: The Park Investment Story," *University of Toledo Law Review* 7 (Spring 1976): 1125; State ex rel. Swetland v. Kinney, 62 Ohio St. 2d 23 (1980).

33. Richard H. Finan and April M. Williams, "Government Is a Three-Legged Stool," *University of Toledo Law Review* 32 (Summer 2001): 517–28.

Chapter 14: Mighty Truth and the Purity of Elections

1. Elizabeth Cady Stanton, Susan B. Anthony, and Matilda Joslyn Gage, eds., *History of Woman Suffrage* (Rochester, N.Y.: Susan B. Anthony, 1887), 4:880–81.

2. 117 H.J., second spec. sess., 346, 411 (1938).

3. Elizabeth M. Cox, *Women State and Territorial Legislators, 1895–1995: A State-by-State Analysis with Rosters of 6,000 Women* (Jefferson, N.C.: McFarland, 1996), 237–41; Sherry S. Bell, ed., *Ohio Women*, 4th ed. (Columbus: Women's Services Division, Ohio Bureau of Employment Services, 1981), 46–47; 119 H.J. 5, 259–73, 345–46 (1941).

4. "Mrs. O'Neil, Served Legislature 20 Years," *Akron Beacon Journal*, 12 October 1970; Alma Kaufman, "Margaret A. Mahoney, Pioneer State Legislator, Cabinet Officer," *Cleveland Plain Dealer*, 28 March 1981.

5. Kaufman, "Mahoney."

6. Jennifer Ingersoll-Casey et al., "Members Demographics, 108th–121st General Assemblies," Ohio Legislative Service Commission research memorandum R-121-6008, October 1996, Ohio Legislative Service Commission library, Columbus.

7. Capitol Square Review and Advisory Board, "African-American Legislators," *George Washington Williams*, http://www.georgewashingtonwilliams.org.

8. Charles Kurfess, interview by author; Carl B. Stokes, *Promises of Power: A Political Autobiography* (New York: Simon and Schuster, 1973), 67–69; Freddie Charles Colston, "The Influence of Black Legislators in the Ohio House of Representatives" (Ph.D. diss., Ohio State University, 1972), 131–41; Charles William Chance, "Analysis of Legislative Agreements: The Case of Ohio" (Ph.D. diss., Ohio State University 1970), 187–89; C. J. McLin Jr., *Dad, I Served: The Autobiography of C. J. McLin, Jr., As Told to Minnie Fells, Johnson, Ph.D.*, ed. Lillie P. Howard and Sarah Byrn Rickman (Dayton, Ohio: Wright State University Office of Public Relations, 1998), 65–67; Vernal G. Riffe Jr. with Cliff Treyens, *Whatever's Fair: The Political Autobiography of Ohio House Speaker Vern Riffe* (Kent, Ohio: Kent State University Press, 2007), 80–82; Gongwer News Service, "Conference Report on Budget Accepted by the Senate, Rejected by the House," *Ohio Report*, 28 June 1977; Gongwer News Service, "House, Senate Approve $13 Billion Biennial Budget Bill," ibid., 29 June 1977.

9. Capitol Square Review and Advisory Board, "African-American Legislators;" Richard M. Peery, "David Albritton, '36 Olympic Medalist," *Cleveland Plain Dealer*, 18 May 1994; Lee Leonard, "Senior House Lawmakers Mallory, Rankin to Retire," *Columbus Dispatch*, 10 December 1993; Jim Siegel, "Ohio House Democrats Select Beatty to Replace Redfern as Minority Leader," 12 January 2006; Dan Williamson, "Big Ben," *Columbus Monthly*, July 1996, 124; Sandy Theis, "McLin Makes Ohio History—Zimmers Wins Praise as He Vacates Seat," *Dayton Daily News*, 17 November 1994.

10. *American National Biography*, s.v. "Stokes, Carl"; McLin, *Dad, I Served.*

11. Frederic C. Howe, *The Confessions of a Reformer* (New York: Scribner's, 1926), 161; Alan Rosenthal, *Legislative Life: People, Process, and Performance in the State* (New York: Harper and Row, 1981), 57.

12. Elizabeth Arias, "United States Life Tables, 2003," *National Vital Statistics Report* 54, no. 14 (2006): 31; Barbara J. Laughon, "Age Demographics for Members of the Ohio General Assembly 1969–1996 108th through 121st General Assemblies," Ohio Legisla-

tive Service Commission research memorandum, 21 October 1996, Ohio Legislative Service Commission library, Columbus.

13. Jim Provance, "Statehouse Strikes a Youthful Pose; Law Succeeds in Cleaning House, but Many Wind up in Senate," *Toledo Blade*, 28 January 2001; Gongwer News Service, "House Primary Fields Include Nine Former Members: Current Returnees Say Much Has Changed over Years," *Ohio Report*, 12 April 2006; Jennifer Drage Bowser, "The Effects of Legislative Term Limits," in *The Book of the States* 35 (Lexington, Ky.: Council of State Governments, 2003), 88.

14. Earl Everett Warner, "Law-Making through Interest Groups in Ohio: A Study of the Activities of the Ohio Chamber of Commerce, the Ohio Farm Bureau Federation and the Ohio State Federation of Labor in the Eighty-eighth General Assembly" (master's thesis, Ohio State University, 1929), between 17 and 18, tables I and II; ibid., 18; Richard Hofstadter, *The Age of Reform: From Bryan to F. D. R.* (New York: Vintage, 1955), 115–20; William Turner, *Ohio Farm Bureau Story, 1919–1979* (Columbus: Ohio Farm Bureau Federation, 1972).

15. Kermit L. Hall, *The Magic Mirror: Law in American History* (New York: Oxford University Press, 1989), 218–21; Robert Bocking Stevens, *Law School: Legal Education in America from the 1850s to the 1980s* (Chapel Hill: University of North Carolina Press, 1983); Ralph Harry Craft, "The Effects of Institutional Changes on Legislative Process and Performances: The Case of Ohio—1959 to 1974" (Ph.D. diss., Rutgers University, 1977), 41; John Mark Wegner, "Legislative Government in the Progressive Era: The Ohio House of Representatives, 1900–1911" (Ph.D. diss., Bowling Green State University, 1992), 237; U.S. Bureau of the Census, *Historical Statistics of the United States, Colonial Times to 1970*, bicentennial ed. (Washington, D.C.: U.S. Department of Commerce, Bureau of the Census, 1975), 1:380.

16. William K. Weisenberg, Statehouse Connection, *Ohio Lawyer*, March–April 1999, 24–25; ibid., July–August 1999, 28–29; ibid., March–April 2007, 22–23.

17. Vern Riffe, Speaking Out, *Ohioan*, March 1997, back cover.

18. "Legislature's a Little Slow," *Ohio State Journal*, 7 February 1915.

19. *American National Biography*, s.v. "Howe, Frederic Clemson."

20. *American National Biography*, s.v. "Taft, Robert Alphonso."

21. 124 O.L. 873 (1951); Haskell Short, "Sen. Pollock: From Horse 'N Buggy Era to Jet Age," *Columbus Citizen*, 20 February 1955.

22. David Arnold Johnston, "Politics and Policy in Ohio: A Study of Equal Rights, Pollution Control, and Unemployment Compensation Legislation" (Ph.D. diss., Ohio State University, 1972), 33–35; Alan Rosenthal, *Heavy Lifting: The Job of the American Legislature* (Washington, D.C.: CQ Press, 2004), 20; Provance, "Statehouse Strikes a Youthful Pose."

23. "'Citizen' Gus Kasch, Colorful Political Figure, Dies at 78," *Akron Beacon Journal*, 21 January 1946; 118 H.J. 204, 442, 887, 901 (1939); 115 H.J. 78 (1933).

24. Herbert R. Mengert, "House Blocks Vote on Appropriations; Consideration Deferred until Monday," *Cincinnati Enquirer*, 12 January 1933; 115 H.J. 1040–41 (1933);

115 H.J. (1st spec. sess.) 10 (1933); Charles Egger, "Where Shall He Sit, Is Problem for Gus Kasch and Solon Colleagues," *Columbus Citizen*, 8 February 1945.

25. Adrienne Bosworth, "The Legislators," *Columbus Monthly*, September 1982, 120; Adrienne Bosworth, "The Legislators: The Best and the Worst," *Columbus Monthly*, July 1978, 47; Lee Leonard, "Colorful Tony Calabrese Brought Flair and Laughter to Statehouse," *Columbus Dispatch*, 15 July 1991.

26. Bosworth, "Legislators" (1982), 49, 46; Adrienne Bosworth, "Rating the Legislators," *Columbus Monthly*, September 1984, 47.

27. Dan Williamson, "Rating the Legislators," *Columbus Monthly*, December 2003, 35–36.

28. Cliff Treyens, "Speaker Axes Two House Committee Chiefs over Votes," *Columbus Dispatch*, 15 January 1987; Lee Leonard, "Power at the Statehouse: The Riffe Reign," *Columbus Monthly*, August 1989, 56; Riffe, *Whatever's Fair*, 72, 82.

29. Riffe, Speaking Out, March 1997; Leonard, "Power," 56–57.

30. Keith McKnight and Andrew Zajac, "Ohio House GOP Minority Knuckles Under; Republican Leader Won't Confront His Friend, Speaker Vernal Riffe," *Akron Beacon Journal*, 28 May 1989; Jim Sweeney, "Can the GOP Dislodge Vern?" *Columbus Monthly*, May 1991, 94.

31. Vern Riffe, Speaking Out, *Ohioan*, May 1996, back cover; John C. Wahlke et al., *The Legislative System: Explorations in Legislative Behavior* (New York: Wiley, 1962), 56; Riffe, *Whatever's Fair*, 69.

32. 91 O.L. 182 (1894); Alexander Keyssar, *The Right to Vote: The Contested History of Democracy in America* (New York: Basic Books, 2000), 186.

33. Hoyt Landon Warner, *Progressivism in Ohio, 1897–1917* (Columbus: Ohio State University Press, 1964), 325–26; C. L. Martzolff, "Ohio: Changes in the Constitution," Notes on Current Legislation, *American Political Science Review* 6 (November 1912): 574; Clarence E. Walker, rptr., *Proceedings and Debates of the Constitutional Convention of the State of Ohio* (Columbus, 1912–13), 1:600–38; ibid., 2:2113.

34. Carrie Chapman Catt and Nettie Rogers Shuler, *Woman Suffrage and Politics: The Inner Story of the Suffrage Movement* (1926; rpt., Seattle: University of Washington Press, 1969), 189–93; Ellen Carol DuBois, *Harriot Stanton Blatch and the Winning of Woman Suffrage* (New Haven, Conn.: Yale University Press, 1997), 184, 323n1; 107 O.L. 7 (1917); 108 O.L., pt. 2, 1381 (1919); Ohio const. of 1851, art. 5, §§ 4, 6.

35. Keyssar, *Right to Vote*, 280–81.

36. 97 O.L. 185 (1904); 107 S.J. 755 (1917); 113 O.L. 307 (1929); Mayo Fesler, "New Election Code for Ohio," Notes and Events, *National Municipal Review* 18 (June 1929): 427–28.

37. 127 O.L. 305 (1977); Keyssar, *Right to Vote*, 312–14; Ted Virostko, "4 State Amendments Offered Ohio Voters," *Columbus Citizen-Journal*, 1 November 1977; Robert Ruth, "Dems Override Voter Signup Bill Vetoes," *Columbus Dispatch*, 16 July 1977.

38. Albert M. Sturm and Kaye M. Wright, "State Constitutional Developments during 1977," *National Civic Review* 67 (January 1978): 31; "Instant Vote Repealed," *Columbus Citizen-Journal*, 9 November 1977; 137 O.L. 3909 (1978).

39. National Voter Registration Act of 1993, 107 Stat. 77 (1993); 146 O.L. 549 (1995).

40. Michael E. McGerr, *The Decline of Popular Politics: The American North, 1865–1928* (New York: Oxford University Press, 1986), 205–9; Ben A. Arneson, "Non-Voting in a Typical Ohio Community," News and Notes, *American Political Science Review* 19 (November 1925): 816–25.

41. "County Sets New Record in Voting," *Ohio State Journal*, 11 November 1928; Paul Kleppner, *Who Voted? The Dynamics of Electoral Turnout, 1870–1980* (New York: Praeger, 1982); Thomas E. Patterson, *The Vanishing Voter: Public Involvement in an Age of Uncertainty* (New York: Knopf, 2002), 4–9.

42. Robert Dinkin, *Campaigning in America: A History of Election Practices* (New York: Greenwood, 1989), 95–96; Tom L. Johnson, *My Story*, ed. Elizabeth J. Hauser (New York: Huebsch, 1911), 202.

43. Douglas V. Shaw, "Interurbans in the Automobile Age: The Case of the Toledo, Port Clinton and Lakeside," *Ohio History* 103 (Summer–Autumn 1994): 125–26; O. K. Schimansky, "Campaigning by Trolley," *Ohio Illustrated Magazine* 1 (September 1906): 268–72; Johnson, *My Story*, 82–84; Warner, *Progressivism*, 133–34; Joseph Foraker, *Notes of a Busy Life* (Cincinnati: Steward and Kidd, 1916), 1:116–17.

44. "Legislator, 72, Won Place by Tramping," *Ohio State Journal*, 19 January 1927; William Merriman, "State Lawmakers out on the Campaign Trail," *Columbus Citizen-Journal*, 1 May 1972.

45. Dinkin, *Campaigning*, 102, 130–36; McGerr, *Decline*, 159–79; Louise Overacker, *Money in Politics* (1932; rpt., New York: Arno, 1974), 29.

46. Overacker, *Money*, 21.

47. Henry M. Hyde, "Has the Direct Primary Made Good?" *McClure's Magazine* 52 (August 1920): 16, 68; Overacker, *Money*, 91, 102, 125–26; William B. Saxbe with Peter D. Franklin, *I've Seen the Elephant: An Autobiography* (Kent, Ohio: Kent State University Press, 2000), 35, 40; Ohio Secretary of State, *Ohio Election Statistics, 1944*, 211–21; Ohio Secretary of State, *Ohio Election Statistics, 1952*, 228–37; http://www.sos.state.oh.us/sos/ElectionsVoter/Results2004.aspx.

48. Howe, *Confessions*, 91–92, 104–5.

49. Overacker, *Money*, 56–57; Howe, *Confessions*, 91–92, 104–5; "Two Candidates Spend Nothing, One 6 Cents," *Ohio State Journal*, 14 August 1920; "Kinkead Lists $193 Spent in Campaign," ibid., 17 August 1920; "Allread Wins over Page by 7780 Margin," ibid., 19 August 1920; "Byer's Unsuccessful Race Cost Him $654," ibid., 17 August 1924; "Resch Spent $1608.75 to Obtain His Licking," ibid., 13 November 1924; "Bartlett Spent $999 in Political Venture," ibid., 14 November 1924; "Thatcher in Report Lists $937 Expenses," ibid., 10 November 1926.

50. "Republicans Spent $26,175 in County; Democrats, $11,039," *Ohio State Journal*, 15 November 1924; "All Candidates File Financial Reports on Nov. 2 Campaign," ibid., 13 November 1926; 103 O.L. 698 (1913).

51. Stokes, *Promises*, 55–56; Frances McGovern, *Fun, Cheap, and Easy: My Life in Ohio Politics, 1949–1964* (Akron, Ohio: University of Akron Press, 2002), 20–32; Riffe, *Whatever's Fair*, 24; Dinkin, *Campaigning*, 161–64.

52. Robert Schmitz, interview with author, 1 August 2006; William Chavanne, interview with author, 7 November 2005; Riffe, *Whatever's Fair*, 49–50, 96–98, 102–6; Lee Leonard, "Pro among Pros," *State Legislatures*, November–December 1989, 13; Sweeney, "Can the GOP Dislodge Vern?" 93; Alan Rosenthal, *The Decline of Representative Democracy: Process, Participation, and Power in State Legislatures* (Washington, D.C.: CQ Press, 1998), 181–82; Wayne Roper, "Vern Riffe: Ohio's House Power," *Kiplinger Program Report* (Spring 1985): 9 (clipping in Ohio Legislative Service Commission files, Columbus, Ohio).

53. Riffe, *Whatever's Fair*, 107–8; Vern Riffe, Speaking Out, *Ohioan*, March 1995, back cover; 92 O.L. 123 (1896); 95 O.L. 77 (1902); Genevieve B. Gist, "Progressive Reform in a Rural Community: The Adams County Vote-Fraud Case," *Mississippi Valley Historical Review* 48 (June 1961): 60–78; 102 O.L. 321 (1911); 102 H.J. 702–7 (1911); 99 O.L. 23 (1908).

54. James Ripley, "Weak Laws Tempt Candidates," *Columbus Citizen-Journal*, 21 June 1973; Bradley A. Smith, "The Siren's Song: Campaign Finance Regulation and the First Amendment," *Journal of Law and Policy* 6, no. 1 (1997): 1–43; Fred Wertheimer and Susan Weiss Manes, "Campaign Finance Reform: A Key to Restoring the Health of Our Democracy," *Columbia Law Review* 94 (May 1994): 1126–59; 135 O.L. 12 (1974).

55. 135 O.L. 12 (1974).

56. 141 O.L. 3155 (1986); 142 O.L. 2635 (at 2777) (1987); 142 O.L. 3443 (1987); 142 O.L. 4093 (1987).

57. Charles Funderburk and Robert W. Adams, "Interest Groups in Ohio Politics," in *Ohio Politics*, ed. Alexander P. Lamis (Kent, Ohio: Kent State University Press, 1994), 315–17; Citizens League Research Institute Political Campaign Finance Task Force, *Campaign Finance in Ohio: An Introduction* (Cleveland: Citizens League Research Institute, 1990), 13.

58. UAW Local Union 1112 v. Philomena, 121 Ohio App. 3d 760, 770 (1998), appeal dismissed, 82 Ohio St. 3d 1450 (1998); editorial, "Paying to Play Ohio's Growing Legislative Art Form," *Akron Beacon Journal*, 11 July 1990; Citizens League Research Institute Political Campaign Finance Task Force, "Campaign Finance," 13; testimony of the League of Women Voters before Senate Task Force on Campaign Finance Reform, 15 February 1995, S.B. 8 bill file, Ohio Legislative Service Commission library; testimony of Bob Taft before Senate Task Force on Campaign Finance Reform, 15 February 1995, S.B. 9 bill file, Ohio Legislative Service Commission library.

59. 146 O.L. 7830 (1995); 146 O.L. 7902 (1995).

60. Paul Cohan, "Ohio Campaign Finance Law to Get First Real Test in 1998," *Stateline Midwest*, May 1997, rpt. in Paul Cohan, *The Price of Free Speech: Campaign Finance in the Midwest* (Lombard, Ill.: Midwestern Legislative Conference of the Council of State Governments, 1997), 19–20.

61. Ted Wendling, "Campaign-Finance Reform Bill OK'd; Session Ends in Rancor, Party-Line Vote," *Cleveland Plain Dealer*, 18 December 2004; Am. Sub. H.B. 1, 125th General Assembly, spec. sess. (2004).

62. Wendling, "Campaign-Finance Reform Bill"; Common Cause Ohio, "The Trojan Horse: Early Campaign Finance Reports Show That Ohio's New Campaign Finance Law Has Opened the Floodgates to Big Money," November 2, 2005, www.commoncause.org/ Ohio; Joe Hallett and Mark Niquette, "Issue 1 Is Lone Winner," *Columbus Dispatch*, 9 November 2005.

63. William B. Shaw, "Good Ballot Laws and Bad," *Outlook* 81 (December 9, 1905): 863–68; "New York Gets Reforms," *Outlook* 105 (December 27, 1913): 861; "Short Ballot in State and County Urged," *Ohio State Journal*, 21 February 1913; Waldo Schumaker, "Reform of the Election Law in Ohio" (master's thesis, Ohio State University, 1918), 44–53, 72–80.

64. Editorial, "Election Reforms Needed," *Columbus Citizen*, 19 November 1944.

65. William Edward Baldwin, ed., *Throckmorton's Ohio Code Annotated, Baldwin's 1948 Revision, Complete to January 1, 1948* (Cleveland: Banks-Baldwin, 1948), 1636, § 4785–99; "Straight Ballot Outlawed in Ohio," *New York Times*, 9 November 1949; "Ohio Battle Arises on Ballot Change," ibid., 10 November 1949.

66. 93 O.L. 277 (1898); J. C. Rupenthal, "Election Reforms: The Trend Toward Democracy," *American Lawyer* 14 (February 1906): 72; Roy G. Saltman, *The History and Politics of Voting Technology: In Quest of Integrity and Public Confidence* (New York: Palgrave Macmillan, 2006), 11–17; State ex rel. Karlinger v. Bd. of Deputy State Supervisors of Elections, 80 Ohio St. 471 (1909); Walker, *Proceedings*, 2:2106, 2113; Schumaker, "Reform," 32–33; 109 H.J. 304–5 (1921); State ex rel. Automatic Registering Mach. Co. v. Green, 121 Ohio St. 301 (1929).

67. "Election Reforms Needed," *Columbus Citizen*, 19 November 1944; Bees v. Gilronan, 116 N.E.2d 317 (C.P. 1953), appeal dismissed, 159 Ohio St. 156 (1953); Saltman, *Voting Technology*, 162; Daniel P. Tokaji, "Early Returns on Election Reform: Discretion, Disenfranchisement, and the Help America Vote Act," *George Washington Law Review* 73 (August 2005): 1221, 1240; Jim Provance, "Punch-Card Ballots Deemed Biased—Ruling against Ohio May Be Moot by May 2," *Toledo Blade*, 22 April 2006.

68. 106 H.J. 1404 (1915); 107 S.J. 38 (1917); 107 S.J. 677 (1917); 107 S.J. 756 (1917); 107 O.L. 52 (1917); 113 O.L. 307 (at 373–74) (1929); Sub. H.B. 234, 126th General Assembly, 2005.

69. 106 O.L. 552 (1915); 107 O.L. 607 (1917); 102 H.J. 702–5 (1911); James Thurber, *The Thurber Album: A New Collection of Pieces about People* (New York: Simon and Schuster, 1952), 154–63.

70. *Ohio State Journal*, 2 November 1920; editorial, "Radio and Elections," ibid., 10 November 1930.

Chapter 15: Living in Columbus

1. "Doors of Famous Old Neil House to Be Closed Forever Saturday; Last Official Celebration Takes Place Today," *Columbus Citizen*, 20 March 1923.

2. Marc Lee Raphael, *Jews and Judaism in a Midwestern Community: Columbus, Ohio, 1840–1975* (Columbus: Ohio Historical Society, 1979), 89, 241–42; Ed Lentz, *Columbus: The Story of a City* (Charleston, S.C.: Arcadia, 2003), 111, 113.

3. Walter W. Liggett, "Ohio—Lawless and Unashamed," *Plain Talk*, July 1930, 13.

4. George Sessions Perry, "Columbus, Ohio," *Saturday Evening Post*, 3 May 1952, 22, 98–99; John Gunther, *Inside U.S.A.* (New York: Harper and Bros., 1947), 450–51.

5. Raphael, *Jews*, 355; Lentz, *Columbus*, 150; Neal R. Peirce, *The Megastates of America: People, Politics, and Power in the the Great States* (New York: Norton, 1972), 329–30.

6. Francis R. Aumann and Harvey Walker, *The Government and Administration of Ohio* (New York: Crowell, 1956), 338–39; 123 S.J. 473 (1949); 123 H.J. 609 (1949); 124 H.J. 9 (1951); Frances McGovern, *Fun, Cheap, and Easy: My Life in Ohio Politics, 1949–1964* (Akron, Ohio: University of Akron Press, 2002), 38–39, 42.

7. Lentz, *Columbus*, 97–98, 113; Ohio Legislative Service Commission, *A Guidebook for Ohio Legislators* [1st ed.] (Columbus: Ohio Legislative Service Commission, 1970), 83–84.

8. McGovern, *Fun, Cheap, and Easy*, 39; "Hotels Hike Rates for Solons," Columbus Calling, *Columbus Citizen*, 2 December 1956; William B. Saxbe with Peter D. Franklin, *I've Seen the Elephant: An Autobiography* (Kent, Ohio: Kent State University Press, 2000), 40.

9. Ohio Legislative Service Commission, *Guidebook* (1970), 83–84; David Lore, "Ohio Legislators Live in Hotels, Apartments, Trailers," *Columbus Dispatch*, 3 January 1971; Lee Leonard, "Winding down after a Tough Day at the Statehouse," *Columbus Monthly*, May 1983, 82.

10. Cliff Treyens, "Statehouse Hangouts 1995," *Ohioan*, April 1995, 10–14; Leonard, "Winding Down," 79–90; Keith McNamara, e-mail to author, 17 July 2006; Vernal G. Riffe Jr. with Cliff Treyens, *Whatever's Fair: The Political Autobiography of Ohio House Speaker Vern Riffe* (Kent, Ohio: Kent State University Press, 2007), 78–79; Alan Rosenthal, *The Third House: Lobbyists and Lobbying in the States*, 2d ed. (Washington, D.C.: CQ Press, 2001), 95–96.

11. Abraham Hegler to Dolly Hegler, 17 February 1839, Abraham Hegler Papers, Ohio Historical Society; W. D. Howells, "In an Old-Time State Capital," *Harper's Monthly Magazine* 129 (September 1914): 593; Elizabeth L. Plummer, "Tourism at the Ohio Penitentiary," *Timeline* 21 (January–February 2004): 18–25; "Trip to Prison Farm Alters Solons' View," *Ohio State Journal*, 20 January 1921; Douglas McCormick, "Orient Facility Tour 'Lonely,'" *Columbus Citizen-Journal*, 22 March 1973; James Ripley, "Implication Irks Legislators," ibid., 23 March 1973; "Tempers Short as Code Bill Hampers Work of Assembly," Columbus Calling, *Columbus Citizen*, 8 February 1953.

12. Hal Conefry, "Revenue Bill in Deadlock," *Columbus Citizen*, 16 February 1941; "Word Is Lobbying Suites to Be Open for Farewells," Columbus Calling, ibid., 19 July 1953; Hal Conefry, "Ohio Legislators, Lobbyists Descend on Columbus as 101st Session Nears," ibid., 1 January 1955; Columbus Calling, ibid., 10 April 1955; "Sandwiching Sandwiches," Columbus Calling, ibid., 16 June 1957; "Ugly Entertainment Rumors," Columbus Calling, ibid., 24 May 1959; Frederic C. Howe, *The Confessions of a Reformer* (New York: Scribner's, 1926), 167.

13. Randolph C. Downes, *The Rise of Warren Gamaliel Harding, 1865–1920* (Columbus: Ohio State University Press, 1970), 75–77.

14. "One Legislator Is Charged Just a Mere $30 by Marge," Columbus Calling, *Columbus Citizen*, 2 August 1959; Riffe, *Whatever's Fair*, 42; Columbus Calling, *Columbus Citizen*, 1 February 1953; Charles Funderburk, "The Legislator," in C. J. McLin Jr., *Dad, I Served: The Autobiography of C. J. McLin, Jr.*, ed. Lillie P. Howard and Sarah Byrn Rickman (Dayton, Ohio: Wright State University Office of Public Relations, 1998), 135.

15. "Sandwiching Sandwiches"; Vinton McVicker, "Legislators, Cleveland Better Acquainted Now," Eyes on Politics, ibid., 31 August 1947; "Solons Asea," Columbus Calling, ibid., 27 June 1954.

16. Hal Conefry, "Anti-Numbers Bill Revived in House for Early Action," *Columbus Citizen*, 22 April 1943; Ted S. Alexander, "Absenteeism Slows Work of Legislature," ibid., 19 April 1949; "Light Week for Solons," Columbus Calling, ibid., 12 April 1953; "Legislators Have Dodged All the Major Issues," Columbus Calling, ibid., 10 April 1955; "If You Must Meet, May as Well Be the Eve of OSU Grid Game," Columbus Calling, ibid., 7 August 1955; Hal Conefry and Rip Manning, "Baseball Season Openers Slow Down Legislature," ibid., 16 April 1957; Jim Siegel, "Ethics Failings Get Light Penalty," *Columbus Dispatch*, 14 December 2005.

17. 101 H.J. 402 (1910); "Solons Stage a Weird Game," *Columbus Citizen*, 5 May 1911; 102 H.J. 484 (1911); Columbus Calling, *Columbus Citizen-Journal*, 4 April 1970; 136 S.J. 1542 (1976); "House Members Play Ball," *Dayton Daily News*, 18 June 2001.

18. 98 H.J. 828–43 (1906); 106 H.J. 308–9 (1915); 115 H.J 382–83, 485 (1933).

19. William H. Newton, "Ohio Senators and Clerk Bateman Lose Elevator, but Gain Air Conditioning and a Rug," Eyes on Politics, *Columbus Citizen*, 8 June 1941; 123 S.J. 1202 (1949); 124 O.L. 804 (1951); Hal Conefry, Eyes on Politics, *Columbus Citizen*, 21 December 1952; editorial, "Air Conditioning and Fire Traps," ibid., 3 June 1953.

20. C. W. Thomas, "Mumble—Shout: Democracy at Work," *Columbus Citizen*, 13 July 1953.

21. Ibid.

22. James J. Downing, "Ohio Senators Pampered; Representatives Rough It," *Columbus Citizen*, 9 January 1947; Ohio Legislative Service Commission, *Legislative Services, Facilities, and Procedures*, Staff Research Report No. 81 (Columbus: Ohio Legislative Service Commission, 1966), 41–42.

23. 94 S.J. 96–97 (1900); 96 S.J. 726 (1904); 102 H.J. 1217–18 (1911); 103 H.J. 96, 125 (1913); 106 S.J. 841 (1915); 102 S.J. 9 (1911); 107 H.J. 20 (1917); 108 H.J. 41 (1919); 103 S.J., app., 195–99 (1913); Schooley Caldwell Associates, *The Ohio Statehouse Master Plan* (Columbus: n.p., 1989), v.

24. McGovern, *Fun, Cheap, and Easy*, 48; Ohio Legislative Service Commission, *Legislative Services*, 34–33; James Thurber, *The Thurber Album: A New Collection of Pieces about People* (New York: Simon and Schuster, 1952), 120–21.

25. David Johnston, "Testimony of David Johnston, Director, Ohio Legislative Service Commission, re H.B. 118, to State Government Committee, Feb. 8, 1971," in vertical file "Buildings—LSC Quarters," Ohio Legislative Service Commission library, Columbus.

26. James K. Mercer, *Ohio Legislative History*, vol. 4 (Columbus: F. J. Heer, 1922?), 485; Bob Waldron, "Rotunda Refurbished," *Columbus Dispatch Magazine*, 29 January 1967; "Rhodes Opposes Plan to Remodel Statehouse," *Cleveland Plain Dealer*, 14 January 1976; Robert Ruth, "Lawmakers Getting Remodeled Offices," *Columbus Dispatch*, 13 December 1978; Duane St. Clair, "Statehouse Annex Slated for Face Lift," ibid., 19 February 1989; Lee Leonard, "The Pols and Their $130 Million Hideout," *Columbus Monthly*, April 1989, 26.

27. 123 S.J. 473 (1949); 125 H.J. 1092 (1953); "Representatives, Not Senators Hold Capitol Lawn Parking Title," *Columbus Citizen*, 15 May 1953; Ralph H. Burke, Inc., *Report on Underground Garage at Broad and High Streets for City of Columbus, Ohio* (Columbus: n.p., 1954); 126 O.L. 12 (1955); "First Earth Is Moved for Statehouse Parking Garage," *Columbus Dispatch*, 21 June 1963; "Rhodes Pushes Bond Issue, Outlines Building Needs," *Columbus Citizen-Journal*, 17 November 1964.

28. Jane Ware, "The Statehouse, God Bless It," *Ohio Magazine*, July 1986, 68.

29. Ibid., 24–25, 66–72.

30. Richard H. Finan, "The Restoration Project," *OhioGrocer*, Summer 1996, 33; Arnold Berke, "This Is Their Jewel," *Preservation*, September–October 1996, 84; Schooley Caldwell Associates, *Statehouse Master Plan*.

31. Alan Johnson, "Statehouse Move Will Be an Adventure," *Columbus Dispatch*, 22 November 1992; Alan Johnson, "Renovation Sends Voinovich Packing," ibid., 4 March 1993; Alan Johnson, "Grand Opening Preservationists Happy with Ohio Senate Building Renovation," ibid., 7 March 1993; Lee Leonard, "Senate OKs Solid Waste Bill in 'Swan-Song Session,'" ibid., 1 April 1993; Lee Leonard, "Both Parties Try to Salve Wounds of Speaker Fees," ibid., 29 September 1993.

32. Ohio Legislative Service Commission, *A Guidebook for Ohio Legislators*, 9th ed. (Columbus: Ohio Legislative Service Commission, 2005), 130–31; Finan, "Restoration," 33; Berke, "Jewel," 76–85.

33. 127 S.J. 128, 301, 324 (1957); "Pigeons Got Lot of Help," Columbus Calling, *Columbus Citizen*, 21 April 1957; 128 O.L. 625 (1959); Robert Ruth, "Audio Ruse Rousts Birds from Statehouse," *Columbus Dispatch*, 8 January 2006.

34. Alan Johnson, "20,000 Visitors Come Away Awed," *Columbus Dispatch*, 8 July 1996.

35. Lee Leonard, "General Assembly Going Home to 'New' Statehouse," *Columbus Dispatch*, 5 January 1997.

Chapter 16: Glasnost and Perestroika

1. 117 S.J. 117, 131, 173, 216 (1937); 117 H.J. 374, 437, 439, 513, 572 (1937); 117 O.L. 77 (1937); David M. Gold, "Rites of Passage: The Evolution of the Legislative Process in Ohio, 1799–1937," *Capital University Law Review* 30, no. 4 (2002): 652–55.

2. Edward Wakefield Hughes, *Hughes' American Parliamentary Guide Prepared for Ohio General Assembly: The Process of Lawmaking* (Columbus: F. J. Heer, 1922), 376, 380; 115

H.J. 79 (1933); George B. Marshall, "Life History of a Bill in the Ohio Legislature," *Ohio State Law Journal* 11 (Autumn 1950): 450–51, 453.

3. 98 O.L. 412 (1906); 97 S.J. 260 (1906); 97 H.J. 473 (1906); Steven H. Steinglass and Gino J. Scarselli, *The Ohio State Constitution: A Reference Guide* (Westport, Conn.: Praeger, 2004), 357.

4. 135 S.J. 296–309, 311–18 (1973); Bob Schmitz, interview with author, 1 August 2006; Gold, "Rites," 648n142; Ohio const. of 1851, am. 1973, art. 2, § 15.

5. State ex rel. Dix v. Celeste, 11 Ohio St. 3d 141 (1984); State ex rel. Franklin County Bd. of Elections, 62 Ohio St. 3d 145 (1991); In re Nowak, 104 Ohio St. 3d 466 (2004); State ex rel. Ohio Acad. of Trial Lawyers v. Sheward, 86 Ohio St. 3d 451, 533 (1999) (Lundburg Stratton, J., dissenting); 151 S.J., 26 April 2005 (www.legislature.state. oh.us/Journals.cfm).

6. Lee Leonard, "Today's Takeover Nothing Like 'Six-Day War,'" *Columbus Dispatch*, 9 January 1995; Maloney v. Rhodes, 1975 Ohio App. LEXIS 8484 (1975), rev'd, 45 Ohio St. 2d 319 (1976).

7. Leonard, "Six-Day War"; Maloney v. Rhodes, 1975 Ohio App. LEXIS 8484.

8. Maloney v. Rhodes, 45 Ohio St. 2d 319 (1976).

9. State ex rel. Smith v. Ocasek, 1975 Ohio App. LEXIS 7189; Ohio const. of 1851, am. 1979, art. 3, § 1b.

10. State ex rel. City Loan and Savings Co. of Wapakoneta v. Moore, 124 Ohio St. 256 (1931); Riffe, *Whatever's Fair*, 170.

11. Hal Conefry, "Flood of Legislation Is Expected Monday as Deadline Is Reached," *Columbus Citizen*, 11 February 1951; State ex rel. Grendell v. Davidson, 86 Ohio St. 3d 629 (1999).

12. Hughes, *Parliamentary Guide*, 29–30, 99, 457–58.

13. 119 S.J. 817–18 (1941); Thomas Suddes, "Ohio Lawmakers Pass $22.6 Billion Noneducation Budget," *Cleveland Plain Dealer*, 29 June 1999; State ex rel. Grendell v. Davidson, 86 Ohio St. 3d 629 (1999).

14. Hughes, *Parliamentary Guide*, 39–40; 97 H.J. 5–14 (1906); 97 S.J. 4–8 (1906); 123 S.J. 4–5 (1949); Gongwer News Service, "House Welcomes 31 New Members during Opening Ceremony," *Ohio Report*, 2 January 2007, www.gongwer-oh.com.

15. Karl B. Pauly, "Minor Posts in Lower Body Are Named by Republicans," *Ohio State Journal*, 8 January 1935; 116 H.J. 10–16 (1935).

16. 103 H.J. 21, 894, 1358–62 (1913); 102 H.J. 164 (1911); 106 H.J. 123 (1913); 114 H.J. 48 (1931).

17. Hughes, *Parliamentary Guide*, 377–78; Marshall, "Life," 450; Frances McGovern, *Fun, Cheap, and Easy: My Life in Ohio Politics, 1949–1964* (Akron, Ohio: University of Akron Press, 2002), 49.

18. H. W. Dodds, *Procedure in the State Legislatures* (Philadelphia: Amercian Academy of Political and Social Sciences, 1918), 69; Harvey Walker, *The Legislative Process: Law Making in the United States* (New York: Ronald, 1948), 261; Gongwer News Service, Report No. 15, 5 February 1935, 1, www.gongwer-oh.com.

19. Walker, *Legislative Process*, 266–67; 44 H.J. 250 (1846); 45 H.J. 83 (1846); 119 H.J. 526 (1941).

20. Douglas W. Jones, "Technologists as Political Reformers: Lessons from the Early History of Voting Machines," paper presented at the Society for the History of Technology Annual Meeting, Las Vegas, Nevada, 13 October 2006, 2–3; 76 H.J. 923, 925 (1880); 90 H.J. 270–71, 994 (1893); Robert Luce, *Legislative Procedure: Parliamentary Practices and the Course of Business in the Framing of Statutes* (Boston: Houghton Mifflin, 1922), 376–79; 113 O.L. 794 (1929), 113 H.J. 23, 263 (1929), 113 S.J. 472–73 (1929); 122 H.J. 885 (1947).

21. "House Will Resemble a Pinball Machine," Columbus Calling, *Columbus Citizen*, 2 January 1955; Richard L. Maher, Hal Conefry, and Don Strouse, "Ohio Solons Face Rough Law Session," ibid., 4 January 1955; William Merriman, "Capital Punishment Repeal Rejected," *Columbus Citizen-Journal*, 3 March 1972.

22. Jane Ware, "The Statehouse, God Bless It," *Ohio Magazine*, July 1986, 67; 134 H.J. 849 (1971).

23. Richard G. Zimmerman, *Plain Dealing: Ohio Politics and Journalism Viewed from the Press Gallery* (Kent, Ohio: Kent State University Press, 2006), 29; 106 H.J. 58 (1915); 139 S.J. 29 (1981); 140 S.J. 6–7, 96 (1983); 150 S.J. 32 (2003).

24. Harvey Walker, *Law Making in the United States* (New York: Ronald, 1934), 207; Walker, *Legislative Process*, 232; Dodds, *Procedure* 53.

25. Walker, *Law Making*, 325–27; Walker, *Legislative Process*, 234–35; 109 H.J. 31 (1921); 102 H.J. 39, 67–68 (1911); 111 H.J. 1012 (1925); Roscoe Baker, "The Reference Committee of the Ohio House of Representatives," American Government and Politics, *American Political Science Review* 34 (April 1940): 306–10; Earl Everett Warner, "Law-Making through Interest Groups in Ohio: A Study of the Activities of the Ohio Chamber of Commerce, the Ohio Farm Bureau Federation and the Ohio State Federation of Labor in the Eighty-eighth General Assembly" (master's thesis, Ohio State University, 1929), 56.

26. Johnston, "Politics and Policy," 23; Charles Egger, Politics, *Columbus Citizen*, 16 May 1945; Eyes on Politics, ibid., 2 March 1947; Hal Conefry, "Solons Refuse to Force Measures from Committee," ibid., 18 March 1951; 127 H.J. 1315–16 (1957).

27. 134 S.J. 202–3 (1971); 136 S.J. 14 (1975); 138 S.J. 690–91 (1979); 140 S.J. 96 (1983); 141 S.J. 180, 183 (1985); 143 S.J. 109–10 (1989); 150 S.J. 32, 35 (2003).

28. 124 S.J. 342–43 (1951); Don Strouse, "Senate Expected to Okay Turnpike Officials Today," *Columbus Citizen*, 29 March 1951; Vernal G. Riffe Jr. with Cliff Treyens, *Whatever's Fair: The Political Autobiography of Ohio House Speaker Vern Riffe* (Kent, Ohio: Kent State University Press, 2007), 74–75.

29. Luce, *Legislative Procedure*, 110, 153, 163–64, 195.

30. Emmet O'Neal, "Distrust of State Legislatures—The Cause; The Remedy," *North American Review* 199 (May 1914): 693–94.

31. 109 H.J. 7 (1921); 99 H.J. 6 (1908); 102 H.J. 7 (1911); 114 H.J. 8 (1931).

32. "House Votes to Bar Public from Committee Meetings," *Ohio State Journal*, 21 January 1931; 113 H.J. 849 (1929); 114 H.J. 54 (1931); 115 H.J. 1270 (1933); Riffe, *Whatever's Fair*, 65–66.

33. 118 S.J. 53 (1939); William Merriman, "GOP Majority Pushing Legislative Secrecy Rule," *Columbus Citizen-Journal*, 12 January 1971; Tom LaRochelle, "Secrecy Voted in Legislature," ibid., 13 January 1971; Charles Egger, "Stay in the Open with Us, Fellows," ibid., 16 January 1971; Dennis J. Willard and Mike Rutledge, "Lawmakers Giving Lobbyists More Say," *Lancaster Eagle-Gazette*, 22 July 1992; Ohio const. of 1851, art. 2, § 13; 145 O.L. 3215 (1993).

34. 101 H.J. 6 (1910); 114 H.J. 8 (1937); 112 H.J. 7 (1927); 102 H.J. 7 (1911); 109 H.J. 6–7 (1921); 119 H.J. 6 (1941); 110 H.J. 7–8 (1923).

35. 117 H.J. 970, 989 (1937); 123 H.J. 49–50, 145–46 (1949); Hal Conefry, "Bill to Hike Solons' Pay Popular—at Least With Solons," *Columbus Citizen*, 21 January 1951.

36. 102 H.J. 1246 (1911); 102 S.J. 827–28 (1911); 114 H.J. 53 (1931); 114 S.J. 32–33 (1931); 124 H.J. 36–37 (1951); 124 S.J. 24 (1951); 134 H.J. 55 (1971); 134 S.J. 201 (1971); 135 O.L., pt. 1, 1860 (1973); 137 O.L. 1405 (1978); 140 O.L. 4937 (1984); 141 H.J. 24–25 (1985); 146 S.J. 13 (1995); Riffe, *Whatever's Fair*, 54–55.

37. 151 H.J., 11 January 2005 (www.legislature.state.oh.us/Journals.cfm); 151 S.J., 6 January 2005 (www.legislature.state.oh.us/Journals.cfm); www.senate.state.oh.us/committees/; www.legislature.state.oh.us/Committee/special_committees.pdf.

38. 111 H.J. 410 (1925); Herbert R. Mengert, "Ohio House Cuts Five Millions, for Highways, from Budget; Senate Passes 'Gas' Tax Bill," *Cincinnati Enquirer*, 11 March 1925; 115 H.J., pt. 2, 2d spec. sess. 346–50, 355–62, 364–66 (1934); Marshall, "Life," 454; Hughes, *Parliamentary Guide*, 108n1, 109n1.

39. 116 O.L. 612, 614, 625 (1935); 116 H.J. 98–99, 204–5, 208–9 (1935); 116 S.J. 373, 387, 537–39 (1935); David A. Johnston, "The Ohio Legislative Service Commission—A Nonpolitical Political Institution," memorandum P-116-8511, 31 January 1986, Ohio Legislative Service Commission library, 5.

40. 108 O.L. 1338, 539 (1919); 109 O.L. 618, 631 (1921); 110 O.L. 644 (1923); 113 O.L. 784 (1929); 111 S.J. 140–41, 161 (1925); 115 O.L. 678 (1933).

41. 118 H.J. 403–4 (1939); 118 S.J. 113–14, 192, 345–46, 363, 371–72, 379, 388, 398 (1939); editorial, "Forget It," *Columbus Citizen*, 30 March 1939; William H. Newton, "Fate of Red Hunt Rests in Senate Group," ibid., 31 March 1939; editorial, "The Red Hunt Dies," ibid., 4 April 1939.

42. 121 H.J. 1059 (1945); Warren P. Hill, "A Critique of Recent Ohio Anti-Subversive Legislation," *Ohio State Law Journal* 14 (Autumn 1953): 439–93; James Truett Selcraig, *The Red Scare in the Midwest, 1945–1955: A State and Local Study* (Ann Arbor, Mich.: UMI Research Press, 1982), 30–35.

43. Hill, "Critique," 444–49; Selcraig, *Red Scare*, 33–38; 124 O.L. 881 (1951); 124 O.L. 795 (1951); 125 O.L. 10, 675 (1953).

44. "Students Rip Spas to Shreds," *Columbus Citizen-Journal*, 5 July 1965; "Guardsmen Leave as Rioting Ends," ibid., 6 July 1965; 131 S.J. 812 (1965); 131 O.L. 1627 (1965).

45. Memorandum, Legislative Service Commission to Criminal Codes Study Committee, 16 November 1966, Select Committee to Investigate Campus Disturbances files, State Archives Series 4195, Box 2951, Folder 17, Ohio Historical Society, Columbus; 132 O.L. 2802 (1968); Steve Bulkley, "OSU Students Swarm to Strike Scene," *Columbus*

Dispatch, 5 October 1967; 132 S.J. 1377, 1564, 1669–70 (1968); 132 H.J. 2130–31, 2181 (1968); 132 O.L. 2394 (1968).

46. 133 O.L. 3022 (1970); 133 S.J. 1522–23 (1970); 133 H.J. 2207–8, 2255–57 (1970).

47. Interim Report of the Select Committee to Investigate Campus Disturbances to the 108th General Assembly Pursuant to Am. Sub. S. Con. R. No. 34, 5 October 1970, Ohio Legislative Service Commission library, 2–3, 27, 30; David Lore, "University Reforms Urged," *Columbus Dispatch*, 5 October 1970.

48. Second Interim Report of the Select Committee to Investigate Campus Disturbances to the 109th Ohio General Assembly Pursuant to Amended Sub. Senate Concurrent Resolution No. 34 as Adopted June 1, 1970 (no date–1970?); *Proposed Ohio Criminal Code*, Final Report of the Technical Committee to Study Ohio Criminal Laws and Procedures (Columbus: Ohio Legislative Service Commission, 1971), 143–46, 221–22; minutes of Criminal Law Technical Committee meetings, Criminal Law Revision Study, vol. 4, minutes of 17 July 1968 and 14 August 1968, Ohio Legislative Service Commission library; 134 O.L 2102 (1971); "Senate Approves Use of Patrol at Riots," *Columbus Dispatch*, 13 November 1971.

49. 119 S.J. 222 (1941).

50. 117 H.J. 91–93 (1937).

51. Columbus Calling, *Columbus Citizen*, 14 June 1953; 134 H.J. 57 (1971); 139 S.J. 30 (1981).

52. Warner, "Law-Making through Interest Groups," 20.

53. 114 H.J. 54, 111 (1931); 114 S.J. 33 (1931); 117 H.J. 40 (1937); 124 H.J. 38 (1951).

54. Donald Axelrod, "Staffing Needs of the Ohio Legislature," app. to Ohio Legislative Service Commission, *Legislative Services, Facilities, and Procedures*, Staff Research Report No. 81 (Columbus: Ohio Legislative Service Commission, 1966), 93–94; John Burns, *The Sometime Governments: A Critical Study of the 50 American Legislatures* (New York: Bantam, 1971), 104–9.

55. C. W. Chance and Higdon C. Roberts, "Staffing Legislative Standing Committees: The Ohio Experience," *State Government* 43 (Winter 1970): 31–38.

56. Burns, *Sometime Governments*, 279–82; 137 O.L. 487 (1977).

57. 146 H.J. 69 (1995).

58. Ralph G. Wright, *Inside the Statehouse: Lessons from the Speaker* (Washington, D.C.: CQ Press, 2005), 29; McGovern, *Fun*, 62.

59. 111 H.J. 514–15 (1925); 111 S.J. 355–56 (1925); 124 H.J. 22, 33–34, 103–4, 125–27, 158–59, 165 (1951); 131 H.J. 1877–78 (1965); 133 S.J. 1051 (1969).

Chapter 17: The Transformation of Legislative Life

1. Donna Pope to Mary Fassingeo, 12 January 1979, Donna Pope Papers, Ohio Historical Society.

2. 94 H.J., app., 3–5 (1900); 94 S.J., app., 3 (1900); 1940 Ohio House of Representatives and Ohio Senate rosters; H. W. Dodds, *Procedure in the State Legislatures* (Philadelphia: American Academy of Political and Social Sciences, 1918), 100; 98 H.J. 6–7 (1906); Frederic C. Howe, *The Confessions of a Reformer* (New York: Scribner's, 1926), 161.

3. William B. Saxbe with Peter D. Franklin, *I've Seen the Elephant: An Autobiography* (Kent, Ohio: Kent State University Press, 2000), 39; S. Gale Lowrie, "The Making of Our Laws," *University of Cincinnati Law Review* 17 (March 1948): 144–49.

4. 132 O.L., 11 (1968); Ohio const. of 1851, am. 1973, art. 2, § 14.

5. 26 U.S.C. § 162(h); Jim Siegel, "'Skeletons' Keep Tax Break Rolling," *Columbus Dispatch*, 25 December 2007.

6. Gongwer News Service, *Ohio Report*, 18 March 1985; 141 S.J. S4, S6 (1985).

7. John P. Green, *Fact Stranger Than Fiction: Seventy-five Years of a Busy Life, with Reminiscences of Many Great and Good Men and Women* (Cleveland: Riehl, 1920), 173; Robert A. Taft, *The Papers of Robert A. Taft: Vol. I, 1889–1939*, ed. Clarence E. Wunderlin Jr. (Kent, Ohio: Kent State University Press, 1997), 302; Edward Ivan Sidlow, "Professionalism in a State Legislature: The Case of Ohio" (Ph.D. diss., Ohio State University, 1979), 81–82; Pope to Fassingeo.

8. Vernal G. Riffe Jr. with Cliff Treyens, *Whatever's Fair: The Political Autobiography of Ohio House Speaker Vern Riffe* (Kent, Ohio: Kent State University Press, 2007), 42; Charles Egger, Politics, *Columbus Citizen*, 16 May 1945; Tim Schaffer, "Sen. Schaffer's Office Handles Many Constituent Services," *Lancaster Eagle-Gazette*, 3 February 2007.

9. "Legislative Compensation," *Cincinnati Post*, 22 February 1999; Linda D. Taylor, "The Ohio Legislator: Part-Time or Full-Time?" policy paper, Ohio State University, 1974, 12; "What Happened to the 'Citizen' in the 'Citizen Legislature?'" *State Legislatures*, July–August 2003, 7; Alan Rosenthal, *Heavy Lifting: The Job of the American Legislature* (Washington, D.C.: CQ Press, 2004), 21–22; Connie Schultz, "Linked by Love, Social Issues Union Activist, State Legislator a Fiery Pair, but Ideal Match," *Cleveland Plain Dealer*, 2 March 1997.

10. Jim Siegel, "Many Ohio Legislators Holding Other Jobs," *Columbus Dispatch*, 9 May 2005; 98 O.L. 287 (1906); "Wow! Here's a Solon Who Seeks Salary of $2500," *Ohio State Journal*, 6 May 1911; 106 H.J. 378–79 (1915).

11. 114 O.L., pt. 2, 3d spec. sess. 65 (1932); State ex rel. Boyd v. Tracy, 128 Ohio St. 242 (1934); 116 O.L. 419 (1935); Frank H. Howe, "Legislator's Pay," letter to the editor, *Ohio State Journal*, 30 March 1934.

12. State ex rel. Harbage v. Ferguson, 68 Ohio App. 189, appeal dismissed, 138 Ohio St. 617 (1941); 124 H.J. 65 (1951); 124 O.L. 825 (1951); Belle Zeller, *American State Legislatures: Report of the Committee on American Legislatures, American Political Science Association* (New York: Thomas Y. Crowell, 1954), 76–78; Frances McGovern, *Fun, Cheap, and Easy: My Life in Ohio Politics, 1949–1964* (Akron, Ohio: University of Akron Press, 2002), 51; 126 O.L. 194 (1955); Hal Conefry, "Bill to Hike Solons' Pay Popular —at Least With Solons," *Columbus Citizen*, 21 January 1951; "Hotels Hike Rates for Solons," Columbus Calling, ibid., 2 December 1956; U.S. Bureau of the Census, *Historical*

Statistics of the United States, Colonial Times to 1970, bicentennial ed. (Washington, D.C.: U.S. Department of Commerce, Bureau of the Census, 1975), 1:166–67, 175–76.

13. Editorial, "There's Work To Do, Ohio Legislators," *Columbus Citizen*, 25 May 1959.

14. "Absentees Lashed at House Session in Verbal Battle," *Ohio State Journal*, 19 March 1927; "40 House Members Absent Today," *Columbus Citizen*, 30 April 1943; Hal Conefry, "15 Ohio Legislators Won't Answer Next Roll Call," ibid., 9 January 1944; Hal Conefry, "Fair Employment Bill Will Bring Fireworks," ibid., 20 March 1949; "An Early Fade," *Columbus Calling*, ibid., 27 March 1955; "Legislators Have Dodged All the Major Issues," *Columbus Calling*, ibid., 10 April 1955; O. F. Knippenburg, "Your Legislator: He's Earning More, Working Less," *Columbus Citizen-Journal*, 26 March 1965; "Legislators Touchy about Being Tagged Chronic Absentees," *Columbus Calling*, ibid., 3 April 1965; Haskell Short, "Ohio's Legislators Off to Slow Start," ibid., 2 February 1973; "Legislator's Attendance Improves—Slightly," ibid., 4 February 1980.

15. Vinton McVicker, "Freshmen Members of Assembly Air Views on More Efficient Legislating," Eyes on Politics, *Columbus Citizen*, 15 July 1951; "'Can't Hardly Get Them . . . '," *Columbus Calling*, 27 February 1955; Sidlow, "Professionalism," 97–99; Dennis J. Willard and Mike Rutledge, "A Look at the Ohio Legislature," *Lancaster Eagle-Gazette*, 19–22 July 1992; Alan Johnson, "State Representative Is Headed for Saudi Arabia," *Columbus Dispatch*, 3 January 1991; Lee Leonard, "Duty Calls Lawmaker to Service Overseas," ibid., 12 December 2003; Jim Siegel, "Lawmaker Returns from Guard Duty in Middle East," ibid., 7 December 2005; Aaron Marshall, "State Rep. Josh Mandel Heads Back to Iraq with Marines for 8 Months," *Cleveland Plain Dealer*, 20 July 2007; Jon Craig, "Duty Calls, Rep. Bubp Answers," *Cincinnati Enquirer*, 7 November 2007.

16. 130 O.L. pt 2 5 (1964); 137 O.L. 1405 (1978); Taylor, "Ohio Legislator," 53; 140 O.L. 1937 (1984); 142 O.L. 1639 (1988); Economic History Association, "How Much Is That?" *EH.Net*, http://www.eh.net/hmit; 148 O.L. 7756 (2000).

17. George B. Galloway, *History of the House of Representatives*, 2d ed., rev. Sidney Wise (New York: Crowell, 1976), 135–40.

18. "Republicans of Senate and House Choose New Officials," *Ohio State Journal*, 3 January 1904; "Make Bid for Economy with State's Money," ibid., 2 January 1906; "Assembly All Ready to Open New Session," ibid., 5 January 1908; Edward Wakefield Hughes, *Hughes' American Parliamentary Guide Prepared for Ohio General Assembly: The Process of Lawmaking* (Columbus: F. J. Heer, 1922), 34; 107 H.J. 5–6, 45, 926–27 (1917); 107 S.J. 4–5, 47, 558 (1917).

19. Robert Luce, *Legislative Procedure: Parliamentary Practices and the Course of Business in the Framing of Statutes* (Boston: Houghton Mifflin, 1922), 501–2; "Senator Charles Curtis: Kansas Furnishes a Floor Leader to Succeed Henry Cabot Lodge," *Current Opinion* 78 (January 1925): 26; Harvey Walker, *The Legislative Process: Law Making in the United States* (New York: Ronald, 1948), 177.

20. 126 O.L. 369 (1955); 129 O.L. 570 (1961); 136 O.L. 47 (1975); 2003 R.C. 101.27.

21. Tom LaRochelle, "Ohio Lawmakers Want New Week," *Columbus Citizen-Journal*, 1 March 1971; Dennis J. Willard and Mike Rutledge, "Legislators' Absences Detour Law-

making," *Lancaster Eagle-Gazette*, 19 July 1992; Columbus Calling, *Columbus Citizen-Journal*, 13 November 1971.

22. "Women on Rise in New Assembly; Top Snag Schools," *Cleveland Plain Dealer*, 3 January 1979; Lee Leonard, "Davidson Wins Top GOP Job—She's First Woman Picked as House Leader," *Columbus Dispatch*, 25 November 1992; Lee Leonard, "State Senate, House Leadership Jobs Change," ibid., 19 April 1996.

23. Lee Leonard, "As Tough as They Come," *State Legislatures*, May 1999, 18–21; Riffe, *Whatever's Fair*, 75–76; Jane Campbell, interview with author, 5 November 2006; Randy Ludlow, "Minority Leader a Woman," *Cincinnati Post*, 25 November 1992; Dave Ghose, "Quitting the Boys' Club," *Columbus Monthly*, March 2003, 130; Lesley Dahlkemper, "Growing Accustomed to Her Face," *State Legislatures*, July–August 1996, 41–42.

24. Norman Nadel, "Roses Sweeten Dull, Tobacco-Filled Premier of 101st Ohio Assembly," *Columbus Citizen*, 4 January 1955; Karl B. Pauly, "About Something Else," Mostly about People, *Ohio State Journal*, 15 March 1934; "Parochial Aid Defeat Feared," *Columbus Citizen*, 16 March 1935; 115 S.J. 354 (1933); Martha Carpenter, letter to the editor, *Ohio State Journal*, 15 April 1935.

25. Riffe, *Whatever's Fair*, 66; Lee Leonard, "Ohio's Finan Follows the Rules," *State Legislatures*, July–August 2002, 28.

26. "Pensions for Mothers Get Solons' O.K.," *Ohio State Journal*, 12 April 1913; "Rushing House Rules Brings Fistic Clash," *Ohio State Journal*, 19 January 1927; 112 H.J. 74–77 (1927); Richard L. Maher, "Rebellion in Senate Threat to Tax Plan," *Columbus Citizen*, 28 May 1959; Columbus Calling, ibid., 31 May 1959; "Senate Hearing Flares into Hot Squabbles," ibid., 25 March 1955.

27. 124 H.J. 264 (1951).

28. 101 H.J. 6 (1910); Dodds, *Procedure*, 75–76, 97–98; Howe, *Confessions*, 165–66; Walker, *Legislative Process*, 296; Clarence E. Walker, rptr., *Proceedings and Debates of the Constitutional Convention of the State of Ohio*, 2 vols. (Columbus: F. J. Heer, 1912–13), 1:570.

29. Walker, *Legislative Process*, 296; Vinton McVicker, "Ohio Solons Ditch School Aid Bill," *Columbus Citizen*, 4 June 1951; Vinton McVicker, "Freshmen Members of Assembly Air View on More Efficient Legislating," Eyes on Politics, ibid., 15 July 1951; Hal Conefry and Don Strouse, "Lawmakers Sing Off Key Swan Song and It's Nothing to Brag About," ibid., 26 June 1955; Walker, *Proceedings*, 1:571; Albert H. Rose, *Ohio Government State and Local*, 3d ed. (Dayton, Ohio: University of Dayton Press, 1966), 305; Albert H. Rose, *Ohio Government State and Local*, 4th ed. (Dubuque, Ia.: Kendall/Hunt, 1974), 323.

30. Dodds, *Procedure*, 98; 101 H.J. 6 (1910); Short, "Ohio's Legislators Off to Slow Start," *Columbus Citizen-Journal*, 2 February 1973; Columbus Calling, ibid., 3 March 1973; Hal Conefry, "Bars Go up in House on Bill Introduction; 246 Heard Final Day," *Columbus Citizen*, 11 February 1947; Hal Conefry, "Flood of Legislation Is Expected Monday as Deadline Is Reached," ibid.,11 February 1951; Hal Conefry, "Assembly, in Session 26 Days, Has Passed Two Measures," ibid., 18 February 1951; 134 H.J. 324–60 (1971).

31. Howe, *Confessions*, 165–66; James T. Patterson, *Mr. Republican: A Biography of Robert A. Taft* (Boston: Houghton Mifflin, 1972), 103; "House Playful, While Senate Pushes Pet Bills Till Close," *Columbus Citizen*, 19 May 1911; Karl B. Pauly, "Solons Quit amid Riotous Scene," *Ohio State Journal*, 5 June 1935.

32. "Legislators Make Good Comedians," ibid., 3 June 1951; Richard L. Maher, "Legislature Quits in Raucous Finale," ibid., 25 July 1959; Robert Ruth, "Lancione Retiring after 32 Years in Ohio House," *Columbus Dispatch*, 13 December 1978; Dan Williamson, "Out with a Clang," *Other Paper* (Columbus), 21 December 2006.

33. Columbus Calling, *Columbus Citizen-Journal*, 26 January 1974.

34. 106 H.J. 136 (1915); 119 H.J. 136 (1941); information provided by House fiscal officer Mike Lundell and House clerk Laura Clemens, 13 July 2006; Jim Siegel, "House Wants Preachers to Tone It Down," *Columbus Dispatch*, 18 May 2007; Riffe, *Whatever's Fair*, 178.

35. Michael Les Benedict, "Civil Liberty in Ohio," in *The History of Ohio Law*, ed. Michael Les Benedict and John F. Winkler (Athens: Ohio University Press, 2004), 2:708–9; 108 O.L. 614 (1919); Meyer v. Nebraska, 262 U.S. 390 (1923); 108 O.L. 514, 34 (1919); 108 O.L. 1391–92 (1920); 108 O.L. 57, 189 (1919); 109 H.J. 303–4 (1921), 109 S.J. 507 (1921); 109 O.L. 629 (1921).

36. 199 O.L. 586 (1941); 119 H.J. 136–37, 139 (1941); Richard J. Ellis, *To the Flag: The Unlikely History of the Pledge of Allegiance* (Lawrence: University Press of Kansas, 2005), 124–37; 126 H.J. 26 (1955); 129 S.J. 154, 161 (1961); 152 H.J., 2 January 2007.

37. 119 H.J. 18–19 (1941); "Gus Kasch Loses Favorite Seat in Lower House," *Columbus Dispatch*, 7 February 1945; Charles Egger, "Where Shall He Sit, Is Problem for Gus Kasch and Solon Colleagues," *Columbus Citizen*, 8 February 1945; 122 H.J. 26–27 (1947); 124 H.J. 17–18 (1951); 125 H.J. 44 (1953).

38. 122 H.J. 90, 194–95, 368–69, 400–401, 676–77, 1776–79, 1811–12 (1947); 122 H.J., 2d spec. sess., 4–7, 28–29 (1948); 138 H.J. 687–88 (1979); "Auto Crash Kills Toledo Legislator," *Columbus Dispatch*, 24 April 1979.

39. Editorial, "Smoking in the Senate," *Ohio State Journal*, 19 May 1911; James J. Downing, "Ohio Senators Pampered; Representatives Rough It," *Columbus Citizen*, 9 January 1947; Nadel, "Roses."

40. "Senate Goes Smoke-Free," 4 July 1985; Richard G. Zimmerman, *Plain Dealing: Ohio Politics and Journalism Viewed from the Press Gallery* (Kent, Ohio: Kent State University Press, 2006), 31–32.

41. Harlan Spector, "Sweeping Prohibition on Smoking Is Adopted," *Cleveland Plain Dealer*, 8 November 2006; "94th Legislature Convenes as Friends, Foes Look On," *Columbus Citizen*, 6 January 1941; Exec. Order (Ohio) No. 99–03T (1999); 142 S.J. 139 (1987); 147 S.J. 13 (1997); 151 S.J. 36 (2005), http://www.legislature.state.oh.us/Journal-Text126/SJ-01-18-05.pdf.

42. Gongwer News Service, "Trouble Percolating? Coffee, Other Drinks and Food Barred in Senate Hearing Rooms," *Ohio Report*, 21 February 2007.

43. "Fight Telephone Abuse," *Ohio State Journal*, 2 January 1906; 98 H.J. 65 (1906); 107 S.J. 149–50 (1917); 118 S.J. 21 (1939); 119 S.J. 15–16 (1941); 120 S.J. 14–15 (1943);

123 H.J. 65 (1949); 123 H.J. 347, 354 (1949); Ohio Legislative Service Commission, *A Guidebook for Ohio Legislators* [1st ed.] (Columbus: Ohio Legislative Service Commission, 1970), 81; Dean Schott, "Phone Calls Billed to State Are 'Illegal,'" *Columbus Citizen*, 4 August 1977.

44. 101 H.J. 388–89 (1910); 103 H.J. 93–94, 99–100, 106 (1913); 107 H.J. 79–80 (1917), 108 H.J. 73–74 (1919), 108 H.J. 72–73 (1919)

45. 98 H.J. 121–22 (1906); 103 H.J. 25 (1913); 107 S.J. 28 (1917); 109 S.J. 20 (1921); 119 H.J. 1117–18 (1941); 125 H.J. 1890–91 (1953); Jane Ware, "The Statehouse, God Bless It," *Ohio Magazine*, July 1986, 72; Lee Leonard, "A Retirement at the Statehouse," *Columbus Monthly*, October 1988, 10–11; Lee Leonard, "Bell Tolls Dec. 24 for Statehouse's Noted Snack Bar," *Columbus Dispatch*, 6 December 1992.

46. Downing, "Ohio Senators Pampered"; C. W. Thomas, "Mumble—Shout: Democracy at Work," *Columbus Citizen*, 13 July 1953; 117 H.J. 456, 692 (1937), 123 H.J. 698–99 (1940); "Mikes in Legislature," Columbus Calling, *Columbus Citizen*, 21 November 1954.

47. Ohio Legislative Service Commission, *Legislative Services, Facilities, and Procedures*, Staff Research Report No. 81 (Columbus: Ohio Legislative Service Commission, 1966), 29, 35–36; Columbus Calling, *Columbus Citizen-Journal*, 6 February 1965; Sidlow, "Professionalism," 29–31; Ohio Legislative Service Commission, *A Guidebook for Ohio Legislators* [3d ed.] (Columbus: Ohio Legislative Service Commission, 1985), 95–96.

48. 112 H.J. 77 (1927); O. F. Knippenburg, "It'll Be Republican Legislature, 2–1," *Columbus Citizen-Journal*, 10 November 1966; Short, "Ohio's Legislators off to Slow Start"; Ohio Legislative Service Commission, minutes, 14 December, 1972, Ohio Legislative Service Commission library; Dave Johnston to LSC staff, 9 December 1980, Ohio Legislative Service Commission library; Lee Leonard, "State Officials Expanding Orientation for New Legislators," *Columbus Dispatch*, 19 March 2000; Michael Hawthorne, "Ohio Prepares for New Lawmakers," *Cincinnati Enquirer*, 6 September 1999; Lee Leonard, "As Tough as They Come," *State Legislatures*, May 1999, 20; Bruce Feustel and Rich Jones, "Legislator Training 101," *State Legislatures*, September 2001, 16–19; printed programs and other information provided by Kathy Luikart, Ohio Legislative Service Commission.

49. Rex Mitchell Baxter, "The Legislative Reference Library," *Arena* 39 (June 1908): 675; J. H. Kennedy, "Alfred Kelley," *Magazine of Western History* 3 (March 1886): 552.

50. Baxter, "Library," 676; Earl Everett Warner, "Law-Making through Interest Groups in Ohio: A Study of the Activities of the Ohio Chamber of Commerce, the Ohio Farm Bureau Federation and the Ohio State Federation of Labor in the Eighty-eighth General Assembly" (master's thesis, Ohio State University, 1929), 59–60; "Legislative Investigations," Legislative Notes and Reviews, *American Political Science Review* 8 (May 1914): 238–39.

51. Hoyt Landon Warner, *Progressivism in Ohio, 1897–1917* (Columbus: Ohio State University Press, 1964), 386–89; John J. Kulewicz, "Reinventing the Governor: A History of Executive Power under Ohio Law," in Benedict and Winkler, *History of Ohio Law*, 1:173–74; 109 H.J. 933 (1921).

52. Walker, *Legislative Process*, 71–75.

53. Vinton McVicker, "Assembly Lobbyist List Longer Than Its Roster," Eyes on Politics, *Columbus Citizen*, 24 December 1950; Columbus Calling, "Unfair to Lobbyists," ibid., 12 May 1957; Warner, "Law-Making through Interest Groups," 109–12; McVicker, "Freshmen Members."

54. Columbus Calling, *Columbus Citizen*, 17 May 1953.

55. David A. Johnston, "The Ohio Legislative Service Commission—A Nonpolitical Political Institution," memorandum P-116–8611, 31 January 1986, Legislative Service Commission library; Karl T. Kurtz, "The History of Us," *State Legislatures*, July–August 1999, 16–21.

Chapter 18: From Patronage to Professionalism

1. H. B. Crafts [?] to Warren G. Harding, 18 November 1899, D. W. Ayers to Harding, 11 November 1899, B. F. Sullivan to Harding, 18 November 1899, W. Clay Huston to Harding, 24 December 1901, [?] Hensley to Harding, 27 December 1901, Warren G. Harding Papers (microfilm), Ohio Historical Society.

2. 116 H.J. 22–24, 1297, 1304–5 (1935).

3. 116 H.J. 22–24, 1297 (1935); Frances McGovern, *Fun, Cheap, and Easy: My Life in Ohio Politics, 1949–1964* (Akron, Ohio: University of Akron Press, 2002), 43.

4. 116 S.J. 1378 (1935).

5. 116 S.J. 706 (1935); 109 S.J. 85–86 (1921); 121 S.J. 11–12 (1945).

6. 116 S.J., pt. 2, first spec. sess., 91 (1935).

7. 116 H.J. 71 (1935); 102 H.J. 1057–58 (1911); 117 H.J. 148 (1937); James K. Mercer, *Ohio Legislative History*, vol. 5 (Columbus: F. J. Heer, [1925?]), 620–21.

8. 98 H.J. 93 (1906); Charles B. Nuckolls Jr., "The Governorship of Martin L. Davey of Ohio" (master's thesis, Ohio State University, 1952), 44; "Davey 'Expose' [illegible] Football Fans," *Cleveland Plain Dealer*, 12 October 1935; 116 H.J. 1233–34 (1935); 117 S.J. 1298 (1937).

9. William J. Baker, *Jesse Owens: An American Life* (New York: Free Press, 1986), 59–62.

10. McGovern, *Fun, Cheap, and Easy*, 49–50.

11. 126 H.J. 1128 (1955); 129 H.J. 1237 (1961); 130 H.J. 1168 (1963).

12. James K. Mercer, *Ohio Legislative History*, vol. 1 (Columbus: F. J. Heer, [1918?]), 666; 97 H.J. 939 (1904); 101 H.J. 9 (1910); 107 H.J. 14 (1917); *Ohio State Journal*, 1 January 1878.

13. 127 H.J. 900 (1957); 126 H.J. 68 (1955); 129 H.J. 183 (1961); 134 S.J. 476–77 (1971).

14. Editorial, "The Unelected 'Senator,'" *Columbus Citizen*, 9 January 1955; Don Strouse, "Clerk Tom Bateman Is an Important Cog When Upper House Machinery Turns," ibid., 17 May 1953; Jane Ware, "The Statehouse, God Bless It," *Ohio Magazine*, July 1986, 72; Bob Schmitz, interview with author, 1 August 2006.

15. Lauren A. Glosser, "The Administrative Aspects of the Legislature of State of Ohio" (master's thesis, Ohio State University, 1932), 12–18.

16. Glosser, "Administrative Aspects," 6–7, 19–29.

17. William Parker Blair III, "The Ohio Senate: Problems in Legislative Reform" (master's thesis, Ohio State University, 1967), 48–62.

18. Ohio Legislative Service Commission, A Guidebook for Ohio Legislators [1st ed.] (Columbus: Ohio Legislative Service Commission, 1970), 78–79.

19. Ohio Legislative Service Commission, A Guidebook for Ohio Legislators [3d ed.] (Columbus: Ohio Legislative Service Commission, 1985), 102; Ohio Legislative Service Commission, 1985–1986 Supplement to A Guidebook for Ohio Legislators (Columbus: Ohio Legislative Service Commission, [1985?]), 7–8; Ohio Legislative Service Commission, 1989–1990 Supplement to A Guidebook for Ohio Legislators (Columbus: Ohio Legislative Service Commission, [1989?]), 8–9.

20. "Armed Officers to Replace Assistant Sergeants-at-Arms," Columbus Dispatch, 28 January 2000.

21. Marion Casey, Charles McCarthy: Librarianship and Reform (Chicago: American Library Association, 1981), 28–37.

22. Zane L. Miller, Boss Cox's Cincinnati: Urban Politics in the Progressive Era (New York: Oxford University Press, 1968), 155–57; Casey, McCarthy, 43.

23. Casey, McCarthy, 43; James K. Mercer, Ohio Legislative History, vol. 4 (Columbus: F. J. Heer, 1923[?]), 54; Hoyt Landon Warner, Progressivism in Ohio, 1897–1917 (Columbus: Ohio State University Press, 1964), 389, 414n13; 101 O.L. 221 (1910); 103 O.L. 8 (1913); James M. Cox, Journey through My Years (New York: Simon and Schuster, 1946), 137.

24. Mercer, Ohio Legislative History, 4:183; ibid., 1: 261; ibid., vol. 2 (Columbus: F. J. Heer, 1918[?], 244; 103 O.L. 8 (1913); Mercer, Ohio Legislative History, vol. 5 (Columbus: F. J. Heer, [1925?]), 283; Michael Burns, "The Legislative Reference Movement in Ohio: From Progressive Ideal to Session Satisfying," University of Toledo Law Review 32 (Summer 2001): 489–91; Warner, Progressivism, 425; Orenna Louise Evans, "The Children's Code of Ohio," Notes on Current Legislation, American Political Science Review 7 (November 1913): 647–50; S. Gale Lowrie, "Ohio Model Charter Law," Notes on Current Legislation, American Political Science Review 7 (August 1913): 422–24.

25. Casey, McCarthy, 33; Rex Mitchell Baxter, "The Legislative Reference Library," Arena 39 (June 1908): 679; Cox, Journey, 137; Warner, Progressivism, 427, 431.

26. 115 O.L., pt 2, 62 (1933); Burns, "Legislative Reference Movement," 491–92.

27. "Legislative Moves Run in Cycles, Champion Drafter of Bills Says," Ohio State Journal, 24 April 1921; Mercer, Ohio Legislative History, 5:282; George B. Marshall, "Life History of a Bill in the Ohio Legislature," Ohio State Law Journal 11 (Autumn 1950): 447; Arthur A. Schwartz, "The Ohio Legislative Reference Bureau and Its Place in the Legislative Process," Ohio State Law Journal 11 (Autumn 1950): 439; Burns, "Legislative Reference Movement," 493–97.

28. Millard H. Ruud, "The Ohio Legislative Service Commission," Ohio State Law Journal 14 (Autumn 1953): 404, 407; David A. Johnston, "The Ohio Legislative Service

Commission—A Nonpolitical Political Institution," memorandum P-116-8611, 31 January 1986, Legislative Service Commission library, 8, 14–15, 18–19, 29, 36.
    29. H. P. Howard to Warren G. Harding, 27 November 1899, Harding Papers; Capitol Square Review and Advisory Board, "African-American Legislators," *George Washington Williams*, http://www.georgewashingtonwilliams.org; James K. Mercer, *Ohio Legislative History*, vol. 3 (Columbus, F. J. Heer. 1921[?]), 292, 450; ibid., 4:474; ibid., 5:618; James K. Mercer, *Ohio Legislative History*, vol. 6 (Columbus, F. J. Heer. 1927[?]), 591.
    30. 116 S.J. 1375, 1378 (1935); 116 H.J. 1297, 1304–6 (1935); 116 S.J., spec. sess., 6–7 (1935); 109 S.J. 74 (1921).
    31. 99 O.L. 30 (1908); 103 O.L. 864 (1913); 135 O.L. 7 (1973); 137 O.L. 3602 (1978); George Roberts, "Ohio Senate in Teenage Dilemma," *Columbus Citizen-Journal*, 21 July 1971; Columbus Calling, ibid., 23 March 1974.

Chapter 19: Milkers, Wild Women, and Pancakes

    1. Harvey Walker, *Law Making in the United States* (New York: Ronald, 1934), 326; 100 H.J. 7, spec. sess. (1909); 102 H.J. 7 (1911); 98 O.L. 342 (1906); Hoyt Landon Warner, *Progressivism in Ohio, 1897–1917* (Columbus: Ohio State University Press, 1964), 204n17, 235–36; 103 O.L. 3 (1913); 102 O.L. 129 (1911); Linda Furney, "Fair Hearing: Balancing Lobby Regulation with Free Speech in Ohio," *University of Toledo Law Review* 32 (Summer 2001): 529–30.
    2. 98 H.J. 829 (1906); George Creel and Sloane Gordon, "What Are You Going to Do about It?" Part 9: "The Shame of Ohio," *Cosmopolitan Magazine* 51 (October 1911): 607.
    3. Creel and Gordon, "Shame of Ohio," 608.
    4. Warner, *Progressivism*, 275–77; Creel and Gordon, "Shame of Ohio," 606–10; "'Some Ohio Solons Would Steal a Bucket of Coal,' Says Burns," *Columbus Citizen*, 8 May 1911.
    5. 108 H.J. 1134–36 (1919); 110 S.J. 351–52, 360–62, 465–66 (1923); "Turn on the Light and Let the Truth Be Revealed," *Columbus Citizen*, 19 March 1923; "Senate to Probe Scandal Rumors," ibid., 20 March 1923; "Senate 'Scandal' Probe under Way," ibid., 21 March 1923; "Speed Scandal Probe," ibid., 22 March 1923; "Senate Probe Is Near Its End," ibid., 23 March 1923; "Marshall and Rowe to Be Cleared," ibid., 24 March 1923.
    6. 115 H.J. 166–67, 246–48, 691–93 (1933); "House Calls on Legislator to Prosecute Man He Says Offered Him $1000 Bribe," *Ohio State Journal*, 26 January 1933; "Solon Balks Jury's Bribe Quiz," ibid., 31 January 1933; "Hall's Bribery Charge Ignored," ibid., 11 May 1933.
    7. "Jury Indicts Senator Herner on Charge of Soliciting Bribe," *Columbus Citizen*, 1 November 1933; "Senator Herner Is Acquitted on Court's Directed Verdict," ibid., 24 January 1934; 115 S.J., 2d spec. sess., 87 (1934).
    8. Editorial, "Investigating Lobbies," *Columbus Citizen*, 1 November 1933; "House Lobbyists Must Sign," Columbus Calling, ibid., 19 April 1953; "Lobbyists 'Hurt,'" Columbus Calling, ibid., 21 November 1954; Hal Conefry, "FEPC, Oleo Measures Coming up

for Vote," ibid., 27 February 1949; "Lobbyist on Job for Every Member of Assembly!" *Ohio State Journal*, 28 January 1933; 125 S.J. 255 (1953).

9. Marda Liggett Woodbury, *Stopping the Presses: The Murder of Walter W. Liggett* (Minneapolis: University of Minnesota Press, 1998), 26–30; Walter W. Liggett, "Ohio— Lawless and Unashamed," *Plain Talk*, July 1930, 1, 5, 9–10.

10. Hal Conefry, "Rule-Breaking Lobbyists to Be Barred from House Floor at Future Sessions," *Columbus Citizen*, 28 January 1933; Belle Zeller, "State Regulation of Lobbying," in *The Book of the States* (Chicago: Council of State Governments, 1948), 128; Belle Zeller, "The State Lobby Laws," in *The Book of the States* 14 (Chicago: Council of State Governments, 1962), 83; 115 H.J. 185 (1933); 120 H.J. 737–38 (1943); 125 H.J. 834–35 (1953); Don Strouse, "'Tip' Hiner Wants Lobby Law with Teeth in It," *Columbus Citizen*, 10 May 1953; "Dept. of Ho-Hum or How 'bout the Lobby Probe!" Columbus Calling, ibid., 4 April 1954; "Ugly Entertainment Rumors," Columbus Calling, ibid., 24 May 1959.

11. Belle Zeller, *American State Legislatures: Report of the Committee on American Legislatures, American Political Science Association* (New York: Thomas Y. Crowell, 1954), 215–16; 125 H.J. 1777–78, 1798 (1953).

12. "Dept. of Ho-Hum."

13. Report of the Committee to Study Lobbying in Ohio (Raymond E. Hildebrand, Chairman) (1954), Ohio Legislative Service Commission library, Columbus; Charles H. Weston Jr., *Lobby Laws in Ohio*, Research Report No. 13 (Columbus: Ohio Legislative Service Commission, 1955), 13.

14. William B. Saxbe with Peter D. Franklin, *I've Seen the Elephant: An Autobiography* (Kent, Ohio: Kent State University Press, 2000), 39; "Legislators Expect to Dig for Their Hotel Expenses," Columbus Calling, *Columbus Citizen*, 9 August 1959; Columbus Calling, ibid., 16 August 1959; Zeller, "Lobby Laws," 83.

15. Saxbe, *Autobiography*, 39.

16. Vinton McVicker, "Freshmen Members of Assembly Air Views on More Efficient Legislating," Eye on Politics, *Columbus Citizen*, 15 July 1951; "Lobbyists 'Hurt'"; Cliff Treyens, "Statehouse Hangouts 1995," *Ohioan*, April 1995, 13; 115 H.J. 1154 (1933); 125 S.J. 255 (1953); 129 H.J. 2002 (1961).

17. 115 H.J. pt 2, 2d spec. sess., 20 (1933); 117 S.J. 705–6 (1937); 119 H.J. 95–96 (1941); 121 H.J. 925 (1945); 9 April 1953; "House Lobbyists Must Sign"; Columbus Calling, *Columbus Citizen*, 9 January 1955; "House, Senate Rap Lobbyists," ibid., 15 May 1957, 127 S.J. 526–27 (1957); 131 S.J. 58 (1965); Lee Leonard, interview with author, 12 January 2007.

18. Joseph S. Nye Jr., Philip D. Zelikow, and David C. King, eds., *Why People Don't Trust Government* (Cambridge, Mass.: Harvard University Press, 1997); J. Todd Segal, "Why Americans Don't Trust Government, and Why They Sometimes Do: Trust in Government in the United States from the 1960s to the Present" (Ph.D. diss., Johns Hopkins University, 2003); Zeller, *American State Legislatures*, 87; 129 H.J. 1990 (1961).

19. Model Code of Legislative Conduct (A Staff Proposal), prepared for submission to the Committee on Legislative Rules, National Legislative Conference, November 1,

1968; Committee of State Officials on Suggested State Legislation of the Council of State Governments, *Suggested State Legislation*, vol. 27 (Chicago: Council of State Governments, 1967), A-3–A-5; 129 H.J. 1987–90 (1961); 134 O.L. 481 (1972).

20. Columbus Calling, *Columbus Citizen-Journal*, 11 March 1972.

21. William Merriman, "'High-on-the-Hog' Day for Ohio's Lawmakers," *Columbus Citizen-Journal*, 14 February 1973; William Merriman, "Lobbyists Outnumber Legislators by 2–1 Margin," ibid., 12 March 1973.

22. William Merriman, "House Approves Ethics Legislation," *Columbus Citizen-Journal*, 3 May 1973; Jack P. DeSario and David E. Freel, "Ohio Ethics Law Reforms: Tracing the Political and Legal Implications," *Akron Law Review* 30 (Fall 1996): 130–31; 135 O.L. 1160 (1973).

23. 136 O.L. 738 (1976).

24. Editorial, "Tougher Ethics Laws," *Columbus Dispatch*, 7 April 1984; Sandy Theis and Nancy McVicar, "An Administration under Fire," *Columbus Citizen-Journal*, 3 September 1985; James Bradshaw, "Ethics Revisions Backed," *Columbus Dispatch*, 27 February 1986; Mary Anne Sharkey, "Celeste Backs Bill on Ethics," *Cleveland Plain Dealer*, 28 February 1985; 141 O.L. 3155 (1986).

25. Vindu P. Goel, "House Chairman Meets for a Fee," *Cleveland Plain Dealer*, 16 September 1993; Tim Miller, "McLin Paid $500 to Speaker," *Dayton Daily News*, 30 September 1993.

26. Vindu P. Goel and Mark Tatge, "Jones Wants to 'Clear the Air'; Lawmaker Requests Ethics Panel Probe of Himself," *Cleveland Plain Dealer*, 1 October 1993; Lee Leonard and Jonathan Riskind, "Ethics Questions Swirl around Lawmaker," *Columbus Dispatch*, 31 October 1993.

27. James Bradshaw, "Petro Says Honorarium Scheme Is 'Offensive,'" *Columbus Dispatch*, 22 December 1995; Catherine Candisky, "Special Prosecutor to Be Picked to Examine Legislator Payments," ibid., 6 June 1994; Catherine Candisky, "Honorariums Probe Clears Legislators," ibid., 27 January 1995.

28. Mike Curtin and Jonathan Riskind, "Riffe, Aronoff Don't List Speaking Fees," *Columbus Dispatch*, 10 October 1993.

29. T. C. Brown, "'Maybe I Made a Mistake,'" *Cleveland Plain Dealer*, 28 September 1993; Lee Leonard, "Stampede toward Ethics Reform Jars House Leadership," *Columbus Dispatch*, 11 October 1993; 145 O.L. 6195 (1994).

30. Lee Leonard, "Ethics Probe Sought—Speaking Fees at Issue," *Columbus Dispatch*, 1 October 1993; Lee Leonard, "Lawmaker Resigns as Chairman—Ethics Fight Dogged Head of Health Panel," ibid., 15 March 1994; Catherine Candisky, "Watts, Aronoff Convicted," ibid., 3 February 1996; Lee Leonard, "Indictment Won't Stop Payments to Legislators," ibid., 5 February 1996; Catherine Candisky, "Ailing Riffe Pleads Guilty, Receives Fine," ibid., 2 July 1996; rosters 1995, 1997.

31. Greg Davies, "The Junkyard Dog of the Ohio Senate," *Columbus Monthly*, November 1997, 112–13.

32. Thomas Suddes, "How Honoraria Data Piled Up," *Cleveland Plain Dealer*, 8 February 1996; Zeller, "Lobby Laws," 83; Jim Siegel, "Rules for Lobbyists Mostly Toothless—

Punishments Amount to Nothing When Someone Breaks Ohio Law," *Columbus Dispatch,* 12 February 2006.

33. Ohio const. of 1851, am. 1973, art. 2, § 4; 87 O.L. 241 (1890); 104 H.J. 47–49, 341–58 (1914); 104 O.L. 252 (1914); 106 O.L. 306 (1915).

34. Lee Leonard, "College Changes Miller's Title after Ethics Decision," *Columbus Dispatch,* 21 July 1992; Lee Leonard, "Miller Forced to Leave Columbus State Job," ibid., 3 October 1992.

35. Lee Leonard, "State Senator Faces Inquiry," *Columbus Dispatch,* 29 March 2005; Lee Leonard, "State Senator Offers His Side," ibid., 30 March 2005; Jim Siegel, "Ethics Failings Get Light Penalty," ibid., 14 December 2005.

36. 119 H.J. 336 (1941); Columbus Calling, *Columbus Citizen,* 7 June 1953; "Thompson Loses Harassment Appeal," *Cleveland Plain Dealer,* 14 January 1992; "Sexual Harassment Lawsuit vs. Van Vyven Dismissed," *Cincinnati Post,* 29 April 1994; Dean Schott, "Phone Calls Billed to State Are 'Illegal,'" *Columbus Citizen-Journal,* 4 August 1977; "Rep. Mallory Is Cleared of Misconduct," *Columbus Dispatch,* 31 July 1980; Sandy Theis, "Fox Loses House Post," *Cincinnati Enquirer,* 27 June 1997; Thomas J. Sheeran, "Jury Convicts State Senator of Extortion in Cleveland," *Columbus Dispatch,* 21 November 1998; Jim Siegel, "Ex-Senator to Direct Legislative Black Caucus," *Columbus Dispatch,* 17 May 2007.

37. Dan Williamson, "Lonesome Larry," *Other Paper* (Columbus), 27 May–2 June 2004; "Scandals Inspire Reforms," *Cleveland Plain Dealer,* 30 July 2004; Dan Williamson, "It's Not Easy Being Mean," *Columbus Monthly,* September 2004, 40–45; Jim Siegel and Joe Hallett, "No Charges as Householder Inquiry Ends," *Columbus Dispatch,* 17 June 2006; Joe Hallett, "Householder Aims at Run for Governor Down the Road," *Columbus Dispatch,* 1 June 2003; Randy Ludlow, "Householder to Bow Out of Political Life," *Columbus Dispatch,* 22 August 2006.

Chapter 20: The Rise and Fall of the Cornstalk Brigade

1. Thomas Suddes, "Gays Were an Easy Target for Ohio's GOP Bullies," *Cleveland Plain Dealer,* 14 November 2001.

2. Justin Steuart, *Wayne Wheeler, Dry Boss: An Uncensored Biography of Wayne B. Wheeler* (New York: Fleming H. Revell, 1928), 67.

3. Michael F. Curtin in collaboration with Julia Barry Bell, *The Ohio Politics Almanac,* 2d ed. (Kent, Ohio: Kent State University Press, 2006), 70.

4. Ibid., 194–95; Eugene H. Roseboom and Francis P. Weisenburger, *A History of Ohio* (Columbus: Ohio Historical Society, 1996), 376–77; George W. Knepper, *Ohio and Its People,* 3d ed. (Kent, Ohio: Kent State University Press, 2003), 303–6.

5. Curtin, *Almanac,* 194–95; Roseboom and Weisenburger, *History,* 377, 388.

6. Jon C. Teaford, *The Twentieth-Century American City,* 2d ed. (Baltimore: Johns Hopkins University Press, 1993), 69–70; Curtin, *Almanac,* 183–95; information supplied by Dr. Todd Gardner, Population Distribution Branch, Population Division, U.S. Census Bureau.

7. B. H. Pershing, "Membership in the Ohio General Assembly," *Ohio Archaeological and Historical Quarterly* 40 (April 1931): 255–58, 267–70.

8. Herbert Waltzer, "Apportionment and Districting in Ohio: Components of Deadlock," in *The Politics of Reapportionment*, ed. Malcolm E. Jewell (New York: Atheron, 1962), 176; 90 O.L. 382 (1893); Steven H. Steinglass and Gino J. Scarselli, *The Ohio State Constitution: A Reference Guide* (Westport, Conn.: Praeger, 2004), 356; Pershing, "Membership," 270–72.

9. Pershing, "Membership," 279–82; F. R. Aumann, "'Rotten Borough' Representation in Ohio," *National Municipal Review* 20 (February 1931): 84–86.

10. Reynolds v. Sims, 377 U.S. 533, 564–64, 581 (1964); Gray v. Sanders, 372 U.S. 368, 381 (1963).

11. Nolan v. Rhodes, 378 U.S. 556 (1964); Don E. Weaver, "What One Man? What One Vote?" *Columbus Citizen-Journal*, 7 August 1965; Nolan v. Rhodes, 251 F. Supp. 584 (S.D. Ohio 1965), aff'd, 383 U.S. 104 (1966); 132 O.L. 2842 (1967).

12. Ohio const. of 1851, am. 1956 and 1967, art. 2, § 2; ibid., art. 11, § 6a (adopted 1956, repealed 1967).

13. Richard G. Zimmerman, *Plain Dealing: Ohio Politics and Journalism Viewed from the Press Gallery* (Kent, Ohio: Kent State University Press, 2006), 36.

14. Richard Lehne, "Shape of the Future," *National Civic Review* 58 (September 1969): 351–55; William J. D. Boyd, "Suburbia Takes Over," *National Civic Review* 54 (June 1965): 294–98; Neal R. Peirce, *The Megastates of America: People, Politics, and Power in the Ten Great States* (New York: Norton, 1972), 316.

15. Malcolm E. Jewell, "The Political Setting," in *State Legislatures in American Politics*, ed. Alexander Heard (Englewood Cliffs, N.J.: Prentice Hall, 1966), 71–72, 81; Robert S. Erikson, "The Partisan Impact of State Legislative Reapportionment," *Midwest Journal of Political Science* 15 (February 1971): 57–71.

16. Francis R. Aumann and Harvey Walker, *The Government and Administration of Ohio* (New York: Crowell, 1956).

17. Louis Masotti and Kathleen Barber, "'Better Men' Running?" *National Civic Review* 56 (October 1967): 506, 511.

18. Yong Hyo Cho and H. George Frederickson, *Measuring the Effects of Reapportionment in the American States* (New York: National Municipal League, 1976), 93; Charles Egger, "Ohio Democrats Owe Thanks to GOP," *Columbus Citizen-Journal*, 11 November 1972; Curtin, *Almanac*, 93–94; Vernal G. Riffe Jr. with Cliff Treyens, *Whatever's Fair: The Political Autobiography of Ohio House Speaker Vern Riffe* (Kent, Ohio: Kent State University Press, 2007), 113–14.

19. Lawrence Baum and Samuel C. Patterson, "Ohio: Party Change without Realignment," in *Party Realignment in State Politics*, ed. Maureen Moakley (Columbus: Ohio State University Press, 1992), 207–8.

20. Riffe, *Whatever's Fair*, 118–19; Steve Hoffman, "Campaigning from the Middle of the Spectrum," *Akron Beacon Journal*, 18 August 2005.

21. Joe Hallett, "Ohio's Stacked Districts Yield Few Competitive Races," *Columbus Dispatch*, 2 January 2005; Thomas A. Flinn, "Continuity and Change in Ohio Politics,"

Journal of Politics 21 (August 1962): 521–44; Thomas A. Flinn, "The Outline of Ohio Politics," Western Political Quarterly 13 (September 1960): 702–21; John H. Fenton, Midwest Politics (New York: Holt, Rinehart and Winston, 1966), 118–32; David Arnold Johnston, "Politics and Policy in Ohio: A Study of Equal Rights, Pollution Control, and Unemployment Compensation Legislation" (Ph.D. diss., Ohio State University, 1972), 40–42; Heinz Eulau, "The Ecological Basis of Party Systems: The Case of Ohio," Midwest Journal of Political Science 1 (August 1957): 125–35, rpt. in Democracy in the Fifty States, ed. Charles Press and Oliver P. Williams (Chicago: Rand McNally, 1966), 179–88; Ohio Secretary of State, Ohio Election Statistics, 1944, 217–21; Ohio Secretary of State, Ohio Election Statistics, 1952, 233–37.

22. Flinn, "Continuity and Change," 521–44; Fenton, Midwest Politics, 118–32.

23. Flinn, "Outline," 720–21; John M. Wegner, "Partisanship in the Ohio House of Representatives, 1900–1911: An Analysis of Roll-Call Voting," Ohio History 106 (Summer-Autumn 1997): 146–70; Charles William Chance, "Analysis of Legislative Agreements: The Case of Ohio" (Ph.D. diss., Ohio State University 1970), 428–30.

24. Robert A. Taft, The Papers of Robert A. Taft: Volume 1, 1889–1939, ed. Clarence E. Wunderlin Jr. (Kent, Ohio: Kent State University Press, 1997), 288–89; James T. Patterson, Mr. Republican: A Biography of Robert A. Taft (Boston: Houghton Mifflin, 1972), 90; Haskell Penn Short, "Robert Alphonso Taft: His Eight Years in the Ohio General Assembly" (master's thesis, Ohio State University, 1951); Walter W. Liggett, "Ohio— Lawless and Unashamed," Plain Talk, July 1930, 21–22.

25. Clayton Fritchey, "Relief in Ohio," American Mercury 50 (May 1940): 78; Richard L. Maher, "Oxcart Government!" in Our Sovereign State, ed. Robert S. Allen (New York: Vanguard, 1949), 169–70; John Gunther, Inside U.S.A. (New York: Harper and Bros., 1947), 440; William B. Saxbe with Peter D. Franklin, I've Seen the Elephant: An Autobiography (Kent, Ohio: Kent State University Press, 2000), 40; 125 H.J. 1560–61 (1953); John C. Wahlke et al., The Legislative System: Explorations in Legislative Behavior (New York: Wiley, 1962), 424–27.

26. Flinn, "Outline," 716; Cho and Frederickson, Measuring, 16; Patterson, Taft, 97; Richard G. Zimmerman, Call Me Mike: A Political Biography of Michael V. DiSalle (Kent, Ohio: Kent State University Press, 2003), 167; Other Paper, 21–27 April 2005.

27. David Dabelko, "The Urban-Rural Conflict in the Ohio House of Representatives: 1957–1964" (master's thesis, Ohio University, 1965), 61–66, 79; Johnston, "Politics and Policy," 471.

28. Lloyd Sponholtz, "The Politics of Temperance in Ohio, 1880–1912," Ohio History 85 (Winter 1976): 9; 99 H.J. 341–42 (1908); 99 S.J. 195 (1908); U.S. Bureau of the Census, Religious Bodies, 1906, Part I: Summary and General Tables (Washington, D.C.: GPO, 1910), 346–47, table 4; U.S. Bureau of the Census, Religious Bodies, 1916, Part I: Summary and General Tables (Washington, D.C.: GPO, 1919), 298–99, table 63.

29. Paul Kleppner, Continuity and Change in Electoral Politics, 1893–1928 (New York: Greenwood, 1987), 183–213; U.S. Bureau of the Census, Religious Bodies, 1906, 346–47, table 4.

30. 106 O.L. 560 (1915); 107 O.L. 784 (1917); 106 H.J. 1125 (1915); 106 S.J. 786 (1915); K. Austin Kerr, *Organized for Prohibition: A New History of the Anti-Saloon League* (New Haven, Conn.: Yale University Press, 1985), 173.

31. 108 H.J. 30 (1919); 108 S.J. 19 (1919).

32. 111 H.J. 322 (1925); Francis R. Aumann, "Ohio Government in the Twentieth Century: From Nash to White (1900–1931)," in *Ohio in the Twentieth Century*, comp. Harlow Lindley, vol. 6, *The History of the State of Ohio*, ed. Carl Wittke (Columbus: Ohio State Archaeological and Historical Society, 1942), 45; Francis R. Aumann, "Rural Ohio Hangs On," *National Municipal Review* 46 (April 1957): 192; 111 H.J. 177–78, 857–65 (1925); 111 S.J. 328 (1925).

33. 100 O.L. 89 (1909); 109 O.L. 307 (1921); 109 S.J. 473 (1921); David M. Chalmers, *Hooded Americanism: The History of the Ku Klux Klan*, 3d ed. (1981; rpt., Durham, N.C.: Duke University Press, 1987), 177; 111 H.J. 322 (1925); 111 S.J. 698 (1925).

34. Norman H. Clark, *Deliver Us from Evil: An Interpretation of American Prohibition* (New York: Norton, 1976), 180–208; Liggett, "Ohio—Lawless and Unashamed," 9–10; Leslie H. Stegh, "A Paradox of Prohibition: Election of Robert J. Bulkley as Senator from Ohio, 1930," *Ohio History* 83 (Summer 1974): 170–82; 115 H.J. 441 (1933); 115 S.J. 220 (1933).

35. David J. Maurer, "Relief Problems and Politics in Ohio," in *The New Deal*, ed. John Braeman, Robert Bremner, and David Brody, vol. 2, *The State and Local Levels* (Columbus: Ohio State University, 1975), 98–99; Aumann, "Rural Ohio," 192–93; Vinton McVicker, "Cities Partially at Fault in Trouble over Finances," Eye on Politics, *Columbus Citizen*, 30 March 1947; Gordon E. Baker, *Rural versus Urban Political Power: The Nature and Consequences of Unbalanced Representation* (Garden City, N.Y.: Doubleday, 1955), 28, 30; Ohio const. of 1851, am. 1953, art. 8, § 2(c); "Rural-Urban Fight Looms over Highway Program," Columbus Calling, *Columbus Citizen*, 6 December 1953.

36. Stephen Ansolabehere, Alan Gerber, and Jim Snyder, "Equal Votes, Equal Money: Court-Ordered Redistricting and Public Expenditures in the American States," *American Political Science Review* 96 (December 2002): 767–77; Cho and Frederickson, *Measuring*, 65, 95; U.S. Bureau of the Census, *Census of Governments: 1962*, vol. 4, *Governmental Finances*, no. 4, *Compendium of Government Finances* (Washington, D.C.: GPO, 1964), 502–9, table 53; U.S. Bureau of the Census, *Census of Governments: 1977*, vol. 4, *Governmental Finances*, no. 5, *Compendium of Government Finances* (Washington, D.C.: GPO, 1979), 282, table 53; U.S. Bureau of the Census, *Census of Governments: 1962*, vol. 4, *Governmental Finances*, no. 3, *Finances of Municipalities and Township Governments* (Washington, D.C.: GPO, 1964), 240–45, table 21; U.S. Bureau of the Census, *Census of Governments: 1977*, vol. 4, *Governmental Finances*, no. 4, *Finances of Municipalities and Township Governments* (Washington, D.C.: GPO, 1979), 293–301, table 22.

37. Fenton, *Midwest Politics*, 117–54; Samuel C. Patterson, "Legislative Politics in Ohio," in *Ohio Politics*, ed. Alexander P. Lamis (Kent, Ohio: Kent State University Press, 1994), 250, 244, 246.

38. Hofstadter, *Age of Reform*, 121–30; Arthur M. Schlesinger, "The City in American History," *Mississippi Valley Historical Review* 27 (June 1940): 43; Aumann, "Rural Ohio," 194, 222; Robert S. Friedman, "The Urban-Rural Conflict Revisited," *Western Political Quarterly* 14 (June 1961): 485; Baker, *Rural versus Urban*, 24, 56–59.

39. Frances McGovern, *Fun, Cheap, and Easy: My Life in Ohio Politics, 1949–1964* (Akron, Ohio: University of Akron Press, 2002), 46; Carl B. Stokes, *Promises of Power: A Political Autobiography* (New York: Simon and Schuster, 1973), 63.

40. McGovern, *Fun, Cheap, and Easy*, 52; 130 H.J. 782–83 (1963); 130 S.J. 1033 (1963); 130 S.J. 377 (1963); 130 H.J. 1546 (1963); Gongwer News Service, "House to Begin Recess Wednesday, Action Ready on August Appropriations, Workmen's Comp," *Ohio Report*, 27 July 1971; Gongwer News Service, "House Passes Workmen's Compensation Bill, August Appropriations," ibid., 28 July 1971; Gongwer News Service, "Unity Prevailed in Senate; House Passes Interim Budget," ibid., 31 August 1971; Warren Van Tine et al., *In the Workers' Interest: A History of the Ohio AFL-CIO, 1958–1998* (Columbus: Center for Labor Research, Ohio State University), 106; 134 H.J. 828–29, 1215 (1971); 134 S.J. 305, 664 (1971); 136 S.J. 61 (1975); 136 H.J. 102–3 (1975); 145 H.J. 593–94, 1278 (1993); 145 S.J. 696, 1278 (1993).

41. Lee Leonard, "Rhodes's Second Eight Years, 1975–1983," in Lamis, *Ohio Politics*, 111–12; Van Tine, *Workers' Interest*, 132–34, 147–49; 136 S.J. 586, 1201 (1975); 136 H.J. 2009, 2050 (1975); 137 S.J. 561, 1363 (1977–78), 137 H.J. 1599 (1977), Gongwer News Service, "Senate Overrides Veto of Collective Bargaining Bill," *Ohio Report*, 25 January 1978; 140 S.J. 243 (1983); 140 H.J. 746 (1983).

42. 146 H.J. 1971 (1996); 146 S.J. 2332 (1996); 150 S.J. 493, 2756–57 (2004); 150 H.J. 2743 (2004).

43. Lee Leonard, "Conservatives' Affinity for Divisive Issues Stymies All Other Work," *Columbus Dispatch*, 13 December 2004.

44. 146 O.L. 2123 (1995); 146 H.J. 869 (1995); 146 S.J. 869 (1995); 148 H.J. 1388 (1999); 150 H.J. 2475–76 (2004); 150 H.J. 1375 (2004); 150 H.J. 255–56 (2003); Dave Ghose, "Quitting the Boys' Club," *Columbus Monthly*, March 2003, 129–30.

45. Dan Williamson, "Are You a Democrat or a Republican? Are You Sure?" *Other Paper* (Columbus), 25 November–1 December 2004.

Chapter 21: The Feds, the Bureaucrats, and the Scope of Legislation

1. Jonathan H. Adler, "Fables of the Cuyahoga: Reconstructing a History of Environmental Protection," *Fordham Environmental Law Journal* 14 (Fall 2002): 94, 99–101.

2. Lawrence M. Friedman, *A History of American Law*, 3d ed. (New York: Simon and Schuster, 2005), 505–8.

3. Robert Wilkin, "A Study in Administrative Law: The Conservancy Act of Ohio," *Ohio State University Law Journal* 3 (December 1936): 33–34.

4. 134 O.L. 1866 (1972); Edward Lindsey, "Historical Sketch of the Indeterminate Sentence and Parole System," *Journal of the American Institute of Criminal Law and Criminology* 16 (May 1925): 10, 34, 38–39.

5. Burt W. Griffin and Lewis R. Katz, "Sentencing Consistency: Basic Principles Instead of Numerical Grids: The Ohio Plan," *Case Western Reserve Law Review* 53 (Fall 2002): 38–39; Fritz Rauschenberg, "Sentencing Reform Proposals in Ohio," *Federal Sentencing Reporter* 6 (November–December 1993): 166–68; Ohio Criminal Sentencing Commission, *A Plan for Felony Sentencing in Ohio: A Formal Report of the Ohio Criminal Sentencing Commission* (Columbus: Ohio Criminal Sentencing Commission, 1993), 20, 27.

6. Ohio Criminal Sentencing Commission, *Plan for Felony Sentencing*, 19–20, 53–71; Rauschenberg, "Sentencing Reform," 168; 146 O.L. 7136 (1995).

7. Henry E. Sheldon II, "From Commandments to Consent: Ohio in the Divorce Reform Era," *Northern Kentucky State Law Forum* 2 (Winter 1974–75): 144–71; Alan E. Norris, "Ohio's Divorce Reform Act—Expectation and Realization," *Ohio Northern University Law Review* 13, no. 2 (1986): 182–87; 108 O.L. 219 (1919); 115 O.L., pt. 2, 306 (1934); 134 O.L. 1485 (1971); Richard G. Zimmerman, "Rhodes's First Eight Years, 1963–1971," in *Ohio Politics*, ed. Alexander P. Lamis (Kent, Ohio: Kent State University Press, 1994), 72–73; Francis R. Aumann, "Ohio Government in the Twentieth Century: From White to Bricker (1931–1940)," in *Ohio in the Twentieth Century*, comp. Harlow Lindley, vol. 6, *The History of the State of Ohio*, ed. Carl Wittke (Columbus: Ohio State Archaeological and Historical Society, 1942), 63, 75–77; 134 H.J. 1534 (1971); 134 S.J. 1251 (1971).

8. John Gunther, *Inside U.S.A.* (New York: Harper and Bros., 1947), 454; Ohio Board of Regents, *Basic Data Series: Ohio Higher Education System* (Columbus: Ohio Board of Regents, 1981), 5; 123 O.L. 329 (1949); 129 O.L. 13 (1961); 124 O.L. 112 (1951); 137 O.L. 359 (1977).

9. John J. Esch, "Our Second Line—the National Guard," *North American Review* 177 (August 1903): 294–96; 95 O.L. 293 (1902); 107 O.L. 382, 579, 604 (1917).

10. David J. Maurer, "Relief Problems and Politics in Ohio," in *The New Deal*, ed. John Braeman, Robert Bremner, and David Brody, vol. 2, *The State and Local Levels* (Columbus: Ohio State University, 1975), 77–102.

11. 115 O.L. 601 (1933); 116 O.L. 555 (1935); 116 O.L. 94 (1935); 116 O.L. pt. 2, 86, 188, 195, 201 (1935–36).

12. H. Roger Grant, *Ohio on the Move: Transportation in the Buckeye State* (Athens: Ohio University Press, 2000), 13–17, 21; Gary T. Schwartz, "Urban Freeways and the Interstate System," *Southern California Law Review* 49 (March 1976): 422–27, 465; 23 U.S.C. 158 (1984); 142 O.L. 3605 (1987).

13. Robert Stevens and Rosemary Stevens, *Welfare Medicine in America: A Case Study of Medicaid* (New York: Free Press, 1974); 131 O.L. 1989 (1965); Ohio Commission to Reform Medicaid, *Transforming Ohio Medicaid: Improving Health, Quality, and Value* (Columbus: Ohio Commission to Reform Medicaid, 2005), 6, 62.

14. Tom Raga, letter to the editor, *Cincinnati Enquirer*, 18 July 2002; 150 O.L. 396, 2375–76 (2003); Ohio Commission to Reform Medicaid, *Transforming Ohio Medicaid*,

63; Am. Sub. H.B. 66, 126th General Assembly, §§ 206.66.52, 206.66.53, 206.87; Ohio Revised Code, § 101.391 (2005); 42 C.F.R. Part 430-end (2004).

15. Ohio Revised Code Chapter 2905 (1953); Ohio Legislative Service Commission, *Criminal Law and Procedures: An Interim Report*, Staff Research Report No. 82 (Columbus: Ohio Legislative Service Commission, 1967); 134 O.L. 1866 (1972).

16. Youngstown v. DeLoreto, 19 Ohio App. 2d 267 (1969); 133 O.L. 1816 (1970); Final Report of the Technical Committee to Study Ohio Criminal Laws and Procedures (Columbus: Ohio Legislative Service Commission, March 1971), 116; 135 O.L. 982 (1974); Am. H.B. 23, 126th General Assembly (2005); Women's Med. Prof'l Corp. v. Voinovich, 130 F.3d 187 (6th Cir. 1997), cert. denied, Voinovich. v. Women's Med. Prof'l Corp., 523 U.S. 1036 (1998) (146 O.L. 2123 [1995]); Women's Med. Prof'l Corp. v. Taft, 353 F.3d 436 (6th Cir. 2003) (148 O.L. 3604 [2000]).

17. David L. Hoeffel, "Ohio's Death Penalty: History and Current Development," *Capital University Law Review* 31, no. 3 (2003): 660–67, 682–83.

18. Nelson L. Bossing, *The History of Educational Legislation in Ohio from 1851 to 1925* (Columbus: F. J. Heer, 1931), 38–39 [previously published in *Ohio Archaeological and Historical Quarterly* 39 (January 1930): 78–291 and 39 (April): 223–399]; 94 O.L. 317 (1900); 97 O.L. 344 (1904); 104 O.L. 133 (1914); James M. Cox, *Journey through My Years* (New York: Simon and Schuster, 1946), 146; William D. Overman, "Education in Ohio since 1900," in *Ohio in the Twentieth Century*, comp. Harlow Lindley, vol. 6, *The History of the State of Ohio*, ed. Carl Wittke (Columbus: Ohio State Archaeological and Historical Society, 1942), 254–55.

19. Ohio Revised Code, Title 47; Superior Films, Inc. v. Dept. of Educ. of Ohio, Div. of Film Censorship, 346 U.S. 587 (1954); R.K.O. Radio Pictures, Inc. v. Dept. of Educ. of the State of Ohio, Div. of Film Censorship, 162 Ohio St. 263 (1954); 126 O.L 655 (1955); 147 O.L. 909, 6542 (1997); 149 O.L. 8 (2001).

20. John M. Weed, "The Traveled Ways," in Lindley, *Ohio*, 148–49; 97 O.L. 511 (1904); 102 O.L. 333 (1911); Francis R. Aumann and Harvey Walker, *The Government and Administration of Ohio* (New York: Thomas Y. Crowell, 1956), 338–42.

21. Aumann and Walker, *Government*, 127–28, 338–41; "Bonus, Amendments Highlight Election," Eye on Politics, *Columbus Citizen*, 2 November 1947.

22. Grant, *Ohio on the Move*, 21–25; Aumann and Walker, *Government*, 335–36, 340–41; Ohio Revised Code, chap. 4561.

23. Paul B. Sears, "History of Conservation in Ohio," in Lindley, *Ohio*, 227–29; William J. Novak, *The People's Welfare: Law and Regulation in Nineteenth-Century America* (Chapel Hill: University of North Carolina Press, 1996), 191–227; Adler, "Fables," 98–100; Sherwood Anderson, "Ohio: I'll Say We've Done Well," *Nation*, 9 August 1922, 146–47.

24. Sears, "History of Conservation," 228–31; 73 O.L. 87 (1876); 91 O.L. 380 (1894); 93 O.L. 142 (1898).

25. 119 O.L. 812 (1941); 122 O.L. 730 (1947); 123 O.L. 634 (1949); 123 O.L. 84 (1949).

26. 124 O.L. 855 (1951); 123 O.L. 199 (1949); 127 O.L. 257 (1957); 127 O.L. 296 (1957).

27. Jonathan H. Adler, "The Fable of Federal Environmental Regulation: Reconsidering the Federal Role in Environmental Protection," *Case Western Reserve Law Review* 55 (Fall 2004): 93–113; 129 O.L. 1350 (1961); 130 O.L. 1412 (1963); 130 O.L. 866 (1963); 132 O.L. 1269 (1967); 130 O.L. 1403–4 (1963); 131 O.L. 474 (1965); 132 O.L. 681 (1968); 128 O.L. 1231 (1959); 132 O.L. 2724 (1967); 133 O.L. 1250 (1970); 133 O.L. 1260 (1970).

28. Adler, "Fables," 94–104; Richard J. Lazarus, *The Making of Environmental Law* (Chicago: University of Chicago Press, 2004), 48–49.

29. Hugh C. McDiarmid, "The Gilligan Interlude, 1971–1975," in Lamis, *Ohio Politics*, 92; 134 O.L. 695 at 727–28 (1972).

30. Lazarus, *Making of Environmental Law*, 70; R.C. 1504.02.

31. 142 O.L. 4418 (1988); 145 O.L. 2211 (1994).

Chapter 22: The Foreseeable Future

1. Ohio Citizens' Committee on the State Legislature, Final Report, 30 June 1972.

2. Ibid., 5–6.

3. Thad Kousser, *Term Limits and the Dismantling of State Legislative Professionalism* (New York: Cambridge University Press, 2005), 65–66, 203, 208.

4. Jennifer Drage Bowser, "Legislative Term Limits," *Legisbrief* [National Conference of State Legislatures] 11, no. 15 (2003); Jennifer Drage Bowser, "States Respond to Term Limits," *Legisbrief* [National Conference of State Legislatures] 12, no. 14 (2004); Rhine L. McLin, "The Hidden Effects of Term Limits: Losing the Voices of Experience and Diversity," *University of Toledo Law Review* 32 (Summer 2001): 542–43.

5. Richard H. Finan and April M. Williams, "Government Is a Three-Legged Stool," *University of Toledo Law Review* 32 (Summer 2001): 519–20.

6. Finan and Williams, "Government," 519–21; McLin, "Hidden Effects," 539–41; Garry Boulard, "Enter the New Breed," *State Legislatures*, July–August 1999, 43–46.

7. Brian Weberg, "Whom Do You Trust?" *State Legislatures*, July–August 1999, 34–37; Samuel C. Patterson, "Legislative Politics in Ohio," in *Ohio Politics*, ed. Alexander P. Lamis (Kent, Ohio: Kent State University Press, 1994), 244–45; McLin, "Hidden Effects," 541–42.

8. Lee Leonard, "Term Limits Won't End Anytime Soon, Forum Reports—In Some States, Governor Controls New Legislatures," *Columbus Dispatch*, 2 May 2004; James T. O'Reilly, "Tort Reform and Term Limits: the 2004 Ohio Experience," *Capital University Law Review* 33 (Spring 2005): 529–30.

9. Jennifer Drage Bowser, "The Effects of Legislative Term Limits," in *The Book of the States* 37 (Lexington, Ky.: Council of State Governments, 2005), 115.

10. Alan Rosenthal, *Heavy Lifting: The Job of the American Legislature* (Washington, D.C.: CQ Press, 2004), 244; Rick Farmer and Thomas H. Little, "Legislative Power in the Buckeye State: The Revenge of Term Limits," Joint Project on Legislative Term Limits

(Denver and Washington: National Conference of State Legislatures, 2005), 18; Joe Hallett, "Officials to Push for Extra Terms—Ohio Parties Have Strickland's Support in Seeking 4 More Years," *Columbus Dispatch*, 13 January 2007; Mark Niquette, "Term Limits Are Bad, Ex-Governors Agree," ibid., 12 March 2007; editorial, *Cleveland Plain Dealer*, 19 January 2007; editorial, *Akron Beacon Journal*, 17 January 2007; editorial, *Toledo Blade*, 19 January 2007; Gongwer News Service, "Survey: 62% of Ohioans Support Existing Legislative Term Limits," *Ohio Report*, 1 May 2007.

11. Cliff Treyens, "Statehouse Hangouts 1995," *Ohioan*, April 1995, 12–13.

12. W. Bennett Rose, interview with author, 17 April 2006.

13. Robert Vitale, "State Law Overrides Local Gun Controls," *Columbus Dispatch*, 15 March 2007; Martin Rozenman, "Few Municipal Officials Opt to Make Leap to Statehouse," ibid., 30 July 2007; Gongwer News Service, "Democrats Forced to Swallow Some Bitter Pills on the 126th General Assembly's Final Workday," *Ohio Report*, 20 December 2006; "Divided Senate Approves Abortion Limit, Capital Bill in Marathon Session," ibid., 19 December 2006; Mark Niquette and Jim Siegel, "Sudden Veto Has GOP in Uproar," *Columbus Dispatch*, 9 January 2007; Gongwer News Service, "Bipartisan Group Hug Marks End of Relatively Harmonious Budget Deliberations," *Ohio Report*, 28 June 2007; "Legislature Sends Eminent Domain Protection Bill to Governor; Proposed November Ballot Issue Falls Short," ibid., 27 June 2007; 101 H.J. 6 (1910); H.J., 15 February 2007, www.legislature.state.oh.us/JournalText127/HJ-02–15–07.pdf.

14. William Hershey, "Survey: Ohioans Are OK with Term Limits," *Dayton Daily News*, 1 March 2007.

15. Rosenthal, *Heavy Lifting*, 246–47.

Note on Ohio Legislative Publications

1. James Monroe, *Oberlin Thursday Lectures, Addresses and Essays* (Oberlin, Ohio: E. J. Goodrich, 1897), 96–97.

2. 103 O.L. 983 (1913).

BIBLIOGRAPHY

Interviews by Author (2003–7)

Stanley Aronoff
Lou Blessing
Jane Campbell
William Chavanne
Laura Clemens
Bill Cohen
Andy DiPalma
Theodore W. Gray
Jeff Jacobson
Charles Kurfess
Lee Leonard
Keith McNamara
Priscilla Mead
W. Bennett Rose
Robert Schmitz
Sandra Stabile-Harwood
Dan Williamson

Newspapers

Akron Beacon Journal
Atkinson's Saturday Evening Post
Centinel of the North-Western Territory
Cincinnati Commercial
Cincinnati Enquirer
Cleveland Gazette
Cleveland Plain Dealer
Columbus Citizen
Columbus Citizen-Journal
Columbus Daily Dispatch
Columbus Daily Dispatch and Daily Ohio Statesman
Columbus Democratic Call

Columbus Dispatch
Columbus Monthly
Columbus Tax-Killer
Crisis (Columbus, Ohio)
Dayton Daily News
Evangelical Magazine and Gospel Advocate (Utica, N.Y.)
Lancaster Eagle-Gazette
National Police Gazette (New York, N.Y.)
New Constitution (Columbus, Ohio)
New York Times
Niles' National Register
Niles' Weekly Register
Ohio Report (Gongwer News Service)
Ohio State Journal
Ohio State Journal and Columbus Gazette
Ohio Statesman
Other Paper (Columbus, Ohio)
Philanthropist (Cincinnati, Ohio)
Saturday Evening Post
Semi-Weekly Eagle (Brattleboro, Vt.)
Toledo Blade
Western Hemisphere and Ohio Monitor
Western Reserve Chronicle
Workingman's Advocate (New York, N.Y.)
Youngstown Vindicator

Manuscript Collections

Grover Cleveland Papers (microfilm), Ohio Historical Society
Calvin Fletcher Papers, Indiana Historical Society
Joshua R. Giddings Papers, Ohio Historical Society
Warren G. Harding Papers (microfilm), Ohio Historical Society
Abraham Hegler Papers, Ohio Historical Society
Isaac Appleton Jewett Papers, Cincinnati Museum Center
Larwill Family Papers, Ohio Historical Society
DeWitt Clinton Loudon Papers, Ohio Historical Society
Northwest Territory Collection. Ohio Historical Society
Donna Pope Papers, Ohio Historical Society
Charles Elmer Rice Papers, Ohio Historical Society
John Armstrong Smith Papers, Ohio Historical Society
Thomas Worthington Papers, Ohio Historical Society

Government Documents

Ohio Constitutional Convention Proceedings

Adel, J. G., rptr. *Official Report of the Debates and Proceedings of the Third Constitutional Convention of Ohio.* 2 vols. Cleveland: W. S. Robison, 1873–74.

Journal of the Convention, of the Territory of the United States North West of the Ohio. . . . , Reprinted in Daniel J. Ryan, "From Charter to Constitution. . . . " *Ohio Archaeological and Historical Publications* 5 (August 1897): 80–132.

Smith, J. V., rptr. *Report of the Debates and Proceedings of the Convention for the Revision of the Constitution of the State of Ohio.* 2 vols. Columbus: S. Medary, 1851.

Walker, Clarence E., rptr. *Proceedings and Debates of the Constitutional Convention of the State of Ohio. . . .* Columbus: F. J. Heer, 1912–13.

Ohio Statutory Compilations

Baldwin, William Edward, ed. *Throckmorton's Ohio Code Annotated, Baldwin's 1948 Revision, Complete to January 1, 1948.* Cleveland: Banks-Baldwin, 1948.

Bates, Clement, ed. *The Annotated Revised Statutes of the State of Ohio, Including All Laws of a General Nature in Force January 1, 1898.* 3 vols. Cincinnati: W. H. Anderson, 1897.

Chase, Salmon P., ed. *The Statutes of Ohio and of the Northwestern Territory, Adopted or Enacted From 1788 to 1833 . . . and acts of Congress.* 3 vols. Cincinnati: Corey and Fairbank, 1833–35.

Daugherty, M. A., John S. Brasee, and George B. Okey, eds. *The Revised Statutes and Other Acts of a General Nature of the State of Ohio, in Force January 1, 1880.* 2 vols. Columbus: H. W. Derby, 1879.

Ellis, Wade H. *The Municipal Code of Ohio.* 3d ed. Revised by Challen B. Ellis. Cincinnati: W. H. Anderson, 1907.

Page, William Herbert, ed., *Page's Desk Edition of the Ohio General Code Containing All Ohio Statutes of a General Nature in Force January 1, 1931.* Cincinnati: W. H. Anderson, 1930.

Pease, Theodore Calvin, ed. *The Laws of the Northwest Territory, 1788–1800.* Springfield: Trustees of the Illinois State Historical Library, 1925.

Swan, Joseph R., ed. *Statutes of the State of Ohio, of a General Nature, In Force August, 1854: With References to Prior Repealed Laws.* Cincinnati: H. W. Derby, 1854.

Ohio Legislative Documents and Publications

Axelrod, David. "Staffing Needs of the Ohio Legislature." Appendix to Ohio Legislative Service Commission, *Legislative Services, Facilities, and Procedures,* Staff Research Report No. 81. Columbus: Ohio Legislative Service Commission, 1966.

Ingersoll-Casey, Jennifer et al. "Members Demographics, 108th–121st General Assemblies." Ohio Legislative Service Commission research memorandum R-121-6008, October 1996, Ohio Legislative Service Commission Library, Columbus.

Johnston, David. "The Ohio Legislative Service Commission: A Nonpolitical Political Institution." Memorandum P-116-8511. 1986. Columbus: Ohio Legislative Service Commission library.

———. "Testimony of David Johnston, Director, Ohio Legislative Service Commission, re H.B. 118, to State Government Committee, Feb. 8, 1971." In vertical file "Buildings—LSC Quarters." Columbus: Ohio Legislative Service Commission library.

Journal of the Senate, of the State of Ohio, in Cases of Impeachment. Chillicothe, Ohio: 1809.

Laughon, Barbara J. "Age Demographics for Members of the Ohio General Assembly 1969–1996 108th through 121st General Assemblies." Ohio Legislative Service Commission research memorandum. 21 October 1996. Columbus: Ohio Legislative Service Commission library.

Manual of Legislative Practice, in the General Assembly of Ohio, Containing the Rules, the Statutes, and that Portion of the Constitution Relating to the Duties and Rights of Members of the Legislature. Columbus: G. J. Brand, 1882.

Ohio Legislative Service Commission. *1985–1986 Supplement to A Guidebook for Ohio Legislators.* Columbus: Ohio Legislative Service Commission, [1985?].

———. *1989–1990 Supplement to A Guidebook for Ohio Legislators.* Columbus: Ohio Legislative Service Commission [1989?].

———. *Criminal Law and Procedures: An Interim Report.* Staff Research Report No. 82. Columbus: Ohio Legislative Service Commission, 1967.

———. *A Guidebook for Ohio Legislators.* Columbus: Ohio Legislative Service Commission, 1970–2005.

———. *Legislative Services, Facilities, and Procedures,* Staff Research Report No. 81. Columbus: Ohio Legislative Service Commission, 1966.

———. *Lobby Laws in Ohio.* Research Report No. 13. Columbus: Ohio Legislative Service Commission, 1955.

Report of the Committee to Study Lobbying in Ohio (Raymond E. Hildebrand, Chairman). 1954. Ohio Legislative Service Commission library.

Select Committee to Investigate Campus Disturbances. Files. State Archives Series 4195. Ohio Historical Society.

———. Interim Report to the 108th Ohio General Assembly. 5 October 1970.

———. Second Interim Report to the 109th Ohio General Assembly. [December 1970?]

Technical Committee to Study Ohio Criminal Laws and Procedures. *Proposed Ohio Criminal Code.* Final Report. Columbus: Ohio Legislative Service Commission, 1971.

Ohio Executive Documents

Awl, William M. "Annual Report of the Superintendent of State House, to the Governor of the State of Ohio, for the Year 1863." In *Annual Reports Made to the Governor of the State of Ohio, for the Year 1863,* pt. 2. Columbus: Richard Nevins, 1864.

Oglevee, John F. "Annual Report of the Auditor of State, to the Governor of the State of Ohio, for the Fiscal Year ending November 15, 1883," In *Executive Documents. Annual Reports for 1883, Made to the Sixty-sixth General Assembly of the State of Ohio, at the Regular Session, Commencing January 7th, 1884*, pt. 2 Columbus: G. J. Brand, 1884.

Ohio Board of Regents. *Basic Data Series: Ohio Higher Education System.* Columbus: Ohio Board of Regents, 1981.

Ohio Secretary of State. *Ohio Election Statistics.* [1944, 1952, 1959–60, 1979–80, and 1989–90].

Smith, Samuel B. "Annual Report of the Adjutant General to the Governor of the State of Ohio, for the Year 1883." In *Executive Documents. Annual Reports for 1883, Made to the Sixty-sixth General Assembly of the State of Ohio, at the Regular Session, Commencing January 7th, 1884*, pt. 1. Columbus: G. J. Brand, 1884.

Wilson, W. T. "Report of the Comptroller of the Treasury." In *Executive Documents. Message and Annual Reports for 1876, Made to the Sixty-sixth General Assembly of the State of Ohio, at the Adjourned Session, Commencing January 2th, 1877*, pt. 1. Columbus: Nevins and Myers, 1877.

Other Ohio Government Documents

Ohio Criminal Sentencing Commission. *A Plan for Felony Sentencing in Ohio: A Formal Report of the Ohio Criminal Sentencing Commission.* Columbus: 1 July 1993.

Ohio Commission to Reform Medicaid. *Transforming Ohio Medicaid: Improving Health, Quality, and Value.* 2005.

United States Documents

Arias, Elizabeth. "United States Life Tables, 2003." *National Vital Statistics Reports* 54, no. 14 (2006): 1–40.

Biographical Directory of the United States Congress, 1774–Present. http://bioguide.congress.gov.

Compilation of Senate Election Cases from 1789 to 1913. 62d Cong., 3d sess, S. Doc. 1036. Washington, D.C.: GPO, 1913.

Congressional Research Service. *History of the House of Representatives, 1789–1994.* Washington, D.C.: GPO, 1994.

DeBow, J. D. B. *The Seventh Census of the United States: 1850.* Washington, D.C.: Robert Armstrong, 1853.

National Archives and Records Service. *The Territorial Papers of the United States.* Edited by Clarence Edwin Carter. Vols. 2 and 3. Washington, D.C.: GPO, 1934.

Richardson, James D., ed. *A Compilation of the Messages and Papers of the Presidents, 1787–1897.* Vols. 2 and 3. Washington, D.C.: GPO, 1896.

United States Bureau of the Census. *Historical Statistics of the United States, Colonial Times to 1970.* 2 vols. Washington, D.C.: U.S. Department of Commerce, Bureau of the Census, 1975.

———. *Religious Bodies, 1906, Part I: Summary and General Tables*. Washington, D.C.: GPO, 1910.

———. *Religious Bodies, 1916, Part I: Summary and General Tables*. Washington, D.C.: GPO, 1919.

———. *Census of Governments: 1962*. Vol. 4, *Governmental Finances*. No. 3, *Finances of Municipalities and Township Governments*. Washington, D.C.: GPO, 1964.

———. *Census of Governments: 1962*. Vol. 4, *Governmental Finances*. No. 4, *Compendium of Government Finances*. Washington, D.C.: GPO, 1964.

———. *Census of Governments: 1977*. Vol. 4, *Governmental Finances*. No. 4, *Finances of Municipalities and Township Governments*. Washington, D.C.: GPO, 1979.

———. *Census of Governments: 1977*. Vol. 4, *Governmental Finances*. No. 5, *Compendium of Government Finances*. Washington, D.C.: GPO, 1979.

———. *Thirteenth Census of the United States Taken in the Year 1910*. Vol. 1, *General Report and Analysis*. Washington, D.C.: GPO, 1913.

Miscellaneous

Swindler, William F., ed. *Sources and Documents of United States Constitutions*. 12 vols. Dobbs Ferry, N.Y.: Oceana, 1973–88.

Theses, Dissertations, and Unpublished Papers

Blair, William Parker, III. "The Ohio Senate: Problems in Legislative Reform." Master's thesis, Ohio State University, 1967.

Bowers, Douglas E. "The Pennsylvania Legislature, 1815–1869: A Study of Democracy at Work." Ph.D. diss., University of Chicago, 1974.

Chance, Charles William. "Analysis of Legislative Agreements: The Case of Ohio." Ph.D. diss., Ohio State University, 1970.

Colston, Freddie Charles. "The Influence of Black Legislators in the Ohio House of Representatives." Ph.D. diss., Ohio State University, 1972.

Cottom, Robert I. "To Be Among the First: The Early Career of James A. Garfield, 1831–1868." Ph.D. diss., Johns Hopkins University, 1975.

Craft, Ralph Harry. "The Effects of Institutional Changes on Legislative Process and Performances: The Case of Ohio—1959 to 1974." Ph.D. diss., Rutgers University, 1977.

Cummings, Abbott Lowell. "Ohio's Capitols at Columbus, 1810–1861" Typescript, Columbus Metropolitan Library, 1948.

Dabelko, David. "The Urban-Rural Conflict in the Ohio House of Representatives: 1957–1964." Master's thesis, Ohio University, 1965.

Glosser, Lauren A. "The Administrative Aspects of the Legislature of State of Ohio." Master's thesis, Ohio State University, 1932.

Johnston, David Arnold. "Politics and Policy in Ohio: A Study of Equal Rights, Pollution Control, and Unemployment Compensation Legislation." Ph.D. diss., Ohio State University, 1972.

Jones, Douglas W. "Technologists as Political Reformers: Lessons from the Early History of Voting Machines." Paper presented at the Society for the History of Technology Annual Meeting, Las Vegas, Nev., 13 October 2006.

Nuckolls, Charles B., Jr. "The Governorship of Martin L. Davey of Ohio." Master's thesis, Ohio State University, 1952.

Pierce, Michael Cain. "The Plow and Hammer: Farmers, Organized Labor and the People's Party in Ohio." Ph.D. diss., Ohio State University, 1999.

Saladino, Carl A. "The Ohio Statehouse: Its Design Sources and Architectural History." Computer printout. Columbus: Ohio Legislative Service Commission Library, n.d.

Schumaker, Waldo. "Reform of the Election Law in Ohio." Master's thesis, Ohio State University, 1918.

Segal, J. Todd. "Why Americans Don't Trust Government, and Why They Sometimes Do: Trust in Government in the United States from the 1960s to the Present." Ph.D. diss., Johns Hopkins University, 2003.

Shadle, Kurt P. "Consensus and the Decline of the Second Party System: Ohio 1848–1854." Seminar paper, University of Virginia, 1978.

Short, Haskell Penn. "Robert Alphonso Taft: His Eight Years in the Ohio General Assembly." Master's thesis, Ohio State University, 1951.

Sidlow, Edward Ivan. "Professionalism in a State Legislature: The Case of Ohio." Ph.D. diss., Ohio State University, 1979.

Taylor, Linda D. "The Ohio Legislator: Part-Time or Full-Time?" Policy paper, Ohio State University, 1974.

Warner, Earl Everett. "Law-Making through Interest Groups in Ohio: A Study of the Activities of the Ohio Chamber of Commerce, the Ohio Farm Bureau Federation and the Ohio State Federation of Labor in the Eighty-eighth General Assembly." Master's thesis, Ohio State University, 1929.

Wegner, John Mark. "Legislative Government in the Progressive Era: The Ohio House of Representatives, 1900–1911." Ph.D. diss., Bowling Green State University, 1992.

Books and Articles

Adler, Jonathan H. "The Fable of Federal Environmental Regulation: Reconsidering the Federal Role in Environmental Protection." *Case Western Reserve Law Review* 55 (Fall 2004): 93–113.

———. "Fables of the Cuyahoga: Reconstructing a History of Environmental Protection." *Fordham Environmental Law Journal* 14 (Fall 2002): 89–146.

Alton, Edmund. *Among the Law-Makers*. New York: Charles Scribner's Sons, 1886.

Amer, Francis J. "The Growth and Development of the Ohio Judicial System." In A History of the Courts and Lawyers of Ohio, edited by Carrington T. Marshall. Vol. 1. New York: American Historical Society, 1934.

Anderson, Sherwood. "Ohio: I'll Say We've Done Well." Nation, 9 August 1922, 146–48.

Andrews, Carol Rice. "A Right of Access to Court under the Petition Clause of the First Amendment: Defining the Right." Ohio State Law Journal 60, no. 2 (1999): 557–691.

Ansolabehere, Stephen, Alan Gerber, and Jim Snyder. "Equal Votes, Equal Money: Court-Ordered Redistricting and Public Expenditures in the American States." American Political Science Review 96 (December 2002): 767–77.

Arneson, Ben A. "Do Representatives Represent?" News and Notes. National Municipal Review 16 (December 1927): 751–54.

———. "Non-Voting in a Typical Ohio Community." American Political Science Review 19 (November 1925): 816–25.

Audretsch, Robert W., ed. The Salem, Ohio 1850 Women's Rights Convention Proceedings. Salem, Ohio: Salem Area Bicentennial Committee, 1976.

Aumann, F. R. "The Course of Judicial Review in the State of Ohio." Judicial Organization and Procedure. American Political Science Review 25 (May 1931): 367–76.

———. "'Rotten Borough' Representation in Ohio." National Municipal Review 20 (February 1931): 82–86.

Aumann, Francis R. "Ohio Government in the Twentieth Century: From Nash to White (1900–1931)." In Ohio in the Twentieth Century, compiled by Harlow Lindley. Vol. 6, The History of the State of Ohio, edited by Carl Wittke. Columbus: Ohio State Archaeological and Historical Society, 1942.

———. "Rural Ohio Hangs On." National Municipal Review 46 (April 1957): 189–94.

Aumann, Francis R., and Harvey Walker. The Government and Administration of Ohio. New York: Crowell, 1956.

Bailyn, Bernard. The Ideological Origins of the American Revolution. Cambridge, Mass.: Harvard University Press, Belknap Press, 1967.

Baker, Gordon E. Rural versus Urban Political Power: The Nature and Consequences of Unbalanced Representation. Garden City, N.Y.: Doubleday, 1955.

Baker, Roscoe. "The Reference Committee of the Ohio House of Representatives." Ameri-can Government and Politics. American Political Science Review 34 (April 1940): 306–10.

Baker, William J. Jesse Owens: An American Life. New York: Free Press, 1986.

Bates, James L. Alfred Kelley: His Life and Work. Columbus: Robert Clarke, 1888.

Baum, Lawrence, and Samuel C. Patterson. "Ohio: Party Change without Realignment." In Party Realignment in State Politics, edited by Maureen Moakley. Columbus: Ohio State University Press, 1992.

Baxter, Rex Mitchell. "The Legislative Reference Library." Arena 39 (June 1908): 674–81.

Belmont, Perry. "Publicity of Election Expenditures." North American Review 180 (February 1905): 166–85.

Beatty, John. "The Diary of John Beatty, January-June 1884." Part 3. Edited by Harvey S. Ford. *Ohio State Archaeological and Historical Quarterly* 59 (January 1950): 58–91.

Beer, Thomas. *Hanna*. New York: Knopf, 1929.

Bell, Sherry S., ed. *Ohio Women*. 4th ed. Columbus: Women's Services Division, Ohio Bureau of Employment Services, 1981.

Benedict, Michael Les. "Civil Liberty in Ohio." In *The History of Ohio Law*, edited by Michael Les Benedict and John F. Winkler. Athens: Ohio University Press, 2004.

———. "The Party Going Strong." *Congress and the Presidency* 9 (Winter 1981–82): 37–60.

Benedict, Michael Les, and John F. Winkler, eds. *The History of Ohio Law*. 2 vols. Athens: Ohio University Press, 2004.

Bennett, Henry Halcomb, ed. *The County of Ross: A History of Ross County from the Earliest Days, with Special Chapters on the Bench and Bar, Medical Profession, Educational Development, Industry and Agriculture and Biographical Sketches*. Madison, Wisc.: Selwyn A. Brant, 1902.

Berke, Arnold. "This Is Their Jewel." *Preservation*, September–October 1996, 76–85.

Bigelow, H. S. "From Pulpit to Stump." *Independent* 61 (1 November 1906): 1036–37.

Bird, Isabella Lucy. *The Englishwoman in America*. 1856. Reprint, Madison: University of Wisconsin Press, 1966.

Blackmore, Josiah H., II. "Not From Zeus's Head Full-Blown: The Story of Civil Procedure in Ohio." In *The History of Ohio Law*, edited by Michael Les Benedict and John F. Winkler. Athens: Ohio University Press, 2004.

Blake, Henry T. "The Official Ballot in Elections." *New Englander and Yale Review* 19 (December 1891): 513–18.

Bliven, Bruce, Jr. *The Wonderful Writing Machine*. New York: Random House, 1954.

Bogart, Ernest Ludlow. *Financial History of Ohio*. Urbana-Champaign: University of Illinois Press, 1912.

———. *Internal Improvements and State Debt in Ohio: An Essay in Economic History*. New York: Longmans, Green, 1924.

———. "Taxation of the Second Bank of the United States by Ohio." *American Historical Review* 17 (January 1912): 312–31.

Bond, Beverley W., Jr. *The Foundations of Ohio*. Vol. 1, *The History of the State of Ohio*, edited by Carl Wittke. Columbus: Ohio State Archaeological and Historical Society, 1941.

Bossing, Nelson L. *The History of Educational Legislation in Ohio from 1851 to 1925*. Columbus: F. J. Heer Printing, 1931.

Bosworth, Adrienne. "The Legislators." *Columbus Monthly*, September 1982, 45–49, 120–32.

———. "The Legislators: The Best and the Worst." *Columbus Monthly*, July 1978, 42–52.

———. "Rating the Legislators." *Columbus Monthly*, September 1984, 44–47, 116–28.

Boulard, Garry. "Enter the New Breed." *State Legislatures*, July–August 1999, 43–46.

Bowser, Jennifer Drage. "The Effects of Legislative Term Limits." In *The Book of the States* 35. Lexington, Ky.: Council of State Governments, 2003.
———. "The Effects of Legislative Term Limits." In *Book of the States* 37. Lexington, Ky.: Council of State Governments, 2005.
———. "Legislative Term Limits." *Legisbrief* [National Conference of State Legislatures] 11, no. 15 (2003).
———. "States Respond to Term Limits." *Legisbrief* [National Conference of State Legislatures] 12, no. 14 (2004).
Boyd, William J. D.. "Suburbia Takes Over." *National Civic Review* 54 (June 1965): 294–98.
Bradley, Cyrus P. "Journal of Cyrus P. Bradley." With introductory and concluding notes by George H. Twiss. *Ohio Archaeological and Historical Publications* 15 (April 1906): 207–70.
"Bribery Cases." *Ohio Legal News* 4 (17 October 1896): 3.
Brown, Marion A. *The Second Bank of the United States and Ohio (1803–1860)*. Lewiston, N.Y.: Edward Mellen, 1998.
Bruchey, Stuart. *Enterprise: The Dynamic Economy of a Free People*. Cambridge, Mass.: Harvard University Press, 1990.
Burnet, Jacob. *Notes on the Early Settlement of the North-Western Territory*. Cincinnati: Derby, Bradley, 1847.
Burns, John. *The Sometime Governments: A Critical Study of the 50 American Legislatures*. New York: Bantam, 1971.
Burns, Michael. "The Legislative Reference Movement in Ohio: From Progressive Ideal to Session Satisfying." *University of Toledo Law Review* 32 (Summer 2001): 485–507.
Burtoft, Ada Judkins, and Clyde Hollingsworth Judkins. *Biographical Sketch of Hon. David A. Hollingsworth, Cadiz, Ohio*. [Cleveland?]: privately printed, 1920.
Byrd, Robert C. *The Senate, 1789–1989: Addresses on the History of the United States Senate*. Bicentennial ed. Vol. 2. Washington, D.C.: GPO, 1991.
C.B.S. "The Reform of Primaries." *Current Literature* 37 (July–December 1904): 22–24.
Calhoun, Ballard C. "Public Policy and State Government." In *The Gilded Age: Essays on the Origins of Modern America*, edited by Charles W. Calhoun. Wilmington, Del.: Scholarly Resources, 1996.
Carter, Alfred G. W. *The Old Court House: Reminiscences and Anecdotes of the Courts and Bar of Cincinnati*. Cincinnati: Peter G. Thomson, 1880.
Casey, Marion. *Charles McCarthy: Librarianship and Reform*. Chicago: American Library Association, 1981.
Catt, Carrie Chapman, and Nettie Rogers Shuler. *Woman Suffrage and Politics: The Inner Story of the Suffrage Movement*. 1926. Reprint, Seattle: University of Washington Press, 1969.
Cayton, Andrew R. L. *The Frontier Republic: Ideology and Politics in the Ohio Country, 1780–1825*. Kent, Ohio: Kent State University Press, 1986.
———. "'Language Gives Way to Feelings': Rhetoric, Republicanism, and Religion in Jeffersonian Ohio." In *The Pursuit of Public Power: Political Culture in Ohio, 1787–1861*,

edited by Jeffrey P. Brown and Andrew R. L. Cayton. Kent, Ohio: Kent State University Press, 1994.

——. "'A Quiet Independence': The Western Vision of the Ohio Company." *Ohio History* 90 (1981): 5–32.

Cayton, Andrew R. L., and Paula R. Riggs. *City into Town: The City of Marietta, Ohio, 1788–1988*. Marietta, Ohio: Marietta College Dawes Memorial Library, 1991.

Chalmers, David M. *Hooded Americanism: The History of the Ku Klux Klan*, 3d ed. 1981. Reprint, Durham, N.C.: Duke University Press, 1987.

Chance, C. W., and Higdon C. Roberts, "Staffing Legislative Standing Committees: The Ohio Experience." *State Government* 43 (Winter 1970): 31–38.

Cheek, William, and Aimee Lee Cheek. *John Mercer Langston and the Fight for Black Freedom, 1829–65*. Urbana: University of Illinois Press, 1989.

"Chillicothe Court-House, Barracks, Etc." *American Pioneer* 6 (June 1842): 203–8.

Cho, Yong Hyo, and H. George Frederickson. *Measuring the Effects of Reapportionment in the American States*. New York: National Municipal League, 1976.

Citizens League Research Institute Political Campaign Finance Task Force. *Campaign Finance in Ohio: An Introduction*. Cleveland: Citizens League Research Institute, 1990.

Clark, Norman H. *Deliver Us from Evil: An Interpretation of American Prohibition*. New York: Norton, 1976.

Clark, Victor S. *History of Manufactures in the United States*. Vol. 1. New York: McGraw-Hill, 1929.

Clonts, Forrest William. "The Political Campaign of 1875 in Ohio." *Ohio Archaeological and Historical Quarterly* 31 (January 1922): 38–97.

Cohan, Paul. "Ohio Campaign Finance Law to Get First Real Test in 1998." *Stateline Midwest*, May 1997. Reprinted in Paul Cohan, *The Price of Free Speech: Campaign Finance in the Midwest*. Lombard, Ill.: Midwestern Legislative Conference of the Council of State Governments, 1997.

Cole, Charles C., Jr. *A Fragile Capital: Identity and the Early Years of Columbus, Ohio*. Columbus: Ohio State University Press, 2001.

"The Columbus Orange Girl—A Real Life Romance." *Saturday Evening Post*, 26 May 1860, 7.

Commemorative Historical and Biographical Record of Wood County, Ohio. Chicago: Beers, 1897.

Committee of State Officials on Suggested State Legislation of the Council of State Governments. *Suggested State Legislation*. Vol. 27. Chicago: Council of State Governments, 1967.

Common Cause Ohio. "The Trojan Horse: Early Campaign Finance Reports Show That Ohio's New Campaign Finance Law Has Opened the Floodgates to Big Money." http://www.commoncause.org/Ohio. 2 November 2005.

Conrad, Ethel, ed. "Touring Ohio in 1811: The Journal of Charity Rotch." *Ohio History* 99 (Summer–Autumn 1990): 135–65.

Cotton, John. "From Rhode Island to Ohio in 1815." *Journal of American History* 16 (July–September 1922): 249–60.

Cox, Elizabeth M. *Women State and Territorial Legislators, 1895–1995: A State-by-State Analysis with Rosters of 6,000 Women*. Jefferson, N.C.: McFarland, 1996.

Cox, James M. *Journey through My Years*. New York: Simon and Schuster, 1946.

Cox, Samuel S. *Eight Years in Congress, from 1857–1865. Memoirs and Speeches*. New York: D. Appleton, 1865.

Creel, George, and Sloane Gordon. "What Are You Going to Do About It?" Part 9: "The Shame of Ohio." *Cosmopolitan Magazine* 51 (October 1911): 599–610.

Croly, Herbert. *Marcus Alonzo Hanna: His Life and Work*. New York: Macmillan 1923.

Cross, Ira. "Direct Primaries." *Arena* 35 (June 1906): 587–90.

Cummings, Abbott Lowell. *The Alfred Kelley House of Columbus, Ohio: The Home of a Pioneer Statesman. With Mrs. Kelley's Recollections and Some Family Letters*. Columbus: Franklin County Historical Society, 1953.

Cunningham, Noble E., Jr. "The Jeffersonian Republican Party." In *History of U.S. Political Parties: Volume I*, edited by Arthur M. Schlesinger Jr. 1973. Reprint, Philadelphia: Chelsea House, 2002.

Curl, Donald Walter. "The Long Memory of the United States Senate." *Ohio History* 76 (Summer 1967): 103–13.

Curtin, Michael F., in collaboration with Julia Barry Bell. *The Ohio Politics Almanac*. 2d ed. Kent, Ohio: Kent State University Press, 2006.

Cushing, Luther Stearns. *Elements of the Law and Practice of Legislative Assemblies in the United States of America*. 1856. Reprint, South Hackensack, N.J.: Rothman Reprints, 1971.

Cushman, Robert E. "Voting Organic Law: The Action of the Ohio Electorate in the Revision of the State Constitution in 1912." *Political Science Quarterly* 28 (June 1913): 207–29.

Cutler, Julia Perkins. *Life and Times of Ephraim Cutler Prepared from His Journals and Correspondence*. 1890. Reprint, New York: Arno Press, 1971.

Dahlkemper, Lesley. "Growing Accustomed to Her Face." *State Legislatures* 22 (July–August 1996): 36–45.

Dallinger, Frederick W. *Nominations for Elective Office in the United States*. New York: Longmans, Green 1897.

Dalzell, Private [James M.]. *Private Dalzell, His Autobiography, Poems and Comic War Papers; Sketch of John Gray, Washington's Last Soldier, Etc*. Cincinnati: Robert Clarke, 1888.

Dannenbaum, Jed. "Immigrants and Temperance: Ethnocultural Conflict in Cincinnati, 1845–1860." *Ohio History* 87 (Spring 1978): 125–39.

Davies, Greg. "The Junkyard Dog of the Ohio Senate." *Columbus Monthly*, November 1997, 108–16.

Davies, Margery W. *Woman's Place Is at the Typewriter: Office Work and Office Workers, 1870–1930*. Philadelphia: Temple University Press, 1982.

Davis, Joseph Stancliffe. *Essays in the Earlier History of American Corporations*. 2 vols. 1917. Reprint, New York: Russell and Russell, 1965.

Davis, Oscar K. "Can You Trust the Primaries?" *Collier's Weekly* 73 (29 March 1924): 8–9. Reprinted in *The Direct Primary*, compiled by Lamar T. Beman. New York: H. W. Wilson, 1926.

Dawes, Henry L. "Has Oratory Declined?" *Forum* 18 (October 1894): 146–60.

Denning, Brannon P., and Brooks R. Smith. "Uneasy Riders: The Case for a Truth-in-Legislation Amendment." *Utah Law Review* 1999, no. 4:957–1025.

Dennis, Donna I. "Obscenity Law and the Conditions of Freedom in the Nineteenth-Century United States." *Law and Social Inquiry* 27 (Spring 2002): 369–99.

DeSario, Jack P., and David E. Freel. "Ohio Ethics Law Reforms: Tracing the Political and Legal Implications." *Akron Law Review* 30 (Fall 1996): 129–53.

Dial, George White. "The Construction of the Ohio Canals." *Ohio Archaeological and Historical Society Publications* 13 (October 1904): 460–82.

Dickens, Charles. *American Notes, & Pictures from Italy*. Philadelphia: George W. Jacobs, 1868.

Dickoré, Marie. *General Joseph Kerr of Chillicothe, Ohio, "Ohio's Lost Senator," from the Carrel Manuscript Collection*. Oxford, Ohio: Oxford Press, 1941.

Dillon, Merton L. *Benjamin Lundy and the Struggle for Negro Freedom*. Urbana: University of Illinois Press, 1966.

Dinkin, Robert. *Campaigning in America: A History of Election Practices*. New York: Greenwood, 1989.

Dodds, H. W. *Procedure in the State Legislatures*. Philadelphia: American Academy of Political and Social Sciences, 1918.

Downes, Randolph C. *The Rise of Warren Gamaliel Harding, 1865–1920*. Columbus: Ohio State University Press, 1970.

DuBois, Ellen Carol. *Harriot Stanton Blatch and the Winning of Woman Suffrage*. New Haven, Conn.: Yale University Press, 1997.

Dunn, James Taylor, ed. "'Cincinnati Is a Delightful Place': Letters of a Law Clerk." *Bulletin of the Historical and Philosophical Society of Ohio* 10 (October 1952): 256–77.

Eaton, Clement. "Southern Senators and the Right of Instruction, 1789–1860." *Journal of Southern History* 18 (August 1952): 303–19

Eckels, James H. "The Menace of Legislation." *North American Review* 165 (August 1897): 240–46.

Ellis, Richard J. *To the Flag: The Unlikely History of the Pledge of Allegiance*. Lawrence: University Press of Kansas, 2005.

Entin, Jonathan L. "Judicial Supermajorities and the Validity of Statutes: How Mapp Became a Fourth Amendment Landmark Instead of a First Amendment Footnote." *Case Western Reserve Law Review* 52 (Winter 2001): 441–70.

Erickson, Leonard. "Politics and Repeal of Ohio's Black Laws, 1837–1849." *Ohio History* 82 (Summer–Autumn 1973): 154–75.

Erickson, Robert S. "The Partisan Impact of State Legislative Reapportionment." *Midwest Journal of Political Science* 15 (February 1971): 57–71.

Ershkowitz, Herbert, and William T. Shade. "Consensus or Conflict? Political Behavior in the State Legislatures during the Jacksonian Era." *Journal of American History* 58 (December 1971): 591–621.

Esch, John J. "Our Second Line—the National Guard." *North American Review* 177 (August 1903): 288–96.

Etcheson, Nicole. *The Emerging Midwest: Upland Southerners and the Political Culture of the Old Northwest, 1787–1861*. Bloomington: Indiana University Press, 1996.

———. "Private Interest and Public Good: Upland Southerners and Antebellum Midwestern Political Culture." In *The Pursuit of Public Power: Political Culture in Ohio, 1787–1861*, edited by Jeffrey P. Brown and Andrew R. L. Clayton. Kent, Ohio: Kent State University Press, 1994.

Eulau, Heinz. "The Ecological Basis of Party Systems: The Case of Ohio." *Midwest Journal of Political Science* 1 (August 1957): 125–35. Reprinted in *Democracy in the Fifty States*, edited by Charles Press and Oliver P. Williams. Chicago: Rand McNally, 1966.

Evans, Elden Cobb. *A History of the Australian Ballot System in the United States*. Chicago: University of Chicago Press, 1917.

Evans, Lyle S., ed. *A Standard History of Ross County, Ohio*. 1917. Reprint, Baltimore: Gateway Press, 1987.

Evans, Nelson W. *A History of Taxation in Ohio*. Cincinnati: Robert Clarke, 1906.

Evans, Orenna Louise. "The Children's Code of Ohio." Notes on Current Legislation. *American Political Science Review* 7 (November 1913): 647–50.

Everstine, Carl N. *The General Assembly of Maryland, 1776–1850*. Charlottesville, Va.: Michie, 1982.

Farkas, Sándor Bölöni. *Journey in North America, 1831*. Translated and edited by Arpad Kadarkay. Santa Barbara, Calif.: ABC-Clio, 1978.

Farmer, Rick, and Thomas H. Little. "Legislative Power in the Buckeye State: The Revenge of Term Limits." Joint Project on Legislative Term Limits. Denver and Washington, D.C.: National Conference of State Legislatures, 2005.

Feller, Daniel. "Benjamin Tappan: The Making of a Democrat." In *The Pursuit of Public Power: Political Culture in Ohio, 1787–1861*, edited by Jeffrey P. Brown and Andrew R. L. Cayton. Kent, Ohio: Kent State University Press, 1994.

Fenton, John H. *Midwest Politics*. New York: Holt, Rinehart and Winston, 1966.

Fesler, Mayo. "New Election Code for Ohio." Notes and Events. *National Municipal Review* 18 (June 1929): 427–28.

Feustel, Bruce, and Rich Jones. "Legislator Training 101." *State Legislators*, September 2001, 16–19.

Finan, Richard H. "The Restoration Project." *OhioGrocer*, Summer 1996, 33.

Finan, Richard H., and April M. Williams. "Government Is a Three-Legged Stool." *University of Toledo Law Review* 32 (Summer 2001): 517–28.

Finkelman, Paul. "Exploring Southern Legal History." *North Carolina Law Review* 64 (November 1985): 77–116.

———. "Race, Slavery, and Law in Antebellum Ohio." In *The History of Ohio Law*, edited by Michael Les Benedict and John F. Winkler. Athens: Ohio University Press, 2004.

Finnarn, Theodore O. "Property Taxes and Farmers in Ohio: The Park Investment Story." *University of Toledo Law Review* 7 (Spring 1976): 1125–95.

Flinn, Thomas A. "Continuity and Change in Ohio Politics." *Journal of Politics* 21 (August 1962): 521–44.

———. "The Ohio General Assembly: A Developmental Analysis." In *State Legislative Innovation: Case Studies of Washington, Ohio, Florida, Illinois, Wisconsin, and California*, edited by James A. Robinson. New York: Praeger, 1973.

———. "The Outline of Ohio Politics." *Western Political Quarterly* 13 (September 1960): 702–21.

Flower, B. O. "Is the Republic Passing?" *Arena* 30 (November 1903): 3–21.

Foner, Eric. *Free Soil, Free Labor, Free Men: The Ideology of the Republican Party before the Civil War*. New York: Oxford University Press, 1970.

Foraker, Joseph Benson. *Notes of a Busy Life*. 2 vols. Cincinnati: Stewart and Kidd, 1916.

Ford, Harvey S. "Seabury Ford." In *Governors of Ohio*. 2d ed. Columbus: Ohio Historical Society, 1969.

Fox, Stephen C. "The Bank Wars, the Idea of 'Party,' and the Division of the Electorate in Jacksonian Ohio." *Ohio History* 88 (Summer 1979): 253–76.

Franklin, John Hope. *George Washington Williams: A Biography*. Durham, N.C.: Duke University Press, 1998.

Friedman, Lawrence M. *A History of American Law*. 3d ed. New York: Simon and Schuster, 2005.

Friedman, Robert S. "The Urban-Rural Conflict Revisited." *Western Political Quarterly* 14 (June 1961): 481–95.

Fritchey, Clayton. "Relief in Ohio." *American Mercury* 50 (May 1940): 74–81.

Funderburk, Charles, and Robert W. Adams. "Interest Groups in Ohio Politics." In *Ohio Politics*, edited by Alexander P. Lamis. Kent, Ohio: Kent State University Press, 1994.

Furney, Linda. "Fair Hearing: Balancing Lobby Regulation with Free Speech in Ohio." *University of Toledo Law Review* 32 (Summer 2001): 529–38.

Galloway, George B. *History of the House of Representatives*. New York: Crowell, 1962.

———. *History of the House of Representatives*. 2d ed. Revised by Sidney Wise. New York: Crowell, 1976.

Garfield, James A. *The Diary of James A. Garfield*. Edited by Harry James Brown and Frederick D. Williams. Vol. 1, *1848–1871*. East Lansing: Michigan State University Press, 1967.

Garrett, Betty. *Columbus: America's Crossroads*. Tulsa, Okla.: Continental Heritage Press, 1980.

Geiser, Karl F. "Defects in the Direct Primary." *Annals of the American Academy of Political and Society Science* 106 (March 1923): 31–39. Reprinted in *The Direct Primary*, compiled by Lamar T. Beman. New York: H. W. Wilson, 1926.

Gerber, David A. *Black Ohio and the Color Line, 1860–1915*. Urbana: University of Illinois Press, 1976.

———. "Lynching and Law and Order: Origins and Passage of the Ohio Anti-Lynching Law of 1896." *Ohio History* 83 (Winter 1974): 33–50.

Ghose, Dave. "Quitting the Boys' Club." *Columbus Monthly*, March 2003, 127–30.

Gienapp, William E. *The Origins of the Republican Party, 1852–1856.* New York: Oxford University Press, 1987.

"The Girl at the Typewriter." *Ladies' Home Journal* 21 (February 1904): 24.

Gist, Genevieve B. "Progressive Reform in a Rural Community: The Adams County Vote-Fraud Case." *Mississippi Valley Historical Review* 48 (June 1961): 60–78.

Gittes, Frederick M. "Paper Promises: Race and Ohio Law after 1860." In *The History of Ohio Law*, edited by Michael Les Benedict and John F. Winkler. Athens: Ohio University Press, 2004.

Goebel, Thomas. *A Government by the People: Direct Democracy in American, 1890–1940.* Chapel Hill: University of North Carolina Press, 2002.

Gold, David M. "The General Assembly and Ohio's Constitutional Culture." In *The History of Ohio Law*, edited by Michael Les Benedict and John F. Winkler. Athens: Ohio University Press, 2004.

———. "Public Aid to Private Enterprise under the Ohio Constitution: Sections 4, 6, and 13 of Article VIII in Historical Perspective." *University of Toledo Law Review* 16 (Winter 1985): 405–64.

———. "Rites of Passage: The Evolution of the Legislative Process, 1799–1937." *Capital University Law Review* 30, no. 4 (2002): 631–55.

Graham, A. A. "The Beginnings of the Buckeye Capital." *Magazine of Western History* 1 (March 1885): 411–31.

Grant, H. Roger. *Ohio on the Move: Transportation in the Buckeye State.* Athens: Ohio University Press, 2000.

Greene, Mary A. "Results of the Woman-Suffrage Movement." *Forum* 17 (June 1894): 413–24.

Green, John P. *Fact Stranger Than Fiction: Seventy-five Years of a Busy Life, with Reminiscences of Many Great and Good Men and Women.* Cleveland: Riehl Printing, 1920.

Griffin, Burt W. and Lewis R. Katz. "Sentencing Consistency: Basic Principles Instead of Numerical Grids: The Ohio Plan." *Case Western Reserve Law Review* 53 (Fall 2002): 1–75.

Griffith, Ernest S. *A History of American City Government: The Conspicuous Failure, 1870–1900.* New York: Praeger, 1974.

Griggs, John W. "Lawmaking." *American Law Review* 31 (September–October 1897): 701–20.

Grossberg, Michael. *Governing the Hearth: Law and the Family in Nineteenth-Century America.* Chapel Hill: University of North Carolina Press, 1985.

Gunderson, Robert Gray. "The Dayton Log-Cabin Convention of 1840." *Bulletin of the Historical and Philosophical Society of Ohio* 7 (October 1949): 202–10.

Gunther, John. *Inside U.S.A.* New York: Harper and Bros., 1947.

Hall, Kermit L. *The Magic Mirror: Law in American History.* New York: Oxford University Press, 1989.

Hamilton, Gail [Mary Abigail Dodge]. "Prohibition in Politics." *North American Review* 140 (June 1885): 509–20

Harlow, Ralph Volney. *The History of Legislative Methods in the Period before 1825.* New Haven, Conn.: Yale University Press, 1917.

Harris, Joseph P. *Registration of Voters in the United States.* Washington, D.C.: Brookings Institution, 1929.

Hayes, Rutherford Birchard. *Diary and Letters of Rutherford Birchard Hayes, Nineteenth President of the United States.* 5 vols. Edited by Charles Richard Williams. Columbus: Ohio Archaeological and Historical Society, 1922.

Heffernan, W. O. "State Budget Making in Ohio." *Annals of the American Academy of Political and Social Science* 62 (November 1915): 91–100.

Higginson, Stephen A. "A Short History of the Right to Petition Government for the Redress of Grievances." *Yale Law Journal* 96 (November 1986): 142–66.

Hill, David B. "We Are Too Much Governed." *North American Review* 170 (March 1900): 367–83.

Hill, Warren P. "A Critique of Recent Ohio Anti-Subversive Legislation." *Ohio State Law Journal* 14 (Autumn 1953): 439–93.

History of Geauga and Lake Counties, Ohio, with Illustrations and Biographical Sketches of Its Pioneers and Most Prominent Men. 1878. Reprint, Evansville, Ind.: Unigraphic, 1973.

History of Washington County, Ohio, with Illustrations and Biographical Sketches. Cleveland: H. Z. Williams and Bro., 1881.

Hitchman, James J., ed. "John Jay Janney and His 'Recollections of Thomas Corwin.'" *Ohio History* 73 (Spring 1964): 100–110.

Hoadly, George. "Methods of Ballot Reform." *Forum* 7 (August 1889): 623–33.

Hoeffel, David L. "Ohio's Death Penalty: History and Current Development." *Capital University Law Review* 31, no. 3 (2003): 659–90.

Hofstadter, Richard. *The Age of Reform: From Bryan to F. D. R.* New York: Vintage Books, 1955.

Holt, Edgar Allan. *Party Politics in Ohio, 1840–1850.* Columbus: F. J. Heer, 1931.

Holt, Michael F. *Political Parties and American Political Development from the Age of Jackson to the Age of Lincoln.* Baton Rouge: Louisiana State University Press, 1992.

———. *The Rise and Fall of the American Whig Party: Jacksonian Politics and the Onset of the Civil War.* New York: Oxford University Press, 1999.

Howe, Henry. *Historical Collections of Ohio. . . .* Ohio centennial ed. Vol. 2. Cincinnati: State of Ohio, 1904.

Howe, Frederic C. *The Confessions of a Reformer.* New York: Scribner's, 1924.

Howells, William Dean. *Selected Letters.* Edited and annotated by George Arms, Richard H. Ballinger, Christoph K. Lohmann, and George K. Reeves. Vol. 1, *1852–1872.* Boston: Twayne, 1979.

Howells, W. D. "In an Old-Time State Capital." *Harper's Monthly Magazine* 129 (September 1914): 593–603.

Hughes, Edward Wakefield. *Guide to Parliamentary Practice in the Ohio House of Representatives.* Columbus: State of Ohio, 1912.

———. *Hughes' American Parliamentary Guide Prepared for Ohio General Assembly: The Process of Lawmaking.* Columbus: F. J. Heer Printing, 1922.

———. *Hughes' American Parliamentary Guide: Mechanics of Lawmaking.* Rev. new ed. Columbus: Heer, 1932.

Huntington, C. C. "A History of Banking and Currency in Ohio before the Civil War." *Ohio Archaeological and Historical Society Quarterly* 24 (July 1915): 235–539.

Hyde, Henry M. "Has the Direct Primary Made Good?" *McClure's Magazine* 52 (August 1920): 15–16, 68–69.

Insley, Edward. "How to Reform the Primary-Election System (with Particular Reference to Reforms in Operation or Proposed)." *Arena* 17 (June 1897): 1013–23.

Jefferson, Thomas. *Jefferson's Parliamentary Writings: "Parliamentary Pocket-Book" and A Manual of Parliamentary Practice.* Edited by Wilbur Samuel Howell. Princeton, N.J.: Princeton University Press, 1988.

Jensen, Richard. *The Winning of the Midwest: Social and Political Conflict, 1888–1896.* Chicago: University of Chicago Press, 1971.

Jewell, Malcolm E. "The Political Setting." In *State Legislatures in American Politics*, edited by Alexander Heard. Englewood Cliffs, N.J.: Prentice Hall, 1966.

Johnson, Tom L. *My Story.* Edited by Elizabeth J. Hauser. New York: Huebsch, 1911.

Jordan, Philip D. *Ohio Comes of Age, 1873–1900.* Vol. 5, *The History of the State of Ohio*, edited by Carl Wittke. Columbus: Ohio State Archaeological and Historical Society, 1943.

Julian, George W. *Political Recollections 1840 to 1872.* Chicago: Jansen, McClurg, 1884.

Kahn, Jonathan. *Budgeting Democracy: State Building and Citizenship in America, 1890–1928.* Ithaca, N.Y.: Cornell University Press, 1997.

Kalette, Linda Elise. *The Papers of Thirteen Early Ohio Political Leaders: An Inventory to the 1976–77 Microfilm Editions.* Columbus: Ohio Historical Society, 1977.

Kaylor, R. S. "Ohio Railroads." *Ohio Archaeological and Historical Society Publications* 9 (October 1900): 189–92.

Keefe, William J. "The Functions and Powers of the State Legislatures." In *State Legislatures in American Politics*, edited by Alexander Heard. Englewood Cliffs, N.J.: Prentice Hall, 1966.

Keller, Morton. *Affairs of State: Public Life in Late Nineteenth Century America.* Cambridge, Mass.: Harvard University Press, Belknap Press, 1977.

Kennan, George. "The Direct Rule of the People." *North American Review* 198 (August 1913): 145–60.

Kennedy, J. H. "Alfred Kelley." *Magazine of Western History* 3 (March 1886): 550–57.

Kenny, John T. "The Legislature That Elected Mr. Hanna." *Arena* 21 (March 1899): 311–26.

Kerber, Linda K. "The Federalist Party." In *History of U.S. Political Parties: Volume I*, edited by Arthur M. Schlesinger Jr. 1973. Reprint, Philadelphia: Chelsea House, 2002.

Kerr, K. Austin. *Organized for Prohibition: A New History of the Anti-Saloon League*. New Haven, Conn.: Yale University Press, 1985.

Key, V. O., Jr. *American State Politics: An Introduction*. New York: Knopf, 1967.

Keyssar, Alexander. *The Right to Vote: The Contested History of Democracy in America*. New York: Basic Books, 2000.

Kinney, Muriel "John Cary, An Ohio Pioneer." *Ohio Archaeological and Historical Publications* 46 (April 1937): 166–98.

Klement, Frank. *The Limits of Dissent: Clement L. Vallandigham and the Civil War*. Lexington: University Press of Kentucky, 1970.

Kleppner, Paul. *Continuity and Change in Electoral Politics, 1893–1928*. New York: Greenwood, 1987.

———. *The Cross of Culture: A Social Analysis of Midwestern Politics, 1850–1900*. New York: Free Press, 1970.

———. *Who Voted? The Dynamics of Electoral Turnout, 1870–1980*. New York: Praeger, 1982.

Knepper, George W. *Ohio and Its People*. 3d ed. Kent, Ohio: Kent State University Press, 2003.

Kousser, Thad. *Term Limits and the Dismantling of State Legislative Professionalism*. New York: Cambridge University Press, 2005.

Kramer, Larry D. *The People Themselves: Popular Constitutionalism and Judicial Review*. New York: Oxford University Press, 2004.

Kruman, Marc W. *Between Authority and Liberty: State Constitution Making in Revolutionary America*. Chapel Hill: University of North Carolina Press, 1997.

Kulewicz, John J. "Reinventing the Governor: A History of Executive Power under Ohio Law." In *The History of Ohio Law*, edited by Michael Les Benedict and John F. Winkler. Athens: Ohio University Press, 2004.

Kurfess, Charles F. "From the Leader's Position . . ." In *Strengthening the States: Essays on Legislative Reform*, edited by Donald G. Hertzberg and Alan Rosenthal. Garden City, N.Y.: Anchor Books, 1972.

Kurtz, Karl T. "The History of Us." *State Legislatures*, July–August 1999, 16–21.

Lapp, John A. "Actual State Legislation." *Annals of the American Academy of Political and Social Science* 43 (September 1912): 49–64.

Lazarus, Richard J. *The Making of Environmental Law*. Chicago: University of Chicago Press, 2004.

Lee, A. E. *History of the City of Columbus*. 2 vols. New York: Munsell, 1892.

"Legislative Investigations." Legislative Notes and Reviews. *American Political Science Review* 8 (May 1914): 238–40.

Lehne, Richard. "Shape of the Future." *National Civic Review* 58 (September 1969): 351–55.

Lentz, Ed. *Columbus: The Story of a City*. Charleston, S.C.: Arcadia, 2003.

Leonard, Lee. "As Tough as They Come." *State Legislatures*, May 1999, 18–21.

———. "Ohio's Finan Follows the Rules." *State Legislatures*, July–August 2002, 25–28.

———. "The Pols and Their $130 Million Hideout." *Columbus Monthly*, April 1989, 25–29.

———. "Power at the Statehouse: The Riffe Reign." *Columbus Monthly*, August 1989, 54–59.

———. "Pro among Pros." *State Legislatures*, November–December 1989, 13–15.

———. "A Retirement at the Statehouse." *Columbus Monthly*, October 1988, 10–11.

———. "Rhodes's Second Eight Years, 1975–1983." In *Ohio Politics*, edited by Alexander P. Lamis. Kent, Ohio: Kent State University Press, 1994.

———. "Winding Down after a Tough Day at the Statehouse." *Columbus Monthly*, 79–90.

Lieber, Francis. *On Civil Liberty and Self-Government.* 2d ed. Philadelphia: J. B. Lippincott, 1859.

Liggett, Walter W. "Ohio—Lawless and Unashamed." *Plain Talk*, July 1930, 1–22.

Lindsey, Edward. "Historical Sketch of the Indeterminate Sentence and Parole System." *Journal of the American Institute of Criminal Law and Criminology* 16 (May 1925): 9–69.

Long, Alexander. "The Autobiography of Alexander Long." Edited by Louis R. Harlan. *Bulletin of the Historical and Philosophical Society of Ohio* 19 (April 1961): 98–127.

"The Longest Ballot?" Editorial comment. *National Civic Review* 52 (January 1963): 5.

Lowrie, S. Gale. "The Makers of Our Laws." *University of Cincinnati Law Review* 17 (March 1948): 144–58.

———. "Ohio Model Charter Law." Notes on Current Legislation. *American Political Science Review* 7 (August 1913): 422–24.

Luce, Robert. *Legislative Assemblies: Their Framework, Make-Up, Character, Characteristics, Habits, and Manners.* Boston: Houghton Mifflin, 1924.

———. *Legislative Principles: The History and Theory of Lawmaking by Representative Government.* Boston and New York: Houghton Mifflin, 1930.

———. *Legislative Procedure: Parliamentary Practices and the Course of Business in the Framing of Statutes.* Boston: Houghton Mifflin, 1922.

Lutz, Donald S. "The Colonial and Early State Legislative Process." In *Inventing Congress: Origins and Establishment of the First Federal Congress*, edited by Kenneth R. Bowling and Donald R. Kennon. Athens: Ohio University Press, 1999.

———. "The Theory of Consent in the Early State Constitutions." *Publius* 9, no. 2 (1979): 11–42.

Magrath, C. Peter. *Yazoo: Law and Politics in the New Republic: The Case of Fletcher v. Peck.* Providence: Brown University Press, 1966.

Maher, Richard L. "Oxcart Government!" In *Our Sovereign State*, edited by Robert S. Allen. New York: Vanguard, 1949.

Maienknecht, Theresa A., and Stanley B. Maienknecht. *Monroe County, Ohio: A History.* Mt. Vernon, Ind.: Windmill Publications, 1989.

Main, Jackson Turner. *The Sovereign States, 1775–1783.* New York: New Viewpoints, 1973.

Maizlisch, Stephen E. *The Triumph of Sectionalism: The Transformation of Ohio Politics, 1844–1856*. Kent, Ohio: Kent State University Press, 1983.

Mark, Gregory A. "The Vestigial Constitution: The History and Significance of the Right to Petition." *Fordham Law Review* 66 (May 1998): 2153–231.

Marshall, George B. "Life History of a Bill in the Ohio Legislature." *Ohio State Law Journal* 11 (Autumn 1950): 447–55.

Marshall, John A. *American Bastile. A History of the Arbitrary Arrests and Imprisonment of American Citizens in the Northern and Border States. . . .* Philadelphia: Thomas W. Hartley, 1885.

Martin, William T. *History of Franklin County: A Collection of Reminiscences of the Early Settlement of the County; with Biographical Sketches and a Complete History of the County to the Present Time.* 1858. Reprint, Columbus: Linden Heights Kiwanis Club, 1969.

Martzolff, C. L. "Ohio: Changes in the Constitution." Notes on Current Legislation. *American Political Science Review* 6 (November 1912): 573–76.

Mason, W. L. "Women's Chances as Bread Winners: II—Women as Stenographers." *Ladies' Home Journal* 8 (February 1891): 8.

Masotti, Louis, and Kathleen Barber. "'Better Men' Running?" *National Civic Review* 56 (October 1967): 504–11, 531.

Maurer, David J. "Relief Problems and Politics in Ohio." In *The New Deal*, edited by John Braeman, Robert Bremner, and David Brody. Vol. 2, *The State and Local Levels*. Columbus: Ohio State University, 1975.

Maxwell, Samuel. "The Evils of Lobbying, and Proposed Remedy." *American Law Review* 30 (May–June 1896): 398–403.

McCabe, Lida Rose. *Don't You Remember?* Columbus: A. H. Smythe, 1884.

McDiarmid, Hugh C. "The Gilligan Interlude, 1971–1975." In *Ohio Politics*, edited by Alexander P. Lamis. Kent, Ohio: Kent State University Press, 1994.

McGerr, Michael E. *The Decline of Popular Politics: The American North, 1865–1928*. New York: Oxford University Press, 1986.

McGovern, Frances. *Fun, Cheap, and Easy: My Life in Ohio Politics, 1949–1964*. Akron, Ohio: University of Akron Press, 2002.

McGrane, Reginald C. "Orator Bob and the Right of Instruction." *Bulletin of the Historical and Philosophical Society of Ohio* 11 (October 1953): 251–73.

———. "The Veto Power in Ohio." In "Proceedings of the Mississippi Valley Historical Association, 1915–1916," special issue, *Mississippi Valley Historical Review* 9, extra number (April 1917): 177–89.

McLin, C. J., Jr. *Dad, I Served: The Autobiography of C. J. McLin, Jr., As Told to Minnie Fells Johnson, Ph.D.*, edited by Lillie P. Howard and Sarah Byrn Rickman. Dayton, Ohio: Wright State University Office of Public Relations, 1998.

McLin, Rhine L. "The Hidden Effects of Term Limits: Losing the Voices of Experience and Diversity." *University of Toledo Law Review* 32 (Summer 2001): 539–48.

Meckstroth, J. A. "A. Victor Donahey." In *The Governors of Ohio*. 2d ed. Columbus: Ohio Historical Society, 1969.

Meeks, James E. "The Evolution of the Public Utility Commission of Ohio (PUCO): (Almost) One Hundred Years of Service to the People of Ohio." In *The History of Ohio Law*, edited by Michael Les Benedict and John F. Winkler. Athens: Ohio University Press, 2004.

Melhorn, Donald F., Jr. *"Lest We Be Marshall'd": Judicial Power and Politics in Ohio, 1806–1812*. Akron, Ohio: University of Akron Press, 2003.

Melish, John. *Travels through the United States of America, in the Years 1806 & 1807, 1810, & 1811; Including an Account of Passages Betwixt America and Britain, and Travels Through Various Parts of Britain, Ireland, & Canada*. Philadelphia: printed for the author; London: reprinted for George Cowie, 1818.

Mercer, James K. *Ohio Legislative History*. 6 vols. Columbus: Edward T. Miller (vol. 1), F. J. Heer (vols. 2–6), [1914–27?].

Middleton, Stephen. *The Black Laws: Race and the Legal Process in Early Ohio*. Athens: Ohio University Press, 2005.

Miller, Edward Alanson. *The History of Educational Legislation in Ohio from 1803 to 1850*. Chicago: University of Chicago, 1920.

Miller, Zane L. *Boss Cox's Cincinnati: Urban Politics in the Progressive Era*. New York: Oxford University Press, 1968.

Milligan, Fred J. *Ohio's Founding Fathers*. New York: iUniverse, 2003.

Milligan, William M., and Joseph E. Pohlman. "The 1968 Modern Courts Amendment to the Ohio Constitution." *Ohio State Law Journal* 29 (Fall 1968): 811–48.

Model Code of Legislative Conduct (A Staff Proposal), prepared for submission to the Committee on Legislative Rules, National Legislative Conference. 1 November 1968.

Mohr, James C. *Abortion in America: The Origins and Evolution of National Policy, 1800–1900*. New York: Oxford University Press, 1978.

Monroe, James. *Oberlin Thursday Lectures, Addresses and Essays*. Oberlin, Ohio: E. J. Goodrich, 1897.

Monsell, Margaret E. "Stars in the Constellation of the Commonwealth: Massachusetts Towns and the Constitutional Right of Instruction." *New England Law Review* 29 (Winter 1995): 285–309.

Mooney, Christopher Z. "Measuring U.S. State Legislative Professionalism: An Evaluation of Five Indices." *State and Local Government Review* 26 (Spring 1994): 70–78.

Morgan, Edmund S. *Inventing the People: The Rise of Popular Sovereignty in England and America*. New York: Norton, 1988.

Morris, B. F., ed. *The Life of Thomas Morris: Pioneer and Long a Legislator of Ohio, and United States Senator from 1833 to 1839*. Cincinnati: Moore, Wistach, Keys and Overend, 1856.

Morris, Richard B. *The Forging of the Union, 1781–1789*. New York: Harper and Row, 1987.

Morris, Thomas D. *Free Men All: The Personal Liberty Laws of the North, 1780–1861*. Baltimore: Johns Hopkins University Press, 1974.

Morton, Marian J. "Homes for Poverty's Children: Cleveland's Orphanages, 1851–1933." *Ohio History* 98 (Winter–Spring 1989): 5–22.

Myers, Allen O. *Bosses and Boodle in Ohio Politics: Some Plain Truths for Honest People.* Cincinnati: Lyceum, 1895.

Nevins, Allen. *The American States During and After the Revolution, 1775–1789.* 1924. Reprint, New York: Augustus M. Kelley, 1969.

"New York Gets Reforms." *Outlook,* 27 December 1913, 861.

Newman, J. H., ed. *Organic Law of Ohio and Proposed Amendments or Helps to Constitution Makers.* Columbus: F. J. Heer Printing, 1913.

Norris, Alan E. "Ohio's Divorce Reform Act—Expectation and Realization." *Ohio Northern University Law Review* 13, no. 2 (1986): 172–202.

Norris, James D., and Arthur H. Shaffer. *Politics and Patronage in the Gilded Age: The Correspondence of James A. Garfield and Charles E. Henry.* Madison: State Historical Society of Wisconsin, 1970.

Novak, William J. *The People's Welfare: Law and Regulation in Nineteenth-Century America.* Chapel Hill: University of North Carolina Press, 1996.

Nye, Joseph S., Jr., Philip D. Zelikow, and David C. King, eds. *Why People Don't Trust Government.* Cambridge, Mass.: Harvard University Press, 1997.

Obhof, Larry J. "DeRolph v. State and Ohio's Long Road to an Adequate Education." *Brigham Young University Education and Law Journal* 2005, no. 1:83–149.

Odegard, Peter H. *Pressure Politics: The Story of the Anti-Saloon League.* New York: Columbia University Press, 1928.

Ohio Citizens' Committee on the State Legislature. Final Report. June 30, 1972.

"One Means of Regulating the Lobby." *Century Illustrated Magazine* 41 (February 1891): 628–29.

O'Neal, Emmet. "Distrust of State Legislatures." *North American Review* 199 (May 1914): 684–98.

Onuf, Peter S. "From Constitution to Higher Law: The Reinterpretation of the Northwest Ordinance." *Ohio History* 94 (Winter–Spring 1985): 5–33.

O'Reilly, James T. "Tort Reform and Term Limits: The 2004 Ohio Experience." *Capital University Law Review* 33 (Spring 2005): 529–49.

"Organize for Short Ballot Campaign." Citizen Action. *National Civic Review* 51 (September 1962): 463.

Orth, Samuel P. *The Centralization of Administration in Ohio.* New York: Columbia University Press, 1903.

———. "The Cleveland Plan of School Administration." *Political Science Quarterly* 19 (September 1904): 402–16.

Overacker, Louise. *Money in Politics.* 1932. Reprint, New York: Arno Press, 1974.

Overman, William D. "Education in Ohio since 1900." In *Ohio in the Twentieth Century,* compiled by Harlow Lindley. Vol. 6, *The History of the State of Ohio,* edited by Carl Wittke. Columbus: Ohio State Archaeological and Historical Society, 1942.

Owen, Robert L. "The Restoration of Popular Rule: The Greatest of All Non-Partisan Issues." *Arena* 39 (June 1908): 643–50.

Oyos, Matthew. "The Mobilization of the Ohio Militia in the Civil War." *Ohio History* 98 (Summer–Autumn 1989): 147–74.

Papke, David Ray. "Pondering Past Purposes: A Critical History of American Adoption Law." *West Virginia Law Review* 102 (Winter 1999): 459–76.

Pasley, Jeffrey L. "Private Access and Public Power: Gentility and Lobbying in the Early Congress." In *The House and Senate in the 1790s: Petitioning, Lobbying, and Institutional Development*, edited by Kenneth R. Bowling and Donald R. Kennon. Athens: Ohio University Press, 2002.

Paterson, Robert G. "The Role of the 'District' as a Unit in Organized Medicine in Ohio." *Ohio State Archaeological and Historical Quarterly* 49 (October 1940): 367–77.

Patterson, Isaac Franklin. *The Constitutions of Ohio . . . and Historical Introduction.* Cleveland: Arthur H. Clark, 1912.

Patterson, James T. *Mr. Republican: A Biography of Robert A. Taft.* Boston: Houghton Mifflin, 1972.

Patterson, Samuel C. "Legislative Politics in Ohio." In *Ohio Politics*, edited by Alexander P. Lamis. Kent, Ohio: Kent State University Press, 1994.

Patterson, Thomas E. *The Vanishing Voter: Public Involvement in an Age of Uncertainty.* New York: Knopf, 2002.

Pauly, Karl B. *Bricker of Ohio: The Man and His Record.* New York: G. P. Putnam's Sons, 1944.

Peabody, A. P. "The Voting of Women in School Elections." *Journal of Social Science*, no. 10 (1 October 1879): 42–54.

Pegram, Thomas R. *Battling Demon Rum: The Struggle for a Dry America, 1800–1933.* Chicago: Ivan R. Dee, 1998.

Peirce, Neal R. *The Megastates of America: People, Politics, and Power in the Great States.* New York: Norton, 1972.

Perry, George Sessions. "Columbus, Ohio." *Saturday Evening Post*, 3 May 1952, 22–23, 96–100.

Pershing, B. H. "Membership in the Ohio General Assembly." *Ohio Archaeological and Historical Quarterly* 40 (April 1931): 222–83.

Peskin, Alan. *Garfield: A Biography.* Kent, Ohio: Kent State University Press, 1978.

Piott, Steven L. *Giving Voters a Choice: The Origins of the Initiative and Referendum in America.* Columbia: University of Missouri Press, 2003.

Pitcavage, Mark. "'Burthened in Defence of Our Rights': Opposition to Military Service in Ohio during the War of 1812." *Ohio History* 104 (Summer–Autumn 1995): 142–62.

Pitcher, M. Avis. "John Smith, First Senator from Ohio and His Connections with Aaron Burr." *Ohio State Archaeological and Historical Quarterly* 45 (January 1936): 68–88.

Piven, Frances Fox, and Richard A. Cloward. *Why Americans Still Don't Vote and Why Politicians Want It That Way.* Boston: Beacon, 2000.

Plummer, Elizabeth L. "Tourism at the Ohio Penitentiary." *Timeline* 21 (January–February 2004): 18–25.

Pocock, Emil. "'A Candidate I'll Surely Be': Election Practices in Early Ohio, 1798–1825." In *The Pursuit of Public Power: Political Culture in Ohio, 1787–1861*, edited by Jeffrey

P. Brown and Andrew R. L. Cayton. Kent, Ohio: Kent State University Press, 1994.

Pohlman, William J. "The Continued Viability of Ohio's Procedure for Legislative Review of Agency Rules in the Post-*Chadha* Era." *Ohio State Law Journal* 49, no. 1 (1988): 251–73.

Pollack, Ervin H. ed., *Ohio Unreported Judicial Decisions Prior to 1823*. Indianapolis: Allen Smith, 1952.

"Popular vs. Delegated Government." *Independent* 69 (25 August 1910): 429–30

Porter, George H. *Ohio Politics during the Civil War Period*. 1911. Reprint, New York: AMS Press, 1968.

Postle, Herman R. *The Government of Ohio and an Outline of the Government of the United States*. Columbus: published by the author, 1901.

Presser, Stephen B. "The Historical Background of the American Law of Adoption." *Journal of Family Law* 11, no. 3 (1971): 443–516.

P. T. "Reform in Senatorial Elections." Under the Rose. *Arena* 21 (March 1899): 391–93.

Purviance, David. *The Biography of Elder David Purviance . . . Written by Himself*. Dayton, Ohio: privately printed, 1848.

Quillin, Frank U. *The Color Line in Ohio: A History of Race Prejudice in a Typical Northern State*. 1913. Reprint, New York: Negro Universities Press, 1969.

Ralph H. Burke, Inc. *Report on Underground Garage at Broad and High Streets for City of Columbus, Ohio*. Columbus: n.p., 1954.

Raphael, Marc Lee. *Jews and Judaism in a Midwestern Community: Columbus, Ohio, 1840–1975*. Columbus: Ohio Historical Society, 1979.

Ratcliffe, Donald J. *Party Spirit in a Frontier Republic: Democratic Politics in Ohio, 1793–1821*. Columbus: Ohio State University Press, 1998.

———. *The Politics of Long Division: The Birth of the Second Party System in Ohio, 1818–1828*. Columbus: Ohio State University Press, 2000.

Rauschenberg, Fritz. "Sentencing Reform Proposals in Ohio." *Federal Sentencing Reporter* 6 (November–December 1993): 166–68.

Reemelin, Charles. *Life of Charles Reemelin, In German: Carl Gustav Rümelin, From 1814–1892*. Cincinnati: Weier and Daiker, 1892.

Reid, John Phillip. *The Concept of Representation in the Age of the American Revolution*. Chicago: University of Chicago Press, 1989.

Reinsch, Paul S. *American Legislatures and Legislative Methods*. New York: Century, 1907.

Remini, Robert V. *Andrew Jackson and the Course of American Freedom, 1822–1832*. New York: Harper and Row, 1981.

———. *Henry Clay: Statesman for the Union*. New York: Norton, 1991.

———. *The House: The History of the House of Representatives*. New York: Smithsonian Books, 2006.

Riddle, A. G. "B. F. Wade, The Politician." Part 5. *Magazine of Western History* 3 (March 1886): 471–84.

———. "Recollections of the Forty-seventh General Assembly of Ohio, 1847–48 [*sic*]." *Magazine of Western History* 6 (August 1887): 341–51.

Riffe, Vern. Speaking Out. *Ohioan*, March 1997, back cover.

————. Speaking Out. *Ohioan*, May 1996, back cover.

————. Speaking Out. *Ohioan*, March 1995, back cover.

Riffe, Vernal G., Jr., with Cliff Treyens, *Whatever's Fair: The Political Autobiography of Ohio House Speaker Vern Riffe*. Kent, Ohio: Kent State University Press, 2007.

"The Rights of a Voter, Given by the Constitution, Cannot be Abridged." *Weekly Law Bulletin and the Ohio State Law Journal* 36 (7 September 1896): 110–11.

Rodabaugh, James H., ed., "From England to Ohio, 1830–1832: The Journal of Thomas K. Wharton." Pt. 2. *Ohio Historical Quarterly* 65 (April 1956): 111–51.

Rokicky, Catherine M. *James Monroe: Oberlin's Christian Statesman & Reformer, 1821–1898*. Kent, Ohio: Kent State University Press, 2002.

Roper, Wayne. "Vern Riffe: Ohio's House Power." *Kiplinger Program Report*, Spring 1985, 7–9.

Rose, Albert H. *Ohio Government State and Local*. 3d ed. Dayton, Ohio: University of Dayton Press, 1966.

————. *Ohio Government State and Local*. 4th ed. Dubuque, Ia.: Kendall/Hunt, 1974.

Roseboom, Eugene H. *The Civil War Era, 1850–1873*. Vol. 4, *The History of the State of Ohio*, edited by Carl Wittke. Columbus: Ohio State Archaeological and Historical Society, 1944.

Roseboom, Eugene H., and Francis P. Weisenburger. *A History of Ohio*. Columbus: Ohio Historical Society, 1996.

Rosenthal, Alan. *The Decline of Representative Democracy: Process, Participation, and Power in State Legislatures*. Washington, D.C.: CQ Press, 1998.

————. *Heavy Lifting: The Job of the American Legislature*. Washington, D.C.: CQ Press, 2004.

————. *Legislative Life: People, Process, and Performance in the State*. New York: Harper and Row, 1981.

————. *The Third House: Lobbyists and Lobbying in the States*. 2d ed. Washington, D.C.: CQ Press, 2001.

Rosenthal, Alan, and Rich Jones. "Trends in State Legislatures." In *The Book of the States* 36. Lexington, Ky.: Council of State Governments, 2004.

Rotella, Elyce J. *From Home to Office: U.S. Women at Work, 1870–1930*. Ann Arbor, Mich.: UMI Research Press, an imprint of University Microfilms International, 1981.

Rubin, Irene S. "Who Invented Budgeting in the United States?" *Public Administration Review* 53 (September–October 1993): 438–44.

Rupenthal, J. C. "Election Reforms; The Trend Toward Democracy." *American Lawyer* 14 (February 1906): 72–75.

Russell, Francis. *The Shadow of Blooming Grove: Warren G. Harding in His Times*. New York: McGraw-Hill, 1968.

Ruud, Millard H. "'No Law Shall Embrace More Than One Subject.'" *Minnesota Law Review* 42 (January 1958): 389–455.

————. "The Ohio Legislative Service Commission." *Ohio State Law Journal* 14 (Autumn 1953): 393–407.

Ryan, Daniel J. "From Charter to Constitution: Being a Collection of Public Documents Pertaining to the Territory of the Northwest and the State of Ohio, from the Charters of James I, to and Including the First Constitution of Ohio, and the State Papers Relating to Its Admission to the Union, Showing Thereby the Historical Chain of Title of Said State from 1606 to 1803." *Ohio Archaeological and Historical Publications* 5 (August 1897): 1–164.

————. *History of Ohio: The Rise and Progress of an American State.* Vols. 3 and 4. New York: Century History Company, 1912.

————. "The Influence of Socialism on the Ohio Constitution." *North American Review* 196 (November 1912): 665–72.

————. Letter to the editor, *North American Review* 197 (February 1913): 279–80.

————. "The State Library and Its Founder." *Ohio Archaeological and Historical Quarterly* 28 (January 1919): 98–107.

Saltman, Roy G. *The History and Politics of Voting Technology: In Quest of Integrity and Public Confidence.* New York: Palgrave Macmillan, 2006.

Sandles, A. P., and E. W. Doty. *The Biographical Annals of Ohio, 1906–1907–1908: A Handbook of the Government and Institutions of the State of Ohio.* Springfield, Ohio: Allied Printing, [1908?].

Sawyer, Charles. Letter to the editor. *North American Review* 197 (February 1913): 275–79.

Saxbe, William B., with Peter D. Franklin. *I've Seen the Elephant: An Autobiography.* Kent, Ohio: Kent State University Press, 2000.

Schaffner, Margaret A. *Lobbying.* Comparative Legislation Bulletin No. 2. Madison: Wisconsin Free Library Commission, Legislative Reference Department, 1906

Scheiber, Harry N. "Alfred Kelley and the Ohio Business Elite, 1822–1859." *Ohio History* 87 (Autumn 1978): 365–92.

————. *Ohio Canal Era: A Case Study of Government and the Economy, 1820–1861.* 1968. Reprint, Athens: Ohio University Press, 1987.

Schimansky, O. K. "Campaigning by Trolley." *Ohio Illustrated Magazine* 1 (September 1906): 268–72.

Schlesinger, Arthur M. "The City in American History." *Mississippi Valley Historical Review* 27 (June 1940): 43–66.

Schneider, Norris F. *Y Bridge City: The Story of Zanesville and Muskingum County, Ohio.* Cleveland: World, 1950.

Schooley Caldwell Associates. "The Ohio Statehouse Master Plan." Columbus: n.p., 1989.

Schudson, Michael. *The Good Citizen: A History of American Civil Life.* Cambridge, Mass.: Harvard University Press, 1998.

Schultz, Martin. "Divorce in Early America: Origins and Patterns in Three North Central States." *Sociological Quarterly* 25 (Autumn 1984): 511–25.

Schwartz, Arthur A., comp. *Amendment and Legislation: Proposed Constitutional Amendments, Initiated Legislation, and Laws Challenged by Referendum, Submitted to the Electors.*

Updated through 2006 by Jennifer Brunner. Columbus: Ohio Secretary of State, 2007. (http://www.sos.state.oh.us/sos/ElectionsVoter/issueHist.pdf.)

———. "The Ohio Legislative Reference Bureau and Its Place in the Legislative Process." *Ohio State Law Journal* 11 (Autumn 1950): 436–46.

Schwartz, Gary T. "Urban Freeways and the Interstate System." *Southern California Law Review* 49 (March 1976): 406–513.

Sears, Alfred Byron. *Thomas Worthington: Father of Ohio Statehood.* Columbus: Ohio State University Press, 1958.

Sears, Barnas, B. B. Edwards, and C. C. Felton. *Classical Studies: Essays on Ancient Literature and Art. With the Biography and Correspondence and Eminent Philologists.* 1843. Reprint, Boston: Gould, Kendall and Lincoln, 1849.

Sears, Paul B. "History of Conservation in Ohio." In *Ohio in the Twentieth Century,* compiled by Harlow Lindley. Vol. 6, *The History of the State of Ohio,* edited by Carl Wittke. Columbus: Ohio State Archaeological and Historical Society, 1942.

Selcraig, James Truett. *The Red Scare in the Midwest, 1945–1955: A State and Local Study.* Ann Arbor, Mich.: UMI Research Press, 1982.

"Selections from the Follett Papers, III." *Quarterly Publication of the Historical and Philosophical Society of Ohio* 10 (January–March 1915): 1–33.

"Senator Charles Curtis: Kansas Furnishes a Floor Leader to Succeed Henry Cabot Lodge." *Current Opinion* 78 (January 1925): 26–28.

Shade, William Gerald. *Banks or No Banks: The Money Issue in Western Politics, 1832–1865.* Detroit: Wayne State University Press, 1972.

Sharp, James Roger. *The Jacksonians versus the Banks: Politics in the States after the Panic of 1837.* New York: Columbia University Press, 1970.

Shaw, Douglas V. "Interurbans in the Automobile Age: The Case of the Toledo, Port Clinton and Lakeside." *Ohio History* 103 (Summer–Autumn 1994): 125–51.

Shaw, John, ed. *Crete and James: Personal Letters of Lucretia and James Garfield.* East Lansing: Michigan State University Press, 1994.

Shaw, William B. "Good Ballot Laws and Bad." *Outlook* 81 (December 9, 1905): 863–68.

Shedd, Carlos B. *Tales of Old Columbus.* Columbus: n.p., 1951.

Sheldon, Henry E., II. "From Commandments to Consent: Ohio in the Divorce Reform Era." *Northern Kentucky State Law Forum* 2 (Winter 1974–75): 119–83.

Sheppard, John S., Jr. "Concerning the Decline of the Principle of Representation in Popular Government." *Forum* 44 (June 1910): 642–50.

Sheridan, Richard G. *Follow the Money: Ohio State Budgeting.* Cleveland: Federation for Community Planning, 2000.

Shibley, George H. "The Progress of the Campaign for Majority Rule." *Arena* 29 (June 1903): 625–37.

Silbey, Joel H. *The American Political Nation, 1838–1893.* Stanford, Calif.: Stanford University Press, 1991.

Singer, Norman J. *Statutes and Statutory Construction.* 5th ed. Vol. 1. St. Paul, Minn.: West Group, 1994.

Bibliography

Skeen, C. Edward. "An Uncertain 'Right': State Legislatures and the Doctrine of Instruction." *Mid-America* 73 (January 1991): 29–47.

————. "*Vox Populi, Vox Dei:* The Compensation Act of 1816 and the Rise of Popular
Politics." *Journal of the Early Republic* 6 (Fall 1986): 253–74. Reprinted in *The
United States Congress in a Transitional Era, 1800–1841*. Vol. 2. Edited by Joel H.
Silby. Brooklyn, N.Y.: Carlson, 1991.

Smith, Bradley A. "The Siren's Song: Campaign Finance Regulation and the First
Amendment." *Journal of Law and Policy* 6, no. 1 (1997): 1–43.

Smith, S. Winifred. "Thomas Kirker." In *The Governors of Ohio*. 2d ed. Columbus: Ohio
Historical Society, 1969.

. Smock, Raymond W. "The Institutional Development of the House of Representatives,
1791–1801." In *The House and Senate in the 1790s: Petitioning, Lobbying, and Institutional Development*, edited by Kenneth R. Bowling and Donald R. Kennon.
Athens: Ohio University Press, 2002.

Spahr, Charles B. "Direct Primaries." In *Proceedings of the Rochester Conference for Good
City Government and Seventh Annual Meeting of the National Municipal League*,
edited by Clinton Rogers Woodruff. Philadelphia: National Municipal League,
1901.

Sponholtz, Lloyd. "The Politics of Temperance in Ohio, 1880–1912." *Ohio History* 85
(Winter 1976): 4–27.

Squire, Peverill. "Historical Evolution of Legislatures in the United States." *Annual
Review of Political Science* 9 (2006): 19–44.

Srole, Carole. "'A Blessing to Mankind, and Especially to Womankind': The Typewriter
and the Feminization of Clerical Work, Boston, 1860–1920." In *Women, Work,
and Technology: Transformations*, edited by Barbara Drygulski Wright, Myra Marx
Ferree, Gail O. Mellow, Linda H. Lewis, Maria-Luz Daza Sampler, Robert Asher,
and Kathleen Claspell. Ann Arbor: University of Michigan Press, 1987.

St. Clair, Arthur. *The St. Clair Papers. The Life and Public Services of Arthur St. Clair*.
Edited by William Henry Smith. 2 vols. Cincinnati: Robert Clarke, 1882

Stanton, Elizabeth Cady, Susan B. Anthony, and Matilda Joslyn Gage, eds. *History of
Woman Suffrage*. Vol. 4. Rochester, N.Y.: National American Woman Suffrage
Association, 1887.

Stegh, Leslie H. "A Paradox of Prohibition: Election of Robert J. Bulkley as Senator from
Ohio, 1930." *Ohio History* 83 (Summer 1974): 170–82.

Steinglass, Steven H., and Gino J. Scarselli. *The Ohio State Constitution: A Reference
Guide*. Westport, Conn.: Praeger, 2004.

Steuart, Justin. *Wayne Wheeler, Dry Boss: An Uncensored Biography of Wayne B. Wheeler*.
New York: Fleming H. Revell, 1928.

Stevens, Harry R. *The Early Jackson Party in Ohio*. Durham, N.C.: Duke University Press,
1957.

Stevens, Robert Bocking. *Law School: Legal Education in America from the 1850s to the
1980s*. Chapel Hill: University of North Carolina Press, 1983.

Stevens, Robert and Rosemary Stevens. *Welfare Medicine in America: A Case Study of Medicaid*. New York: Free Press, 1974.

Stewart, Gilbert H. "Politics and Politicians." *Ohio Illustrated Magazine* 2 (April 1907): 346–51.

Still, John S. "Ethan Allen Brown and Ohio's Canal System." *Ohio Historical Quarterly* 66 (January 1957): 22–56.

Stimson Henry L., and McGeorge Bundy. *On Active Service in Peace and War*. New York: Harper and Bros., 1948.

Stokes, Carl B. *Promises of Power: A Political Autobiography*. New York: Simon and Schuster, 1973.

Storey, Moorfield. "The American Legislature." *American Law Review* 28 (September–October 1894): 683–707.

Studer, Jacob H., comp. *Directory of the 58th General Assembly, Including State Officers, of the State of Ohio, 1868*. Columbus: Columbus Printing, 1868.

Sturm, Albert M., and Kaye M. Wright. "State Constitutional Developments during 1977." *National Civic Review* 67 (January 1978): 31–36.

Suddes, Thomas. "Panorama of Ohio Politics in the Voinovich Era, 1991–." In *Ohio Politics*, edited by Alexander P. Lamis. Kent, Ohio: Kent State University Press, 1994.

Sweeney, Jim. "Can the GOP Dislodge Vern?" *Columbus Monthly*, May 1991, 91–94.

Sydnor, Charles S. *The Development of Southern Sectionalism, 1819–1848*. Baton Rouge: Louisiana State University Press, 1948.

Szymanski, Ann-Marie E. *Pathways to Prohibition: Radicals, Moderates, and Social Movement Outcomes*. Durham, N.C.: Duke University Press, 2003.

Taft, Robert A. *The Papers of Robert A. Taft: Volume 1, 1889–1939*. Edited by Clarence E. Wunderlin Jr. Kent, Ohio: Kent State University Press, 1997.

Taylor, W. A. *Hundred-Year Book and Official Register of the State of Ohio, from 1789 to 1891, Inclusive*. Columbus: Westbote, 1891.

Teaford, Jon C. *The Twentieth-Century American City*. 2d ed. Baltimore: Johns Hopkins University Press, 1993.

Thompson, Jack M. "James R. Garfield: The Making of a Progressive." *Ohio History* 74 (Spring 1965): 79–89.

Thurber, James. *The Thurber Album: A New Collection of Pieces about People*. New York: Simon and Schuster, 1952.

Thurston, Helen M. "The 1802 Constitutional Convention and the Status of the Negro." *Ohio History* 81 (Winter 1972): 15–37.

Tokaji, Daniel P. "Early Returns on Election Reform: Discretion, Disenfranchisement, and the Help America Vote Act." *George Washington Law Review* 73 (August 2005): 1206–53.

Trefousse, H. L. *Benjamin Franklin Wade: Radical Republican from Ohio*. New York: Twayne, 1963.

Trester, Delmer J. "David Tod and the Gubernatorial Campaign of 1844." *Ohio State Archaeological and Historical Quarterly* 62 (April 1953): 162–78.

Treyens, Cliff. "Statehouse Hangouts 1995." *Ohioan*, April 1995, 10–14.

Trimble, Allen. *Autobiography and Correspondence of Allen Trimble, Governor of Ohio, with Genealogy of the Family*. Edited by Mary McA. T. Tuttle and Henry P. Thompson. Columbus: n.p., 1909.

Trollope, Frances. *Domestic Manners of the Americans*. Edited by Donald Smalley. 1832. Reprint, New York: Knopf, 1949.

Turner, William. *Ohio Farm Bureau Story, 1919–1979*. Columbus: Ohio Farm Bureau Federation, 1972.

Tuttle, A. H. "The Bronson Primary Law in Ohio." *Publications of the Michigan Political Science Association* 6 (March 1905): 106–17.

Tuttle, Alonzo H. "History of the Executive Veto in the Ohio Constitution." *Ohio State Law Journal* 2 (March 1936): 99–114.

Usher, Brian. "The Lausche Era, 1945–1957." In *Ohio Politics*, edited by Alexander P. Lamis. Kent, Ohio: Kent State University Press, 1994.

Utter, William T. *The Frontier State, 1803–1825*. Vol. 2, *The History of the State of Ohio*, edited by Carl Wittke. Columbus: Ohio State Archaeological and Historical Society, 1942.

Vallandigham, Clement L. *Speeches, Arguments, Addresses, and Letters of Clement L. Vallandigham*. New York: J. Walter, 1864.

Van Tine, Warren, C. J. Slanicka, Sandra Jordan, and Michael Pierce. *In the Workers' Interest: A History of the Ohio AFL-CIO, 1958–1998*. Columbus: Center for Labor Research, Ohio State University, 1998.

Volpe, Vernon L. *Forlorn Hope of Freedom: The Liberty Party in the Old Northwest, 1838–1848*. Kent, Ohio: Kent State University Press, 1990.

Wahlke, John C., Heinz Elau, William Buchanan, and LeRoy C. Ferguson. *The Legislative System: Explorations in Legislative Behavior*. New York: Wiley, 1962.

Walker, Harvey. *Law Making in the United States*. New York: Ronald Press, 1934.

———. *The Legislative Process: Law Making in the United States*. New York: Ronald Press, 1948.

———. "Municipal Government in Ohio before 1912." *Ohio State Law Journal* 9, no. 1 (1948): 1–17.

Walsh, Justin E. *The Centennial History of the Indiana General Assembly, 1816–1978*. Indianapolis: Select Committee on the Centennial History of the Indiana General Assembly in cooperation with the Indiana Historical Society, 1987.

Waltzer, Herbert. "Apportionment and Districting in Ohio: Components of Deadlock." In *The Politics of Reapportionment*, edited by Malcolm E. Jewell. New York: Atheron, 1962.

Ware, Alan. *The American Direct Primary: Party Institutionalization and Transformation in the North*. Cambridge: Cambridge University Press, 2002.

Ware, Jane. "The Statehouse, God Bless It." *Ohio Magazine*, July 1986, 24–25, 66–72.

Warner, Hoyt Landon. *Progressivism in Ohio, 1897–1917*. Columbus: Ohio State University Press, 1964.

Watson, Harry L. *Liberty and Power: The Politics of Jacksonian America*. New York: Hill and Wang, 1990.

Watkins, Albert. "The Primary Election Movement." *Forum* 33 (March 1902): 92–102.

Weberg, Brian. "Whom Do You Trust?" *State Legislatures*, July–August 1999, 34–37.

Webster, Homer J. "History of the Democratic Party Organization in the Northwest, 1824–1840." *Ohio Archaeological and Historical Publications* 24 (January 1915): 1–120.

Weed, John M. "The Traveled Ways." In *Ohio in the Twentieth Century*, compiled by Harlow Lindley. Vol. 6, *The History of the State of Ohio*, edited by Carl Wittke. Columbus: Ohio State Archaeological and Historical Society, 1942.

Wegner, John M. "Partisanship in the Ohio House of Representatives, 1900–1911: An Analysis of Roll-Call Voting." *Ohio History* 106 (Summer–Autumn 1997): 146–70.

Weisenberg, William K. Statehouse Connection. *Ohio Lawyer*, March–April 1999, 24–25.

———. Statehouse Connection. *Ohio Lawyer*, July–August 1999, 28–29.

Weisenburger, Francis P. "A Life of Charles Hammond: The First Great Journalist of the Old Northwest." *Ohio Archaeological and Historical Quarterly* 43 (October 1934): 337–427.

———. *The Passing of the Frontier, 1825–1850.* Vol. 3, *The History of the State of Ohio*, edited by Carl Wittke. Columbus: Ohio State Archaeological and Historical Society, 1941.

Wertheimer, Fred, and Susan Weiss Manes. "Campaign Finance Reform: A Key to Restoring the Health of Our Democracy." *Columbia Law Review* 94 (May 1994): 1126–59.

"What Happened to the 'Citizen' in the 'Citizen Legislature?'" *State Legislatures*, July–August 2003, 7.

Whitaker, F. M. "Ohio WCTU and the Prohibition Campaign of 1883." *Ohio History* 83 (Spring 1974): 84–102.

Whitlock, Brand. *Forty Years of It.* New York: D. Appleton, 1914.

Wigmore, John H. "Ballot Reform: Its Constitutionality." *American Law Review* 23 (September–October 1889): 719–32.

Wilcox, Delos F. *Municipal Government in Michigan and Ohio: A Study in the Relations of City and Commonwealth.* New York: Columbia University Press, 1896.

Wilentz, Sean. *The Rise of American Democracy: Jefferson to Lincoln.* New York: Norton, 2005.

Wilhelmy, Robert W. "Senator John Smith and the Aaron Burr Conspiracy." *Cincinnati Historical Society Bulletin* 28 (Spring 1970): 38–60.

Wilkin, Robert. "A Study in Administrative Law: The Conservancy Act of Ohio." *Ohio State University Law Journal* 3 (December 1936): 33–47.

Williams, Samuel. "Governor Tiffin." In James B. Finley, *Sketches of Western Methodism: Biographical, Historical, and Miscellaneous. Illustrative of Pioneer Life.* Cincinnati: privately printed, 1855.

Williams, W. W. *History of the Fire Lands, Comprising Huron and Erie Counties, Ohio, with Illustrations and Biographical Sketches of Some of the Prominent Men and Pioneers.* 1879. Reprint, Evansville, Ind.: Whippoorwill Publications, 1985.

Williamson, Chilton, *American Suffrage from Property to Democracy, 1760–1860.* Princeton, N.J.: Princeton University Press, 1960.

Williamson, Dan. "Big Ben." *Columbus Monthly*, July 1996, 117–25.

———. "It's Not Easy Being Mean." *Columbus Monthly*, September 2004, 40–45.

———. "Rating the Legislators." *Columbus Monthly*, December 2003, 34–45.

Winkle, Kenneth J. "Ohio's Informal Polling Place: Nineteenth-Century Suffrage in Theory and Practice." In *The Pursuit of Public Power: Political Culture in Ohio, 1787–1861*, edited by Jeffrey P. Brown and Andrew R. L. Cayton. Kent, Ohio: Kent State University Press, 1994.

———. *The Politics of Community: Migration and Politics in Antebellum Ohio*. New York: Cambridge University Press, 1988.

Wittke, Carl. "Ohio's Germans, 1840–1875." *Ohio Historical Quarterly* 66 (October 1957): 339–54.

Wood, Gordon S. *The Creation of the American Republic, 1776–1787*. Chapel Hill: University of North Carolina Press, 1969.

———. *The Radicalism of the American Revolution*. New York: Knopf, 1991.

Woodbury, Marda Liggett. *Stopping the Presses: The Murder of Walter W. Liggett*. Minneapolis: University of Minnesota Press, 1998.

Wright, Ralph G. *Inside the Statehouse: Lessons from the Speaker*. Washington, D.C.: CQ Press, 2005.

Zagarri, Rosemarie. *The Politics of Size: Representation in the United States, 1776–1850*. Ithaca, N.Y.: Cornell University Press, 1987.

Zainaldin, Jamil S. "The Emergence of a Modern American Family Law: Child Custody, Adoption, and the Courts, 1776–1851." *Northwestern University Law Review* 73 (February 1979): 1038–89.

Zeller, Belle. *American State Legislatures: Report of the Committee on American Legislatures, American Political Science Association*. New York: Thomas Y. Crowell, 1954.

———. "The State Lobby Laws." In *The Book of the States* 14. Chicago: Council of State Governments, 1962.

———. "State Regulation of Lobbying." In *The Book of the States* 7. Chicago: Council of State Governments, 1948.

Zimmerman, Richard G. *Call Me Mike: A Political Biography of Michael V. DiSalle*. Kent, Ohio: Kent State University Press, 2003.

———. *Plain Dealing: Ohio Politics and Journalism Viewed from the Press Gallery*. Kent, Ohio: Kent State University Press, 2006.

———. "Rhodes's First Eight Years, 1963–1971." In *Ohio Politics*, edited by Alexander P. Lamis. Kent, Ohio: Kent State University Press, 1994.

INDEX

Page numbers in italics indicate illustrations.

Householder, Larry, 281, 417
House Un-American Activities Committee
(HUAC), 344
Howe, Frederic C., 58, 229–30, 277, 291; on
fellow legislators, 272–73, 357; political
principles of, 231; on session-end chaos,
370
Howells, William Dean, 165
Huffman, Isaac E., 406
Hughes, Edward Wakefield, 328, 388
Hundred-Year Book, 49
Huntington, Samuel, 33, 55

Ide, W. D., 162
immigrants, politics and, 21–22, 69–70,
196–97, 288, 373, 432; growth of cities
and, 420
Independent, 233
instruction, people's right of, 17–18; direct
primaries and, 241; Massachusetts and,
26–27; U.S. senators and, 27–29, 234

Jackson, Andrew, 27, 28, 181–82, 187–88
Jefferson, Thomas, 5, 10, 118; *Manual of Par-
liamentary Practice*, 118, 122
Jefferson County, 69, 75
Jeffersonian Republican Party, 9–10, 181
Jennings, David, 85
Jewett, Isaac Appleton, 84, 144
Johnson, Jeffrey, 417
Johnson, Tom, 252, 277, 288
Johnston, David A., 319, 431
Joint Legislative Ethics Committee, 414–15,
416
Jones, Paul, 413, 414–15
judicial branch: 1850–51 constitutional convention and, 32–34, 43, 46; 1912 constitutional convention and, 262–63; Fifty
Dollar Act and, 32–33; judicial review
and, 32–34, 259–60, 262–64; labor and
tax regulation, 262; licensing decisions and, 258; Modern Courts Amendment of 1967 and, 262–64; municipal
classification and, 262; Progressivism and,
231; property taxes, uniform rule and,
264–65; relative power of, 265; Sweeping
Resolution and, 34, 80. *See also specific
laws and cases*

Kansas-Nebraska Act of 1854 (U.S.), 182,
194, 197
Karmol, Irma, 375
Kasch, Gus, 279–80, 325, 374
Kasich, John, 397
Keller, Morton, 230
Kelley, Alfred, 54–55, 83, 87, 190, 283, 381;
home of, 88
Kent State University, 345–46
Kentucky, legislative supremacy and, 31
Kerr, Joseph, 67
Kiefer, Horace, 343
King, E. R., 330
Kinney, Coates, 168
Kirker, Thomas, 52, 54, 55–56
Knight, Howard A., 289
Know-Nothing Party, 182, 196–97. *See also*
political parties
Kousser, Thad, 461
Kraemer, Adolphus, 21
Ku Klux Klan, 373, 433
Kurfess, Charles, 259, 385

Lamar, Lucius Q. C., 205
Lancaster Eagle-Gazette, 362–63, 365
Langston, John Mercer, 69
Larwill, William, 165
Lausche, Frank, 252, 260, 344
Layman, Amos, 163–64
LeFever, Ruth, 402
legislation, xvi–xvii, 382, 442; 1825 session
and, 210; 1849–50 session and, 209; 1872
notification rule and, 131–32; 1904
session and, 209–10; air pollution and,
453–54; air travel and, 450–51; amendments, reporting of, and, 128; automobiles
and, 450; business incorporations, bank
charters and, 35–38, 183–86, 215; canal
projects and, 36, 210–12; capital punishment and, 447–48; commercial regulation
and, 12; criminal law and, 346–47,
441–42; divorces and, 215–17, 442–43;
drafting of bills and, 381–82; early
framework of government and, 11–12;
education and, 44, 212, 218, 443, 449;
engrossment and, 121–22; environment
and, 451–55; ethics law of 1974, 412;
matters and, 217; federal government and,

444–48; focus of, changes in, 224–25; Great Depression and, 444–45; health care and, 446; highway construction and, 434, 435, 445–46, 450; income tax and, 262, 365, 427, 443; initiative and referendum and, 237–38, 240; labor issues and, 336, 437–38; liquor measures and, 206–7; lobby regulation law of 1976, 412; milking bills and, 405–6; motions for leave and, 119–20; municipalities and, 12, 220–21; occupational health and safety and, 451; one-subject rule and, 124, 326; origination of, 119; path of, 1937, 324–25; petition process and, 119, 213–14, 224–25; pigeonhole veto and, 336–37, 340; postponement and, 127; professional fitness and, 451; Progressivism and, 330–31; promotionalism and, 35–38, 46, 443; public education and, 44, 210, 256; quantity of, 136–37; readings of, 121, 122–25, 325–26; resolutions and, 12, 353–55; sales tax and, 443; sexual behavior and, 12, 222–25, 438–39, 447; sources of, 382–85; Speaker of the House and, 335–36; special laws and, 212–18; special sessions and, 137, 358–59; taxation and, 210–12; uniform laws and, 443–44; urban versus rural areas and, 430–39; voting on, 332–33, 334; water conservation and, 453. See also specific issues and laws

legislative committees, 121, 125–33, 335, 340–41, 348, 349, 460; anticommunism and, 343–45; assignments per member and, 341; checking in and, 348–49; Citizens Conference on State Legislatures and, 351; committee of the whole and, 342; German propaganda and, 342; House Speaker and, 335–36; Legislative Service Commission (LSC) and, 342, 351; pigeonhole veto and, 336–37; public transparency and, 338–39; Reference Committee and, 336–37; Rules Committee and, 337–38; scheduling problems and, 347–50; Speaker of the House and, 335–36; special committees and, 129, 342; standing committees and, 129–30, 335, 340–41; writing legislation and, 353

Legislative Reference and Information Department, 382, 398
Legislative Reference Bureau (LRB), 400
Legislative Reference Department (LRD), 398–99
Legislative Research Commission, 400–401
Legislative Service Commission (LSC), 379, 384–85, 401, 460; legislative committees, mock memo and, 352; legislative committees and, 342, 351

legislators: absenteeism and, 153–55, 361–63; African Americans as, 148–50, 270–72; age of, 50, 272–74; alcohol and, 84–85, 100, 144; becoming conduct and, 148–51; bribery and, 173–79, 405–7; collegiality and, 465–66; compensation of, 120, 151–55, 360–66, 461; constituent services and, 359; corruption and, 170–79; covering the clock and, 369, 370; dual office-holding and, 415–17; eligibility for office and, 58–59; gender and race of, 51–52; individual offices and, 378–79; influence of, 48–58, 150–51, 280–84; leadership structure and, 364–66; legal profession and, 274–75; living arrangements and, 82–83, 98, 305–13; mutual trust and interpersonal relationships and, 465; native Ohioans and, 49–50; nomination of, 59–64; occupations of, 50–51, 274–76; orientation programs and, 379, 381; pancaking and, 413–14; part-time versus full-time, 356–60; quality of debate and, 143–44, 331–32; sense of public duty and, 86–87; session-end chaos and, 147, 370–71; smoking and, 144–45, 375–76; social lives of, 84–87, 99–100, 313–16; sports events and, 315–16; swearing-in of House members, 1947, 372; telephones and, 376–77; tenures of, 278–79; term limits and, 238, 240, 273–74, 278–79, 461–64; travel and, 78–80; turnover of, 52–54, 276, 379, 441; unbecoming conduct and, 143–47, 366–71; urban versus rural areas and, 430–39; women as, 266–70, 366. See also legislative committees; lobbyists
Leland, David, 281
Leonard, Lee, 281, 282, 438
LeVeque Tower, 304, 307

National Conference of State Legislatures
    (NCSL), 385
National Environmental Policy Act, 454
National Industrial Recovery Act, 445
National Minimum Drinking Age Act, 446
National Order of Women Legislators, 267
National Road, 79, 82
National Voter Registration Act of 1993, 287
Negro Protective Party, 64
Neil House, 83, 85, 302–3, 312–13
Netzley, Robert, 381
New Constitution, 39–40
Niles' National Register, 141
Nineteenth Amendment (U.S.), 286
Nixon, Corwin, 282–83
Northwest Ordinance, 3; democracy and,
    5; divorces and, 215; employees and,
    159–60; General Assembly and, 4–5;
    House of Representatives and, 6; Legisla-
    tive Council and, 5–6
Northwest Territory, 3; Indiana Territory
    and, 11
Norton, James A., 168
*Notes on the Early Settlement of the North-
    Western Territory* (Burnet), 9
Novak, William, 222

Oberlin-Wellington fugitive slave case, 198
Ocasek, Oliver, 345
O'Connor, John, 146
Ohio Canal, 36
Ohio Citizens' Committee on the State Legis-
    lature, 459
Ohio Commission to Reform Medicaid, 446
Ohio Criminal Sentencing Commission, 442
Ohio Environmental Protection Agency
    (EPA), 454
Ohio Life Insurance and Trust Company, 197
Ohio Magazine, 280
Ohio Manufacturers Association, 406, 411
Ohio Program Commission, 400–401
Ohio Revised Code of 1953, 447
Ohio State Journal, 20, 71, 99, 131, 154, 165,
    197, 276; campaign finance and, 291
Ohio Statesman, 141, 146, 154, 173
Ohio Trucking Association, 314, 411
Ohio Un-American Activities Commission
    (OUAC), 344–45
Olds, Edson B., 200–201

O'Neal, Emmet, 338
O'Neil, Anna F., 267
Onuf, Peter, 13
Oregon, slavery and, 189
Orth, Samuel P., 255
Ott, Adelaide S., 268
Overmire, Jacob, 216
Owen, Frank, 100
Owens, Jesse, 388–89

pancaking, 295, 413–15
Panic of 1837, 37, 185, 215
Payne, Henry B., 175–76, 229
Pease, Calvin, 32–34
Peirce, Neal, 305
Pendleton, George, 175
Pennington, Miller, 38
Perry, George Sessions, 304
Pierce, Michael, 205
Pike, Jarvis, 90
Poland, Luke P., 173–74
political parties, 207–8, 287–88; Andrew
    Jackson and, 182–83; Antimasons, 181;
    Anti-Saloon League and, 419, 433; appor-
    tionment revolution of 1966 and, 426–27;
    banking and currency and, 36–37, 41,
    183–86, 192; Catholic Church and, 196,
    204, 432; Civil War and, 182, 197; eco-
    nomic issues and, 438; election campaigns
    and, 65–67; ethnocultural issues and, 66,
    194–97, 203–4; growth of cities and,
    420–23; highway construction and, 434,
    435, 445–46; immigrants and, 429, 432;
    importance of, 429, 436; labor issues and,
    437–38; liquor bills and, 431–33; Mexican
    War and, 189–90; moral issues and, 207–8;
    nomination of candidates and, 60–64; orga-
    nizational structure and, 10; partisan shifts
    and, 427; prohibition and, 195–96, 204–7,
    432–33; religion and, 196–97; Rose local-
    option law of 1908 and, 431–32; Senatorial
    elections and, 183; slavery and, 187–89,
    194–95; systems of, 36–37, 181–83,
    194–95; tradition and, 429; twentieth cen-
    tury and, 418–20, 438–39; urban versus
    rural interests and, 430–39; voter registra-
    tion and, 70–71; Western Reserve and,
    198; women's suffrage and, 267. *See also*
    specific issues and laws; specific parties

Polk, James K., 189–90
Pollock, Robert A., 278, 343
Polly, Peyton, 194
Pope, Donna, 356, 359
Prentiss, C. J., 271
primary elections, 63–64
Progressivism, 276–77; gubernatorial veto
    and, 251–52; initiative and referendum
    and, 232–34; results of, 236–44; social
    change and, 230–31
prohibition, 434–35; crime and corruption
    and, 304, 408, 430; Eighteenth Amend-
    ment (U.S.), 433–34; legislation and, 206;
    political parties and, 195, 204–7, 432–33;
    religion and, 207; urban versus rural areas
    and, 431–33, 434–35
Prohibition Party, 205, 207; convention,
    1892, 208. See also political parties
property taxes: Taft, Robert A., on, 431; uni-
    form rule and, 43–44, 211–12, 264–65
Public Utilities Commission of Ohio, 255–56
Purviance, David, 51, 52

Randall, Brewster, 39, 193
Rankin, Helen, 271
Ratcliffe, Donald J., 10
Reagan, Ronald, 454
Reemelin, Charles, 21, 23–25; on daily prayer,
    141–42; on prohibition, 195
Reighard, Frank H., 364
Reinsch, Paul S., 178
religion, political parties and, 196–97, 203–5.
    See also Catholic Church
representation: methods of, 22–26; single-
    member districts and, 24–25, 243, 424–25,
    426–27. See also apportionment
Republican Party, 9–11, 418–20; Bank of the
    United States (BUS) and, 184; Civil War
    and, 197–99; direct primaries and, 235–36,
    242–43; domination of, 54, 419–20; judi-
    cial review and, 32; nomination of candi-
    dates and, 60–61; prohibitionists and, 207;
    rise of the cities and, 420–23; single-mem-
    ber districts and, 426–27; statehood and,
    14; women in politics and, 267. See also
    political parties
retrenchment, 120, 151–152, 161
Revised Code of 1953, 285, 442, 446, 447, 451;
    environmental protection and, 454–55

Rhodes, James A., 252–53, 254, 260, 326–27,
    330, 388, 426, 436; capital construction
    and, 443; collective bargaining and, 437;
    environmental regulation and, 454; voter
    registration and, 287
Riddle, Albert G., 39, 56, 90, 137, 148, 198
Riffe, Vernal G. (Vern), Jr., 260, 281–84, 313,
    315, 436; on behavior of legislators, 367;
    black caucus and, 270–71; campaign
    finance and, 292, 295; death of members
    and, 375; floor debate and, 333–34; House
    procedure and, 328; pancaking and, 413,
    414, 415; on term limits, 276
Rockefeller, John D., 452
Roe v. Wade, 447
roll-call studies, limitations of, 430–31
Roosevelt, Theodore, 233
Rose local-option law of 1908, 431–32
Rosenthal, Alan, 273, 464, 467
Ross, Joseph W., 209
Ross County courthouse, 1801, 8
Russell, Howard, 207
Russell, Robert, 83
Rutherford v. M'Faddon, 33
Ryan, Daniel J., 212, 233, 237

Sankey, Ira D., 142
Sargent, Winthrop, 5, 6
Saxbe, William, 290, 310
Scheiber, Harry N., 54
Schorr, Ed, 384
Scott, James, 97
Scrivens, Ella, 391
Seaver, Derrick, 274, 439
Second Bank of the United States (BUS), 184
sergeants at arms, 158–66, 329–30, 386–90
Seventeenth Amendment (U.S.), 234
Shaw, Robert, 321–22
Sheppard, Carl, 337
Sherman, John, 176
Shields, James, 53
Shkurti, Bill, 397
Shoemaker, Myrl, 413
Six Day War of 1975, 326–27
Skinner, William, 82
Slaughter, Robert F., 52, 53
slavery: Black Laws and, 129, 186–87, 189,
    193, 203; fugitive slave laws and, 188,
    198; Louisiana Purchase and, 187;